++

JOSEPH CAMPBELL

THE MASKS OF GOD: ORIENTAL MYTHOLOGY

++

PENGUIN BOOKS

PENGUIN BOOKS
Viking Penguin Inc., 40 West 23rd Street,
New York, New York 10010, U.S.A.
Penguin Books Ltd, 27 Wrights Lane, London W8 5TZ
(Publishing & Editorial) and Harmondsworth,
Middlesex, England (Distribution & Warehouse)
Penguin Books Australia Ltd, Ringwood,
Victoria, Australia
Penguin Books Canada Limited, 2801 John Street,
Markham, Ontario, Canada L3R 1B4
Penguin Books (N.Z.) Ltd, 182–190 Wairau Road,
Auckland 10, New Zealand

First published in the United States of America by
The Viking Press 1962
First published in Great Britain by
Souvenir Press Ltd 1973
Viking Compass Edition published 1970
Reprinted 1971, 1972, 1973, 1974
Published in Penguin Books 1976
Reprinted 1977, 1979, 1981, 1982 (twice), 1984, 1985, 1986, 1987

Library of Congress catalog card number: 59-8354
ISBN 0 14 00.4305 5

Printed in the United States of America by
Offset Paperback Mfrs., Inc., Dallas, Pennsylvania
Set in Times Roman

*The author wishes to acknowledge with gratitude the generous
support of his researches by the Bollingen Foundation.*

CONTENTS

v

REFERENCE NOTES AND INDEX

ILLUSTRATIONS

Sketches for Figures 2, 3, 4, 5, 7, 8, 14, 15, 16,
17, 18, 19, 20, 21, 22, 23, are by John L.
Mackey.

THE MASKS OF GOD:
ORIENTAL MYTHOLOGY

ON COMPLETION OF
The Masks of God

Looking back today over the twelve delightful years that I spent on this richly rewarding enterprise, I find that its main result for me has been its confirmation of a thought I have long and faithfully entertained: of the unity of the race of man, not only in its biology but also in its spiritual history, which has everywhere unfolded in the manner of a single symphony, with its themes announced, developed, amplified and turned about, distorted, reasserted, and, today, in a grand *fortissimo* of all sections sounding together, irresistibly advancing to some kind of mighty climax, out of which the next great movement will emerge. And I can see no reason why anyone should suppose that in the future the same motifs already heard will not be sounding still—in new relationships indeed, but ever the same motifs. They are all given here, in these volumes, with many clues, besides, suggesting ways in which they might be put to use by reasonable men to reasonable ends—or by poets to poetic ends—or by madmen to nonsense and disaster. For, as in the words of James Joyce in *Finnegans Wake:* "utterly impossible as are all these events they are probably as like those which may have taken place as any others which never took person at all are ever likely to be."

THE SEPARATION
OF EAST AND WEST

++

Chapter 1

THE SIGNATURES OF THE
FOUR GREAT DOMAINS

++

1. The Dialogue in Myth of East and West

The myth of eternal return, which
is still basic to Oriental life, displays an order of fixed forms
that appear and reappear through all time. The daily round of the
sun, the waning and waxing moon, the cycle of the year, and the
rhythm of organic birth, death, and new birth, represent a miracle
of continuous arising that is fundamental to the nature of the universe. We all know the archaic myth of the four ages of gold, silver,
bronze, and iron, where the world is shown declining, growing
ever worse. It will disintegrate presently in chaos, only to burst
forth again, fresh as a flower, to recommence spontaneously the
inevitable course. There never was a time when time was not.
Nor will there be a time when this kaleidoscopic play of eternity
in time will have ceased.

There is therefore nothing to be gained, either for the universe
or for man, through individual originality and effort. Those who
have identified themselves with the mortal body and its affections
will necessarily find that all is painful, since everything—for them
—must end. But for those who have found the still point of eternity,
around which all—including themselves—revolves, everything is
acceptable as it is; indeed, can even be experienced as glorious
and wonderful. The first duty of the individual, consequently, is
simply to play his given role—as do the sun and moon, the various
animal and plant species, the waters, the rocks, and the stars—
without resistance, without fault; and then, if possible, so to order

his mind as to identify its consciousness with the inhabiting principle of the whole.

The dreamlike spell of this contemplative, metaphysically oriented tradition, where light and darkness dance together in a world-creating cosmic shadow play, carries into modern times an image that is of incalculable age. In its primitive form it is widely known among the jungle villages of the broad equatorial zone that extends from Africa eastward, through India, Southeast Asia, and Oceania, to Brazil, where the basic myth is of a dreamlike age of the beginning, when there was neither death nor birth, which, however, terminated when a murder was committed. The body of the victim was cut up and buried. And not only did the food plants on which the community lives arise from those buried parts, but on all who ate of their fruit the organs of reproduction appeared; so that death, which had come into the world through a killing, was countered by its opposite, generation, and the self-consuming thing that is life, which lives on life, began its interminable course.

Throughout the dark green jungles of the world there abound not only dreadful animal scenes of tooth and claw, but also terrible human rites of cannibal communion, dramatically representing—with the force of an initiatory shock—the murder scene, sexual act, and festival meal of the beginning, when life and death became two, which had been one, and the sexes became two, which also had been one. Creatures come into being, live on the death of others, die, and become the food of others, continuing, thus, into and through the transformations of time, the timeless archetype of the mythological beginning; and the individual matters no more than a fallen leaf. Psychologically, the effect of the enactment of such a rite is to shift the focus of the mind from the individual (who perishes) to the everlasting group. Magically, it is to reinforce the ever-living life in all lives, which appears to be many but is really one; so that the growth is stimulated of the yams, coconuts, pigs, moon, and breadfruits, and of the human community as well.

Sir James G. Frazer, in *The Golden Bough,* has shown that in the early city states of the nuclear Near East, from which center all of the high civilizations of the world have been derived, god-

kings were sacrificed in the way of this jungle rite,[1]* and Sir
Leonard Woolley's excavation of the Royal Tombs of Ur, in
which whole courts had been ceremonially interred alive, revealed that in Sumer such practices continued until as late as c.
2350 B.C.[2] We know, furthermore, that in India, in the sixteenth
century A.D., kings were observed ceremoniously slicing themselves
to bits,[3] and in the temples of the Black Goddess Kali, the terrible
one of many names, "difficult of approach" (durgā), whose stomach
is a void and so can never be filled and whose womb is giving
birth forever to all things, a river of blood has been pouring continuously for millenniums, from beheaded offerings, through chan-
nels carved to return it, still living, to its divine source.

To this day seven or eight hundred goats are slaughtered in
three days in the Kalighat, the principal temple of the goddess in
Calcutta, during her autumn festival, the Durga Puja. The heads
are piled before the image, and the bodies go to the devotees, to
be consumed in contemplative communion. Water buffalo, sheep,
pigs, and fowl, likewise, are immolated lavishly in her worship,
and before the prohibition of human sacrifice in 1835, she received from every part of the land even richer fare. In the towering Shiva temple of Tanjore a male child was beheaded before
the altar of the goddess every Friday at the holy hour of twilight.
In the year 1830, a petty monarch of Bastar, desiring her grace,
offered on one occasion twenty-five men at her altar in Dantesh-
vari and in the sixteenth century a king of Cooch Behar immolated
a hundred and fifty in that place.[4]

In the Jaintia hills of Assam it was the custom of a certain royal
house to offer one human victim at the Durga Puja every year.
After having bathed and purified himself, the sacrifice was dressed
in new attire, daubed with red sandalwood and vermilion, arrayed
with garlands, and, thus bedecked, installed upon a raised dais
before the image, where he spent some time in meditation, repeating sacred sounds, and, when ready, made a sign with his finger.
The executioner, likewise pronouncing sacred syllables, having
elevated the sword, thereupon struck off the man's head, which
was immediately presented to the goddess on a golden plate. The

* Numbered reference notes begin on page 517.

lungs, being cooked, were consumed by yogis, and the royal family partook of a small quantity of rice steeped in the sacrificial blood. Those offered in this sacrifice were normally volunteers. However, when such were lacking, victims were kidnaped from outside the little state; and so it chanced, in 1832, that four men disappeared from the British domain, of whom one escaped to tell his tale, and the following year the kingdom was annexed—without its custom.[5]

"By one human sacrifice with proper rites, the goddess remains gratified for a thousand years," we read in the Kalika Purana, a Hindu scripture of about the tenth century A.D.; "and by the sacrifice of three men, one hundred thousand. Shiva, in his terrific aspect, as the consort of the goddess, is appeased for three thousand years by an offering of human flesh. For blood, if immediately consecrated, becomes ambrosia, and since the head and body are extremely gratifying, these should be presented in the worship of the goddess. The wise would do well to add such flesh, free from hair, to their offerings of food." [6]

In the garden of innocence where such rites can be enacted with perfect equanimity, both the victim and the sacrificial priest are able to identify their consciousness, and thereby their reality, with the inhabiting principle of the whole. They can truly say and truly feel, in the words of the Indian Bhagavad Gita, that "even as worn out clothes are cast off and others put on that are new, so worn out bodies are cast off by the dweller in the body and others put on that are new." [7]

For the West, however, the possibility of such an egoless return to a state of soul antecedent to the birth of individuality has long since passed away; and the first important stage in the branching off can be seen to have occurred in that very part of the nuclear Near East where the earliest god-kings and their courts had been for centuries ritually entombed: namely Sumer, where a new sense of the separation of the spheres of god and man began to be represented in myth and ritual about 2350 B.C. The king, then, was no longer a god, but a servant of the god, his Tenant Farmer, supervisor of the race of human slaves created to serve the gods with unremitting toil. And no longer identity, but relationship, was the paramount concern. Man had been made not to *be* God but to know, honor, and serve him; so that even the king, who, according to the earlier mythological view, had been the chief embodiment of divinity on earth, was now but a priest offering sacrifice in tendance to One above—not a god returning himself in sacrifice to Himself.

In the course of the following centuries, the new sense of separation led to a counter-yearning for return—not to identity, for such was no longer possible of conception (creator and creature were not the same), but to the presence and vision of the forfeited god. Hence the new mythology brought forth, in due time, a development away from the earlier static view of returning cycles. A progressive, temporally oriented mythology arose, of a creation, once and for all, at the beginning of time, a subsequent fall, and a work of restoration, still in progress. The world no longer was to be known as a mere showing in time of the paradigms of eternity, but as a field of unprecedented cosmic conflict between two powers, one light and one dark.

The earliest prophet of this mythology of cosmic restoration was, apparently, the Persian Zoroaster, whose dates, however, have not been securely established. They have been variously placed between c. 1200 and c. 550 B.C.,[8] so that, like Homer (of about the same span of years), he should perhaps be regarded rather as symbolic of a tradition than as specifically, or solely, one man. The system associated with his name is based on the idea of a conflict between the wise lord, Ahura Mazda, "first father of the Righteous Order, who gave to the sun and stars their path," [9] and an independent evil principle, Angra Mainyu, the Deceiver, principle of the lie, who, when all had been excellently made, entered into it in every particle. The world, consequently, is a compound wherein good and evil, light and dark, wisdom and violence, are contending for a victory. And the privilege and duty of each man—who, himself, as a part of creation, is a compound of good and evil—is to elect, voluntarily, to engage in the battle in the interest of the light. It is supposed that with the birth of Zoroaster, twelve thousand years following the creation of the world, a decisive turn was given the conflict in favor of the good, and that when he returns, after another twelve millennia, in the person of the messiah Saoshyant, there will take place a final battle and cosmic conflagration, through which the principle of darkness and the lie will be undone. Whereafter, all will be light, there will be no further history, and the Kingdom of God (Ahura Mazda) will have been established in its pristine form forever.

It is obvious that a potent mythical formula for the reorientation of the human spirit is here supplied—pitching it forward along the way of time, summoning man to an assumption of autonomous responsibility for the renovation of the universe in God's name, and thus fostering a new, potentially political (not finally contemplative) philosophy of holy war. "May we be such," runs a Persian prayer, "as those who bring on this renovation and make this world progressive, till its perfection shall have been achieved." [10]

The first historic manifestation of the force of this new mythic view was in the Achaemenian empire of Cyrus the Great (died 529 B.C.) and Darius I (reigned c. 521–486 B.C.), which in a few decades extended its domain from India to Greece, and under the protection of which the post-exilic Hebrews both rebuilt their temple (Ezra 1:1–11) and reconstructed their traditional inheritance. The second historic manifestation was in the Hebrew application of its universal message to themselves; the next was in the world mission of Christianity; and the fourth, in that of Islam.

"Enlarge the place of your tent, and let the curtains of your habitations be stretched out; hold not back, lengthen your cords and strengthen your stakes. For you will spread abroad to the right and to the left, and your descendants will possess the nations and will people the desolate cities" (Isaiah 54:2–3; c. 546–536 B.C.).

"And this gospel of the kingdom will be preached throughout the whole world as a testimony to all nations; and then the end will come" (Matthew 24:14; c. 90 A.D.).

"And slay them wherever you catch them, and turn them out from where they have turned you out; for tumult and oppression are worse than slaughter. . . . And fight them on until there is no more tumult or oppression and there prevail justice and faith in Allah; but if they cease, let there be no hostility except to those who practice oppression" (Koran 2:191, 193; c. 632 A.D.).

Two completely opposed mythologies of the destiny and virtue of man, therefore, have come together in the modern world. And they are contributing in discord to whatever new society may be in the process of formation. For, of the tree that grows in the garden where God walks in the cool of the day, the wise men westward of Iran have partaken of the fruit of the knowledge of good and evil, whereas those on the other side of that cultural divide, in India and the Far East, have relished only the fruit of eternal life. However, the two limbs, we are informed,[11] come together in the center of the garden, where they form a single tree at the base, branching out when they reach a certain height. Likewise, the two mythologies spring from one base in the Near East. And if man should taste of both fruits he would become, we have been told, as God himself (Genesis 3:22)—which is the boon that the meeting of East and West today is offering to us all.

II. The Shared Myth of the One That Became Two

The extent to which the mythologies—and therewith psychologies—of the Orient and Occident diverged in the course of the period between the dawn of civilization in the Near East and the present age of mutual rediscovery appears in their opposed versions of the shared mythological image of the first being, who was originally one but became two.

"In the beginning," states an Indian example of c. 700 B.C., preserved in the Brihadaranyaka Upanishad,

> this universe was nothing but the Self in the form of a man. It looked around and saw that there was nothing but itself, whereupon its first shout was, "It is I!"; whence the concept "I" arose. (And that is why, even now, when addressed, one answers first, "It is I!" only then giving the other name that one bears.)
> Then he was afraid. (That is why anyone alone is afraid.) But he considered: "Since there is no one here but myself, what is there to fear?" Whereupon the fear departed. (For

what should have been feared? It is only to a second that fear refers.)

However, he still lacked delight (therefore, we lack delight when alone) and desired a second. He was exactly as large as a man and woman embracing. This Self then divided itself in two parts; and with that, there were a master and a mistress. (Therefore this body, by itself, as the sage Yajnavalkya declares, is like half of a split pea. And that is why, indeed, this space is filled by a woman.)

The male embraced the female, and from that the human race arose. She, however, reflected: "How can he unite with me, who am produced from himself? Well then, let me hide!" She became a cow, he a bull and united with her; and from that cattle arose. She became a mare, he a stallion; she an ass, he a donkey and united with her; and from that solid-hoofed animals arose. She became a goat, he a buck; she a sheep, he a ram and united with her; and from that goats and sheep arose. Thus he poured forth all pairing things, down to the ants. Then he realized: "I, actually, am creation; for I have poured forth all this." Whence arose the concept "Creation" [Sanskrit *sṛṣṭiḥ:* "what is poured forth"].

Anyone understanding this becomes, truly, himself a creator in this creation.[12]

The best-known Occidental example of this image of the first being, split in two, which seem to be two but are actually one, is, of course, that of the Book of Genesis, second chapter, where it is turned, however, to a different sense. For the couple is separated here by a superior being, who, as we are told, caused a deep sleep to fall upon the man and, while he slept, took one of his ribs.[13] In the Indian version it is the god himself that divides and becomes not man alone but all creation; so that everything is a manifestation of that single inhabiting divine substance: there is no other; whereas in the Bible, God and man, from the beginning, are distinct. Man is made in the image of God, indeed, and the breath of God has been breathed into his nostrils; yet his being, his self, is not that of God, nor is it one with the universe. The fashioning of the world, of the animals, and of Adam (who then became Adam and Eve) was accomplished not within the sphere of divinity but outside of it. There is, consequently, an *intrinsic,* not merely *formal*, separation. And the goal of knowledge cannot be to *see* God here and now in all things; for God is not in things. God is transcendent. God is beheld only by the dead. The goal of knowledge has to be, rather, to know the *relationship* of God to his creation, or, more specifically, to man, and through such knowledge, by God's grace, to link one's own will back to that of the Creator.

Moreover, according to the biblical version of this myth, it was only after creation that man fell, whereas in the Indian example creation itself was a fall—the fragmentation of a god. And the god is not condemned. Rather, his creation, his "pouring forth" (*sṛṣṭiḥ*), is described as an act of voluntary, dynamic will-to-be-more, which anteceded creation and has, therefore, a metaphysical, symbolical, not literal, historical meaning. The fall of Adam and Eve was an event within the already created frame of time and space, an accident that should not have taken place. The myth of the Self in the form of a man, on the other hand, who looked around and saw nothing but himself, said "I," felt fear, and then desired to be two, tells of an intrinsic, not errant, factor in the manifold of being, the correction or undoing of which would not improve, but dissolve, creation. The Indian point of view is metaphysical, poetical; the biblical, ethical and historical.

Adam's fall and exile from the garden was thus in no sense a metaphysical departure of divine substance from itself, but an event only in the history, or pre-history, of man. And this event in the created world has been followed throughout the remainder of the book by the record of man's linkage and failures of linkage back to God—again, historically conceived. For, as we next hear, God himself, at a certain point in the course of time, out of his own volition, moved toward man, instituting a new law in the form of a covenant with a certain people. And these became, therewith, a priestly race, unique in the world. God's reconciliation with man, of whose creation he had repented (Genesis 6:6), was to be achieved only by virtue of this particular community— in time: for in time there should take place the realization of the Lord God's kingdom on earth, when the heathen monarchies would crumble and Israel be saved, when men would "cast forth their idols of silver and their idols of gold, which they made to themselves to worship, to the moles and to the bats." [14]

> Be broken, you peoples, and be dismayed;
>   give ear, all you far countries;
> gird yourselves and be dismayed;
>   gird yourselves and be dismayed.
> Take counsel together, but it will come to nought;
>   speak a word, but it will not stand,
>   for God is with us.[15]

In the Indian view, on the contrary, what is divine here is divine there also; nor has anyone to wait—or even to hope—for a "day of the Lord." For what has been lost is in each his very self (*ātman*), here and now, requiring only to be sought. Or, as they say: "Only when men shall roll up space like a piece of leather will there be an end of sorrow apart from knowing God." [16]

The question arises (again historical) in the world dominated by the Bible, as to the identity of the favored community, and three are well known to have developed claims: the Jewish, the Christian, and the Moslem, each supposing itself to have been authorized by a particular revelation. God, that is to say, though conceived as outside of history and not himself its substance (transcendent: not immanent), is supposed to have engaged himself miraculously in the enterprise of restoring fallen man through a covenant, sacrament, or revealed book, with a view to a general, communal experience of fulfillment yet to come. The world is corrupt and man a sinner; the individual, however, through engagement along with God in the destiny of the only authorized community, participates in the coming glory of the kingdom of righteousness, when "the glory of the Lord shall be revealed, and all flesh shall see it together." [17]

In the experience and vision of India, on the other hand, although the holy mystery and power have been understood to be indeed transcendent ("other than the known; moreover, above the unknown"),[18] they are also, at the same time, immanent ("like a razor in a razorcase, like fire in tinder").[19] It is not that the divine is every*where:* it is that the divine is every*thing.* So that one does not require any outside reference, revelation, sacrament, or authorized community to return to it. One has but to alter one's psychological orientation and recognize (re-cognize) what is within. Deprived of this recognition, we are removed from our own reality by a cerebral shortsightedness which is called in Sanskrit *māyā*, "delusion" (from the verbal root *mā*, "to measure, measure out, to form, to build," denoting, in the first place, the power of a god or demon to produce illusory effects, to change form, and to appear under deceiving masks; in the second place, "magic," the production of illusions and, in warfare, camouflage, deceptive tactics; and finally, in philosophical discourse, the illusion superimposed upon reality as an effect of ignorance). Instead of the biblical exile from a geographically, historically conceived garden wherein God walked in the cool of the day,[20] we have in India, therefore, already c. 700 B.C. (some three hundred years before the putting together of the Pentateuch), a *psychological* reading of the great theme.

The shared myth of the primal androgyne is applied in the two traditions to the same task—the exposition of man's distance, in his normal secular life, from the divine Alpha and Omega. Yet the arguments radically differ, and therefore support two radically different civilizations. For, if man has been removed from the divine through a historical event, it will be a historical event that leads him back, whereas if it has been by some sort of psychological displacement that he has been blocked, psychology will be his vehicle of return. And so it is that in India the final focus of concern is not the community (though, as we shall see, the idea of the holy community plays a formidable role as a disciplinary force), but yoga.

III. The Two Views of Ego

The Indian term *yoga* is derived from the Sanskrit verbal root *yuj*, "to link, join, or unite," which is related etymologically to "yoke," a yoke of oxen, and is in sense analogous to the word "religion" (Latin *re-ligio*), "to link back, or bind." Man, the creature, is by religion bound back to God. However, religion, *religio*, refers to a linking historically conditioned by way of a covenant, sacrament, or Koran, whereas yoga is the psychological linking of the mind to that superordinated principle "by which the mind knows." [21] Furthermore, in yoga what is linked is finally the self to itself, consciousness to consciousness; for what had seemed, through *māyā,* to be two are in reality not so; whereas in religion what are linked are God and man, which are not the same.

It is of course true that in the popular religions of the Orient the gods are worshiped as though external to their devotees, and all the rules and rites of a covenanted relationship are observed. Nevertheless, the ultimate realization, which the sages have celebrated, is that the god worshiped as though without is in reality a reflex of the same mystery as oneself. As long as an illusion of ego remains, the commensurate illusion of a separate deity also will be there; and vice versa, as long as the idea of a separate deity is cherished, an illusion of ego, related to it in love, fear, worship, exile, or atonement, will also be there. But precisely that illusion of duality is the trick of *māyā.* "Thou art that" (*tat tvam asi*) [22] is the proper thought for the first step to wisdom.

In the beginning, as we have read, there was only the Self; but it said "I" (Sanskrit, *aham*) and immediately felt fear, after which, desire.

It is to be remarked that in this view of the instant of creation (presented from within the sphere of the psyche of the creative being itself) the same two basic motivations are identified as the leading modern schools of depth analysis have indicated for the *human* psyche: aggression and desire. Carl G. Jung, in his early paper on *The Unconscious in Normal and Pathological Psychology* (1916),[23] wrote of two psychological types: the introvert, harried by fear, and the extrovert, driven by desire. Sigmund Freud also, in his *Beyond the Pleasure Principle* (1920),[24] wrote of "the death wish" and "the life wish": on the one hand, the will to violence and the fear of it (*thanatos, destrudo*), and, on the other hand, the need and desire to love and be loved (*eros, libido*). Both spring spontaneously from the deep dark source of the energies of the psyche, the *id,* and are governed, therefore, by the self-centered "pleasure principle": *I* want: *I* am afraid. Comparably, in the Indian myth, as soon as the self said "I" (*aham*), it knew first fear, and then desire.

But now—and here, I believe, is a point of fundamental importance for our reading of the basic difference between the Oriental and Occidental approaches to the cultivation of the soul—in the Indian myth the principle of ego, "I" (*aham*), is identified completely with the pleasure principle, whereas in the psychologies of both Freud and Jung its proper function is to know and relate to external reality (Freud's "reality principle"): not the reality of the metaphysical but that of the physical, empirical sphere of time and space. In other words, spiritual maturity, as understood in the modern Occident, requires a differentiation of *ego* from *id,* whereas in the Orient, throughout the history at least of every teaching that has stemmed from India, ego (*aham-kāra:* "the making of the sound 'I' ") is impugned as the principle of libidinous delusion, to be dissolved.

Let us glance at the wonderful story of the Buddha in the episode of his attainment of the goal of all goals beneath the "tree of awakening," the Bo- or Bodhi-tree (*bodhi,* "awakening").

The Blessed One, alone, accompanied only by his own resolve, with his mind fixed only on attainment, rose up like a lion at nightfall, at the time when flowers close, and, proceeding along a road that the gods had hung with banners, strode toward the Bodhi-tree. Snakes, gnomes, birds, divine musicians, and other beings of numerous variety did him worship with perfumes, flowers, and other offerings, while the choirs of the heavens poured forth celestial music; so that the ten thousand worlds were filled with delightful scents, garlands, and shouts of acclaim.

And there happened to come, just then, from the opposite direction, a grass-cutter named Sotthiya, bearing a burden of cut grass, and when he saw the Great Being, that he was a holy man, he presented to him eight handfuls. Whereafter, coming to the Bodhi-tree, the one who was about to become the Buddha stood on the southern side and faced north. Instantly the southern half of the world sank until it seemed to touch the lowest hell, while the northern rose to the highest heaven.

"Methinks," then said the Buddha-to-be, "this cannot be the

place for the attainment of supreme wisdom"; and walking round the tree with his right side toward it, he came to the western side and faced east. Thereupon, the western half of the world sank until it seemed to touch the lowest hell, while the eastern half rose to the highest heaven. Indeed, wherever the Blessed One stood, the broad earth rose and fell, as though it were a huge cartwheel lying on its hub and someone were treading on the rim.

"Methinks," said the Buddha-to-be, "this also cannot be the place for the attainment of supreme wisdom"; and walking further, with his right side toward the tree, he came to the northern side and faced south. Then the northern half of the world sank until it seemed to touch the lowest hell, while the southern half rose to the highest heaven.

"Methinks," said the Buddha-to-be, "this also cannot be the place for the attainment of supreme wisdom"; and walking round the tree with his right side toward it, he came to the eastern side and faced west.

Now it is on the eastern side of their Bodhi-trees that all the Buddhas have sat down, cross-legged, and that side neither trembles nor quakes.

Then the Great Being saying to himself, "This is the Immovable Spot on which all the Buddhas have established themselves: this is the place for destroying passion's net," he took hold of his handful of grass by one end and shook it out there. And straightway the blades of grass formed themselves into a seat fourteen cubits long, of such symmetry of shape as not even the most skillful painter or carver could design.

The Buddha-to-be, turning his back to the trunk of the Bodhi-tree, faced east, and making the mighty resolution, "Let my skin, sinews, and bones become dry, and welcome; and let all the flesh and blood of my body dry up; but never from this seat will I stir until I have attained the supreme and absolute wisdom!" he sat himself down cross-legged in an unconquerable position, from which not even the descent of a hundred thunderbolts at once could have dislodged him.[25]

Having departed from his palace, wife, and child some years before, to seek the knowledge that should release all beings from sorrow, the prince Gautama Shakyamuni had come thus at last to the midpoint, the supporting point, of the universe—which is described here in mythological terms, lest it should be taken for a physical place to be sought somewhere on earth. For its location is psychological. It is that point of balance in the mind from which the universe can be perfectly regarded: the still-standing point of disengagement around which all things turn. To man's secular view, things appear to move in time and to be in their final character concrete. I am here, you are there: right and left; up, down; life and death. The pairs of opposites are all around, and the wheel of the world, the wheel of time, is ever revolving, with our lives engaged in its round. However, there is an all-supporting midpoint, a hub where the opposites come together, like the spokes of a wheel, in emptiness. And it is there, facing east (the world direction of the new day), that the Buddhas of past, present, and future—who are of one Buddhahood, though manifest in series in the mode of time—are said to have experienced absolute illumination.

The prince Gautama Shakyamuni, established in his mind in that spot and about to penetrate the last mystery of being, was now to be assailed by the lord of the life illusion: that same self-in-the-form-of-a-man who, before the beginning of time, looked around and saw nothing but himself, said "I," and immediately experienced first fear, and then desire. Mythologically represented, this same Being of all beings appeared before the Buddha-to-be, first as a prince, bearing a flowery bow, in his character as Eros, Desire (Sanskrit *kāma*), and then as a frightening maharaja of demons, charging on a bellowing war-elephant, King Thanatos (Sanskrit *māra*), King Death.

"The one who is called in the world the Lord Desire," we read in a celebrated Sanskrit version of the Buddha-Life, composed by one of the earliest masters of the so-called "poetic" (*kāvya*) style of literary composition, a learned Brahmin who had been converted to the Buddhist Order, Ashvaghosha by name (fl. c. 100 A.D.),

the owner of the flowery shafts who is also called the Lord Death and is the final foe of spiritual disengagement, summoning before himself his three attractive sons, namely,

Mental-Confusion, Gaiety, and Pride, and his voluptuous daughters, Lust, Delight, and Pining, sent them before the Blessed One. Taking up his flowery bow and his five infatuating arrows, which are named Exciter of the Paroxysm of Desire, Gladdener, Infatuator, Parcher, and Carrier of Death, he followed his brood to the foot of the tree where the Great Being was sitting. Toying with an arrow, the god showed himself and addressed the calm seer who was there making the ferry passage to the farther shore of the ocean of being.

"Up, up, O noble prince!" he ordered, with a voice of divine authority. "Recall the duties of your caste and abandon this dissolute quest for disengagement. The mendicant life is ill suited for anyone born of a noble house; but rather, by devotion to the duties of your caste, you are to serve the order of the good society, maintain the laws of the revealed religion, combat wickedness in the world, and merit thereby a residence in the highest heaven as a god."

The Blessed One failed to move.

"You will not rise?" then said the god. He fixed an arrow to his bow. "If you are stubborn, stiff-necked, and abide by your resolve, this arrow that I am notching to my string, which has already inflamed the sun itself, shall be let fly. It is already darting out its tongue at you, like a serpent." And, threatening, without result, he released the shaft—without result.

For the Blessed One, by virtue of innumerable acts of boundless giving throughout innumerable lifetimes, had dissolved within his mind the concept "I" (*aham*), and along with it the correlative experience of any "thou" (*tvam*). In the void of the Immovable Spot, beneath the tree of the knowledge beyond the pairs-of-opposites beyond life and death, good and evil, as well as beyond I and thou, had he so much as thought "I" he would have felt "they," and, beholding the voluptuous daughters of the god who were displaying themselves attractively before him as objects in the field of a subject, he would have been, to say the least, required to control himself. However, there being no "I" present to his mind, there was no "they" there either. Absolutely unmoved, because himself absolutely not there, perfectly established on the Immovable Spot in the unconquerable (psychological) position of all the Buddhas, the Blessed One was impervious to the sharp shaft.

And the god, perceiving that his flowery stroke had failed, said to himself: "He does not notice even the arrow that set the sun aflame! Can he be destitute of sense? He is worthy neither of my flowery shaft, nor of my daughters: let me send against him my army."

And immediately putting off his infatuating aspect as the Lord Desire, that great god became the Lord Death, and around him an army of demonic forms crystallized, wearing frightening shapes and bearing in their hands bows and arrows, darts, clubs, swords, trees, and even blazing mountains; having the visages of boars, fish, horses, camels, asses, tigers, bears, lions and elephants; one-eyed, multi-faced, three-headed, pot-bellied, and with speckled bellies; equipped with claws, equipped with tusks, some bearing headless bodies in their hands, many with half-mutilated faces, monstrous mouths, knobby knees, and the reek of goats; copper red, some clothed in leather, others wearing nothing at all, with fiery or smoke-colored hair, many with long, pendulous ears, having half their faces white, others having half their bodies green; red and smoke-colored, yellow and black; with arms longer than the reach of serpents, their girdles jingling with bells: some as tall as palms, bearing spears, some of a child's size with projecting teeth; some with the bodies of birds and faces of rams, or men's bodies and the faces of cats; with disheveled hair, with topknots, or half bald; with frowning or triumphant faces, wasting one's strength or fascinating one's mind. Some sported in the sky, others went along the tops of trees; many danced upon each other, more leaped about wildly on the ground. One, dancing, shook a trident; another crashed his club; one like a bull bounded for joy; another blazed out flames from every hair. And then there were some who stood around to frighten him with many lolling tongues, many mouths, savage, sharply pointed teeth, upright ears, like spikes, and eyes like the disk of the sun. Others, leaping into the sky, flung rocks, trees, and axes, blazing straw as voluminous as mountain peaks, showers of embers, serpents of fire, showers of stones.

And all the time, a naked woman bearing in her hand a skull, flittered about, unsettled, staying not in any spot, like the mind of a distracted student over sacred texts.

But lo! amidst all these terrors, sights, sounds, and odors, the mind of the Blessed One was no more shaken than the wits of Garuda, the golden-feathered sun-bird, among crows. And a voice cried from the sky: "O Mara, take not upon thyself this vain fatigue! Put aside thy malice and go in peace! For though fire may one day give up its heat, water its fluidity, earth solidity; never will this Great Being, who acquired the merit that brought him to this tree through many lifetimes in unnumbered eons, abandon his resolution."

And the god, Mara, discomfited, together with his army, disappeared. Heaven, luminous with the light of the full moon, then shone like the smile of a maid, showering flowers, the petals of flowers, bouquets of flowers, freshly wet with dew, on the Blessed One; who, that night, during the remainder of the night, in the first watch of that wonderful night, acquired the knowledge of his previous existence, in the second watch acquired the divine eye, in the last watch fathomed the law of Dependent Origination, and at sunrise attained omniscience.

The earth quaked in its delight, like a woman thrilled. The gods descended from every side to worship the Blessed One that was now the Buddha, the Wake. "O glory to thee, illuminate hero among men," they sang, as they walked around him in reverential sunwise ambulation. And the daemons of the earth, even the sons and daughters of Mara, the deities who roam the sky and those that walk the ground—all arrived. And after worshiping the victor with the various forms of homage suitable to their stations, they returned, radiant with a new rapture, to their sundry abodes.[26]

In sum: the Buddha in his dissolution of the sense of "I" had moved in consciousness back past the motivation of creation— which, however, did not mean that he had ceased to live. Indeed, he was to remain half a century longer within the world of time and space, participating with irony in the void of this manifold, seeing duality yet knowing it to be deceptive, compassionately teaching what cannot be taught to others who were not really other.

For there is no way to communicate an experience in words to those who have not already had the experience—or at least something somewhat like it, to be referred to by analogy. Furthermore, where there is no ego, there is no "other"—either to be feared, to be desired, or to be taught.

In the classic Indian doctrine of the four ends for which men are supposed to live and strive—love and pleasure (*kāma*), power and success (*artha*), lawful order and moral virtue (*dharma*), and, finally, release from delusion (*mokṣa*)—we note that the first two are manifestations of what Freud has termed "the pleasure principle," primary urges of the natural man, epitomized in the formula "I want." In the adult, according to the Oriental view, these are to be quelled and checked by the principles of *dharma,* which, in the classic Indian system, are impressed upon the individual by the training of his caste. The infantile "I want" is to be subdued by a "thou shalt," socially applied (not individually determined), which is supposed to be as much a part of the immutable cosmic order as the course of the sun itself.

Now it is to be observed that in the version just presented of the temptation of the Buddha, the Antagonist represents all three of the first triad of ends (the so-called *trivarga:* "aggregate of three"); for in his character as the Lord Desire he personifies the first; as the Lord Death, the aggressive force of the second; while in his summons to the meditating sage to arise and return to the duties of his station in society, he promotes the third. And, indeed, as a manifestation of that Self which not only poured forth but permanently supports the universe, he is the proper incarnation of these ends. For they do, in fact, support the world. And in most of the rites of all religions, this triune god, we may say, in one aspect or another, is the one and only god adored.

However, in the name and achievement of the Buddha, the "Illuminated One," the fourth end is announced: release from delusion. And to the attainment of this, the others are impediments, difficult to remove, yet, for one of purpose, not invincible. Sitting at the world navel, pressing back through the welling creative force that was surging into and through his own being, the Buddha actually broke back into the void beyond, and—ironically

—the universe immediately burst into bloom. Such an act of self-noughting is one of individual effort. There can be no question about that. However, an Occidental eye cannot but observe that there is no requirement or expectation anywhere in this Indian system of four ends—neither in the primary two of the natural organism and the impressed third of society, nor in the exalted fourth of release—for a maturation of the personality through intelligent, fresh, individual adjustment to the time-space world round about, creative experimentation with unexplored possibilities, and the assumption of personal responsibility for unprecedented acts performed within the context of the social order. In the Indian tradition all has been perfectly arranged from all eternity. There can be nothing new, nothing to be learned but what the sages have taught from of yore. And finally, when the boredom of this nursery horizon of "I want" against "thou shalt" has become insufferable, the fourth and final aim is all that is offered—of an extinction of the infantile ego altogether: disengagement or release (*mokṣa*) from both "I" and "thou."

In the European West, on the other hand, where the fundamental doctrine of the freedom of the will essentially dissociates each individual from every other, as well as from both the will in nature and the will of God, there is placed upon each the responsibility of coming intelligently, out of his own experience and volition, to some sort of relationship with—not identity with or extinction in—the all, the void, the suchness, the absolute, or whatever the proper term may be for that which is beyond terms. And, in the secular sphere likewise, it is normally expected that an educated ego should have developed away from the simple infantile polarity of the pleasure and obedience principles toward a personal, uncompulsive, sensitive relationship to empirical reality, a certain adventurous attitude toward the unpredictable, and a sense of personal responsibility for decisions. Not life as a good soldier, but life as a developed, unique individual, is the ideal. And we shall search the Orient in vain for anything quite comparable. There the ideal, on the contrary, is the quenching, not development, of ego. That is the formula turned this way and that, up and down the line, throughout the literature: a systematic, steady, continually drumming devaluation of the "I" principle, the reality function—which has remained, consequently, undeveloped, and so, wide open to the seizures of completely uncritical mythic identifications.

IV. The Two Ways of India and the Far East

Turning from India to the Far East, we read in the opening lines of the Tao Te Ching, "The Book (*ching*) of the Virtue or Power (*tê*) of the Way (*tao*)":

The Tao that can be discussed is not the enduring eternal Tao;
The name that can be named is not the enduring, eternal name.

From the unnamed sprang heaven and earth;
The named is the Mother of the ten thousand things.

Verily: Only he that is desireless can discern the secret essences.
Unrelieved of desire, we see only shells.[27]

The word *tao*, "the way, the path," is in as much equivalent to *dharma* as it refers to the law, truth, or order of the universe, which is the law, truth, order, and way of each being and thing within it, according to kind. "It means a road, path, way," writes Mr. Arthur Waley; "and hence, the way in which one does something; method, principle, doctrine. The Way of Heaven, for example, is ruthless; when autumn comes 'no leaf is spared because of its beauty, no flower because of its fragrance.' The Way of Man means, among other things, procreation; and eunuchs are said to be 'far from the Way of Man,' *Chu Tao* is 'the way to be a monarch,' i.e. the art of ruling. Each school of philosophy had its *tao*, its doctrine of the way in which life should be ordered. Finally in a particular school of philosophy whose followers ultimately came to be called Taoists, *tao* meant 'the way the universe works'; and ultimately, something very like God, in the more abstract and philosophical sense of that term." [28]

The Sanskrit equivalent certainly is *dharma,* from the root *dhṛ,* meaning to hold up, support, carry, bear, sustain, or maintain. *Dharma* is the order that supports the universe, and therewith every being and thing within it according to kind. And as the

Tao Te Ching has said of the *tao,* so say the Indians of *dharma:* its yonder side is beyond definition; its hither side is the mother, support, and bearer of all things.

The Chinese diagram symbolic of the *tao* represents geometrically an interplay of two principles: the *yang,* the light, masculine or active, hot, dry, beneficent, positive principle; and its opposite, the *yin,* dark, feminine, passive, cold, moist, malignant, and negative. They are enclosed in a circle of which each occupies half, representing the moment (which is forever) when they generate the ten thousand things:

"The separating line of this figure," as Professor Marcel Granet has observed, "which winds like a serpent up one diameter, is composed of two half-circumferences, each having a diameter equal to half that of the large circle. *This line therefore is equal to one half-circumference.* The outline of the *yin,* like that of the *yang,* is equal to the outline around both. And if one now draws, instead of the separating line, a line composed of four half-circumferences with diameters half again as large, these will still be equal to one half-circumference of the main circle. Furthermore, it will always be the same if the operation is continued, and the winding line meanwhile will be approaching and tending to coalesce with the diameter. Three will be coalescing with two. . . . In the Sung period [1127–1279 A.D.] this diagram was considered to be a sign of the phases of the moon." [29]

What this diagram represents geometrically is the mystery of the one circumference that becomes two and yields, then, the ten thousand things of creation. The unnamed, ineffable, yonder aspect of the same mystery, on the other hand, is represented simply by a circle:

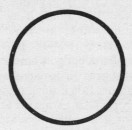

In all things the *yang* and *yin* are present. They are not to be separated; nor can they be judged morally as either good or evil. Functioning together, in perpetual interaction, now the one, now the other is uppermost. In man the *yang* preponderates, in woman the *yin*—yet in each are both. And their interaction is the universe of the "ten thousand things." So that we read, next, in the Tao Te Ching:

> In source, these two are the same, though in name different;
> The source we call the Great Mystery:
> And of the Mystery the yet darker Mystery is the portal of all
>   secret essences.[30]

It is surely obvious that this Chinese conception of the one beyond names, which, becoming two, produced of itself the ten thousand things and is therefore within each as the law—the *tao,* the way, the sense, the order and substance—of its being, is a conception much closer to the Indian than to the biblical view of the one that became two. The symbol of the *tao* provides an image of the dual state of Adam before Eve was separated from his side. However, in contrast with the biblical figure and in harmony with the Indian of the Self that split in two, the *tao* is immanent as well as transcendent: it is the secret essence of all things, yet the darkest mystery.

Moreover, in the Far East as well as in India, the art of meditation as a way to recognition of the mystery has been practiced, apparently, from of old. "We know," states Mr. Waley, that many different schools of Quietism existed in China in the fourth and third centuries before Christ. Of their literature only a small part survives. Earliest in date was what I shall call the School of Ch'i. Its doctrine was called *hsin shu,* "The Art of the Mind." By "mind" is meant not the brain or the heart, but "a mind within the mind" that bears to the economy of man the same relation as the sun bears to the sky.[31] It is the ruler of the body, whose component parts are its ministers.[32] It must remain serene and immovable like a monarch upon his throne. It is a *shen,* a divinity, that will only take up its abode where all is garnished and swept. The place that man prepares for it is called its temple (*kung*). "Throw open the gates, put self aside, bide in silence, and the radiance of the spirit shall come in and make its home." [33] And a little later: "Only where all is clean will the spirit abide. All men desire to know, but they do not enquire into that whereby one knows." And again: "What a man desires to know is *that* (i.e. the external world). But his means of knowing is *this* (i.e. himself). How can he know *that?* Only by the perfection of *this.*" [34]

Thus we find a native Chinese counterpart not only of the Indian myth of the one that became two, but also of the method by which the mind is readied for reunion with the one. However, and even though with the coming of Buddhism to China in the first century A.D. an almost overwhelming transformation of the mythologies and rituals of the Far East was effected, there is always manifest in the two civilizations of the Pacific—the Japanese, no less than the Chinese—a cultural, spiritual stance very different from that of their Indian master, who, when sitting, as we have seen, cross-legged beneath the Bodhi-tree in an unconquerable position, "broke the roof beam of the house and passed in consciousness to the void beyond." [35]

The classical Indian work on the rudiments of yoga is the Yoga Sutra, "Guiding Thread to Yoga," of the legendary saint and sage Patanjali—who is supposed to have dropped (*pata*) in the form of a small snake from heaven into the hands of another saint, Panini, as the palms were being brought together in the posture of worship (*añjali*).[36] The word *sūtra,* meaning "thread," etymologically related to our English "suture," connotes throughout the Orient a type of extremely concise handbook summarizing the rudiments of a discipline or doctrine, to which commentaries greatly swelling the bulk have been added by later writers. In the Yoga Sutra the basic text is a very thin thread of only one hundred and ninety-five brief sentences supporting a prodigious mass of such commentary, the two most important layers of which are: 1. "The Elucidation of Yoga" (*Yoga-bhāsya*), which is supposed to have been composed in prehistoric times by the legendary author of the Mahabharata, the poet Vyasa, of whose miraculous birth and life we shall read in a later chapter, but which is far more likely to have been written c. 350–650 A.D., or even later; [37] and 2. "The Science of Reality" (*Tattva-vaiśrādī*), by a certain Vachaspatimishra, who appears to have flourished c. 850 A.D.[38] The firm thin thread itself has been variously dated by modern scholarship anywhere from the second century B.C.[39] to the fifth A.D.; [40] but since the disciplines that it codifies were known to both the Buddha (563–483 B.C.) and the Jain savior Mahavira (died c. 485 B.C.) and seem even to have been practiced before the coming of the Aryans,* all that can be said is that no matter what the dates of this problematical document may be, both its aim and its means are of indeterminable age.

The key to the art is presented in the opening aphorism: *yogaś cittavṛtti-nirodhyaḥ:* "Yoga is the (intentional) stopping of the spontaneous activity of the mind stuff." [41]

The archaic psychological theory implied in this definition holds that within the *gross* matter of the brain and body there is an extremely volatile *subtle* substance, continually active, which assumes the forms of everything presented to it by the senses, and that by virtue of the transformations of this subtle matter we become aware of the forms, sounds, tastes, odors, and pressures of the outer world. Furthermore, the mind is in a continuous ripple of transformation—and with such force that if one should try without yogic training to hold it to a single image or idea for as long, say, as a minute, almost immediately it would be seen to have already broken from the point and run off into associated, even remote, streams of thought and feeling. The first aim of yoga,

* Cf. infra, pp. 168–70.

therefore, is to gain control of this spontaneous flow, slow it down, and bring it to a stop.

The analogy is given of the surface of a pond blown by a wind. The images reflected on such a surface are broken, fragmentary, and continually flickering. But if the wind should cease and the surface become still—*nirvāṇa:* "beyond or without (*nir-*) the wind (*vāṇa*)"—we should behold, not broken images, but the perfectly formed reflection of the whole sky, the trees along the shore, the quiet depths of the pond itself, its lovely sandy bottom, and the fish. We should then see that all the broken images, formerly only fleetingly perceived, were actually but fragments of these true and steady forms, now clearly and steadily beheld. And we should have at our command thereafter both the possibility of stilling the pond, to enjoy the fundamental form, and that of letting the winds blow and waters ripple, for the enjoyment of the play (*līlā*) of the transformations. One is no longer afraid when this comes and that goes; not even when the form that seems to be oneself disappears. For the One that is all, forever remains: transcendent—beyond all; yet also immanent—within all. Or, as we read in a Chinese text about contemporary with the Yoga Sutra:

The True Men of old knew nothing either of the love of life or of the hatred of death. Entrance into life occasioned them no joy; the exit from it awakened no resistance. Composedly they went and came. They did not forget what their beginning had been, and they did not inquire into what their end would be. They accepted their life and rejoiced in it; they forgot all fear of death and returned to their state before life. Thus there was in them what is called the want of any mind to resist the Tao, and of all attempts by means of the Human to assist the Heavenly. Such were they who are called True Men. Being such, their minds were free from all thought; their demeanor was still and unmoved; their foreheads beamed simplicity. Whatever coldness came from them was like that of autumn; whatever warmth came from them was like that of spring. Their joy and anger assimilated to what we see in the four seasons. They did in regard to all things what was suitable, and no one could know how far their action would go.[42]

But whereas the usual point of view and goal of the Indian has always been typically that of the yogi striving for an experience of the water stilled, the Chinese and Japanese have tended, rather, to rock with the ripple of the waves. Compared with any of the basic theological or scientific systems of the West, the two views are clearly of a kind; however, compared with each other in their own terms, they show a diametric contrast: the Indian, bursting the shell of being, dwells in rapture in the void of eternity, which is at once beyond and within, whereas the Chinese or Japanese, satisfied that the Great Emptiness indeed is the Mover of all things, allows things to move and, neither fearing nor desiring, allowing his own life to move with them, participates in the rhythm of the Tao.

> Great, it passes on.
> Passing on, it becomes remote.
> Having become remote, it returns.
> Therefore the Tao is great; Heaven is great.
> Earth is great; and the sagely King is also great.
> Man's law is from the Earth; the Earth's from Heaven;
>   Heaven's from the Tao.
> And the law of the Tao is its being what it is.[43]

Instead of making all stand still, the Far Eastern sage allows things to move in the various ways of their spontaneous arising, going with them, as it were, in a kind of dance, "acting without action." Whereas the Indian tends to celebrate the catalepsy of the void:

> For me, abiding in my own glory:
>   Where is past, where is future,
>   Where is present,
>   Where is space,
>   Or where even is eternity? [44]

These, then, are the signatures of the two major provinces of the Orient, and although, as we shall see, India has had its days of joy in the ripple of the waves and the Far East has cocked its ear to the song of the depth beyond depths, nevertheless, in the main, the two views have been, respectively, "All is illusion: let it go," and "All is in order: let it come"; in India, enlightenment (*samādhi*) with the eyes closed; in Japan, enlightenment (*satori*) with the eyes open. The word *mokṣa,* release, has been applied to both, but they are not the same.

v. The Two Loyalties of Europe and the Levant

Turning our eyes briefly, now, to the West, where a theology derived largely from the Levant has been grafted upon the consciousness of Europe, as in the Orient the doctrine of the Buddha upon that of the Far East, we find again that the fusion has not been without flaw. Indeed, the flaw here, which was apparent from the start, has now widened to a full and vivid gap. And the preparation for this breach we may see already illustrated in a variant—once again—of the mythological image of the first being that became two: the version in the *Symposium* of Plato.

The reader recalls the allegorical, humorously turned anecdote, attributed to Aristophanes, of the earliest human beings, who, in the beginning, were each as large as two are now. They had four hands and feet, back and sides forming a circle, one head with two faces, two privy members, and the rest to correspond. And the gods Zeus and Apollo, fearful of their strength, cut them in two, like apples halved for pickling, or as you might divide an egg with a hair. But those divided parts, each desiring the other, came together and embraced, and would have perished of hunger had the gods not set them far apart. The lesson reads: that "human nature was originally one and we were a whole, and the desire and pursuit of the whole is called love. . . . And if we are friends of God and reconciled to him we shall find our own true loves, which rarely happens in this world." Whereas, "if we are not obedient to the gods there is a danger that we shall be split up again and go about in basso-relievo." [45]

As in the biblical version of the image, the being here split in two is not the ultimate divinity itself. We are again securely in the West, where God and man are separate, and the problem, once again, is of relationship. However, a number of contrasts are to be noted between the Greek and Hebrew mythological accents; for "Greek theology," as F. M. Cornford has observed, "was not formulated by priests nor even by prophets, but by artists, poets and philosophers. . . . There was no priestly class guarding from innovating influence a sacred tradition enshrined in a sacred book. There were no divines who could successfully claim to dictate the terms of belief from an inexpugnable fortress of authority." [46] The mythology, consequently, remains fluid, as poetry; and the gods are not literally concretized, like Yahweh in the garden, but are known to be just what they are: personifications brought into being by the human creative imagination. They are realities, in as much as they represent forces both of the macrocosm and of the microcosm, the world without and the world within. However, in as much as they are known only by reflection in the mind, they partake of the faults of that medium—and this fact is perfectly well known to the Greek poets, as it is known to all poets (though not, it would appear, to priests and prophets). The Greek tales of the gods are playful, humorous, at once presenting and dismissing the images; lest the mind, fixed upon them in awe, should fail to go past them to the ultimately unknown, only partially intuited, realities and reality that they reflect.

From the version of the myth of the one that became two presented in the *Symposium,* we learn that the gods were afraid of the first men. So terrible was their might, and so great the thoughts of their hearts, that they made an attack upon the gods, dared to scale heaven, and would even have laid hands upon the gods. And those gods were in confusion; for if they annihilated the men with thunderbolts, there would be an end of sacrifice and the gods themselves would expire for lack of worship.

The ironic lesson of this moment of heavenly indecision is of the mutual dependency of God and man, as, respectively, the known and the knower of the known—which is a relationship in which not all the initiative and creativity is on one side. Throughout the religions of the Levant this relativity of the idea of God to the needs, capacity, and active service of the worshiper seems never to have been understood, or, if understood, conceded; for there, God, however conceived—whether as Ahura Mazda, Yahweh, the Trinity, or Allah—has always been supposed to be, in that particular character, absolute, and the one right God for all, whereas among the Greeks, in their high period, such literalism and impudence were inconceivable.

Moreover, in relation to whatever conflict of values might arise between the inhuman, cosmic forces symbolized in the figures of the gods and the highest principles of humanity represented in their heroes, the loyalty and sympathy of the Greeks, typically, were on the side of man. It is true that the boldest, greatest thoughts of the human heart inevitably come against the cosmic counterforce, so that there is ever present the danger of being cut in half. Wherefore, prudence is to be observed, lest we should go next in basso-relievo. However, never do we hear from the Greek side any such fundamental betrayal of the human cause as is normal and even required in the Levant. The words of the sorely beaten, "blameless and upright" Job, addressed to a god who had "destroyed him without cause," [47] may be taken to represent the pious, submissive, priestly ideal of all of the great religions of that zone. "Behold, I am of small account. . . . I lay my hand upon my mouth. . . . I know that thou canst do all things. . . . I despise myself and repent in dust and ashes." [48] The Greek Prometheus, in contrast, likewise terribly tortured by a god who could fill the head of Leviathan with harpoons, yet standing by his human judgment of the being responsible for this torment, shouts, when ordered to capitulate: "I care less than nothing for Zeus. Let him do what he likes." [49]

On the one hand: the power of God who is great, against whom all such merely human categories break as mercy, justice, goodness, and love; and, on the other: the titanic builder of the City of Man, who has stolen heavenly fire, courageous and willing to bring upon himself the responsibility of his own decisions. These are the two discordant great themes of what may be termed the orthodox Occidental mythological structure: the poles of experience of an ego set apart from nature, maturing values of its own, which are not those of the given world, yet still projecting on the universe a notion of anthropomorphic fatherhood—as though it should ever have possessed, or might ever come to possess, either in itself or in its metaphysical ground, the values, sensibilities and intelligence, decency and nobility of a man!

Whereas in the greater Orient of India and the Far East, such a conflict of man and God, as though the two were separate from each other, would be thought simply absurd. For what is referred to there by the terms that we translate "God" is not the mere mask that is defined in scripture and may appear before the meditating mind, but the mystery—at once immanent and transcendent—of the ultimate depth of man's own being, consciousness of being, and delight therein.

vi. The Age of Comparison

When the bold square-riggers of the West, about 1500 A.D., bearing in their hulls the seeds of a new, titanic age, were coming to port, sails furled to yardarms, along the coasts not only of America but also of India and Cathay, there were flowering in the Old World the four developed civilizations of Europe and the Levant, India and the Far East, each in its mythology regarding itself as the one authorized center, under heaven, of spirituality and worth. We know today that those mythologies are undone—or, at least, are threatening to come undone: each complacent within its own horizon, dissolving, together with its gods, in a single emergent new order of society, wherein, as Nietzsche prophesied in a volume dedicated to the Free Spirit, "the various world views, manners, and cultures are to be compared and experienced side by side, in a way that formerly was impossible when the always localized sway of each culture accorded with the roots in place and time of its own artistic style. An intensified aesthetic sensibility, now at last, will decide among the many forms presenting themselves for comparison: and the majority will be let die. In the same way, a selection among the forms and usages of the higher moralities is occurring, the end of which can be only the downfall of the inferior systems. It is an age of comparison! That is its pride—but more justly also its grief. Let us not be afraid of this grief!" [50]

The four representatives, respectively, of human reason and the responsible individual; supernatural revelation and the one true community under God, yogic arrest in the immanent great void, and spontaneous accord with the way of earth and heaven—Prometheus, Job, the seated Buddha, eyes closed, and the wandering Sage, eyes open—from the four directions, have been brought together. And it is time, now, to regard each in its puerility, as well as in its majesty, quite coldly, with neither indulgence nor disdain. For although life, as Nietzsche declares, "wants to be deceived and lives on deception," [51] there is need also, at certain times, for a moment of truth.

THE CITIES OF GOD   -

++

1. The Age of Wonder

Two mighty motives run through the mythologies and religions of the world. They are not the same. They have different histories. The first and the earlier to appear we may term *wonder* in one or another of its modes, from mere bewilderment in the contemplation of something inexplicable to arrest in daemonic dread or mystic awe. The second is *self-salvation:* redemption or release from a world exhausted of its glow.

Rudolf Otto, in his important work on *The Idea of the Holy*,[1] writes of a non-rational factor, essential to the religious experience, which cannot be characterized by any of the terms traditionally applied by theologians to the deity: Supreme Power, Spirit, Reason, Purpose, Good Will, Selfhood, Unity, and the rest. Indeed, credos composed of such rational terms tend rather to preclude than to produce religious experience; and accordingly, any scientific study of religion or mythology dealing only with such concepts and their gradual evolution is simply missing the essence of its topic. "For," as Professor Otto writes,

> if there be any single domain of human experience that presents us with something unmistakably specific and unique, peculiar to itself, assuredly it is that of the religious life. In truth the enemy has often displayed a keener vision in this context than either the champion of religion or the neutral and professedly impartial theorist. For the adversaries on their side know very well that the entire "mystical unrest" has nothing to do with "reason" and "rationality."
>
> And so it is salutary that we should be moved to notice that religion is not exclusively contained and exhaustively

35

comprised in any series of "rational" assertions. And it is well worth while to attempt to bring clearly before the mind the relation to each other of the different "moments" of religion, so that its nature may become more clearly manifest.[2]

This statement I shall take as the motto and assignment of our task, only adding that in the history of the higher cultures, following a period of common development in the nuclear Near East, the two branches of the Orient and Occident went apart and the "moments" (or, as I would say, "psychological stages") of their experiences of the holy also went apart. Furthermore, following the crucial moment that I shall term *the great reversal*— when, for many in the Orient as well as in the West, the sense of holiness departed from their experience both of the universe and of their own nature, and a yearning for release from what was felt to be an insufferable state of sin, exile, or delusion supervened—the ways of self-salvation that were followed in the two worlds were, in every sense, distinct. In the West, owing to the emphasis noted in our last chapter on the man/God dissociation, the agony was read as a divorce from God, largely in terms of guilt, punishment, and atonement; whereas in the Orient, where a sense of the immanence of divinity in all things remained, even though occluded by wrong judgment, the reading was psychological and the ways and imageries of release there have the character, consequently, rather of alternative therapies than of the authoritative directives of a supernatural father. In both spheres, however, the irony of the case lies in the circumstance that precisely those who desire and strive for salvation most earnestly are in their zeal bound the more, since it is exactly their self-seeking that is giving them their pain. We have just read that when the Buddha extinguished ego in himself, the world burst into flower. But that, exactly, is the way it has always appeared to those in whom wonder—and not salvation—is religion.

II. Mythogenesis

A galaxy of female figurines that comes to view in the archaeological strata of the nuclear Near East c. 4500 B.C. provides our first clue to the focus of wonder of the earliest neolithic farming and pastoral communities. The images are of bone, clay, stone, or ivory, standing or seated, usually naked, often pregnant, and sometimes holding or nursing a child. Associated symbols appear on the painted ceramic wares of the same archaeological strata; and among these a prominent motif (e.g., in the so-called Halaf ware of the Syro-Cilician corner) [3] is the head of a bull, seen from before, with long, curving horns—suggesting that the widely known myth must already have been developed, of the earth-goddess fertilized by the moon-bull who dies and is resurrected. Familiar derivatives of this myth are the Late Classical legends of Europa and the Bull of Zeus, Pasiphaë and the Bull of Poseidon, Io turned into a cow, and the killing of the Minotaur. Moreover the earliest temple compounds of the Near East—indeed, the earliest temple compounds in the history of the world—reinforce the evidence for the bull-god and goddess-cow as leading fertility symbols of the period. Roughly dated c. 4000–3500 B.C., three such primary temple compounds have been excavated in the Mesopotamian south, at Obeid,[4] Uruk,[5] and Eridu; [6] two a little to the north, at Khafajah [7] and Uqair,[8] respectively north and south of Baghdad; while a sixth, far away, at Tell Brak, in the Khabur valley of northeastern Syria,[9] suggests a broad diffusion of the common form from that Syro-Cilician (so-called Taurean) corner. Two of these six compounds are known to have been dedicated to goddesses: that of Obeid to Ninhursag, that of Khafajah to Inanna; the deities of the others being unknown. And three of the compounds (at Obeid, Khafajah, and Uqair), each enclosed by two surrounding high walls, were of an oval form designed, apparently, to suggest the female genitalia (Figure 1).[10] For, like Indian temples of the mother-goddess, where the innermost shrine has a form symbolic of the female organ, so were these symbolic of the generative force of nature by analogy with the bearing and nourishing powers of the female.

The chief building in each compound was placed upon a platform of packed clay, from ten to twenty feet high and approached by stairs. All were made of brick, in a trim, boxlike, somewhat "modern" style, corners oriented to the quarters, and decorated with polychrome tiles and a colored wash. Other structures within the oval compounds were the residences of priests, service areas, kitchens, etc., and notably, also, cattle barns. Polychrome mosaics found among the ruins at Obeid show a company of priests at their holy task of milking the sacred cows, straining and stor-

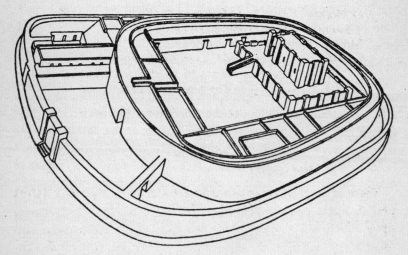

Figure 1. Early Temple Compound, Oval Type: Iraq, c. 4000–3500 B.C.

ing the milk; and we know from numerous later written documents that the form of the goddess honored in that temple, Ninhursag, the mother of the universe and of all men, gods, and beasts, was in particular the patroness and guardian of kings, whom she nourished with her blessed milk—the actual milk being that of the animals through which she functioned here on earth.

To this day in India all who visit temples of the goddess are fed a milk-rice, or other such dairy-made food, which is ritually dispensed as her "bounty"' (prasad). Furthermore, in South India, in the Nilgiri hills, there is an enigmatic tribe, the Todas, unrelated racially to its neighbors, whose little temple compounds are dairies, where they keep cattle that they worship; and at their chief sacrifice—which is of a calf, the symbolic son of the mother —they address to their goddess Togorsh a prayer that includes the word Ninkurshag, which they cannot interpret.[11] There can be no doubt that in the royal cattle barns of the goddesses Ninhursag of Obeid and Inanna of Khafajah, a full millennium and a half before the first signs of any agrarian-pastoral civilization eastward of Iran, we have the prelude to the great ritual symphony of bells, waved lights, prayers, hymns, and lowing sacrificial kine, that has gone up to the goddess in India throughout the ages:

> O Mother! Cause and Mother of the World!
> Thou art the One Primordial Being,
> Mother of innumerable creatures,
> Creatrix of the very gods: even of Brahma the Creator,
>   Vishnu the Preserver, and Shiva the Destroyer!
> O Mother, in hymning Thy praise I purify my speech.
>
> As the moon alone delights the white night lotus,
> The sun alone the lotus of the day,
> As one particular thing alone delights one other thing,
> So, dear Mother, dost Thou alone delight the universe
>   by Thy glances.[12]

There is an early Sumerian cylinder seal of c. 3500 B.C. (Uruk period, phase A: just before the invention of the art of letters) upon which two mouflon rams are to be seen, confronting each other above a mound of earth, from the side of which a doubleheaded serpent arises that appears to be about to bite them (Figure 2). A flower is above their noses, and clutching at their rumps, which come together on the reverse of the cylinder, is an eagle. Professor Henri Frankfort has observed in his discussion of this piece that every one of its elements was related in later art and cult to the mythology of the dead and resurrected god Tammuz (Sumerian Dumuzi), prototype of the Classical Adonis, who was

Figure 2. The Self-Consuming Power: Sumer, c. 3500 B.C.

the consort, as well as son by virgin birth, of the goddess-mother of many names: Inanna, Ninhursag, Ishtar, Astarte, Artemis, Demeter, Aphrodite, Venus.[13] Throughout the ancient world, such a mound of earth as that in the center of this composition was symbolic of the goddess. It is cognate with the Classical omphalos and the early Buddhist reliquary mound (*stūpa*). Magnified, it is the mountain of the gods (Greek Olympos, Indian Meru) with the radiant city of the deities atop, the watery abyss beneath, and the ranges of life between. The goddess-mother supports them all. She is recognized in the star-studded firmament as well as in the sown earth, and in the seal is to be seen not only in the mound, but also in the plain background as well as upper and lower margins, into the last of which the mound merges.

The serpent emerging from this hillock appears to be about to bite the rams; and the rams, in turn, appear to be about to eat the flower. Turning to the reverse, we see the pouncing bird of prey. A cycle of life-in-being-through-mutual-killing is indicated. And since all of the figures represent the power of the same god, the mythological theme represented is that of the self-consuming, ever-dying, ever-living generative energy that is the life and death in all things.

In a second Sumerian seal of c. 3500 B.C. a priest perhaps symbolic of the god is holding the tree to his chest in such a way that its two stems go in the four directions (Figure 3). The beasts now are clearly browsing on its blossoms, while on the reverse

Figure 3. The Lord of Life: Sumer, c. 3500 B.C.

there is a calf between two tall bundles of reed such as in this art always represent the gate to the precincts of a temple of the goddess. The calf is there for sacrifice and yet, as it were, safely within the womb. In the Christian idea that Christ, the Sacrificial Lamb, Fruit of the Tree of Jesse, while in the womb of the Virgin Mother was already virtually the Crucified, we have a comparable birth-death amalgamation.

Between the period of the earliest female figurines of c. 4500 B.C. and that of the seals of Figures 2 and 3, a span of a thousand years elapsed, during which the archaeological signs constantly increase of a cult of the tilled earth fertilized by that noblest and most powerful beast of the recently developed holy barnyard, the bull—who not only sired the milk-yielding cows, but also drew the plow, which in that early period simultaneously broke and seeded the earth. Moreover, by analogy, the horned moon, lord of the rhythm of the womb and of the rains and dews, was equated with the bull; so that the animal became a cosmological symbol, uniting the fields and laws of sky and earth. And the whole mystery of being could thus be poetically illustrated through the metaphor of the cow, the bull, and their calf, liturgically rendered within the precincts of the early temple compounds—which were symbolic of the womb of the cosmic goddess Cow herself.

During the following millennium, however, the basic village culture flowered and expanded into a civilization of city states, particularly in lower Mesopotamia; and, as Sir James G. Frazer has amply shown in *The Golden Bough,* the poetic liturgy of the cosmic sacrifice now was enacted chiefly upon kings, who were periodically slain, sometimes together with their courts. For it was the court, not the dairy, that now represented the latest, most impressive, magnification of life. The art of writing had been invented c. 3200 B.C. (Uruk period, phase B); the village was definitively supplanted by the temple-city; and a full-time professional priestly caste had assumed the guidance of the civilization. Through astral observations, the five visible planets were identified (Mercury, Venus, Mars, Jupiter, and Saturn), moving in courses along the ways already marked by the moon and sun

among the fixed stars (seven voyagers in all); a mathematically
correct calendar was invented to regulate the seasons of the
temple-city's life according to the celestial laws so revealed; and,
as we know from numerous sources, the concept of the order of
the state was to such a degree identified with those celestial laws
that the death and resurrection of the moon, the cycle of the
year, and the greater cycles of the mathematically forecast cosmic
eons, were as far as possible literally imitated in the ritual patterns
of the court, so that the cosmic and the social orders should be
one.

Two Sumerian seals of c. 2300 B.C. will suffice to illustrate the
new order of the symbolic royal courts. The first (Figure 4), from

Figure 4. The Sacrifice: Sumer, c. 2300 B.C.

the ruins of the city of Lagash, shows a naked woman squatting
on a man who is lying on his back, while a second male, having
seized her arm, is threatening with a staff or dirk. At the proper
right of the scene is an inscription of which the first two lines
are damaged. The next line, however, yields the words: "King of
Ghisgalla"—which, as Ernest de Sarzec has observed, refers to
"a divinity that is termed in other texts the 'king-god' or 'god-
king' of that locality." [14] There was a temple of the cosmic goddess

at Ghisgalla, and what we seem to have here is a ritual of sacrifice in connubium, wrought upon a priestess and a king.[15]

The second seal (Figure 5) is of similar theme, with the female

Figure 5. The Ritual Bed: Sumer, c. 2300 B.C.

again above the male. It represents, in the words of Professor Henri Frankfort,

> the ritual marriage, which, according to various texts, was consummated by the god and goddess during the New Year's Festival and immediately followed by a feast in which the whole population enjoyed the abundance now ensured by the completion of the rites. . . . The couch supporting the two figures has animal-shaped legs, either bull's hoofs or lion's claws. The scorpion beneath it may symbolize Ishara, the goddess of love,[16] and the figure at the foot of the couch . . . the officiating priest who is said in the description of the ceremony in the time of Idin Dagan [king of Isin, c. 1916–1896 B.C.] [17] to purify the god and the goddess before their connubium. . . .
>
> The scene . . . formed part of [a] ritual, which we know was enacted by the king or his substitute and a priestess. It represents the death of the god and his resurrection, followed by reunion with the goddess. It is said in Gudea's description of this festival that after the completion of the marriage a feast took place in which the gods, the ruler and the population of the city partook together; [18] [and in the seal, proper left] a jar with projecting drinking tubes indeed stands near the couch upon which the ritual marriage is consummated.[19]

A great many seals depict this banquet scene. "The participants in the feast—often a man and woman—face each other on either side of a large jar from which they imbibe through tubes, and this seems to have been the usual manner of enjoying beer in the Ancient Near East." [20] Many such seals were found among the skeletons of the royal tombs of Ur, where proof enough appears of the realization of the ritual love-death in the period represented by Figures 4 and 5. The account of these amazing tombs given in my earlier volume I need not review,[21] but only note, in summary, that within the temple compound of that city of the moon-god, Sir Leonard Woolley, in the early twenties, unearthed a series of some sixteen burials of what appeared to be entire royal courts. The most impressive was the dual entombment of a lady named Shub-ad and her lord A-bar-gi, wherein the death-pit of the latter, which contained some sixty-five attendants and two wagons drawn by three oxen each, lay beneath that of the heavily ornamented queen or priestess, who, with an entourage of only twenty-five and a sledge drawn by two asses, had followed her lord into the netherworld—fulfilling, thereby, the myth of the goddess who followed the dead god Dumuzi into the netherworld to effect his resurrection.

The skeleton of Shub-ad lay on a wooden bier in a vaulted tomb chamber of brick, with a gold cup at hand from which her potion of death may have been drunk. And there was a diadem nearby of a strip of soft white leather worked with lapis-lazuli beads, against which were set a row of exquisitely fashioned animals of gold: stags, gazelles, bulls, and goats, with between them clusters of three pomegranates, fruit-bearing branches of some other tree, and at intervals gold rosettes. The analogy with the seal of Figure 2 is evident. The head of a cow in silver lay on the floor; while among the bones of the girl musicians in attendance on her lord in the pit beneath were two beautiful harps, each ornamented with the head of a bull: one of copper, the other of gold, with lapis-lazuli horn-tips, eyes, and beard.

The silver cow in the chamber of Shub-ad and the golden bearded bull in the burial pit of A-bar-gi point backward a full

two thousand years to the dairy temples of the cosmic goddess
Cow, the early female figurines, and the painted ceramic wares
showing the head of the mythological lunar bull with long curving
horns. Professor Anton Moortgat in his survey of these same
two thousand years of the birth of civilization remarks that "the
mother-goddess and sacred bull—the earliest tangible, significant,
spiritual expressions of farming village culture—represent thoughts
that were to retain their form in the Near East through millenniums." [22] And not alone, we can add, in the Near East. For the
motifs pictorially announced in these earliest symbols of the
focus of wonder of the creators of civilization survive, in some
measure, even in the latest theologies of the modern East and
West. In fact, we shall hear echoes of their song throughout the
mythological past of what has now become the one great province
of our dawning world civilization. Although announced very
simply in these earliest neolithic forms, their music swelled to a
great and rich *fortissimo,* c. 500–1500 A.D., in a full concert of
cathedral and temple art, from Ireland to Japan.

III. Culture Stage and Culture Style

Following Rudolf Otto, I shall assume the root of mythology
as well as of religion to be an apprehension of the numinous.

This mental state [he writes] is perfectly *sui generis* and
irreducible to any other; and therefore, like every absolutely
primary and elementary datum, while it admits of being discussed, it cannot be strictly defined. There is only one way to
help another to an understanding of it. He must be guided
and led on by consideration and discussion of the matter
through the ways of his own mind, until he reach the point
at which "the numinous" in him perforce begins to stir, to
start into life and into consciousness. We can cooperate in this
process by bringing before his notice all that can be found
in other regions of the mind, already known and familiar, to
resemble, or again to afford some special contrast to, the particular experience we wish to elucidate. Then we must add:
"This X of ours is not precisely *this* experience, but akin to
this one and opposite to that other. Cannot you now realize

for yourself what it is?" In other words our X cannot, strictly speaking, be taught, it can only be evoked, awakened in the mind; as everything that comes "of the spirit" must be awakened.[23]

The symbolism of the temple and atmosphere of myth are, in this sense, catalysts of the numinous—and therein lies the secret of their force. However, the traits of the symbols and elements of the myths tend to acquire a power of their own through association, by which the access of the numinous itself may become blocked. And it does, indeed, become blocked when the images are insisted upon as final terms in themselves: as they are, for example, in a dogmatic credo.

Such a formulation, Dr. Carl G. Jung has well observed, "protects a person from a direct experience of God as long as he does not mischievously expose himself. But if he leaves home and family, lives too long alone and gazes too deeply into the dark mirror, then the awful event of the meeting may befall him. Yet even then the traditional symbol, come to full flower through the centuries, may operate like a healing draught and divert the final incursion of the living godhead into the hallowed spaces of the church." [24]

With the radical transfer of focus effected by the turn of mankind from the hunt to agriculture and animal domestication, the older mythological metaphors lost force; and with the recognition, c. 3500 B.C., of a mathematically calculable cosmic order almost imperceptibly indicated by the planetary lights, a fresh, direct impact of wonder was experienced, against which there was no defense. The force of the attendant seizure can be judged from the nature of the rites of that time. In *The Golden Bough,* Frazer has interpreted the ritual regicide rationally, as a practical measure, practically conceived, to effect a magical fertilization of the soil; and there can be no question but that it was applied to such an end—just as in all religious worship, prayer is commonly applied to the purchase of desired boons from God. Such magic and such prayer, however, do not represent the peculiar specificity of that experience of the numinous which authorities closer than Frazer to the core of the matter universally recognize in religion. We cannot assume that early man, less protected than ourselves from the numinous, had a mind somehow immune to it and consequently, in spite of being defenseless, was rather a sort of primitive social scientist than a true subject of numinous seizure. "It is not easy," as Professor Otto has said, "to discuss questions of religious psychology with one who can recollect the emotions of his adolescence, the discomforts of indigestion, or, say, social feelings, but cannot recall any intrinsically religious feelings." [25] Assuming that my reader is no such heavyweight, I shall make no further point of this argument, but take it as obvious that the appearance c. 4500–2500 B.C. of an unprecedented constellation of sacra— sacred acts and sacred things—points not to a new theory about how to make the beans grow, but to an actual experience in depth of that *mysterium tremendum* that would break upon us all even now were it not so wonderfully masked.

The system of new arts and ideas brought into being within the precincts of the great Sumerian temple compounds passed to Egypt c. 2800 B.C., Crete and the Indus c. 2600 B.C., China c. 1600 B.C., and America within the following thousand years. However, the religious experience itself around which the new elements of civilization had been constellated was not—and could not be —disseminated. Not the seizure itself, but its liturgy and associated arts, went forth to the winds; and these were applied, then, to alien purposes, adjusted to new geographies, and to very different psychological structures from that of the ritually sacrificed godkings.

We may take as example the case of the mythologies of Egypt, which for the period of c. 2800–1800 B.C. are the best documented in the world. Frazer has shown that the myths of the dead and resurrected god Osiris so closely resemble those of Tammuz, Adonis, and Dionysos as to be practically the same, and that all were related in the period of their prehistoric development to the rites of the killed and resurrected divine king. Moreover, the most recent findings of archaeology demonstrate that the earliest center from which the idea of a state governed by a divine king was diffused was almost certainly Mesopotamia. The myth of Osiris, therefore, and his sister-bride, the goddess Isis, must be read as

Egypt's variant of a common, late neolithic, early Bronze Age theme.

Dr. E. A. Wallis Budge, on the other hand, in his many works on Egyptian religion, has argued for an African origin of the Osirian mythology,[26] and Professor John A. Wilson, more recently, while attesting to "outside contacts which must have been mutually refreshing to both parties," likewise argues for the force of the native Nilotic "long, slow change of culture" in the shaping of Egyptian mythology and civilization.[27] The argument of native against alien growth dissolves, however, when it is observed that two problems—or rather, two aspects of a single problem—are in question. For, as a broad view of the field immediately shows, in every well-established culture realm to which a new system of thought and civilization comes, it is received creatively, not inertly. A sensitive, complex process of selection, adaptation, and development brings the new forms into contact with their approximate analogues or homologues in the native inheritance, and in certain instances—notably in Egypt, Crete, the Indus valley, and, a little later, the Far East—prodigious forces of indigenous productivity are released, in native *style,* but on the level of the new *stage.* In other words, although its culture stage at any given period may be shown to have been derived, as an effect of alien influences, the particular style of each of the great domains can no less surely be shown to be indigenous. And so it is that a scholar concerned largely with native forms will tend to argue for local, stylistic originality, whereas one attentive rather to the broadly flung evidence of diffused techniques, artifacts, and mythological motifs will be inclined to lime out a single culture history of mankind, characterized by well-defined general stages, though rendered by way of no less well-defined local styles. It is one thing to analyze the genesis and subsequent diffusion of the fundamental mythological heritage of all high civilizations whatsoever; another to mark the genesis, maturation, and demise of the several local mythological styles; and a third to measure the force of each local style in the context of the unitary history of mankind. A total science of mythology must give attention, as far as possible, to all three.

IV. The Hieratic State

The earliest known work of art exhibiting the characteristic style of Egypt is a carved stone votive tablet bearing on each side the representation of a conquering pharaoh (Figures 7 and 8). The site of its discovery was Hierakonpolis in Upper Egypt, which appears to have been the native place of coronation of a line of kings devoted to the solar-falcon, Horus. About 2850 B.C. these kings moved north, into Lower Egypt, and established the first dynasty of the united Two Lands. A second discovery at the site was a brick-lined subterranean tomb-chamber, one of the plastered walls of which was ornamented with hunting, boating, and combat scenes in the comparatively childish style of late neolithic decorated pottery (Figure 6).[28] And this tomb is notable not only for its

Figure 6. Mortuary Mural at Hierakonpolis: Egypt, c. 2900? B.C.

mural, which is the earliest known to Egyptology, but also for its bricks, which in that period represented a new idea derived from the mud-land of Mesopotamia.

Graves in Egypt had formerly been of a simple "open-pit" variety, rectangular in outline with round corners, or, in smaller burials, oval. The body, wrapped in hide, in loose folds of linen, or in both, was placed in a contracted posture on its left side, head south, facing west, and, after household ceramic vessels had been stowed along the sides, the excavation was filled and the surplus earth heaped above in a mound, upon which offerings could be set.[29] Brick, however, made it possible for an earth-free chamber to be constructed in the open pit below ground (the

substructure), as well as for the mound above to be raised and
magnified into a large, or even huge, brick-faced mastaba (the
superstructure), to serve both as a memorial to the personage
dwelling beneath and as a chapel for his mortuary cult. But such
superstructures do not endure like stone. "Massive structures of
this kind," states Professor George Reisner in his fundamental
study of early Egyptian tombs, "have been proved to have disappeared within a few years in the last half-century." [30] Consequently, in time the mastabas vanished; the subterranean chambers,
in which the kings were to have slept forever, were looted; and
the sands poured in through shattered roofs.

The chamber at Hierakonpolis was of considerable size: 15
feet long, 6½ feet wide, 5 feet deep, divided in two equal parts
by a low partition. The floor and walls were of unfired bricks
averaging 9 inches by 4½ inches by 3½ inches, plastered with
a layer of mud mortar and coated with a yellow wash. Its upper
margin was flush with the desert surface and its contents were
gone.[31] The painting, however, remained. And the high-hulled
ships that it shows are impressive: they are of a Mesopotamian
type. Furthermore, among its numerous figures we note a man
dompting two balanced animals rampant (fourth figure from lower
left) and, over his shoulder, a merry-go-round of five antelopes;
also, at the other end of the long boat rightward, two more antelopes, facing in opposite directions (upward and downward),
joined by the legs; all of which motifs had come to Egypt from the
Southwest Asian sphere, where they had appeared as stock motifs
on the painted pottery (Samarra ware) as early as c. 4500 B.C.

And yet, though obviously influenced by a tide of cultural discoveries flowing in from Mesopotamia,[32] Egyptian art in the period
of the Narmer palette reveals suddenly—and, as far as we know,
without precedent—not only an elegance of style and manner
of carving stone but also a firmly formulated mythology that are
characteristically and unquestionably its own. The monarch depicted is the pharaoh Narmer, whom a number of scholars now
identify with Menes,[33] the uniter of the two lands of Upper and
Lower Egypt, c. 2850 B.C.[34] And the deed commemorated seems
to be exactly that of his conquest of the North.

"The priests say," wrote the Father of History, Herodotus
(484–425 B.C.), "that Menes was the first king of Egypt and
that it was he who raised the dike that protects Memphis from
the inundation of the Nile. Before his time the river flowed entirely along the sandy range of hills skirting Egypt on the side
of Libya. He, however, by banking up the river at the bend that
it forms about a hundred furlongs south of Memphis, laid the
ancient channel dry, while he dug a new course for the stream
halfway between the two lines of hills. . . . Menes, the first
king, having thus, by turning the river, made the tract where it
used to run dry land, proceeded in the first place to build the city
now called Memphis, which lies in the narrow part of Egypt;
after which he further excavated a lake outside the town, to the

Figure 7. Narmer Palette (obverse): Egypt,
c. 2850 B.C.

north and west, communicating with the river, which was itself the eastern boundary." [35]

Figure 8. Narmer Palette (reverse): Egypt,
c. 2850 B.C.

On both sides of the Narmer palette there appear two heavily horned heads of the cow-goddess Hathor in the top panels, presiding at the corners: four such heads in all. Four is the number of the quarters of sky, and the goddess, thus pictured four times, was to be conceived as bounding the horizon. She was known as Hathor of the Horizon, and her animal was the cow—not the domestic cow, however, as in the cult of Ninhursag, the Sumerian dairy goddess, but the wild cow living in the marshes.[36] Thus a regional differentiation is evident, so that the two cults, learnedly scrutinized, are not the same. And yet, intelligently scrutinized, they are indeed the same; namely, of the neolithic cosmic goddess-

Cow. Hathor stood upon the earth in such a way that her four legs were the pillars of the four quarters. Her belly was the firmament. Moreover, the sun, the golden solar falcon, the god Horus, flying east to west, entered her mouth each evening, to be born again the next dawn. Horus, thus, was the "bull of his mother," his own father. And the cosmic goddess, whose name, *hat-hor,* means the "house of Horus," accordingly was both the consort and the mother of this self-begetting god, who in one aspect was a bird of prey.[37] In the aspect of father, the mighty bull, this god was Osiris and identified with the dead father of the living pharaoh; but in the aspect of son, the falcon, Horus, he was the living pharaoh now enthroned. Substantially, however, these two, the living pharaoh and the dead, Horus and Osiris, were the same.

In Egyptian, furthermore, according to Professor Frankfort, " 'house,' 'town,' or 'country,' may stand as symbols of the mother." [38] Hence the "house of Horus," the cow-goddess Hathor, was not only the frame of the universe, but also the land of Egypt, the royal palace, and the mother of the living pharaoh, while, as we have just seen, he, the dweller in the house, self-begotten, was not only himself but also his own father.

All of which may seem a little complicated, as of course it is if one thinks of the pharaoh simply as this or that mortal being, born at such and such a time, known for such and such a deed, and buried circa so and so B.C. However, that pharaoh—when so described—is not the Pharaoh of whom mythology treats. That is not the falcon who is the bull of his own mother. The pharaonic principle, Pharaoh with a capital P, was an eternal, not mortal, being. Hence the reference of mythology and symbology was always to *that* Pharaoh, as incarnate in these mortal pharaohs of whom we write when determining dates, dynasties, and other matters of historical interest.

It is a bold attribution, this of one immortal substance to a sequence of mortal men; but in those days the madness could be overlooked simply by dressing up and regarding not the man but the costume, as we do at a play, while the incumbent himself no longer acted of his own will but according to his part, "so that the scripture might be fulfilled." For as Thomas Mann once very well explained in a discussion of the phenomenon of "lived myth," "The Ego of antiquity and its consciousness of itself was different from our own, less exclusive, less sharply defined. It was, as it were, open behind; it received much from the past and by repeating it gave it presentness again." And for such an imprecisely differentiated sense of ego, " 'imitation' meant far more than we mean by the word today. It was a mythical identification. . . . Life, or at any rate significant life, was the reconstitution of the myth in flesh and blood; it referred to and appealed to the myth; only through it, through reference to the past, could it approve itself as genuine and significant." And as a consequence of this solemn play of life as myth, life as quotation, time was abrogated and life became a festival, a mask: the scenic reproduction with priestly men as actors of the prototypes of the gods—as for instance, the life and sufferings of the dead and resurrected Osiris.[39]

The pharaoh on the Narmer palette, therefore, though executing a historical act in time, at a certain date, and in space, in the land of Egypt, is depicted not as a merely successful warrior king, but as the manifestation in history of an eternal form. This form is to be known as the "truth" or "right order" (*maat*), and it supports the king while being realized in his deed.

Truth, *maat*, right order, is the principle mythologically personified as the cow-goddess Hathor. She is an eternally present, world-supporting principle: at once the frame of the world and a maternal force operating within it, bringing forth the realized god while at the same time fructified in her productivity by his act. That is why it is said that the god is the bull of his mother. And that is why the mythologized historical event of the Narmer palette is framed by the four visages of the goddess Hathor.

"The conquest completed," states Professor Frankfort, "it became possible to view the unification of Egypt, not as an ephemeral outcome of conflicting ambitions, but as the revelation of a predestined order. And thus kingship was, in fact, regarded throughout Egyptian history . . . as the vindication of a divinely ordered state of affairs." [40] So that war and its cruelty were not violences against nature when prosecuted by the god-king, but works in realization of an eternal moral norm, *maat,* of which the king with lifted mace was the earthly force and revelation. Of such a king it is said: "Authoritative utterance (*hu*) is in thy mouth. Understanding (*sia*) is in thy breast. Thy speech is the shrine of the right order (*maat*)." [41]

The godly ceremonial costume of the king and the high stylization of the art of the Narmer palette throw the mind into mythological focus: hence the gods appear who supported the event. We behold on one side Pharaoh wearing the tall white crown of Upper Egypt and with lifted mace (the Horus posture) murdering the chieftain of the Delta marshes. Behind the head of this unfortunate man (who is here in the mythological role of the dark antagonist, the enemy of Osiris slain by Horus, the god Seth) is the sign of the seventh Lower Egyptian nome, a harpoon, horizontal, above a lake: heraldic device of the fishing folk whose ancient capital was the holy city of Buto in the Western Delta. Their chief deity, the cobra-goddess Wadjet (after the manner of such local goddesses, who, after all, are but specifications of the general force of the cosmic goddess-mother of *maat*), would now become the patroness and protectress of the victor, having been brought by his work into amplified manifestation. Behind him we observe his sandal-bearer. Before him, over the victim's head, is a falcon (Horus, the force here in operation) holding a rope tied through the nose of a human head shown as though it were emerging from the earth of a papyrus marsh. An inscription reads, "6000 enemies." And in the lowest panel are two floating corpses.

The reverse shows the same King Narmer, now, however, wearing the flat red crown, with symbolic coil, of Lower Egypt, which he has conquered. Followed again by his sandal-bearer, preceded by four symbolic standards, the victor approaches ten beheaded enemies, each with his head between his feet. At the bottom of the composition is a mighty bull demolishing a fortress: Pharaoh in his character as the consort of Hathor; while in the center is a marvelous symbol of the uniting of the Two Lands, the serpent-necked lions or panthers of which were derived from Mesopotamia, where examples from c. 3500 B.C. have necks identically interlaced.[42] And as there, so here, the interlaced forms symbolize the union of a pair of opposites meant for union; for such was the concept of the two Egypts, heroically joined.

Examining the representations of the king closely, we perceive that over the front of his skirt there hang four decorated panels, each ornamented on top with a head of Hathor; so that again she appears four times, suggesting the quarters. This royal belt represents the horizon, which Pharaoh fills in his character as god. There is also hanging from this belt a kind of tail. And the figures on the standards carried before him, left to right, represent 1. the royal placenta, 2. the wolf-god Upwaut, standing on a form known as the *shedshed,* who goes before the king in victory as the Opener of the Way, 3. a solar falcon, and 4. a second solar falcon; so that again the number is four. These four standards are to be conspicuous throughout the history of the royal cult. They represent manifest aspects of the dweller in the house of Horus, who is incarnate in this pharaoh, the World King, from whom support and force go out to the four quarters.

Now it is evident that although the concept of the universal monarch here represented entered Egypt in the Late Gerzean period, along with the idea and institution of kingship itself, and although it is equally evident that the same concept entered India centuries later, and, later still, China and Japan, nevertheless the particular style of adaptation in each domain is peculiar to itself. Moreover, in each case the new style seems to have appeared suddenly, without prelude. Spengler in his *Decline of the West* has pointed to this problem, little treated by historians, of the sudden appearance of such culture styles at certain critical moments within limited horizons, and their persistence, then, for centuries, through many phases of development and variation. The Narmer palette already is Egypt. The little painted tomb, just earlier, is not yet Egypt. The interlaced necks of the beasts on the Narmer palette are from Mesopotamia, as are also the motifs to which I pointed in the tomb. However, in the Narmer palette they have been caught in a field of force that has transformed them into functions of an Egyptian mythopoetic reading of the place and destiny of man in the universe; whereas on the tomb wall they were not yet so engaged. They remained there rather in the condition of an uncoordinated miscellany—perhaps telling a story, perhaps not; we do not know. In any case, they were not yet telling that particular story which for the following three millenniums was to be the great myth of Egypt—variously stressed, yet ever the same.

And we shall be forced to recognize similar moments both in India and in the Far East—moments when, as it would seem, the character of the culture became established. They were the moments in which a new reading of the universe became socially operative. And they first took form, not through a great broad field, but in specific, limited foci, which then became centers of force, shaping first an elite and then gradually a more broadly shared and carried structure of civilization—the folk, meanwhile, remaining essentially on the pre-literate, neolithic level, rather as the objects and raw matter than as the subjects and creative vitality of the higher history.

What the psychological secret of the precipitating moment of an unprecedented culture style may be, we have not yet heard—at least, as far as I know. Spengler wrote of a new sense and experience of mortality—a new death-fear, a new world-fear—as the catalytic. "In the knowledge of death," he declared, "that world outlook is originated which we possess as being men and not beasts." [43]

Spengler continued: "The child suddenly grasps the lifeless corpse for what it is, something that has become wholly matter, wholly space, and at the same time it feels itself as an individual *being* in an alien extended world. 'From the child of five to myself is but a step. But from the newborn baby to the child of five is an appalling distance,' said Tolstoy once. Here, in the decisive moments of existence, when man first becomes man and realizes his immense loneliness in the universal, the world-fear reveals itself for the first time as the essentially human fear in the presence of death, the limit of the light-world, rigid space. Here, too, the higher thought originates as meditation upon death." [44]

And thereafter, "everything of which we are conscious, what-

ever the form in which it is apprehended—'soul' and 'world,' or
life and actuality, or History and Nature, or law and feeling,
Destiny or God, past and future or present and eternity—has for
us a deeper meaning still, a final meaning. And the one and only
means of rendering this incomprehensible comprehensible must be
a kind of metaphysics which regards *everything whatsoever* as
having significance as a *symbol*." [45]

The apparition of the Narmer palette marks the epochal moment, for Egypt, when the culture organism, so to say, reached
the age of five. Something—definitely—had taken place: deeper,
and of more intimately human, more infinitely cosmic, worth than
the political slaughter of six thousand enemies and establishment
of a new Reich. Indeed, the presence of a new art style—the art
style, *de facto,* of Egypt, and of an integrated mythopoetic micro-
macrocosmic vision wherein the pharaoh is already perfectly placed
in his role—would seem to indicate, not that a new political or
economic crisis had brought forth a new idea for a civilization,
but precisely the reverse. The idea already *in being* in the Narmer
palette was destined to survive as an effective culture-building
and -sustaining force through millenniums of new and old, familiar and alien, unfavorable and favorable political and economic
crises, until supplanted and liquidated, not by a new army or
economy, but by a new myth, in the period of Rome.

v. Mythic Identification

An awesome series of tombs was unearthed beneath the sands
outside of Abydos, in Upper Egypt, during the last years of the
last century, and although all had been thoroughly plundered,
enough scraps of evidence remained to supply an insight into the
character of the mythology they had been designed to serve.[46] The
two earliest were of the late predynastic period, c. 2900 B.C.,
larger than the chamber at Hierakonpolis but without either plaster
within or painting. Each was some 20 feet long, 10 wide, 10
deep, and with walls no thicker than the length of one brick: 11
inches. The next tomb, however, was of a new and marvelous
size: 26 by 16 feet and with walls from 5 to 7 feet thick. Five

wooden pillars along each side and one at each end had served
as backing for an interior wooden paneling, while auxiliary to this
formidable chamber, running off some eighty yards toward the
northeast, was a new and somewhat chilling discovery: a subterranean real-estate development of thirty-three small, subsidiary,
brick-lined graves in eleven rows of three graves each, with a
terminal larger burial at the farther end and two, quite a bit larger,
at the nearer: thirty-six subsidiary graves in all. Something—definitely—had happened. And we know what it was. For this was
the tomb and necropolis of King Narmer.[47] The neighboring tomb,
of a certain King Sma, though equally formidable, lacked an associated necropolis. However, the one next to that, of about the
same size, had beside it two very large subsidiary graves—and the
name of its pharaoh, Aha-Mena, has been identified by some
authorities with Menes.[48] There is therefore some question as to
which of these three was the actual first pharaoh, uniter of the
Two Egypts; no question, however, as to who were interred in the
additional dwellings of these subterranean estates.

Overwhelming evidence of the nature of the rites that in the
period of Old Kingdom Egypt (c. 2850–2190 B.C.) attended the
obsequies of a king came to light in the years 1913 to 1916, when
Professor George Reisner unearthed a relatively undisturbed
Egyptian cemetery, some two hundred acres in extent, far up the
Nile, in Nubia, where an extremely prosperous Egyptian provincial
government, c. 2000–1700 B.C., had controlled the trade routes,
and notably the gold supply, coming north. These dates, it will be
observed, fall within the period of Middle Kingdom Egypt (2052–
1610 B.C.), when rituals of this kind were no longer practiced (as
far as we know, at least) in the main centers of Egyptian civilization. However, in those days, as now, people dwelling in the
provinces, far from the wickedness of great cities, tended to favor
and foster the good old-fashioned religion with its good old-
fashioned ways.

The cemetery in question was an immense necropolis, which
had been in service some three hundred years, and it contained
both a multitude of small modest graves and an impressive number of great tumuli, one of which was over one hundred yards

in diameter. And what the excavator found, without exception, was a pattern of burial with human sacrifice—specifically, female sacrifice: of the wife and, in the more opulent tombs, the entire harem, together with attendants.

The chief body—always male—always lay on its right side on the south side of the grave, usually on a bed with a wooden head-rest, head east, facing north (toward Egypt), and with the legs slightly bent at the knees, the right hand beneath the cheek and the left hand on or near the right elbow, as though in sleep. Beside and around it were the usual weapons and personal adornments, certain toilet articles and bronze implements, an ostrich-feather fan, and a pair of rawhide sandals. A hide (usually ox-hide) covered the whole body, and the legs of the bed had the form of those of a bull. The body had been clothed in linen, and there were numerous large pottery vessels stowed nearby and around the walls.

Of considerable interest and importance here is the detail of the bull legs, together with the covering of hide. Sir Flinders Petrie, in his account of the cluster of plundered tombs that he opened in the sands of Abydos, reported that among the shattered bits of grave gear left to be classified were numerous parts of furniture (stools, beds, caskets, etc.) with legs carved to simulate the legs of bulls; [49] whereas toward the close of Dynasty V (c. 2350 B.C.), lion legs began to supplant bull. By that time, also, the custom of human sacrifice at royal burials had been abandoned. Tombs, furthermore, were then being constructed of stone, not of brick, and sanctuaries were being erected to a new sun-god Re, to whom the pharaoh himself paid worship as to his father above, in heaven —not below, in the grave. The pharaoh, from that period on, was known as the "good god," whereas in the period of Dynasties I–IV he was the "great god" who paid worship to none, being himself the supreme manifestation of godhead in the universe.[50] Thus it appears that during the epochal half-millennium that elapsed between the founding of Dynasty I, c. 2850 B.C., and the fall of Dynasty V, c. 2350 B.C., a coming to climax and transformation of the pharaonic cult of the mighty bull took place that is registered in no written text, but only in the mute forms and contents of the tombs of the dead-yet-ever-living pharaohs and their buried courts.

In each of the graves of the Nubian necropolis it was observed that the chief body and its furniture occupied only a very small part of the excavation. The rest was taken up by other human bodies, ranging in number from one to a dozen or more in the lesser burials and from fifty or so to four or five hundred in the larger. The colossal tumulus already mentioned, no less than one hundred yards in diameter, had a long corridor running east-to-west through its center, from which a sort of buried city of brick walls, literally packed with skeletons, fanned out to the periphery. The remains of numerous rams were also found in the graves. And in contrast to the always peaceful posture of the chief body, the disposition of the others followed no rule. Most were on the right side, indeed, heads east, but in almost every possible attitude, from the half-extended posture of the chief body to the tightest possible doubling up. The hands were usually over the face or at the throat, but sometimes wrung together and sometimes clutching the hair. "These extra bodies," writes Professor Reisner, "I call sacrifices." [51]

By far their greater number, whether in the smaller graves or in the larger, were female, and of these one particularly well equipped with jewelry and grave gear was always placed either directly in front of or on the bed, beneath the hide. "The group," declares Professor Reisner, after many years of careful excavation and study of these graves, "represents a family group . . . made up from the members of one family although not necessarily including the whole family." And in the greater tumuli, where the number of occupants increased approximately in proportion to the magnitude of the monument, even the four or five hundred sometimes present would not have been too many to represent the harem of an Egyptian governor of the Sudan. They would have included a large proportion of women and children, but also male bodyguards and harem servants, and that some of the latter were eunuchs is of course possible but indeterminable.

The man [Professor Reisner reminds us] was the governor of a country which controlled the main trade lines and the gold supply of Egypt, and at the distance of so many days' journey from Thebes and Memphis, must have held the position of a nearly independent but tribute-paying viceroy to the king of Egypt. Under such circumstances, a harem with all its dependents, servants, and miscellaneous offspring would in the Orient easily amount to five hundred persons or more. Thus all the statements in regard to the extra bodies in the smaller graves apply in equal degree to those of the great tombs. These enormous burials also represent family interments made on one and the same day, differing only in scale, which was proportionate to the place and power of the chief personage.

Concluding that the burial represents a family group of attendants, females, and children together with the chief body; that all were buried in one day and in the same grave; that this occurred not in one grave but in every grave in a vast cemetery, containing in the Egyptian part alone about four hundred graves; and that the practice must cover a period of several hundred years: it may well be asked of human experience under what conditions such a custom can exist. The chances of war become at once an absurdity; the possibility of the continual extermination of family after family by execution for criminal or political offences cannot be seriously considered; and there is certainly no microbe known to modern science which could act in so maliciously convenient a manner as to deliver family after family through so many generations simultaneously at the graveside. In all the range of present knowledge, there is only one custom known which sends the family or a part of it into the other world along with the chief member. That is the custom, widely practiced but best known from the Hindoo form called *satī* or *suttee*, in which the wives of the dead man cast themselves (or are thrown) on his funeral pyre. Some such custom as this would explain fully the facts recorded in the graves of Kerma, and after several years of reflection I can conceive of no other known or possible custom which would even partially explain these facts.[52]

We are brought, thus, directly to an interesting enigma, which must strike the minds of all who seriously compare the antiquities of Egypt with those of India and the Far East; namely, the enigma of the numerous analogues that appear, and continue to appear, at every turn.

For example, in the mythology of the Narmer palette the figure of the cow is, of course, obvious. The range of religious and emotional reference of the cow throughout Indian literature and life is enormous; always, however, in the way of a gentle, beloved maternal image—a "poem of pity," to use Gandhi's phrase.[53] Already in the Rig Veda (c. 1500–1000 B.C.) the goddess Aditi, mother of the gods, was a cow.[54] In the rites a cow was ceremonially addressed in her name.[55] She was the "supporter of creatures," [56] "widely expanded," [57] mother of the sun-god Mitra and of the lord of truth and universal order, Varuna; [58] mother, also, of Indra, king of the gods, who is addressed constantly as a bull [59] and is the archetype of the world monarch. In the later Hinduism of the Tantric and Puranic periods (c. 500–1500 A.D.), when the rites and mythologies of Vishnu and Shiva came to full flower, Shiva was identified with the bull, Vishnu with the lion. Shiva's animal vehicle was the white bull Nandi, whose gentle form is a prominent figure in all of his temples, and in one celebrated case, at Mamallapuram, near Madras (the Shore Temple, c. 700–720 A.D.),[60] Nandi appears, multiplied many times, in the way of a kind of fence surrounding the compound. Shiva's consort, furthermore, the goddess Sati (pronounced suttee), who destroyed herself because of her love and loyalty, is the model of the perfect Indian wife. And finally, the Indian mythological figure and ideal of the universal king (*cakravartin*), the bound of whose domain is the horizon, before whose advance the sun-wheel (*cakra*) rolls (*vartati*) as a manifestation of divine authority and as opener of the way to the four quarters, who at birth is endowed with thirty-two great marks and numerous additional secondary marks, and who, when buried, is to have a huge mound (*stūpa*) erected over his remains,[61] without doubt is a perfect counterpart of the old Egyptian image and ideal of the pharaoh.

Such parallels are not accidental concatenations, but related, deeply meaningful, culture-structuring mythological syndromes that represent the very nucleus of the paramount problem of any seriously regarded science of comparative culture, mythology, religion, art, or philosophy.

As in India to this day, therefore, so also in the deep Egyptian past, we find this appalling, apparently senseless, certainly very cruel, rite of suttee—and we shall discover it again in earliest China. The royal tombs of Ur show it in Mesopotamia, and there is evidence in Europe as well. What can it mean, that man, precisely at the moments of first flowering of his greatest civilizations, should have offered his humanity and common sense (indeed, even, one can say, his fundamental, biological will to live) on the altar of a dream?

Were these willing victims, or were they forced, whom we have broken in upon in the cities of their sleep?

"If the victims had been killed before entering the grave," wrote Professor Reisner, "they would have been placed all in the same position, neatly arranged on the right side, head east, with the right hand under the cheek and the left hand on or near the right elbow." However, although a few were approximately in this posture, the greatest number were in other attitudes, which—to quote the professor—"could only be the result of fear, resolution under pain or its anticipation, or of other movements which would naturally arise in the body of perfectly well persons suffering a conscious death by suffocation."

The most common thing was for the person to bury the face in the hands, or for one hand to be over the face and the other pressed between the thighs. In three cases one arm was passed around the breast, clasping the back of the neck from the opposite side. Another skeleton showed the head bent into the crook of the elbow—"in a manner," states Professor Reisner, "most enlightening as an indication of her state of mind at the moment of being covered." Another was on the right side, head west, but with the right shoulder turned on the back and the right hand clutching an ostrich-feather fan pressed against the face bent toward the breast, while the left arm was passed across to clutch the right forearm. Two skeletons were unearthed with their foreheads pressed against each other, as for comfort. Another had the fingers of the right hand clenched in the strands of the bead head circlet; and this was an attitude not uncommon. The principal sacrifice in one of the graves, the woman on the bed, beneath the oxhide, was turned on her back, legs spread wide apart, left hand clenched against her breast, right grasping tightly the right pelvic bone, and with her head bent against the left shoulder. Another grave revealed a poor thing who had crawled beneath the bed and so had suffocated slowly. The position of her legs showed that she had placed herself there on her right side, properly, head east, but had then turned on her stomach with the head so twisted as to lie on its left cheek, facing south instead of north. The arms were stretched down with the left hand on the buttocks and the right apparently grasping the left foot. For, owing to the lowness of the bed, she could not turn over without straightening her legs—and this was impossible, since they would project beyond the foot of the bed, where they were blocked by the filling. And still another woman, again the principal sacrifice in her grave, lying at the foot of the bed, under the oxhide, had turned on her back with the right hand against the right leg and the left hand, in her agony, clutching her thorax.[62]

However, in spite of these signs of suffering and even panic in the actual moment of the pain of suffocation, we should certainly not think of the mental state and experience of these individuals after any model of our own more or less imaginable reactions to such a fate. For these sacrifices were not properly, in fact, individuals at all; that is to say, they were not particular beings, distinguished from a class or group by virtue of any sense or realization of a personal, individual destiny and responsibility, to be worked out in the way of an individual life. They were parts, only, of a larger whole; and it was only by virtue of their absolute submission to that in its unalterable categorical imperative that they were anything at all.

The full sense of the Indian term suttee (*satī*) will expose, I think, something of the quality and character of the mind and heart absolutely opened in this way to an identification with a role. The word is from the Sanskrit verbal root *sat,* "to be." The noun form, *satya,* means "truth; the real, genuine and sincere, the faithful, virtuous, pure and good," as well as "the realized, the fulfilled," while the negative, *a-sat,* "un-real, un-true," has the connotations, "wrong, wicked and vile," and in the feminine parti- cipial form, *a-satī,* "unfaithful, unchaste wife." *Satī,* the feminine participle of *sat,* then, is the female who really *is* something in as much as she is truly and properly a player of the female part: she is not only good and true in the ethical sense but true and real ontologically. In her faithful death, she is at one with her own true being.

An illuminating, though somewhat appalling, glimpse into the deep, silent pool of the Oriental, archaic soul suffused by this sense of the transcendence of its own reality is afforded by an al- most incredible tale of a suttee-burial from recent India, which took place on March 18, 1813. The report was communicated by a certain British Captain Kemp, an eyewitness of the living sacri- fice, to an early missionary in India, the Reverend William Ward. One of the Captain's younger and best workmen, Vishvanatha by name, who had been sick but a short time, was said by an astrol- oger to be on the point of death, and so was taken down to the side of the Ganges to expire. Immersed to the middle in the mud- laden stream, he was kept there for some time, but when he failed to die was returned to the bank and left to broil in the sun. Then he was placed again in the river—and again returned to the bank; which activity continuing for some thirty-six hours, he did, in- deed, finally expire; and his wife, a young, healthy girl of about sixteen, learning of the death, "came to the desperate resolution," writes the captain, "of being buried alive with the corpse." The British officer tried in vain to persuade first the girl, then her mother, that a resolution of this kind was madness, but encountered not the slightest sign anywhere of either hesitation or regret. And so the young widow, accompanied by her friends, proceeded to the beach where the body lay, and there a small branch of the mango tree was presented to her, which, when she took it, set the seal upon her resolution.

> At eight p.m. [then writes the Captain] the corpse, accom- panied by the self-devoted victim, was conveyed to a place a little below our grounds, where I repaired, to behold the

perpetration of a crime which I could scarcely believe possible to be committed by any human being. The corpse was laid on the earth by the river till a circular grave of about fifteen feet in circumference and five or six feet deep was prepared and was then (after some formulas had been read) placed at the bottom of the grave in a sitting posture, with the face to the north, the nearest relation applying a lighted wisp of straw to the top of the head. The young widow now came forward, and having circumambulated the grave seven times, calling out Huree Bul! Huree Bul! * in which she was joined by the surrounding crowd, descended into it. I then approached within a foot of the grave, to observe if any reluctance appeared in her countenance, or sorrow in that of her relations. She placed herself in a sitting posture, with her face to the back of her husband, embracing the corpse with her left arm, and reclining her head on his shoulders; the other hand she placed over her own head, with her forefinger erect, which she moved in a circular direction. The earth was then deliberately put around them, two men being in the grave for the purpose of stamping it round the living and the dead, which they did as a gardener does around a plant newly transplanted, till the earth rose to a level with the surface, or two or three feet above the heads of the entombed. As her head was covered some time before the finger of her right hand, I had an opportunity of observing whether any regret was manifested; but the finger moved round in the same manner as at first, till the earth closed the scene. Not a parting tear was observed to be shed by any of her relations, till the crowd began to disperse, when the usual lamentations and howling commenced without sorrow.[63]

We may compare with this Professor Reisner's reconstruction of the burial rites of the great provincial governor, Prince Hepzefa, in the largest of the tumuli of the Nubian cemetery at Kerma, which must have taken place, according to his calculation, some time between 1940 and 1880 B.C.[64] The procession would have started from a large rectangular edifice, the ruins of which were excavated some thirty-five yards from the prodigious tumulus.

I imagine the procession filing out of the funerary chapel [he writes] and taking the short path to the western entrance of the long corridor of the tumulus; the blue-glazed quartzite

---

* "Hari [i.e., Vishnu], hail! Hari, hail!" For the Indian woman, her husband is her manifestation of God.

bed, on which the dead Hepzefa probably already lay covered with linen garments, his sword between his thighs, his pillow, his fan, his sandals in their places; the servants bearing alabaster jars of ointments, boxes of toilet articles and games, the great blue faïence sailing boats with all their crews in place, the beautifully decorated faïence vessels and the fine pottery of the prince's daily life; perhaps the porters straining at the ropes which drew the two great statues set on sledges, although these may have been taken to the tomb before this day; the bearers who had the easier burden of the statuettes; the crowd of women and attendants of the harem decked in their most cherished finery, many carrying some necessary utensil or vessel. They proceed, not in the ceremonial silence of our funerals, but with all the "ululations" and wailings of the people of the Nile. The bed with the body is placed in the main chamber, the finer objects in that chamber and in the anteroom, the pottery among the statues and statuettes set in the corridor. The doors of the chambers are closed and sealed. The priests and officials withdraw. The women and attendants take their places jostling in the narrow corridor, perhaps still with shrill cries or speaking only such words as the selection of their places required. The cries and all movements cease. The signal is given. The crowd of people assembled for the feast, now waiting ready, cast the earth from their baskets upon the still, but living victims on the floor and rush away for more. The frantic confusion and haste of the assisting multitude is easy to imagine. The emotions of the victims may perhaps be exaggerated by ourselves; they were fortified and sustained by their religious beliefs, and had taken their places willingly, without doubt, but at that last moment, we know from their attitudes in death that a rustle of fear passed through them and that in some cases there was a spasm of physical agony.

The corridor was quickly filled. With earth conveniently placed a few hundred men could do that work in a quarter of an hour; a few thousands with filled baskets could have accomplished the task in a few minutes. The assembled crowd turned then probably to the great feast. The oxen had been slaughtered ceremonially to send their spirits with the spirit of the prince. The meat must be eaten, as was ever the case. If I am right in my interpretation of the hearths, consisting of ashes and red-burned earth, which dot the plain to the west and south of the tumulus, the crowd received the meat in portions and dispersed over the adjacent ground in family or village groups to cook and eat it. No doubt the wailing and the feasting lasted for days, accompanied by games and dances. Day after day, the smoke of the fires must have drifted southwards. . . .[65]

There can be no question but that in viewing these two rites, so different in degree, we are in the field of the same spiritual belief. The mythology and ritual of suttee, which so greatly shocked the early Western visitors to India and fundamentally outraged the Western moral sense, is older by far than the Indian Brahminical tradition to which it is generally ascribed and by which it was maintained until suppressed in 1829. In our volume on Primitive Mythology we have discussed at length the mythology of the ritual love-death, first as it has been practiced up to the present on the culture level of the primitive planting village communities of the tropical equatorial zone, from the Sudan eastward to Indonesia and across the Pacific even to the New World; and then as it appeared in a considerably elevated form in the royal rites of the earliest hieratic city states of the Near East—whence the awesome custom of a periodic ritual regicide was diffused, together with the institution of kingship itself, into Egypt, inner Africa, and India, and to Europe and China as well.[66] We shall not repeat the argument here, but only point once again to the royal tombs of Sumerian Ur, excavated by Sir Leonard Woolley, where it appeared that when a royal personage died (or was perhaps ritually slain) the members of the court—or at least the female members and the body servants—in full regalia, entering the grave with the bier, were buried alive.[67] And there were found in one of the royal chambers at Ur two model boats, one of silver, one of copper, with high stem and stern and with leaf-bladed oars. The boat models of blue-glazed faïence in the prince's tumulus at Kerma, therefore, were not mere toys or whimsies, but elements of a symbolism of the yonder world: the boats of the ferryman of death. There is a rock picture from the Nubian desert south of Kerma showing such a boat, complete with sail and ferryman, so placed on the back of a bull that the boat and galloping animal are one (Figure 9). There is also, on a coffin in the British Museum, the picture of Osiris in the form of a galloping bull with crescent horns bearing the dead to the underworld.[68] And now let us recall the funeral beds with legs like those of a bull—and the oxhide covers placed over the dead. We have already discussed the

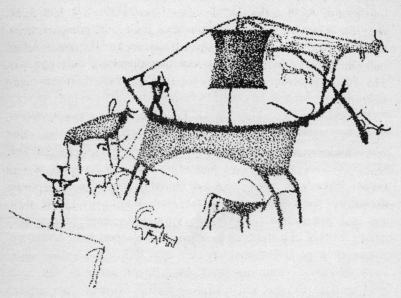

Figure 9. Petroglyph: The Ship of Death: Nubia, c. 500–50 B.C.?

cylinder seal from Mesopotamia showing the couple on a couch having legs suggesting those of a bull.[69] And in far-away Bali, at the remotest reach into Indonesia of the influence of the Indian culture complex, the bodies of the wealthy, waiting to be burned, are placed in sarcophagi with the shapes of bulls.

Returning now to ancient Abydos with eyes better able to see, we observe again the royal palaces, silent for millenniums beneath the sands. We may recall that in the little painted tomb at Hierakonpolis there were two parts, divided by a low wall. We view again the necropolis of King Narmer, the uniter of the two lands, the mighty bull of his mother, who on a day overthrew six thousand enemies. And we ask who were in those other graves: or in the two large subsidiary chambers near the tomb of that other possible first pharaoh, Aha-Mena. Then we look at the next burial: that of Zer, the immediate follower of the pharaoh Aha-Mena, and probably his son. There is no more grandiose subterranean city of the dead anywhere in the world. The main tomb, some 20 feet under ground, was 43 feet long, 38 feet wide, 9 feet deep; and within there had been a large wooden chamber divided into rooms. Against the outside of its heavy walls, 8½ feet thick, were the lesser brick walls of numerous additional compartments, while beyond this many-chambered royal palace there reached out—in the way of an underground Versailles—a vast court of 318 subsidiary graves, arranged in outbuildings, annexes, and wings.

The likely occupants suggested by Reisner were as follows. In the most stately annex of seventeen subsidiary chambers: six chief wives and eleven second-rank women of the harem. In the barracks just behind these: forty-four of the harem retinue, two harem keepers, and two harem keepers' servants. In a large separate dormitory: some thirty-eight male (perhaps eunuch) harem servants and twenty-one bodyguards, chair bearers, etc. In a second wing or annex: twenty members of what appears to have been a separate, secondary harem. In a vast service dormitory, quite apart: a service company, variously ordered, of about one hundred and seventy-four souls. And amid the ruins of the chamber itself, which in the course of its forty-seven hundred years had been thoroughly sacked, there was found a piece of the torn-off arm of a mummy in its wrappings, still bearing four elegant bracelets of gold of the favorite or chief queen.[70]

A schedule of crude statistics will suffice to illustrate the suttee pattern of the remaining First Dynasty graves at Abydos, in chronological order.

King Zet: a court of 174 subsidiary graves, besides chambers within the main hall.

Queen Merneith (Zet's queen?): 41 subsidiary graves, besides chambers within the main hall.

King Den-Setui: an extremely elegant mausoleum, with a broad stairway descending to an entrance in the side of the substructure (a new idea, copied by all who followed, which allowed the subterranean palace to be completed, roofed, and furnished by the

monarch himself before his death): in the main chamber, a paving
of large, pink, well-cut granite blocks and a portcullis of dressed
white limestone, affording the earliest evidence of a mastery of
stone that was soon to lead to imposing consequences; grouped
around the central palace, a court of 136 subsidiary graves, of
which one, very large and with a stair, may have been of a queen.

King Azab-Merpaba: the main hall a mere 22 feet by 14 feet
with only 64 subsidiary graves. ("It is to be concluded," is Reisner's
comment, "that either his means were considerably diminished or
his reign was very short.") [71]

King Mersekha-Semempses (Semerkhat): a new style: not a
lot of wings and separate annexes, out beyond the spread of the
main mastaba, but a single mighty substructure, with a large number of rooms within and 63 subsidiary cells packed around, so that
one prodigious superstructure would cover all.

King Qa: another tomb in this new style, with 26 subsidiary
cells, built, however, in haste and covered before the bricks dried,
so that many of the chambers collapsed when the weight of the
sands above pressed down—completely proving, as Petrie notes,
that all within had been buried simultaneously with the king, possibly in confusion; for the time was that of the fall of the line of
Menes and rise of Dynasty II.[72]

And now, one more detail: It must be told that another series of
fully appointed suttee palaces, built by the pharaohs of Dynasty I,
has recently been discovered, far down the Nile from the necropolis
of Abydos, at Sakkara, near Memphis—a second set of tombs,
that is to say, *of precisely the same pharaohs.* "The Sakkara Tombs
are, in every case, far larger and more elaborate than their counterparts in Abydos," states Mr. Walter Emery, a director of the
excavations. Furthermore, he declares, "the excavations have
shown that civilization at the dawn of Egypt's pharaonic period
was far higher than we have hitherto supposed." [73]

VI. Mythic Inflation

"In Upper Egypt," wrote Sir James G. Frazer in *The Golden
Bough,* citing the observations of a German nineteenth-century
voyager, "on the first day of the solar year by Coptic reckoning,

that is, on the tenth of September, when the Nile has generally reached its highest point, the regular government is suspended for three days and every town chooses its own ruler. This temporary lord wears a sort of tall fool's cap and a long flaxen beard, and is enveloped in a strange mantle. With a wand of office in his hand and attended by men disguised as scribes, executioners, and so forth, he proceeds to the Governor's house. The latter allows himself to be deposed; and the mock king, mounting the throne, holds a tribunal, to the decisions of which even the governor and his officials must bow. After three days the mock king is condemned to death; the envelope or shell in which he was encased is committed to the flames, and from its ashes the Fellah creeps forth. The custom points to an old practice of burning a real king in grim earnest." [74]

It is surely worth observing, that, although in the period of the great tombs of the pharaohs of Dynasty I those mighty bulls when departing drew with them into the underworld all of their numerous herds of cows—"poems of pity"—nevertheless, they were themselves not committed to any such identification with their mythological role as should have required of them—mighty kings—a like submission to ritual death. In the earliest centuries of the prehistoric hieratic city states—for which we have ample circumstantial evidence, and which I am dating schematically and hypothetically c. 3500–2500 B.C.[75]—the kings in their mythical identification were to such an extent "open behind" (to use the apt phrase of Thomas Mann) that they gave their bodies to be slain or even slew themselves in the festival mime: as, indeed, kings in India continued to be slain as late as the sixteenth century and in Africa into the twentieth.[76] In Egypt, however, already in the period of the Narmer palette (c. 2850 B.C.), their individualities had to a certain extent "closed," so that the holy death-and-resurrection scenes were no longer being played with all the empathy of yore—at least by the players in the leading part. Those warrior kings, strategists and politicos, fashioners of the first compound political state in the history of the world, were not offering themselves like actual bulls, pigs, rams, or goats, to the local priestly guardians who in former days had derived their solemn knowledges of the right order (*maat*) from a watch of the cycling stars.[77] Somewhere, sometime, at some point on the prehistoric map not yet brought into focus by research, the king had taken *maat* unto himself; so that by the time the earliest datable royal actors come striding in upon the scene for us, they are already rendering a new reading of the well-known role of Character A.

Instead of that old, dark, terrible drama of the king's death, which had formerly been played to the hilt, the audience now watched a solemn symbolic mime, *the Sed festival,* in which the king renewed his pharaonic warrant without submitting to the personal inconvenience of a literal death. The rite was celebrated, some authorities believe, according to a cycle of thirty years, regardless of the dating of the reigns;[78] others have it, however, that the only scheduling factor was the king's own desire and command.[79] Either way, the real hero of the great occasion was no longer the timeless Pharaoh (capital P), who puts on pharaohs, like clothes, and puts them off, but the living garment of flesh and bone, this particular pharaoh So-and-so, who, instead of giving himself to the part, now had found a way to keep the part to himself. And this he did simply by stepping the mythological image down one degree. Instead of Pharaoh changing pharaohs, it was the pharaoh who changed costumes.

The season of year for this royal ballet was the same as that proper to a coronation: the first five days of the first month of the "Season of Coming Forth," when the hillocks and fields, following the inundation of the Nile, were again emerging from the waters. For the seasonal cycle, throughout the ancient world, was the foremost sign of rebirth following death, and in Egypt the chronometer of this cycle was the annual flooding of the Nile. Numerous festival edifices were constructed, incensed, and consecrated: a throne hall wherein the king should sit while approached in obeisance by the gods and their priesthoods (who in a crueler time would have been the registrars of his death); a large court for the presentation of mimes, processions, and other such visual events; and finally a palace-chapel into which the god-king would retire for his changes of costume. Five days of illumination, called the "Lighting of the Flame" (which in the earlier reading of this miracle play would have followed the quenching of the fires on the dark night of the moon when the king was ritually slain),[80] preceded the five days of the festival itself; and then the solemn occasion (*ad majorem dei gloriam*) commenced.

The opening rites were under the patronage of Hathor. The king, wearing the belt with her four faces and the tail of her mighty bull, moved in numerous processions, preceded by his four standards, from one temple to the next, presenting favors (not offerings) to the gods. Whereafter the priesthoods arrived in homage before his throne, bearing the symbols of their gods. More processions followed, during which the king moved about—as Professor Frankfort states in his account—"like the shuttle in a great loom" to re-create the fabric of his domain, into which the cosmic powers represented by the gods, no less than the people of the land, were to be woven.[81]

All this pomp and circumstance, however, was but preliminary to the central event; for, as in all traditional rites, so in this: the period of ceremonious approach and preparation was to be followed by an act of consummation (formerly, the killing of the king), after which a brief series of terminal meditations, blessings, etc., would lead to an exit march. Normally five stages are represented in such a program:

1. Preparatory vestings, blessings, and consecrations
2. Introductory processions
3. Rites approaching the consummation
4. *The consummating sacrifice (or its counterpart)*
5. *The application of the benefits*
6. Thanksgiving, final blessing, and dismissal

In our present summary sketch of a Sed festival we have already arrived at Stage Number 4.

The king, wearing now a short, stiff archaic mantle, walks in a grave and stately manner to the sanctuary of the wolf-god Upwaut, the "Opener of the Way," where he anoints the sacred standard and, preceded by this, marches to the palace chapel, into which he disappears.

A period of time elapses during which the pharaoh is no longer manifest.

When he reappears he is clothed as in the Narmer palette, wearing the kilt with Hathor belt and bull's tail attached. In his right hand he holds the flail scepter and in his left, instead of the usual crook of the Good Shepherd, an object resembling a small scroll, called the Will, the House Document, or Secret of the Two Partners, which he exhibits in triumph, proclaiming to all in attendance that it was given him by his dead father Osiris, in the presence of the earth-god Geb.

"I have run," he cries, "holding the Secret of the Two Partners, the Will that my father has given me before Geb. I have passed through the land and touched the four sides of it. I traverse it as I desire." [82]

There is an amusing, extremely early engraving on a broken piece of ebony from the tomb of King Den-Setui, the fifth pharaoh of Dynasty I (that pious Bluebeard whose palace with the pink granite pavement, once full of murdered wives, we have already noted),* which shows the king just following his reception of the Will (Figure 10). He is striding nimbly away with it. The flail is

Figure 10. The Secret of the Two Partners: Egypt, c. 2800 B.C.

over his shoulder and the Will is in his left hand. "The scene," writes Petrie in his report of the discovery, ". . . is the earliest example of a ceremony which is shown on the monuments down to Roman times." [83] Both Osiris and the pharaoh wear the double crown of the two lands, which is a compound of the tall tiara-like

* Supra, pp. 71–72.

white crown of Upper Egypt and the low red crown, with symbolic coil, of the North.

It has been suggested that within the palace court an area must have been marked out to symbolize the two lands of Lower and Upper Egypt and that the pharaoh traversed this in some sort of formal, striding, ceremonious slow dance. Later accounts and pictures indicate that a female, probably a priestess representing the goddess Mert, who was symbolic of the land, faced the dancer and clapped accompaniment, calling, "Come! Bring it!" while the wolf-standard of the "Opener of the Way" was born before him by an attendant clothed archaically in a kilt of hide.[84]

Such, then, or somewhat such, was the rite by which the literal killing of the old king and transfer of power to the new had been transformed into an allegory. The king died not literally, but symbolically, in the earliest passion play of which we have record. And the plot of the sacred mime was the old, yet ever new, formula of the Adventure of the Hero, which is known to the later arts and literatures of all the world.[85] Analyzed in terms of its component folkloristic motifs, the plot might be summarized as follows:

> Pharaoh (the Hero), when it became known to him that the time had come for him to be slain, set forth to procure a token of his qualification for continued possession of his throne (Call to Adventure). Led by the "Opener of the Way" (Guide to Adventure: Magical Aid), he entered the palace of the underworld (Threshold of Adventure: Labyrinth: Land of the Dead), where he touched the four sides of the land of Egypt (Difficult Task: Micro-macrocosmic correspondence), and with the goddess of the land of Egypt assisting (Magical Aid: Ariadne Motif: Supernatural Bride), was thereupon acknowledged by his dead father, Osiris (Father At-one-ment). He received the Will (Divine Designation: Token: Elixir), and in new attitre (Apotheosis), reappeared before his folk (Resurrection: Return), to resume his throne (Adventure Achieved).

Thus in a marvelously subtle way the work commenced of Art, which in the course of the following long, cruel centuries was gradually to alleviate the force of the earlier, literally enacted mythic seizures, releasing man thereby from their inhumanity,

while opening through the figures of their inspiration new ways to
an understanding of humanity itself.

The fifth stage of the Sed festival, that of the Application of
Benefits, was devoted to the installation of the pharaoh on his dual
throne, which he now had properly achieved. In his character,
first, as King of Lower Egypt, he was carried in a boxlike litter on
the shoulders of the Great Ones of the Realm to the chapel of
Horus of Libya with the Lifted Arm, where the high priest bestowed on him the shepherd crook, the flail and "welfare" scepter,
and two dignitaries of the holy city of Buto in the Delta sang a
hymn four times to the quarters; the command "Silence!" four
times repeated, having preceded each declamation. In his character, then, as King of Upper Egypt he was carried in a litter shaped

Figure 11. The Dual Enthronement:
Egypt, c. 2800 B.C.

like a basket to the chapel of Horus of Edfu and Seth of Ombos,
where the high priest bestowed the bow and arrows of his royal
rule. Releasing an arrow in each of the four directions, the king
assumed his throne and was crowned four times, once facing each
quarter, whereafter, in the terminating stage of the festival, the
sixth, he moved in procession to the Court of the Royal Ancestors,
where he offered homage in a rite in which the four royal standards
—called "the gods who follow Horus"—played a leading role.[86]

The earliest extant representation of the dual enthronement of
the Sed festival appears on a royal sealing (Figure 11) found by

Petrie in the ravaged tomb of King Zer, the second pharaoh (according to Petrie's count) of Dynasty I, to whose monstrous suttee-burial we have already had occasion to refer.* And this returns us to our point. For although it is perfectly clear that these pharaohs had taken *maat* unto themselves, away from the stars and their gods and priests, forgoing the holy ritual death and assuming the much lighter part of a ritual dance—thus no longer playing the role of pivotal sacrifice in an awesome hieratic order governed by heaven, but saving themselves for the mastery of a religiously rationalized and costumed, yet actually political, order governed by their own fiat—on the other hand, when they finally did expire in nature's own good (nonsymbolic) time, they required their wives, concubines, harem keepers, palace guards, and dwarfs to carry out the heavier part, following the corpse into an underworld prepared for them by himself.

Such obsequies cannot be interpreted, like those of the archaic ritual regicide, as giving evidence of any quenching of ego in the godly role of king. Indeed, on one level—let us say, the merely personal—they would have been celebrated adequately and nobly enough in Tennyson's unexciting last stanza of *Enoch Arden:*

> So passed the strong heroic soul away.
> And when they buried him the little port
> Had seldom seen a costlier funeral.

Historically regarded, however, the great suttee-tombs are of enormous interest. For their moment at the dawn of Egyptian history was precisely that when—to use Spengler's figure—the knowledge of death struck the mind. It was the moment—to manipulate the figure of Thomas Mann—when the sense of individuality, which formerly had been "open behind," closed, and the knowledge of death struck home. Or, again, it was the moment when—to use the evidence of our recent science of archaeology—the invention of the sun-hardened mud brick made it possible to line the substructure of a grave with a roof-supporting wall and thus create an earth-free chamber within, where the body, and with the body the individual corporeal soul (Egyptian, *ha*), could be preserved. "The

* Supra, pp. 70–71.

body of the dead man," as Spengler has said, with reference to Egypt's mortuary cult, "was made everlasting." [87] And the function of the cult was to reunite by magic the corporeal soul (the *ba*) and the incorporeal energetic principle (the *ka*) which had slipped away at death. This done, it was supposed, there would be no death.

And so we are now to recognize in the history of our subject a secondary stage of mythic seizure: not *mythic identification,* ego absorbed and lost in God, but its opposite, *mythic inflation,* the god absorbed and lost in ego. The first, I would suggest, characterized the actual holiness of the sacrificed kings of the early hieratic city states, and the second, the mock holiness of the worshiped kings of the subsequent dynastic states. For these supposed that it was in their temporal character that they were god. That is to say, they were mad men. Moreover, they were supported in this belief, taught, flattered, and encouraged, by their clergy, parents, wives, advisers, folk, and all, who also thought that they were god. That is to say, the whole society was mad. Yet out of that madness sprang the great thing that we call Egyptian civilization. Its counterpart in Mesopotamia produced the dynastic states of that area; and we have adequate evidence, besides, of its force in India, the Far East, and Europe as well. In other words, a large part of the subject-matter of our science must be read as evidence of a psychological crisis of inflation, characteristic of the dawn of every one of the great civilizations of the world: the moment of the birth of its particular style. And if I am correct in my notion of the earlier hieratic stage, a certain sequence appears to be indicated; namely: 1. mythic identification and the hieratic, pre-dynastic state, and 2. mythic inflation and the archaic dynastic styles.

The pharaohs in their cult were no longer simply imitating the holy past, "so that the scripture might be fulfilled." They and their priests were creating something of and for themselves. We are in the presence here of a line of grandiose, highly self-interested, prodigiously inflated egos. Furthermore, as we have seen, these megalomaniacs were not satisfied to be merely one god; they were two, and, as such, had two burial palaces apiece. On the Narmer palette, which was worked on two sides, two crowns appeared, one on each face; and they represented the two Egypts, which again were represented by the interlaced necks of two symbolic beasts. On one side of the palette the pharaonic principle was represented in the bird form of the falcon Horus, on the other as a mighty bull. And in the pageantry of the Sed festival two coronations were celebrated. In the royal sealing of King Zer, the monarch is shown twice, while in the little scratched picture of King Den-Setui nimbly stepping from the presence of his father (with whom, though they were two, the king was one) we have seen that both wear the double crown.

Moreover, the ceremonial name of the Will, the final symbolic warrant of pharaonic rule, is the "Secret of the Two Partners." What are we to think of that?

The answer appears beneath the sands of Abydos, in the tombs of the pharaohs of Dynasty II, which are enormous and exhibit every evidence of a lavish display of suttee. For the fourth pharaoh of this line is always represented by two cartouches and two names, over one of which, Sekhemab, there is shown the usual Horus falcon of the royal house, while over the other name, Perabsen, there appears the curiously characteristic quadruped somewhat resembling an okapi that always stands for the arch-enemy of both Horus and Osiris—namely, Seth. And on the seals of the seventh and last pharaoh of this line, Khasekhemui, the two antagonists, Horus the hero and Seth the villain of the piece, stand side by side, together and co-equal (Figure 12), while the monarch himself is termed "the appearing of the dual power in which the two gods are at peace." [88]

The name of the Will, then, "the Secret of the Two Partners," was a reference to the hidden understanding of the two gods, who, though they appear to be implacable enemies, are of one mind behind the scenes. And we are forced to revise—or at least to amplify—our view of the wisdom of the pharaoh's madness. Mythologically representing the inevitable dialectic of temporality, where all things appear in pairs, Horus and Seth are forever in conflict; whereas in the sphere of eternity, beyond the veil of time and space, where there is no duality, they are at one; death and life are at one; all is peace. And there it is known, also, that that same transcendent peace abides even in the cruelties of war. So

that in the Narmer palette, where the pharaoh, with the lifted arm
of Horus, slays the chieftain of the harpoon folk, together with
six thousand enemies, who are here in the role of Seth, the scene
is one of peace. And of this peace, which is the inhabiting reality
of all things, all history and sorrow, the living god Pharaoh is the

Figure 12. The Dual Power:
Egypt, c. 2650 B.C.

pivot. He is an epitome of the field—the universe itself—in which
the pairs-of-opposites play. Hence, to follow him in death is to
remain in life, there being in fact no death in the royal pasture beyond time, where the two gods are at one and the shepherd crook
gives assurance.

And this secret knowledge that there is the peace of eternal being
within every aspect of the field of temporal becoming is the signature of this entire civilization. It is the metaphysical background of
the majesty of its sculpture as well as of the nobility of its pharaonic
cult of death, which in itself was madness, but, in the way of a
sign, was a metaphor of the mystery of being.

Pharaoh was known as "The Two Lords":

"The Two Lords" [wrote Professor Frankfort] were the
perennial antagonists, Horus and Seth. The king was identified
with both of these gods but not in the sense that he was con-

sidered the incarnation of the one and also the incarnation of the other. He embodied them as a pair, as opposites in equilibrium. . . .

Horus and Seth were the antagonists per se—the mythological symbols for all conflict. Strife is an element in the universe which cannot be ignored; Seth is perennially subdued by Horus but never destroyed. Both Horus and Seth are wounded in the struggle, but in the end there is a reconciliation: the static equilibrium of the cosmos is established. Reconciliation, an unchanging order in which conflicting forces play their allotted part—that is the Egyptian's view of the world and also his conception of the state.[89]

This, then, was the madness of the pharaoh and of Egypt—as it is of the Orient, to this day.

VII. The Immanent Transcendent God

A battered stone, tossed up like jetsam on a beach, reached the British Museum from Egypt in the year 1805, to be catalogued as Stela No. 797. Its difficult inscription was abraded, for it had served for some time as a nether millstone. The light in the museum gallery was poor; Egyptologists are human; and the manner of arrangement of the hieroglyphs was peculiar. In the earliest published copies of its text, therefore, the lines were not only inaccurately rendered but also numbered in reverse. And it was the grand old Professor James Henry Breasted, whose Ancient Histories we all have read in school, who, while gradually working his meticulous way through the British Museum collection of inscriptions for the preparation of the Berlin Egyptian Dictionary, was the first to realize what had happened to the lines: whereupon a revelation stood suddenly before him. He wrote a paper: "The Philosophy of a Memphite Priest." [90]

Professor G. Maspero followed, and he also wrote a paper: "Sur la toute puissance de la parole." [91]

Professor Adolf Erman then composed a paper, "Ein Denkmal memphitischer Theologie," [92] which fixed the date of the text as at the beginning of the Old Kingdom; and this early assignment has now been confirmed.[93] The tossed-up bit of battered rock had received its literary cargo from an earlier document "devoured by worms," which had been copied for preservation in the eighth century B.C. on the order of a certain pharaoh Sabakos. And the reason for all the excitement when its message was deciphered was that the text was found to have anticipated by two thousand years that idea of creation by the power of the Word which appears in the Book of Genesis, where God said, "Let there be light," and there was light. Moreover, in this Old Egyptian version of that unwitnessed scene, the point of view (like that of the Indian account of the Self who said "I" and became two) was interior to the divinity and psychological; not, like the biblical version, an account merely of the sequence of commands and their effects, plus a refrain: "And God saw that it was good." In the Memphite text of the mummy-god Ptah we are told that it was the *heart* of God that brought forth every issue and the *tongue* of God that repeated what the heart had thought:

"Every divine word came into existence by the thought of the heart and the commandment of the tongue."

"When the eyes see, the ears hear, and the nose breathes, they report to the heart. It is the heart that brings forth every issue, and the tongue that repeats the thought of the heart. Thus were fashioned all the gods: even Atum and his Ennead."

The priestly minds of the great temple of Ptah, in the capital city founded by the first pharaoh,* display in this text a view of the nature of deity (c. 2850 B.C.) that is at once psychological and metaphysical. The organs of the human body are associated with psychological functions: the heart with creative conception; the tongue with creative realization. And these functions, then, are *cosmologized*. In the way of a micro-macrocosmic correspondence, they are conceived to be man's portion of universally operative powers. And these principles or powers are what are personified in the figures of the gods, who are thus manifestations (imaged realizations) of the various recognized aspects of the mystery of being. The gods participate, as such, in the numinous aspect of reality. But, on the other hand, in as much as they have been recognized and named, they represent, also, the measure of man's penetration of the mystery of being. And their characters conse-

* Cf. supra, pp. 51–52.

quently partake not only of the ultimate mystery that inhabits every sanctuary of contemplation whatsoever, but also of the measures of insight represented in the priesthoods by which their natures have been defined.

Thus the Memphite priesthood of the creator-deity Ptah deepened the meaning and force of their god's name when they penetrated psychologically to a new depth in their understanding of the nature of creativity itself. And by this philosophical feat they went past the neighboring priesthood of the ancient city of On (Heliopolis), whose concept of creation had been rendered in the myth of their own local creator-deity, the sun-god Atum.

We have two accounts of the creative acts of Atum, both from the Pyramid Texts—which are the earliest known body of religious writings preserved anywhere in the world, inscribed on the walls of a series of nine tombs (c. 2350–2175 B.C.) in the vast necropolis of Memphis, at Sakkara.

According to the first of these accounts:

> Atum created in Heliopolis by an act of masturbation.
> He took his phallus in his fist, to excite desire thereby.
> And the twins were born, Shu and Tefnut.[94]

According to the second version, creation was from the spittle of his mouth, the god standing at the time on the summit of the cosmic maternal mound,* symbolized as a pyramid:

> O Atum-Khepri, when thou didst mount the hill,
> And didst shine like the phoenix on the ancient pyramidal
>   stone in the Temple of the Phoenix in Heliopolis,
> Thou didst spit out what was Shu, sputter out what was Tef-
>   nut.
> And thou didst put thine arms about them as the arms of a
>   ka, that thy ka might be in them.[95]

Atum, therefore, like the Self in the Indian Upanishad, poured himself physically into creation. However, there is no developed psychological analogy indicated in either of these two Egyptian texts—which are certainly much older than the inscriptions in which they are preserved. What they present is simply a primary

* Cf. supra, p. 40.

image of physical creation on the level almost of an unadorned dream symbol.

The twins Shu and Tefnut were a male and female, and it was from them that the rest of the pantheon derived. So we read:

> Shu together with Tefnut created the gods, begat the gods, established the gods.[96]

And the gods begotten of them were the heaven-goddess Nut and her spouse, the earth-god Geb, who in turn begot two divine sets of opposed twins, Isis and Osiris, Nephthys and her brother-consort Seth. So that already in the priestly system of the temple of the sun-god of Heliopolis, a late—and far from primitive—syncretic mythology had been developed, wherein nine gods (known as the Ennead of Heliopolis) were brought together in a hierarchic order, symbolized as a genealogy:

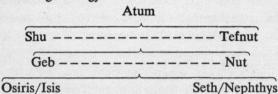

> O great Ennead who are in Heliopolis,
> Atum, Shu, Tefnut, Geb, Nut, Osiris, Isis, Seth, Nephthys,
> Children of Atum . . . your name is the Nine Bows.[97]

Compare, now, the Memphite insight by which this theology was surpassed. The brief text can be readily followed in full.

> *There came into being on the heart and tongue of Ptah, something in the image of Atum.*

The rival creator in a physical sense here is shown as the mere agent of an antecedent spiritual force.

> *Mighty and great is Ptah, who rendered power to the gods and their* kas: *through his heart, by which Horus became Ptah; and through his tongue, by which Thot became Ptah.*

Thot was an ancient moon-god of the city of Hermopolis, who had been brought into the syncretic system of Heliopolis in the role of scribe, messenger, master of the word and of the magic of the resurrection. In the great hall in which the dead are judged he records the weights of their hearts. His animal forms are the ibis and baboon. As an ibis, he sails over the sky. As a baboon, he greets the rising sun. As symbolic of the creative word, however, he is in the Memphite system identified with the power of the *tongue* of Ptah. Likewise, the solar power that Thot greets in its rising, namely Horus, the living son and resurrection of the creative power of Osiris, here is identified with the power of the *heart* of Ptah. The gods are thus functioning members of the larger body, or totality, of Ptah, who dwells in them as their eternal vital force, their *ka*.

> *Thus the heart and tongue won mastery over all the members, in as much as he is in every body and every mouth of all gods, all men, all beasts, all crawling things, and whatever lives, since he thinks and commands everything as he wills.*

The idea is here announced unmistakably of the immanent God that is yet transcendent, which lives in all gods, all men, all beasts, all crawling things, and whatever lives. The Indian image of the Self that became creation is thus anticipated by a full two thousand years.

> *His Ennead is before him in his own teeth and lips. These correspond to the semen and hand of Atum. But whereas the Ennead of Atum came into being by his semen and fingers, that of Ptah consists in the teeth and lips of his mouth, which pronounced of every thing its name—whence Shu and Tefnut came forth; and which was thus the creator of the Ennead.*

The teeth and lips as the agents of the tongue's speech here stand in the roles elsewhere represented by Shu, Tefnut, and the rest. The whole pantheon, as well as the world, thus becomes organically assimilated to the cosmic body of the creator.

And now we come to the psychological analogy already cited:

> *When the eyes see, the ears hear, and the nose breathes, they report to the heart. It is the heart that brings forth every issue, and the tongue that repeats the thought of the heart. Thus were fashioned all the gods: even Atum and his Ennead.*
>
> *Every divine word has come into existence through the heart's thought and tongue's command.*

Thus it was—by such speech—that the kas *were created and the maid servants of the* kas.

The "maid servants of the *kas*" are a constellation of fourteen qualities, identified as the primary effects and signs of creative force; namely: might, radiance, prosperity, victory, wealth, plenty, augustness, readiness, creative action, intelligence, adornment, stability, obedience, and taste.[98]

It is these that make all sustenance, all food; all that is liked and all that is loathed.

Thus it was he who gave life to the peaceful and death to the transgressor.

Thus it was he who made every work, every craft, the action of the arms, the movement of the legs and the activity of each member, according to commands thought by the heart and issuing from the tongue, communicating its significance to each thing.

Therefore it is said of Ptah: "It is he who made all and brought the gods into being." He is verily The Risen Land that brought forth the gods, for everything came forth from him, sustenance and food, the offerings of the gods, and every good thing. Thus it was discovered and understood that his strength was greater than that of all the gods. And Ptah was satisfied when he had made all things and every divine word.

He had fashioned the gods, made the cities, founded the nomes, installed the gods in their shrines, established their offerings and equipped their holy places. He had made likenesses of their bodies to the satisfaction of their hearts, and the gods had entered into these bodies made of every wood, stone, and clay thing that grows upon him, wherein they have taken form. And in this way all the gods and their kas *are at one with him, content and united with the Lord of the Two Lands.*[99]

"One can see," comments Eduard Meyer, on this text, "how really old these speculations of 'Egyptian Wisdom' really are. . . . The myths can no longer be taken simply in their literal sense. They have to be understood as a rendition of deeper thoughts, striving to comprehend the world spiritually, as a unit." [100]

Whereas, however, such cosmic speculations in later ages have been rendered, for the most part, in verbal terms, the normal medium of archaic thought was presentational, in visual terms. And it is surely curious to consider that, although no scholar worth his mortarboard would be likely to eat the menu instead of the dinner, mistaking the printed word for its reference, elementary lapses of this sort are normal in works of learning treating of the ancient gods. It is true that both clergy and layfolk commonly make this mistake in relation to their own religious symbols nowadays, and that everywhere and through all time there have been men who thought their gods were supernatural "celebrities" who might be met somewhere in person. Nevertheless, our battered glimpse of the Wisdom of Stela No. 797 has let us know that in the view, at least, of the priesthood in his temple, the god Ptah was not so quaintly conceived.

He is represented in his glyph as a mummy with a tassel at the back of his collar and the bald head of a tonsured priest; and he was said to be incarnate in a black bull miraculously engendered by a moonbeam. This so-called Apis bull, when ceremonially slain upon attaining the age of twenty-five, was embalmed and buried in the necropolis of Sakkara in a rock cut tomb known as the Serapeum; whereupon, immediately, a new incarnation of the god was born, which could be recognized by certain signs: among others, peculiar white marks on its neck and rump resembling a falcon's wings, and a scarab-like knot beneath its tongue.

The symbolism of the Apis bull thus carried, by way of animal (instead of human) imagery, the basic theme of the sacrificed god that was essential to the pharaonic cult; and the emphasis placed upon it in the capital founded by the founder of Dynasty I suggests very strongly that the metaphor of the sacrificed bull must have been felt to be an adequate substitute for that of the sacrificed king. In the pre-dynastic age, the moon-king had been ritually slain, but in this later age it was the bull—so that the king, relieved of numinous weight, was released for his political ballet.

Ptah is depicted as a mummy; and the Apis bull is black, save for the lighter marking of the falcon wings. Both the mummy and the blackness of the bull refer to the dark moon, the dead moon, into which the old moon dies and from which the new is born. The visible cycle of waning and waxing is but a manifestation in time of aspects of that deeper, timeless stratum. Analogously, the

mythology of the death of Osiris and birth of Horus is no more
than a manifestation in time of a deeper, timeless Ptah.

Likewise in India, in the late Tantric imagery of the period of c.
500–1500 A.D., there is an important order of symbols linked to
the worship of the goddess mother of the world, where she is
shown seated upon Shiva in a manner suggesting the posture of the
early Sumerian seal discussed previously (Figure 4), while beneath
the form of Shiva, as he lies upon his back, there is another aspect
of the god, linked to the first but turned away from the goddess
and with eyes closed (Figure 21; page 335). Shiva in this second
form is known as Shava, "the Corpse," and the analogy with Ptah
as the mummy is obvious.

The analogy is enlarged when it is considered that the animal of
Shiva is the bull Nandi whereas that of Ptah is the Apis bull. It is
enlarged still further when it is realized that the reference of both
symbolic systems is to the mystery of the god who is transcendent
(the Self before it said "I") yet simultaneously immanent (the Self,
split in two, begetting the universe). And the analogy goes beyond
all mere chance when it is known that the animal vehicle of the
goddess consort of Shiva is the lion, whereas the goddess consort
of Ptah is the great and terrible lion-goddess Sekhmet, whose name
means the "Powerful One." Her Indian counterpart is called the
"power" (*śakti*) of Shiva, and, as we have seen (pages 5–6), she
is insatiable in her thirst for the ambrosia of blood.

There is an Egyptian document of c. 2000–1800 B.C. which
tells of the wrath of the lion-goddess Sekhmet, who, according to
this text, came into being as an aspect of the cow-goddess Hathor,
to wreak chastisement on the people of Seth. She could not be
stayed when her work was done, however, and so the gods, to save
mankind, caused their slave girls to brew seven thousand jars of
beer, which they infused with powdered mandrake, to make it resemble human blood. "And in the best part of the night," we read,
"this sleeping draught was poured out until the fields were flooded
four spans by that liquid. And when the goddess appeared in the
morning [as the blazing morning sun], she beheld this inundation:
her face, reflected in it, was beautiful. She drank and, liking it,

returned to her palace drunk. And it was thus that the world of mankind was saved." [101]

In the early mythologies of the moon-bull the sun was always conceived as a warlike, blazing, destructive deity; and in the fierce heat of the tropics it is indeed a terrible force, well likened to a lioness or to a pouncing bird of prey; whereas the moon, dispenser of the night dews by which the world of vegetation is refreshed, represents the principle of life: the principle of birth and death that is life. Symbolically, the moon—the moon-bull—like all living things, dies and is reborn; and whereas, on the one hand, its death is a function of its own nature, on the other hand, it is brought about by the pounce of the lioness, or of the solar bird of prey. So that the solar bird or lioness actually is only an agent of a principle of death that inheres already in the nature of life itself. Hence, the sun must be conceived to be a manifestation of only one aspect of the life/death principle, which is more fully symbolized in the moon: in the moon-bull attacked by the lion. Sekhmet is a manifestation, therefore, of one aspect of Hathor. And whereas Ptah, in his creative, phallic aspect, sends his moon-beam to fertilize a cow, the animal of Hathor, and thus generates the moon-bull; in his punitive, death-dealing, pharaonic aspect, his consort is Sekhmet. His son by Sekhmet is the ruling pharaoh— symbolized in the human-headed, lion-bodied Sphinx, among the pyramids wherein the Osiris-bodies of the pharaohs silently reside. And finally, to clinch the argument by analogy for an identity in origin of the symbols of Ptah and Shiva, it is to be observed that the Uraeus Serpent of pharaonic authority appears from the mid-point of the brow of the Sphinx, which in the Shivaite symbolism of India is the point of the third eye, known as the center of "command" (*ājñā*), whence the annihilating blaze of the so-called Serpent Power of the god flashes in his wrath.

VIII. The Priestcraft of Art

The subtle lore of the greatest capital city of Old Egypt can be understood in its proper force only when it is realized that those by whom it was developed were a priesthood of practicing creative artists. The tombs at Abydos, in Upper Egypt, had been dug into gravel; those of the Memphis area, on the high plateau at Sakkara, where the limestone stratum lay much closer to the surface, had to be cut down into bed rock.[102] Already in the late predynastic period the harder stones had been brought into use in Egypt for mace heads, slate palettes, and various types of vessel, worked by means of hand drills and by rubbing. At the time of the Narmer palette, the bow drill and weighted crank borer were introduced, and with such effect that by the time of King Zer * stone vessels were being produced in such quantity that all but the finer types of ceramic wares were being displaced.[103] Hence, already in the period of the pharaoh Sekhemab/Perabsen of Dynasty II, copper chisels in the hands of the craftsmen of the Memphite nome were not only quarrying and finishing huge blocks, but even carving at will into living rock.

The period of Khasekhemui, at the close of the reign of Dynasty II (c. 2650 B.C.), was one of sudden advance in all the arts. The potter's wheel had recently been introduced (which in Southwest Asia had appeared as early as c. 4000 B.C.), copper was coming abundantly into use, a new corpus of stone vessels made an appearance, and the art of carving stone, both in relief and in the round, began to move toward mastership. As Eduard Meyer wrote of this period in his great *History of Antiquity:* "We are already approaching the blossom time of early Egyptian culture." [104] And with the fall of Dynasty II the time of that blossoming arrived. For with Dynasty III (c. 2650–2600 B.C.), there came a decisive shift of political emphasis north to Memphis, the grim series of suttee tombs at Abydos terminated, and in the Memphite necropolis at Sakkara there appeared, c. 2630 B.C., the fabulous Step Pyramid of the pharaoh Zoser.

This lovely monument was not of brick, as the great tombs before it had been, but of a white limestone, with a beautifully polished finish that was admired by tourist visitors until as late as c. 600 B.C. (as their exclamations written on its surface show). The superstructure was a tall stepped monument of six progressively diminishing stone mastabas, piled one upon the other to a

* Supra, p. 71.

height of some 200 feet, being at the base about 230 feet long by 223 wide. The burial chamber (the substructure) was cut far down into the limestone beneath, into which immense blocks of hardest granite were lowered for the construction of the mausoleum, and surrounding the precincts of the pyramid (which was about as tall as a modern twenty-story building) there was a fortified wall 30 yards long east to west, 596 yards north to south, and 30 feet high, faced with a fine white limestone masonry of small brick-like blocks, to imitate the mud brick walls of an archaic fortified town. Along this wall at regular intervals great square bastions stood, and between two of these, larger than the rest, was the main, very narrow entrance, with a width of only 3 feet. Within were to be seen rows of gleaming temples, secondary tombs and chapels, galleries and colonnades, in perfectly worked, perfectly finished, perfectly beautiful white stone: columns, fluted and unfluted, free-standing and engaged; rectangular capitals and bases, circular capitals and bases, papyrus capitals, capitals with pendant leaves; caryatids; stairways of stone; walls inlaid in mat patterns with tiles of blue faïence; walls carved in wattle-mat patterns in bas-relief; walls carved with figures in high relief: bas-relief figures of the pharaoh Zoser nimbly striding, holding the flail over his shoulder and in his left hand the document of the Sed festival, the Secret of the Two Partners, wearing the archaic kilt and belt with the heads of the cow-goddess Hathor of the Horizon.

When the ruins were systematically excavated during the twenties and thirties of the present century, tons of alabaster fragments lay all about; for the precious area had been murderously plundered before the cool science of the West arrived to register for mankind—not appropriate and destroy—as much as possible of our common past. And among the fragments there was found the monolithic base of a throne, ornamented by fourteen lion (not bull) heads, carved in the round.[105]

An age had passed: that of the bull. Another had dawned: that of the lion. The mythology of the lunar bull was henceforth to be overlaid, and not alone in Egypt, by a solar mythology of the lion. The lunar light waxes and wanes. That of the sun is forever bright. Darkness inhabits the moon, where its play is symbolic of that of death in life here on earth; whereas darkness attacks the sun from without and is thrown off daily in defeat by a force that is never dark. The moon is the lord of growth, the waters, the womb, and the mysteries of time; the sun, of the brilliance of the intellect, sheer light, and eternal laws that never change.

It is noteworthy that with the coming to flower in Memphis of an art in durable stone, the mythology arose also of a god who never dies. Moreover, it is also to be noted that the priesthood now known to have been responsible for Egypt's art and architecture in stone was that of the temple compound of Ptah. Within the precincts of that temple a multitude of master craftsmen chipped and polished away, throughout the pyramid age, under supervision of a high priest who bore the title *wr ḥrpw ḥmwt,* "master of the master craftsmen." The prodigious stone elements of the monuments to the glory of the pharaohs were fashioned there apart and, at the times of the annual inundation, when all the fieldwork ceased, the field hands of the whole country came to Memphis to float the perfectly trimmed huge blocks over the waters and haul them up ramps into place. The quarries, too, were owned by the god Ptah, so that both the material and the work were ordered by the king from the priesthood of his temple. And since the royal projects, both for the pharaoh himself and for those of his court whom he favored with funeral plots and tombs near his own, were infinitely numerous, the greatest art school of the ancient world until the brief period of Athens in its prime was developed from the heart and tongue, so to say, of the master of the diligent, perfectly competent master craftsmen of Ptah.[106]

The mummy-god was thus, indeed, a god not only of creation, but also of creative art. The Greeks identified him with Hephaistos. He was the god who had fashioned the world, and the secrets of his craft, therefore, were those of the form and formation of the world. Would it be too bold to suggest, then, that the knowledge of the nature of creation rendered in his mythology must have derived its depth from the actual creative experience and knowledge of the priesthood by which it was conceived? It is entirely to them that the civilized world owes the noble ruins not only of the Step Pyramid of Dynasty III (c. 2650 B.C.) but also of the Pyramid

Age of Dynasties IV–VI (c. 2600–2190 B.C.), and therewith the earliest manifestation in firmly datable stone of practically all of the basic rules, techniques, and formulae upon which the arts of architecture and sculpture in stone have been grounded ever since.

IX. Mythic Subordination

Throughout the reigns of Dynasties I–IV (c. 2850–2480 B.C.) every calorie of Egyptian manpower not required for the tilling of the fields was thrown into the mythological enterprise of keeping the pharaohs happy for all eternity; and such a cult of the dead, as Eduard Meyer has observed, "never had to do with the worship of a god from whom help and protection were desired, or whose wrath was to be appeased (as all theories deriving the origins of religion from ancestor worship would presume), but, on the contrary, was concerned only with the artificial respiration of a spirit, impotent in itself, that was to be made equivalent to a god, yet was no such thing." [107] The myth was directly, and without irony, breach, or distance, assumed to himself by the pharaoh; so that the paramount divinity, focus of religious life, and proposed object of highest concern for all mankind was that mighty summary of the Secret of the Two Partners, this individual, somewhat "open behind": the god-king. And the magnitude of Cheops' pyramid (six and a quarter million tons: "the mightiest structure that the earth has to bear," as Meyer remarks) [108] illustrates the proportions to which an untrammeled ego may grow under such manuring.

However, at the high period of the Pyramid Age itself, a new, comparatively humane, benevolent, fatherly quality began to be apparent in the character and behavior of the pharaohs of Dynasty IV. "The harsh stress on the omnipotence of Pharaoh," Meyer notes, "and the unbridled satisfaction of his whims, belonged to a distant past, even though in the language of the magical texts it might seem to have survived. He was to be approached only as a god, yet even the gods had become kind. Time and time again we read in the tomb inscriptions of how the king looked graciously upon his servants, loved them, praised them, and gave them rich awards. And when the grave inscriptions in the middle of the IVth Dynasty began to become talkative, they gave praise to the deceased for never having perpetrated evil, taken from anyone his property or servant, never having abused his power, but having always behaved justly: and there were even mentions of filial piety and marital love." [109] Whereas, of yore, in the period of the awesome palaces of the dead sacrificed to this god-king, the Lord of Life and Death had taken wives from their husbands just as he wished, according to the heat of his own lust; men had approached him trembling, kissing the dust of his feet, only the most privileged being allowed his knees; and even the naming of his name was shunned, there being used a screening term instead, to wit: the "Great House" (par'o), Pharaoh.[110]

One can only try to imagine, in the light of this description of the masters of those underground palaces built by the living gods themselves while yet alive, what the feelings must have been of the herd of young women, dwarfs and eunuchs, bodyguards and masters of the court, who watched and knew the meaning of the rooms and corridors being constructed to receive them. And one can only ask what the sobering influences might have been by which those monsters of the great big "I" were rendered human and humane.

My own first guess, already named, is that it was by the influence of art. For since mythology is born of fantasy, any life or civilization brought to form as a result of a literal mythic identification or inflation, as a concrete *imitatio dei,* will necessarily bear the features of a nightmare, a dream-game too seriously played— in other words, madness; whereas, when the same mythological imagery is properly read as fantasy and allowed to play into life as art, not as nature—with irony and grace, not fierce daemonic compulsion—the psychological energies that were formerly in the capture of the compelling images take the images in capture, and can be deployed with optional spontaneity for life's enrichment. Moreover, since life itself is indeed such stuff as dreams are made on, such a transfer of accent may conduce, in time, to a life lived in noble consciousness of its own nature.

It is completely obvious that in the ancient valley of the Nile, in the third millennium B.C., a lived myth—or rather, a myth living itself out in the bodies of men—was turning a neolithic folk culture into one of the most elegant and enduring of the world's high civilizations, literally moving mountains to become pyramids, and filling the earth with the echoes of its beauty. Yet the individuals in its ban were so bewitched that, titans though they were in deed, in sentiment they were infantile. A number of long wooden royal barges were recently discovered buried in deep rock-cut slots around the mighty pyramids at Giza: five around the pyramid of Cheops (Khufu) and five around that of Chephren (Khafre).[111]

First, suttee burial; and then, this? The great man sailing in his toy to eternity, like an infant in an airplane without wings?

"Never on this earth," wrote Eduard Meyer, in comment on the mortuary cult of the Pyramid Age,

> was the task of turning the impossible into the possible addressed with so much energy and persistence: the task, that is to say, of extending the brief span of a man's years, together with all of its delights, into eternity. The Old Empire Egyptians believed in this possibility with the deepest fervor; otherwise they would never have gone on, generation after generation, squandering upon it the whole wealth of the state and civilization. Nevertheless, behind the enterprise there lurked the feeling that all of the splendor was only illusory; that all the massive means that were being employed would even under the most favorable circumstances be able to produce only a haunting dreamlike state of existence and not really change the facts the least bit. The body, in spite of the magic, still would not be alive; could neither move nor take nourishment to itself. And so a statue would suffice in its stead; as would, also, pictures on the tomb wall instead of actual offerings and living sacrifices; or even dolls would do, for example of women grinding and baking, placed near the dead; in fact, finally, simply offering-formulae would be sufficient, pronounced and inscribed around the tomb door. In the period of Dynasty IV things had not yet gone so far that the implications of this line of reasoning were carried to their logical end and the presentation of actual offerings abandoned. However, the formulae and the picture world were already supplementing

the offerings and would eventually take their place. And so it came to be supposed that the painted and sculpted forms of his servants, particularly if their names were inscribed, would be assured the same continued existence as the deceased himself.[112]

The final breakthrough, for Egypt, came with the fall of Dynasty IV and appearance of the priest-founded Dynasty V (2480–2350 B.C.). For at that moment, and from that moment onward, the pharaoh, though still a god, was to know and comport himself as a god not of first but of second rank. A new myth sprang to the fore: of a new and glorious divinity, the sun-god named Re, who was not, like Horus, the son, but himself the father of the pharaoh, as well as of all else. The earlier history of this divinity is unknown. He was identified with Atum, but has a different quality and force. Nor do we know the background of the royal house by which he was brought forward. There is, however, a legend of the virgin birth of the first three pharaohs of the reign, where they are represented as sons of the god Re; and, although preserved in a late papyrus of c. 1600 B.C., it is almost certainly the basic origin myth of the dynasty itself. Its sunny atmosphere of play is characteristic of the mythic mood of solar as opposed to lunar thought. In it the old, deep, vegetal melancholy of a dark destiny of death and of birth out of decay has disappeared and a fresh, blithe breath of clean air has come blowing into the field, scattering shadows all away. A masculine spirit has taken over: boyish, somewhat; comparatively superficial, one might say; but with a certain distance from itself that makes a play of intellect possible where before all had been depth and woe.

The tale is of the good lady Ruditdidit, spouse of a certain high priest, Rausir by name, of the temple of the sun-god Re; who had conceived three sons of Re that were to be born to her as triplets. And when the pangs of childbirth approached, the god himself, on high, called out urgently to Isis, Nephthys, Hiqait (the frog-headed midwife who had been present at the birth of the world), Maskhonuit (goddess of childbirth and of the cradle), and the god Khnum (who fashions forms): "Hie there! Make haste! Deliver the lady Ruditdidit of those babes that are in her womb, which are to fulfill in the Two Lands the beneficent kingly function, building temples for you and bringing offerings to your altars, provisions to your tables, and increasing your temple-estates."

And having heard that command of the Majesty of Re, those five deities made off. The four goddesses changed themselves into musicians, and Khnum accompanied them as a porter, in which guise they arrived at the domicile of Rausir, where they discovered him unfolding linen. And when they passed before him with their castanets and sistrums, he called to them: "Ladies! Ladies! Please! There is a woman here in the pains of childbirth." But they answered: "Allow us, then, to see her; for we are skilled in the midwife's art." And he said to them: "Well then, do come in!" So they entered. And they closed the door on the lady Ruditdidit and themselves.

Isis placed herself before the woman where she was crouching upon a mat; Nephthys stood behind to clasp her round the body during the pains; and Hiqait hastened the delivery by massaging. "O child," said the goddess Isis, "in thy name of Usir-raf, 'He whose mouth is mighty,' be not mighty in her womb!" Whereupon the child came out upon her hands: an infant of a cubit's length, powerful of bone, with members the color of gold, and lapis lazuli hair. The attendant goddesses washed him, cut the umbilical cord, and placed him on a brick bed, whereupon Maskhonuit approached and prophesied: "This will be a king who will exercise royalty in the Two Lands." And Khnum infused health into his members.

Isis again placed herself before the woman, Nephthys stood behind, and Hiqait assisted the second birth. "O child," said Isis, "in thy name of Sahuriya, 'He who is Re journeying in heaven,' do not journey longer in the womb!" Whereupon the child came out upon her hands, etc. . . . And a third time, assisting, she said: "O child, in thy name of Kakui, 'The Dark One,' do not tarry longer in the dark womb!" And this little pharaoh too came out upon her hands: of a cubit's length, powerful of bone, with members the color of gold, and lapis lazuli hair. The deities washed him, cut the cord, laid him on a brick bed, Maskhonuit approached and made her prophecy, and Khnum infused health into his members.

Departing, they said to the good man outside: "Rejoice, Rausir, for behold, three sons have now been born to thee." And he said to them, "O Ladies, what can I do for you?" And he said to them again: "Here, give this corn to your porter, that he may take it in payment to your silos." And the god took up the corn, and those five returned to the place whence they had come.[113]

We take note of the virgin-birth motif. In the earlier mythology the pharaoh had been the bull of his mother; he is not to be so any more. An eternal, higher principle of pure light has been turned against the earlier, fluctuating principle of both darkness and light, death and resurrection, as the sun against the moon. The sun never dies. The sun descends into the netherworld, battles the demons of the night sea, is in danger, but never dies.

Superficially regarded [wrote Professor Meyer], the cult of Re might be said to represent only one more god added to the rest. The pharaoh attended no less zealously to the service of those others, with offerings and grants of land, than to the building of his new temples to Re; and in these temples themselves, furthermore, worship was paid to Re's double, the god of light, 'Horus on the Horizon,' and to the heaven-goddess Hathor, as well as to Re himself. In this the cult differed essentially from the later sun religion of Ikhnaton. But already, even the form of the cult reveals the profound distinction between Re and all the other deities. An otherworldly element and a more elevated idea of God enter Egyptian life; and therewith a counterweight is brought to bear against the idea of the god-king, which exclusively dominated Dynasty IV. Along with the task of building his own colossal tomb, the pharaoh now assumes, immediately upon coming to the throne, the no less important, no less costly duty of erecting to the sun-god a new place of worship. . . . Local deities maintain the respect of the educated and retain their place in theology only as forms of the manifestation of Re, while the goddesses become heaven-goddesses and mothers of the sun. And the kingship itself also is reinterpreted. On the one hand, exalted as the son of the heavenly ruler of the world, the pharaoh is, on the other hand, subordinated to a new and higher religious idea. The king no longer stands on a footing or equality with his father, as formerly the living Horus among the gods, but is now his obedient son who accomplishes his will. That is why the pharaoh of the following centuries is no longer the "great god," as before, but the "good." [114]

And with this I would end our present viewing of the documents of the Nile, where the record is preserved of a sequence of psychological transformations, progressing:

1. from an antecedent pre-dynastic stage of mythic identification, characterized by the submission of all human judgment to the wonder of a supposed cosmic order, announced by a priesthood, and executed upon a sacrificed god-king;

2. through an early dynastic stage of mythic inflation (Dynasties I–IV, c. 2850–2480 B.C.), when the will of the god-king himself became the signal of destiny and a vastly creative, daemoniac pathology conjured into being a symbolic civilization;

3. to a culminating stage of mythic subordination (Dynasty V, c. 2480–2350 B.C. and thereafter), where the king, though still in his mythic role, no longer played the untrammeled part of a *mysterium tremendum* made flesh, but brought to bear against himself the censorship of an order of human judgment.

Thus, in the way of a communal psychoanalytic cure, the civilization was brought, through the person of its symbolic king, from a state of fascinated cosmic seizure to one of reasonably balanced humanity. Human values projected upon the universe—goodness, benevolence, mercy, and the rest—were attributed to its creator, and the taming of the pharaoh was achieved as a reflection of this supposed humanity of the universal god. The pharaoh was "Good," no longer "Great" in the archaic sense; and yet he still was God —true God as well as true Man. He retained his power and special place among men as a divinity, and yet was subordinated through the imagery of myth to a power higher, not than himself, but than those aspects of himself that appear—like the Apis bull—in the field of time. Furthermore, the land of Egypt in which he ruled was paradise: the sense remained of a divinity immanent in the world. Man was not cut off. There had been no Fall. The individual at death would stand before the judgment seat of Osiris, but that was to be an affair touching the virtues of only that particular case. Mankind itself was not ontologically condemned, nor was the universe. So that Egypt—definitely—is to be recognized as belonging to the context rather of a certain aspect of the Orient than of the West. The inhabiting spirit of the mythology is wonder, not guilt.

And finally it is surely appropriate to ask, now, whether it may not have been through the magic of its wonderful art that the cure of Egypt from its seizure was effected, without breaking the bond of wonder and yet humanizing its force. In Mesopotamia the bond broke; but in Mesopotamia there was no such glorious art as in Egypt. Indeed, there was no match for Egyptian art anywhere in the world until the Classic period of Greece; and after that the Gupta period of India, c. 400 A.D., whence the magic passed with Mahayana Buddhism to China and Japan. We have noted homologies, more than superficial, associating the mythologies of Ptah and Shiva. Let us now point to those also of the arts. In the rock-cut cave temple of Abu Simbel built by Ramses II (1301–1234 B.C.), not only the craft, but also the whole idea and even the basic architectural plan, organization of the façade, and conception of the interior anticipate by over a millennium and a half the rock-cut Indian temples of both Shiva and the Buddha at Elura and elsewhere. So that, if the relationship of an art style to its informing myth is a matter of any moment, there is a problem here of considerable interest, waiting to be explored; namely, the passage of inspiration from both the arts and the mysteries of Egypt to those that came to flower c. 400–1250 A.D. in India, Tibet, China, and Japan.

✦✦✦✦✦✦✦✦✦✦✦✦✦✦✦✦✦ *Chapter 3* ✦✦✦✦✦✦✦✦✦✦✦✦✦✦✦✦✦

THE CITIES OF MEN

✦✦✦

I. Mythic Dissociation

In the almost perfectly protected, readily defended valley of the Nile, with the sea to the north and deserts east, west, and south, the ruling dynasties remained in power, for the most part, over long periods and with no interference from without—save in the century of Hyksos rule, when a mixed horde of Asiatic aliens, equipped with the war chariot and compound bow, shattered the northeast frontier and took possession, c. 1670–1570 B.C. "They ruled without Re and did not act by divine command," declared Queen Hatshepsut (1486–1468 B.C.), when those whom the gods abominate had been made distant and the earth had carried off their footprints.[1] New protective imperial outposts for Egypt then were established deep within Asia, as far north even as Syria; and while the people of the Nile returned to their own old ways of toil, peace, and prosperity under *maat,* the influence of their thought and civilization spread abroad.

Throughout the Southwest Asian Near East, on the other hand, fluctuating swarms of races and traditions of altogether differing backgrounds were continually colliding; so that a pell-mell of battle, massacre, general disorder, and mutual vituperation, held in check only momentarily by petty kings who at best were never more secure in their seats than the man temporarily on top of a battle royal, produced an atmosphere little conducive to belief or confidence in the wholesomeness of God's world. In addition, the two holy rivers themselves were undependable; as were also the comings and goings of the clouds. The annual, desirable inundations of the Nile were in perfect accord with the normal hopes and expectations of the populace. Occurring at the time of the annual appearances of Sothis (Sirius), the beautiful star of Isis, on the dawn horizon, they afforded a relatively dependable sign and schedule of the right order of the goddess-mistress of the cosmos. Whereas the flash floods and even sudden shiftings of course of the Tigris and Euphrates were as undependable, unmanageable, and terrible as everything else in that harsh terrain. Hence in Mesopotamia the priestly art of knowing the will and order of creation required a much more constant watch given to immediate phenomena than its counterpart in Egypt, and a development of numerous, very seriously studied techniques of divination was a consequence of this necessity; as, for example: hepatoscopy (examining the livers of sacrificed beasts), oleography (judging the configurations of oil poured into water), astroscopy (an observation of the visible appearances of the stars, planets, moon, and sun, not yet, as in astrology proper, a judgment of their relative placements in the zodiac); also a judgment of meteorological conditions (cloud formations, varieties of thunder and lightning, rains, winds, earthquakes, etc.); further, an observation of the behavior of animals, the flights of birds, births of prodigies, etc.[2] And just as the tumult of the social and political scene led in time to a development throughout Southwest Asia of increasingly powerful governments and orders of civil law, so the necessity to keep a strict watch on nature conduced—especially in astronomy —to the beginnings of a systematic science.

Hence, whereas in Africa, in the protected oasis of the Nile valley, an archaic civilization retained its form in essential purity from c. 2850 B.C. until the dawn of the Christian era, Southwest Asia, where the earliest high neolithic culture forms had appeared as early as c. 4500 B.C. and the earliest considerable city states a millennium later, retained not its *form,* but its *leadership* as the chief growing point of all civilization whatsoever—until precisely 331 B.C., when the brilliant European youth Alexander the Great (356–323 B.C.), broke the army of the King of Kings, Darius III (r. 336–330 B.C.), and sounded the prelude to the modern age of intercultural syncretism under the leadership of the European West.

We have already taken note of the forms of the earliest known temple compounds anywhere in the world: those at Brak, Khafajah, Uqair, Obeid, Uruk, and Eridu, whose general date was c.

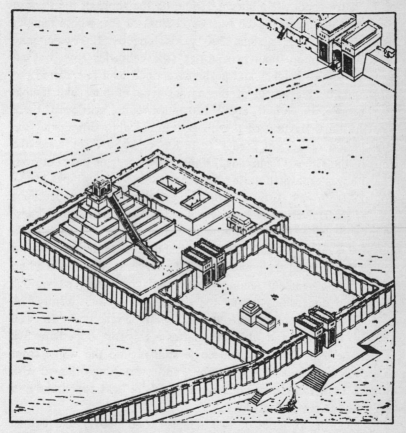

Figure 13. The Ziggurat at Nippur (Reconstruction): Iraq, c. 2000 B.C.

4000–3500 B.C. During the subsequent millennium a new type of Mesopotamian temple arose in the form of the towering many-terraced ziggurat (Figure 13). Oriented with its four angles to the quarters, rising from an immense precinct within which numerous subsidiary buildings harbored a busy administrative priesthood, the symbolic mountain of packed clay and brick carried a palace on its summit furnished for the chief god of the city. For each of the Mesopotamian city states was in this period conceived to be the earthly manor of one of the world-controlling gods: Ur, of the moon-god Nannar; and nearby Obeid, as we have seen, of the dairy-goddess Ninhursag. Eridu, on the shore of the Persian Gulf, was the manor of the water-god Enki or Ea, whose temple, rising from a terrace some 200 yards long by 120 wide, may have had no more than two stories (the centuries have washed away its proper height) and perhaps retained to a late period the form, greatly magnified, of the earlier type of houselike temple on a terrace. In Nippur, about 110 miles to the northwest, there rose the huge ziggurat of the air-god Enlil, who, throughout the high period of ancient Sumer (c. 3500–c. 2050 B.C.) was, like Zeus of the Greek Olympians, *primus inter pares* of the pantheon. The site was excavated during the years 1889–90, 1890–91, 1893–96, and 1896–1900, by a series of greatly troubled expeditions sent by the University of Pennsylvania. Harassed by Arabs, illness, clumsy methods, and everything else, the courageous spadesmen amassed a haul of some thirty thousand cuneiform tablets,[3] but somewhat bungled their analysis of the ziggurat,[4] so that we find today little agreement among the learned concerning its various forms and dimensions during the periods of its long history.[5] A large forecourt fronting the river and a larger rear court are well assured, however, and within the latter a ziggurat of perhaps five stories, perhaps three, with a single stairway up the whole front to a probable temple at the summit, and everything oriented with corners to the quarters. Furthermore, there was, apparently, a large "lower temple" at the base.

In fact, the formula of two temples, one above, one below, appears to have been essential to the ziggurat from its earliest period; and the mythological background of this circumstance has been sensitively interpreted by the architect W. Andrae.[6] Very briefly, his argument suggests that the deity dwelt in the temple at the summit and was revealed in that below. There were furnished apartments in the upper, to accommodate not only the chief god or goddess, but also an entourage of divine attendants; and at certain festival times designated by the calendar, the deity, appearing in the lower temple, received the worship of the folk and bestowed boons. So that the ziggurat, on the one hand, supplied the deity with a means of descent to his city on earth and, on the other hand, provided the inhabitants of that city with a means of approach and petition to their god.

For the Mesopotamian kings were no longer, like those of Egypt, gods in themselves. That critical dissociation between the spheres of God and man which in time was to separate decisively the religious systems of the Occident from those of the Orient, had already taken place. The king was no longer a god-king, or even properly a "king" (*lugal*), but only the "vicar" (*patesi*) of the true King, who was the god above.

There is a myth of the creation of man in which some of the implications of this new sense of dissociation come to view. It is from the cycle of the god Enki or Ea of the temple-city of Eridu, one of whose names, *e-a,* means "God of the House of Water," and the other, "the Lord (*en*) of the goddess Earth (*ki*)." His symbolic animal had the foreparts of a goat but the body of a fish: the form still familiar as Capricorn, the symbol of the tenth sign of the zodiac, into which the sun enters at the time of the winter solstice, for rebirth. Enki functioned as a god of purification in the water rituals known as rituals of the "house of baptism" or "of washing"; [7] and there is surely more than a coincidence to be seen in the fact that in the work of a late Babylonian priest Berossos, who wrote in Greek, c. 280 B.C., the name given him was Oannes: compare the Greek *Iōannes,* Latin *Johannes,* Hebrew *Yoḥanan,* English *John:* John the Baptist and the idea of rebirth through water (John 3:5). Enki resided with his spouse, the goddess Ninhursag, in an island paradise known as Dilmun, which has been identified geographically as the island Bahrein in the Persian Gulf, but in its mythological character was a "land of the living," pure and bright, in the midst of the primeval sea:

> In Dilmun the raven does not croak,
> The kite does not utter its shrill cry,

The lion does not kill,
The wolf snatches not the lamb,
Unknown is the kid-devouring wild dog.

There the dove droops not its head,
The sick-eyed says not 'I am sick-eyed,'
The sick-headed says not 'I am sick-headed,'
Its old woman says not 'I am an old woman,'
Its old man says not 'I am an old man.' [8]

Dr. Samuel Noah Kramer has shown through comparative studies of innumerable Sumerian tablets in the libraries of Europe, the Near East, and America, that the goddess Nammu, whose name is written with the pictograph for "primeval sea," was the ultimate "mother, who gave birth to Heaven and Earth," [9] and that these two were pictured in the single form of a cosmic mountain, the base of which, hovering above the watery abyss, was the bottom of the earth, while its summit was heaven's zenith. The lower portion, Earth (*Ki*), was female, and the upper, Heaven (*An*), a male; so that their nature was again that of the dual primordial being we already know.

An begot the air-god Enlil, who separated Earth and Heaven, tore them apart just as, in the well-known Classical myth of Hesiod, Gaia (Earth) and Uranos (Heaven) were separated by their son Kronos (Saturn).[10] A numerous pantheon was born, and those gods in their heavenly city lived about as men do on earth, tilling fields of grain.

However, there came a time when their crops failed, owing largely to neglect, and Nammu, the old water-mother, perceiving the plight of her progeny, looked about to find Enki, the cleverest of them all, the lord of her own abyss, whom she discovered in deep slumber on his couch. She woke him up. "My son!" she said. And she told him of the sorrow of the gods. "Arise from thy couch and bring to pass some great work of wisdom. Fashion servants for the gods who will assume their tasks." And the wise Enki, rising, said to her: "O Mother, it can be done."

"Reach up," he said, "and take a handful of clay from the bottom of the earth, just above the surface of our watery abyss, and shape it to the form of a heart. I shall produce good and princely craftsmen who will bring that clay to the right consistency. And then do thou shape the limbs. Above thee the Earth-mother, my goddess-spouse, will be in labor, and eight goddesses of birth will be at hand to assist. Thou shalt name the newborn's fate. The Earth-mother will have fixed the image of the gods upon it. And what it will be is Man."

The work came to pass. The Earth-goddess, spouse of Enki, stood above the goddess of the watery abyss, and with the eight birth goddesses in attendance, the clay was taken, severed as one severs an infant from its mother. Good and princely craftsmen brought it to the right consistency, and Nammu shaped first the heart, then the body and limbs.

Whereupon, to celebrate, Enki made a feast for his spouse and his mother, to which he invited all the gods; for it was a great and wonderful idea that he had brought to realization, as the gods were quick to perceive. They praised him fulsomely for his invention of a race that would serve as slaves, to work diligently the farms from which they would now derive the rich fats and nourishment of sacrifice forever. Each deity would have his own estate and manor, with an overseer, his tenant farmer, who would imitate on earth the kingly role of Enlil among the gods. His dwelling would be a symbol on earth of the world-mountain of Enlil. His queen would be his counterpart of the lovely goddess Ninlil, the planet Venus. And all would be on earth as it is in heaven. There would be a doorkeeper and chief butler of the palace-temple, just as in the palace of the god above; a counselor and body servant, chamberlain, coachman, drummer, and chief musician, seven daughters (ladies-in-waiting), armorers and palace guards; and beyond the walls of the temple citadel, in the fields and villages round about, a bailiff, inspector of fisheries, gamekeeper, sheriff, and—here the wonder!—multitudes of toiling serfs.

It was a glorious party, and both Enki and his wife soon were hilariously drunk. The text from here on is worth close attention:

Their hearts became elated and the goddess called over to the god:
"How good, really, or how bad, can a human body be?

As my heart now prompts me, I shall make the body good,
    or make it bad."

And Enki, broad of understanding, answered:
"Whatever body comes from thy hand, I shall find a place for
    it."

She took a mess of that clay, and fashioned of it six defective
wights, each of which had some great bodily lack: a woman unable
to give birth, a being with neither male nor female organ. . . .
But for each, as it came, Enki was able to suggest a place:

Enki, upon seeing the woman who could not give birth,
Decreed her fate: to be stationed in the harem.
Enki, upon seeing the one with neither male nor female organ,
Decreed its fate: to stand before the king. . . .

Four others such were created—the description of which no
one has yet been able to interpret from the cuneiform. However,
the game had not yet reached an end; for Enki, feeling that he had
won, challenged the goddess to change sides: he would now
create, and she name the place.

He made a creature called "My Birthday Is Remote," with
liver and heart in great pain, eyes diseased, trembling hands,
spirit gone. Then he called to his goddess:

"For each of those whom thou hast fashioned, I have readily
    named a place;
So now do thou name the place for this that I have fashioned,
Wherein he may subsist."

She approached the being and spoke to him. He was unable to
reply. She offered him bread. He was unable to reach for it. He
could neither sit, stand, nor bend his knees. She was unable to
name for him any fate.

And so Enki created more. Once again, however, the cuneiform
becomes illegible. Apparently disease, madness, and everything
else of the sort came into being as Enki maliciously drove his
goddess to a corner. All we know is that in the end she was
screaming:

"My city is destroyed, my house wrecked;
My children have been taken captive.

I have been exiled from the mountain city of the gods:
Even I escape not thy hand!
Henceforth thou shalt dwell neither in heaven nor on earth."

And Enki, thus indignantly condemned by the goddess-mother of mankind, was indeed exiled from the earth to the abyss. "A command issuing from thy mouth," he said, "who can change it?" And with that line the tablet breaks off.[11] The drunken party fades in uproar. Its effects, however, abide.

"Man's mime," as we read in *Finnegans Wake;* "God has gest."

It is worth remarking that, whereas in the Mesopotamian myth of the separation of the joined heaven-earth parent-mountain by their son Enlil, heaven (*An*) is male and the earth (*Ki*) female, in the corresponding Egyptian myth precisely the opposite was the case. Heaven, there, was first (in the period of the Narmer palette) the cow-goddess Hathor, then (in the period of the Pyramid Texts) the anthropomorphic goddess Nut, who is depicted as overarching the world, hands and feet to ground. In the Pyramid Texts this goddess Nut is called "the brilliant, the great," [12] "the great protectress," [13] "she of the long hair, she of the hanging breasts." [14] "She cannot be fertilized," it is said, "without putting down her arms." [15] And the earth-god, her spouse, Geb, sits beneath her. "One arm reaches to heaven," we read, "his other arm rests on the earth." [16] The two were separated, furthermore, by Shu, the air-god, who was not their offspring—as Enlil is the offspring of Anki—but their sire; * so that, whereas in one case a violent Freudian, Oedipal deed is suggested of a son spurning the father, taking the mother to himself ("After An carried off the heaven, After Enlil carried off the Earth"),[17] in the other system the separation is seen rather as an effect of parental solicitude. Also, we note the coarse image of creation. Man is to be fashioned of clay taken from the bottom of the earth, where it overspreads the water of the abyss; and the figure is given of the goddess Earth standing above the goddess Sea, the clay being taken from her "as an infant from its mother"—which is an image, obviously, of the creation of mankind from excre-

* Supra, p. 86.

ment: another infantile Freudian theme, anticipating the sentiment of the oft repeated biblical phrase, "What is man that thou art mindful of him?" (Job 7:17; 15:14; Psalms 8:4; 144:3; Hebrews 2:5).

We turn back to the early Sumerian seals of c. 3500 B.C. (Figures 2 and 3) and recall the idea rendered in these of a self-producing, self-consuming divinity, immanent in all things. We observe that this idea is in essence the same as that of the Memphite view of Ptah, who is "in every body and in every mouth of all gods, all men, cattle, creeping things, and everything that lives." * We look next at the two Sumerian seals of c. 2500 B.C. (Figures 4 and 5), where the female forms are placed above the male, and we note the correspondence of this placement with that of Egypt's Nut and Geb.

It would appear, therefore, that the earlier, neolithic order was of the female above the male, the cosmic mother above the father, and that at some date, which we must now attempt to indicate, the parental assignments in Mesopotamia became fixed in opposite senses and therewith, too, their psychological effects—with interesting philosophical as well as mythological results. For, whereas the body buried in Egyptian soil returned to and became identified with the god-man Osiris in the underworld of his father Geb, that buried in Mesopotamian soil went not to the father but to the mother. And with the progressive devaluation of the mother-goddess in favor of the father, which everywhere accompanied the maturation of the dynastic state and patriarchy but was carried further in Southwest Asia than anywhere else (culminating in the mythology of the Old Testament, where there is no mother-goddess whatsoever), a sense of essential separation from the supreme value symbol became in time the characteristic religious sentiment of the entire Near East. And the rising ziggurats, striving to reach upward in tendance, while at the same time offering to the heavenly powers a ladder by which to come graciously down to the cut-off race of man, were the earliest signals of this spiritual break.

* Supra, p. 87.

II. Mythic Virtue

After An, Enlil, Enki, and Ninhursag
Had fashioned the blackheaded people,
Vegetation burgeoned from the earth,
Animals, quadrupeds of the plain, were brought artfully
    into existence: [18]

and the world as we know it, or as the people of Sumer knew it
in the fourth millennium B.C., was in being, precisely in the form
that it was expected to retain without change. For there is no idea
in any archaic mythology of an evolution either of society or of
species. The forms produced in the beginning were to endure until
the end of time. And the virtue of each class of things, each
manner of man, thereafter, was to represent the god-given natural
patterning of its kind—which in Egypt, as we have learned, was
known as *maat*, in India as *dharma,* in the Far East, as *tao,* and
in Sumer, now, was to be known as *me.*

Dr. Kramer has drawn from an ancient Sumerian clay tablet an
interesting partial list of the virtues (*me's*) that in those earliest
days of systematic thought were supposed to constitute the order
of the universe. Perusing the list, the modern reader must try to
forget his own ideas not only of nature but also of common sense,
and let his imagination pore submissively upon each category, as
though it were a permanent, structuring element of God's world,
representing perfectly His design; as follows: (1) supreme lordship; (2) godship; (3) the exalted and enduring crown; (4) the
throne of kingship; (5) the exalted scepter; (6) the royal insignia;
(7) the exalted shrine; (8) shepherdship; (9) kingship; (10) last-
ing ladyship; (11) the priestly office known as "divine lady";
(12) the priestly office known as *ishib;* (13) the priestly office
known as *lumah;* (14) the priestly office known as *gutug;* (15)
truth; (16) descent into the nether world; (17) ascent from the
nether world; (18) the office of the eunuch known as *kurgarru;*
(19) the office of the eunuch known as *girbadara;* (20) the office
of the eunuch known as *sagursag;* (21) the battle standard; (22)
the flood; (23) weapons; (24) sexual intercourse; (25) prostitution; (26) legal procedure; (27) libel; (28) art; (29) the cult

chamber; (30) the role of the "hierodule of heaven"; (31) the musical instrument called *gusilim;* (32) music; (33) eldership; (34) heroship; (35) power; (36) enmity; (37) straightforwardness; (38) the destruction of cities; (39) lamentation; (40) rejoicing of the heart; (41) falsehood; (42) the rebel land; (43) goodness; (44) justice; (45) the art of woodworking; (46) the art of metal working; (47) scribeship; (48) the craft of the smith; (49) the craft of the leatherworker; (50) the craft of the builder; (51) the craft of the basket weaver; (52) wisdom; (53) attention; (54) holy purification; (55) fear; (56) terror; (57) strife; (58) peace; (59) weariness; (60) victory; (61) counsel; (62) the troubled heart; (63) judgment; (64) decision; (65) the musical instrument called *lilis;* (66) the musical instrument called *ub;* (67) the musical instrument called *mesi;* (68) the musical instrument called *ala.*[19]

These were the archetypes of being and experience fixed in the fourth millennium B.C. for all time. And the emphasis upon music is interesting. It will be recalled that there were a number of harps found among the suttee-burials of the royal tombs of Ur that bore as ornament the figure of the dead and resurrected moon-bull, Tammuz, with lapis-lazuli beard.* For the inaudible "music of the spheres," which is the hum of the cosmos in being, becomes audible through music; it is the harmony, the meaning, of the social order; and the harmony of the soul itself discovers therein its accord. This idea is basic to Confucian music, to Indian music as well; it was, of course, the Pythagorean belief; and it was a fundamental thought, also, of our own Middle Ages: whence the continuous chanting of the monks, who were diligently practicing in accord with the choir of the angels.

Not only music, however; all art—all archaic and Oriental art —partakes of this mystique. It is an epiphany of the Form of forms. "Where European art," wrote Dr. Ananda K. Coomaraswamy, "naturally depicts a moment of time, an arrested action or an effect of light, Oriental art represents a continuous condition." [20] So also, it might be added, does every aspect, mode, experience, and condition of Oriental life. And so, likewise, throughout the

* Supra, p. 44.

Middle Ages all forms of life were conceived to subsist substantially as ideas (fixed species) in the radiant mind of God. Indeed, we can even say that for most of the modern Western world this ancient belief still is held at least on Sundays when it is not Charles Darwin's *Origin of Species* but the Book of Genesis (first millennium B.C.: fixed species, Adam's rib, serpent in the Garden, Noah's ark, and everything else) that is the preferred scientific text.

"All things whatsoever have order among themselves, and this is the form that makes the universe like unto God," wrote the poet Dante; [21] and in the same vein, Saint Thomas Aquinas: "God in Himself neither gains nor loses anything by the act of man; but man, for his part, takes something from God, or offers something to Him, when he observes or does not observe the order instituted by God." [22] And this order, of course, whether in the second millennium A.D. or in the fourth millennium B.C., is ever that of the local social structure and state of accepted learning, brought into being by the work—and even brutal, murderous work—of man himself (as, for example, the Egyptian Narmer's uniting of the two lands): all to be read, however, as precisely, totally, and eternally *maat, me, dharma, tao,* and the archetypology of God's will.

III. Mythic Time

From all that we know of ancient Mesopotamia, it is evident that certain numbers were supposed to give access to a knowledge of the cosmic order, and as early as c. 3200 B.C., with the first appearance of written tablets, two systems of numeration were employed, the decimal and the sexigesimal. The latter was based on the *soss* (60), by which unit we still both measure circles and calculate time. Sixty seconds make one minute, 60 minutes one degree, 360 degrees one circle. The heavens and the earth are measured in degrees. And in the circle of time: 60 seconds make a minute, 60 minutes an hour. The Mesopotamian year was reckoned as 360 days; so that the circles of time and space were in accord, as two prospects of the same principle of number. And in the center of the circle of space were the 5 points of

the sacred ziggurat—four angles to the quarters and summit to
the sky—by way of which divinity was brought into the world;
while in the circle of time, likewise, besides the secular 360 days,
there was an added festival week of 5 days, during the course of
which the old year died, the new was born, and the principle
of divinity in the world was restored. Furthermore, as the day in
proportion to the year, so was the year in proportion to the great
year; and at the close of each such eon or great year there was a
deluge, a cosmic dissolution and return.

A Sumerian tablet, now in Oxford (Weld-Blundell, 62), gives a
list of ten mythological kings who ruled for a total of 456,000
years in the period between the first descent of kingship from the
courts of heaven upon the cities of men and the coming of the
Flood. A second tablet (Weld-Blundell, 144) names only eight of
these kings, with a total of 241,200 years; and a third list, very
much later, composed in Greek c. 280 B.C. by the learned Babylonian priest Berossos, whom we have already had occasion to
name, gives all ten kings again, but with a total of 432,000 years—
which is an extremely interesting sum. For in the Icelandic Poetic
Edda it is told that in Odin's heavenly warrior hall there were
540 doors:

> Five hundred doors and forty there are,
> I ween, in Valhall's walls;
> Eight hundred fighters through each door fare
> When to war with the Wolf they go.[23]

The "war with the Wolf" in that mythology was the recurrent
cosmic battle of the gods and antigods at the end of each cosmic
round (the *Götterdämmerung* of Wagner's Ring), and as the
reader—ever alert—has no doubt already realized, 540 times 800
is 432,000, which is the number given by Berossos for the sum
of years of the antediluvian kings. Furthermore, in the Indian
Mahabharata, and numerous other texts of the Puranic period
(c. 400 A.D. and thereafter), the cosmic cycle of four world ages
numbers 12,000 "divine years" of 360 "human years" each, which
is 4,320,000 human years; and our particular portion of that
cycle, the last and worst, the so-called Kali Yuga, is exactly one-
tenth of that sum.[24] So that we have found this number, now, in

Europe, c. 1100 A.D., in India, c. 400 A.D., and in Mesopotamia, c. 300 B.C., with reference in each case to the measure of a cosmic eon.

But there is another interesting circumstance associated with this number, which came to notice just before the First World War, provoked a good deal of acrid controversy at the time, and then dropped completely out of sight; but which I should like now to bring right back onto the table, since I cannot find that it was ever settled, but only dropped. It concerns the observable fact that at the moment of the spring equinox (March 21) the heavens are never in quite the position they were in the year before, since there is a very slight annual lag of about 50 seconds, which in the course of 72 years amounts to 1 degree ($50'' \times 72 = 3600'' = 60' = 1°$) and in 2160 years amounts to 30 degrees, which is one sign of the zodiac. The sun at the spring equinox stands today in the constellation of the Fish (Pisces), but in the century of Christ was in the Ram (Aries), and in the period of earliest Sumer in the constellation of the Twins (Gemini). This considerable slippage is known as the "precession of the equinoxes," and is generally supposed to have been first reported by an Asiatic Greek, Hipparchus of Bithynia (fl. 146–126 B.C., one hundred and fifty years later than the period of Berossos), in a work "On the displacement of the solstitial and equinoctial signs" —in which, however, his calculations arrived at the figure, slightly wrong, of about 45 to 46 seconds a year.[25] The correct reckoning is supposed to have had to wait for the century of Copernicus, c. 1526 A.D. However, if we continue the Sumerian reckoning already commenced, we shall find the following.

In one year, as we have seen, the precessional lag is 50 seconds, in 72 years it is 1 degree, and in 2160 years, 30 degrees; hence, in 25,920 years it would be 360 degrees, one complete cycle of the zodiac, or, as it is called, one "Great" or "Platonic Year." But 25,920 divided by 60 (one *soss*) yields the figure 432. And so, there we are again. There is an exact relationship between the number of years assigned by Berossos to the cycle of his ten antediluvian kings and the actual sum of years of one equinoctial cycle of the zodiac.

Can it be, then, that the Babylonians had already observed and correctly calculated the precession of the equinoxes centuries before Hipparchus got it wrong? Professor H. V. Hilprecht, in Philadelphia, at The University Museum, poring over literally thousands of clay fragments on which mathematical reckonings appeared, wrote in 1906 that "all the multiplication and division tables from the temple libraries of Nippur and Sippar and from the library of Ashurbanipal are based upon 12,960,000." [26] And, as he pointed out, $12,960 \times 2 = 25,920$, which is our figure for the Great or Platonic Year. Alfred Jeremias was inclined to accept Hilprecht's discovery as showing the likelihood of a recognition of the precession in Mesopotamia as early as the third or perhaps even fourth millennium B.C. "If this interpretation is correct and the figure really does refer to the precession," he wrote, "then it proves that before Hipparchus an exact reckoning of the precession had been achieved, which later was forgotten." [27] And he wrote again: "It is, in fact, incredible that the Babylonians, experienced as they were in the observation of the heavens, should not have deduced from the difference between earlier and later observations a shift of the equinoctial point. . . . As soon as the position of the sun at the time of the spring equinox became a point of observation, the precession during centuries *must* have been noticed . . . indeed in the course of one year it comes to 50 seconds, and during longer periods cannot possibly have been ignored." [28]

A French Assyriologist, V. Scheil, however, pointed out in 1915 that Professor Hilprecht's discovery cannot be taken as proof of precise astronomical observation, since the sexagesimal system would itself have provided the number as the fourth power of 60: $60 \times 60 \times 60 \times 60 = 12,960,000$.[29]

And so we have now to ask, I suppose, whether one should marvel the more at the sexagesimal system or at the Sumerians who invented it. Their ancient calendric festival-year was reckoned in the purely mathematical, not natural, terms of 72 five-day weeks, plus 5 intercalated festival days, $5 \times 72 = 360$. But $360 \times 72 = 25,920$: yielding, thus, a *mathematically* found "great year" whose coincidence with the observable *astronomical* "great year" might indeed have been the result only of a sheer (but then how really wonderful!) accident.

In any case, it is evident that Berossos took the number seriously as, in some sense, the sum of years between the descent of kingship from heaven and the coming of the Flood.

And so, now, let us compare the two very early Sumerian king lists with the much later list of Berossos and add, for good measure, the ten antediluvian patriarchs of the Book of Genesis.

The tables are as follows:

SUMERIAN W-B. 144			SUMERIAN W-B. 62	
	KING	YEARS	KING	YEARS
1.	Alulim	28,800	Alulim	67,200
2.	Alagar	36,000	Alagar	72,000
3.	Enmenluanna	43,200	Kidunnushakinkin	72,000
4.	Eumengalanna	28,800	. . . ?	21,600
5.	Divine Dumuzi	36,000	Divine Dumuzi	28,800
6.	Ensibzianna	28,800	Enmenluanna	21,600
7.	Enmenduranna	21,000	Enzibzianna	36,000
8.	Ubardudu	18,600	Eumenduranna	72,000
9.			Arad-gin	28,000
10.			Ziusudra	36,000
		241,200		456,000

BEROSSOS			THE BIBLE (GENESIS 5) *	
	KING	YEARS	PATRIARCH	YEARS
1.	Aloros	36,000	Adam	130
2.	Alaparos	10,800	Seth	105
3.	Amelon	46,800	Enoch	90
4.	Ammenon	43,200	Kenan	70
5.	Megalaros	64,800	Mahalel	65
6.	Daonos	36,000	Jared	162
7.	Euedoraches	64,800	Enoch	65
8.	Amempsinos	36,000	Methuselah	187
9.	Opartes	28,800	Lamech	182
10.	Xisuthros	64,800	Noah: until Flood	600
		432,000		1656

* The numeration here is according to the Hebrew (King James), not the Septuagint (Vulgate) or Samaritan versions.

The first point to notice is that although Berossos considerably differs from the earlier lists and they between themselves, there is enough to indicate that all are variants of a common legacy, which therewith is proved to have persisted in essential continuity for at least two thousand years. And we can readily see that although their year assignments greatly vary, all are of the same mythological order and could not possibly be read today by anybody in his right mind as referring accurately to historical events. These accounts, therefore, represent precipitates not of sober history, but of legend; that is to say, history interpreted as a manifestation of myth.

Nor can it be said that the mythology here in question arose, or can possibly have arisen, spontaneously from the psyche in the manner of a dream. Neither is it to be read in terms simply of the typical neolithic theme and concern of fertility, which, while perhaps present, cannot be claimed to account for the evident emphasis throughout this mythology, and through all mythologies derived from it, upon numbers—immense numbers; and not merely numbers helter-skelter, but numbers carefully worked out, based upon the laws, themes, and correspondences of a certain shared, seriously regarded mathematical order—as we immediately see when it is recognized that in all three of the previously noted Mesopotamian schedules the final sums are multiples of that same integer, 1200, which in India represents to this day the sum of "divine years" in a cosmic cycle: $1200 \times 201 = 241,200$; $1200 \times 380 = 456,000$; $1200 \times 360 = 432,000$.

The indication would seem to be, therefore, that the highest concern of the mythology from which these king-lists derived can have been neither history nor fertility, but some sort of order: some sort of mathematically ordered, astronomically referred notion about the relationship of man and the rhythms of his life on earth, not simply to the seasons, the annual mysteries of birth, death, and regeneration, but beyond those to even greater, very much larger cycles: the great years. The earlier, comparatively simple neolithic folk and village fertility themes have been amplified colossally and opened to a totally new, elite, poetic vision of man in the universe—man as an organ *of* the universe, together with the gods and all those "virtues" (*me's*), which, as we have seen, are the permanent structuring elements of God's world.

Or rather, I do not think that we can say "God" in this context, since the only gods named and recognized in this mythology are themselves functions and functionaries of the order. Nor can the Deluge in this mythology have been originally conceived as sent to punish man. The whole idea of the cosmic rhythm involves intrinsically death and resurrection; so that an anthropomorphized reading in terms of punishment or the willfulness of an unpredictable god can represent only a foreground view; the deeper, holier ground being illustrated in those awful graves of Ur, where, when the time came, literally hundreds of noble human beings put off their bodies. The cosmic order (*me*), which, as we have seen, is manifest in the categories of (1) supreme lordship, (2) godship, etc., including (22) the Flood, is known even more deeply and essentially through number, which becomes audible— as Pythagoras held and the harps of Ur suggest—in the harmonies and rhythms of music; specifically, the number system of:

60—the *soss*
600—the *ner*
3600—the *sar*
216,000—the *great sar* ($= 60 \times 3600$)

two *great sars* yielding that interesting 432,000 of Berossos' eon.

iv. The Mythic Flood

A number of scholars have thought that actually there may have been some devastating flood that all but annihilated civilization in the area of the early cities, and some have even thought that in their excavations they had discovered the evidence. However, the flood strata unearthed in the various Mesopotamian city sites do not correspond to one another in date. Those at Shuruppak [30] and Uruk [31] were laid down at the close of the Jemdet Nasr period, c. 3000 B.C., while that of Ur [32] occurred at the close of the Obeid period, half a millennium before, and that of Kish [33] two or three centuries later; so that each can be interpreted only as a local, not as a general Mesopotamian (let alone universal) catastrophe. It is of course possible that in each little city state itself the local flood was overinterpreted as a cosmic event, rendering present the mythological Deluge. However, as modern students of this subject we cannot allow ourselves to go along with such obvious misjudgments, crying like the little hen when the pea fell on her tail, "Run, run, the sky is falling!"

The earliest deluge story yet found is on a badly damaged fragment of baked clay, 7 inches long by 5⅝ inches wide, that was transported to the University of Pennsylvania, among thousands of other trophies, from the expedition to Nippur of 1895–96. Catalogued and filed away in 1904 as "Incantation 10673 (III Exp. Box 13)," it was critically examined only in 1912, by Professor Arno Poebel of the University Museum, and, as had the Memphite stone under Breasted's lens two or three years before, it suddenly opened to view—like the wan beam of a distant star that on closer watching proves to be an immeasurable galaxy—another unsuspected revelation of the great third millennium B.C.

The opening lines of the cuneiform text are greatly damaged. A god is talking, or perhaps a goddess; either Enlil, Enki, or the goddess Nintu (an aspect of Ninhursag):

"My human kind, in its destruction I will . . ."

Is this the voice of Enlil, threatening? For it is he who is going to send the flood: ". . . in its destruction I will engage!" Or is the voice that of either Enki or the goddess, already contemplating rescue? ". . . in its destruction I will give rescue!" We cannot tell.

The next line also is obscure:

"My, Nintu's creations . . . I will . . ."

Or perhaps, rather:

"O Nintu, what I have created . . . I will . . ." [34]

The remainder, however, is comparatively clear:

"The people to their settlements I will restore;
Cities . . . they shall build. . . .
Their shade [or shelter] I will make restful.
The bricks of our temples they will lay in pure places.
Our . . . places they will establish in pure places." [35]

There follow a couple of mangled lines and then the four that I have already cited on page 113, after which—in Column II—there is named a list of the five cities to be destroyed: Eridu, Larak, Badtibira, Sippar, and Shuruppak.

We are next—Column III—listening to the goddess who has realized what is about to happen. The first name given her is Nintu; the second, however, Inanna. It is not clear whether we are to see in these differing designations one goddess or two, since multiple namings of this kind need not be separately personified:

> The . . . place . . .
> The people . . .
> A rainstorm . . .
> At that time Nintu screamed like a woman in travail;
> The pure Inanna wailed because of her people.
> Enki in his own heart took counsel.
> An, Enlil, Enki, and Ninhursag . . .
> The gods of heaven and earth invoked the names of An
>   and Enlil.

There is apparently dissension among the gods, and it is evident that the cosmic Deluge is to be treated in this text not as a cool, mathematically determined, inevitable occurrence, but as the consequence of a god's wrath, against which certain other deities are about to connive; and this would seem to represent an altogether different theology from that considered in connection with the king lists.

Or should we think of this text, rather, as a popular, exoteric presentation of the same tradition? We know that in India an attitude of devotional love and fear of God is cultivated in numerous popular cults where the personality of some deity is emphasized, while in depth the ultimate teaching is of an absolute law. Likewise, among the Greeks, where the gods in the tales so well known to us appear to be self-moving and willful, there was a deeper teaching of divine destiny, *moira,* personified in the Fates, against which not even Zeus himself could strive. And in the Bible we have God surprised, or pretending to be surprised, repenting of his creation, coming to new decisions—in dialogue, so to say, with his creatures; whereas we are taught, also, of his eternity, omnipotence, and foreknowledge. The problem is of the pairs-of-opposites, destiny and free will, justice and mercy, etc., which in themselves cannot be reconciled, and which, when we find them in our own tradition, we tend to recognize as reconciled in God. However, when we find them in alien traditions, we tend to speak, rather, of inconsistency.

In the present case we are not in an alien tradition but in an early chapter of our own: an early, Sumerian variant of the same deluge tale that has come down to us in the Book of Genesis in two late Semitic versions: the "Jehovistic" of perhaps the ninth century B.C., in which Noah is told to take into his ark "of every living thing of all flesh two of every sort" (Genesis 6:19), and the "Priestly" of the fifth century B.C., where it is to be "seven pairs of all clean animals and a pair of the animals that are not clean" (Genesis 7:2). We have to ask, therefore, whether those who have learned to recognize the signs of a higher wisdom in biblical inconsistencies should not, in the name of consistency itself, run their learning back to the antecedent Sumerian sources; or whether, on the other hand, there may not have been, at some period, a change in point of view; a change, in the present case, from an earlier mythology of impersonal law to a later, more anthropomorphic, of the will of a personal god.

As in the Bible, so in this text of c. 1750 B.C., there is to be saved only one good man (apparently with his family) in a huge boat full of beasts. He is the tenth and last of the long-lived antediluvian kings (in the Bible they have become patriarchs), good old King Ziusudra of the ancient city state of Shuruppak. We are still reading Column III:

> At that time Ziusudra was King, the lustral priest of . . .
> He built a huge . . .
> Humbly, prostrating himself, reverently . . .
> Daily and perseveringly, standing in attendance . . .
> Auguring by dreams such as never were seen before . . .
> Conjuring in the name of heaven and earth . . .

The column breaks off, and we look to Column IV. The king's effort to know the will of the gods now is already being rewarded; for he is standing by the wall of a shrine that he has built, when a voice—the voice of the god Enki—is heard:

> . . . the gods a wall . . .
> Ziusudra standing at its side, heard:

That is the setting. Now comes the voice:

> At the wall, at my left hand, stand. . . .
> At the wall, I will speak to thee a word.
> O my holy one, open thine ear to me.
>
> By our hand a rainstorm . . . will be sent,
> To destroy the seed of mankind . . .
> Is the decision, the word of the assembly of the gods,
> The command of An and Enlil. . . .
> Its kingdom . . . its rule . . .

There is again a break. On the lost portion the building and boarding of the boat must have been accomplished; for at the beginning of Column V we are already witnessing the Flood, which is described in two brief, vivid stanzas:

> All the windstorms of immense power, they all came together.
> The rainstorm . . . raged along with them.
> And when for seven days and seven nights
> The rainstorm in the land had raged,
> The huge boat on the great waters by the windstorm had
>   been carried away,
> Utu, the sun, came forth, shedding light over heaven and
>   earth.
>
> Ziusudra opened a window of the huge boat.
> He let the light of the sun-god, the hero, come into the in-
>   terior of the huge boat.
> Ziusudra, the king,
> Prostrated himself before Utu.
> The king: he sacrifices an ox, slaughters a sheep. . . .

And now, finally, Column VI: We do not know for certain who is talking, but it may be the sun-god Utu, who has gone before An and Enlil in Ziusudra's favor:

> "By the soul of heaven, by the soul of earth, do ye conjure
>   him, that he may . . . with you.
> By the soul of heaven, by the soul of earth, O An and Enlil,
>   do ye conjure, and he will . . . with you."

Vegetation, coming out of the earth, rises.
Ziusudra, the king,
Before An and Enlil prostrates himself.

And the gods bestow on the hero life immortal in that happy
land of which we have already heard:

Life like that of a god they bestow on him.
An eternal soul like that of a god they create for him.
Whereupon Ziusudra, the king,
Bearing the title, "Preserver of the Seed of Mankind,"
On a . . . mountain, the mountain of Dilmun, they caused
    to dwell. . . .[36]

The date of the tablet on which this earliest known version of the
Flood appears—which in the West is known as Noah's flood and in
India as Manu's—actually, in Sumerian terms, is late: c. 1750 B.C.[37]
"The Sumerian idiom of our text," states Professor Poebel, "is no
longer that of the classical period." [38] In fact, Sumer as a political
force had already collapsed, and the lead in civilization had passed
to the largely Semitic peoples of Akkad, for whom Sumerian was
an archaic, learned tongue, somewhat like the Latin of the Middle
Ages. Indeed, even the final Sumerian period of Ur III, c. 2050–
1950 B.C., had itself been a backward-looking, neo-Sumerian
century of restoration, whose last three kings, Amar-Sin, Shu-Sin,
and Ibbi-Sin, bore Semitic names.

For, as a glance at a physical map will show, there is a great
desert westward of Mesopotamia, reaching from Syria in the north
to the southern extremities of Arabia, which, from as remote a
period as the end of the paleolithic, has been the matrix from
which all the numerous Semitic tribes of history have emerged;
notably:

1. The Akkadians, who conquered the land of Sumer and took
the kingship to their city of Agade (Sargon of Agade) c. 2350 B.C.
(The restoration period of Ur III followed, c. 2050–1950 B.C.);

2. the Amoritic Babylonians, who gave the *coup de grâce* to
both Sumer and Akkad, c. 1850 B.C. (Hammurabi, c. 1700 B.C.);

3. the later Amorites, who conquered the ancient city of Jericho,
c. 1450 B.C., and left it in ruins;

4. the Canaanites, who followed them in Syria and Palestine;

5. the closely related Phoenicians of the coast;

6. the Hebrews (Saul, c. 1010 B.C.);

7. the Assyrians, who conquered Babylon c. 1100 B.C. and at the height of their power, in the period of Ashurbanipal (668–626 B.C.), dominated the whole of Southwest Asia;

8. the Chaldeans, who were briefly the masters, from 625 to c. 550 B.C.;

9. the Aramaeans—obscurely defined—whose speech was general from Sinai to Syria, and, as a language of trade, as far as to India, in the centuries just before and after Christ; and

10. finally, the Arabs, who, with the victories of Islam (seventh to sixteenth centuries A.D.), became the masters of the most broadly flung cultural domain in the history of the archaic world.

But even before the victories of Sargon, nomadic Semitic warrior tribes were already raiding and occasionally plundering Sumer; so that from an early date there were, in the classic domain of the earliest hieratic states, contributions from the primitive sphere of herding desert nomads for whom the subtleties of the mathematical star watch meant not a thing. Hence we cannot rule out the probability that in our tale of the Deluge of Ziusudra, Semitic influences already were at work. The sudden stress given to the role of Utu, Sumerian counterpart of the great Semitic sun-god Shamash, points to a bit of such doctoring as priestly hands always allow themselves. And the whole idea of the Flood rather as the work of a god of wrath than as the natural punctuation of an eon of say 432,000 years seems, indeed, to be an effect of later, secondary, comparatively simple cerebration.

Thus the evidence from a number of quarters suggests very strongly that in the earliest known Sumerian mythological texts the basic, mathematically inspired priestly vision has already been overlaid by an intrusive anthropomorphic view of the powers that motivate the world, far more primitive than that from which the earliest high civilization had emerged; so that the myths that have survived to us represent a certain drop or devolution of tradition, which was either intentional, in the way of all devotional popularization, or else unintentional, following a loss of realization.

And the latter is the more likely, since, as Professor Poebel has let us know, the Sumerian idiom of these texts "is no longer that of the classical period." They are already of a late, epigonous age.

I would suggest, therefore, that the mathematics still evident in certain of the earliest known, yet late, Sumerian documents suffice to show that during the formative period of this potent tradition (which has by now reshaped mankind) an overpowering experience of order, not as something created by an anthropomorphic first being but as itself the all-creative, beginningless, and interminable structuring rhythm of the universe, supplied the wind that blew its civilization into form. Furthermore, by a miracle that I have found no one to interpret, the arithmetic that was developed in Sumer as early as c. 3200 B.C., whether by coincidence or by intuitive induction, so matched the celestial order as to amount in itself to a revelation. The whole archaic Oriental world, in contrast to the earlier primitive and later Occidental, was absolutely hypnotized by this miracle. The force of number was of far greater moment than mere fact; for it seemed actually to be the generator of fact. It was of greater moment than humanity; for it was the organizing principle by which humanity realized and recognized its own latent harmony and sense. It was of considerably greater moment than the gods; for in the majesty of its cycles, greater cycles and ever greater, more majestic, infinitely widening cycles, it was the law by which gods came into being and disappeared. And it was greater even than being; for in its matrix lay the law of being.

Thus, mathematics in that crucial moment of cultural mutation met the earlier-known mystery of biological death and generation, and the two joined. The lunar rhythm of the womb had already given notice of a correspondence between celestial and terrestrial circumstance. The mathematical law now united both. And so it is that, in all of these mythologies, the principle of *maat, me, dharma,* and *tao,* which in the Greek tradition became *moira,* was mythologically felt and represented as female. The awesome, wonderfully mysterious Great Mother, whose form and support dominate all the ritual lore of the archaic world, whom we have seen as the cow-goddess Hathor at the four quarters of the festival palette of

Narmer, and whose dairyland goddess of the cow, Ninhursag, was the nurse of the early Sumerian Kings, is equally present in the heavens above, in the earth beneath, in the waters under the earth, and in the womb. And the law of her generative rhythm was represented for the entire ancient world in those units and multiples of 60 of the old Sumerian sexagesimal arithmetic, which had caught the measure at once of time and of space.

Indeed, even the Book of Genesis may carry her secretly throughout, in the mathematics of the destiny of its People of God—as a comparison of the matched schedules of the Babylonian ten kings and Hebrew ten patriarchs appears to suggest. There is, at first glance, of course, considerable difference between the sums of years given by Berossos and the Bible—respectively, 432,000 and 1656. However, as a distinguished Jewish scholar of the last century, the "Nestor of Assyriology," [39] Julius Oppert (1825–1906), pointed out in a fascinating paper on "The Dates of Genesis," [40] both sums contain 72 as a factor: $432,000 \div 72 = 6000$, and $1656 \div 72 = 23$; so that the relationship is of 6000 to 23. (It will be recalled that 72 is the number of years it takes for the precession to advance one degree.) Furthermore, in the Jewish calendar one year is reckoned as 365 days, which in 23 years, plus the 5 leap-year days contained in such a period, amounts to 8400 days, or 1200 seven-day weeks; and the latter sum multiplied by 72, to find *the number of Jewish seven-day weeks in 1656* (23×72) *years,* yields 86,400 (1200×72). Whereas, on the other hand, in the Babylonian calendar the year was composed of 72 five-day weeks: so that, if now—following a practice normal to calculations of this kind—we count each Babylonian year as one day, and then reckon *the number of Babylonian five-day weeks in 432,000 days,* the result is again 86,400 ($432,000 \div 5$). But $86,400 = 86,400$—Q.E.D. Clearly, a point-for-point correspondence of calendric systems is here implied: and since a mathematical order is antithetic to a doctrine of free will, one can only wonder by what transcendent thought the two theologies were reconciled.

Professor Oppert imagined, when he wrote his paper in 1877, before anything was known of Sumer, that the Hebrew figures had been the original and those of Berossos the "falsified"; [41] however, the opposite now appears. Nor can there have been any "falsification" either way, since there were no facts, properly speaking, anywhere in this pliant story to be falsified, but only a way of interpreting the universe—and who wants the other fellow's way? Just as Egypt, India, and China, Crete, Greece, and Rome, the Germans and the Celts, inherited and restyled the civilizing legacy of the nuclear Near East, so too the authors of the Book of Genesis. And "re-creation," not "falsification," is the word to use when discussing the reconstruction of a myth.

v. Mythic Guilt

A paradox now becomes apparent, which is to remain throughout the history of our subject, to set the Orient and Occident apart; for as the cosmic vision fades into the background and gods are no longer mere administrators of a mathematical order, but themselves omnipotent, freely willing creators of a comparatively arbitrary order—personifications of fatherhood writ large, subject to whims, wrath, love, and all the rest—a certain mystical sophistication characterized by dignity and maturity, majesty of prospect and spiritual assurance, disappears; but, on the other hand, a personal, ethical, humanizing factor comes to view that is absolutely missing on the other side of the wall. Over there one finds nonduality, peace of soul—and inhumanity; here, tension, duality, and a sense of exile—yet the face not of the mere functionary, but of the freely willing, autonomous individual, competent to change destiny and so responsible to himself, humanity, and the future, not to the cosmos, metaphysics, and the past. That is the wall that cuts the two hemispheres right apart, East and West, from here to heaven, hell, and beyond.

As the Japanese Zen Buddhist philosopher Dr. Daisetz T. Suzuki once said, summarizing what seemed to him to be the characteristic Western spiritual situation: "Man is against God, Nature is against God, and Man and Nature are against each other." Whereas, in contrast, according to his argument: "If God created the world, he created Man as part of it, as belonging to it, as or-

ganically related to it. . . . There is something divine in being
spontaneous and being not at all hampered by human conventionalities and their artificial sophisticated hypocrisies. There is
something direct and fresh in this not being restrained by anything
human." [42] And indeed there is. But the whole spiritual history of
the West, since c. 2350 B.C., has been the long weaning of its
own part of humanity away from this sublime daemonism.

A strain of criticism is implicit already in the Sumerian myth
of creation, where the virtue of man is described as that of a slave
made for the pleasure of the gods. Such a myth represents not
worship essentially, but a comment; and in such comment the
Orient is lost, the Occident born. The metaphysical *tremendum,*
the deep awe before the great, unchanging truth, and the full submission of all human judgment to a mystery unnamed, which is
infinite, impersonal, yet intimately within all beings, all things, and
in death too: these have been the sentiments that in the Orient
have remained honored as the most holy. And from the point of
view of the knowledge in rapture of that full void, the dedication
of the Occidental mind to the merely personal affairs of men and
women living in the world appears to represent only the loss of the
fruit of life—which that little girl found beside the Ganges when
she went with her husband into the earth.*

We have seen that in Egypt a sequence of psychological stages
progressed (or, if the reader prefers, declined) from a state of
mythic identification, through inflation, to mythic subordination,
and that in the last of these a certain standard of human decency
not inherent in the order of nature was by projection attributed to
God. The Pharaoh—that great "Nature Boy"—was thereby subdued to human virtue without damage to his sense of participation
in the virtue of divinity. But in Mesopotamia this highly flattering
sense of participation in divinity dissolved. The king was no longer
the Great God, nor even, as in Egypt, the Good God, but the Tenant Farmer of the God. And this mythological rupture set the two
orders of nature and humanity apart, without converting man
fully, however, to the courage of his own rational judgments. As a

* Supra, pp. 66–67.

consequence, a pathos of anxiety developed in which all the nursery agonies of a child striving to gain parental favor were translated into a cosmological nightmare of mythic dependency, characterized by alternate gains and loss of divine support, and finally a mordant, rat-toothed sense of intrinsic human guilt.

There is an important, rather well-known little epic lay of a certain King Etana of the city of Kish, in which the import of this transit from the earlier mythology of man's (or at least the king's) intrinsic divinity to the later mythology of absolute dissociation, dependency, and guilt, comes so vividly to view that it may well serve as our milestone to mark the point of no return between the earlier and later spiritual fields.

In the old Sumerian king lists, of which we have already surveyed the portions dealing with the time before the Flood, the name of Etana appears among the kings of the first dynasty following that catastrophe, where he is termed "a shepherd, the one who ascended to heaven, the one who consolidated all the lands, became king, and reigned for 1560 years." [43] This notation makes it apparent that, although no actual Sumerian version of his flight to heaven has come down to us, Etana's adventure was known to the early chronicler; and it would also appear that he was supposed to have succeeded in his flight. The legend must have served, in fact, to validate the king's divine mandate. However, in the versions of his flight that have survived, all of which are of late Semitic vintages—Babylonian or Assyrian, mostly from the shattered library of the last Assyrian monarch, Ashurbanipal (668–635 B.C.) —the entire theme has been turned into its negative, so that the lesson rendered is not of the virtue of aspiration, but of guilt.

The prologue of this little epic, as it now stands, tells of the guilt even of the mighty bird, the Solar Eagle, who was to serve in the main adventure as the vehicle of the world's first astronaut.

"Come," said this bird to his neighbor, the Serpent, "let us swear an oath of peace and friendship; and may the curse of the sun-god Shamash fall heavily upon the one who fails to honor it."

Before the sun-god they took their oath, sealing it with a curse. "And may Shamash with the mighty hand of a smiter smite calamitously the one that transgresses the boundary of Shamash! May the mountain of the dead close its entrance against him!"

Their young thereafter were conceived and born: the serpent's in the shade of an elm; those of the bird on a mountain peak. And when the bird caught a wild bull or ass, the serpent ate, drew back, and its children ate; when the serpent caught a wild goat or ante-lope, the great eagle ate, drew back, and its children ate; until, on a certain day, when its eaglets had been fledged, an evil thought entered the bird's mind.

"Lo," it said, "let me devour the offspring of that serpent."

"O my father," said one of its own young, "do not do so, lest the net of Shamash entrap thee."

The bird plunged nevertheless, devoured the young of the ser-pent, tore apart its nest, and when the serpent looked, its offspring had disappeared. Whereupon it went before Shamash.

"Surely, O Shamash," it prayed, "thy net is the wide earth; thy trap, the distant sky! And from thy net, who shall escape?"

"Make ready!" said the sun-god. "Ascend the mountain! Let a wild bull be thy place of hiding. Tear open its belly, enter, and set up there thy residence. Every bird of the sky will descend, and among them, your eagle, unsuspecting, with a single thought: to get inside. Seize a wing. Tear away his wings and claws. Strip him, cast him into a pit, and let him die there of hunger and thirst."

The serpent did so, and the broken bird in the pit cried to Shamash: "O Lord, am I to expire in this pit? O Lord, thy punish-ment is indeed upon me. However, do but allow me to live—thine eagle—and forever I shall celebrate thy name."

The sun-god said to him: "Thou hast been evil, causing grief, which is a thing forbidden by the gods. It is a disgraceful thing that thou hast done: for thou didst swear. And verily, I shall now visit upon thee the recompense of thine oath. Give thyself to whatever man I shall send to thee, and let him take thee by the hand."

The man to come was to be the old, very feeble shepherd king, Etana of the city of Kish.

"O my Lord Shamash," this old man had prayed; "thou hast

consumed the strength of my sheep and, in the whole realm, the young of my lambs; yet have I honored the gods, given thought to the dead, caused priestesses to immolate my offerings. By thy command, therefore, O Lord, let someone obtain for me the plant of birth; for I am old and without issue. Let the plant of birth be revealed to me. Tear out its fruit, O God, and grant me a child."

"Ascend the mountain," the sun-god had said. "Seek out the pit. Look therein. The bird there will show thee the plant of birth." And Etana did so. . . .

The fragmentary tablets break at this point; and when the tale resumes, the old king, riding his eagle, is already arriving at the gate of the lowest heaven, wherein are the sun, moon, storm, and planet Venus. The bird is speaking to its rider.

"Come, my friend, let me carry thee farther still, to the higher heaven of Anu [Sumerian An]. Press thy bosom against me. Upon the feathers of my wings place thy hands and upon the shoulders of my wings thine arms."

Two hours more they climbed. The bird exclaimed: "Look below, my friend, at the earth, how it appears! The salt sea is surrounded by an ocean. The land in its midst is a mountain."

Two hours more they climbed. The bird said: "Look below, my friend, at the earth, how it appears! The salt sea is but a broad band around the land."

Two hours more, and again: "Look below, my friend, at the earth, how it appears! The salt sea is no more than a gardener's irrigation ditch."

They reached the high gate of the gods Anu, Bel, and Ea [Sumerian An, Enlil, and Ea]. . . . Etana and his eagle . . .

The tablet again breaks off. Turning it over, we recognize the bird:

"Come, my friend, let me carry thee farther still, to the heaven of the goddess Ishtar [Inanna]. Let me set thee down at her feet. Press thy bosom against me. Upon the feathers of my wings place thy hands."

Two hours more, and the bird said: "Look below, my friend, at the earth, how it appears. The land seems flat, and the broad salt sea no more than a barnyard."

Two hours more: "Look below, my friend, at the earth, how it appears. The land is a mere clod and the broad salt sea a wicker basket."

Two hours more they climbed. But this time, when Etana looked, he could see below neither sea nor land. "O my friend, do not climb farther!" he cried; and with that, they fell.

For two hours they fell; two hours more . . .

The fragmentary document and its characters go to pieces together at the bottom. All that remains are a few broken lines:

> A third two hours . . .
> The eagle fell and he was . . .
> It was shattered on the earth . . .
> The eagle fell and he was . . .
> . . . eagle . . .

A further scattering of words suggests that the king's widow is mourning and his ghost is being invoked in a time of need.[44]

Professor Morris Jastrow, in his discussion of this piece, already observed half a century ago that "in the original tale of Etana, there is every reason to suppose that he was actually placed among the gods."

"This is shown," he wrote, "by the success of the first flight, in which the goal is attained, since the heaven of Anu—the highest part of heaven—is reached. The second flight is clearly a duplicate of the first and betrays in the language used its dependence upon the former.* It is a favorite theme with the Babylonian theologies to whom we owe the preservation and final form in which the old folk tales and popular myths were cast, that man cannot come to the gods, nor can he find out what is in store for him after death, beyond the certainty that he will be condemned to inactivity in a gloomy subterranean cavern. There may be exceptions but that is the general rule." [45]

Professor Jastrow discerned in this version of the legend, fur-

---

* "That the 2nd flight is merely a duplicate of the first is seen in the persistence of the 'three double hours' as the distance traversed. In reality the two flights cover six double hours and the eagle ought to fall this distance before reaching the earth." (Jastrow's note.)

thermore, two entirely distinct tales combined: the first, of a king and his city abandoned by its gods, and the second, of an eagle and serpent allied. In the first, he believed, the well-being of the community must have been restored through the intervention of the goddess and god of fertility—namely Ishtar (Inanna) and Bel (Enlil)—after which Etana appealed to Shamash (or perhaps originally to Ishtar) to be shown the plant of birth through which his flocks might again bear young.[46]

The animal tale, on the other hand, was a piece of folklore, to which a moral had been added. And it would have been quite in keeping with the later Babylonian spirit, if, in the combination of the two pieces, Etana should have been prevented from attaining his goal.

"Instead of being brought into the presence of Ishtar, he is thrown down to the earth. Just as he appears to be approaching his goal, the eagle with Etana on his back falls through the great space of three double hours that he has traversed. . . ."[47] And the adventure is unattained.

Jastrow concludes: "The two tales thus combined are made to teach a lesson, or rather two lessons: (a) one that the laws of Shamash cannot be transgressed without entailing grievous punishment, and secondly—and more important—(b) that man cannot be immortal like the gods. It is this lesson which the Babylonian theologians made the burden of the composite Gilgamesh epic . . . and it is this same lesson which, as it seems to me, the Etana myth in its final form was intended to convey."[48]

Thus it appeared to one of the leading students of this field already in 1910 that the idea of man's absolute separation from the gods belongs properly not to Sumer but to the later Semitic mind. However, it also belongs to the Greeks, in their idea of *hybris,* and is the inhabiting principle of tragedy. It underlies the Christian myth, also, of the Fall and Redemption, Tree and Cross. Indeed, throughout the literature of the Occident defeat is typical of such superhuman adventures; whereas it is not so in the Orient, where, as in the legend of the Buddha, the one who sets forth to gain immortality almost invariably wins.

In the West the sense of tragedy is of such force that the word "catastrophe" (Greek *kata,* "down," *strophein,* "to turn"), which primarily means simply the final event, denouement, of a drama, whether sorrowful or not, has come to mean for us, in normal speech, only calamity; and even our highest symbol of spirituality, the crucifix, shows God himself at that tragic moment when his body is delivered to the power of death.

Our concept of the hero, that is to say, is of the actual, particular individual, who indeed is mortal and so doomed. Whereas in the Orient the true hero of all mythology is not the vainly striving, empirical personality, but that reincarnating one and only trans-migrant, which, to quote a celebrated passage, "is never born; nor does it ever die; nor, having once been, does it ever cease to be. Unborn, eternal, changeless and of great age, it is not slain when the body is slain." [49]

The fall of Etana and his eagle has the character of an Occidental, not Oriental, "catastrophe." So that, with this legend, we have left innocence, tasted the fruit of the knowledge of good and evil, and moved out the Western gate to that great field of the psyche and destiny where the task of man has been conceived, for the most part, not psychologically, as a quest within for a principle already there, but historically, as the progressive establishment of accord between the moral and empirical orders.

VI. The Knowledge of Sorrow

Many scholars have observed, like Professor John A. Wilson, that the earliest Egyptian tomb murals and reliefs "do not stress burial and mortuary services; they stress the pleasure in an abounding harvest, delight in nature, enjoyment of the hunt, and the excitement of feasts and games." The total impression, as he remarks, is confident, lively, and gay. "Self-assurance, optimism, and a lust for life produced an energetic assertion of eternally continuing life." [50]

However, in the first centuries of the second millennium B.C. a new note of dissonance becomes apparent in the writings of Egypt and, more emphatically, Mesopotamia. For example, we read in a celebrated papyrus of c. 2000 B.C. the following melancholy "Dialogue of a Misanthrope with His Soul."

Lo, my name is abhorred:
   Lo, more than the odor of birds
   On summer days, when the sky is hot.
Lo, my name is abhorred:
   Lo, more than the odor of fishermen
   By the marshes when they have fished.
Lo, my name is abhorred:
   Lo, more than a woman,
   Against whom a lie is told her husband.

To whom can I speak today?
   Brothers are evil;
   The friends of today do not love.
To whom can I speak today?
   The gentle man has perished;
   The bold-faced goes everywhere.
To whom can I speak today?
   With wretchedness I am laden,
   Without one friend of good faith.
To whom can I speak today?
   Wickedness smites the land;
   It has no end.

Death is before me today:
   Like the recovery of a sick man,
   Like going forth into a garden after sickness.
Death is before me today:
   Like the odor of myrrh,
   Like sitting under a sail in a good wind.
Death is before me today: '
   Like the course of a stream;
   Like the return of a man from the war-galley to his house.
Death is before me today:
   Like the home that a man longs to see,
   After years spent as a captive.

He who is yonder *
   Will seize the culprit, like a living god,
   Inflicting punishment on the wicked.
He who is yonder
   Will stand in the celestial bark,
   Causing the choicest offerings to be given to the temples.

* "He who is yonder": the *Ka* of the unhappy one himself, when it shall
have been joined by his *Ba* in the boat of Re. For *Ka* and *Ba,* cf. p. 80.

He who is yonder
    Will be a sage who is not rebuffed
    When he speaks in prayer to Re.[51]

Do we not hear in this the prelude to the Buddha's First Noble
Truth: "All life is sorrowful," and to the judgment of Aquinas: "It
is impossible for man's happiness to be in this life"? [52] As Nietzsche has observed: "The sick and perishing: it was they who despised the body and the earth, and invented the heavenly world
and the redeeming drops of blood. . . . Beyond the sphere of
their body and this earth they now fancied themselves transported,
these ungrateful ones. Yet to what did they owe the convulsion and
rapture of their transport? To their body and this earth." [53]

I shall term this crisis *The Great Reversal,* whereby death was no
longer viewed as a continuance of the wonder of life but as a
rescue from its pain: "like the recovery of a sick man," "like the
home that a man longs to see."

But what can have caused this inversion of values?

In Egypt, apparently, a period of social disintegration following the fall of Dynasty VI, c. 2190 B.C., and in Mesopotamia the
frightfulness of an age during which the warcraft, first of city
against city, but then, with mounting force, of desert and steppe
tribesmen (Semites and Aryans) against the hearths of civilization
itself, strewed ruins on every hand.

"Sargon, King of Agade," we read in a royal chronicle of
c. 2350 B.C., "Viceregent of Inanna, King of Kish, pashishu of
Anu, King of the Land, great ishakku of Enlil: the city of Uruk
he smote and its wall he destroyed. With the people of Uruk he
battled and he routed them. With Lugal-zaggisi, King of Uruk, he
battled and he captured him and in fetters he led him through the
gate of Enlil. Sargon of Agade battled with the man of Ur and
vanquished him; his city he smote and its wall he destroyed.
E-Ninmar he smote and its wall he destroyed, and its entire territory, from Lagash to the sea, he smote. And he washed his weapons
in the sea. With the man of Umma he battled and he routed him
and smote his city and destroyed its wall. Unto Sargon, King of
the Land, Enlil gave no adversary; from the upper sea to the lower
sea, Enlil subjected to him the lands." [54]

Moreover, there were also the inevitable disappointments of those pious souls who, like Job, had fulfilled even beyond the call of duty all the duties of religion, only to find themselves struck down horribly, as was the case of an aged, pious king, Tabi-utul-Enlil, of c. 1750 B.C., who is known as The Babylonian Job. His lament and testimony are worth quoting at a certain length:

Mine eyeballs he obscured, bolting them as with a lock;
Mine ears he bolted, like those of one deaf.
A king, I have been turned into a slave,
And as a madman I am maltreated by those around me.
The allotted time of life I had reached and passed;
Wherever I turned there was evil upon evil.
Misery increased, justice departed,
I cried to my god, but he did not show his countenance;
I prayed to my goddess, she did not raise her head.

The diviner-priest could not determine the future by an inspection,
The necromancer through an offering failed to justify my suit.
I appealed to the oracle-priest: he revealed nothing.
The chief exorciser with his rites failed to release me from the ban.
The like of this had never been seen:
Wherever I turned, there was trouble in pursuit.

As though I had not always set aside the portion for the god
And had not invoked the goddess at the meal,
Had not bowed my face and brought my tribute:
As though I were one in whose mouth there is not constantly prayer and supplication;
Had not set aside the day of the god; had neglected the new-moon feast;
Been negligent, or had spurned their images,
Not taught his people reverence and fear,
Not invoked his deity, or had eaten the god's food,
Neglected his goddess and had failed to proffer a libation:
I am rated with the oppressor that has forgotten his lord
And profaned the sacred name of his god.

Whereas I thought only of prayer and supplication;
Prayer was my practice, sacrifice my law,
The day of worship of the gods, the joy of my heart,
The day of devotion to the goddess, more to me than riches;

Royal prayer—that was my joy;
Its celebration—my delight.
I taught my country to guard the name of the god,
Accustomed my folk to honor the name of the goddess.
The glorification of the king, I made like unto that of a god,
And in the fear of the palace, I instructed the people.
I thought such things were pleasing to a god. . . .

Thus the problem of this poor old man. And now comes the usual answer, already known to Babylon c. 1750 B.C.

What, however, seems good to oneself, is to a god displeasing,
What is spurned by oneself finds favor with a god.
Who is there that can grasp the will of the gods in heaven?
The plan of a god, full of mystery—who can understand it?
How can mortals learn the way of a god?

For man is but a puny thing, whereas gods are great.

The man who was alive yesterday is today dead;
In a trice he is given to grief, of a sudden, crushed.
For a day he sings and plays;
In a moment he is wailing like a mourner.

Men's spirits change like day and night;
When hungry, they are like corpses;
Filled, they count themselves equal to their god;
When things go well, they prate of mounting to heaven,
When in distress, they groan of descending to hell.

Like Job, however, who would be facing this same problem some 1500 years later, old king Tabi-utul-Enlil, though terribly tested, was finally not abandoned by his god, but rendered even greater in fortune than before. First, however, to make clear the extent of this miracle of his god we must hear the whole litany of his ills:

An evil demon came out of its lair,
And from yellowish my sickness turned white.
It struck my neck, crushed my whole spine,
Bent my tall stature like a poplar;
So that I was uprooted like a plant of the marsh and thrown
    upon my back.
Food became bitter—putrid.
And the malady dragged out its course. . . .

I took to my bed, unable to leave it,
And my house became my prison.
Like fetters for my body, my hands were powerless,
Like pinions for my person, my feet were stretched out,
My discomfiture was great, the pain severe.

A strap had struck me of many twists,
A lance, sharply pointed, pierced me.
And the pursuer followed me all day;
All night granted me no respite:
As though wrenched, my joints were torn apart,
My limbs shattered, rendered helpless.
In my stall I passed the night like an ox,
Saturated like a sheep in my excrements.

The disease of my joints baffled the chief exorciser,
To the diviner my omens were obscure;
The exorciser could not read the character of my disease,
Nor the diviner fix the limit of my malady.

Yet no god came to my aid, taking me by the hand,
No goddess had compassion for me, coming to my side.
The grave was open, my burial ordered,
Though not dead, I was already mourned.
The folk of my land already had said "alas" over me.
My enemy learning of it, his face shone;
When the tidings were announced his liver rejoiced,
And I knew the day had come when my whole family,
Resting under the protection of our deity, would be in
    distress.

But then, when all was lost and the old king, bedridden, paralyzed, blind, deaf, unable to eat and racked with unceasing pain,
had been brought to the brink of despair, why lo! that righteous
sufferer was not abandoned, but in his darkest hour there came
in a dream the messenger of his deity—"a strong hero decked
with a crown"—and all that had been taken away was restored.

The god sent a mighty storm to the foundation of the heavenly
    mountain,
To the depths of the earth he drove it
And he forced back that evil demon into the abyss. . . .

On the tide of the sea he swept away the ague.
He tore out the root of my disease like a plant.

The bad sleep, which had disturbed my rest, filled and darkened the heavens, like smoke. . . .

And my eyes, which had been covered with a veil of night,
Through a mighty wind that drove away the veil he made to
   shine.
My ears, which had been closed and bolted, like those of a
   person deaf,
He cleared of the deafness, opening their hearing.

The mouth that had been covered, so that with difficulty it
   uttered sounds,
He purified: like copper he made it shine.
The teeth that had been seized, so that they were pressed to-
   gether,
He opened, strengthening their roots.
From the tongue swollen so that it could not move,
He took away the coating, so that speech returned.
My throat, which had been compressed, closed like that of a
   corpse,
He cured so that my breast resounded like a flute. . . .

My neck had been twisted and bent low:
He made it erect and like a cedar raised up.
My stature he made as one of perfect strength;
And as one released from a demon, he polished my nails.
He cured my scurvy, healed me of the itch. . . .
My whole body he restored.

For the old king, clinging to his faith, had been carried, like a
believer brought to Lourdes, or to the Ganges, to a sacred water
where the power of the god had immediately healed him:

He wiped away the blemish, making the entire body radiant.
The crippled frame regained its splendor.
On the banks of the stream where judgment is held over men
The brand of slavery was erased and the fetters removed.

Whence the following lesson:

Let him who sins against the temple learn from me:
Into the jaw of the lion about to devour me, Enlil inserted a
   bit.
Enlil seized the noose of my pursuer:
Enlil encompassed the demon's lair.[55]

And so, at last, after all those myths about immortality and of kings who set and rose as the moon; millenniums of ritualized inhumanity, when man, participating in the animal, vegetal, and mathematical orders of nature, had so little thought of his own judgment that the law (*maat, me*) which had been projected upon the universe from his own temporally conditioned imagination was accepted without question, not only as supernaturally ordained, but also as superior to what, even in the fourth millennium B.C., must occasionally have been acknowledged as common sense; after the high and holy fairy tales of creation from nothing, magical verbalization, masturbation, or the intercourse of divine beings, the early pranks of the gods upon each other and their creatures, floods, miscreations, and the rest—now, at last: the one point not previously conceded even so much as a place on the agenda, namely the moral problem of suffering, moved to the center of the stage, where it has remained ever since.

For when the sensibilities of man himself—or rather, of certain notable high persons—developed from the cold-blooded, reptilian level of the early kings to the humanity of such as later wrote to their sons: "Make thyself innocent before God. . . . Show kindness to the city; God will praise thee for regard. . . . Good is to work for the future . . ." [56] it inevitably became presently apparent that man himself had more kindness than God, more love, honor, justice, and more heart. And as the realization of this truth increased and the second axiom of the Buddha came gradually to mind—"There is release from sorrow!"—the highest concern of mythology, ritual, and human wisdom shifted from the old magical interests of the nature cult, which were in fact now being gradually assumed by an improved agrarian technology anyhow, to the more intimately psychological task of achieving peace, harmony, and depth of soul in this vale of tears.

THE MYTHOLOGIES
OF INDIA

++

ANCIENT INDIA

++

1. The Invisible Counterplayer

"A belief in the origin of life in the waters," states a work of Dr. Ananda K. Coomaraswamy, "was common to many ancient cultures and must have arisen very naturally in the case of peoples, like those of the Nile, the Euphrates, or the Indus Valley, amongst whom water, in the form either of seasonal rains or of ever-flowing rivers, was the most obvious prerequisite of vegetative increase." [1]

The implication of this suggestion is that analogous mythologies might have developed independently in various parts of the world according to common psychological laws; and this was a favored view of much nineteenth- and early twentieth-century scholarship. However, since the most recent archaeological discoveries indicate specific culture hearths from which shared varieties of grain, domesticated beasts, techniques of fashioning new artifacts, etc., have been diffused to the corners of the earth, the old argument for a parallel development of originally isolated civilizations through the operation of "natural" economic, sociological, or psychological "laws" has now been generally abandoned. As already remarked: the ultimate origin of the peasant barnyard economy of grain agriculture and stock breeding on which the earliest river civilizations rested was not in the great valleys themselves of the Nile, lower Tigris-Euphrates, and the Indus, but in the rain-watered hilly grasslands and mountain valleys flanking the Fertile Crescent. And in this unique zone of cultural transformation a sub-area of particular moment both for India and for the West was southwest

Iran, where a characteristic fine buff ware appeared c. 4500 B.C. that can be traced in its influence both westward into lower Mesopotamia, c. 4000 B.C. (initial settlement of the Sumerian zone: Early Eridu and Obeid) and eastward, about a millennium later, to Baluchistan (Quetta, Nal, and Kulli assemblages) and the Indus Valley (Amri and Kalepar wares).[2]

The immigrants pressing toward India from this southwest Asian matrix were supplied with the elements of an advanced neolithic culture: domesticated goats, sheep, and cattle, covered ox-carts and the potter's wheel, copper and bronze, and even, apparently, glass. They built towns of crude brick, stone, or brick on stone foundations, planted fields of grain, and fashioned ceramic figurines of the goddess and of bulls. Moreover, the ornamentation of their pottery comprised motifs already familiar in the West: swastikas betray the influence of Iran; double axes, distant Syria; meanders, hatched and wavy lines, checker patterns, triangles, chevrons, lozenges, etc., with animals, plants, fish, and birds among them, stylized or naturalistically rendered, reproduce, often precisely, features known from the high neolithic sites of southwest and northern Iraq (Susa I, II, and Samarra ware), Syria (Halaf ware), and the earliest strata of riverine Mesopotamia (Obeid and Jemdit Nasr): in fact, to such a degree that, as Professor V. Gordon Childe has observed: "Baluchistan . . . must once have formed part of a cultural continuum extending from the Tigris to the Indus." [3]

Furthermore, since it was from the same nuclear Near East, and particularly Syria—where the bull, double ax, and goddess appeared as early as c. 4500 B.C.—that the basal civilization of Crete and of much of the early Mediterranean was derived, we need no longer be amazed or metaphysically edified when homologies amounting to identities appear in the myths and rituals of the Orient and the West. As Dr. Robert Heine-Geldern has well observed: "However original and unique each of the ancient civilizations may appear to be, not one of them came into being independently. . . . We are confronted with a great historical movement or, more precisely, with a concatenation of movements which, in the last analysis, radiated all from a common source." [4]

And yet, if we now look not for analogies but for differences, a number of traits immediately strike the eye at the Oriental edge of the broadly spreading Near Eastern neolithic continuum, which seem to point to an order of Indian civilization not entirely dependent upon the inspiration or contributions of the new arrivals from the West. The beautiful bulls depicted on the pottery and modeled in ceramic figurines are of the humped Indian (*Bos indicus*) variety. Decorative motifs based on the forms of the leaves of the Indian pipal (*Ficus religiosa*) tree indicate that a plant worshiped throughout India today and associated particularly with native Indian earth genii (*yakṣas* and *yakṣīs*) was already held in reverence. And there is an interesting series of ceramic goddess-figurines from the Zhob Valley of north Baluchistan with features that are matched nowhere in the whole broad domain of the Near Eastern goddess cult. Like a number of examples from Iran, these end below the waist in pedestals; and like goddess figurines everywhere, they are endowed with ornate necklaces. But as Professor Stuart Piggott has observed, the faces are totally different from any known in other parts of the world.

"Hooded with a coif or shawl," he writes, "they have high, smooth foreheads above their staring, circular eye-holes, their owl-beak nose and grim slit mouth. The result is terrifying, even in a tiny model not more than 2 inches high, and in two from Dabar Kot all pretense is thrown aside and the face is a grinning skull. . . . These can hardly be toys, but seem rather to be a grim embodiment of the mother-goddess who is also the guardian of the dead—an underworld deity concerned alike with the corpse and the seed-corn buried beneath the earth." [5]

Others have goggle eyes, such as are prominent to this day in South Indian images of the goddess, where she is known affectionately as "The Fish-eyed One" (*minakṣī*). Furthermore, at Dabar Kot in Baluchistan, one of the excavated altars revealed a fired-brick drain, and in the Quetta Valley, somewhat to the west, figurines of the mother goddess and bull appeared on a mud-brick platform containing such drains, which had in its foundations a disarticulated human skull.[6]

These drains we recognize. They are those that in present-

day Indian shrines carry the blood of beheaded victims immediately back to their source in the Goddess; for, as we have read,
"blood, if immediately consecrated, becomes ambrosia." * And
to complete the picture of a particularly Indian line of stress in
these remains: from a site known as Moghul Ghundai in South
Baluchistan there has come a phallus carved in stone, while from
another—Periano Ghundai—not only a phallus in rough pottery
but a figurine consisting of "an enormously exaggerated female
vulva and thighs." [7] It is true that phallic traits are prominent also
in Western cults of the neolithic goddess. However, in India they
preponderate even to the present hour; and in combination with the
above remarked motifs of the goddess of death, the fish-eyed goddess, altars with drains, altars built upon sacrificed human beings,
humped bulls, and pipal leaves, they suggest that there may have
been in India a separate culture center of some kind, with features of its own, related to the Western, yet not entirely its imitation.

A real challenge confronts the prehistorian with this evidence,
however; for when the archaeological spade goes an inch below
these earliest village and town settlements, it breaks abruptly upon
a much more primitive stratum, indicating a vast cultural hiatus;
namely, very simple pre-neolithic materials of the late Capsian
hunting age, the characteristic feature of which is a type of tiny
flint (microlith) that has been found distributed over the whole
western portion of the late paleolithic culture field, from South
Africa to northern Europe and from Morocco to Ceylon, the homeland of which was certainly not India. And if one digs, then,
deeper still, the next cultural drop is the whole abyss, to the very
bottom of the human cultural scale in the period of the lower
paleolithic.

India, that is to say, in terms of hard goods—stone, ceramic,
and metal—offers an extremely spotty, disarticulated picture. For
the lower-paleolithic assemblage to which we have now arrived
dates from the last phase of the second glacial age or beginning of
the second interglacial, somewhat before and up to c. 400,000 B.C.
and about contemporary with Pithecanthropus erectus, old Professor Haeckel's celebrated "Missing Link." [8] A type of large

* Cf. supra, p. 6.

rough stone flake tool known as a chopper, found in Northwest and Central India, represents the Indian variant of the paleolithic industry of that fumbling, dim-witted day. And these earliest known Indian tools, called Pre-Soan Chopping-Choppers, are followed in the northwest—the so-called *Soan Culture Zone*—during the course of the second interglacial age, from c. 400,000 to perhaps c. 200,000 B.C., by two additional types of extremely primitive stone implement: 1. a massive rounded "pebble tool," showing affinities with the contemporary and earlier, crudest implements of South and East Africa, and 2. a new type of thick, heavy chopper flake, and the cores from which such rough implements were detached. Tools and cores of the latter sort have been discovered also in Burma (Anyathian industry), Malaya (Tampanian), Java (Pajitanian), and China (in association with the remains of Peking Man at Choukoutien), so that a broad East Asian early paleolithic culture zone is indicated, in which the northwestern quarter of India shared.

During this long period, however, a much more advanced type of stone core tool had already been developed in the West, in the vast Eurafrican domain of the so-called Acheulean hand-ax culture —and in this development only Western, Central, and Southeastern India participated. Two interacting, yet distinct, earliest Indian culture zones can therefore be recognized from as early as c. 500,000 B.C., namely:

A. The Soan Culture Zone of the Northwest, employing
    1. "pebble tools" with early South African affinities, and
    2. "choppers" with later East Asian affinities;
B. The Madras-Acheul Zone of Western, Central, and Southeastern India (Bombay to Madras); represented by
    3. "hand-axes" of Acheulean type.

During the middle paleolithic (third interglacial and last glacial age, from c. 200,000 to perhaps 30,000 B.C., when Neanderthal Man, who now had entered the freezing regions of the north, was pursuing the woolly mammoth throughout Europe) the two basal Indian provinces above defined remained true to their respective, very slowly developing, lower-paleolithic traditions. And that is the end, as far as we know, of the paleolithic history of India; for nothing has yet been found to indicate any advance on Indian soil to the cultural level of the upper paleolithic, that is to say to a "true blade" type of industry, such as appeared in Europe in the period of the painted Crô-Magnon caves (Lascaux and the rest, c. 30,000–c. 10,000 B.C.) and progressed in Africa during the late Capsian (c. 10,000–c. 4000 B.C.) to that microlithic, terminal phase just mentioned.

However, as Professor Piggott notes, stone tools do not tell the whole story, by any means.

"We seem to have," he writes, "the imperishable remnant of the material culture of nomadic hunting groups, who may have been well equipped with other objects made of such impermanent substances as wood, fiber, grass, leaves, or other organic materials such as skin and leather." [9]

And Leo Frobenius, many years ago, made the interesting point that in our reconstructions of the earliest periods of mankind, of which only the most durable skeletal parts remain, the visible evidence must be understood to represent only a precipitation out of an otherwise unknown, invisible, once living reality.[10] Moreover, throughout the broad equatorial zone of man's earliest origins and diffusion, where the natural materials most available for use are perishable, nothing but the forms survive according to which materials are traditionally shaped; whereas in the northern, temperate zones, stone, and then pottery and metals, play a proportionately much greater part in the material constitution of a culture. So that, whereas the influence of a northern upon a southern neighbor may be represented by a visible, measurable intrusion, the impact of an equatorial upon a stone-, ceramic-, or metal-using temperate-zone tradition can be revealed only by symptomatic modifications of the artifacts of that northern tradition itself—which the unwary philosopher then may be led to interpret as an illustration of some vaguely conceived "natural law" of cultural evolution.

> Our understanding of ancient history [Frobenius writes] depends on documents from cultural contexts first manifest in archaeological and then later in historical forms. But all of these reports are of an essentially egoistic kind: they give information about themselves and their own little egos. Each

domain—Sumer here, Egypt there—tells me about its own affairs. Whatever takes place, exists, or functions, beyond the bounds of these narrow provinces is completely ignored, and if a cultural influence springs from without, it matters not whence it came and from what alien circumstance it derived. All that matters is the fact of its arrival, never the history of its preparation elsewhere. And so we are led to believe that the great West Asiatic–Egyptian culture cycle developed alone and cut off from the world, first coming into being and then developing all of itself. It is not directly evident from these monuments that beyond this realm there were silently working forces. The outer world does not appear in the mirror of these documents.

As long as scholarship was satisfied to investigate the historical character of the higher cultures—in other words, as long as the criterion adopted from the Roman period of a classification into "civilized people" and "barbarian" was accepted—this limitation was allowed. However, in the last few decades [Frobenius was writing in 1929], when the necessity of inquiring into the destiny of mankind forced upon us the question of the ultimate character and sense of culture, everything changed. Archaeology on the one hand and modern ethnology on the other demonstrate that the high cultures are the pinnacles of pyramids, the lower parts and bases of which can be reconstructed only through a search for miserable fragments. And yet such discoveries show that a brilliant cultural life has animated the world from of yore, beyond the pale of the ruins of the higher cultures.

The grandiose high cultures of antiquity occupied, according to our knowledge, no more of the world than a belt reaching from about 20 to 45 degrees north; that is, they were confined to an area north of the Tropic of Cancer. Over against this demonstration of archaeology, the ethnological branch of our science could not fail forever to recognize that southward of this belt, from West Africa, through India, the Malay Archipelago and Melanesia, cultures have survived to this day whose traits not only cannot be derived from those of the historical cultures, but also represent a world of their own, which is no less distinct from the other than the plant world from the animal. This domain of *a second kind of culture* is a fact. This second kind is in all and everything so different from the character of the historical cultures that it is not possible to associate it with any historical circumstance; for it offers no external key or clue to its age. Externally regarded, it exhibits only static vistas and perspectives. It appears to have whiled its life away, like the plant world of its homeland, without spring or winter, heights or depths.

I would term this great group of cultures "the invisible counterplayers" (*die unsichtbaren Gegenspieler*) in the history of the culture of mankind.

And although its existence is seldom attested in historical documents and so can hardly ever be directly demonstrated, nevertheless I have no doubt that its effects may be recognized in the influences that it has worked upon the higher cultures, from the south.[11]

And so it is that, against the hard evidence of the archaeological finds so well described for us in the works of prehistory now appearing, we have to estimate the force, also, of an invisible counterplayer, whose character will be indicated only by such transformations and additions as an eye not alert for signs might overlook. Professor W. Norman Brown has suggested an area some five hundred to a thousand miles east of the Indus as the possible site for a characteristic Indic culture contemporary with the earliest evidences of high culture in the Indus Valley;[12] and as a tentative hypothesis, this idea can still be plausibly offered. However, to rate its possible level of civilization above that, say, of a contemporary Melanesian village complex would be to go considerably beyond the evidence. My own suggestion would be that in the rich peninsula of India a local order of tropical village forms must indeed have developed, related generically to the common equatorial complex that I have described in my Primitive volume, and that this can well have been of a respectable dignity and spiritual depth. But the patriotic idea cherished by many learned Indians today of a timeless wisdom revealed uniquely in India at some undefinable time, perhaps before the Deluge,[13] when, to quote one inspired author, "thought proceeded by other methods than those of our logical reasoning and speech," and the Vedas came into being as "a divine Word that came vibrating out of the Infinite to the inner audience of the man who had previously made himself fit for the impersonal knowledge,"[14] I shall have to leave, I am afraid, to those for whom the intangibility of a thought supplies the measure of its worth. For the present, I am going to ask the reader to let the measured facts of our still developing Western science, not the winds of proud Himalaya, be our guide.

II. The Indus Civilization: c. 2500–1500 B.C.

No one has yet quite explained the sudden appearance in the Indus Valley, c. 2500 B.C., of two large Bronze Age cities in full flower, culturally identical, yet four hundred miles apart and with little but villages between: Harappa, in the Punjab, on the river Ravi; and Mohenjo-daro, in the south, in Sind, on the Indus, to which the Ravi is tributary. Since they are in ground plan alike, the two cannot have been of independent growth. They were colonial emplacements. And what is surprising is the extent of their influence. Sir Mortimer Wheeler, their most recent excavator, has observed that "the Indus Civilization exemplifies the vastest political experiment before the advent of the Roman Empire." [15] Its characteristic artifacts have been found from the Punjab nearly to Bombay. However, what is even more astonishing is the monotony of it all. For the remains exhibit no development or even variation, either from first to last or from north to south; only a slow deterioration of standards following the first spectacular appearance. The cities and their civilization break into view, remain without change for a millennium, fade, and disappear like illusions in the night.

It has been pointed out by Wheeler that in the period of Sargon of Akkad (c. 2350 B.C.) there were ships in the harbor of his Mesopotamian capital which had arrived from two remote ports, Makkan and Meluhha—with a pause for reprovisioning at the island known as Dilmun or Telmun (Bahrein). Somewhat later, in the period of Ur III (c. 2050–1950 B.C.), Makkan was still within direct reach, but not Meluhha, though copper, stone, wood, ivory objects, and certain breeds of animals were somehow being obtained from there. And then finally, in the period roughly of Hammurabi (c. 1700 B.C.), contact was lost also with Makkan. "The implication of this record of dwindling trade," Wheeler writes, "is that Telmun, Makkan and Meluhha lay at successively greater distances from Mesopotamia; and if to this inference be added the association of the ultimate Meluhha with ivory, wood and copper, its identification with the Indus Civilization (with its forests and elephants and its sources of copper in Rajasthan) becomes probable. It matches, too, with the archaeological evidence. Ivory-working was an Indus craft. . . .

"We may imagine," he goes on to suggest, "cargoes of woods and metals and ivory—and why not also apes and peacocks, both familiar to the Indus artist?—setting sail from the Indus ports in the heyday of the civilization; and in the sequel, with the long-drawn-out decline which is evident in later civic standards, it is easy to visualize a corresponding decline in the scope and volume of overseas traffic. Inference from the records and the material evidence are at one." [16]

Racially, the fifty-odd human skeletons found among the Indus ruins have been classified, for the most part, in two groups: 1. those showing Proto-Australoid features, and 2. those of Mediterranean affinity.

The first have been compared with the Veddoid aborigines of Ceylon, the natives of Australia, and numerous native tribes of India itself. "Current opinion tends to the view," writes Professor Stuart Piggott of this strain, "that Australia received her aboriginal population by migration through Ceylon and Melanesia from Southern India, where the type is well represented today. Of small stature, with a dark skin-color approaching black, wavy or curly (but never frizzy) black hair, long heads, broad flat nose and fleshy, protruding lips, these people form the main element in the South and Central Indian aboriginal tribes of the present day, as well as largely constituting the so-called 'exterior castes' of Hindu society." [17]

There is a bronze statuette from Mohenjo-daro of a lanky naked girl who is of this type (Figure 14). Her coiffure, small breasts, and the distribution of her bracelets suggest comparison with a series of figurines from the Kulli culture complex of South Baluchistan, c. 3000 B.C.; "and if, as seems likely," writes Professor Piggott, in his suggestion of this comparison, "she is indeed a representation of a Baluchistan type, one may note in passing that the very dark complexion associated with the Proto-Australoid group would be in accord with the name given to Southern

Baluchistan in classical times—Gedrosia, the country of the dark folk." [18]

It should be noted, further, that the principal languages of South India, which are not Aryan but of Dravidian stock—namely,

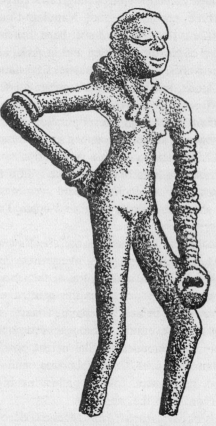

Figure 14. Portrait of a Servant:
Indus Valley, c. 2000 B.C.

Tamil (the chief language of the South, of which the Malayalam of Malabar is a dialect), Telugu (in the neighborhood of Madras), Kanarese (the language of Mysore), Kodagu, Badaga, Kota and Toda (tribal tongues of the Nilgiri hills), Gondi and its dialects, Bhil and Kolam, also Khondi and Oraon (of the Central Provinces, Orissa and Bihar), and finally, Malto (in Rajmahal)—have a close relative to this day in the Brahui tongue of the mountains of East Baluchistan and Sind.[19]

In contrast, the second race, the Mediterranean—once again to quote Professor Piggott—"at the present day includes a large number of groups of peoples stretching from Iberia to India. The characteristic type appears in late Natufian times in Palestine [c. 7500–5500 b.c.] and may have been differentiated in the southern steppes of Northern Africa and in Asia, and spread westwards and eastwards. The predynastic Egyptians certainly belonged to this stock, and the purest representatives at the present day are to be found in the Arabian Peninsula. In India it forms today a dominant element in the population of the north and is widespread elsewhere among the upper social classes. Such people are medium to tall in stature, with a complexion ranging from dark to light olive-brown, a long head and face, and a narrow and relatively pronounced nose; black hair, and eyes ranging from black to brown and characteristically large and open. The body is slenderly built.

"The archaeological evidence shows," he then adds, "that this long-headed Mediterranean type is everywhere in Western Asia associated with the earliest agricultural settlements." And he concludes: "Just as the evidence from the painted pottery of Baluchistan and that lying behind the painted wares in the Harappa Culture points to an eventual homogeneity among these various simple agricultural economies, so the actual physical type shows an ethnic community over the whole area, and the appearance of the early 'Mediterranean' folk in prehistoric India must be related to expansion from the west." [20]

There is a broken statuette from Mohenjo-daro, seven inches high, showing a priestlike figure draped in a shawl with trefoil design that has been drawn over the left shoulder, leaving the right bare (Figure 15)—which is still the proper way to indicate reverence both in India and throughout the Buddhist world when approaching a shrine or holy person. Such a reverent baring of the right shoulder is typical also, however, of the early Sumerian statues of priestly personages, and the trefoil design likewise appears in Mesopotamian art, though not in the later Indian tradi-

tion. Nor is the manner of dealing with the hair in this statuette
duplicated in later Indian art. Brushed back and parted in the
middle, it terminates in short locks at the nape and is bound with
a narrow fillet tied at the back with two long hanging ends, bear-

Figure 15. Portrait of a Priest:
Indus Valley, c. 2000 B.C.

ing a medallion at the middle of the forehead. Beard and mustache
are closely cropped, and beneath each ear is a hole that may have
secured a necklace, while around the right biceps the figure wears
an armlet. The long eyes appear to be half closed. The nose,
well formed, has a high bridge and does not suggest in any way
the derogatory epithet "noseless" (*anāsa*) that was later used by
the invading Aryans in abuse of the native population, whom they
scorned as black-skinned "devils" (*dāsas, dasyus*), "whose god is

the phallus" (*śiśna-deva*).[21] Obviously, this figure is of the culturally and socially superior second race, which by the time the Aryans arrived may already have been to some extent absorbed.

Among the ruins there is much to indicate that the phallic cults of the mother-goddess, despised by the Aryans, were a prominent feature of the civilization. Moreover, as the ethnologist Father Wilhelm Koppers has shown, there survives in India to this day a double fold of mother-goddess worship, namely 1. of the Proto-Australoid stratum, and 2. of the neolithic, while the concept of the ultimate godhead rather as female than as male has nowhere else in the world been so elaborately developed.[22] It is, therefore, not to be marveled that human sacrifice, which is everywhere characteristic of the worship of the Goddess, whether in the tropical or in the neolithic sphere, should have survived in force in India, both in temples and in village groves, until suppressed by law in 1835. Furthermore, it must be assumed that in the Indus Valley period rites of essentially the same kind were celebrated, not only in the native villages and workers' quarters, but also in the high calendric ceremonies of state. And what such rites entailed in the way both of suffering for the victim and of excitement for the people may be learned from what we know of India in modern times on the village level.

A vivid typical lesson is supplied, for example, by the Khonds—a folk of Dravidian, Proto-Australoid stock, of Orissa, Bengal, and Bihar *—who had victims known as *meriah,* set apart and often kept for years, who were to be offered to the Earth Goddess to ensure good crops and immunity from disease, and in particular a fine, deep, rich red for the turmeric harvest. To be acceptable, such a figure had to have been either purchased or else born as the child of a *meriah.* The Khonds, according to report, occasionally sold their own children for this sacrifice, supposing that in death their souls would be singularly blessed. More often, however, the purchase was from the neighboring Pans, a criminal weaving tribe, who procured children for this purpose from the plains. In youth, the *meriah* was generally given as spouse another *meriah,* and their offspring then would be *meriahs* too. They were regarded as consecrated beings and treated with extreme affection and respect, and were available for sacrifice either on extraordinary occasions or at the periodic feasts, before the sowing; so that each family in the village might procure at least once a year a shred of flesh to plant in its field for the boosting of its crop.

Ten or twelve days before the offering, the victim was dedicated, shorn of his hair, and anointed with oil, butter, and turmeric. A season of wild revelry and debauchery followed, at the end of which the *meriah* was conducted with music and dancing to the *meriah* grove, a little way from the village, a stand of mighty trees untouched by the ax. Tied there to a post and once more anointed with oil, butter, and turmeric, the victim was garlanded with flowers, while the crowd danced around him, chanting to the earth: "O Goddess, we offer to thee this sacrifice; give to us good seasons, crops, and health"; and to the victim: "We bought thee with a price, we did not seize thee, and now, according to custom, we sacrifice thee: no sin rests upon us." A great struggle to secure magical relics from the decorations of his person—flowers or turmeric—or a drop of his spittle, ensued, and the orgy continued until about noon the following day, when the time came, at last, for the consummation of the rite.

The victim was again anointed with oil [writes Sir James G. Frazer in his summary of four separate accounts of eye-witnesses] and each person touched the anointed part, and wiped the oil on his own head. In some places they took the victim in procession round the village, from door to door, where some plucked hair from his head, and others begged for a drop of his spittle, with which they anointed their heads. As the victim might not be bound nor make any show of resistance, the bones of his arms and, if necessary, his legs were broken; but often this precaution was rendered unnecessary by stupefying him with opium. The mode of putting him to death varied in different places. One of the commonest modes seems to have been strangulation, or squeezing to death. The branch of a green tree was cleft several feet down the middle; the victim's neck (in other places, his chest) was inserted in the cleft, which the priest, aided by his assistants, strove with all his force to close. Then he wounded the victim slightly with his ax, whereupon the crowd rushed at the wretch and hewed the flesh from the bones, leaving the head and bowels untouched. Sometimes he was cut up alive. In Chinna Kimedy he was dragged along the fields, surrounded by the crowd, who, avoiding his head and intestines, hacked the flesh from his body with their knives till he died. Another very common mode of sacrifice in the same district was to fasten the victim to the proboscis of a wooden elephant, which revolved on a stout post, and, as it whirled round, the crowd cut the flesh from the victim while life remained. In some villages Major Campbell found as many as fourteen of these wooden elephants, which had been used at sacrifices. In one district the victim was put to death slowly by fire. A low stage was formed, sloping on either side like a roof; upon it they laid the victim, his limbs wound round with cords to confine his struggles. Fires were then lighted and hot brands applied, to make him roll up and down the slopes of the stage as long as possible; for the more tears he shed the more abundant would be the supply of rain. Next day the body was cut to pieces.

The flesh cut from the victim was instantly taken home by the persons who had been deputed by each village to bring it. To secure its rapid arrival, it was sometimes forwarded by relays of men, and conveyed with postal fleetness fifty or sixty miles. In each village all who stayed at home fasted rigidly until the flesh arrived. The bearer deposited it in the place of public assembly, where it was received by the priest and the heads of families. The priest divided it into two portions, one of which he offered to the Earth Goddess by burying it in a hole in the ground with his back turned, and without looking. Then each man added a little earth to bury it, and the priest poured water on the spot from a hill gourd. The other portion of flesh he divided into as many shares as there were heads of houses present. Each head of a house rolled his shred of flesh in leaves, and buried it in his favorite field, placing it in the earth behind his back without looking. In some places each man carried his portion of flesh to the stream which watered his fields, and there hung it on a pole. For three days thereafter no house was swept; and, in one district, strict silence was observed, no fire might be given out, no wood cut, and no strangers received. The remains of the human victim (namely, the head, bowels, and bones) were watched by strong parties the night after the sacrifice; and next morning they were burned, along with a whole sheep, on a funeral pile. The ashes were scattered over the fields, laid as paste over the houses and granaries, or mixed with the new corn to preserve it from insects. Sometimes, however, the head and bones were buried, not burnt. After the suppression of the human sacrifices, inferior victims were substituted in some places; for instance, in the capital of Chinna Kimedy a goat took the place of the human victim. Others sacrifice a buffalo. They tie it to a wooden post in a sacred grove, dance wildly round it with brandished knives, then, falling on the living animal, hack it to shreds and tatters in a few minutes, fighting and struggling with each other for every particle of flesh. As soon as a man has secured a piece he makes off with it at full speed to bury it in his fields, according to ancient custom, before the sun has set, and as some of them have far to go they must run very fast. All the women throw clods of earth at the rapidly retreating figures of the men, some of them taking very good aim. Soon the sacred grove, so lately a scene of tumult, is silent and deserted except for a few people who remain to guard all that is left of the buffalo, to wit, the head, the bones, and the stomach, which are burned with ceremony at the foot of the stake.[23]

To this day, among the Nagas of Assam, one may see a live bull, running about in a bull ring, hacked gradually to bits by a tribe of shouting savages, and among the gentle-eyed Burmese, in the north of the Upper Chindwin district, little children purchased for the purpose used to be sacrificed annually at a festival in August, to ensure a hearty crop of rice.

"A rope having been placed round his neck, the victim was taken to the houses of all the relatives of his purchaser. At each house a finger joint was cut off, and all persons in the house were smeared with the blood. They also licked the joint and rubbed it on the cooking tripod. The victim was then tied to a post in the middle of the village and killed by repeated stabs of a spear, the blood from each stab being caught in a hollow bamboo, to be used afterwards for smearing on the bodies of the purchaser's relatives. The entrails were then taken out and the flesh removed from the bones, and the whole was put in a basket and set on a platform near by as an offering to the god. After the blood had been smeared on the purchaser and his relatives, who danced and wept meanwhile, the basket and its contents were thrown into the jungle " [24]

Such rites are endemic to the culture zone of the Invisible Counterplayer and have already been considered in my Primitive volume.[25] The underlying myth is of a divine being, slain, cut up, and the parts buried, which thereupon turn into the food plants on which the community lives; and the leading theme, as I have said in my earlier work, is the coming of death into the world: the particular point being that it comes by way of a murder. The second point is that the food plants on which man lives derive from that death. And finally, the sexual organs, according to this mythology, appeared at the time of that coming of death; for reproduction without death would have been a calamity, as would death without reproduction. Hence we may state now, once again, "that the interdependence of death and sex, their import as the complementary aspects of a single state of being, and the necessity of killing—killing and eating—for the continuance of this state of being, which is that of man on earth, and of all things on earth, the animals, birds, and fish, as well as man—this deeply moving, emotionally disturbing glimpse of death as the life of the living is the fundamental motivation supporting the rites around which the social structure of the early planting villages was composed." And it was also, we have now to add, the fundamental motive out of which the entire mythology, civilization, and philosophy, of India has grown.

For the calmly ruthless power of the jungle and consequent orientation of its folk (the Proto-Australoid aborigines of that world of static vistas, with no history but duration) has supplied the drone base of whatever song has ever been sung in India of man, his destiny, and escape from destiny. New civilizations, races, philosophies, and great mythologies have poured into India and have been not only assimilated but greatly developed, enriched, and sophisticated. Yet, in the end (and, in fact, even secretly throughout), the enduring power in that land has always been the same old dark goddess of the long red tongue who turns everything into her own everlasting, awesome, yet finally somewhat tedious, self.

"Oh, she plays in different ways," we have been told, for instance, by her greatest devotee of recent times, Shri Ramakrishna (1836–1886).

It is she alone who is known as Maha-Kali (Mighty Time), Nitya-Kali (Endless Time), Shmashana-Kali (Kali of the Burning-ground), Raksha-Kali (Guardian Kali), and Shyama-Kali (the Black One). Maha-Kali and Nitya-Kali are mentioned in the Tantra philosophy. When there were neither the creation, nor the sun, the moon, the planets, and the earth, and when darkness was enveloped in darkness, then the Mother, the Formless One, Maha-Kali, the Great Power, was one with Maha-Kala, the Absolute.

Shyama-Kali has a somewhat tender aspect and is worshiped in the Hindu households. She is the Dispenser of boons and the Dispeller of fear. People worship Raksha-Kali, the Protectress, in times of epidemic, famine, earthquake, drought, and flood. Shmashana-Kali is the embodiment of the power of destruction. She resides in the cremation ground, surrounded by corpses, jackals, and terrible female spirits. From her mouth flows a stream of blood, from her neck hangs a garland of human heads, and around her waist is a girdle made of human hands.

After the destruction of the universe, at the end of the great cycle, the Divine Mother garners the seeds for the next creation. She is like the elderly mistress of the house, who has a hotchpotch-pot in which she keeps different articles for household use. . . . After the destruction of the universe, my Divine Mother, the Embodiment of Brahman, gathers together the seeds for the next creation. After the creation this Primal Power dwells in the universe itself. She brings forth this phenomenal world and then pervades it. . . .

Is Kali, my Divine Mother, of a black complexion? She appears black because she is viewed from a distance; but when intimately known she is no longer so. . . . Bondage and liberation are both of her making. By her Maya worldly people become entangled in "women and gold," and again, through her grace they attain their liberation. She is called the Savior, and the Remover of the bondage that binds one to the world. . . . She is self-willed and must always have her own way. She is full of bliss." [26]

As Exhibit A, in evidence of the role of this mighty goddess in the early Indus Valley, we may take a sealing discovered in Harappa, to which Sir John Marshall, director of the first excavation of the site, early drew attention (Figure 16). It exhibits, on the right of the obverse face, a nude female, upside down, legs apart, and with a plant issuing from her womb. On the left of the same

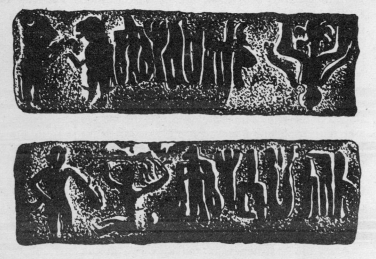

Figure 16. The Sacrifice: Indus Valley, c. 2000 B.C.

face is an opposed pair of animal genii. And between these and the nude female is an undeciphered inscription of six signs. On the reverse, the inscription is repeated, and to its left, as Marshall points out, are "the figures of a man and woman, the former standing with a sickle-shaped knife in his right hand, the latter seated on the ground with hands raised in an attitude of supplication.

"Evidently," Marshall observes, "the man is preparing to kill the woman, and it is reasonable to suppose that the scene is intended to portray a human sacrifice connected with the Earth Goddess depicted on the other side, with whom we must also associate the two genii, whom I take to be ministrants of the Deity. Although unique, as far as I am aware, in India, this striking representation of the Earth Goddess with a plant growing from her womb is not unnatural, and is closely paralleled by a terracotta relief of the early Gupta age [c. 330–650 A.D.], from Shītā in the United Provinces, on which the Goddess is shown with her legs in much the same posture, but with a lotus issuing from her neck instead of from her womb." [27]

A second sealing (Figure 17) carries the matter further. It shows again our nude goddess, but she is now standing between the

Figure 17. The Goddess of the Tree: Indus Valley, c. 2000 B.C.

parted limbs of a sacred pipal tree, which, as Marshall has pointed out, "is the tree of knowledge (*bodhi-* or *bo*-tree), under which the Buddha gained enlightenment." A sort of sphinx, part bull, part goat or ram, with human face, stands behind the half-kneeling figure of what appears to be a suppliant before her, while in the field below there is a line of seven female attendants, each with a plume, or perhaps branch, in her hair and a long braid falling down her back. Many Mesopotamian seals show a votary led by a god into the presence of a higher god. I take it that this seal is of the same order. We note, also, that both here and in Meso- potamian seals horned crowns embellish certain figures who in the Mesopotamian series always represent divinities. On this analogy, the present scene would represent a god conducting a sphinx into the presence of the nude goddess of the tree. And since we know that in Egypt the sphinx was symbolic of the

Pharaoh (capital P), it is difficult not to see in this scene the presentation of a divine king (ritual regicide) to the goddess who is to be fructified. In which case the seven would perhaps be suttee maids. And has the tree been split, as for the ritual murder of the Khonds?

No burials have been found in association with the Indus Valley complex, so that we cannot state with certainty that a regicide was practiced. However, as already noted, in Malabar, as late as the sixteenth century A.D., a king was observed standing on a platform, slicing himself to bits and tossing the pieces about to his waiting folk, until, when about to faint, he slit his throat.*

The first observation to be made with respect to Indian mythology, therefore, is that its deepest root is in the soil of the timeless equatorial world of the ritual death from which life proceeds. And in the period of the enigmatic Indus Valley cities, a neolithic counterpart of this primitive reading of the mystery of being arrived with its own version of the goddess from the Near East, together with the arts of a literate civilization: writing and, no doubt, calendric mathematics, kingship, and the rest. Furthermore, unless the evidences of both archaeology and ethnology have deceived us, there was practiced in these cities a ritual of regicide and suttee, from which at least some, and possibly all, of those major Indian traditions of human sacrifice are to be traced, records and accounts of which abound not only in the notes of Western voyagers but also in the monuments, chronicles, myths, and fashionable tales of India itself.

A second theme, no less typical of timeless India, strikes the eye in the imagery of a series of about half a dozen Indus seals showing *figures in yoga posture,* of which two examples will suffice for our present view. The first (Figure 18) shows a personage, apparently with three faces, seated in yoga on a low dais, before which stand two opposed gazelles. Four beasts surround him in the four directions: a tiger, elephant, rhinoceros, and water buffalo. His immense headdress of horns with its towering crown between

* Cf. supra, p. 73, and *The Masks of God: Primitive Mythology,* pp. 165–66.

suggests (like the headdress of the goddess in the tree) the form of a trident (*triśūla*). And the phallus, exposed, is erect.

All who have commented on this figure have perceived in it a prototype of Shiva, the god who in India to this day is the consort

Figure 18. The Lord of Beasts: Indus Valley, c. 2000 B.C.

of the goddess Kali; for Shiva is the lord of yoga, of cremation grounds, of the beasts of the wilderness, who are quelled in their ferocity by his meditating presence, and of the lingam (the phallus). His symbol is the trident. In his character as Maheshvara, the Great Lord, he has three faces. Moreover, his particular animal is the bull; and, among the numerous beasts represented on the Indus Valley seals, the bull preponderates by far, frequently standing before a censor, which suggests that, like the Apis bull of Ptah, it was regarded as divine.

However, Shiva is not the only great figure of later Indian myth suggested by this form; for the two gazelles before the dais are posed as in the classic imagery of the Buddha preaching his first sermon in the Deer Park of Benares. The form of the headpiece, furthermore, is familiar in Buddhist art as symbolic of the so-called "Three Jewels": the Buddha, the Law, and the Order.

In the second seal of this yoga series (Figure 19) a pair of serpents lift their bodies at either side of the meditating form to the height precisely of the crown of his head, while kneeling worshipers pay him honor at either hand.

Figure 19. The Serpent Power: Indus Valley, c. 2000 B.C.

Numerous phallic symbols have been found among the Indus ruins, ranging from half an inch to a foot or thereabouts in length; and with these are associated a curious series of so-called ring stones. "In size," wrote Marshall of the latter, "they range from half an inch to nearly four feet in diameter. All the larger specimens are of stone; the smaller ones of the same material or of faïence, shell, or imitation carnelian. The most typical of them have their upper and lower surfaces undulating; in others, the lower surface is flat, and the top takes a quatrefoil form." In ring stones of much later date unearthed at Taxila, which is also in the Indus Valley, he adds, "nude figures of a goddess are significantly engraved inside the central hole, thus indicating . . . the connection between them and the female principle." [28]

The classic Indian lingam and yoni symbols—which are the most numerous sacred objects by far in the whole range of contemporary Indian religion—are clearly anticipated in these Late Stone and High Bronze Age representations. And when the figures, on the one hand, of the meditating divine yogi, and, on the other, of the goddess mother of the plant world, are added to this evidence, there can be no doubt of the antiquity in India of the

great god and goddess known today as Shiva and his blood-con-
suming consort, Kali, "the dark one," Durga, "difficult of approach," to whom sacrifices pour. Their cult, moreover, is two-
ply; on one level, of an extremely primitive order, Proto-Australoid
and joined in affinity with the village cults of Melanesia, New
Guinea, and the other jungle areas of the world; but on the other,
derived from the Near Eastern matrices of civilization, where the
leading concept was of the goddess of an eon mathematically
marked by the passages of the seven spheres, and the king, ritually
slain, was the incarnate god, her ever-living, ever-dying spouse.

Now it has been found that along the western edge both of
Harappa and of Mohenjo-daro—guarding the quarter from which
the builders of this culture province had arrived and from which,
in time, the Aryan warrior folk also would come who were to terminate their day—there stood a formidable citadel of packed
earth, well faced with brick, about a quarter of a mile long, north
to south, 50 feet high, and 200 yards wide. On top were gates and
platforms (suggesting processions), fortifications, watch towers,
halls and areas of various sort and, at Mohenjo-daro, a public
bath, 39 feet long, 23 feet wide, and 8 feet deep, complete with
dressing rooms. Two major avenues, 30 feet wide, ran eastward
from each end of these great citadels, cut across in each case by
three broad streets running north to south, at intervals of about
250 yards. So that the cities, quadratically planned, were neatly
blocked in twelve precincts, within each of which a rat's maze
of narrow alleys threaded between unrelieved brick walls.

In certain quarters of the cities considerable luxury is suggested
by the floored bathrooms, covered wells, and elaborate systems of
sanitation, which are roughly comparable, though on a larger
scale, to those unearthed in Crete. Certain other quarters, however, have suggested to the excavators comparison with the coolie
quarters of modern Oriental slums. The workers' quarters at
Harappa, for example, consisted of ranges of identically planned
structures, each 20 feet by 12 feet internally and divided into two
rooms, one twice the size of the other. Nearby were the metal
workers' furnaces and the circular grain-pounding areas of well-
fired brick, where a barley was ground that is generally thought

to have been derived from the Near East; but also, a bread wheat of twenty-one chromosomes developed in or near the valley itself. Comparably, although the species of pig, goat, ox, sheep, and ass here known had already belonged for three millenniums to the Fertile Crescent Complex, a number of local breeds and beasts were also domesticated: the humped bull or zebu already noted for Baluchistan, the camel and horse (also, apparently, from that zone), the elephant, water buffalo, and barnyard fowl (which are definitely of Indian and Southeast Asiatic provenance) and, finally, a large dog akin to the Indian pariah dog and Australian dingo.[29] Add to all this the evidence of the two races, already remarked, and the main historic situation is apparent. There was no defense needed eastward; for the natives were undeveloped, mesolithic or even paleolithic primitives. They could be trained, however, to labor. And so we find in India, as nowhere else in the ancient world, not only a two-ply cult of the goddess, but also the preconditions of caste. Nowhere else was there such a racial and cultural breach between the upper, conquering, and lower, subjugated races. And to this day that breach—with its characteristic heritage mixed of inhumanity and tolerance—remains.

III. The Vedic Age: c. 1500–500 B.C.

It is difficult to realize that before the second millennium B.C., wherever man went, unless by coracle or boat, he traveled on his own two feet. The cultural drift, therefore, was centrifugal: a trend away and into distance, there to remain. And the result for mythology was continuous differentiation. Themes, characters, episodes, entire systems, were carried to new lands, where, by a sensitive process that I have termed (following Dr. Ananda K. Coomaraswamy) *lánd-náma,* "land naming" or "land taking," [30] the features of the newly entered world were assimilated to the imported heritage of myth.

With the mastery of the horse, however, all things changed; and we see the first signs of the new force in the sudden appearance, shortly following c. 2000 B.C., of the light two-wheeled chariot drawn by a pair of well-trained steeds. The wheel, as we know, had already appeared in Sumer c. 3200 B.C., and there is a quaint

mosaic of shell, lapis lazuli, and red sandstone from the royal
tombs of Ur that shows—as Sir Leonard Woolley, who discovered
it, declares—"the armament and the organization of the earliest
field army of which we have any knowledge." [31] Chariots are to
be seen on this piece; but they were clumsy four-wheeled affairs
drawn by teams of four donkeys or onagers. "The wheels were
solid," writes Professor V. Gordon Childe, describing the vehicles
of that time, "being formed of solid pieces of wood fixed together
by struts and bound with leather tires attached with copper nails.
They turned in one piece with the axle which was fastened to
the body of the car by leather thongs." [32] Obviously, not an easy
vehicle to maneuver! At some point in place and time, however,
roughly c. 2000 B.C. and probably north of the Caucasus range,
the light two-wheeled chariot drawn by two swift horses came
into use, and the wheels, which now were spoked, revolved freely
on their axles, so that the cars could be readily turned. And with
the advantage of this mobile military arm, new empires suddenly
came into being in unforeseen parts of the world, as, for instance,
the empire of the Hittites in Anatolia, c. 1650 B.C.—who, moreover, had already moved ahead to the use of iron; or that of the
Shang, in China, c. 1523 B.C., still using bronze. The Hyksos,
who "ruled without Re," brought the vehicle to Egypt, c. 1670–
1570 B.C., and it came with the Indo-Aryans to India c. 1500–
1250 B.C. Furthermore, in Southeastern Europe, c. 1500 B.C., a
new weapon, the sword, appeared, contrived for slashing from
the saddle.[33] From somewhere men were coming who had learned
to ride.

Now to all who acquired the use of them these new weapons
gave a powerful horizontal thrust that carried all before it, and
the older, basically peasant, land-rooted civilizations were simply
helpless. But not only a new striking power, a new arrogance, too,
had arrived: for is there anything more flattering to a man of
simple character than a good seat on a splendid horse? The words
cavalier, caballero, chevalrie, and *chivalrous* tell the tale. The
day of the peasant afoot and the nobleman ahorse had dawned,
which the machine age, only now, has ended. And it was to last
for about four thousand years, gradually welding by violence and

empire the far-flung provinces of the earlier, centrifugal ages; so that the world that formerly had been dividing was now gradually being brought together—but with a radical split horizontally between those who cry "Victory!" and those who weep. All the way from the Nile to the Yellow River the lesson of the inevitability of sorrow thus was learned by those in the role of the anvil from those with the mettle to be hammers, and with that, the golden age of the children of the Earth Mother was of yore.

Groups of skeletons left lying, skeletons of men, women, and children, some bearing sword and ax cuts, have been found on the topmost level of the Mohenjo-daro site. A raiding party had passed through—and it was of a race so little interested in cities that once they had gained the mastery there were no cities more in the Indus for a thousand years. At Chanhu-daro, some eighty miles to the south, and at several other sites, a squatter folk of lower grade raised shoddy shacks upon the ruins (the so-called Jhukar culture), and in the most southerly reaches of the once vast cultural domain, the peninsula of Kathiawar, there remained a sort of vestigial pocket. However, as far as "the vastest political experiment before the advent of the Roman Empire" was concerned: *fuit Ilium,* its day was done.

Some sense of the brilliance of the new nomadic fighting race that had arrived, chanting magically potent verses to a pantheon of chariot-driving, fighting gods, can be gained from the following typical hymn from the Rig Veda:

> I call upon Agni, first, for welfare;
> I call upon Mitra-Varuna, here, for aid.
> I call upon Night, who brings the world to rest;
> I call upon the god Savitri for support.
>
> Rolling this way through a darkling space,
> Laying to rest both the immortal and the mortal,
> In his golden car Savitri comes,
> The god beholding all beings.

Savitri's name is from the Sanskrit verbal root *sū,* "to excite, stimulate, incite, impel," and denotes, according to an ancient commentator, "the stimulator of everything."

Golden-handed Savitri, the active one,
Fares between heaven and earth.
He banishes disease, directs the sun,
And through the spaces of darkness reaches heaven.

By a downward path, by an upward path he goes;
Adorable he goes, with his two bright steeds.
From afar comes the god Savitri,
Dispelling all tribulation.

By thine ancient paths, O Savitri,
Dustless and well made in the air,
Faring by those paths readily traversed,
Protect and speak for us, O God, this day.[34]

For about a century and a half scholars of immense learning have been arguing the origin of the Aryans who thus arrived; and although a number of important points remain unsolved, the main lines of a general theory of the prehistory of the so-called Aryan, Indo-European, or Indo-Germanic family of peoples, languages, and mythologies have pretty well emerged.

Briefly, two prehistoric stages of development from what may or may not have been, at first, a fairly homogeneous nuclear community are to be distinguished:

1. A stage of common origins, somewhere in the broad grazing lands, either between the Rhine and Don, or between the Rhine and Western Turkestan.

2. A stage of division between a) a Western congeries of tribes, centered possibly in the plains between the Dnieper and Danube, from which there were presently derived the earliest Greek, Italic, Celtic, and Germanic diffusions; and b) an Eastern division, centered possibly north of the Caucasus, possibly around the Aral Sea, from which there stemmed, in time, the Armenians and various Balto-Slavic tribes (Old Prussians, Latvians, and Lithuanians; Czechs, Poles, Russians, etc.), as well as the early Persians and their close relatives, the Indo-Aryans, which latter, pressing through the passes of the Hindu Kush, broke into the broadly spreading, rich, and waiting Indian plain.

No one knows when the separation of the two main divisions,

a) and b), occurred, or where the group was when it went apart —if, indeed, it can be said to have gone apart at all or even to have been at any time a single, homogeneous group. For the broad northern grasslands from which they appeared had been a paleolithic hunting ground for some 200,000 years before the new arts of the nuclear Near East arrived, gradually and spottily, to make herdsmen out of hunters. One may think of a toiling peasantry pressing eastward and westward from the early centers of the neolithic, c. 4500–2500 B.C., and the older paleolithic tribes pressed back. But after assimilating a portion of the new arts in their own way, the latter turned, and, with their mastery of the chariot, became terrific. Herds, primarily of cattle, were their chief possession. They were polygamous, patriarchal, proud of their genealogies, tent dwellers, filthy, and tough. And since the women of their conquests were added gladly to their baggage trains, the Aryan races—if they can be called such—can have been evolved only by a process of constant mixing, blending, and splitting. Indeed, as Professor C. C. Uhlenbeck has shown, even before the two divisions went apart, their mother tongue was mixed of elements that suggest affinities, on the one hand with the peoples of the Caucasus, and on the other with the Eskimo.[35]

The gods of the various Aryan pantheons are, for the most part, disengaged from local associations. They are not specifically identified with this or that particular tree, pond, rock, or local scene, like so many divinities both of primitive and of advanced, settled cultures, but are the powers made manifest rather in such phenomena as the ranging nomads could experience or transport here, there, and everywhere. For example, of the 1028 hymns of the Indo-Aryan Rig Veda, no less than 250 were addressed to Indra, king of the gods, who was the wielder of the lightning bolt and giver of rain; 200 to Agni, the deity of fire, who in the fires of their hearths guarded the families and in the fires of their altars received the homage of their sacrifices, which he carried in his mouth of flame to the gods; and 120 went to Soma, the liquor of the sacrifice poured into Agni's mouth.

Hymns addressed to the sun, the wind, the rain god, and gods of storm were numerous. The brilliant Father Heaven and the broadly spreading Mother Earth, together with their daughters, lovely Dawn and Night, also were celebrated. However, in majesty above all, though hardly a dozen hymns were addressed to him exclusively, was the deity Varuna.

Varuna's name is from the verbal root *vr,* "to cover, to encompass"; for he encompasses the universe, and his attribute is sovereignty. Varuna placed fire in the waters; made the golden swing, the sun, to fly above; regulates and keeps day and night apart; and the rhythm of his order (*rta*) is the order of the world. Standing in air, he measures out the earth through his occult creative force (*māyā*), using as instrument the sun. He has made in this way three worlds, in all of which he abides: heaven, earth, and the interspace of air, where the wind that resounds is Varuna's breath. His golden abode is in the zenith: a mansion of a thousand doors, where he sits, observing all deeds, while around him sit his spies, who survey the world and are undeceived. The Fathers, also, see him there, and the all-observing sun, rising from his own shining house, proceeds to that high dwelling to report the deeds of men.[36]

Manifestly, this deity is by no means such a mere "nature god" as many have wished to see in the figures of the Vedic (as well as the Greek) pantheon. Nor is it proper to apply systematically any theory of religious evolution to this collection of poetic hymns, and accordingly to classify as early all those addressed to the *actual* fire burning on the altar, the shining sun itself, the lightning flashing from the cloud, or the rain pouring from the sky, and then, as of later growth, those in which the powers *behind* these phenomena have been personified. For, in the first place, there is no firm evidence anywhere in the world of any such tendency of mythology to evolve from a direct view of the phenomenon to a personification of its inhabiting power. Already in the myths of the pigmies of the Andamans—which are about as simple as any known—personifications appear throughout, as, for example, in the figure of Biliku, the northwest monsoon. And, in the second place, the Aryans, already possessed of domesticated beasts,

chariots, and bronze, were far indeed from primitive. The fundamental, structuring forms of their Vedic order show that they were
derived, together with agriculture, animal husbandry, and the
decimal system of mathematical reckoning, from the primary
center of all higher civilization whatsoever, namely Sumer. Heaven,
earth, and the air between are the realms of An, Ki, and Enlil.
Soma, the sacrifice, is a counterpart of Tammuz and even carries
the same associations; for this god, too, is identified with the waning and waxing moon, the bull tethered to the sacrificial post, the
fructifying sap that flows through all life and in the form of an
intoxicating drink fermented from the juice of the soma-plant is
the ambrosia of immortal life. Moreover, the principle of order
(*rta:* "course, or way") according to which Varuna governs all
things is the Vedic counterpart, exactly, of Egyptian *maat,* Sumerian *me.* And, like *maat* and *me,* the term designates not only a
physical, but also a moral, order.

Wrote Professor Hermann Oldenberg of this governing principle
of the universe in his classic study of Vedic thought:

> "*Rta* makes the rivers flow." "According to *rta* the heaven-
> born Dawn arises." The world-governing Fathers "according
> to *rta* have raised into the sky the sun," which is itself "the
> radiant visible countenance of *rta"*; while the darkness of an
> eclipse, which obscures the sun in violation of the natural
> order, is a thing "contrary to law." Around the sky there rolls
> the twelve-spoked wheel of *rta,* which never grows old—the
> year. And the force of *rta* is particularly visible where any sur-
> prising, apparently contradictory circumstance becomes an
> ever-renewed occurrence; as, for example, in that marvel to
> which man is indebted for his nourishment, that the dark-
> colored cow should produce white milk, the raw cow a drink
> already cooked—which is by the Vedic poet celebrated as
> "the *rta* of the cow, controlled by *rta.*"
>
> "*Rta*-and-Truth" are terms in constant combination; and
> as antonym to "true" the term *anrta,* "what is not *rta,*" is
> often used. The man who does injury to his fellow through
> deceit or malicious magic is placed in opposition to the hon-
> orable man, who "strives according to *rta.*" "For the one who
> follows *rta* the path is lovely underfoot and without
> thorns." . . .

It is true that a certain tinge of concreteness inheres in *rta*. There even are touches of a sort of vague localization, as when we read that the dawns come awakening from the residence of *rta;* or when the place of the sacrifice is represented as the seat of *rta.* There are paths of *rta*—and this, understandably, is a favorite expression, since *rta* in fact implies the idea of a direction in events; there are charioteers of *rta,* boats of *rta,* cows and the milk of *rta.* Yet with a few inconsequential exceptions, no one has ever prayed to *rta* or brought to it sacrificial gifts.[37]

It is to be remarked, however, that although an obviously massive influence from the primary culture matrices of the Near East is responsible for the architectural grandeur of the mythology of the Vedas, there is a totally different spirit and line of interest throughout these hymns from anything known to the prayers and myths either of Sumer or of Egypt. For like the Semites, the Aryans were a comparatively simple lot, and when they borrowed from the priestly orders of the great temple cities of the settled states, they applied the material to their own purpose, which was not the articulation of a complex social unit, since they governed no such state, but, specifically, power: victory and booty, aggressive productivity and wealth.

Now, as we have seen, the mythological foundation of the Indus Civilization overthrown by the Aryans appears to have been a variant of the old High Bronze Age vegetal-lunar rhythmic order, wherein a priestly science of the calendar required of all submission without resistance to an ungainsayable destiny. The goddess mother in whose macrocosmic womb all things were supposed to live their brief lives was absolute in her sway; and no such puny sentiment as heroism could hope, in the field of her dominion, to achieve any serious result. "She is self-willed," said Ramakrishna, "and must always have her own way." Yet for those children who submit without tumult to their mother's will, "she is full of bliss." All life, all moments, terminate in her insatiable maw; yet in this frightening return there is ultimately rapture for the one who, in trust, can give himself—like the perfect king: the son and yet the bull of his cosmic mother.

> Is Kali, my Mother, really black?

So chants an Indian devotee.

> The Naked One, of blackest hue,
> Lights the Lotus of the Heart.[38]

In the hymns of the Veda, on the other hand, there rings a totally different song. With a vivid, colorful delight in the bounty of life's onward flow, these magical verses reach for it with the brilliance of a sunrise or of their favorite young goddess, Dawn, who is celebrated in some twenty hymns:

> Glorious to behold, she wakes the world of men,
> Riding ahead, opening the way
> In her lofty car, majestic, delighting all,
> Spreading light at the break of day.

> As though proud of the loveliness of her body,
> Freshly bathed, the young Dawn stands upright,
> To be seen. Darkness, the Enemy, is expelled
> When Heaven's Child appears, spreading light.

> Heaven's Daughter, like a fair bride, lets fall the veil
> From her breast: reveals brilliant delight
> To him who adores her. As of old she came, so
> The young Dawn stands again, spreading light.[39]

One hears the rumble of war chariots, crack of whips, and the clang of bronze on bronze in the cadences of these potent verses, in which the power of the gods themselves was felt to have been caught. A recognition of fate as something that a manly spirit can well bear in true and patient devotion, with a prospect of a good result in the end, ignites each line; and as the sunrise, the flash of lightning, and the blaze of Agni's fire tongues on the altars are their prime symbolic images, so throughout these hymns there is a confidence in the capacity of aggressive fire to make way everywhere for its own victory over darkness. The gained speed of the newly harnessed horse, the new weapons, and the power therewith achieved to ride without defeat over cities, plains, everywhere at will, had given to the warrior folk a new sense of autonomy. So that even the lesson of the cosmic sacrifice now was read as a lesson not in submission but in gained strength. Soma, the lunar victim, was poured into the fire in the form of the juice of the plant soma as a drink fit for the gods; but the same intoxicating brew was poured also into the warrior's own gullet, where it ignited the warrior courage of his heart in a manner all its own. "Wisely," we hear:

Wisely have I partaken of the sweet food that stirs
Good thoughts: best banisher of care.
To which all gods and mortals,
Calling it honey, come together.

We have drunk Soma; we have become immortal.
We have gone to the light; we have found the gods.
What can hostility do to us now?
And what the malice, O Immortal One, of mortal man?

O you glorious, freedom-giving drops!
You have knit me together in my joints, as straps a car.
May these drops protect me against breaking a leg,
And save me from disease.

Like fire kindled by friction, do inflame me!
Illumine us! Make us rich!
For in the intoxication that you render, O Soma,
I feel rich. Now entering into us, make us really rich as well.[40]

The Aryans, we have said, were, like the Semites, a comparatively simple lot. And just as, in the mythology of the Semites, the priestly concept of the irresistible eon became transformed into a function of the pliant will of a personal god, subject to wrath but also to petition, so likewise in the Vedic sphere: the cyclic order (*rta*) of Varuna, though recognized with piety, was not allowed to stand in the foreground of the system. As hunters, herders, and warriors, the Aryans knew too well the power of the autonomous deedsman to shape destiny to have allowed the dead and killing weight of a mathematical, priestly vision to grind them into pap with all the rest. The rhythmic order of Varuna, consequently, moved back. And to the foreground of their mythic cosmic scene there drove, in a battle chariot drawn by two snorting, tawny steeds with flowing manes of peacock-feather hue, the greatest Soma drinker of them all, the god of battle, battle courage, battle power, and battle victory, hurler of the many-angled bolt, whose tawny beard was violently agitated when he had quaffed and was full of Soma, like a lake: Indra, like the sun, whose long arms flung the bolt by which the cosmic dragon Vritra was undone.

A snorting serpent, hissing, having thunder, lightning, mist, and hail at his command, Vritra, the archdemon without hands or feet, reposed amid distant fortresses, couching on the mountains—having hoarded to himself the waters of the world, so that the universe, deprived for centuries of all fluid whatsoever, had become a waste land.

But of Indra's deed, who has not already heard?

> Like a vehement bull, he took to himself the Soma,
> Drank the pressed drink from three mighty bowls,
> Picked up his weapon, the fiery bolt,
> And slew the first-born dragon.[41]

The deed is sung, as we have said, in at least one-quarter of the hymns of the collection.

Moreover (and here is a point that, I believe, has not been sufficiently stressed in the commentaries), the name of the dragon exploded by the bolt is from the verbal root vr, "to cover, to encompass," which, the reader recalls, is the root from which the name Varuna also was derived.

In other words:

1. The antagonist in this Aryan mythology is the negative aspect of the priestly cosmic order itself, as it affects the world of life.

2. The drought brought about by the coiled serpent Vritra, "the Enveloper," is the counterpart in this mythology of the Deluge in the Mesopotamian system.

3. As in the Semitic version of the Deluge, so in this Aryan version of the Drought: the cosmic catastrophe is interpreted not as the automatic effect of an impersonal rhythmic order, but as the work of an autonomous will.

4. In contrast to the Semitic view, however, the Indo-Aryan myth has portrayed Vritra, the worker of the negative deed, not as a god to be honored, but as a thing to be despised:

Footless, handless, he gave battle to Indra,
Who flung the bolt onto his back.
And the gelded bull, who had sought to equal the virile bull,
Vritra, lay scattered in many places.

And over him, who lay there like a slaughtered offering,
The flood of the waters climbed,
Which he, by his might, had formerly enclosed:
Beneath its course, now, the great dragon lay.[42]

5. Accordingly, whereas in the Mesopotamian development
the highest god may be unfavorable to man—a jealous, dangerous, touchy god who, if displeased, becomes malignant; the Vedic
gods, in the main, are genially disposed, readily pleased, and if
neglected, simply turn away. As Professor Winternitz states the
contrast:

> The Vedic singer looks up to the god whom he celebrates,
> neither with the profound awe, nor with the stone-hard be-
> lief, of the psalmist of Jehovah. Nor do the prayers of the
> priestly singers of ancient India leap up to Heaven, like the
> psalms, from the innermost depths of the soul. These poets
> stand on a more familiar footing with the gods they cele-
> brate. When they sing praise to a god, they expect that he
> will reciprocate with a wealth of cows and hero sons, and do
> not hesitate to let him know it. "I give, that thou shouldst
> give (*do, ut des*)," is their stand; and so there sings a Vedic
> singer to Indra:
>> If I, Indra, like thee,
>> Were the sole lord of all goods,
>> The singer of my praise
>> Would never be without cows.
>>
>> I would aid him gladly;
>> Give the wise singer his due:
>> If, O Bounteous God, I
>> Were, like thee, the Lord of Cows.[43]

But now there is one more point to be made; namely, that in
the buoyant life and will to earthly power of these hymns we find
nothing either of the spirit or of the mythological world image of
the later Hinduism, which, ironically, is supposed to have been derived from the Vedas. There is, for example, no idea of reincarna-

tion; no yearning for release from the vortex of rebirth; no yoga; no mythology of salvation; no vegetarianism, non-violence, or caste. The old Vedic word for war, *gaviṣṭi,* means "desire for cows"—and the cows of the Aryan herdsmen were slaughtered, flayed fo₁ leather, and eaten, as well as milked. (All of which would be difficult to explain, if inconsistency and both wishful and willful misreadings were not normal to religious traditionalism throughout the world.)

However, the meaning is simply that the mythology of later India is not in substance Vedic at all, but Dravidian; stemming in the main from the Bronze Age complex of the Indus. For in the course of years the Aryans were assimilated (though not, unfortunately, their cows); and the principle of order of the cosmic god Varuna—which had been derived, like the Indus forms themselves, from the mathematics of the Near East—assumed supremacy over the principle of the autonomous will of Indra. Varuna's *ṛta* became *dharma.* Varuna's creative *māyā* became Vishnu's creative *māyā.* And the cycles of eternal return—ever turning —returned to grind on forever. So that the act of will and virtue of the greatest hero god of the Vedas became only something that should not have occurred.

For that dragon, as we now are to hear, had been a Brahmin. And since the killing of a Brahmin—according to later Indian thought—is the most heinous of all crimes, Indra's killing of the Brahmin Vritra was a crime that he would be able to expiate only by the performance of an odious penance.

We read, therefore, in the Mahabharata, a full millennium (at least) later than the period of our Vedic hymns, the following transformed account of the killing of the cosmic dragon by the Vedic god.

"Let us hear, O Sage!" So runs the invocation to the storyteller at the opening of this passage: "Let us hear of the great dedication to virtue (*dharma*) of that immeasurably brilliant Vritra, whose wisdom was unequaled and devotion to Vishnu beyond account!"

In those days [the transformed tale now begins] the puissant chariot-riding King of Gods, surrounded by his army of celestials, saw before him the great titan, standing mighty as a mountain, 4500 miles tall and in girth a full 1500. Whereupon, perceiving that prodigious form, which the powers of all three worlds together would have been impotent to undo, the entire celestial host was paralyzed with fear, and their leader, discerning the contour of his foe, lost the use of his limbs from the waist down.

A noise of beaten drums, trumpets, and other sounding instruments went up on all sides, and the titan, taking notice of the army of the gods and its king before him, was neither astonished nor appalled. Nor did he feel that he would be called upon to make use of all his powers in this fight.

The war commenced. And it terrified all three worlds. For the entire sky was covered with the warriors of both sides, wielding swords, javelins, dirks and axes, spears and heavy clubs, rocks of various size, bows of loud sound, numerous types of celestial weapon, fires and burning brands. And there assembled to watch, gathering in their best chariots, all of those blessed seers to whom the Vedas had in times of yore been revealed, likewise yogis fully realized, and heavenly musicians in their own fair cars, wherein were also celestial mistresses; moreover, shining above all was the creator and governor of the world, the great god Brahma himself.

Then dharma-supporting Vritra deftly overwhelmed both the King of Gods and the entire world of air with a dense shower of rocks. And the gods, burning with anger, pouring a shower of arrows at those rocks, dissolved them. But the titan, mighty in his maya-power as well as in his strength, completely stupefied the King of Gods by virtue of his maya. And when the god of a hundred sacrifices, numbed by that maya-power, stood without moving, the Vedic sage Vasishtha —who in contemplation had heard, and so composed, all the hymns of the seventh book of the Rig Veda—restored him to his senses by chanting at him Vedic verses. "You are the leader of the gods," said the sage. "Within you is the power of all three worlds. Why, therefore, do you falter? Brahma the Creator, Vishnu the Preserver, and Shiva the Destroyer of Illusion, as well as glorious, divine Soma, and all the Vedic seers, are watching. Do not collapse here like a mere mortal. All three of Shiva's eyes are upon you. And do you not hear the Vedic saints lauding you in your victory with hymns?"

Thus recalled to his senses, the god, becoming confident, applied himself to yoga, and so dispelled the maya by which he had been stupefied. Whereupon the seers, who had now

been witness to the prowess of the titan, turned to Shiva, lord
of the universe, in prayer. And that Great God, in response,
sent his energy into Vritra in the form of a terrific fever.
Simultaneously Vishnu entered Indra's weapon. And the
whole company of seers, turning to Indra, bade him attack
his foe. The god Shiva himself addressed him:

"Before you is your foe, Vritra, supported by his army:
the very Self (*ātman*) of the universe, ubiquitous, and of immense deluding power. For 60,000 years that titan applied
himself to severe ascetic austerities for the acquisition of this
strength, until, in the end, Brahma was compelled to grant
the boons he wished. And these were the greatest to be gained
by yoga, namely, the power of creating illusions at will, unconquerable force, and energy without end. However, I am
now committing to you *my* energy and force. Therefore, with
yoga to assist you, slay the enemy with your bolt."

Said then the King of Gods: "O Greatest God, before thy
blessed eyes, endowed with the boon of thy grace, I shall now,
with this my thunderbolt, slay that invincible son of the
mother of demons."

And the gods and all the saints, seeing the enemy struck with
that fever, lifted a roar of great joy. Rolling drums, kettle
drums, conchs and trumpets, thousands upon thousands,
everywhere began to beat and blow. The demons lost their
wits. Their powers of delusion left them. And the form that
the King of Gods then assumed, on the point of the great
moment of his victory, seated in his car, amid the shouts of
acclaim of the Vedic seers, was such that none could look
at it without fear.

But let us tell, first, of the stricken titan. When he had
been filled with that burning fever, his immense mouth gave
forth a blast of flame. His color disappeared. Everywhere
he trembled, he could scarcely breathe, and each hair on his
body stood erect. His mind came through his jaws in the
shape of an evil, hideous jackal, and meteors burst blazing
from his sides, both right and left.

And the King of Gods, praised and worshiped by the gods,
handling his bolt, watched the monster, who, when he had
been ravished by that fever, yawned wide with a great howl;
and while his great mouth was open still the god let fly into
it his bolt, filled with no less energy than the fire that consumes the universe at the end of a cosmic cycle—which blasted
Vritra prodigiously, forthwith. The gods were in ecstasy. And

the King of Gods, recovering his bolt, made away in haste in his chariot toward the sky.

But that heinous crime, Brahminicide, dreadful, ominous, striking fear into all the worlds, came forth from the body of the murdered titan with teeth projecting terribly, of an aspect furiously contorted, tawny and black, with disheveled hair, appalling eyes, and a garland of skulls around her neck, bathed in blood, clad in rags and in the bark of trees. And she went after the Master of the Bolt, overtook his chariot, seized him, and from that moment Brahminicide was stuck to him. Terrified, he fled into a lotus stalk, where he stayed for years with it clinging to him still, trying every way to be quit of her. But all his attempts were in vain until, at last, with that fiend still attached, the miserable King of Gods approached in obeisance Brahma the Creator, who, knowing the crime, commenced to ponder the question of how the King of Gods might be set free.[44]

Now, surely, there is nothing Vedic about this episode but the names—and names alone—of its two contenders. Their characters are changed; their powers, too; even their virtues are reversed. We cannot but note that the puppet-hero's courage is derived not from soma but from yoga, which, as we have learned from the Indus seals, was a feature of the Indus civilization. Furthermore, the final credit for the victory has been assigned to Shiva, the lord of yoga, likewise prefigured in those seals. So that, manifestly, in the course of the centuries between the entry of the Aryans and the composition of this piece, the Vedic pantheon was adjusted to a theology derived, in certain features at least, from the earlier, native Indian system in which yoga played a paramount role. Indeed, even the power of the antagonist is here attributed to an exercise in yoga in which he persisted for sixty thousand years.

We note, further, an emphasis on *dharma,* which is interpreted as virtue in accord with cosmic law: precisely *maat, me, ṛta, tao.* The Bronze Age principle of order, in other words, has come again to the foreground, fading out the Vedic hero theme of the individual deed. And in fact, a contrary, unheroic theme has become paramount in this account, which is strongly stressed throughout the Mahabharata; namely of an alternation of power between a company of titans and a company of gods, in illustration of the principle of the cycle of dark and light. So that, much as in certain modern views of history—as, for example, that of Tolstoi or of Marx—it is the tide of history itself that is represented as bearing apparent heroes (Napoleons, Bismarcks, Indras, etc.) upon its irresistible crest; not the hero who makes history. However, in contrast to the somewhat Levantine system of Marx, there is to be in this mythology no Messianic Age in which the laws of history as we know them cease to function. For, according to this view, there inheres in the victory of each side an intrinsic limitation. Alternation is of the essence. Brahma, the creator of the world illusion, gives the power of illusion to the villain of the piece. Shiva gives to Indra his energy and force for the destruction of that illusion. But when the hero god has then slain his man, he finds that he has become—so to say—a war criminal, though still the savior of the world.

There is thus an echo, here, of Prometheus; an echo, also, of Christ crucified, with the sins of the world upon his shoulders. Christ on his cross; Prometheus nailed to the world mountain; Indra in his lotus stem! We have touched, once again, that archaic mythological vein which first appeared to us in the figures of Horus, Seth, and their Secret of the Two Partners,* beyond good and evil.

Yoga and the principle of the cycle, then, were already, apparently, features of the earlier system of the Indus. The motif, however, of the chanting Vedic seers belongs to the Vedic side of the picture presented in this myth; and the notion of a trinity of gods, comprising Brahma, as creator of the world illusion; Vishnu, its preserver; and Shiva with three eyes, the lord of yoga, as destroyer of the world illusion, is a late, very late, conception, which does not appear in Indian art and myth until c. 400 A.D.

We treat of this later age in Chapter VI; and meanwhile shall follow the course by which the sunny Vedic gods first were joined to the unheroic system of the phallic worship they despised, and then, ironically, converted to the service of that world-negating doctrine of what Nietzsche termed the Dwarfing Virtue,

* Supra, pp. 81–83.

by which the great are made small, the little, great, and the teachers
of resignation gain the glory—for themselves.

IV. Mythic Power

The means by which the priestly caste in India gained the
mastery over the nobles—gradually, perhaps, but surely and
securely—was the awe that they managed to inspire in all around
them by the chanting, and apparent power, of their Vedic charms.
In the earliest period the gods were implored. But when it was
reasoned that since the gods could be conjured to man's will the
power of the conjuring rites must be greater than that of the gods,
the deities were no longer implored but compelled to yield their
boons to the warrior clans; and the magic of the Brahmins, the
knowers of the potent spells, became recognized as the mightiest,
and most dangerous, in the world.

The word *veda,* "knowledge," is from the root *vid* (compare
Latin *video,* "I see"), which means, "to perceive, to know, to
regard, to name, to find out, to acquire, to grant." The Vedic
hymns, it was supposed, had not been humanly composed, but
"heard" (*śruti*), as by revelation, by the great seers (*ṛsis*) *of the*
mythic past. They were therefore a treasury of divine truth, and
consequently power, to be studied, analyzed, and contemplated.
The works of theology devoted to their interpretation are the so
called "Works of the Brahmins" (*Brāhmaṇas*), the earliest of
which may be dated c. 800 B.C. In these the Vedic hymns and rites
are treated, not as products of man's thought and action, but as
fundamental factors of the universe. In fact, the Vedas, it was
now supposed, anteceded the universe; for they contained those
potent, creative, eternal syllables out of which the gods and the
universe had proceeded. "OM!" we read, for example:

> This imperishable Syllable is all this.
> That is to say:
> All that is Past, Present, and Future is OM;
> And what is beyond threefold Time—that, too, is OM.[45]

Through his knowledge and control of the power in the Vedic
hymns, the learned Brahmin could bring about, just as he pleased,

either benefits to his friends or disaster to his foes, simply by appropriate manipulations of the verses. For instance:

> If he desire of a man, "Let me deprive him of expiration," he should recite the triplet to Vayu (the wind-god) in confusion, he should pass over a verse or line; thereby it is confused: verily thus he deprives him of expiration. If he desire of a man, "Let me deprive him of expiration and inspiration," he should recite for him the triplet to Indra and Vayu in confusion, he should pass over a verse or line; thereby it is confused; verily thus he deprives him of expiration and inspiration. . . . If he desire of a man, "Let me deprive him of strength," he should recite for him the triplet to Indra in confusion. . . . If he desire of a man, "Let me deprive him of limbs," he should recite for him the triplet to the All-gods in confusion. . . . But if he desire of a man, "with all his members, with all the self, let me make him prosper," verily let him recite for him thus in due and proper order; verily thus he makes him prosper with all his members, with all his self. With all his members, with all his self, he prospers who knows thus.[46]

The gods derived their strength from the sacrifice. "The sacrifice," it was said, "is the chariot of the gods." [47] Consequently, the Brahmins were the masters, not of men alone, but also of the gods. "There are verily," we read, "two kinds of god. That is to say, the gods are gods, and the learned, well-instructed Brahmins are human gods. Between these two, the offering is shared: the sacrifices are for the gods and the fees are for the human gods, the learned, well-instructed Brahmins. The person giving the sacrifice gives pleasure to the gods with the sacrifice and to the human gods, the learned, well-instructed Brahmins, with the fees. And when they are well pleased, these two kinds of god translate him to the beatitude of heaven." [48]

Should the question arise, however, as to which of the two kinds of god is the greater, the answer is at hand. "The Brahmin descended from a great rishi is himself, verily, all the gods"; [49] and again: "The Brahmin is the highest god." [50]

Now of all the mighty ceremonies through which the Brahmins were prepared to magnify their patrons, the greatest was the pageant-filled Horse Sacrifice (*aśva-medha*), designed and reserved for kings, and for which a vast number of skilled Brahmins were required. These Brahmins were of four classes:

1. The Hotri, or "Invoker," who in the earlier period (c. 1000 B.C.) may have been both chanter and sacrificer, but in the high period of the later Brahmanas (c. 800–600 B.C.), had the particular task of calling to the gods, summoning them from their several stations to participate in the feast and receive the offered morsels from the fire;

2. The Adhvaryu, or "Sacrificer," whose task was to supervise the offerings; and whereas the Hotri is praised as "beautiful-tongued," the Adhvaryu is "beautiful-handed"; the handbook of the Hotri was the Rig Veda, that of the Adhvaryu the Yajur Veda; and at all great rites these two were the chief functionaries, each with a number of assistants, depending on the magnitude of the occasion;

3. The Udgatri, or "Chanter," who intoned selections from another collection, the Sama Veda, where the hymns (many of which are the same as those of the Rig) are accented for his use; and finally:

4. The Supervising Brahmin, who was often, but not necessarily, the chief house priest of the king.

The symbolism of the Horse Sacrifice was in many parts coarsely sexual; for the rite was derived by adaptation from the earlier Bronze Age rituals of the bull, which had served in cults primarily of vegetal fertility. However, even the most overt of the phallic aspects were here supposed to yield, not fertility alone, but, above all, supreme royal power and authority over—in the best case—the entire world. The rite commenced either in spring or in summer; and the animal had to be a stallion of pure breed, distinguished by special marks. When chosen, he was set apart ceremonially, tethered to a sacrificial post.

"The sacrificial post," we read, "is yonder sun, the altar is the earth; the strew of sacred grass represents the plants; the kindling wood, the trees; the sprinkled waters are the waters; the enclosing sticks, the four quarters." [51]

Every aspect of the sacrifice had its counterpart in the structure of the universe; every act a cosmic reference: and the power of the rite to work effects upon the world derived from the precision of these analogies. The power of the Brahmin caste, in fact, lay in its knowledge of such accords. Basically, the principle involved was that of Frazer's "imitative magic." [52] However, whereas on the primitive level the implied analogies of magic are usually obvious to the eye, those of the Brahmins were extremely recondite and often brilliantly poetic.

The horse, following its tethering at the post, was driven with a broom into the water to be bathed, while the son of a whore clubbed a "four-eyed" dog to death (that is to say, a dog with a dark patch above each eye, suggesting the guardian dogs of the land of the dead), which then was floated off in a southerly course beneath the belly of the horse and away, toward the land of the dead.

"Let Varuna advance against anyone who would presume to attack this steed," cries the killer of the dog. "Away the man! Away the dog!" [53]

The killed dog in this curious rite is symbolic of misfortune, which is magically dispelled by a being who not merely represents but actually is an effect of the power of sheer sex: the offspring of a whore. The power of sex, then, is to play its part in this rite, no less than the powers of military arms and the knowledge of Brahminical lore.

The horse now is released and allowed to run at will for one year in the company of a hundred nags but no shining mares, followed by a cavalry of a hundred princes, another hundred sons of officers of high rank, and a hundred sons of lower rank; so that if anyone should offer to make off with the gallant mount or prohibit its entrance into his kingdom, that king would have to fight. Whereas, on the other hand, if any king submitted to the passage of this horse, he therewith conceded overlordship to the great monarch who had set him loose—and who was now very busy at home with a ceremony of considerable magnitude and magical importance.

Gifts were being offered daily to the god Savitri, in the way of sacrifice. Daily, also, at a festive gathering before the king and his court, the Hotri priest was staging recitals with dramatic presentations, song and music, dance and the recitation of epic tales, together with impromptu verses sung by a noble bard in honor of the king. And in accord with the matter of the day the audiences were chosen: whether for old or for young; for snake-charmers, fishermen and bird-catchers; for robbers and usurers; or for sages.[54] Moreover, as the horse, during this year, was to have no joy of sex, so too the king—for whom, however, the austerity was rendered the more difficult through his requirement to sleep every night between the legs of his favorite queen. And a college of thirty-six Adhvaryu priests, every fortnight or so, sitting each on a bench of ashvatta wood (a pun is involved here on the word *aśva,* "horse") whiled away the night by pouring products of the field and dairy into a fire: butter, barley, milk, and rice.[55]

The year ended with a festival of three days, when the horse with his fellowship, returning, galloped gallantly into the fair ground and sang out the Sama Veda chant. This wonder of animal voice was achieved when the Udgatri priest broke off his own chant, a mare was trotted forth, and the perfect stallion neighed. That was known as the Udgitha of the stallion. The perfect mare replied. And that was the Udgitha of the mare.[56]

Apparently in earlier Vedic times, the only beast sacrificed in this rite besides the horse was a ram, representing the god Pushan, messenger of the sun. However, in the Mahabharata, the following spectacle is described:

> The priests, learned in the Vedas, performed accurately all the rites, duly moving about in all directions, perfectly trained and all perfectly wise. Nor was there any infringement of ordinance: nothing was improperly done. Among the multitude, furthermore, none could be found who was without cheer, none poor, none starved, none in grief, and none who was vulgar: food was available to all who wished to eat.
> Every day, the priests, versed in every category of sacrificial lore, precisely following scriptural injunctions, performed the necessary acts for the consummation of a mighty rite, and there was none who was neither a master of Vedic lore nor perfectly an observer of his vows. And when the time had come for the setting up of stakes, six were of vilva wood, six of khadira, six of sarvavarnin, two of devadaru, and one of shleshmataka [twenty-one stakes in all]. Furthermore, for the

sake of beauty only, others were lifted that were of gold. And those stakes, adorned with pennants given by the king, shone as Indra surrounded by the deities of his court, together with seven celestial seers standing round about. Moreover, bricks of gold were supplied for the building of a tower, beautiful as any built in heaven, eighteen cubits high and of four stories, upon the pinnacle of which a large triangular bird of gold was placed in the shape of Garuda, the sun-bird.

Whereupon the priests, following perfectly all scriptural injunctions, tied animals and birds to those stakes in accordance with the deity of each. Bulls of proper mark, as indicated in the Scriptures, aquatic animals too, were affixed properly to those stakes after the kindling of the sacrificial fire. And in preparation for that sacrifice, three hundred beasts were thus fastened to those stakes—including that foremost of all perfect steeds.

And the entire sacrificial field therewith was gloriously bedight, like a place alive with celestial seers, together with troops of celestial musicians and their mistresses, the dancing girls. . . .[57]

The king's three (or four) wives, one of whom could be of the Shudra caste,* now approach and circumambulate the horse, after which they prepare it for immolation, oiling, rubbing down the beast, and hanging garlands about its neck, while the Hotri priest and supervising Brahmin perform a symbolic, comical enigma play. The horse thereafter is led back to its post, covered with a cloth, and suffocated, whereupon the king's chief queen approaches, and the curious, almost incredible archaic rite begins of a queen's marriage to a dead beast, symbolic of the ever-living great god Varuna, master of the order of the world.

She lies down beside the dead horse, and the Adhvaryu priest covers the two with a cloth. He prays: "In heaven be ye covered, both. And may the manfully potent stallion, seed bestower, bestow the seed within." The queen is to grasp and draw forth the sexual organ of the stallion, pressing it to her own.

"O Mother Mother Mother!" she cries out. "Nobody will take

---

* "Three kinds of wife are for the Brahmin, two for the Kshatriya, the Vaishya must wed only from his own caste. . . . Let the Brahminic wife be the first of a Brahmin and the Kshatriya of a Kshatriya. For the pleasure a Shudra also is allowed. Others, however, disallow this" (*Mahābhārata* 13.44.12.).

me! The poor nag sleeps! Me, this wonderful little thing all dressed
in the leaves and bark of the kampila tree!"

The priest: "I shall incite the procreator. Do thou, too, incite the
procreator."

Whereat the queen says to the stallion: "Come, let the two of us
stretch out our limbs."

The priest prays to incite the god: "Come, lay thy seed well
in the channel of the one who has opened to thee her thighs. O thou,
potent of manhood, set in motion the organ that is to women the
nourisher of life. It darts into the sheath, their hidden lover, darkly
buffeting, back and forth."

The queen: "O Mother Mother Mother! No one is taking me!"

The king adds an enigmatic metaphor: "Heave it high, like
someone leaning a load of reeds against a hill. It will then be at
ease in the midst, like someone winnowing in a fresh wind."

The priest turns to an attendant princess, pointing to her sex:
"The poor little hen there is splashing about, in a flurry. The yard
runs deep into the cleft; eagerly the sheath swallows."

And the princess says to the priest, pointing to his sex: "The
poor little cock there is splashing about, in a flurry, just like thy
great big talkative mouth. Priest, hold thy tongue."

Once again the queen: "O Mother Mother Mother! No one is
taking me!"

The Supervising Brahmin calls down to her: "Thy father and
thy mother once climbed to the top of the tree. 'Now,' called thy
father, 'I am going to come across,' and he worked the yard in the
deep cleft, going back and forth."

The queen: "O Mother Mother Mother! No one is taking me!"

The Hotri priest, turning to one of the other queens: "When
that big thing in that narrow cleft bumps against the little thing, the
two large lips stir like two little fish in a puddle in a cow path."

The addressed queen turns to the Adhvaryu priest: "If the gods
grant joy to that dripping, spotted bull, the woman's lifted knees
will show it as clearly as a truth before your eyes."

And the queen again: "O Mother Mother Mother! No one is
taking me!"

The lord high steward, now, to the fourth wife, the Shudra:

"When the noble antelope feeds on the barley seed, no one thinks of the village cow that fed upon it before. When the Shudra's lover is an Aryan, she forgets the prostitute's fee." [58]

Crude and difficult to associate with the fine titles of those from whose noble mouths they issue, these ritualized obscenities are entirely in keeping with the magic lore of the archaic Bronze and Iron Age religion. For, as Professor J. J. Meyer, in his massive study of the vegetation cults of India, writes: "Thanks to the principle of analogy, such verbal coitus works no less salubriously in its magic than actual ritual intercourse, or indeed sexual intercourse of any kind." [59] The symbolized act of the sacrificed dead horse corresponds to that of Osiris dead, begetting Horus, the young Apis bull.* And the rite of a queen united with a beast is readily matched, as Meyer notes, "in the hieros gamos of the Queen of Athens with the fertility god Dionysos, celebrated in 'the cattle stall'—where the god must have approached her in his bull form, just as here Varuna came to the Great Queen (*mahiṣī*) in his stallion manifestation." [60]

All the queens, including the one who has lain with the sacrificial horse, now stand and recite in unison a verse from the Rig Veda, addressed to a divine, flying steed named Dadhikravan ("He who scatters curdled milk"):

> Of Dadhikravan the praises let me sing:
> The potent, swift steed of many victories:
> May he lend fragrance to our mouths.
> May he give length of days to our life! [61]

They wash themselves ceremonially, addressing with the following words, likewise from the Veda, the waters, which are to be conceived as rushing, like all the waters of the world, to Varuna:

> O thou Water, be to us quickening,
> And bring to us fresh power,
> That there may be known to us great joy.
>
> What fluent benison is thine!
> Let us partake of it here,
> Like the loving, divine goddess-mothers.

* Supra, p. 53, and *The Masks of God: Primitive Mythology*, pp. 424–26.

> Thee we approach in the name of him
> To whose dwelling thou dost speeding go.
> Give us, O Water, of thy strength! [62]

"After butchering the horse," we next read in the version of the Mahabharata, "they caused the queen of high intelligence—who was endowed with sacred knowledge, also property, and equally devotion: which are the prime qualities of a queen—to sit beside the cut up beast, while the Brahmins, cool and composed in mind, taking the marrow, duly cooked it. Whereupon the king, still following scripture, sniffed the steam of that marrow so cooked, which is potent to purge sin. The remaining limbs of the beast were then cast into the fire by the sixteen learned priests, and the Horse Sacrifice of that World Monarch was complete." [63]

Homer's legend of the Trojan Horse, by rebirth through which the Greek heroes conquered Troy, must have been a reflex of some such potent rite as this. A greatly simplified Horse Sacrifice, involving also the killing of a white ram as the "messenger" of the god but with omission of the sexual as well as imperial motifs, was observed as recently as 1913 among the Finnic Cheremiss people of the Volga region.[64] The rite is of the heritage of the northern steppe folk, among whom the horse was first mastered and of whom the Vedic Aryans were a branch. And in the context of the later Indian tradition, it is a prime token of the Brahminical Aryan strain, as the rites of human sacrifice are of the older, non-Vedic mythic order of the Goddess and her spouse.

v. Forest Philosophy

Brahmavarta, the classic Holy Land of the Vedas, was in the northeast portion of the plain between the rivers Jumna and Sutlej, roughly, between Delhi and Lahore; while Brahmarshidesha, "the Country of the Holy Seers," where the hymns were collected and arranged, lay a little southeastward of this zone, in the upper portion of the Doab (the land between Jumna and Ganges) and in the regions around Mathura.[65] The tiger of Bengal is not mentioned in the Rig Veda; nor is rice, which is a product of the south. The place of honor goes to the lion, which at that time prowled the vast deserts eastward of the Sutlej; and the grain of the cattle-herders appears to have been wheat.[66]

The classic country of the Buddhists, on the other hand, lies far eastward of these early Aryan centers, down the Ganges, below Benares, in the neighborhood of Oudh and Bihar, reaching northward to Nepal and southward to the dangerous Chota Nagpur jungles: the lands of the Bengal tiger and of rice.

We may let these two worlds stand as symbolic poles representing the interplay of the contrary mythologies of the newcomers and the older inhabitants of the land. For not only the Buddhists and Jains, but also a considerable galaxy of unaffiliated, world-negating forest sages, had their own classic Holy Land in this latter part of India. Benares was the city of the god Shiva, "The Lord of Yoga." And there is, in fact, a possibility—as noted earlier *—that this may have been the center from which the yoga postures represented in the Indus Valley seals ultimately derived. We may take it, hypothetically, to be a mythogenetic zone of unfathomed past.

Now the Brahmins, we have heard, were the greatest of the gods. However, there was a considerable breach in the magical fortress of their Olympus; and this breach did not become known to them until the Aryan mastery of the Gangetic plain had reached the neighborhood of Benares—say, about 700–600 B.C. As we read in the earliest of the Upanishads:

> There was once a proud and learned Brahmin of the Gargya family, Balaki by name, who went before the king Ajatashatru of Benares. "I will tell you," said he, "about brahman." The king replied: "For such instruction I will give you a thousand cows." And the Brahmin Gargya said: "That person who is in the sun I honor as brahman." But Ajatashatru said: "Do not talk to me about him: I already revere him as the supreme head and king of all beings. Anyone revering him as such becomes the supreme head and king of all beings." Gargya said: "That person who is in the moon, I honor as brahman." But Ajatashatru said: "Do not talk to me about him: I already revere him as the great white-robed king Soma. Anyone revering him as such receives abundant soma continually pressed out every day: his food does not fail."

* Supra, p. 154.

The Brahmin tried in the same way to preach of lightning, space, the wind, fire and water, the being beheld in a mirror, the sound of a man walking, the four quarters, the shadow, and the body; to each of which suggestions he received the same rebuff; whereupon he became suddenly silent.

The king said: "Is that all?"

Gargya said: "That is all."

The king said: "But that is not enough for the knowledge of brahman."

The Brahmin said: "I approach you as a pupil."

And the king said: "But surely it is extraordinary that a Brahmin should come to a Kshatriya, thinking, 'He will tell me about brahman.' Nevertheless, I shall instruct you." And the king rose, took Gargya by the hand, and walked with him to a man asleep. Ajatashatru said to that sleeping man: "Oh thou great, white-robed King Soma." He did not rise. The king pushed him till he woke. The man got up. And Ajatashatru said: "Where, when this man slept, was the person who consists of understanding; and whence did he come when he returned?"

Gargya could not say.

Ajatashatru said: "When a man sleeps, the person who consists of understanding rests in the space within the heart, having through his understanding taken to himself the understanding of the senses. And when that person has in this way absorbed the senses, one is said to be asleep. The breath is absorbed; the voice, and the faculties of eye, ear, and intellect. And when a man thus sleeps, the whole world is his. He becomes a maharaja, as it were. He becomes a great Brahmin, as it were. He enters the high, as it were, and the low. For, just as a maharaja, taking with him his people, moves around in his own country as he pleases, so this person asleep, taking with him his senses, moves around [in dream] in his own body as he pleases.

"But when he then goes further and falls sound asleep, knowing nothing at all, he is at rest throughout his body, having crept out of that space within the heart through 72,000 veins, which lead from the heart into the body. And then, as a maharaja might rest, a great Brahmin, or a child, when he has reached the summit of bliss, that person rests.

"For as a spider comes out along its thread or as sparks pour from a fire, even so, from this Self (*ātman*) come forth all the senses, the worlds, the gods, and all being. And the secret name (*upaniṣad*) thereof is the reality of reality (*satya-sya satya:* the being of being, the truth of truth). The sense-world is a reality, indeed. And its reality is this. . . ." [67]

A striking feature of this teaching is that of the nerves or veins going out from the heart, together with the mystical association of this interior anatomy with the states of dream sleep and dreamless sleep. This lore of the Being of being belongs without question to a psychosomatic doctrine of yoga—already well developed here, c. 700–600 B.C., although we have heard nothing of it in the Vedas. The doctrine of *ātman,* the spiritual "Self," also is fully formed in this text, and associated, furthermore, not with the Brahminical lore of the sacrifice, but with a doctrine of introverted dream and dreamless states.

Let me call attention, further, to the number 72,000. The Mesopotamian year, we have seen, was composed of 72 five-day weeks. Moreover, in Plutarch's account of the killing of Osiris, the dead-and-resurrected god who is identical with the Self * was clapped into his coffin (sent, that is to say, into the state of deep sleep) by 72 associates of his brother Seth. [68] The number is of a Mesopotamian context in which macro- and microcosmic equivalences are assumed. It is a mythic magnitude, related to a science rather of a symbolic than of a strictly factual order.

The ideas, then, of 1. ātman, 2. deep sleep, dream, and the waking state, 3. yoga, and 4. a psychosomatic system symbolically related to 5. a cosmic system derived, apparently, from Bronze Age Mesopotamia, come suddenly to view in the first Upanishad—out of a clear sky. They are to remain as basic thoughts of the entire subsequent development of Oriental philosophy and religion. And they are introduced to the world history of thought, let us note, neither by a Brahmin nor by a monk, but by a king—non-Aryan, possibly—to whom the proud Gargya had gone as a missionary, and, like many of the best missionaries, learned what he should have taught, namely, that he was not in control, after all, of the entire field of truth.

A second, rather charming Brahmin, who is a favorite of all teachers of the wisdom of the Orient, received a like surprise when

* Cf. supra, pp. 90–91.

he sent his son to a certain royal house to attend an assembly of sages. The learned youth, Shvetaketu, arrived; and the king, Pravahana Jaibali, said to him:

"Young man, has your father instructed you?"

"Yes sir; he has."

"Do you know where creatures go when they pass away?"

"No sir."

"Do you know how they come back?"

"No sir."

"Do you know where the two ways separate: one going to the gods, the other to the fathers?"

"No sir."

"Do you know why the yonder world never is filled?"

"No sir, I do not."

"Do you know how it is that in the fifth libation water comes to be called Man?"

"No sir; no indeed."

"Then, pray, why did you tell me that you were instructed? How could anyone ignorant of such matters call himself instructed?"

Distressed, the young man returned to his father.

"Venerable sir, you let me think you had instructed me, when you had not. That fellow of the princely class put to me five questions, of which I could not answer one."

The father, told the questions, said to him: "But I do not know a single answer either. Had I known, I should have taught you."

And he went, therefore, to the palace of the king.

The king said to his guest: "Venerable Gautama, you may choose for yourself any boon you wish of human wealth."

But he answered: "Human wealth be yours, O King! I have come to ask, rather, of those questions you put to my son."

And the king thereupon became troubled.

"Wait," said he. "This knowledge has never before been given to a Brahmin. That is why, in all the world, up to now, sovereignty has remained with the Kshatriya caste alone."

Nevertheless, the king Jaibali proceeded to instruct; and the doctrine that he taught is one of those most central to Oriental mythic thought. It is termed here the doctrine of flame and smoke, or the parting of the two spiritual ways: on the one hand, the road of flame, which leads to the sun and therewith the gods, there to abide; but on the other hand, the road of smoke, to the moon, the fathers, and reincarnation.

"Those who know this lore," said the king, "and those, who, dwelling in the forest, meditate with faith and austerity, pass into the flame of the cremation fire, and from the flame into the day; from the day into the fortnight of the waxing moon; from that into the six months of the sun trending north; thence, into the year and from the year into the sun; from the sun into the moon; and from the moon into the lightning, where there is a non-human (*a-manāva*) Person (*puruṣa*), who leads them beyond, to Brahma. This is the way to the gods.

"But those who in the village reverence sacrifice, merit, and almsgiving, pass into the smoke of the sacrificial fire and from the smoke into the night; from the night, into the latter fortnight of the month; from that into the six months of the sun trending south—which do not culminate the year; from those months, into the world of the fathers; from the world of the fathers, into space; from space into the moon. That is King Soma. That is the food of the gods. That is what the gods eat.

"And so remaining in that place just as long as the merit of their good works lasts, they return along the course by which they came. They move into space, and from space, into wind. Having been wind, they become smoke, and after being smoke, they become mist. After mist, they become cloud. After being cloud, they fall as rain, and are born as rice or barley, herbs, trees, sesame or beans, from which condition it is difficult indeed to emerge. For only if someone or other eats him as food and then emits him as semen, can anyone so caught develop further.

"For those who have been of pleasant conduct here on earth the prospect then is, however, that they will enter a pleasant womb, either of a Brahmin, Kshatriya, or Vaishya. But for those who are of stinking conduct here the prospect is, indeed, that they will enter a stinking womb, either of a dog, a pig, or an outcaste.

"But then, finally, on neither of these ways go those small, continually returning creatures, of whom it is said: 'Be born and die.' Theirs is a third state. And that is why the yonder world never is filled. That is why one should be ever on one's guard. . . .

"He who knows this never is stained with evil. . . . He

becomes pure, clean, the possessor of a pure world, he who knows this—yea, he who knows this!" [69]

And there we have it; the whole thing: caste, karma, the wheel of rebirth and escape from it; an association of the moon with the cycle of death and birth, and of the solar door with release; disciplines of secular piety (sacrificial rites, almsgiving, etc.) as the means to a favorable birth, as well as to a pleasant heavenly sojourn among the fathers, and, on the other hand, disciplines of austerity practiced in the forest, as the means to release. Add to this the teaching of yoga, atman, deep sleep, dream, and waking, given by the other king, and there is little more of basic Hinduism to seek.[70]

As Professor Paul Deussen remarked in his classic discussion of this topic: "When it is considered that in these passages on the knowledge of brahman as atman, of atman as the all-ensouling principle, and of the destiny of the soul beyond death, the most important points of the doctrine of the Upanishads are announced, and that in these not only are the kings portrayed as the knowers, but the Brahmins specifically shown to have been the non-knowers or wronger-knowers (the texts, moreover, being communicated by the Vedic schoolmen, who were Brahmins themselves), then one can only draw the conclusion—if not with absolute surety, at least with considerable likelihood—that the doctrine of atman, which is actually opposed to the whole spirit of Vedic ritual lore, even though it may at first have been designed by Brahmins, nevertheless was taken up and cultivated not in the circles of Brahmins, but of Kshatriyas, and only later adapted by the Brahmins." [71]

Deussen wrote in the late nineteenth century, before anything was known of the Indus Civilization; yet he recognized already—as no Indians seem ever to have seen—that between the Vedic and Upanishadic views the difference is so great that the latter could not possibly have been developed out of the former. One was outward-turned and liturgical, the other inward and psychological. One was Aryan; the other, not.

Indeed, as one further text will show, the patriarchal Aryan gods were now to be exposed as mere punies in wisdom in contrast even to the Goddess. The old neolithic Bronze Age Goddess! She appears for the first time in any Indo-Aryan document in the following Upanishad of c. 600 B.C.

THE LEGEND OF THE GODDESS AND THE
VEDIC-ARYAN GODS

Brahman had won a victory for the gods: brahman, the holy power. They, however, exulting in that victory of brahman, imagined it to have been their own, thinking: "Ours, indeed, is this victory! Ours the glory!" Brahman, therefore, understood their pride and appeared before them; but they did not know what brahman was. "What sort of specter (*yakṣa*) can this thing be?" they asked. And they said to Agni: "O thou Almost Omniscient One, find out what this thing is." "Yes," said he, and he ran to it. Brahman asked: "Who are you?" "I am the famous Agni, the Almost Omniscient One," he said. Brahman asked: "What power in you warrants such fame?" And the god replied: "I can burn things up, whatever there is on earth." Brahman put a straw down before him. "Burn that!" Agni came at it with all his force. He was unable to burn it. He returned to the gods. "I have not been able to learn," said he, "what that specter is."

The gods then said to Vayu: "O thou Wind, find out what this specter is." "Yes," said he, and he ran to it. Brahman asked: "Who are you?" "I am the famous Vayu, the One Who Moves Through the Sky," he said. Brahman asked: "What power in you warrants such fame?" and the god replied: "I can carry things away, whatever there is on earth." Brahman put a straw down before him. "Carry that away!" said brahman. Vayu came at it. With all his force he was unable to carry it away. He returned to the gods. "I have not been able to learn," said he, "what that specter is."

Then the gods said to Indra: "O thou Worshipful One, find out what that specter is." "Yes," he answered; and he ran toward it, but it vanished before him. In that very place he came upon a woman of great beauty, Uma Haimavati, the Daughter of the Snowy Mountain. He asked her: "What was that specter?" She answered: "Brahman. Through the victory of that brahman you attained the glory in which you take such pride." From this, Indra learned of brahman.[72]

"The Goddess was no initiate in Vedic wisdom," wrote Heinrich Zimmer in comment on this allegorical legend;

nevertheless she—not the Vedic gods—knew brahman. And she taught them to know that divine essence, so that these three then became the greatest of the gods, "because they were the first to know brahman." [73] By this text we see that already at a comparatively early period (c. seventh century B.C.) it was the Goddess, and not the seemingly dominant masculine divinities of the Vedic pantheon, who was the real knower of that hidden, central, holy power of the universe by which all victories are won in the unending drama of the world-process. For she herself was that selfsame power. She is brahman, the life-force of the universe that secretly dwells within all things.

In this episode in the Kena Upanisad, where the mother goddess appears for the first time in the orthodox religious and philosophical tradition of India, she—womanhood incarnate—becomes the guru of the male gods. She is represented as their mystagogue, their initiator into the most profound and elementary secret of the universe, which is, in fact, her own essence. [74]

When the term *brahman*, "holy power," from the root *brh*, "to grow, to increase, to roar," [75] appears in Vedic hymns, it is only with reference to the power inherent in the words and meter of the prayer; its meaning is specifically "this stanza, verse, or line"; as, for example, "By this stanza (*anena brahmaṇā*) I make you free from disease." [76] The god Brihaspati, priest of the gods, is therefore "the lord (*pati*) of the roaring power (*brh*)," the power of the magical stanzas; and the Brahmins are his counterpart among men: great gods because they have the knowledge and control that apply that power. The employment of the term *brahman*, however, with reference to a metaphysically conceived ground of all being, antecedent to and independent of the Brahminical utilization of that power, we do not encounter until the period of the Brahmanas, and even then only rarely and in the later, so-called "Forest Books."

There can be no doubt about it: an alien constellation has made itself known to the Brahmins and is in the process of being assimilated. Nor can it be doubted that the background of this influence stands revealed in the cities of the Indus Valley. In contrast to the liturgical, outward-directed, imitative magic of the Brahmins, first imploring and then conjuring the powers of heaven, earth, and the air between, through the world-controlling focal center of the fire altar, this other was an essentially inward-turned, psychological system of thought, magic, and experience, in which much of what today is known of the unconscious was anticipated and even to a certain extent, along a certain line, surpassed.

vi. The Immanent Transcendent Divinity

We have already compared two components of the Indian mythic complex: that of the early Indus Valley, in which the bull was the foremost symbolic beast and the figures of both Shiva and the Great Goddess were anticipated; and the system of the Vedas, where the place of honor went to the lion—which eats up the bull, as the warrior drinks soma and the sun consumes the light of the moon. We have now to regard a third component: yoga, which, in terms of our present subject, may be defined as a technique for inducing mythic identification.

The appearance of figures in a classic yoga posture on the Indus Valley seals suggests a connection of the system with the early Bronze Age mythology of the ritual regicide, where the king was identified with the dying and resurrected moon; and the association of yogic thought in later centuries with the idea of the ever-returning cycle, as well as with Shiva and the Goddess, tends to enforce this indication. Numerous signs, in fact, suggest a particularly close connection with the world feeling and symbolic system of the priestly order of the great Egyptian Ptah; so that it might be arguable that the Indian development of yoga was colonial to Memphis. However, in view of the fact that every line of yogic literature betrays a depth of psychological insight surpassing anything of which we have direct knowledge from Egypt, and of the further fact that there is no archaic evidence anywhere westward of the Indus of such a yogic posture as that of the little figures on those seals, it would seem more sensible to assume—tentatively, at least—that yoga must have been indigenous to India, and to treat it, consequently, as a third and separate force.

Hypothetically, yoga might be supposed to have been developed

from local shamanistic techniques for inducing trance and possession. For, as Professor Mircea Eliade has shown, the production
of "inner heat" (*tapas*) by retention of breath is a widely disseminated technique among primitive peoples, which is commonly
associated with the mastery of fire, "a feat of fakirdom that must,"
as he declares, "be regarded as the most archaic and most generally disseminated element of the magical tradition. . . ." Aboriginal India, then, as he concludes, "may have known a number
of immemorial traditions regarding the means for obtaining magical
heat, ecstasy, or divine possession." [77]

The Indus Valley seals, in that case, would mark an assimilation
of the yogic tradition to the mythic order of the early Bronze Age,
when the latter reached the Indus Valley c. 2500 B.C. And the passages previously cited from the Upanishads would mark a similar
affiliation of its technique to the iconography of the Vedic Aryans.
In association with the Indus system, the ultimate term of identification would have been the ever-dying lunar god, the *object* of
destiny, the sacrifice (the sacrificed King Soma), whereas in the
Aryan system, on the contrary, the ultimate term of identification
was the *subject* of destiny, the fiery power by which the sacrifice is
consumed. Identified with the former, the yogi or devotee dies and
returns by the "way of smoke," continuing in the round; whereas
the one identified with the latter moves to the realm of eternity by
the way of a consummate mythic identification either with an all-
consuming sun-, lightning-, or fire-god, or with some such abstrac-
tion as, for example, brahman, the pure subject (*ātman*), or (as in
Buddhism) the void.

A number of points of support for an immediate organic graft of
the Vedic, outturned hemisphere of myth and the inward non-
Vedic of yoga were supplied by numerous deities and principles of
the Vedic system itself, and the Brahmins (who at this juncture
proved themselves to be the most creatively alert interpreters of
myth the world had ever known) were quick to perceive the possibility.

The Vedic god Savitri, for example, celebrated in the first hymn
cited on page 174, who suggests in many ways the sun, is actually

a power beyond the sun. As Professor Oldenberg has stated of this god and the Vedic system of which he is to this day a leading symbol:

"Since in itself the sun epitomizes the chief moving force in the universe, and so, controls every other movement, Savitri naturally stands to it in a particularly close relationship, and there is a tendency to transfer to him the attributes of a solar deity. However, to attempt therefore to interpret the original and even the Rig-Vedic Savitri as a sun-god is to misunderstand the structure of this entire complex of ideas. The essential point in the conception of Savitri is not the idea of the sun; nor is it the idea of the sun serving a certain function in as much as it stimulates life and movement. On the contrary, the main thing here is the abstract thought of this stimulation itself. This supplies the frame that includes all of the ideas associated with this god." [78]

The name Savitri, as we have seen, is from the root *sū*, "to excite, incite, stimulate, and impel," and means, according to an ancient commentator, "the stimulator of everything." [79] We read in a verse addressed to him:

> All immortal things rest upon him,
> As on the axle-end of a chariot.[80]

And again:

> In the lap, forever, of Savitri,
> The God, the settlers and all peoples rest.[81]

Savitri bestows length of life on man, immortality on the gods; the waters and winds obey his ordinance; no being, not even the greatest god, can resist his will, and he is the lord both of what moves and of what stands. With bonds he has fixed the earth: he made the sky firm in rafterless space. And he observes fixed laws.[82]

A second Vedic figure who supplied a point of juncture with the other system was the fierce god Rudra, to whom but three Vedic hymns are assigned, and whose name, from the root *rud*, "to cry out," seems to mean "Howler." He became identified in later cult with the meditating Lord of Beasts (Figure 18), discussed above as a proto-Shiva. The epithet Shiva, "Auspicious

One," is itself a Sanskrit word and so cannot have been the name
of that god in pre-Vedic times. It is addressed in the Vedas, however, to the god Rudra, who, though terrible and destructive, is
beneficent as well. He is called a bull and is the father of a great
golden troop of young male gods, the Maruts, whose mother was a
cow. These hold the lightning in their hands, are decked richly
with ornaments, and are as broad as the sky through which their
chariots thunder, spilling rain.

> O Rudra, Wielder of the Bolt, the best of what
> Is born, in glory, mightiest of the mighty:
> Transport us in all safety to the farther shore,
> Beyond distress, warding off all threats of mischief.[83]

The yonder shore beyond ill, the mighty bolt, the howling host, the
bull and cow, the fierce and yet protective character, and the universal rule of the god Rudra, ever young: these are all attributes of
the Shiva of later days. However, the emphatically phallic character
of the later Hindu god cannot have been derived by any argument
from the Vedas; nor his character as the lord of yoga.

Likewise, the minor Vedic deity Vishnu, to whom but half a
dozen hymns are addressed, is in later cult developed into one of
the richest, most sophisticated deities of the Hindu pantheon. In
the Veda, as a conqueror of demons, he is allied with Indra and
celebrated particularly for his three strides, two of which are visible
to men, whereas the last is beyond the flight of birds. With these he
measured (i.e., brought into being) the earth, the air, and heaven.
Moreover, his name, from the root *vis,* "to be active," is allied in
sense to that of Savitri. And so, in him, once again, we may see by
what readings in depth, beyond their poetically imaged mythic
forms, the Vedic gods became eligible to be viewed as manifestations of the all-inhabiting brahman of the native faith.

> To Vishnu let my inspiring hymn sing forth,
> To that widely pacing, mountain dwelling bull,
> Who alone, with but three paces, measured out
> This immense, far extended gathering place.
>
> O would that I might go to that dear domain of his,
> Where those devoted to the gods are dwelling in joy:

> For that place, supremely akin to the wide-strider,
> Is a wellspring of ambrosia: Vishnu's highest step.[84]

And, finally, the god Soma, the sacrifice, was another Vedic figure well fitted for adaptation to the idea of an all-suffusing self. Cut up, yet living in all things, he is consumed by Agni in the fire of the altar. Analogously, when food is eaten the fire of the stomach digests (i.e., "cooks") it. The fire in the stomach is Agni. The food, therefore, is Soma. And when the individual dies, he, in turn, becomes Soma; for Agni consumes him on the funeral pyre, and in the maggots. So that this entire world is a never-ending Soma sacrifice: immortality poured forever into the fire of time.

"All things, O priests," said the Buddha in his famous Fire Sermon, "are on fire. . . . And with what are they on fire? With the fire of passion, say I, the fire of hatred, infatuation, birth, old age, death, sorrow, lamentation, misery, grief, and despair. . . . And perceiving this, O priests, the learned and noble disciple conceives an aversion. . . ." [85]

But that was not the mood of the earlier Vedic-Upanishadic view of the dancing flames. There we read, rather:

> Oh, wonderful! Oh, wonderful! Oh, wonderful!
> I am food! I am food! I am food!
> I am a food-eater! I am a food-eater! I am a food-eater!
> I am a fame-maker! I am a fame-maker! I am a fame-maker!
> I am the first-born of the world-order [rta],
> Antecedent to the gods, in the navel of immortality!
> Who gives me away, he indeed had aided me!
> I, who am food, eat the eater of food!
> I have overcome the whole world!
>
> He who knows this, has a brilliantly shining light.
> Such is the mystic upanishad.[86]

And so we are brought to the great theme and problem of the fourth component of the Indian mythic view of life: the rejection with loathing by the forest sages of the period of the Buddha of all that had formerly been affirmed, even the wonder of that immanent transcendent divinity of being which had been the glory of the late Vedic view.

VII. The Great Reversal

"OM. The dawn is the head of the sacrificial horse; the sun, its eye; the wind, its breath; cosmic fire, its open mouth. The year is the body of the sacrificial horse; heaven, its back; the interspace, its belly; the earth, the under part of its belly; the quarters, its flanks; the intermediate quarters, its ribs; the seasons, its limbs; the months and half-months, its joints; days and nights, the feet; stars, the bones; clouds, the flesh. Sand, moreover, is the food in its stomach; rivers, the entrails. Mountains are its liver and lungs; herbs and trees, its hair. The rising sun is its fore-part; the setting sun, its hind part. Its yawn is lightning; the shivering of its body, thunder; its urination is rain; and its voice, the creative Word. . . ." [87]

Identified as the horse, the universe, like the horse, is now to be sacrificed by the sage in his mind and heart. This we shall term *the interiorization of the sacrifice*. It is a fundamental yogic act. And as the Horse Sacrifice both fructified the king's realm and established him as a World Monarch, so this sacrifice, interiorized, fructifies the Self, brings the lotus of the Self to flower, and establishes the sage on its corolla as king.

"O priests," declared the Buddha in his Fire Sermon,

the learned and noble disciple conceives an aversion for the eye, conceives an aversion for forms, conceives an aversion for eye-consciousness, conceives an aversion for the impressions received by the eye; and whatever sensation, pleasant, unpleasant, or indifferent, originates in dependence on impressions received by the eye, for that also he conceives an aversion. He conceives an aversion for the ear, conceives an aversion for sounds, . . . conceives an aversion for the nose, conceives an aversion for odors, . . . conceives an aversion for the tongue, conceives an aversion for tastes, . . . conceives an aversion for the body, conceives an aversion for things tangible, . . . conceives an aversion for the mind, conceives an aversion for ideas, conceives an aversion for mind-consciousness, conceives an aversion for the impressions received by the mind; and whatever sensation, pleasant, unpleasant or indifferent, originates in dependence on impressions received by the mind, for this also he conceives an aversion. And in conceiving this aversion, he becomes divested of passion, and by the absence of passion he becomes free, and when he is free he becomes aware that he is free; and he knows that rebirth is exhausted, that he has lived the holy life, that he has done what it behooved him to do, and that he is no more for this world.[88]

The way is consummated therewith to the gaining of absolute security through introversion; however, it is by no means certain that the earliest aim of yoga was to bear the sage along this road to release from the vortex of rebirth. Yoga is not intrinsically, necessarily, or even usually, associated with negation. It is by no means certain, therefore, that because the earliest scriptures known to us in which yoga is analyzed describe it as a discipline of disengagement, the figures on the Indus Valley seals were in their time associated with any such ideal. In fact, in the popular mind to this day yoga is largely associated rather with the acquisition of "powers" (*siddhi*) than with the forcing of an exit from the world arena; and these powers by which the concrete obstacles of the world are magically overcome are eight, as follows: 1. the power to become small or invisible; 2. the power to swell to immense size and so to reach even the most distant object—for example, the moon with the tip of one's finger; 3. the power to become light, and so, to walk on air, to walk on water; 4. the power to become as heavy as the world; 5. the power of obtaining everything at will, including knowledge of others' thoughts and of the past and future; 6. the power of infinite enjoyment; 7. the power of mastering all things, including death; and 8. the power of bewitching, fascinating, and subduing by magical means.*

In fact, even a little yoga practiced by a man who knows the proper means can bring about these miraculous effects. For example, as we read in the last chapters of the classic Indian work of politics, Kautilya's Arthashastra, "The Textbook of the Art of Gaining Ends":

"Having fasted for three nights, one should obtain, on the day of the constellation known as Pushya, the skull of a man who has

---

* The Sanskrit terms are: 1. *aṇimā*, 2. *mahimā*, 3. *laghimā*, 4. *garimā*, 5. *prāpti*, 6. *prakāmya*, 7. *īsitva*, and 8. *vasitva*.

been murdered with a weapon or put upon the gallows. And having
filled that skull with soil and barley seed, one should irrigate these
with the milk of goats and sheep; then, putting on a garland made
from the shoots of that barley crop, one can walk invisible to
others." [89]

Or again:

"Having fasted four nights, one should, on the fourteenth day
of the dark fortnight of the moon, obtain the figure of a bull
fashioned from a human bone, and worship it with the following
mantra:

" 'With the god of fire, I take refuge, and with all the goddesses
of the ten quarters: * may all obstructions vanish, and may all
things come under my power! Oblation!'

"A cart drawn by two bullocks then will come before the worshiper, who, mounting it, can drive in the sky and everywhere about
the sun and the other celestial orbs." [90]

The chronicles are full of accounts of magic of this kind, practiced by yogis throughout the history of India. Moreover, the power
to which a really great dedication to yoga may lead—say, after
some sixty thousand years—we have already seen.† However, in
the light of the wisdom of those who are truly wise—as the following anecdote will prove—all power, natural or supernatural,
that adds to one's enjoyment of the world is but straw added to the
fire that one should be striving with all zeal to quench.

The tale I would tell is of a great sage, Saubhari by name, who,
like all of the great sages of India, was learned in the Vedas and
devoted only to the highest virtue. He had spent years, therefore,
immersed in a certain piece of water, far from the world of man.
Nor was it any man, king, woman, or fiend who lured him back
to the world of delusion, but the presence only of a certain fish, of
considerable size, who inhabited the water of the saint's element.

With his numerous progeny of children and grandchildren flocking around him in all directions, this fish lived among them very
happily, playing with them night and day. And Saubhari, the sage,

* Four points of the compass, four points between, the zenith above, and
the nadir below.
† Supra, p. 186.

being disturbed in his concentration by their splashing, noted the patriarchal felicity of the monarch of the lake and allowed himself to think: "How enviable, this creature, who, though born in such a modest state, is nevertheless sporting cheerfully among his off-spring and their young! He wakens in my mind the wish to partake likewise of such pleasure, making merry thus among my children." And having so resolved, Saubhari left the water and went to the palace of a certain mighty King Mandhatri, to ask for one of his daughters.

The king, told of the saint's arrival, rose from his throne and offered the usual hospitality, treating him with profound respect; and Saubhari then said to the king: "I have determined, O King, to marry. Do you, therefore, give me one of your daughters. It is not the practice of the princes of your race to refuse the wishes of those who come to them for aid, and so I know that you will not disappoint me. Other kings dwell upon the earth, to whom daugh-ters have been born, but your family is above all renowned for its practice of liberality. You have fifty daughters. Give to me but one."

And the king, regarding the person of the sage, emaciated by austerity and old age, felt disposed to refuse consent; but dreading to incur the anger and imprecation of the holy man, he was much perplexed, and, declining his head, remained lost a while in thought.

Whereupon the sage, observing that hesitation, said: "On what, O Raja, do you meditate? What have I asked that cannot be readily accorded? If I am pleased by the daughter whom you now must give to me, furthermore, there will be nothing in the world for which you may wish that you will not gain."

But the king, greatly afraid of his displeasure, replied, "Grave Sir, it is the usage of our house to wed our daughters only to such as they themselves choose from suitors of fitting rank; and since your request has not yet been made known to my children, I can-not say whether it will be as welcome to them as it is to me. That is the reason for my thought; I do not know what to do."

The sage understood. "This," he thought, "is merely a device of the king to evade me. He sees that I am old, having no charms for women and not likely to be chosen by any of his daughters. Well, so be it! I shall be a match for him." And he said: "Since that, O mighty prince, is the custom of your house, command that I be led into the harem. Should any of your daughters be willing to take me as her bridegroom, I shall have her for my bride; and if none be willing, then let the blame attach to the years that I have numbered, and to them alone."

Mandhatri, greatly fearing him, was thus obliged to command the eunuch to lead him to the inner chambers, where the sage, as he entered, put on a form of such beauty that he far exceeded anything mortal, or indeed even the charms of the heavenly beings. And the eunuch said, "Your father sends to you this pious sage, young ladies, who has come to him for a bride. And the king has promised him that he will not refuse to him any one of you who shall choose him for her husband." The girls, beholding him and hearing this announcement, were inspired immediately with desire and like a troop of female elephants disputing the favors of the master of the herd, cried out, pushing at each other: "Away, sister, away! He is my choice. He is mine. He is not for you. He has been created by Brahma for me, and I for him. I saw him first. You cannot come between us." So that a violent feud arose and as the blameless sage was thus fought for by the many screaming princesses, the eunuch returned to the king and with downcast eyes reported the quarrel. The king was amazed. "What!" he exclaimed. "Can it be possible? And what am I to do now? What was it that I promised?" And in keeping with his promise, he had now to marry to the old visitor all fifty.

And so, having wedded, according to the law, all fifty of the king's daughters, the sage went off with them to his forest, where he caused the master craftsman of the gods, Vishvakarman himself, to build for him fifty palaces, one for each of his wives, providing each luxuriously with couches, elegant seats, and other furniture, gardens, pleasant groves, and reservoirs of water, where the wild duck and other water fowl should play among the lotuses; and finally, in each there was an inexhaustible larder and treasury, so that the princesses could entertain their guests and waiting maids with choice drinks and viands of all kinds.

Then, after a time, the king Mandhatri, yearning for his daughters and concerned to know how they were faring, set off on a visit to the hermitage of Saubhari. He saw before him, however, when he arrived, a galaxy of crystal palaces, shining in a row as brilliantly as fifty suns, amid lovely gardens and reservoirs of pellucid water. Entering one, he found and joyfully embraced one of his daughters. "Dear child," he said, with affectionate tears trembling in his eyes, "tell me how it is? Are you happy? Does the great sage treat you kindly? Or do you brood with regret on your early home?"

She answered: "Father, you see yourself in what a beautiful palace I am living, surrounded by lovely gardens and lakes where the lotus blooms and the wild geese call. I have the most delicious food, the rarest unguents, costly ornaments and beautiful clothes, soft beds, and every enjoyment that affluence can afford. Why then should I call to memory the palace of my birth? To your favor I owe all that I now possess. I have only one anxiety, however, which is this: that since my husband is never absent from my palace but is solely attached to me and ever at my side, it must be that he never goes near my sisters. I am concerned to think that they must feel mortified by his neglect. That is the only thing to give me cause for worry."

The king proceeded, one by one, to his other daughters, embracing each in turn, and sitting down, put the same question—to which all gave the same reply. And the king, with his heart overflowing with wonder and delight, then repaired to the wise Saubhari, whom he found alone. He bowed before the sage, and gratefully addressed him.

"O holy sage, I have beheld this marvelous evidence of your mighty power: the like miraculous faculties I have never known any other to possess. What a great reward for your devout austerities!"

The king, greeted respectfully by the sage, remained with him for some time, partaking abundantly of the pleasures of the marvelous resort, and then returned, well pleased, to his capital. The daughters bore, in time, thrice fifty sons, and day by day Saubhari's affection for his children grew, so that his heart was wholly occupied with the sentiment of self (*mamatā:* "mineness"). "These my sons," he loved to think, "charm me with their infant prattle. They will learn to walk. They will grow to youth and manhood. I shall see them married and they will have children. And then I shall see the children of those children."

He perceived, however, that every day his anticipations outstripped the course of time; so that at last, he thought, "What a fool! There is no end to my desires. Even though for ten thousand years or a hundred thousand years, all that I wish should come to pass, there would still be new wishes springing to my mind. For I now have seen my infants walk, beheld their youth, manhood, marriages, and progeny, yet expectations still arise and my soul yearns to behold the progeny of their progeny. As soon as I see those a new wish will arise, and when that is accomplished how am I to prevent the birth of still further desires? I have at last discovered that there is no end of hope until it terminates in death, and that the mind perpetually engrossed in expectation cannot be attached to the supreme spirit. My devotions, when I was immersed in water, were interrupted by attachment—to my friend the fish. The result of that connection was my marriage, and the result of my married life is insatiable desire. . . . Separation from the world is the only path of the sage to final liberation; from commerce with the world there can arise only innumerable errors. I now, therefore, shall exert myself for the rescue of my soul."

And having thus communed with himself, Saubhari abandoned his children, his home, and all his splendor and, accompanied by his wives, entered the forest, where he daily practiced the observances prescribed for those authorities having families, until he had cleansed away all attachments. Then, his intellect having attained maturity, he concentrated in his spirit the holy fires and became a religious mendicant—after which, consigning all his acts to the supreme, he won to the condition of Solidity (*acyuta:* "not dripping, not leaking, not perishable"), which knows no change and is not subject to the vicissitudes of birth, transmigration, and death.[91]

The moral is obviously that for your true Indian the world is not enough—even at its best, even beyond its best. His paramount aim, therefore, is beyond this world. And yet the creatures and doings of

the world have for him certain fascinating allures, which take hold
of his faculties like snares. The forest, therefore, is the first resort
of his yearning heart. But even the forest teaches delight. Hence,
the doors of the senses themselves must be closed. Within, however, even the breathing teaches delight—and further within?

Let us seek and follow the yogi on his road of flame.

VIII. The Road of Smoke

First, to understand from what sea of pain the Indian sage desires
release, let us consider in some detail one of the several Indian
versions of the archaic, mathematically structured myth of the ever-
returning cycle. Let us choose, because of its clarity, the world
cycle of the Jains, who, though today a sect small in number, were
in the past both numerous and of great influence. Their most celebrated teacher, Mahavira, who died c. 485 B.C., was a contemporary and formidable rival of the Buddha. Both were natives of
that lower Ganges country below Benares that we have called the
classic Holy Land of the forest sages. Both were of Kshatriya, not
Brahmin, descent and, after marriage, left the world to become
the wandering saviors of ascetic companies of disciples. And both
taught doctrines of release (*mokṣa*) from desire (*kāma*) and death
(*māra*), by way of a gradually progressed system of vows. However, whereas the Buddha's was in every sense a Middle Way, that
of the Mahavira could not have been more extreme. It bore the
traits in every aspect of an archaic, dualistic notion of absolutely
opposed matter and spirit, extreme loathing toward the mixture
of the two principles in the organism of the universe, an unrelent-
ing will to extricate one's own immortal spirit from the vortex, and
yet an extraordinary gentleness toward all things whatsoever, since
all (sticks, stones, air, water, and all) were living spirits trapped
by their own misdirected will in the profitless, cruel round of rebirth in the ever-revolving vortex of this world of pain.

The Buddha preached a new doctrine; Mahavira, however,
taught one that in his time was already old. His parents before him
had been Jains, followers of the teachings of an earlier savior, the
Lord Parshva, whose symbolic animal had been the serpent—because, at the moment of his achievement of perfection, standing

absolutely naked ("sky clad": *digambara*) in the upright posture known as "dismissing the body" (*kāyotsarga*), having pulled out with his own hands every bit of his hair and torn out by the root every impulse to exist, he was attacked by a demon, but protected on each side by an immense pair of cosmic serpents.

The demon, whose name was Meghamalin ("Cloud-enveloped"), had sent tigers, elephants, and scorpions against the inwardly absorbed saint, which, however, slunk away ashamed when they entered the field of his immobile presence. Then a dense and terrible darknes. was conjured up. A cyclone arose. Trees, shattering, hurtled through the air. Peaks fell. The earth, with a roar, opened and rain descended, becoming a torrent. Yet the figure of the saint remained unmoved. The monster, wrathful, became hideous: face black, mouth vomiting fire. With a garland of skulls, he resembled that god of death, Mara, who assailed the Buddha in a like situation. But when he came rushing, shining in the night, shouting "Kill! Kill!" the Lord Parshva remained, as ever, absolutely unmoved.

Then it was that the serpent king beneath the earth, whose heads with many hoods support the plane of the earth, emerged from beneath this earth, together with his queen, the goddess Shri Lakshmi, who, like himself, was now in serpent form. The two snakes made obeisance before the lord, who remained unaware of the arrival, and, stationing themselves at either hand, spread their hoods above him. Whereupon the demon, terrified by their magnitude, turned in his chariot and fled, when the two, once again bowing to the lord, returned to their abode.

The scene suggests the Indus seal with the two serpents (Figure 19), and there may, in fact, be a connection. For the Lord Parshva, whose dates have been estimated to have been c. 872–772 B.C.,[92] was not the first world savior of the Jains, but—according to Jain tradition—the twenty-third. And if there were really twenty-two before him, or even only a quarter of that sum, the line could easily have stemmed from the period of those seals. However, the Jain style of mathematical reckoning does little to assure us of the accuracy of their calculations. For, according to to their legend, Arishtanemi, the savior before Parshva, anteceded him by 84,000 years, which lands him in the period of Neanderthal Man. Nami, number twenty-one, is placed c. 134,000 B.C., and Suvrata, number twenty, c. 1,234,000 B.C.—which is a good 800,-000 years before Pithecanthropus erectus. With saviors earlier still we pass beyond even geological time, and the fact becomes clear that, as in the case of the Mesopotamian kings and biblical patriarchs before the flood, the reckoning now is in mythical, not in earthly terms.

In the cosmic image of the Jains the order of time is depicted as a wheel of six descending (*avasarpinī*) and as many ascending (*utsarpinī*) spokes. During those descending—of which the long age of the twenty-four world saviors was the fourth, and our own age (following the death of Mahavira) constitutes the fifth—good gives place to bad; but on the other hand, during the subsequent ascending ages, bad gives place to good and the whole world returns inevitably to virtue.

At the beginning of the first descending period people attained a stature of 6 miles, had 256 ribs, and were born as twins, always boy and girl, who became man and wife and lived for three *palyas:* three "periods of countless years." Ten wish-fulfilling trees answered all desires, one abounding with delicious fruits, another with leaves that formed pots and pans, while the leaves of a third continually rendered sweet music. A fourth shone at night with a bright light, and a fifth with the radiance of many little lamps. The flowers of a sixth were not only glorious but filled the air with a lovely scent, and a seventh gave food both of great beauty and of many interesting tastes. An eighth produced jewelry. A ninth was a many-storied palace, and the bark of the tenth supplied clothes. The earth then was sweet as sugar; the waters were delicious wine. And when each couple in its time, gave birth to one pair of twins, the elders, after a period of seven times seven days, passed directly to the regions of the gods without ever having heard of religion.

This age, known as Very Beautiful, Very Beautiful (*suṣamā-suṣamā*), lasted 400,000,000,000,000 oceans of years * and gave place to that known as Very Beautiful (*suṣamā*), which—as the

* An "ocean of years" consists of 100,000,000 times 100,000,000 *palyas,* a *palya* being a period of countless years.

name suggests—was exactly half as fortunate as the former. The wish-fulfilling trees, the earth, and the waters were only half as bountiful as before. Men and women were only 4 miles tall, had only 128 ribs, lived for only two periods of countless years, and passed to the world of the gods when their twins were only 64 days old. This period lasted 300,000,000,000,000 oceans of years, declining gradually but inevitably to the stage called Sorrowfully Very Beautiful (*susamā-duḥsamā*), when joy became mixed with grief. The twins now were 2 miles tall, with 64 ribs, and lived for only one period of countless years. Furthermore, the wish-fulfilling trees had become so sparing in their yield that people laid claim to them severally as property, and so a need for government arose. A law giver was therefore appointed, Vimalavahana by name, and the last patriach of his long line, Nabhi, was the father of the first Jain Savior, Rishabhanatha. For there was need now not only for government but also for a guide to release from this already sorrowing round.[93]

Rishabhanatha, whose name means the "Lord (*nātha*) Bull (*ṛṣabha*)," was born in the capital, Ayodhya, of his venerable father, enjoyed as a young prince the pleasures of the court for 1,000,000 times 2,000,000 years, and when he became king, perceiving that the wish-fulfilling trees would presently be insufficient in their yield, he taught, during the 1,000,000 times 6,300,000 years of his reign, the 72 sciences, of which the first, we are told, is writing, arithmetic the most important, and the science of divination the last; also, 100 useful arts, 3 masculine occupations, and 64 feminine perfections. He had 100 sons, to each of whom he gave a kingdom, and then, turning to his final work, he renounced the world, gave himself to the practice of austerities for 1000 times 1,000,000 years, and, achieving in the end illumination beneath a banyan tree in the park known as Dirty Face (*sakaṭamukha*) near the town of Purimatala, he preached to 84 chief disciples throughout the remaining 99,000 times 1,000,000 years of his life, saw the growth of an order of 84,000 monks, 300,000 nuns and 859,000 lay disciples (305,000 male and 554,000 female), departed, finally, to the summit of Mount Octopod (*aṣṭapada*), where, after a full career of 8,400,000 times 1,000,000 years, his golden body was let drop by its monad, precisely three years, eight months and a half before the end of the Sorrowfully Very Beautiful period of the world and beginning the Very Beautifully Sorrowful (*duḥṣamā-suṣamā*).

For with the fourth age of the descending series, the unpleasant aspects of existence began to preponderate over the pleasant and this circumstance got worse with every passing million years. The age before had lasted 200,000,000,000,000 oceans of years; this would last only 100,000,000,000,000 oceans, minus 42,000 common years. And whereas people at the opening of the period were 1000 yards tall, had 32 ribs, and lived for 10,000,000,000 years, at the close (which is precisely dated, 522 B.C.), they were but 9½ feet tall and lived no more than a miserable century. The Jain religion, however, was during this time renewed repeatedly for their rescue by the long line of twenty-four World Saviors or "Passage Makers (*tīrthaṅkaras*) to the Yonder Shore," the last of whom passed away three years, eight months and a half before the commencement of the fifth descending age, which is our own, when the gate to release is gradually closing, the religion of the Jains will soon disappear, and there will come no more Tirthankaras to preach to a deteriorating humanity now below the level of capacity necessary for achievement.

This is the age known as Sorrowful (*duḥṣamā*). And though to certain foreigners and aborigines it may appear to be a period of auspicious change and opening horizons, to the wise (who have been devoting themselves to the reading of sacred texts rather than to the vain learning of the world, and who therefore know, not only what a wonderful thing life was millions of oceans of years ago, but also that even that blessed state, bound to the wheel of delusion, is surpassed infinitely in the unconditioned condition of nirvana) this world with all its tawdry glory of merely visible trees, mountains, oceans, stars, and galaxies of amazement, is a miserable vale of tears indeed. For, look now! The tallest men are but 10½ feet tall, and their life spans no more than 125 years. People have only 16 ribs, and they are selfish, unjust, violent, lustful, proud, and avaricious. The age is to endure for 21,000 years, and before its close the last Jain monk, who will have been named Dup-

pasahasuri, the last Jain nun, Phalgushri, the last Jain layman,
Nagila, and the last laywoman, Satyashri, will have died unil-
luminated, and then the last descending age, to be known as
Sorrowfully Sorrowful (*duhsamā-duhsamā*), will arrive.

The longest life then will be 20 years, 18 inches the greatest
stature, and a mere 8 the number of ribs. The days will be terribly hot, the nights freezing, disease will be rampant and chastity
non-existent. Tempests will sweep over the earth, and toward the
conclusion of the period these will increase. In the end all life,
human and animal, and all vegetable seeds, will be forced to seek
shelter in the Ganges, in caves, and in the sea.

The descending series of six ages will terminate, and the ascending (*utsarpinī*) begin, when the tempest and desolation will have
reached the point of the unendurable. Then for seven days it will
rain; seven different kinds of rain will fall; the soil will be refreshed and seeds will begin to grow. This improvement will commence during the dark fortnight of the moon in the month of
Shravana (July–August). Out of their caves the horrible dwarf-
like creatures of the arid earth will venture and very gradually there
will be perceptible a slight improvement in their morals, health,
stature, and beauty; until, in time, they will be living in a world
such as the one we know today. A savior named Padmanatha
("Lord Lotus") will be born to announce again the religion of the
Jains; the stature of mankind will approach again the superlative
and the beauty of man will surpass the splendor of the sun. At last,
the earth will sweeten and the waters turn to wine, the wish-
fulfilling trees will yield their bounty of delights to a blissful population of perfectly wedded twins; and the happiness of this community again will be doubled, and the wheel, through ten millions
of ten millions of one hundred millions of one hundred million
periods of countless years, will approach the point of beginning
the downward revolution, which again will lead to the extinction of the eternal religion and the gradually increasing tumult
of unwholesome merrymaking, warfare, and pestilential winds.

The earliest recorded mythology of such a cycle of world ages
we have found in ancient Mesopotamia, where, however, no
signs appear of any such systematic rationalization of world-

loathing as in this mythology of the Jains. Nor am I aware of any early Mesopotamian concept of the shape of the universe that quite matches that of the Jains—which is of a colossal human form, usually female, with the earth plane at the level of the waist; seven hells beneath, in the pelvic cavity, legs and feet, stratified as in Dante's vision; fourteen celestial stories above, in the chest cavity and shoulders, neck and head; while soaring above, in the shape of an umbrella of luminous white gold, 14,230,250 yojanas * [94] in circumference, 8 yojanas thick at the center and tapering to the tenuity of a gnat's wing at the edge, is a place of unalloyed perfection called "Slightly Tilted" (iṣat-prāgbhāra), to which the released soul ascends when the last least taint of a trace even of heavenly attachment has been burned away through the practice of yoga.

On the plane at the level of the waist, a number of circular continents, arranged like the rings of a target with oceans between, are thought to circumscribe an axial mountain, Mount Meru. The circular continent of the Rose Apple Tree is the innermost. It has two suns and as many moons and in its southernmost part is India. It is surrounded by the Salty Ocean, which has four suns and four moons. Next is the continent of the Purple Willow Tree, with twelve suns and moons, surrounded by the Black Ocean, with forty-two. The Circle of the Lotus, which is next, has seventy-two pairs of luminaries and is the ultimate continent inhabited by man. Beyond is the Ocean of the Lotus and thereafter, in expanding series, the Circle of the God Varuna and the Ocean of Varuna, the Circle of Milk and the Ocean of Milk, Circle of Clarified Butter and Ocean of Clarified Butter, Circle of Sugarcane and Ocean of Sugarcane, on through many more to, finally, the Land of the Joy of Being Oneself and, beyond, the Ocean of the Joy of Being Oneself, which has a diameter of one infinitude (rajju) and fills the breadth of the waist of the cosmic being.

Now this great being has no will, no joy, no power, indeed no being of its own; for it is merely a magnitude of matter (a-jīva) blown into shape, so to say, by the force and vitality of an in-

* One yojana is variously described as equivalent to about 2½, 4 or 5, 9, or 18 miles.

finite number of deluded monads (*jīvas*), swarming, like maggots, through every particle of its otherwise inert substance. Trapped and circulating through the vast limbs and organs, these put on and off the forms of the various orders that we know as life, seemingly born, seemingly passing away, yet actually merely transmigrating from one state to another in a piteous, helpless round. And these numerous, greatly differing orders of appearance are classified by the Jains minutely in what is really an amazing system of psychologically graded categories, a little tedious to review, perhaps, but of consequence for not only Jainism but also Buddhism, Hinduism, the whole Orient touched by the Buddhist law, Zoroastrianism—and even Dante. As an image of *la condition humaine*, furthermore, it is about as dismal and bizarre as anything the mad mind of man has ever conceived.

At the level of the waist of the great cosmic being, where the passage of time is marked by the ever-returning cycle of twelve stages already reviewed, the incarnations through which we all have passed many times and are still passing are as follows:

I. Earth Incarnations:
1. numerous varieties of dust particle
2. sand, pebbles, boulders, and rock
3. the various metals
4. the various precious stones
5. clays, sulphur, and the various salts (talc, alum, realgar, saltpeter, natron, orpiment, cinnabar, etc.)

Monads endure in these forms for periods of from less than a second to some 22,000 years and while remaining on this level may experience as many as 700,000 incarnations. Besides appearances in gross matter (*sthūla*) others occur in subtle matter (*sukṣma*); for example, in the scenery of the heavens and the apparitions of dream.

II. Water Incarnations:
1. seas, lakes, rivers, etc., and rains of various sort
2. dew and other exudations
3. hoarfrost

    4. snow, hail, and ice

    5. clouds and fog

Such may last from less than a second to 7000 years and for a single monad may number as many as 700,000, whether gross or subtle.

III. Plant Incarnations:

    1. plants propagating by gemmation (lichens, mosses, onions, and other bulbous roots, aloes, spurges, saffron, bananas, etc.): 1,400,000 incarnations may be experienced by a single monad in this sphere

    2. individual plants, produced from seed (trees, shrubs and lianas, grasses, grains, and aquatic plants): in these the monad can appear but 1,000,000 times

All incarnations of these three divisions of earth, water, and plant, are known as Immobiles. Another multitude, also in three divisions, are the Mobiles; namely:

IV. Fire Incarnations:

    1. flames

    2. embers

    3. lightning flashes

    4. thunderbolts

    5. meteors and bolides

Such never last longer than three days and are usually briefer than a second. A single monad may experience 700,000.

V. Wind Incarnations:

    1. breezes

    2. gales, squalls, storms, and tempests

    3. whirlwinds

    4. freezing blasts

    5. the inhalations and exhalations of living beings

Whether mobile or immobile, all of the beings so far named possess four life powers: a body, length of life, respirations, and the sense of touch. The following, in ascending scale, have additional life powers:

VI. Organisms: all of which have the power to make a sound (*vāc*):

1. Beings with two senses, touch and taste (worms, leeches, conches, cowries, barnacles, clams and other shellfish)

2. Beings with three senses, touch, taste, and smell (fleas and lice, meal worms, roaches, earwigs, crawling bugs, ants, spiders, etc.): these live no more than 49 days

3. Beings with four senses, touch, taste, smell, and sight (butterflies, bees and wasps, flies and mosquitoes, scorpions, crickets, grasshoppers, and other highly developed insects): these may live as long as six months; and finally:

4. Beings possessed of five senses, which are classified in two categories, each, however, subdivided:

   A. Animals

   i. Aquatic: fish, sharks, dolphins, porpoises, crocodiles, and tortoises

   ii. Terrestrial: mammals (some with hoofs, some claws); lizards and ichneumons, serpents

   iii. Aerial: feather-winged (parrots, swans, etc.); leather-winged (bats); having wings and shape of round boxes (these are never seen by human eye, but dwell on other continents); those never touching the earth but soaring and even sleeping aloft on wings ever extended (these are never seen either)

   B. Mankind:

   i. People of decent lineage (*āryan*): these are of many kinds; for example: handsome and ugly, sickly and well, wise and thoughtless, rich and poor; with few or many relatives, celebrated or unknown, powerful or of low degree; speaking this language or that; owning fields, houses, cattle, slaves, gold, or other goods; merchants, potters, weavers, bankers, scribes, tailors, warriors, priests and kings, great kings, and universal monarchs—the last, furthermore, being subdivided as to either Lunar Dynasty or Solar; and finally, a radical distinction is made between those inhabiting the so-called "realms of action," which are in the extreme south and north as well as center of the Continent of the Rose-Apple Tree, and those inhabiting the "realms of delight," in certain other parts of the earth: in the latter, men are giants, twice as tall as those that we know, but, since they pay no attention to the laws of virtue, are subject to innumerable incarnations

ii. Barbarians (*mlecchas*): these are the residue of mankind, and among them are fabulous races living on remote, unvisited isles, some having horns and tails, others hopping about on one leg, all with monstrous faces, some with immense ears, which, when they sleep, they fold across their eyes.[95]

Incarnations at the level of the waist do not constitute the whole story, however; for the hells and heavens also are alive with monads: those below, suffering the punishments, and those above, the rewards, of their lives on earth.

Below, in the seven hells, are figures terrible to behold, like immense birds deprived of feathers, sexless, and having bodies of a type known as "changeable" (*vaikriyika*); for they are without bones or tendons and very loosely put together. In the lowest hell they are 1000 yards tall; * [96] in the next, 500; the fifth, 250; in the fourth, 125; next, 62½; the second, 31¼; and in the first or uppermost hell, 46 feet, 10½ inches. Those of the lowest three hells are black, the next two, dark blue, and the upper two, the gray of smoke. All being subject to the four cardinal passions of pride, wrath, delusion, and desire, they torment and mangle one another horribly with arrows, javelins and tridents, clubs and axes, knives and razors, tossing one another to beasts and birds endowed with claws and beaks of iron or into rivers of corrosive liquid or of fire; some are hung head downward into boiling vats of blood and filth, others are being roasted alive; more, pinned through the head to great moaning trees, are having their bodies sliced to ribbons. And the food of this company is poison, sizzling grease and ordure, while for drink they have molten metal. The upper three hells are blazing, the next two, mixed of hot and cold, and the deepest, freezing—as in Dante's view.

* Five hundred dhanus, a dhanu being 4 hastas ("hands": the measure from the elbow to the tip of the middle finger, about 18 inches).

Furthermore, to the upper hells, fifteen deities of a coarse and lusty ilk known as *asuras* are assigned, who are not miserable at all in this domain, but, on the contrary, take fiendish delight in administering pain.

But deities, in the Jain view, whether fiends in hell or celestial beings, are themselves merely monads caught in the vortex of rebirth, happy for a time, but destined to pass to other forms. And they are of four chief but finely subdivided categories:

I. Gods supporting the earthly order
  1. Fiends of the upper hells (*asuras*)
  2. Divine serpents
  3. Lightning deities
  4. Golden-feathered sun-birds
  5. Fire deities
  6. Wind deities
  7. Thunder gods
  8. Water gods
  9. Gods of the continents
  10. Gods of the quarters

II. Wilderness or Jungle Sprites
  1. Kinnaras (the name means "what sort of man?"): birdlike musicians having human heads
  2. Kimpurushas (a name also meaning "what sort of man?"): these are of human form with the heads of horses
  3. Mahoragas: "Great Serpents"
  4. Gandharvas: celestial manlike musicians
  5. Yakshas: powerful earth demons, usually benign
  6. Rakshasas: malignant and very dangerous cannibal demons
  7. Bhutas: cemetery vampires
  8. Pishachas: malignant, mighty imps

III. Heavenly bodies
  1. Suns: numbering, in the worlds inhabited by man, 132
  2. Moons: likewise 132
  3. Constellations: for each sun and for each moon 28
  4. Planets: for each sun and for each moon 88

5. Stars: for each sun and for each moon 6,697,500,000,000,-000,000

IV. Dwellers in the Mansions of the Storied Heavens; of two orders, sub-divided in ascending series

1. Those within the Temporal Sphere
   A. Masters of the True Law
   B. The Lordly Powers
   C. The Ever-Youthful
   D. The Great Kings
   E. Dwellers in the Causal World
   F. Lords of the Mystical Sound Va
   G. The Greatly Brilliant
   H. Those of a Thousand Rays
   I. The Pacific
   J. The Revered
   K. Those Delighting in the Abyss
   L. The Imperishable (*acyutas:* "not dripping")

2. Those beyond the Temporal Sphere; in two subdivided classes
   A. Those Residing in the Cosmic Neck
      i. Delightful to See
      ii. Of Noble Achievement
      iii. Delighting the Mind
      iv. Universally Benign
      v. Illustrious
      vi. Well Disposed
      vii. Auspicious
      viii. Giving Joy
      ix. Giving Bliss
   B. Those Residing in the Head
      i. The Victorious
      ii. The Carriers of Banners
      iii. The Conquerors
      iv. The Invincibles
      v. The Fully Realized

Each of these forty-nine sub-orders of divine being is organized, like an Indian kingdom, in ten grades:

1. Kings (*indras*)
2. Princes
3. Thirty-three high functionaries
4. Court Nobles
5. Bodyguards
6. Palace Guards
7. Soldiers
8. Citizens
9. Slaves
10. Criminal Classes

All deities dwelling below the sphere of the neck delight in sexual play, and, as in the hells, so here, the life monads are of colors according to kind: those of categories I, II, and III are black, dark blue, and the gray of smoke; those of IV, sub-orders 1. A and B, flame red; C to E, yellow; and the rest, increasingly white. Gods of orders I, II, and III, furthermore, and of IV. 1. A and B are ten feet six inches tall; IV. 1. K, L, and the gods dwelling in the neck, three feet tall, while the beings at the top—the victors bearing banners, conquerors, invincible, and fully realized—are all less than eighteen inches tall. Contrast the beings in the lowest hell, with a stature of one thousand yards! One of these gods would stand very prettily on one's desk.

And so, above the earth, as well as beneath, there is imagined only a manifold of monads—no God, nor even god, either in the usual Occidental sense of these terms or in the early Vedic sense. For, even in their highest, banner-bearing day of victory in the luminous heavens of the head, these are but souls, monads, temporarily well placed, because of deeds well done in lives before, but destined to move along when their merit has been served. Nor, again, is there any judge numbering those deeds to assign due punishment and reward. The effects of action are automatic. Deeds of violence automatically draw weight and darkness into the soul; those of gentleness lighten both its color and its weight; so that the monad falls and rises of itself. And there was never a creator of this world: it has been as it is from all eternity.

Thus Jainism is a religion without God. One might almost term it mechanistic—scientific—even though it is surely obvious that, in spite of its grand show of meticulous numeration, this image is (to say the least) inaccurate as to fact. Such an effort to read a consistent order into the entire spectacle of nature is far from primitive. It represents an already highly developed search for laws that should be constant throughout time and space. However, in its mad nightmare of a system, the indispensable scientific attitude toward evidence—checking, testing, criticizing, carefully sorting fact from fancy—is absolutely missing; and the result is a world that never was—to which the individual, nevertheless, is urged to shape his life, thoughts, meditations, dreams, and even basic fears and delights.

Moreover, whatever the aim and attitude may have been of the early proto-scientists to whom the origins of this attempt to classify the phenomenology of both the gross world and the visionary in purely psychological terms may be due, in the Jain system, and throughout the later religious usages of such archaic cosmological organizations, there is no interest whatsoever in relevancy to fact. Projected from the mind onto the actual universe, like a movie onto a screen, this image has been for centuries employed not to elicit further research but to blot the universe out. Its function is psychological: the unsettling and dissolution of the will to live and the guidance of the sentiments away from their natural earthly concerns, even past all the usual religious imageries of hope and fear—hells, heavens, and the rest—to an absolutely transcendent, absolutely inconceivable goal, to which every effort of the will is to be turned. No one cares at all whether such a vision, competent to lure the mind and heart away from earth, corresponds, as science, to earthly fact. The judgment of its truth and value is pragmatic: if it works (upon the psyche), it is true enough.

And so we have in this mythology of the Jains an example of something absolutely new in the history of our subject, at least as far as the evidence goes; namely, a mythology designed to break (not foster) the will to live and to blot out (not enhance) the universe.

Among the Greeks, it is true, there was an ascetic strain also, in the line of the Orphics, Pythagoras, Eleatics, and Plato. But there is nothing anywhere in Greek philosophy, or indeed anywhere in the known history of our subject, to match the absolute No! of the religion of the Jains. The peculiar melancholy of their alienation from this life-in-death that will never end goes infinitely farther than the Greek—as does their vision of the reach of time and space, and therewith of cosmic misery. For the Greek view of the world, as Spengler well showed in his discussions of the "Apollonian soul" in *The Decline of the West,* placed all its emphasis on visible, tangible bodies. The Greek tongue possessed no word for space. The far away and the invisible were *ipso facto* "not there." The Greek term *cosmos* referred not to a field of space and force, but to a sum of harmoniously ordered bodies well defined, Euclidean, measurable, and perceptible. Euclidean number was a definition of bounds. "So that, inevitably," as Spengler declared, "the Classical became by degrees the Culture of the small." [97]

The reach into boundlessness of the Indian mind, on the other hand, which is well epitomized in its (to us) ridiculous integer, the *palya* ("a period of countless years") by which even precise numbers are rendered imprecise, has so dilated the cosmic spectacle that the actualities at hand are simply unworthy of the notice of the wise. In contrast to the Greek, whose reading of the cosmos began with the visible and pressed only a little into space, the space of which his eye might become aware, the Indian opened his cosmology with space (*ākāśa*), and produced from that a universe no one had ever seen: moreover, a universe pierced through with such a magnitude of sorrow that the actual sorrow and suffering of those ephemeral beings immediately present to the eye —one's neighbors, for example, of lower caste—hardly merited a thought. The sage, already saturated with his knowledge of the world's sorrow, could see in them only illustrations of a cosmic and incorrigible state. And in the light of this knowledge, all that was surely evident was the infinite importance to the infinite individual of the spiritual task of getting out of this exquisite nightmare, in which even heaven is only a net of perfumed gossamer of gold, to catch and lure the jiva back into the calamitous round.

The peculiar force and melancholy of the Indian alienation

from this life-in-death that will never end is a function of the
Indian mind itself, which, in its fabulous reach, has found infinity
at every hand and filled it, not with rational observation but with
a rationalized nightmare of its own production. There never was
a time when time was not, nor will there come a time when time
will have ceased to be: this sorrowful world—as it is—will go on,
sorrowful, forever. Moreover, the sorrow that meets the eye does
not represent, by any means, the magnitude in depth as well as
breadth of the whole. The misery of man and the beasts around
him, the plant world and supporting earth, the rocks and waters,
fire, wind, and flying clouds, indeed space itself with its luminaries,
constitutes but the least fraction of that ever-living, ever-deluded
body and conglomerate of misery which is the universe in its total
being.

IX. The Road of Flame

"As a large pond," we read in a Jain text, "when its influx of
water has been blocked, dries up gradually through consumption
of the water and evaporation, so the karmic matter of a monk,
which has been acquired through millions of births, is annihilated
by austerities—provided there is no further influx." [98]

The first task of the Jain teacher, therefore, is to block in his
student the karmic influx, which can be achieved only through a
gradual reduction of the sphere of life participation; and the
second task, when the student has finally closed and locked every
door, is to have him burn out through asceticism the karmic matter
already present. The normal Sanskrit term for this discipline is
tapas, a word meaning "heat." The Jain yogi, through his fierce
interior heat, is supposed, literally, to burn out karmic matter and
thus to cleanse and lighten his precious monad, so that, rising
through the planes of the cosmic body, it may ultimately ascend
beyond, to "peace in isolation" (kaivalyam), beneath the Umbrella Slightly Tilted, where the individual life-monad, perfectly
clear, at last, of all coloring matter whatsoever, will shine forever
in its own translucent, crystalline, pure being.

To begin seriously and systematically the great ascent—which may require many future lives—the mere man of the world, the layman, heavily stained and weighted with the matter of the world, yet desiring to be disengaged, must first renounce five faults: 1. doubt concerning the validity of the Jain view of the universe, the achievement of the World Saviors, "Makers of the Crossing to the Other Shore," and the efficaciousness of Jain practice; 2. desire to embrace any other faith; 3. uncertainty concerning the deleterious effects of action; 4. praise of deceivers (i.e., people who have not renounced the five faults); and 5. association with deceivers.

The next step is to assume progressively—according to capacity —twelve vows:

I. The Five Basic Vows of the Jain Layman
  1. non-violence
  2. truthfulness
  3. non-theft
  4. chastity
  5. non-acquisition of possessions

II. Three vows to increase the force of the Basic Five
  6. to limit one's moving about
  7. to limit the number of things used
  8. not to wish evil to anyone or to use one's influence for evil, to endanger life by carelessness, or to keep unnecessary knives and weapons

III. Four vows to initiate positive religious practice
  9. to meditate at least 48 minutes a day
  10. to limit further, for a day, occasionally, the limits already imposed
  11. to engage, four days a month, in a monklike fast and meditation
  12. to support monasteries and monks with donations

And the ideal layman's life toward which one should be striving through all of this is to include the following eleven orders of virtue.

1. *virtues of belief:* firm belief in Jainism, reverence for one's religious teacher (*guru*), worship of the twenty-four Crossing Makers (*tīrthaṅkaras*), and avoidance of seven bad deeds, to wit: gambling, meat-eating, the drinking of intoxicants, adultery, hunting, thieving, and debauchery

2. *virtues of dedication:* strict observance of the twelve vows and the reception of death, when it comes, in absolute peace

3. *virtues of meditation:* the raising of the number of meditation periods to at least three times a day

4. *virtues of monastic effort:* the raising of the periods of monklike fast to at least six times a month

5. *the virtue of non-injury to plants:* avoidance of uncooked vegetables; care never to break a mango from its tree or to eat a mango before someone else has removed the stone, etc.

6. *the virtue of non-injury to minute insects:* never to eat between sunset and sunrise or to sip water before daylight, lest there should be some unseen insect in the drink

7. *the virtue of perfect chastity:* avoidance even of one's wife and of the scenting of the body lest she be aroused; then, avoidance of all gods, human beings, and animals of the opposite sex, in thought and speech as well as in life

8. *the virtue of renounced action:* never beginning any enterprise that might involve the destruction of life; viz., the building of a house or the digging of a well

9. *the virtue of renounced possession:* renunciation of ambition, dismissal of all servants, transfer of property to one's children

10. *the virtue of renounced participation:* one eats no meals but only the remains from the dining of others; one gives no worldly advice, and so, one is prepared at last for the great step

11. *the virtue of retreat:* one dons the garb of an ascetic, withdraws to some religious building or to the jungle, and lives according to the scriptural rules for a monk.

Having said farewell to his kindred [we read in a Jain text], being released by his family, wife, and sons; having applied himself to the practice of knowledge, intuition, conduct, asceticism, and courageous concentration; then, before a

qualified monk, a leader, rich in merits, of distinguished
family and pure complexion, of mature age and highly approved by other monks, he makes a bow and, after saying,
"accept me," receives approval.

Vows, religious observances, restraint of the senses, re-
moval of all hair, daily duties, nakedness, and avoidance of
bathing: these are the fundamentals of monkhood, prescribed
by the best of the Victors (*jinas*); also, sleeping on the
ground, not brushing the teeth, reception of food in a standing posture, and one meal a day.

If the renunciation is not absolute, then there is for the
monk no purification of karmic influx. And in the mind of the
unpure how can karma be annihilated? [99]

During the earliest stages of monastic effort anger is quelled;
pride, deceitfulness, and greed are reduced to mere traces; the
need for sleep is overcome, the power of meditation grows, and
a new joy enters the life.

Presently, pride vanishes and with this, the power of meditation
vastly improves. Women, it is said by some, cannot progress beyond this point; hence, they are not allowed to enter into the so-
called "sky-clothed," naked state. "Infatuation, aversion, fear,
disgust and various kinds of deceit (*māyā*), are ineradicable from
the minds of women," a Jain guidebook to nirvana states; "for
women, therefore, there is no nirvana. Nor is their body a proper
covering; therefore they have to wear a covering. In the womb,
between the breasts, in their navel and loins, a subtle emanation
of life is continually taking place. How then can they be fit for self-
control? A woman may be pure in faith and even occupied with a
study of the sutras or the practice of a terrific asceticism: in her
case there will still be no falling away of karmic matter." [100]

"As deceitfulness is natural to women," states another guide,
"so are standing, sitting down, roaming about, and teaching the
law, natural to sages." [101]

The next passion to be quenched, then, is that urge to play a
part in the game of life which is called deceitfulness by the Jains
and which in women is never overcome. When this disappears, the
character becomes virtually sexless and absolute detachment is

hampered only by the memory of things pleasant or unpleasant that one did and saw before becoming an ascetic.

Meditations grimly pursued, therefore, must now eradicate not only all sense of pleasure in the beauty of forms and sounds, but also revulsion from ugliness and foul smells, and even pain. And when this prodigy of purgation has been accomplished the sage is completely humorless and the last glint of his humanity dead.

And yet the chemistry of the body still is clinging to the first and last, elementary link of the life-monad to matter. The terms "greed," "avidity," or, on the chemical level, "valence," on the physical atomic level, "binding power," might be used to characterize this sheerly physiological grip that must now be loosed. For if it is not broken, but only weakened or relaxed, not only will the final escape to absolute freedom never be achieved, but there will remain the latent danger that with even a slight failure of ascetic concentration the nearly dead fire may burst into flame. Then the whole series, in a chain reaction, will be again ignited— pleasure and pain, memories, pride, anger, and the rest—so that the monad on a blazing tide will be swept again into the maelstrom; as it was in the case of the yogi with the fifty young wives, who had allowed his one-pointedness to be broken by the splash of a fish.

For the one who has achieved this step, on the other hand, and so attained the condition of "annihilated infatuation," only two further stages remain, namely: 1. that of "self-identity in yoga," and 2. that of "self-identity without yoga."

And as the Jain view of the misery of the universe was a mythic, supernormal image designed to inspire revulsion, so is the view, now, of achievement no less mythic, designed, however, to inspire zeal.

We learn, for example, of the World Savior Parshva, that when the demon Meghamalin, who had assailed him with darkness, storm, and the form of the very god of death, had been dispelled by the pair of cosmic serpents, the saint—who, in contrast to the one who had been distracted by a fish, had remained unmoved even when the earth opened, mountains fell, and a forest shattered around him—acquired self-identity in yoga. All connection with the outer world having dissolved, his energy and light were at rest, infinitely radiant, within the monad. Showers of celestial blossoms thereupon descended. The seats of all of the gods of the universe shook. The heavenly choirs sang. And there came pouring from all directions deities with fly whisks, deities of all categories, to build for the World Teacher an assembly hall of twelve parts called the "Flocking Together," in which there was to be an allotted place for every species of being. The lion-shaped throne was furnished for him, the umbrella of world rule, and a shining halo. His royal father, mother, and former queen arrived, chanting hymns in his praise. There was a beating of celestial kettle drums, and he preached to all the Cosmic Sermon, wherein the fourfold discipline was taught of the way to the shore beyond sorrow, namely: charity, piety, asceticism, and character.

Many—including the demon who had assailed him—were converted; some even achieved perfection. Father, mother, and queen took vows. A black, four-armed, elephant-faced demon arrived, riding on a tortoise, protected by the hood of a large cobra, bearing in his two left hands respectively an ichneumon and a serpent, in his right a citron and a serpent, after which a four-handed golden goddess in a chariot drawn by a winged serpent appeared, in her two right hands a noose and lotus, in her left a hook and fruit. And the Lord, followed by the whole vast assembly, began to walk, with the demon on one side and goddess on the other, before him the wheel of the law aloft, and a great drum sounding in the air. Served by an umbrella and by chowries, he went striding upon golden lotuses, which emerged before him as he proceeded, while the trees bowed in homage; diseases fled to great distances; the seasons, birds, and winds were glorious; and throughout the world hostilities ceased.

Then, knowing that his nirvana was at hand, the Lord Parshva ascended a certain mountain, dropping off his great company gradually on the way, till he arrived at the summit with only thirty-three illuminated sages, who, together with him there, practiced yoga for a month. And when no more time remained to him on earth than would have sufficed for the utterance of the five vowels, he passed into the stage of self-identity without yoga.

Seventy years before, his destructive karmas had been destroyed; now the eighty-five ties associated with the four modes of non-destructive karma were annihilated. This took place on the seventh day of the bright fortnight of the moon of the month Shravana (July–August), and the Lord passed immediately to his liberation.

The radiant life-monad rose from the earth, greater and more brilliant than the sun, yet without color, crystalline, immortal, omniscient and omnipotent, boundless and without weight, passing upward through all the heavens within the temporal sphere of the great cosmic thorax, on beyond, through those of the neck and head, out through the cranium, to ascend to, and remain forever in, that more than supernal place "without wind" (nir-vāna) where the great umbrella soars. The released, weightless monad is not to be reached by any prayer. It is indifferent to the cycling maelstrom far beneath. It is all-aware, though unthinking; alone yet everywhere. It is without individual character, personality, quality, or definition. It is simply perfect.

And the body, which had been dismissed, lay deprived of life on the summit of the mountain. The seats of all the gods trembled. Showers of celestial blossoms fell. Heavenly choirs sang; the kettledrums again rolled; deities with fly whisks arrived from every quarter; divine serpents, lightning deities, golden-feathered sun-birds, fiends from the upper hells, carriers of banners from the heavens of the head: all came. They bathed the body in the blessed fluid of the Cosmic Milky Ocean, decked it with godly ornaments, placed it on a pyre of sandal and aloe wood—whereupon, from the head of the god of fire a blaze shot forth and the body was consumed. Cloud youths quenched the pyre.

The gods and goddesses rubbed the ashes upon their heads and persons, built over the bones a pagoda of gems, and finally, with songs and dances, marched in all directions triumphantly back to their hidden homes.[102]

BUDDHIST INDIA

++

I. The Occidental and the Oriental Hero

Four decades ago, Miguel Asín y Palacios, a Catholic priest and professor of Arabic at the University of Madrid, delivered a shock to the European world of scholarship by showing in Dante's *Divine Comedy* an influence of Moslem sources.[1] Reviewing in detail the literature of the legend of Mohammed's nocturnal visit to purgatory, hell, and heaven, he demonstrated parallels enough to prove decisively a relationship; referring, also, to the lore of Zoroastrian Persia and, beyond that, the judgment of the soul before Osiris in the Egyptian Book of the Dead. And of particular interest to our present purpose is the notice in his work of the Persian background of the torture by cold in the lowest Dantean circle. "It need hardly be remarked," states Father Asín, "that Biblical eschatology makes no mention of any torture of cold in hell. The Moslem doctrine, however, places this torture on the same footing as torture by fire. . . . Its introduction into the Moslem scheme of hell was due . . . to the assimilation by Islam of a Zoroastrian belief. . . . It is probable that it had been introduced by Zoroastrians converted to Islam." "Torture by cold," he adds, "also occurs in the Buddhist hell." [2] And, as we have just discovered, it occurs, too, in the Jain.

The ultimate background of both the Oriental and the Occidental storied heavens and pits of hell, with the world mountain between, is the Mesopotamian concept of the architecture of the universe, where, as we have found, there is an axial cosmic mountain symbolized by the ziggurat oriented with its sides to the quarters,

above which, in the highest heaven, sits a supreme god, An, amidst
a brilliant company of deities. The Plant of Birth and the Bread
and Water of Immortality are in that lofty sphere, below which,
in the middle sky, is the divine archetype and lord of royal rule,
whose role, in the long course of Mesopotamian history with its
fluctuation of empire, was played by a number of incumbents:
first, apparently, Enlil (the patron deity of Sumerian Nippur),
then Bel Marduk (of Hammurabi's Babylon), Assur (of Assyria),
and, among numerous others, Yahweh (of the early Hebrews).
In his court of many shining gods (or angels) the Tablets of Fate
were annually indited. And the seven heavens of the planets revolved below, in stages, which in the period of Assyria (c. 1100–c.
630 B.C.) were represented by seven terraced stories on the mountainside of the ziggurat, while beneath the earth, in the abyss, the
terrible goddess Ereshkigal, of the Land of No Return, was approached through seven gates. In her domain of darkness, called
Arallu, a horde of monsters and of unfortunate souls deprived at
death of the last rites of burial wandered horribly in the forms
of unsightly birds.[3]

Thus in the iconography of the earliest centers of civilization,
the Sumerian cities of riverine Mesopotamia, which flourished c.
3500–2000 B.C. and brought into being the symbolic order of the
hieratic city state, is to be seen the common source of both the
Oriental and the Occidental mythological visions of the universe.
A differentiating process clearly separated and transformed the
two, however, in the course of time. For one notes in the West, in
conformity with our characteristic stress on the dignity of the
individual life—for each soul one birth, one death, one destiny, one
maturation of the personality—that whether in heaven, purgatory,
or hell, the visiting visionary readily recognizes the deceased. Mohammed in heaven spoke to his brave and loyal friends, just as
Dante both to the damned and to the saved in the course of his
adventure. And in the Classical Greek and Roman visits to the
underworld as well: both Ulysses and Aeneas talked with their
departed friends. Whereas in the Orient there is no such continuity of the personality. The focus of concern is not the individual, but the monad, the reincarnating jiva, to which no individuality

whatsoever intrinsically pertains, but which passes on, like a ship through waves, from one personality to the next: now a mealworm, now a god, demon, king, or tailor.

Hence we find, as Heinrich Zimmer has remarked, that in the Oriental hells and heavens, though multitudes of beings are depicted in their agonies and joy, none retains the traits of his earthly personality. Some can remember having once been elsewhere and know what the deed was through which the present punishment was incurred; nevertheless, in general, all are steeped and lost in their present state. Just as any dog is absorbed in the state of being precisely whatever dog it happens to be, fascinated by the details of its present life—and as we ourselves are in general spellbound by our present personal existences—so are the beings in the Hindu, Jain, and Buddhist other worlds. They are unable to remember any former state, any costume worn in a previous existence, but identify themselves exclusively with that which they are now. And this, of course, from the Indian point of view, is just what they are not.[4]

Whereas the typical Occidental hero is a personality, and therefore necessarily tragic, doomed to be implicated seriously in the agony and mystery of temporality, the Oriental hero is the monad: in essence without character but an image of eternity, untouched by, or else casting off successfully, the delusory involvements of the mortal sphere. And just as in the West the orientation to personality is reflected in the concept and experience even of God as a personality, so in the Orient, in perfect contrast, the overpowering sense of an absolutely impersonal law suffusing and harmonizing all things reduces to a mere blot the accident of an individual life.

An obscure and as yet completely unsolved problem in the history of the break between the two worlds envelops the figure of the Persian Zoroaster and the origins of his progressive, ethically oriented, strictly dualistic mythology, which, as far as its spirit is concerned, is entirely on the Western side of the cultural watershed, and yet, in its origins, clearly has stemmed, in part at least, from the same mythology as the Vedas. A discussion at some length will be reserved for my Occidental volume. But in relation to India and the influence of Persian thought upon both Buddhism and Hinduism, it is necessary at this time to point out a few of the chief contrasts that immediately set the doctrine of Zoroaster—and therewith the West—apart.

The first and most radical of the innovations—which, as far as I know, appears here for the first time in the history of mythology —is the progressive, not deteriorating world cycle. As already remarked,* the Zoroastrian version of the world course presents a creation by a god of pure light into which an evil principle entered, by nature contrary to and independent of the first, so that there is a cosmic battle in progress; which, however, is not to go on forever, but will terminate in a total victory of the light: whereupon the process will end in a perfect realization of the Kingdom of Righteousness on Earth, and there will be no continuation of the cycle. There is no idea here of eternal return.

A second radical innovation, setting this mythology apart particularly from India, is to be seen in the responsibility that it places upon the individual to choose, of his own free will, whether and how he shall stand for the Light, in thought, word, and deed.

"Hear ye then with your ears; see ye the bright flames with the eyes of the Better Mind. It is for a decision as to religions, man and man, each individually for himself. Before the great effort of the cause, awake ye to our teaching." [5]

And finally, a third principle, essential to the Zoroastrian world view, which sets it not merely apart from, but diametrically opposed to, the Indian, is that of engagement, not disengagement, as the way to the ultimate goal. The individual, who, of his free will, has taken it upon himself to think, speak, and act for the Better, applies himself with all zeal to the work, not of the forest, but of the village. The cause of the world is by no means hopeless. And I think it greatly worth noticing that in the iconography of the later Zoroastrianism the figure epitomizing all evil on earth, the dark antagonist of the moral order, is the tyrant king Azhi Dahaka, the "Fiendish Snake," who is actually represented with serpents springing from his shoulders—like the Lord Parshva in the art of the Jains. I am inclined to see in this no mere accident. For, like

* Supra, pp. 7–8.

Jainism, the religion of Zoroaster is an absolute dualism—without compromise. There is in neither of these opposed systems any sense of an implicit "Secret of the Two Partners" by which the Better and the Bad (in Zoroastrianism), jiva and non-jiva (in Jainism), should ever be reconciled behind the scenes of the world stage on which their drama is being played out. The two religions are opposed twins: for each the other represents perfectly the Deceiver. And whereas in the Indian system the only possible way to salvation lay in a disengagement of the monad from the world in its futile round, the way of the Persian was precisely engagement in the common struggle of God and man toward an attainable —not at all futile—aim of righteousness on earth. We find, in fact, in Zoroastrian literature, an explicit, direct, and intentional attack on the ideals of such a philosophy as that which we have just viewed in our study of the Jains:

> Verily I say unto thee [declared the lord of light, Ahura Mazda, to his prophet Zoroaster], the man who has a wife is far above him who begets no sons; he who keeps a house is far above him who has none; he who has children is far above the childless man; he who has riches is far above him who has none: And of two men, he who fills himself with meat is filled with the good spirit much more than he who does not do so; the latter is all but dead; the former is above him by the worth of a dirhem, by the worth of a sheep, by the worth of an ox, by the worth of a man. It is this man that can strive against the onsets of Death the Bone Divider, Death the Self-moving Arrow; that even with thinnest garment on, can strive against the winter fiend; that can strive against the wicked tyrant and smite him on the head; it is this man that can strive against the ungodly deceiver and deceived, who does not eat.[6]

Zoroaster's dates, as we have said, are unknown. Even the question that Professor James Darmesteter proposed as early as 1880, as to "whether Zoroaster was a man converted into a god, or a god converted into a man," [7] remains unanswered. About all that is secure as to date is the fact that Darius I (reigned 521–486 B.C.), who was an exact contemporary of Mahavira (died c. 485 B.C.) and the Buddha (563–483 B.C.), Aeschylus (525–456 B.C.), and

Confucius (551–478 B.C.), wrote himself down, 520 B.C., in a trilingual cuneiform inscription at Behistun—composed in Persian, Elamite, and Akkadian—as a dedicated Zoroastrian: "By the grace of Ahura Mazda I am king."

At this time the Persian empire reached from the Greek Ionian isles (Satrapy I) to the Punjab and the Indus (Satrapy XX). All the ancient worlds of Egypt, Mesopotamia, Phoenicia, the Asiatic Greeks, and the Indus Valley had been absorbed into one progressively and aggressively inspired, international nation: the first of its kind in the history of the world. The Persian answer to sorrow, therefore—contemporary with the tragic of Aeschylus, ascetic of Mahavira, and prudent of Confucius—was the building of a soundly governed, progressive world empire under God. Viable roads and a lively commerce ran from India to Greece. A general policy of tolerance fostered the rebuilding of the temple in Jerusalem, which the Chaldeans had destroyed. The gods of many broken peoples were restored. The arts flourished. New cities and courts arose throughout the realm. And for a time it looked as though the Universal Monarch had, in the Persian King of Kings, indeed come into being.

II. The New City States: c. 800–500 B.C.

The Aryan warrior herdsmen whose covered wagons rumbled into India during the second millennium B.C. were matched in Greece, as we have seen, by the numerous and various hunting and herding warrior groups, great and small, whose devastations the archaeology of the Aegean has disclosed for the long period from c. 1900 to c. 1100 B.C. Writing of those who left their mark on the shores of southern Greece and in Crete, Professor H. G. L. Hammond writes:

> Some negative conclusions are permissible. The invaders brought no distinctive painted pottery or other mark of a developed civilization. They did not take to urban life. They were probably nomadic at first, living in tents and huts, using wooden utensils, and worshiping wooden statues. Their early village settlements were small. They showed no reverence for the standards of Mycenaean civilization, and therefore presumably came from outside the limits of the Mycenaean area.

They must have been physically tough and ably led in order to overthrow the centers of Mycenaean power. They may have had some superior weapons, but in the arts they were inferior to those they conquered.[8]

Undoubtedly the same general description can be applied to the pastoral tribesmen who entered and crossed through the Indus Valley at the time of the fall into ruins of the two earlier High Bronze Age cities of Harappa and Mohenjo-daro. However, whereas the invaders of the Aegean were entering a world of still powerful archaic empires, those of India, having passed and left behind the two crumbling citadels of an already worn-out colonial establishment of some kind, saw before them only comparatively rude jungle planters, hunters, and collectors, the Dasyus of their deep disdain. Furthermore, the Greeks by 1200 B.C. had iron; the Indian Aryans did not. And finally, the pleasant, open waters of the ship-filled Mediterranean beckoned the Greeks to learn of distant lands and to keep their eyes alert, whereas the land and mountain vastnesses of Asia, never overcome by man, always threatening to reply to his little victories with a force infinitely surpassing anything humanly imaginable, kept before the mind the aspect of the universe that is experienced rather as sublime than as beautiful. So that whereas in the European sphere the gods and myths of the archaic inheritance became—with the increased assurance of man in a world where he could feel at home—increasingly developed on the anthropomorphic side, in India the aspect of awe, great fear and power, superhuman force and transcendent sublimity was carried to such a point that even in the heart of man humanity dissolved and there entered the inhumanity of God.

The old world of the hieratic city states now was a memory, and for the most part very dim. But though many cities had fallen, many also remained—that is to say, in the West. In India, on the other hand, there were none. Hence, the Greeks soon were rebuilding on the ruins of the past, building in brick, plaster, and stone, while the Vedic Aryans of the Punjab and Gangetic plain were building in no material permanent enough to have left to us any physical remains. Their period, to c. 800 B.C., is an archaeological blank. Nor have they left any literary tokens of their way of life. From the *Iliad* and *Odyssey* a fairly dependable image can be drawn of the Greek heroic age, for which we have, besides, considerable archaeological support. From the Indian epics, on the other hand—which, as we have seen, show traits and deep alterations from as late as the fifth century A.D.—only a mirage-like, greatly idealized, priestly vision can be drawn of the world and people of the Vedic age; while tangibly—to let us see, instead of merely hear about, the household, ritual, and battle gear of those for whom Indra slew the dragon, released the seven streams, "made subject the dark Dasa folk and made their color disappear," [9]—we have exactly nothing.

For the period immediately following the Vedic Aryan, however, a promising archaeological breakthrough occurred in the upper Ganges area a little over a decade ago, when a well-stratified mound was explored some eighty miles northeastward of Delhi, at Hastinapura, where a sequence of three distinct ceramic wares appeared, as follows:

1. Ocher-Colored Ware, apparently of c. 1000 B.C., with which copper implements are associated. "The impression for the moment," states Sir Mortimer Wheeler, "is that these precede . . . the full development of urban life in the region." [10]

2. Painted Gray Ware, dated by Wheeler about eighth to fifth centuries B.C.: a distinctive Bronze Age ware concentrated in the "two river" (*doāb*) Jumna-Ganges area, but with extensions westward to the Punjab and southward as far as Ujjain: wheel-turned and well fired with painted linear and dotted patterns, concentric circles, spirals, sigmas and swastikas, generally black but occasionally red. "If Aryans must be dragged into this picture," Wheeler writes, "it is possible to suppose that the P.G. Ware may represent the second phase of their invasion of India, when, from the Punjab, they entered and Aryanized the Middle Country of the Ganges-Jumna *doāb,* after picking up ideas and doubtless craftsmen in the Indus valley and the Baluch borderland." [11]

This was the period of the Brahmanas and chief Upanishads, kings Ajatashatru and Jaibali, and, possibly also, that great war whose echoes have come to us in the Mahabharata—which, like the Wars of the Roses in England, represents the end of an aristocratic feudal age. Following that disaster, the term *vīra,* "hero," was no longer applied primarily to chariot fighters but to yogis; as, for example, in the name Maha-vira, the Great (*mahā*) Hero (*vīra*), the last of the World Saviors of the Jains.

3. *Northern Black Polished Ware,* an elegant, wheel-turned, highly polished ware of steel-like quality, associated with iron; ascribed, schematically and still tentatively, to the fifth to second centuries B.C.—the period from the Buddha (563–483 B.C.) to the Emperor Ashoka (reigned c. 268–232 B.C.): apparently dominant in Bihar, the area of the Buddha's early teaching, whence it may have been carried, by the victories of Ashoka and his immediate predecessors, westward to the upper Punjab (Taxila), eastward to Bengal and Orissa, and southward to Amaravati and Nasik.

It is only with the last two of these wares that the rise of cities in India is to be associated: cities not of brick or stone, but of wood, and with stockades of prodigious beams and logs. In association with the Painted Gray Ware, we may imagine (Wheeler suggests) "a comfortable and organized city life in the Jumna-Ganges basin sometime in the first half of the first millennium B.C. . . . the general urban background of the Mahabharata . . . : a picture of wealthy and jealous dynasties and politics, based upon a limitless and fertile soil and serviceable river-communications." [12] And then, about 500 B.C.—in association with the Northern Black Polished Complex—"a knowledge of iron-working spread through the region, doubtless introduced from Persia where iron smelting had been familiar for five or six centuries. . . . The introduction of coinage, also from Persia, betrays a quickening of the commercial sense," and, as Wheeler concludes, this Ganges civilization, which the Northern Black Polished Ware marks for us, once it had been established, "endured through the centuries with a changelessness which the modern age has not altogether shaken." [13]

We may register, then, with a glance again at Greece beyond the other bound of the Persian empire, a gradual rise and flowering from c. 800 to c. 500 B.C. of a multitude of secular (in contrast to hieratic) monarchic states across the whole domain from Athens to Bengal: literally hundreds of tiny sovereign powers, each with its capital fortress, town, or city, governed by a princely family and with councils of elders, citizen assemblies, palace army, temple clergy, peasantry and trading gentry, shops, dwellings, and—among the more prosperous—monuments and parks. And behold, at a certain time there began appearing in these pleasant little capitals wandering teaching sages, each with his cluster of devotees and each supposing himself to have solved—once and for all—the mystery of sorrow: Kapila (perhaps c. 600 B.C.), Gosala (fl. 535 B.C.), Mahavira (died c. 485 B.C.), the Buddha (563–483 B.C.); Pythagoras (c. 582–500 B.C.), Xenophanes and Parmenides (both, also, of the sixth century), and Empedocles (c. 500–430 B.C.), "the wonder-worker, who went about among men as an immortal God, crowned with fillets and garlands." Behind these there loom more shadowy figures, of whom it cannot be said whether they were men or gods: Parshva (872–772?) and Rishabha, Orpheus (date unknown) and Dionysos. Furthermore, in the teachings of these sages, in both India and Greece, a number of characteristic themes appear that were unknown to the myths of the early Aryans. For example: the idea of the wheel of rebirth, which is fundamental to Orphism as well as to India; the idea of the soul in bondage to the body ("the body a tomb," said the Orphics) and deliverance through asceticism; sin leading to the punishments of hells, virtue to ecstasy and thence to absolute knowledge and release. Heracleitus (fl. 500 B.C.) spoke of life as an ever-living fire, as did the Buddha (same date) in his Fire Sermon. The doctrine of the elements is common to the two traditions: fire, air, earth, and water among the Greeks; ether, air, fire, water, and earth in the Indian series. The Orphics, as well as Indians, knew the image of the cosmic egg, also the cosmic dancer. Already in the words of Thales (c. 640–546 B.C.) the idea is announced that the universe, possessed of a soul, is full of spirits. And in Plato's *Timaeus* the body of the universe is described very much in the way of the Jains, as "a Living Creature of which all other living creatures, severally and in their families, are parts." [14]

We have already remarked among primitive hunting peoples the idea of the immortality of the individual soul, which neither dies nor is born, but simply passes back and forth, as it were through a veil, appearing in bodies and departing. We have observed, also, the development in the ancient Near East of the idea of the hieratic city state, governed in every phase of life by the model of a cosmic, mathematical harmony that is revealed and illustrated by the celestial spheres. And we have noticed, c. 1750 B.C., in the two leading centers of that time, Mesopotamia and Egypt, a literature of lamentation, doubt, and questioning.

A turbulent millennium had intervened. The old, largely rural Bronze Age situation had given place, over a broad domain of maturing civilization, to a galaxy of cities governed by secular, not divine kings. And in these the folk were no longer largely farmers. We hear of merchants, professional thieves, moneylenders, artisans of all kinds, judges and a class of clerks, mariners, caravan personnel, innkeepers, mining supervisors, and military officers. For such, the old rites of a rural religion of the fertile soil, or kingly of the magic of victory, simply had no force; they were out of date. A broad zone of readiness had therefore been established for the reception of a new approach to the problem of man's highest good. Dislodged from the soil as well as from the old necessities of the hunt, a rather sophisticated urban population had appeared, with a certain leisure, considerable luxury, and time, consequently, for neuroses. Inevitably the new initiators appeared, who had, themselves, in their own experience, faced out the new anxieties: the first systematic psychologists of all time and in many ways, perhaps, the best. And their basic tools were everywhere the same: the old ritual lore, inherited from the hieratic past, with its concept of a hidden harmony and equivalence uniting the microcosm and the macrocosm and of a consequent resonance conducive to magical effects. However, now the chief concern was no longer magical (the weather, crops, abundance of goods, and long years), but psychological (the *détente* and harmonization of the psyche) and sociological (the integration of the individual with a new society based on a secular instead of hieratic tradition). Thus a perfect mythogenetic zone had been established: "a limited yet sufficiently broad area of the earth's surface, relatively uniform in character, where a large population of closely related individuals [here those inhabiting the broad domain of the late High

Bronze and early Iron Age societies] became affected simultaneously by roughly comparable imprints [those of an emergent urban
domesticity], and where, consequently, psychological 'seizures' of
like kind were everywhere impending and, in fact, became precipitated in a context of ritualized procedure and related myth." [15]

In such a zone of readiness ideas and practices may appear
spontaneously in more than one place at a time and spread as
quickly as a flash fire.

"Detached from their background of original, tribal-bound,
widely distributed men's rites," states Dr. Karl Kerényi, writing of
the Orphic rites of spiritual initiation, which in Greece became à la
mode in the sixth century B.C., "they offered their arts revised to
the religious requirements of a new age. And in this historical
process both the sense and the character of the initiation changed.
They became divided into a lower, merely ritualistic, and a higher,
purely spiritual direction, where philosophers—first the Pythago-
reans and then others also, and not all in the ceremonial fashion
of an Empedocles—became the initiators." [16]

And so it was in India too: with the old rites of the pre-Aryan
cities furnishing the basic themes of rebirth in death and asceticism,
psychological detachment, and mythic identification. In perfectly
parallel courses the new teachings arose, perhaps—though also
perhaps not—cross-fertilized by way of Persia. All that can now be
affirmed in the light of the very sparse evidence at hand for the
period is that in both India and Greece, as well as in Persia between, the basic motifs of an early dualistic mythological philosophy abruptly appeared in new forms, about simultaneously, and
immediately spread.

III. The Legend of the World Savior

It is impossible to reconstruct the character, life, and actual
teaching of the man who became the Buddha. He is supposed to
have lived c. 563–483 B.C. However, his earliest biography, that
of the Pali Canon, was set down in writing only c. 80 B.C. in Ceylon,
five centuries and fifteen hundred miles removed from the actual
historic scene. And the life, by then, had become mythology—

according to a pattern characteristic of World Saviors of the period from c. 500 B.C. to c. 500 A.D., whether in India, as in the legends of the Jains, or in the Near East, as in the Gospel view of Christ.

Schematically summarized, this archetypal Savior Biography tells of:

1. the scion of a royal line
2. miraculously born
3. amid supernatural phenomena
4. of whom an aged holy man (Simeon: Asita), shortly following the birth, prophesies a world-saving message, and
5. whose childhood deeds proclaim his divine character.

In the Indian series, the world hero then:

6. marries and begets an heir
7. is awakened to his proper task
8. departs, either with the consent of his elders (Jain series), or else secretly (the Buddha)
9. to engage in arduous forest disciplines
10. which confront him, finally, with a supernatural adversary, over whom
11. victory is achieved.

The last-named, the Adversary, is a figure that in Vedic times would have appeared as an anti-social dragon (Vritra), but in accord with the new, psychological stress represents those errors of the mind that the World Savior's plunge into his own depth brings to light and against which he is striving, both for his own victory and for the rescue of the world.

In the Christian legend, the years of youth represented by stages 6 to 8 are unrecorded. However, the culminating episodes 9 to 11 are represented by the fast of forty days in the wilderness and confrontation there with Satan. Further, it might be argued that the earlier infant scenes of King Herod's slaughter of the innocents, the angelic warning to Saint Joseph, and the Holy Family's flight into Egypt correspond symbolically to 6, the efforts of the future Buddha's kingly father to frustrate him in his mission by confining him to his palace and causing him to marry, after which, 7, he was awakened to his task by the sight of an old man, a sick man, a corpse, and a yogi, whereupon, 8, he contrived to escape. For in both cases the narrative is of a kingly enemy of the spirit, striving with all his resources—whether malevolently (King Herod) or benignly (King Suddhodana)—to frustrate the infant Savior in his predestined task, to no avail.

Following his face-to-face encounter with, and conquest of, the Antagonist, the World Savior:

12. performing miracles (walking on water, etc.)
13. becomes a wandering teacher
14. preaching a doctrine of salvation
15. to a company of disciples, and
16. a smaller, elite circle of initiates
17. one of whom, less quick to learn than the rest (Peter: Ananda),[17] is given charge and becomes the model of the lay community, while
18. another, dark and treacherous (Judas: Devadatta), is bent on the Master's death.

In various versions of the legend, different readings are given to the shared motifs, to accord with differences of doctrine. For instance, 2: whereas the Virgin Mary conceived of the Holy Ghost, Queen Maya, the mother of the Buddha, was a true spouse of her consort; nor was the World Savior that she bore an incarnation of God, the Creator of the universe, but a reincarnating jiva, entering upon the last of its innumerable lives. Likewise, items 10–11: whereas the Buddha life reached culmination in the victory over Mara beneath the Bodhi-tree, the Christian legend transfers the Tree of Redemption to 19, the death of the Savior, which in the Buddha life is but a peaceful passage at the end of a long career as teacher. For the main point of Buddhism is not—as in the earlier Soma sacrifice—the physical immolation of the Savior, but his awakening (*bodhi*) to the Truth of truths and therewith release (*mokṣa*) from illusion (*māyā*). And the main point for the individual Buddhist, consequently, is not whether his legend of the Buddha corresponds to what happened actually and historically c. 563–483 B.C., but whether it serves to inspire and guide himself to enlightenment.

IV. Mythic Eternalization

Thus it is told, with little concern for relevancy to fact, that:

There was, once upon a time, a good king Suddhodana, of the Dynasty of the Sun, who ruled in the city of Kapilavastu, where the sage Kapila once had taught (Legendary Episode).

The Dynasty of the Sun, as the reader knows, stands for the principle of sheer light. The light of the sun is pure. The light of the moon, on the other hand, partakes of darkness. The light of the sun, furthermore, is eternal, whereas that of the moon, waning and waxing in counterpoise to its own dark, is at once mortal and immortal. The gods Tammuz and Osiris and, in the Vedic system, Soma, were manifestations of the lunar mystery. And the god Shiva, too, we have seen, was a deity of this context. His animal is the bull; in his hair is the crescent moon; we have linked his iconography with that of the yogi of the Indus seals. The mythology of the Buddha, on the other hand, is of the sun. He is termed the Lion of the Shakya Clan, who sits upon the Lion Throne. The symbol of his teaching is the Sun Wheel, and the reference of his doctrine is to a state that is no state, of which the only appropriate image is light.

In Egypt, with the rise of Dynasty V, c. 2480 B.C., the mythology of the sun superseded the lunar system of Osiris, and the pharaoh, in the lunar role, was called the son of the sun-god Re. Thrones and couches with the legs of bulls were superseded by those with the legs of lions. Among the Semites, the sun-god Shamash (Sumerian Utu) was a deity of supreme power, and among the Aryans everywhere the sun has been a mighty force. In the brilliant city of Persepolis of the Persian King of Kings—built by Darius I, 522 B.C., and destroyed 330 B.C. by Alexander—the solar principle of the Lord of Light of the Aryan prophet Zoroaster shone with the radiance of the sun itself on earth, sending forth its rays. And now we hear, as well, that the good king, father of the Buddha, was of the Dynasty of the Sun, ruling in the city where the sage Kapila once had taught.

Kapila was the founder of the so-called Sankhya philosophy, from which the Buddha took his departure. Like Jainism and Buddhism, the Sankhya is non-Vedic, and like Jainism, but not like Buddhism, it treats of two contrary principles: 1. matter, which it terms *prakṛti;* and 2. the monad, which it terms *puruṣa,* "the person." Whereas in Jainism, however, the monad is conceived to be physically contaminated by matter, in the Sankhya view there is no actual contact. The person—like the sun—stands apart. Its radiance activates the inert principle of matter, which is like an agitated water on which solar light is flashing. And each flash imagines that itself is the person and should therefore be eternal: hence, anxiety is experienced, together with sorrow and the rest. When through yoga, however, the portion of the agitated matter that is within the individual mind (the mind stuff) is stilled—as in the yoga of Patanjali described in our first chapter *— the unbroken image of the true person is beheld, the false idea of the mere reflection (ego: *aham*) disappears, and one's actual identity with that undying, sunlike entity is recognized, which, ironically, one has been—without knowing it—all the while.

The yoga of Patanjali described above—so different in both aim and method from the psycho-physical suicide of the Jains—is the discipline of this philosophy. And the classic fable told to illustrate its central theme is that of the king's son who was removed from his father's palace while a babe and reared in ignorance of his true nature by a primitive hill tribesman. He lived for years, thinking, "I am an outcaste, a primitive tribesman." However, when the king died without other issue, a certain minister of state, ascertaining that the boy was alive, traced him and gave him this instruction: "You are not an outcaste. You are the king's son." Immediately the youth gave up the idea that he was an outcaste and took to himself his royal nature, saying to himself: "I am the king."

"So likewise," runs the lesson, "following the instruction of a merciful being (the guru), who declares: 'Thou didst originate

* Supra, pp. 26–28.

from the Primal Man (*ādipuruṣa*), the universal divine life-monad
that manifests itself through pure consciousness and is spiritually
all-embracing and self-contained; thou art a portion of that,' an
intelligent person abandons the mistake of supposing himself to
be a manifestation or product of mere matter and cleaves to his
own intrinsic being (*svasvarūpam*)." [18]

Kapila's name means the "Red One" and is an epithet of the
sun, which is symbolic of the crystalline, radiant monad. And there
is a legend of him in the Mahabharata, which tells that when the
sixty thousand sons of a certain Universal Monarch named Ocean
(*sagara*) were riding as the armed guard of their father's sacrificial
horse, the beast suddenly vanished from before their eyes, and
when they dug into the earth where it had disappeared, they discovered it far under ground with a saint sitting beside it in meditation—Kapila, to wit; who, when they moved to recapture their
charge without pausing to pay him proper obeisance, with a flash of
his eye burned them all to ashes.[19] Similarly, the vision of the
monad, the "Red One," we might say, annihilates the myriadfold
illusions of the world ocean. The sacrifice of the cosmic horse
therewith becomes an interior sacrifice,* and the false identifications disappear.

In our survey of the early bull-to-lion sequence of Egypt, three
significant psychological stages were noted: 1. Mythic Identification (in the Pre-dynastic Ritual Regicide), 2. Mythic Inflation (in
the Pharaonic Cult of Dynasties I–IV), 3. Mythic Subordination
(in the Re Mythology of Dynasty V).

We have now to register, in connection with the Sankhya philosophy of Kapila, yoga of Patanjali, and earlier, cruder mythology
and yoga of the Jains, a fourth stage or stance; namely: 4. Mythic
Eternalization (in yoga), where, by a shift of association, the
subject learns to identify himself, not with the son of the sun but
with the sun itself, the Father witnessing the Son.

"As serenely as light itself would shine if all that it illuminates—
Heaven, Earth, and Air—were not: just so is the isolated state of
the seeing subject, the pure Self, when the world threefold, you and
I, in short everything visible, is gone." [20]

* Supra, p. 211.

"Even so is the isolation of the seer who remains without see-ing, after the hurly-burly of appearances—I, you, the world, and all—has disappeared." [21]

Just as in Stage 1, so here, a mythic identification has been achieved. It is not, however, with any object perceived, whether mortal or immortal, but with the perceiving subject; not the field but the perceiver of the field; not "matter" (*prakṛti*), in any form, but the "person" (*puruṣa*) alone: consciousness—of nothing—in and of itself.

v. The Middle Way

And so let us skip now to episodes 6–11, the young Gautama's years of marriage, search, and awakening, who was to surpass even Kapila in the power of his introversion; for if Kapila caused the object world to vanish, the Buddha wiped out, also, the subject.

The version of his legend that I shall use, by the poet-monk Ashvaghosha, c. 100 A.D., has already supplied our account of the attack of Mara.* Composed in Sanskrit, from the point of view of the later, Mahayana division of Buddhist thought, it not only provides an occasion for comparison with the more strictly monastic, Sankhya-like point of view of the earlier Hinayana posi-tion, but also devotes more precise attention than the Pali text to the crises of the intellectual search that preceded the finding of the Middle Way. And for our present purpose, which is to define as far as possible in Oriental terms the transformations of Oriental mythic thought, such a summary guide is invaluable. I shall pause along the way, to underline categories—but in the main only strive to render, as well as possible in abridgment, something of the flavor, as well as sense, of this earliest classic of the so-called Kavya ("poetic") style of the Sanskrit literary tongue.

ITEM 6. THE PALACE OF DELIGHTS

When the young prince Gautama had passed childhood and reached middle youth, he learned in a few days the sciences suitable to his race, which others require many years to master; and the king, his father, sought for him from a family of unblemished moral

* Supra, pp. 17–20.

excellence a bride possessed of beauty, modesty, and gentle bearing, Yashodhara by name, after which the prince rejoiced in that princess. Moreover, so that he should see no sight that might trouble his mind, the king had prepared for him a dwelling far from the busy press of the palace and furnished with all delights. With the softly sounding tambourines beaten by the tips of women's hands and dances danced as by heavenly nymphs, that dwelling shone like the mountain of the gods. With their beautiful soft voices, playful intoxications, sweet laughter, and stolen glances half concealed, these women skilled in the ways of love delighted him to such a degree that once, in pursuit on a pavilion roof, he inadvertently stepped off; however, he never reached the ground, but like a holy sage stepping from a heavenly chariot hovered on buoyant air.

In due course, to the fair-bosomed Yashodhara there was born a son, Rahula, and the good king, Gautama's father, rejoicing in this grandson, redoubled those pieties to which he had become devoted since the birth of his own son, Gautama. He offered soma sacrifices to Agni and the other deities of the pantheon, muttering phrases from the Vedas, practiced perfect calm, and observed numerous disciplines appropriate for laymen; yet always asked himself by what further means of sensuous seduction he might prevent his dear son from departing for the forest.

Prudent kings of this earth who cherish prosperity watch over their sons carefully in the world; but this king, though devoted to religion, kept his son away from it, turning him only toward the objects of delight.

However, those whose "being" (*sattva*) is "illumination" (*bodhi*), Bodhisattvas, the Future Buddhas, after knowing the flavor of the world, have always, following the birth of a son, departed to the forest.

ITEM 7. THE FOUR SIGNS

And so, on a certain day when the lotus ponds were adorned and the forests carpeted with tender grass, having heard of the beauty of the city groves beloved of women, the Bodhisattva resolved to go forth, like an elephant long shut up in its barn. And the king, having learned of the wish of his son, ordered a pleasure party prepared, with extreme precautions taken that no afflicted person should appear along the way to unsettle his son's protected mind.

In a golden chariot, with a worthy retinue, and on a road heaped with strewn flowers, the prince set forth, drawn by four gentle horses; and when the word went out ahead of him, "The prince is coming forth," the women, having obtained the permission of their husbands, hastened to the roofs, frightening the flocks of birds among the rooftops with the jingling of their girdles and anklets resounding up the stairs. Some were hindered by the strings of the girdles slipping down, eyes bewildered, just awakening from sleep, and with their ornaments hastily put on; others were hampered in their climbing simply by the weight of their massive hips and full bosoms. Swaying restlessly at the windows, crowding together in the mutual press, earrings polished by continual collision and their ornaments all jingling, the women's lotus faces shone as they looked brightly out and whispered with pure minds and no baser feeling: "Happy, indeed, his wife!"

The gods, however, in their pure abodes, having recognized the moment, sent forth an old man to walk along the road.

The prince beheld him.

The prince addressed his charioteer.

"Who is that man there with the white hair, feeble hand gripping a staff, eyes lost beneath his brows, limbs bent and hanging loose? Has something happened to alter him, or is that his natural state?"

"That is old age," said the charioteer, "the ravisher of beauty, the ruin of vigor, the cause of sorrow, destroyer of delights, the bane of memories and the enemy of the senses. In his childhood, that one too drank milk and learned to creep along the floor, came step by step to vigorous youth, and he has now, step by step, in the same way, gone on to old age."

The charioteer thus revealed in his simplicity what was to have been hidden from the king's son, who exclaimed, "What! And will this evil come to me too?"

"Without doubt, by the force of time," said the charioteer.

And the great-souled one whose mind, through many lives, had

become possessed of a store of merits, was agitated when he heard
of old age—like a bull who has heard close by the crash of a
thunderbolt. He asked to be driven home.

A second day, another outing; and the gods sent a man afflicted
by disease.

The prince said, "Yonder man, pale and thin, with swollen
belly, heavily breathing, arms and shoulders hanging loose and his
whole frame shaking, uttering plaintively the word 'mother' when
he embraces there a stranger: who is that?"

"My gentle lord," said the charioteer, "that is disease."

"And is this evil peculiar to him, or are all beings alike threat-
ened by disease?"

"It is an evil common to all," said the charioteer.

And a second time the prince, trembling, desired to be driven
home.

There came a third time, another outing, and the deities sent
forth a dead man.

Said the prince, "But what is that, borne along there by four
men, adorned but no longer breathing, and with a following of
mourners?"

The charioteer, having his pure mind overpowered by the gods,
told the truth. "This, my gentle lord," he said, "is the final end of
all living beings."

Said the youth, "How can a rational being, knowing these
things, remain heedless here in the hour of calamity? Turn back
our chariot, charioteer. This is no time or place for pleasure."

The driver, this time, however, in obedience to the youth's
father, continued to the festival of women in the groves. And the
young prince, arriving, was met as a bridegroom. Some thought of
him as the god of love himself incarnate; others thought of him
as the moon. Many were so smitten they simply gaped as if to
swallow him. And the son of the family priest urging all to make
use of their charms, their souls were carried away by love. They
assailed the prince with all kinds of stratagems. Pressing him
with their full bosoms, they addressed to him invitations. One
embraced him violently, pretending to have tripped. Another
whispered in his ear, "Let my secret be heard." A third, with

appropriate gestures, sang an erotic song, easily understood; and a fourth, with beautiful breasts, laughed, earrings waving in the wind, and cried, "Catch me, sir, if you can!" But that best of youths, there wandering like an elephant of the forest accompanied by his female herd, only pondered in his agitated mind: "Do these women not know that old age one day will take away their beauty? Not observing disease, they are joyous here in a world of pain. And, to judge from the way they are laughing at their play, they know nothing at all of death."

The party returned to the palace with broken hopes.

Thus the young, tender prince had learned the negative lessons of old age, disease, and death, which in the Buddhist system are the signs of the sorrow of all life. And the circumstance of the impossibly well-protected childhood has given accent to the impact of these negative aspects of existence; for the tale is wholly symbolic, not an actual biography. A gifted, sensitive youth is brought up in a world of complete delusion to that brooding period when deep psychological shocks do, in fact, strike the soul; and a shock in full depth thereby is represented, such as we should call today a trauma. His search, now, is to be for a cure.

But a cure to what end? Back to this world, which had been found (to use Schopenhauer's dreadful phrase) to be "something that should not have been"?

As Nietzsche writes of this problem:

> The everyday world is separated by a gulf of obliviousness from the dionysian reality of life; and when, after a glimpse of that depth, the everyday world comes back into view, it is beheld only with disgust. An ascetic mood, negative toward the will to live, is the consequence of such a state of mind.
>
> In this sense, the dionysian character resembles Hamlet. Each has gained a real glimpse into the essential nature of things. They are enlightened. And it now can only disgust them to act. For their deeds cannot change a thing as far as the eternal nature of existence is concerned. They find it either ridiculous or disgraceful, consequently, that they should be asked to set the world aright—which is out of joint. En-

lightenment paralyzes action, which requires that there should
be a veil of illusion thrown about the truth. That is the moral
of Hamlet. . . .

For, once having beheld the truth of things, bearing this
truth in mind, one can see everywhere only the monstrous-
ness or absurdity of existence: one comprehends the symbolism of the destiny of mad Ophelia. . . . One is filled
with nausea.[22]

It is simply too easy to attribute such a glimpse into the nature
of things and its resultant shock to a pathological trauma, and to
write complacently then of "adjustment." Such banality only
draws a veil of oblivion; and over that, a veil of illusion. Whereas
the problem is, actually, while retaining the gained insight, to
press through it to what Nietzsche had termed a "higher health."

And the call of the young prince Gautama to that end came to
him on his next departure from the nest, when he beheld the fourth
and last of the Four Signs.

He was riding his white steed, Kanthaka, across a field that was
being plowed, when he saw its young grass not only torn and scattered, but also covered with the eggs and young of insects, killed.
Then filled with a deep sorrow, as for his own kindred slaughtered,
he alighted from his horse, going over the ground slowly, pondering birth and destruction, musing, "Pitiable, indeed!" And,
desiring to be alone, he went apart, to sit at the foot of a rose
apple tree in a solitary spot, on the leaf-covered ground. Pondering the origin of the world and destruction of the world, he laid
hold there of the path to firmness of mind. And released therewith
from all such sorrows as attach to desire for the objects of the
world, he attained the first stage of contemplation. He was calm,
and full of thought.

Whereupon he saw standing before him an ascetic mendicant.
"What art thou?" he asked. To which the other answered, "Terrified by birth and death, desiring liberation, I became an ascetic.
As a beggar, wandering without family and without hope, accept-
ing any fare, I live now for nothing but the highest good." Whereupon he rose into the sky and disappeared; for he had been a god.

ITEM 8A. THE GRAVEYARD VISION

The prince, returning home, went to his father in the full assembly of the court, and, prostrating himself, hands joined above his head, said to him, "O Lord of Men, I want to become an ascetic mendicant." But the king, shaken like a tree struck by an elephant, gripped the joined hands of his son and said to him, choked with tears, "O my son, keep back this thought. It is not time for you to be turning to religion. During the first period of life the mind is fickle and the practice of religion full of danger." The prince looked up and answered sharply, "Father, it is not right to lay hold of a person about to escape from a house that is on fire." And he rose and returned to his palace, where he was greeted by his wives. But the king said, "He shall not go!"

The prince, in his palace, sat on a seat of gold, surrounded by those charming women, who desired nothing but to please him with their music. And the gods threw on them a spell, so that as they played they dropped off to sleep with their instruments falling from their hands. One lay with her drum as with a lover. Another, hair disheveled, skirts and ornaments in disarray, was like a woman crushed by an elephant and then dropped. Many were noisily breathing; others, bright eyes wide and motionless, lay as dead. One with her person exposed, with fully developed limbs, drooled saliva as though intoxicated. And all, with their garments variously astray, were lost to shame and helpless, who had before been possessed of all grace. They were like a lake of lotuses broken by a wind.

The prince considered. "Such is the nature of women: impure and monstrous in the world of living beings! Deceived by dress, a man becomes infatuated by their charms. But let him regard their natural state, this change produced in them by sleep!"

And he rose, with a will only to escape into the night.

8B. THE GREAT DEPARTURE

The gods caused the door of the palace to fly open, and the prince descended to the court, going directly to his charioteer. "Quick!" he said; "I am leaving." And the man, knowing the king's command, yet urged in his mind by a stronger force, brought forth the beautiful white steed Kanthaka, whom the prince with his lotus hand caressed. "O best of steeds," said he; "the king, my father, riding thee, has overthrown many foes. So do thou now exert thyself, for thine own good and that of the world, that I too may be a victor." And that steed, when the prince had mounted, galloped forth in silence at full speed. The earth demons received its hoofs upon their palms, so that their clatter should not wake the night. And the charioteer, Chandaka, ran swiftly at the bridle. The city gates, closed with heavy bars, opened of their own accord, without noise. And the rider, having passed them, looking back, roared with the sound of a lion.

"Till I have seen the farther shore of birth and death, I will never enter again the city named for Kapila."

And having heard that mighty lion voice, the troops of the gods rejoiced.

The adventure had begun that was to shape the civilization of the larger portion of the human race. The lion roar, the sound of the solar spirit, the principle of the pure light of the mind, unafraid of its own force, had broken forth in the night of stars. And as the sun, rising, sending forth its rays, scatters both the terrors and the raptures of the night: as the lion roar, sending its warning out across the teeming animal plain, scatters the marvelously beautiful gazelles in fear: so that lion roar of the one who had thus come gave warning of a lion pounce of light to come.

Along the way of the one who had thus broken forth from the palace of nets of gold and gossamer set to catch and trammel lion hearts, heavenly beings strewed light; and at dawn the prince, no longer a prince, arrived at a forest hermitage, for what was to be his first adventure on the road of fire. Its gazelles and deer were still asleep in quiet trust and its birds tranquilly resting. And thus coming suddenly upon it, the Future Buddha, too, became restful, as though his goal had been attained.

He alighted from his steed, stroked him with a few words, and turned to the charioteer. "Good friend, your devotion to me and your courage of soul have been proved by your pacing of this mount." And he gave the man a great jewel, removed from his diadem, requiring him to return with the mount to Kapilavastu. "I am not to be mourned," he said. "Nor have I departed at a wrong time for the forest. There is, in fact, no wrong time for religion."

Chandaka was choked with tears. "O master! What will your poor father say, and your queen with her little son? And O Master, at your feet is my only refuge. What is to become of me?"

The Future Buddha replied, "As birds resort to their roosting tree but depart, so must the meetings of all beings end inevitably in separation. My good friend, do not grieve, but depart; and if your love lingers on, some day return. To those in Kapilavastu say only that I shall either return having slain old age and death, or else myself perish, having failed."

Hearing this, the horse, dropping its head, let fall hot tears and licked its feet. The prince stroked him. "Thy perfect equine nature," he said, "has been proved. Weep not, good Kanthaka. Thy deed shall have its fruit."

Whereupon he drew from its sheath his sharp jeweled sword, dark blue, with gold-ornamented blade. And having drawn it forth, he severed with a single stroke the lordly topknot of his own hair. Together with its diadem, he tossed this high into the air, where the gods, seizing it respectfully, carried it with cries of joy to heaven for adoration.

ITEM 9. THE SEARCH FOR THE WAY

With a stride like a lion, beautiful as a deer, the Future Buddha entered the grove; and all within, pre-eminent in penances, left off their diligences. Delighted, the peacocks uttered cries; the oblation-giving cows poured forth their milk. Ascetics grazing like deer stood still, together with the deer. And the prince said to those who approached, "Good sirs, since this, today, is my first hermit grove, will you explain, please, the purposes of these works?"

"Leaves, water, roots, and fruits, uncultivated food," he was told: "this and this alone is the fare of these good saints. Some, like birds, peck at seeds; others graze, like deer. Some live on air and dwell like snakes among the ants that they have allowed to

pile up hills around them. A few, with immense effort, gain their
nouriture from stones. More eat grain ground with their own teeth.
Some, like fish, dwell in the water, letting turtles scratch their
flesh; while many, with matted hair continually wet, offer oblations
to Agni, chanting hymns. For pain, we say, is the root of merit.
Heaven is gained by greater penances, earthy goals by lesser; but
in either case, it is by the path of pain that eventually bliss will be
attained."

Thought the Future Buddha: "It is at best heaven that they are
gaining. But if pain is religion and happiness irreligion, then by
religion they are gaining irreligion. Since, however, it is only by the
mind that the body acts or acts not, what should be controlled is
not the body, but thought. Without thought, the body is but a log.
Nor will water wash away sin."

That was an argument borrowed by the young prince from the
psychological school of Kapila, by which were refuted both Jainism
and the crude, even more cruel extremes of such sheerly physical,
yogic disciplines as those of this hermit grove. However, a second
thought conceived on this occasion, as presented in our Mahayana
text, points beyond Kapila toward the ultimate founding of the
popular religion that would emerge, one day, from the Buddha's
finding and teaching of his Middle Way. The Future Buddha
mused: "If a place on earth is to be sought that might properly be
termed holy, let it be one where there is something that has been
touched by a virtuous man. I would count as goals of pilgrimage
only the virtues of those who have manifested virtue."

There is already in this thought a rationalization of the later,
popular Buddhist cult of relics; and the broad appeal of a religious,
in contrast to philosophical, way of redemption is prescribed. For
the influence finally intended here is not to be upon thought alone,
but upon character. Thought in itself may transform character;
but even the mere presence of a personage may also work such a
miracle of change. The curious popular eagerness just to see,
touch, and gather souvenirs from "personalities," which in the
West today is not regarded generally as a variety of religious
effort, in the Orient is exactly that, as it was in our own Middle

Ages; and the Future Buddha, in this biography, is supposed to have been prepared to accommodate this desire to his system, as a popular, secondary, but by no means inconsequential adjunct. The Ceylonese relic of the Buddha's Tooth and the relics preserved everywhere in the reliquary mounds (*stūpas*) of the Buddhist world, bring to the mind those thoughts of the virtues of the virtuous by which "sins"—that is to say, wrong thoughts, and, consequently, wrong words and acts—are washed away.

The Future Buddha remained but a few nights in that diligent, peaceful hermit grove, watching the yogis at their penances, and when he turned to go, they all gathered, imploring him not to leave. "With your coming," said one old man, "this hermitage became filled. My son, surely you will not leave us now. In front of us, we have the holy Himalayas to regard, inhabited by saints; their presence multiplies the merit of our penances. Nearby are numerous centers of pilgrimage: ladders to heaven. Or have you perhaps seen someone here neglecting his offices? some outcaste? someone impure? Speak out, and we shall gladly hear!'"

The author of this text, c. 100 A.D., the reader must know, had been of the Brahmin caste himself before joining the Buddhist order, and is humorously satirizing here the pieties of his own earlier belief: the grim austerities of the forest yogis, their reverence for the mighty Himalayas, glorification of pilgrimage, notions of spiritual merit, and reckonings of caste.

"Good saints," said the Future Buddha, "this devotion of yours is to gain heaven, whereas my desire is no further birth. Cessation is not the same as action. Therefore, I cannot dwell longer in this holy wood. All here, like the great Vedic sages, are well established in their religious tasks, which are in perfect accord with the way of former times."

The gathered ascetics paid him due respect; and a certain red-eyed Brahmin lying there in ashes lifted his voice. "You are brave indeed, O sage, in your purpose. Indeed, any man who, pondering the alternatives thoroughly of heaven and liberation, decides for liberation, is brave! And so, go now to the sage Arada. He is one who has gained insight into perfect bliss."

The Future Buddha started on his way, but two interruptions intervened before his arrival at Arada's cell. For when his dismissed charioteer returned to the palace without his lord, but with a steed that refused to eat and turning to the forest neighed repeatedly with mournful sound, the king, who was in the temple at the time, was told the news and fell to the ground. Lifted by attendants, he gazed upon the empty saddle and fell back to the ground. Then a counselor offered to fetch the son and, with the king's blessing, mounting a chariot, reached the hermitage, where they told him that the prince had proceeded to Arada. He overtook the prince, descended, and approached.

"O Prince, consider," he said; and he rehearsed the whole case at home. But the answer gave no hope. "I shall return home," said the Future Buddha, "only with knowledge of the truth. And should I fail in my quest I would enter a blazing fire sooner than my house."

The counselor turned back; and the other, crossing the Ganges, came to the city of Rajagriha, where the king, Bimbisara, noticing from his palace an accumulating crowd slowly moving through the street, asked the reason and was told. The young mendicant left the city and proceeded up the side of a neighboring hill, where Bimbisara followed with a modest retinue and presently saw him sitting as still as the mountain itself. The king, a lion among men, respectfully approached, sat upon the clean surface of a rock, and, at the nod of the other, addressed him.

"Gentle youth, I have a strong friendship with your family; and if, for some reason, you do not wish your father's kingdom, then accept, here and now, one-half of mine. You are a lover of religion: but they say that to the young man belong pleasures; to the middle-aged wealth and goods; religion to the old. You should enjoy your pleasures now. However, if religion is really your sole aim, well then, it behooves you to offer sacrifice according to the manner of your race and in this way merit highest heaven."

The prince replied. And when he had spoken, first of gratitude for the king's friendship, but then of old age, disease, and death, and of the pains of those who desire pleasure, he declared that he had quit the world absolutely, not set his mind on higher goals.

"And as to what you have just said, namely, that I should be diligent in sacrifices worthy of my race, which bring glorious fruit: honor to such. I desire no fruit obtained by causing pain and death. But I have come this way, to visit Arada, the seer; and am on my way to him this very day. So now, therefore, you may guard the world, O King, like Indra; guard it continually, like the Sun; guard its happiness; guard the earth; and guard religion."

Bimbisara lifted his joined hands before his face. "Go!" he said. "You are on the road to your desire. And when, at last, you have gained your victory, come this way and bestow on us your grace."

The king returned to his palace. The prince arose and went his way. And the sage Arada, in his rocky forest cell, perceiving him from afar, bade him welcome with a loud cry. Wide-eyed, he addressed him as he approached.

"It is no marvel when kings retire to the forest in old age, turning over their glory to their sons, a garland dropped after being used. But this to me is indeed a marvel. You are a worthy vessel."

The prince, sitting down, asked to be taught, and the sage rehearsed for him the whole lesson of the master sage, Kapila.

"What is born, must of necessity grow old and die; it is bound by the laws of time and is termed the manifest, from which the unmanifest is to be distinguished by contrariety.

"Now, as to the cause of temporal existence: it is threefold, namely, ignorance, action, and desire, each leading to the other two. No one abiding in this cycle attains to the truth of things.

"Such wrong abiding is the prime mistake, from which derive, in series: egoity, confusion, indiscrimination, false means (rites and the rest are false means), attachment, and the misery of gravitation. One imagines 'This am I,' then 'This is mine,' whereupon one is drawn downward to new births.

"So let the wise know these four things: the manifest and the unmanifest; unenlightenment and enlightenment. Knowing these, one may apprehend the immortal."

The listener asked the means to such knowing, and the old sage, Arada, taught:

"First of all, the mendicant life. The practice there of restraint of the senses leads to contentment, wherein the first stage of contemplation is experienced: a new ecstasy and delight. The wise go on to a second stage: a higher, more luminous ecstasy and delight. Continuing to a third, one arrives at ecstasy without delight, where many take their stand; but there is a fourth stage of contemplation, namely, without ecstasy; and the truly wise go even beyond that, to be rid of all sense of body.

"Now to experience the void of the body, one may first make use in contemplation of all the openings of one's body, proceeding thence to a feeling of void in the solid parts. Or, considering the dweller in the body to be all space, one may develop this consideration beyond space, recognizing a yet more refined void. A third way is to abolish the sense of being a person by considering the supreme Person.

"Then, like a bird from its cage, the person, escaped from the body, is said to be liberated. This we call that supreme Person— eternal, unchanging, void of attributes—the knowledge of which the wise, who know reality, term Release.

"So I have shown you both the goal and the way, and if you have both understood and approved, now act."

The Future Buddha had pondered, but not accepted.

"I have heard your subtle teaching, profound, pre-eminently auspicious; yet it cannot be final, for it does not teach how to be rid of the Person, the supreme Self itself. Though the self purified may be termed free, yet as long as that Self remains, there is no real abandonment of egoity. Moreover, if the Self in its pristine state is free, how did it become bound? I hold that the only absolute attainment is in absolute abandonment."

He rose, and, bowing, departed from the sage Arada.

And he went to another sage, Udraka, who had found his restlessness set at rest in the idea that there is nothing either named or unnamed. This he termed the view beyond name and non-name, beyond the manifest and unmanifest.

Listening and rising, the Future Buddha left the sage Udraka too.

And he came to a pleasant hermitage by the lovely stream

Nairanjana, where he joined five mendicants in a way of discipline based on progressively severe fasting; until, having only skin and bone remaining, emaciated to no purpose, he considered: "But this, certainly, is not the way to passionlessness, knowledge, and liberation, which cannot be attained without strength."

Whereupon he recalled his own earliest meditation at the foot of the rose apple tree, when, having seen death everywhere in a plowed field, he had alighted from his horse and gone apart to ponder alone. "That," he thought, "was the true way." And he thought further: "Perfect calm, the mind's self-possession, can be gained only by the constant, perfect satisfaction of the senses. Contemplation is produced when the mind, self-possessed, is at rest. And through contemplation that supremely calm, undecaying state is eventually gained which is so difficult to attain. All of which is based upon eating food."

And so, once again he arose. And, having bathed, thin as he was, in the lovely stream Nairanjana, supported by the trees along the shore as by a hand, he came back onto the bank.

The lovely daughter, Nandabala, of a leading herdsman of those parts, moved and guided by the gods, approached him where he sat and, bowing before him with a sudden joy arising in her heart, offered him a rich bowl of milk, by which his body was restored; but the five mendicants, considering him to have returned to the world, departed. And he rose and, alone, went to the Bodhi-tree, accompanied only by his own resolve, where he placed himself— as we have heard—on the Immovable Spot.

ITEMS 10 AND 11. THE GREAT AWAKENING

We are told in this Mahayana version of the Acts of the Buddha that when the Lord of Death (*māra*), whom we call in the world Delight (*kāma*), had failed in his effort to unseat him, the Blessed One recalled in the first watch of that night the multitude of his former lives and, thinking, "All existence whatsoever is unsubstantial," felt compassion for all beings. In his search for the pass beyond sorrow he had already marked out the Middle Way between devotion to pleasure (*kāma*) and to pain (*māra*), and now, as the first fruit of his passage between the clashing rocks of those two extremes, he was experiencing a further reach of the Middle Way; namely, on the one hand, a realization that all beings are without a self (*anātman*), and yet, simultaneously, a compassion for all beings (*karunā*).

This we may term the fundamental posture of the Buddhist mind. The serious commitment of the Occidental mind to the concerns and value of the living person is fundamentally dismissed, as it is in Jainism as well, and in the Sankhya too. However, the usual Oriental concern for the monad also is dismissed. *There is no reincarnating hero-monad to be saved, released, or found.* All life is sorrowful, and yet, there is no self, no being, no entity, in sorrow. There is no reason, consequently, to feel loathing, shock, or nausea, before the spectacle of the world; but, on the contrary, the only feeling appropriate is compassion (*karunā*), which is immediately felt, in fact, when the paradoxical, incommunicable truth is realized that all these suffering beings are in reality—no beings.

By what principle of delusion, then, has it come to pass that so many beings—though without a self—are to such a degree self-concerned that they suppose their own and others' sufferings to constitute a cosmic problem, saying, "Life is something that should not have been"?

The answer came to the Blessed One in the second watch of that night, when he received divine sight and beheld the world as in a spotless mirror: the torments of the damned, the transmigration of souls into beasts, and all varieties of birth, impure and pure. He clearly saw then that where there is birth there is inevitably old age, disease, and death; where there has been attachment there is birth; where there is desire there is attachment; where a perception, there desire; where a contact, there perception; where the organs of sense, there contact; where an organism, there organs of sense; where incipient consciousness, there an organism; where inclinations derived from acts, there incipient consciousness; and where ignorance, there inclinations.

Ignorance, therefore, must be declared to be the root.

By the discontinuance of ignorance, the sufferings of all existing beings are discontinued.

The Blessed One considered. "This, then, is the cause of suffering in the world of living beings; and this, therefore, is the method for its discontinuance."

From 1, ignorance, there proceed in series: 2. acts, 3. new inclinations, 4. incipient consciousness (portending further life), 5. an organism, 6. organs of sense, 7. contact, 8. perceptions, 9. desire, 10. attachment, 11. rebirth, and 12. old age, disease, and death.

He had found what he had set forth to seek. He was awake: "the one who had seen." He was the Buddha.

11 (CONTINUED). THE FESTIVAL OF GREAT JOY

A great deal has been written about Buddhist belief, and there is enough disagreement about the meaning of the twelve-linked chain of causation (*pratītya-samutpāda*), just now described, to leave the problem pretty much in the air. The main point of the doctrine is clear enough, however, which is, namely, that, since all things are without a self, no one has to *attain* extinction; everyone is, in fact, already extinct and has always been so. Ignorance, however, leads to the notion and therefore experience of an entity in pain. And not disdain or loathing, but compassion is to be felt for those suffering beings who, if they were only quit of their ego-notion, would know—and experience the fact—that there is no suffering person anywhere at all.

The Buddha, when he had achieved this illumination, thought: "But how shall I teach a wisdom so difficult to grasp?"

This, therefore, is the second point; briefly, that Buddhism cannot be taught. What are taught are simply the ways that lead from various points of the spiritual compass to the Bodhi-tree; and to know those ways is not enough. To see the tree is not enough. Even to go sit beneath the tree is not enough. Each has to find and sit beneath the tree himself and then, in solitary thought, begin the passage into and to himself, who is nowhere at all.

The gods strewed flowers from the sky, and the Buddha, on a throne, ascending in the air to seven times the height of a palm tree, addressed the Bodhisattvas of all time. "Ho! Ho! Listen now to my words," he called, illumining their minds. "It is by meritorious acts that all is achieved. By such acts, through many lives, I became first a Bodhisattva and am now the Victor, All-Wise. Therefore, as long as life remains, acquire merit!"

So that here, then, is a third point, the chief point of the Mahayana, as opposed to Hinayana, way. It is known as the Bodhisattva Way, the way of living in the world, not retiring to the forest: acquiring an experience and thereby knowledge of the truth of egolessness through giving—boundless giving—doing selflessly one's life task.

The Bodhisattvas of all time, having paid worship to the Buddha, disappeared, and the gods arrived, strewing flowers; whereupon the Victor, descending to the level of the earth, stood on his throne, transfixed in thought for seven days, and his only thought was: "I have here attained perfect wisdom."

The earth shook six different ways, like a woman overjoyed; myriads of universes were illumined; and the beings of all the worlds, descending, moved around the Buddha in circumambulation, returning to their homes.

Another seven days, and he was bathed by heavenly beings with jars of the water of the four oceans.

A third period of seven days, and he remained seated with closed eyes.

A fourth period of seven days, and he was standing on his throne, assuming many forms, when a god, descending, asked the name of the meditation of the past four weeks. "It is called, O divine being," the Buddha said, "the Array of the Aliment of Great Joy. It is the festival of an inaugurated king, who, having conquered all his foes, now enjoys prosperity. The former Buddhas, too, remained, as I am here remaining, beneath their Bodhi-trees."

The heavens darkened for seven days, and a prodigious rain descended. However, the mighty king of serpents, Muchalinda, came from beneath the earth and protected with his hood the one who is the source of all protection. When the great storm had cleared, the serpent king assumed his human form, bowed before the Buddha, and returned in joy to his palace.*

The Buddha moved to a large fig tree, where he sat for seven days more; after which he moved gradually to other places. Two wealthy merchants begged for bits of his hair and nails for the building of a reliquary shrine. The four gods of the quarters arrived with the gift of four begging bowls that became one, from which the Victor sipped an offering of milk. And a goddess, daughter of the gods, smiling, brought to him for his investiture a garment of rags.[23]

VI. Nirvana

It is extremely difficult for an Occidental mind to realize how deep the impersonality of the Oriental lies. But if anything at all is ever to be understood of that profoundly alien world into dialogue with which our will to life and abundance now has brought us, the image has to be abandoned, which a considerable company of sentimentalists has been painting for us, of a sort of pre-Raphaelite Buddha-soul sitting harmlessly on a lotus, deliquescing into nirvana with love for all beings in its lotus heart.

Once the Venerable Ananda approached the Lord and said: "It is wonderful, O Master, that while the Conditioned Arising that you have taught is so deep and looks so deep, to me it seems perfectly clear."

"Do not talk like that, Ananda; for this Conditioned Arising that I have taught is deep and looks deep too. It is from not awakening to this truth, Ananda, from not penetrating it, that this generation has become tangled like a ball of thread, covered as with a blight, twisted like a rope of grass, and cannot win release from sorrow, from circumstantiating evil, from the maelstrom, from this cycling round."[24]

The earliest significant meeting of East and West on the level of

* Compare Figure 20 and supra, pp. 218–19. The episode of the serpent in the Parshva life, it will be observed, coincides with that of the breakthrough. Here it comes after enlightenment, and represents a theme of reconciliation with the force of nature that supports the world. The serpent, born from itself anew when sloughing its skin, is symbolic of the lunar principle of eternal return.

an attempt at philosophical exchange occurred when that first and most vivid Westerner of all arrived: the young Alexander the Great. Having smashed the whole Persian empire with a single mighty blow, he came crashing through and appeared in the Indus Valley, 327 B.C., to engage immediately in philosophical as well as political, economic, and geographical observations. We are told by Strabo that in Taxila, the first Indian capital that he entered, Alexander and his officers learned of a set of philosophers sitting in session outside the city; and imagining counterparts of their own teachers and models (Alexander's tutor, Aristotle, or that glorious chatterbox, Socrates), they sent an embassy to invite the learned circle to Alexander's table. And what they found were fifteen stark-naked chaps sitting motionless on a sun-baked stretch of rock so hot that no one could step on it without shoes. The captain of the embassy, Onesicritus, letting one of those gentlemen know through a series of three interpreters that he and his king wished to be taught something of their wisdom, the reply came back that no one arriving in the bravery of top boots, a broad-brimmed hat, and flashing cavalry coat, such as the Macedonian was wearing, could be taught philosophy: the candidate—did he come from God himself—should first be naked and have learned to sit peacefully on broiling rock. The Greek, whose own master had been Diogenes, undaunted by this taunt, talked to a second naked thinker about Pythagoras, Socrates, Plato, and the rest; and the Indian, conceding that such men must have been of great parts, nevertheless expressed regret and surprise that they should have retained so much respect for the laws and customs of their folk as to have denied themselves the higher life by remaining clothed.

Strabo goes on to tell that two of the company, an elder and a younger, nevertheless, were finally persuaded by the raja of Taxila to Alexander's board, but as they left the rock they were followed by the round abuse of their fellows and, when they returned, retired to a place apart. There the elder lay on his back, exposed to sun and rain, while the younger stood on his right and left leg alternately for a whole day, holding up a staff some six feet long in both hands.[25]

Another of the group, whom the Greeks nicknamed Kalanos because when greeting people he used the word *kalyāna,* "luck," actually joined the entourage for a time, where he became a notable figure among the men of war and philosophers around the young king. However, when the army, turning westward, arrived in Persia, he bade Alexander have a great pyre built, to which he was carried on a litter, garlanded in the Indian way and chanting in a tongue the Greeks could not understand. In the sight of the army he mounted and assumed the cross-legged seated posture of a yogi. The construction had been covered with gold and silver vessels, precious stuffs, and other treasures, which he distributed to his friends, after which he ordered the torch to be applied. The Greek trumpets sounded all together. The whole army shouted, as when going into battle. The Indian elephants uttered their peculiar cry. Flames, mounting, enwrapped the figure, which the beholders saw sitting motionless.[26] And Kalanos, taking leave thus of the Greeks, was immediately reborn, we may suppose, in perhaps the Heaven of the Neck, to remain for numerous millions of oceans of indefinite periods of years in some inconceivable state of delight.

Now, it is amazing, but this Greek report is the earliest known tangible evidence of the practice of yoga in Aryan India. For there is not a single piece either of writing or of chiseled stone to mark the whole stretch of time from the ruin of the Indus cities to the year of Alexander's coming. Following that event, however, developments, first political and then in the arts, brought those things to view, as though by sudden magic, from which the whole panorama of the earlier Vedic and first Buddhist centuries has been reconstructed by the no less marvelous magic of philology— to which, in recent years, the wizardry of archaeology has been added.

The expectation of the yogis encountered by Onesicritus that philosophers worthy of the name should reject the laws and customs of their folk, remove their clothes in illustration of this dropping of the world, and retire to a broiling rock, demonstrates that by 327 B.C., at the latest, the fundamental Indian notion of the goal of human life was already developed that inspires to this day all typically Indian thought and is the inspiration, finally, of that bromide about the Indian being "spiritual" and the Westerner "materialistic" which has become a sort of axiom of the international arena—including the fashionable cocktail circuit, where the Indians sip tomato juice. Among the Jains, who represent this dualistic view *in extremis,* the altogether physical reading of the problem of disengagement conduced, as we have seen, to a clean-cut, unequivocal development of progressed vows, graduating from the bound condition of the layman to the freedom, after many lives, of the Victor. "The universe," we read in a typical text, "is constituted of jiva and non-jiva. When these are separated, nothing more is needed; but when united, as they are in the world, the discontinuance and the gradual and then final dissolution of their union are the only possible considerations." [27] And in the Sankhya system, also, as we have learned from the sage Arada, the concept of an essential separation of the spiritual person (*puruṣa*) from the world of matter (*prakṛti*) confirmed the view that the mendicant life, with control of the senses, etc., was the one true way to that state of spiritual isolation (*kaivalyam*) which is the one true goal for man. Likewise, in the earliest body of Buddhist writings, that of the Ceylonese Pali canon of c. 80 B.C., such an ideal, in its purity, is held above all others. And the Buddhist schools derived from this center, the so-called Southern Schools of Burma, Thailand, and Cambodia, give unquestioned primacy to this (from the worldly standpoint) negative ideal, its symbol being the Buddha as a monk. As we read in one of the early psalms of the order:

> Each by himself, we in the forest dwell,
> Like logs rejected by the woodman's craft;
> And many a one doth envy me my lot,
> E'en as the hell-bound him who fares to heaven.[28]

However, in the earliest Buddhist monuments of stone, namely those of the first great layman of the faith, King Ashoka, who reigned c. 268–232 B.C., two centuries earlier than the writing of the canon, it appears that a contrary ideal and mythology were already beginning to develop around the figure of the man living in the world as the Buddha lived for innumerable lifetimes—and is living now in each one of us—gaining nirvana not by the cessation, but by the performance, of acts. And in the course of the following centuries, culminating in the period of the reign of King Kanishka, c. 78–123 A.D. (or, according to another reckoning: c. 120–162 A.D.),[29] this secular theme was developed to such a point that the earlier, monastic, world-negating view was fundamentally challenged as an archaic misinterpretation of the Middle Way. The term bodhisattva, "one whose being (*sattva*) is enlightenment (*bodhi*)," had been employed in the earlier vocabulary of the Ceylonese Pali Canon * to designate one on the way to realization but not yet arrived: a Buddha in his earlier lives, a Future Buddha. In the new vocabulary of the Sanskrit canon, on the other hand, which developed in the north and northwest of India proper in the first centuries A.D., the term was used to represent the sage who, while living in the world, has refused the boon of cessation yet achieved realization, and so remains a perfect knower in the world as a beacon, guide, and compassionate savior of all beings.

For if, as the Buddha announced, there is no self anywhere to be found, if all are already extinct, and if what should be controlled is not the body but thought—then why all this talk about a voyage to and arrival at the yonder shore? We are already there. Some, indeed, to control their minds, may have to shave their heads, pick up bowls, hie away to the country, and look at deer instead of men. But those truly endowed for the wisdom of the Buddha can put their minds in order at home, and at the same time be of help to others in the realization of the wisdom of the Buddha in their own lived lives. For, as Heinrich Zimmer once remarked: "The radio station WOB, Wisdom of the Buddha, is broadcasting all the time: all we need is a receiving set."

We have seen how Ashvaghosha handled the introduction of the Bodhisattva theme into the scene of the night of Enlightenment, where it had not existed before. On a throne, ascending in the

* The actual form of the word in Pali is *bodhisatta;* but I am using Sanskrit forms throughout this work, as sufficient for our purpose.

air to seven times the height of a palm tree, the newly illuminated Buddha addressed the Bodhisattvas of all time: "It is by meritorious acts that everything is achieved." Then he descended to the earth and the normal course of the scene was resumed. Likewise, in a later episode of importance, that of the first turning of the Wheel of the Law in the Deer Park of Benares, Ashvaghosha added to the usual sermon, delivered to the five starved ascetics with whom Gautama had spent the last phase of his years of quest, a second message, delivered not to anyone on earth but to Maitreya, the Future Buddha, who was waiting in the Heaven of the Happy Gods to be born five thousand years after the passing of Gautama, and had come, together with numerous gods and Bodhisattvas, to attend this First Turning of the Wheel of the Law.

"Everything subject to causation," said the Buddha to Maitreya and those about him, "is like a mirage, a dream, the moon beheld in water, an echo: neither removable, nor self-subsistent. And the Wheel of the Law itself is described as neither 'it is' nor 'it is not.' And having heard this Law and welcomed it with joy, go on now forever in happiness. For this, sirs, is the Mahayana, set forth by all the Buddhas. By worshiping the Buddhas, the Bodhisattvas, the Pratyeka Buddhas [Buddhas who do not teach] and the Arhats [illuminated sages], a man will generate in his mind the idea of Buddhahood and proclaim the Law in good works. So that where this pure doctrine prevails, even the householder dwelling in his house becomes a Buddha." [30]

Thus the Mahayana, "The Great (mahā) Ferry (yāna)," is a vessel on which all may ride—and in fact are riding—going absolutely nowhere, since all are already extinct. It is a pleasure ride, a festival of joy. Whereas the Hinayana, "The Abandoned (hīna) Ferry (yāna)," is a comparatively small, diligent work-launch, transporting only yogis across a maelstrom they despise, on the way to nowhere at all! So that they, finally, are on a pleasure voyage too, but seem not to know it.

As the Reverend Hpe Aung, a distinguished master of the Burmese order, recently described the main stages of insight of the Hinayana Buddhist yogi passage, they are as follows.

1. The insight that all is impermanent, sorrowful, and without a self
2. The insight regarding the beginning and ending of things
3. The insight regarding the destruction of things
4. The insight that the world is dreadful
5. The insight that such a dreadful world is full of emptiness and vanity
6. The insight that such a world should be loathed
7. The insight that the world should be forsaken
8. The insight that liberation should be realized
9. The insight that equilibrium should be observed in spite of the vicissitudes of life
10. The insight that adaptation has to be made for the realization of nirvana.

"Buddhists are optimistic," he wrote, "because, though the world is full of sufferings, yet, to a Buddhist, there is a way out of it." [31]

And so, although recognizing that the aim of the Jains to break away from the world of matter and achieve isolation physically, that of the Sankhya to realize the actuality of isolation psychologically, and that of the Buddhist monk to realize the actuality of nonentity psychologically, represent differences of importance to actual practitioners of the art of yoga, we must nevertheless classify all three of these monastic ways as variants of the single mythic category of the Great Reversal.

In the Mahayana, on the other hand, in spite of the fact that a reverence for the monk, the arhat, and the Buddha remains characteristic to the end, a powerful, ever growing theme developed of world wonder and affirmation, symbolized by the image of the Bodhisattva. For whereas the Hinayana represents the mystery of nirvana from the point of view of the normal dualistic thought of the world, where it is supposed that there is a difference between the vicissitudes of the cycle and the peace of eternal liberation, the Mahayana sees the world from the point of view of the realized void, eternity itself, and knows that to experience a distinction between the peace of that void and the tumult of this world, non-being and being, is to remain deluded by the dualistic categories of sense.

The Buddha said, according to one of these Mahayana texts of the Wisdom of the Yonder Shore, "All that has form is deceptive. But when it is seen that all form is no form, the Buddha is recognized. . . . All things are Buddha things." [32]

And with this we have come to the fifth and culminating component of the primary Indian mythic complex.

The first, we have seen, was laid down in the Indus Valley system: a vegetal-lunar mythology of wonder and submission before destiny, in two aspects: a) the proto-Australoid, of a burgeoning tropical plant world, and b) the High-Bronze Age, hieratic, derived from the Near East, of a cosmic order (*maat, me*), mathematically determinable and visually manifest in the planetary cycles.

The second was the leonine Aryan power system of the Vedas, which is also to be noted in two aspects: a) an earlier, in which deities were the final terms of reference, and b) a later, in which the power of the Brahminic liturgy itself was the final term. We have observed, also, that in contrast to the Semitic view, where catastrophe and suffering are read as punishments sent upon guilty men by a god, the Aryan disposition has always been to regard such calamity as the work, rather, of demons, with the gods on the side of man. In the course of time in India the Vedic freely willing gods lost command, and the earlier Bronze Age principle of order (*maat, me, ṛta, dharma*) returned ineluctably. Yet, as masters of the liturgies in which the principle of order was subsumed, the priestly caste retained command—not over destiny itself, but over the distribution of its effects. *Vidyā*, "knowledge," was of the cosmic order and "He who knows thus" (as we read throughout both the Brahmanas and the Upanishads) can do practically anything he wills.

Component three of the Indian mythic complex, then, was yoga, defined, in terms of the present subject, as a technique for achieving mythic identification. A number of its disciplines appear to have been derived from shamanism; as, for example, the regulation of the breath and use of dance, rhythmic sounds, drugs, controlled meditations, etc., for the production of inner heat, ecstasy, and possession. On this primitive level identifications are achieved with various shamanistic birds and beasts (the wolf, bear, fox, raven, eagle, wild gander, etc.), and the powers gained include, besides that of assuming such animal forms, a mastery of and immunity from fire, ecstatic flight, invisibility, passage beyond the bounds of earth and to upper and lower realms, resurrection, knowledge of former lives, and miraculous cures. Much of the character and fame of yoga in the villages of India is on that level to this day. However, in the Indus Valley context we have seen figures in classic yoga posture resembling, on the one hand, Shiva as Lord of Beasts (*paśupati*) and, on the other, Gautama Buddha in the Deer Park of Benares and the Lord Parshva between serpents. The indication is obvious that yoga in its specifically Indian character had already been developed in association with an iconography that remains with it to the present, but we do not know what its aims were at that time. The seal of Figure 17, showing a presentation scene before the goddess of the Tree of Enlightenment, suggests a theme of ritual regicide in the period of the Indus Valley system, and it may be supposed, therefore, that the lord of yoga was the sacrificed king himself; in which case the lunar god would have been the most likely term of identification —but we do not know. In the much later, Vedic-Aryan period of the Upanishads, both lunar and solar mythologies were embraced in the yoga taught to the Brahmins by the learned kings; so that both lunar and solar identifications are firmly documented for a period c. 700–600 B.C. And we know also that with the subsequent juncture of non-Vedic yoga with the Vedic power system in its second stage, stage b), the ultimate term with which the yogi might strive to become identified lay beyond all gods whatever, in the power, *brahman,* of the sacrifice, now recognized as the ground of all being.

The fourth essential component of the Indian mythic complex, the mood of absolute world loathing of the Great Reversal, appears to have been known to the teaching kings of the Upanishads; for they refer in illustration of the solar way, the Way of Flame, to those who have quit the world for the forest. We know also that in both Egypt and Mesopotamia a lamentation literature had

developed as early as c. 1750 B.C.* It can be supposed that in
the Indus Valley, as well, a mood of world- and life-negation
overcame many of the native non-Aryan population in their period
of collapse, when the Vedic warrior folk arrived, c. 1500–1200 B.C.
But whereas in neither Egypt nor Mesopotamia does anyone seem
to have found a practical answer to the problem of escape from
sorrow, in India yoga supplied the means. Instead of striving for
mythic identity with any being or principle of the object world,
the meditating world-deniers now began—perhaps already c. 1000
B.C.—the great (and, I believe, uniquely) Indian adventure of
the negative way: "not that, not that (*neti neti*)." We have named
three stages of this path of exit from the field. The first was that
of the Jains, who strove for the separation physically of jiva and
non-jiva through progressive vows of life-renunciation. The second
was that of the Sankhya philosophy of Kapila and the yoga system
of Patanjali, where the subject of knowledge, Purusha, was conceived to rest forever apart from the object world of matter, and the
crucial task was simply that of achieving in the mind full knowledge of one's identity with Purusha, the subject of all knowledge:
"the energy of intellect grounded in itself." [33] Whereas in the
victory of the Buddha even that subject was erased, and the sole
term became the void: which was—and remains—the posture of
the Hinayana.

However, at this juncture a fifth and final factor entered the
field of Indian thought; for, as every schoolboy knows, two negatives make a positive. The double negative, canceling identification both with object and with subject, led to an ironic return to
life without commitment to anything at all, but with compassion
(*karunā*) equally for all. For all things are void.

Nietzsche in *Thus Spake Zarathustra* describes what he terms
"three metamorphoses of the spirit": the camel, the lion, the
child.

> There is much that is difficult for the spirit, the strong
> reverent spirit that would bear much: but the difficult and
> most difficult are what its strength demands.
> What is difficult? asks the spirit that would bear much, and

* Supra, pp. 137–44.

kneels down like a camel wanting to be well loaded. . . . And like the camel that, burdened, speeds into the desert, the spirit then speeds into the desert.

In the loneliest desert, however, the second metamorphosis occurs. Here the spirit becomes a lion who would conquer his freedom and be master in his own desert. Here he seeks out his last master: he wants to fight him and his last god; for ultimate victory he wants to fight with the great dragon.

Who is the great dragon whom the spirit will no longer call lord and god? "Thou shalt" is the name of the great dragon. But the spirit of the lion says, "I will." "Thou shalt" lies in his way, sparkling like gold, an animal covered with scales; and on every scale shines a golden "Thou shalt."

Values, thousands of years old, shine on these scales; and thus speaks the mightiest of all dragons: "All value of all things shines on me. All value has long been created, and I am all created value. Verily, there shall be no more 'I will.' " Thus speaks the dragon.

My brothers, why is there a need in the spirit for the lion? Why is not the beast of burden, which renounces and is reverent, enough?

To create new values—that even the lion cannot do; but the creation of freedom for oneself for new creation—that is within the power of the lion. The creation of freedom for one-self and a sacred "No" even to duty—for that, my brothers, the lion is needed. To assume the right to new values—that is the most terrifying assumption for a reverent spirit that would bear much. Verily, to him it is preying, and a matter for a beast of prey. He once loved "Thou shalt" as most sacred: now he must find illusion and caprice even in the most sacred, that freedom from his love may become his prey: the lion is needed for such prey.

But say, my brothers, what can the child do that even the lion could not do? Why must the preying lion still become a child? The child is innocence and forgetting, a new beginning, a game, a self-propelled wheel, a first movement, a sacred "Yes." For the game of creation, my brothers, a sacred "Yes" is needed: the spirit now wills his own will, and he who had been lost to the world now conquers his own world.

Of three metamorphoses of the spirit I have told you: how the spirit became a camel; and the camel, a lion; and the lion, finally, a child.[34]

The Lion Roar of the Buddha—a spirit of immense creativity in life, in civilization, in the arts, and of rapture in the game of the gods (an Olympian laugh)—played through all of India in the brilliant centuries now to follow. But a new problem also emerged, which it will be our task to view in some detail, and which, indeed, represents a prime problem in the meeting and mutual comprehension of East and West today. For if all things are Buddha things and nothing is either honored or condemned, what becomes of the social values on which all civilization rests? In the Occident these values have been the high concern of both philosophy and religion, even to the untenable point of attributing ethical values to the universe and its supposed, ethically oriented maker. As Dr. Albert Schweitzer has summarized this view: "According to this ethical explanation of the universe, man by ethical activity enters the service of the divine world aim." [35] In India, however, whether in the idea of *brahman* of the Upanishads or in that of the void (*śunyatā*) and compassion (*karunā*) of the Mahayana Buddhist realization, a fundamental break beyond good and evil is achieved; as it is, also, in fact, though negatively, in the Jain, Sankhya, and Hinayana negative identifications.

The following chapters are going to show, one way or another, the power of India's great Double Nay to bring forth new worlds; but also, the force there, as well, of the continuing "thou shalt" of the ever-living dragon with scales of gold. The dragon and the camel, the lion and the child: those are the four faces, so to say, of Brahma, the creator of the Indian soul. And, if one may summarize at this point the structure of the fundamental spiritual paradox and tension of that soul, even to the present hour, it is between the claims, on the one hand, of the dragon, *dharma,* and, on the other, of the ultimate spiritual aim of absolute release from virtue, *mokṣa:* the child, the wheel rolling of itself.

"The sense of duty," we read in a classic Vedantic text, "is of the world of relativity. It is transcended by the wise, who are of the form of the void, formless, immutable, and untainted.

"The guileless person does whatever comes to be done, whether good or evil; for his action is like that of a child." [36]

VII. The Age of the Great Classics: c. 500 B.C.–c. 500 A.D.

We have now to survey in broadest lines the paradoxical spectacle of a civilization burgeoning from the manifestation of the un-manifest; for it is a fact that the later civilization of India came to flower as an expression of the play through all things of the energy of the void—whether in Buddhist or in Brahminic terms.

The epoch from the century of the Buddha to the middle of the Gupta period (c. 500 B.C. to 500 A.D.) may be termed the age of the Great Classics, not for India alone but for the civilized world. In Europe, between the time of Aeschylus (525–456 B.C.) and that of Boethius (c. 480–524 A.D.), the Greco-Roman heritage was shaped and terminated. In the Levant, between the reigns of Darius I (reigned c. 521–486 B.C.) and Justinian (527–565 A.D.), the Zoroastrian, Hebrew, Christian, various Gnostic, and Manichaean canons were defined. In the Far East, between the lifetime of Confucius (551–478 B.C.) and the legendary date of the coming to China of the Indian Buddhist sage Bodhidharma (520 A.D.), the basic texts and principles of Confucian, Taoist, and Chinese Buddhist thought were established. And in fact, even the civilizations of pre-Columbian America came to flower in this millennium of their so-called Classic Horizon: c. 500 B.C.–c. 500 A.D.[87]

Both overland and by sea, the ways between Rome, Persia, India, and China were opened in this period to an ever-increasing commerce, and to such a degree that nowhere in the hemisphere was there any longer the possibility of a local mythological de-velopment in isolation. The exchange of ideas was multifarious. And yet, there was in each domain a local force (which I have termed the style or signature) * that worked as a transforming factor on every import: in Europe, as above defined, the force of the rational, innovating individual; in the Levant, the idea of the one true community realizing God's aim; in China, the old Bronze Age thought of an accord between heaven, earth, and man; and throughout the history of later India, the sense of an

* Supra, Chapter I.

immanent ground into which all things dissolve and out of which, simultaneously, by a trick of maya, they continually pour.

During the course of this millennium there flowed from the West into India four increasingly massive tides: I. The first, from Achaemenian Persia, after c. 600 B.C., we have already briefly noted.* II. The second, following Alexander's raid of 327 B.C., was of a distinctly Hellenistic cast, supported by a powerful Greek community in the northwestern border province of Bactria, which for a time regained control of the entire Indus Valley, c. 200–c. 25 B.C. III. The next bore the imprint of Rome and flowed to India largely by way of an extremely dangerous but profitable sea trade that developed in the first centuries A.D., through a chain of ports along the western Indian coast, around the Cape, and up the other side. And finally, IV, with the victory in Rome of the Christian cult, the closing of the universities and extirpation of pagans throughout the empire, there turned up in India, c. 400 A.D., a tide of learned refugees, bearing a rich treasure of Late Roman, Greek, and Syro-Egyptian civilization, whose influence immediately inspired many aspects of the subsequent Indian golden age.

Archaeologically, as I have noted,† we have little more than broken shreds of Ocher-Colored, Painted Gray, and Black Polished Wares to mark the centuries of Vedic Aryan culture before the coming of Alexander. A sudden blossoming of elegant stone monuments brought the glory of India out of the dark into the full dress of a documented civilization, however, in the period of the following Maurya Dynasty (c. 322–185 B.C.). The impact of the young Macedonian's blow had reverberated across the north of the subcontinent, and in the moment of shifting political balances an upstart of unknown provenance, Chandragupta Maurya, possibly of low caste, not only overthrew the king of the Nanda dynasty, whose commander-in-chief he had been, but established a native military state on the Persian model, strong enough to confront Seleukos in the year 305 B.C. with half a million men, nine thousand war elephants, and a sea of chariots. A treaty was arranged by which the Greeks acquired five hundred

* Supra, pp. 246 and 249–52.
† Supra, pp. 248–49.

of the elephants and Chandragupta (apparently) a daughter of Seleukos, the Greeks retired to Bactria, and the newly founded Maurya dynasty stood from Afghanistan to Bihar.[38]

VIII. Three Buddhist Kings

ASHOKA MAURYA: C. 268–232 B.C.

Chandragupta's grandson was the great Ashoka, who reigned c. 268–232 B.C., and, continuing the course of victory, conquered the whole east coast of India from Orissa to Madras. When he beheld, however, the havoc of sorrow, misery, and death that his victory had caused, he was filled (like the young prince Gautama) with a deep sorrow, and, repenting of the nature of the world, joined the Buddhist Order as a lay disciple and the first Buddhist king. He is supposed to have supported 64,000 monks and to have built not only countless monasteries but also, in a single night, 84,000 reliquary shrines. Actually, about half a dozen of his fabled reliquary mounds (*stūpas*) survive to this day, increased so greatly in size, however, that we cannot judge of their Ashokan phase.

More instructive survivals from the decades of his reign are a series of seven heraldic stone columns, standing or fallen in various sites, bearing elegantly carved capitals in a highly polished Achaemenid Persian style. With the fall of the Persian empire and the burning of the palace city of Persepolis, "the accumulated artistry of Persia," as Sir Mortimer Wheeler has put it, "was out of work," and, moving eastward to the nearest successor empire, had reached Chandragupta's India,[39] where, in the Buddhist art of Ashoka's time, a colonial flowering of the Achaemenid style produced the first stone monuments of what presently became one of the greatest sculptural traditions in the history of the world.

Let us note at this point, however, that all of the sites of the world's first and foremost stone tradition, that of the Memphite priesthood of Ptah in Egypt, had been embraced, long since, within the bounds of the empires, first of Persia, then of Alexander the Great. Cambyses, the son of Cyrus, conquered Egypt 525 B.C., and the tomb of his successor, Darius I (reigned c. 521–485), may be visited to this day outside the ruins of Persepolis, hewn, like the rock-cut tombs of the pharaohs (Abu Simbel and the rest), into a perpendicular rock wall. Six more such rock-cut mausoleums are in the neighborhood, one of which is unfinished; and these are attributed, respectively, to Xerxes I (485–465), Artaxerxes I (465–425), Darius II (424–404), Artaxerxes II (404–359), Artaxerxes III (359–338), and (the one unfinished) Arses (338–336) or, perhaps, the victim of Alexander, Darius III (336–330).

Shall we be surprised, then, if the earliest rock-hewn monuments in India appear in the period of Ashoka? The most notable of the Ashokan series is a delicately carved little hermit cell near Gaya, the so-called Lomas Rishi cave, cleanly cut into solid rock, with a charming sculptured façade, imitating a lodge of wood and thatch, and having a lively bas-relief showing a file of hustling elephants gracefully arched above its entrance.

The Ashokan reliquary mounds (*stūpas*) likewise suggest a background in the deep past, specifically in the cult of the neolithic goddess Earth. For, as Dr. Heinrich Zimmer has pointed out in his lectures on *The Art of Indian Asia,* clusters of seven little mounds of battered clay are to this day made and worshiped in South Indian villages, not as graves or reliquaries, but as shrines to the seven mother-goddesses.[40] The mound in the Sumerian seal of Figure 2 will also be recalled. Relics of the dead placed in such a sanctuary are returned, as it were, to the womb of the goddess mother for rebirth, like the mummy of the pharaoh in his pyramid. The Buddhist stupa would seem to point, therefore, like the yoga of Buddhism itself, not to the Vedic-Aryan, but to an earlier neolithic system of belief.

Likewise, the rock-cut hermit caves, pointing by way of Persia back to Egypt, let us know that the forms of art and architecture appearing in this period of Ashoka were not exactly new. They were derived from an archaic art that had been first developed in the precincts of the Memphite temple of Ptah, and were now being grafted, after centuries, on a pre-Vedic Indian base of cruder style, yet essentially of the same cultural stock.

And as the forms of Indian art progress from this date, the

evidences increase of just such an organic interplay between traits of the deepest Indian past and affiliated arrivals from the West. So that an extremely complex problem stands to be faced by the student of these works. They represent an organic cultural interaction, where the force of an apparently alien tide emanating from an alien center actually carried traits in strong affinity with a long-hidden aspect of the native spiritual past.

However, not everything coming to view in this period has to be read as an opening of the eyes of a tropical giant who has slept for two thousand years. There was much that was actually new. The use of iron and of coinage, which had arrived from Persia some three centuries before Ashoka's time, was new; so likewise the use of a Semitic alphabet for the writing of royal inscriptions. A number of columns of Ashoka bear inscriptions of this kind, as do also certain surfaces of crude rock; and the type of script (*Karoṣṭhi*) in which the majority were inscribed was an adaptation of the Aramaic of the Near East.

For instance: on a rock wall near Kandahar, South Afghanistan, there is a bilingual text in Greek and Aramaic (Greek above, Aramaic below), celebrating, in the following self-congratulatory, paternally admonitory terms, Ashoka's conversion to the Buddhist faith and subsequent exemplary conduct:

> The King of Gentle Regard, when ten years of his reign had been accomplished, made manifest to mankind the virtue of piety. And from that time, men have been moved to become more pious; whereas on earth everything has prospered. And the King abstains from living beings: so likewise do others; and the hunters and fishers of the King have ceased to hunt.
>
> Moreover, those who were not masters over themselves have ceased, according to their powers, not to be masters over themselves. And they are obedient to their fathers, mothers, and elders, which formerly was not the case. So that in the future, behaving thus, they are going to live in a manner better and more profitable in all ways.[41]

The Greek of this inscription, as Professor A. Dupont-Sommer, in his presentation of the monument, states, "conforms completely to the Hellenistic style of the third century B.C., without exoticisms

or provincialisms. . . . The Aramaic just below it . . . conforms in the main to the 'imperial Aramaic' which had been
current in the Achaemenid chanceries; but shows a certain loosen-
ing of syntax as well as various provincialisms. And, as was the
case in the Achaemenid period itself, it has picked up a number
of Iranian terms, no less than nine of its eighty-odd words being
Iranian." [42]

A comparison can be made between the destiny of Christianity
under Constantine, three centuries after the Crucifixion, and that
of Buddhism under Ashoka, three centuries after the First Turning
of the Wheel of the Law. For in both cases an ascetic doctrine of
salvation, taught to a cluster of mendicant disciples ("If anyone
strikes you on the right cheek, turn to him the other also. . . .
Follow me, and leave the dead to bury their own dead"),[43] became an imperial, secular religion of devotionalized good conduct
for people living in the world, still in the field of history, not by
any means having given up all to shave their heads and carry
bowls. It is also possible to note that in the Rock Edicts of
Ashoka, which are the earliest Buddhist writings we possess, no
mention whatsoever is made of the doctrines of no-self, ignorance,
and extinction, but only of heaven, good works, merit, and the
soul.

"Let all joy be in effort," the king counsels, "because that avails
for both this world and the next." [44]

"The ceremonial of piety is not temporal; for even if it fails to
attain the desired end in this world, it surely begets eternal merit
in the next." [45]

"Even the small man can, if he choose, win for himself by
exertion much heavenly bliss." [46]

"And for what do I toil? For no other end than this, that I may
discharge my debt to animate beings, and that while I make some
happy here, they may in the next world merit heaven." [47]

Or again: "His Majesty thinks nothing of much importance
save what concerns the next world." [48]

"His Sacred and Gracious Majesty," states the most celebrated
of all, with a quality of tolerance that has been typical of India

throughout its long religious history, "does reverence to men of all sects, whether ascetics or householders, by gifts and various forms of reverence. His Sacred Majesty, however, cares not so much for gifts or external reverence as that there should be a growth of the essence of the matter in all sects. The growth of the essence of the matter assumes various forms, but the root of it is restraint of speech, to wit, a man must not do reverence to his own sect by disparaging that of another man without reason. Deprecation should be for specific reasons only, because the sects of other people deserve reverence for one reason or another. . . . Concord, therefore, is meritorious, to wit, hearkening and hearkening willingly to the law of piety as accepted by other people. For it is the desire of His Sacred Majesty that adherents of all sects should hear much teaching and hold sound doctrine." [49]

It was under the patronage of Ashoka that the Buddhist world mission was initiated, with teachers sent not only to Ceylon, where the mission struck fertile soil, but also to Antiochus II of Syria, Ptolemy II of Egypt, Magas of Cyrene, Antigonus Gonatas of Macedonia, and Alexander II of Epirus.[50] We find also in his period the first substantial evidence of a penetration into the south of India by the northern, Gangetic civilization. Excavations conducted, largely in Mysore, in the last years of British directorship, but supplemented and supported by diggings elsewhere since, have shown that until c. 200 B.C. the culture of the Deccan and South was still extremely primitive. The tools were of a late paleolithic, crude microlithic order. Pottery still was handmade, usually of a coarse gray fabric, globular in type, though occasional shards of incised and painted ware occur. Metal was known, but extremely scarce: bits of copper and bronze but none of iron appear among the remains. Post holes suggest houses made of timber, sometimes supplemented by low walls of rough granite blocks. And that is just about the whole story.

It was only after c. 200 B.C. that an extremely interesting late megalithic culture complex arrived, bearing astonishing resemblances to the much earlier Bronze Age megalithic (c. 2000 B.C.) of Spain, France, England, Sweden, and Ireland. However, this complex reached South India in association with iron and seems to have come, not from the west, but from the northeast. Whereafter, suddenly, c. 50 A.D., a far more advanced influence arrived and a brilliant period dawned in the south with the appearance of the merchantmen of Rome.[51]

Thus, for the area south of the Vindhyas, three periods of greatly delayed development seem to be indicated, following the paleolithic: 1. a crude meso-chalcolithic stone ax culture, from perhaps the first millennium B.C. to c. 200 B.C.; 2. an intrusive megalithic culture associated with iron, from c. 200 B.C. to c. 50 A.D.; 3. an arrival of Roman trading and manufacturing stations, c. 50 A.D., by direct sea route from Egyptian Red Sea ports. And it was into this comparatively primitive jungle zone, toward the close of Period 1, that the Northern Black Polished Ware and iron of the Aryan-Buddhist urban centers penetrated, c. 300 B.C., with the victories of the great Mauryan rulers. Three copies of one of Ashoka's edicts have been found as far south as Brahmagiri in Mysore.

So that a vast, culturally well mixed domain is indicated for the period of the earliest Buddhist diffusion: marked in the west by Ashoka's Greek-Aramaic edict in Afghanistan (and beyond that, his missions to Macedonia and Egypt), in the east by his conquest of the Indian coast from Orissa to Madras, and in the south by his mission to Ceylon as well as (on the mainland) his edicts in Mysore. And in this largely Buddhist world a combination of Egypto-Assyro-Persian, Indo-Aryan, Dravidian, and Greek elements can be readily discerned: the whole superintended by a monarch, the greatest in the world in his day, of a tolerance and gentleness seldom matched in the history of states, protecting the myriads of lion-roaring monks of the numerous life-renouncing nirvana cults of his time, yet equally fostering and developing, with the wisdom of a great patriarch, the well-being, both on earth and in heaven, of his children of the world.

And for a time, under the reign of this mighty yet pious king, it actually seemed that something like the golden age of the lion lying with the lamb was about to be realized. However, the laws of history—which in the political textbook of his grandfather had been defined as the "law of fishes" (the big ones eat the little ones, and the little ones have to be fast) [52]—had by no means been undone in the vortex of this world. The empire disintegrated some fifty years after Ashoka's death, when the last of his successors, Brihadratha, was murdered by his own commander-in-chief on the occasion of a review of his troops, and a new non-Buddhist family, stemming from the province of Ujjain (which had formerly been a Maurya fief), assumed the imperial throne. Whereupon the murderer, Pushyamitra, founder of the new Hindu Shunga dynasty, released a horse, in preparation for a classical Vedic sacrifice, to wander at will over the realm, attended by a hundred warrior princes. But somewhere about midway to the Punjab the challenge of the ranging symbolic steed was accepted by a company of Greek cavalry. The Europeans were routed, and the imperial Vedic sacrifice was completed—but the presence of the Greek riders was enough to give notice of something interesting brewing in the West.[53]

MENANDER: C. 125–95 B.C.

For, indeed, in Hellenistic Bactria a Greek tyrant, Euthydemus, had established c. 212 B.C. a Greek military state independent of the Seleucids, and his son Demetrius reconquered the entire Indus Valley for the Greeks, c. 197 B.C.

In this formidable outpost Hindu and Buddhist, as well as Classical, mythologies and beliefs were in play. The Greeks themselves identified Indra with Zeus, Shiva with Dionysos, Krishna with Herakles, and the goddess Lakshmi with Artemis; and one of the greatest of the Greek kings, Menander (c. 125–c. 95 B.C.), appears to have been, if not himself a Buddhist, then at least a lavish patron of the faith. The Buddhist Wheel of the Law appears on his coins.[54] Plutarch states that the cities of his realm contended for the honor of his ashes and agreed on a division among themselves in order that the memory of his reign should not be lost.[55] And there is an important early Buddhist text (in part, perhaps, c. 50 B.C.),[56] "The Questions of King Milinda" (*Milindapañha*), in which this king (Milinda = Menander) is shown arguing with a Buddhist monk, Nagasena, by whom he is defeated and converted.

"The king was learned," we read, "eloquent, wise and able, a faithful observer—and that at the right time—of all the various acts of devotion and ceremony enjoined by his own sacred hymns concerning things past, present, and to come. . . . And as a disputant he was hard to equal, harder still to overcome; the acknowledged superior of all the founders of the various schools of thought. Moreover, as in wisdom, so in strength of body, swiftness, and valor, there was found none equal to Milinda in all India. He was rich, too, mighty in wealth and prosperity, and the number of his armed hosts knew no end."

I shall leave it to the reader to seek out the text itself [57] and learn how this mighty man, when his day of work was done, would ask his five hundred Ionian courtiers to suggest some learned Indian sage with whom he might enjoy an evening's talk and of how, attended by the five hundred, mounting the royal car, he went to the dwellings, one after another, of those suggested, putting questions to them to which they were unable to respond.

Then thought Milinda the king within himself: "All India is an empty thing; it is verily like chaff! There is no one, either recluse or Brahmin, capable of discussing things with me and dispelling my doubts."

Fortunately for the reputation of India, however, there were dwelling in the high Himalayas a company of Buddhist arhats, and one of these, by his divine power of hearing, overheard Milinda's thought. Whereupon a search was instituted for one who would be able to match the Greek, and it was learned—again by telepathy —that he would be found (be not amazed!) in the Heaven of the Happy Gods. The innumerable company of arhats, vanishing from the summit of their mountain, appeared in the Heaven of the Happy Gods and, discovering the god in question, Mahasena by name, learned that he would be pleased to assist the faith by refuting the heresy of Milinda. Whereupon the arhats, vanishing from that heaven, reappeared on their Himalayan slope, and the god was born on earth as the son of a Brahmin.

When he had acquired what Brahminism could teach, Mahasena joined the Buddhist Order under the name Nagasena, learned the Law with ease, and soon was an arhat worthy to be sent against the king, who thereupon met his match. The sage successfully answered every single one of the Greek's 262 questions, the earth shook six times to its boundaries, lightning flashed, a rainfall of flowers fell from heaven, etc., all the inhabitants of the city, and the women of the king's palace, bowed down before Nagasena, raised their joined hands to their foreheads, and departed thence. And the king, with joy in his heart, pride suppressed, became aware of the virtue of the religion of the Buddhas, ceased to entertain doubt, tarried no longer in the jungle of heresy, and, like a poisonous cobra deprived of its fangs, craved pardon for his faults and admission to the faith, to be its true convert and supporter as long as life should last.

KANISHKA: C. 78–123 (OR 120–162?) A.D.

The days of the Greeks on this threshold of nirvana were numbered by the approach of a somewhat enigmatic horde of nomads from the vicinity of the Chinese Wall, called by the Chinese Yueh-Chi, by the Indians the Kushanas, classified by some as Mongols, by others as Turkomen of a sort, and by still others as some kind of Scythian-like Aryan folk. They had been dislodged and set in motion by a group of Huns ranging the country between the southern reaches of the Wall and the mountains of Nan Shan. Their migration across the wastes of Kuku Nor and Sinkiang lasted about forty years (c. 165–125 B.C.), causing major displacements of population in the areas traversed, and therewith new pressures on the borders of Bactria. The Greek defenses broke. First Scythians, then Kushanas, poured through and, crossing the mountains into India, possessed themselves of the greater part of the Gangetic plain, southward as far as to the Vindhya hills.

Kanishka, whose dates are variously reckoned as c. 78–123 or c. 120–162 A.D.,[58] was the greatest of the Kushana kings. There is a portrait statue, 5 feet 4 inches tall to the shoulders (unfortunately, the head is missing), executed in the red sandstone of Mathura, in which the long belted field-coat and heavy riding boots, the vigorous stance, and the readiness of the two hands at the hilts of two immense sheathed swords, announce dramatically the character of the Central Asians who had assumed the leadership of India.[59]

Like Ashoka and Menander, Kanishka was a convert to Buddhism and, as such, a lavish patron both of monks and of the arts of the lay community. Ashvaghosha was a figure of his court—possibly the agent of his conversion. There is a tradition—questionable though generally accepted—that under his patronage a great Buddhist council launched the Mahayana on its career. The cultivation of Sanskrit as an elite literary tongue, and of the classic Kavya ("poetic") style, commenced, apparently, in the Kushana courts.[60] And in the sphere of religious art, a number of developments took place that were among the most notable in the history of the Orient.

Numerous immense reliquary mounds were built in his day; those from Ashoka's time were enlarged; and there were raised around these sanctuaries opulently carved stone gates and railings, on which all of the earth and vegetation genii of the ageless folk tradition appeared in teeming abundance—surrounding in joyous reverence the great silent mounds symbolic of nirvana. But these figures, far indeed from representing the sorrows and loathsomeness of the world as taught by the Teacher and his monks, appear rather to represent its naïve charm. To the pilgrim visitor coming to the shrine, these little scenes and figures seem to say: "Indeed, for thee who hast come, heavy with thy self, all is sorrow; but for us, here in the knowledge that we and all things are without a self, there is the rapture of nirvana even here on earth, in every one of our various lives and manners of being."

Pot-bellied dwarfs support great architraves, whereon are beasts, gods, nature sprites, and human beings adoring symbols of the Buddhas, past and future. Winged lions squat like guardian dogs. Earth demons shouldering heavy clubs guard the Sun Wheel of the Law. Everywhere flowering vines and lianas pour from the mouths and navels of mythological monsters. Conchs, masks, and vases likewise emit lianas, lotuses, and auspicious fruit-and-jewel-bearing plants, from which animals spring or among which birds may hop and earth spirits play. Dryads grasp the boughs of their trees, voluptuously hanging. And among these numerous forms scenes appear both from the life and from the earlier lives of the Buddha: when he was a tortoise, monkey, elephant, or great hare, merchant or world monarch; when he returned to Kapilavastu and performed miracles before his father, mounted miraculously to his mother in heaven, who had died seven days following his birth, or when he walked on water.

Now in monuments of this type built before the period of Kanishka (those of the so-called Early Classic Style of c. 185 B.C.– c. 50 A.D.) the human form of the Buddha himself is never shown. In the scene, for example, of his palace excursions in the chariot, the charioteer is to be seen holding an umbrella over a prince who is not there.[61] The return to Kapilavastu shows the father and his court greeting, and the gods above dropping garlands, but where the Buddha should have stood we see a Bodhi-tree, symbolic of his presence.[62] The Wheel of the Law, the tree, an empty chair, footprints, or a stupa, represent the Buddha in such scenes; for he is the one who has realized extinction, who, like the sun, has set, and is "empty, without being." As we read in a text of the Ceylonese Pali Canon: "There is nothing any more with which he can be compared." [63]

However, in the period and reign of Kanishka a new development took place, in as much as the Buddha himself now was represented—everywhere—and in two contrasting styles: the Greco-Roman of Gandhara, where he is shown as a kind of semi-divine Greek teacher, humanized, as an impressive personality; [64] and a powerful native style developed by the stone craftsmen of the city of Mathura, where he is rendered, vigorously and realistically, as an archetypal Indian sage.[65] And the explanation of this appearance, as Heinrich Zimmer was the first to point out, is that a new conception of the fundamental doctrine had come into being. "And we know," as he states, "precisely what the new conception was: it was the Mahayana, which is documented in the very period of the Gandhara monuments by the Prajna-paramita texts. In these we are told that just as there never has been any world, so, also, there never was a historical Buddha to redeem it. The Buddha and the world are equally void; śūnyam: 'empty, without being.' From the transcendental standpoint of the released consciousness they are on one and the same plane of illusoriness; and this transcendental standpoint, moreover, is the true one. The illusory historical Buddha, who through bodhi entered into nirvana yet until his parinirvana continued to live for the eyes of the world, may consequently be represented as though alive in the illusory world." [66]

One detail more is to be remarked in the art of these early Buddhist stupa railings, which, in the light of what we know of the usual attitude of monks, would appear to represent a direct challenge to their point of view.

Ananda said: "Lord, how should we behave toward women?"

The Master: "Not see them."

Ananda: "And if we have to see them?"

The Master: "Not speak to them."

Ananda: "And if we have to speak to them?"

The Master: "Keep your thoughts tightly controlled." [67]

And yet, the most prominent single figure in the ornamentation of all the early Buddhist monuments, rivaling in prominence even the symbols of the Buddha and nirvana, is the lotus-goddess, Shri Lakshmi, of the popular Indian pantheon. She appears variously standing or sitting on a lotus, elevating lotuses in her hands, with lotus buds and corollas rising around her—on two of which elephants may appear, pouring water from their trunks or from pots lifted in their trunks, over her head and broad-hipped body. Furthermore, although in the earlier renditions (e.g., on the railings of Stupa No. 2, at Sanchi, c. 110 B.C.),[68] her lower body is decently clothed, as are likewise the bodies of the other female forms on the monuments of that period, on the railings and gates of later date (Sanchi Stupa No. 1: first century A.D.),[69] not only is the lower body of the lotus goddess naked, but the leg is often swung wide to reveal the lotus of her sex; and the other female forms, whether crowding on balconies and at windows to watch the prince Gautama ride forth from his palace, or voluptuously swinging as dryads from their trees, wear a type of ornamented girdle that does not conceal, but frames and accents, their sex.[70] In the Buddha life by Ashvaghosha, the scenes just cited of the women on the rooftops, in the pleasure groves and seraglio, are rendered with an erotic stress on detail that in numerous passages covers pages. And in the course of the following centuries, whether in Buddhist, Hindu, or even Jain, art and literature, this accent on the female, and specifically as an erotic object, steadily increases, until by the twelfth and thirteenth centuries there would almost appear to be in Indian mysticism little else.

The Indus Valley goddess of the tree, giving birth to the plant world, has thus dramatically returned (Figures 16, 17); and she is to be known as present or represented, it would seem, in every woman in the world. She is the goddess of the Bodhi-tree—the same who, in the legend of Adam, was Eve. But in the Garden of Eden the serpent, her lover, was cursed, whereas at the scene of the Bodhi-tree the serpent arose from the earth to protect the Savior. Also, in the scene of the trial of Parshvanatha, the serpent together with his consort came forth to protect the yogi. And the consort, in that instance, was expressly the goddess Lotus, Shri Lakshmi, the goddess of the life force, in serpent form.

There is a great mythological context opening out here before us, reaching westward and eastward, like the two arms of the tree: of the knowledge, on the one hand, of good and evil and, on the other, of immortal life. But we shall have to wait for a little more news before this reappearance in the midst of a world of meditating monks of the goddess symbolic of the universe can be appraised. For something really new has occurred.

"The Enlightened One sets forth in the Great Ferryboat," we read in a text of this period, "but there is nothing from which he sets forth. He starts from the universe; but in truth he starts from nowhere. His boat is manned with all the perfections; and is manned by no one. It will find its support on nothing whatsoever and will find its support on the state of all-knowing, which will serve it as a non-support. Moreover, no one has ever set forth in the Great Ferryboat; no one will ever set forth in it, and no one is setting forth in it now. And why is this? Because neither the one setting forth nor the goal for which he sets forth is to be found: therefore, who should be setting forth, and whither?"

The Bodhisattva Subhuti said: "Profound, O Venerable One, is the perfect Transcendental Wisdom."

And the Venerable One replied: "Abysmally profound, like the space of the universe, O Subhuti, is the perfect Transcendental Wisdom."

Subhuti said again: "Difficult to be attained through Awakening is the perfect Transcendental Wisdom, O Venerable One."

To which the Venerable One replied: "That is the reason, O Subhuti, why no one ever attains it through Awakening." [71]

IX. The Way of Vision

Han Ming Ti of China dreamed of a golden man in the west; or so, at least, we have been told.[72] And although he knew that only demons and barbarians dwelt beyond the bounds of his celestial empire—which he held in order, together with the universe, by sitting immovably on his cosmic throne, facing south—he nevertheless sent forth an embassy. This passed into the wilderness along the Old Silk Road, which had been opened between Rome and the Far East, c. 100 B.C. And there indeed, coming eastward along the bleak desert way, were two Buddhist monks conducting a white horse that bore on its back an image of the Buddha and a packet of Mahayana texts. The monastery built to receive them in the capital Lo Yang was named for the animal on whose back the honored cargo had arrived; and it was there, in that White Horse Monastery, c. 65 A.D., that the long task began of rendering Sanskrit into Chinese.

The image, judging from the date, must have been of the Greco-Roman, Gandhara school, possibly of gold, and probably of Gautama teaching. However, the great majority of the Far Eastern Buddha images fashioned since do not represent the Indian Buddha Gautama. They are of purely visionary apparitions, "meditation Buddhas," with no historical reference whatsoever. And of these, by far the most popular and important is Amitabha, the Buddha of "immeasurable (a-mita) light (ābha)"—known also as Amitayus, the Buddha of "immeasurable (a-mita) life duration (āyus)"— who is a product of purely Buddhist thought, yet bears the marks of an ultimate derivation from Iran.

Amida, as this brilliant solar Buddha is termed in the Far East, was known in China by the middle of the second century A.D. and is today in Japan the focus of devotion of the great Jodo and Shinshu sects. In his worship the way taught is not self-reliance (Japanese: *jiriki,* "one's own strength"), but reliance on the grace (*tariki,* "outside strength, another's strength") of Amida—which two ways, however, do not differ as greatly as a Westerner might suppose, since the Buddha, conceived to be without, is symbolic of Buddhahood, which is equally within.

In the Mahayana version of the Buddha life that we have just been reading, by the Indian poet monk Ashvaghosha, a number of scenes are introduced that do not appear in the Hinayana Pali text; one of the most important of which occurs at the end of the fourth week of the festival of the Great Awakening, when, according to this version, the antagonist, Mara, came once again before the Blessed One. "O thou Blessed One," he said, "thou wilt now kindly pass on to nirvana." But the Buddha Gautama replied, "I shall establish, first, innumerable Buddha Realms." And the tempter, with a great cry of horror, disappeared.[73]

The Buddha Realm is an invention of the Mahayana of enormous interest to every student of comparative mythology; for, on one hand, it shows many points of resemblance to the Western idea of paradise, yet, on the other, it is not conceived to be the ultimate goal of the spiritual life, but the penultimate, next to last. It is a kind of port of departure for nirvana. And as numerous ports are to be found along the shoreline of a great sea, so likewise along that of the ocean of the void there have been set up many Buddha Realms. We hear of those of Maitreya, Vairochana, and Gautama, as well as of that of Amida and, theoretically at least, even the Paradise of Christ might be experienced as a Buddha Realm. In fact, as a coupling device by which the paradisiac mythology of any religion can be linked to the Buddhist, the concept of the Buddha Realm makes it possible for the Mahayana mission to enter any religious field whatsoever and not destroy, but augment and supplement the local forms.

The Buddha Realm of Amitabha came into being, we are told, by virtue of the vow that this particular World Savior made when hc was still a Bodhisattva; which was, that he would refuse enlightenment for himself unless by his Buddhahood he might bring to nirvana anyone who appealed to his name—even by so little as its mere repetition ten times. And the power of his yoga was such that a purely visionary land, the Land of Bliss (*sukhāvatī*) thereupon came into being in the West, where he now sits forever, like a setting sun—never, however, setting—forever enduring (*amitāyus*), immeasurably radiant (*amitābha*), on the shore of a great lotus lake. And all who implore his name are reborn on the lotuses of that lake, some on open calyxes, others, however, within buds, according to their various spiritual grades; for not all, at the time of death, are ready for the fullness of the radiant saving light.

When a being of the highest category dies, who has practiced throughout life true compassion (*karunā*), injured none, and fully practiced all the precepts, Amitabha in a blaze of light appears to him, flanked by two Great Bodhisattvas: Avalokiteshvara standing at his left, Mahasthama at his right. Unnumbered historic Buddhas are shining all about, together with their monks and devotees, innumerable gods, and a multitude of jeweled palaces. A diamond seat is offered to the deceased by the two Great Bodhisattvas; all extend to him hands of welcome; the Buddha Amitabha sends over his body rays of light; and, having seen all these, with a leap of joy he finds himself on that diamond throne, being led in a great procession to the Land of Bliss. Everywhere the Doctrine is heard, brilliant rays and jewel forests are beheld. And, living in the presence of all those Buddhas, Bodhisattvas, gods, and luminous sights, bathed continuously in the light of Amitabha, conscious of a spirit of resignation to whatever consequences may arise, he is given countless thousands of meditation-formulae to recite, and obtains nirvana in brief course.[74]

At the opposite moral extreme, the being of no achievement whatsoever, wicked, stupid, full of the guilt of many crimes, who at the time of death was advised by some friend saying, "Even if you cannot imagine the Buddha, at least you can mutter his name," and thereupon pronounced the formula ten times of "Adoration to the Buddha Amitayus," will see, on passing away, a golden lotus, brilliant as the disk of the sun, within the corolla of which he will then find himself enclosed. And on that lake, for twelve great eons, he will remain within that bud, receiving and absorbing all the while the radiant influences of the lake; until, one day, the petals unfold and all the glories of the lake lie around him. He will then hear the voices, raised in great compassion, of the two Great Bodhisattvas, teaching him in detail the real state of all the elements of nature and the law of the expiation of sins. Immediately, rejoicing, he will direct his whole thought to Buddhahood, which, indeed, he will then presently attain.[75]

Obviously, a gentle purgatory has here superseded the usual Indian image of spiritual progress by reincarnation, and were the date of the doctrine not so early, one could suppose that a Christian influence might have come into play. However, as things stand, the more plausible view is that the influence of Iran and the doctrine of Zoroaster, which, as already noted, played a role in the shaping of Dante's vision, had been operative here. "It is not to be forgotten," states an excellent recent monograph on this subject,

> that the first apostle to bring Amida worship to China was a Parthian prince, Ngan Che-Kao, and that the Kushana empire where Amida worship first arose was no less Iranian than Indian, no less Mazdaen than Buddhist. Ngan Che-Kao was an Arsacid who lived in China from 148 to 170 A.D. . . . Furthermore, the work of translating sacred texts and of peddling and fashioning sacred images was in the second and third centuries A.D. carried on principally by the Bactrian and Sogdian subjects of the Yueh-chi. . . . Hence, it is not in India proper that the factors contributing to the victory of Amida must be sought, but in the intermediate Chinese-Indian Zone, where the prevailing influence was of Iran. . . . All of which explains why Amida worship, which in Central Asia and the Far East enjoyed such a great expansion, appears to have been little favored in India proper.[76]

Dr. Marie-Thérèse de Mallmann, the author of this important study, has shown that the names Amitabha and Amitayus correspond to the usual characterizations of the Persian creator-god Ahura Mazda, as the lord both of light and of unending time; furthermore, that throughout the broad domain of Persian religious influence (which, as we know, reached with the Roman army into

Gaul and Britain), divine triads matching that of Amitabha seated
between his two great standing Bodhisattvas appear at many sites.

For example, at Reims a Gallo-Roman altar (Figure 20) has
been found, on the front of which there is shown in high re-

Figure 20. The Lord of Life: France, c. 50 A.D.

lief a horned deity on a low dais, holding on his left forearm a
cornucopia-like bag from which grain pours; and before his dais,
facing each other like the gazelles of the horned Indus Valley deity
of Figure 18, stand a bull and stag feeding on the grain. The pedi-
ment above contains the figure of a large rat, which in India is the
animal vehicle of the god Ganesha, lord (*iśa*) of the hosts (*gaṇa*)

of his father Shiva. While at either hand, right and left, of this Celtic god, who has been identified as Cernunnos (and elsewhere appears, like Shiva, with three heads), stand a pair of gods, Apollo and Hermes-Mercury, much in the manner of the two Great Bodhisattvas.[77]

The resemblances of this symbolic composition to the Buddhist triad and, beyond that, its manifold association with incidental motifs of the Shiva-Buddha context, are much too close to be accidental. And if we now recall that the Persian prophet Mani (216?–276? A.D.), the founder of Manichaeism, sought to synthesize the teachings of the Buddha, Zoroaster, and Christ, and that by the fifth century A.D. Manichaean communities were known from North Africa (where Saint Augustine was a professed Manichaean from 373 to 382 A.D.) to China, it will be evident that the religion of Amida was by no means the only conspicuous example of cross-cultural syncretism in this general period of the rising and falling great military empires of Rome, Persia, India, and Han China.

The religion of Amida, however, is in spirit absolutely different from the Occidental dualism either of the Persian or of the Christian revelation. Superficially, an obvious base for syncretic manipulations was furnished by an affinity not only of traditions but also of imagery and general spiritual aims. For example, if the Christian view of the destiny of man be compared with the Hindu-Buddhist, it will be seen that in both the basic theme and highest concern is the preparation of the temporal being for an experience in eternity of the *summum bonum*. Those who at the time of death are unprepared must undergo beyond death a sort of postgraduate discipline, which in the Christian image is represented by the symbol of purgatory and in the Hindu-Buddhist by reincarnation. Purgatory and reincarnation are thus homologous. Likewise, according to both iconographies, those so confirmed in vice that no influence of divine grace can possibly undo them remain as they are, shut away from their own highest good, either in a permanent hell (the Christian image) or in a round of interminable rebirth.

Significant differences appear, however, when the two systems are more exactly brought together. For when we compare their lower margins we find that in the Christian image of the great theater of salvation the animal, plant, and inanimate realms of being have been omitted from the composition, while at the upper margin the highest integer is God. The Western image, that is to say, is but the torso of the other, reaching neither below man-made-in-the-image-of-God nor above God-in-the-image-of-man: for, no matter how loftily and airily God may be described, he is always finally manlike, either grossly so, as throughout the Bible, or more subtly, as when described as some kind of abstract presence bearing in superlative degree the human qualities of goodness, mercy, justice, wisdom, wrath, and might.

In sum, whereas the Man/God margins of the Occidental system result in a reading of the universe in terms, finally, of an Oedipal situation (a good father creating a bad son who sinned and now must be atoned), in the Orient the anthropomorphic order is but the foreground of a larger structure. And whereas within the anthropomorphic frame an essentially ethical, penal cast is given to the problem of the universe (disease, defeat, storm, and death being punishments and trials: animal suffering, however, unexplained), ethics in the Orient—being good and obeying father—represent only the kindergarten of a higher school. Hence, whereas in the Occidental image of purgatory, the ultimate aim, the *summum bonum* to be achieved, is the beatific vision in the Land of Bliss, in the Mahayana Buddhist imagery of Amida, the beatific vision itself is but the last phase of the purgatorial process; not an ultimate aim but an ultimate step to something beyond. One is to leap beyond God-in-the-image-of-man, man-in-the-image-of-God, and the universe cognized by the mind. The mind itself, indeed, is to break and dissolve in the burning light of a realization both above and below, beyond and yet within, everything it has conceived: an experience of the ineffable, unimaginable no-thing that is the mystery of all being and yet no mystery, since it is actually ourselves and what we are regarding every minute of the whole duration of our lives.

Consequently, man's earthly condition is not interpreted in the Orient as a punishment for something; nor is its end in any sense atonement. The saving power of Amida has nothing whatsoever to

do with atonement. Its function is pedagogical, not penal. The aim
is not the satisfaction of a supernatural father, but an awakening
of the natural man to truth. And its only claim is that the vision of
this Buddha and his eloquent Land of Bliss will effect that aim
more easily and swiftly—and more surely for more types of man—
than any other known pedagogical device.

For example, in the "Guide Book to Meditation on Amida"
from which I have already cited, the method of building in the
mind, step by step, the saving vision of the Buddha, his attendant
Bodhisattvas, and the Land of Bliss itself, is presented in detail—
with the final assurance that the vision is actually not of a being
and place somewhere literally in the West but of the inhabiting
being and nature of oneself and of the whole world, all things
and all that is beyond all things. Furthermore, as we read onward
in this text (which I think it important to present here at some
length) we cannot but recognize in it the source of the imagery
of the Buddhist temple art of the whole Far East—which can be
only misread in Occidental terms. For those images are in no
sense idols: they are supports of meditation. And the Buddha of
meditation himself is not a supreme being somewhere in heaven,
or even in some actual Land of Bliss, but a figure, a mask, a
presentation to the mind, of the inhabiting mystery of all phenomenality whatsoever, whether of the world, of the temple, of
the image, or of the devotee himself.

The lesson is presented in this text in the way of a teaching
rendered by the Buddha Gautama to the queen consort of that
gracious king Bimbisara, who had offered him his realm when,
at the beginning of his youthful quest, he had passed, begging,
through the king's city and retired to a mountainside for a pause.*
The king himself, now an old man, had fallen upon bad times; for
his wicked son, Ajatashatru, had cast him into a prison with seven
walls; and his queen, Vaidehi, the mother of that wicked son, had
also been cast into a jail. She had prayed for consolation, however; and the World Saving Buddha, Gautama Shakyamuni, appeared to her in vision, sitting on a lotus of numerous brilliant

* Supra, pp. 269–70.

jewels, flanked by two disciples, and with deities above, showering flowers. From between the Buddha's brows there flashed a ray that spread to all the worlds of the ten quarters and, returning, rested above his head, where it became a golden pillar, tall as the mountain of the gods, wherein all the Buddha Realms of the ten quarters could be seen at once. And she, regarding them, selected that of the Buddha Amitabha-Amitayus.

Gautama said: Those desiring to be born there, first should be filial, compassionate, and observant of the ten negative precepts, which are as follows: 1. not to kill, 2. not to steal, 3. not to lie, 4. not to be unchaste, 5. not to drink intoxicants.* These are the five that all must observe, following which are five additional, for monks: 6. not to eat at forbidden times, 7. not to dance, sing, or attend theatrical or other spectacles, 8. not to use scents, garlands, or other ornaments, 9. not to use high or broad beds, 10. not to accept money.

Secondly, said the Buddha, those desiring to enter this realm should take refuge in the Buddha, the law, and the order, fulfill all ceremonial observances, and give their whole attention to the attainment of enlightenment, deeply believing in the doctrine of the twelvefold causal chain, studying and reciting the sutras, and leading others to follow the same course.

And when he had rehearsed thus the elementary lore, the Buddha said graciously to the queen: "You are just an ordinary person; the quality of your mind is inferior and feeble. You have not as yet achieved the divine eye and so cannot see anything that is not directly at hand. You will ask, therefore, how the perception of that Buddha Realm is to be formed. I shall now explain." Whereupon he taught the good and pious queen the manner of envisioning Amitayus.[78]

At the time of the setting sun she was to sit facing west, fix her

---

* Compare supra, p. 235, the five basic vows of Jainism. Compare, also, the recent political parody of these five in the "Five Points" (*pañca śila*) for International Coexistence, set forth in April 1954 in the preamble to the Sino-Indian Agreement on Trade with Tibet (discussed by Adda B. Bozeman, "India's Foreign Policy Today: Reflections upon Its Sources," *World Politics*, Vol. X, No. 2, January 1958, pp. 256–73).

mind firmly on the setting sun, and hold the image of that sun in memory. That would be the perception of the sun: the First Meditation.

Next, she would form the perception of pure water, holding this image firmly fixed; and when the water had been perceived, the meditating mind was to envision ice, shining and transparent, after which, lapis lazuli. The earth, then, was to be seen as lapis lazuli, transparent and radiant, both within and without, supported from beneath by a golden banner with seven jewels, reaching to the eight corners of the earth, each corner of the earth consisting of a hundred jewels, each jewel of a thousand rays, and every ray of eighty-four thousand colors, which, being reflected from the lapis lazuli ground, would look like a thousand million suns. Stretching over that ground were to be seen golden ropes, intertwined crosswise, the whole divided by strings of seven jewels, every jewel emitting rays of five hundred colors, resembling flowers, or like the moon and stars. And these rays should form a tower of ten million stories built of jewels, every side of which should be furnished with a hundred million flowery banners and numberless musical instruments, all emitting the sounds signifying "suffering," "non-existence," "impermanence," and "no self." That would be the perception of water: the Second Meditation.

Next, this perception having been formed, each of its constituents, one by one, was to be visualized so clearly that the whole would never be lost, even when the eyes were open—except during sleep. "The one who has realized this perception," said the Buddha, "is declared to have seen dimly the Land of Bliss." And this perception of the Land is Meditation Number Three.

The next meditation was to be of the jewel trees of that Buddha Realm: seven rows of them, each 800 yojanas high, all bearing flowers and leaves of seven jewels. And from the first jewel of each, which is of lapis lazuli, there issues a golden ray; from the second, of crystal, a saffron ray; next, of agate, a diamond ray, etc. Corals, amber, and all other gems follow as ornaments. Moreover, seven nets of pearls are to be visualized, spreading over each tree, and between each set of such nets and its neighbor five hundred million palaces built of excellent flowers, like the palace of the god

Brahma. Heavenly children live in those palaces, and every child has a garland of five hundred million precious gems, the rays of which illuminate a hundred yojanas, as if a hundred million suns and moons were united. "It is difficult," said even the Buddha, "to explain them all in detail." [79]

And we have come only to the Fourth Meditation!

Nirvana is the goal, and the mind is beginning to crack—as it must, if that goal is to be achieved.

However, since the goal of the present work is not nirvana but a cross-cultural view of the imagery by which the peoples of the world have, in time and space, sought to represent their intuitions of that term beyond terms which in the West we personify as God and in the Orient is depersonified either as Being or as Non-Being, I am going to ask the gracious reader wishing to continue with the Buddha to let me say to him, respectfully, in the words of the Antagonist (who was himself—as we now know—a Buddha thing): "O thou Blessed One, thou wilt now kindly pass on to nirvana." For we are going to pause here, a while, to classify. We have come to a point in our study where the whole field is breaking, like a Buddha Realm, into five hundred million varicolored rays, and it certainly is difficult to explain them all in detail.

x. The World Regained—as Dream

The use of visions to lead the mind and sentiments beyond themselves, over thresholds to new realms of realization, has been developed in the Orient during the centuries since the writing of the "Guide Book to Meditation on Amida" into an extremely versatile pedagogical technique; and in its service not only books of meditation, but also works of visual art are employed. We have not yet, in our present systematic survey, arrived at the period of the greatest unfoldment of this visionary methodology. However, the basic principles are already evident. And since these represent not only a mode of Oriental guidance of the soul, but also the deepest, broadest, most thoroughly tested and proved theory of the nature and use of myth that learning anywhere in this field has yet produced, I am going to pause for a brief analysis of its elementary postulates before proceeding.

The first point to be noted is that already recognized in our study of the system of the Jains, namely, the break away from actuality. Whether in the forest voluntarily as a monk, or in jail by *force majeure,* the individual is psychologically dissociated from the field of life normal to his kind. External stimuli are cut off.

Next: with the normal system of sign stimuli cut off (the reality system), a supernormal order is developed (the mythic system), to which the sentiments are addressed.

Whereupon two alternatives arise. The negative method of the Jains, Sankhya, and Hinayana required the extinction, finally, of either part or all of the mythic system of supernormal stimuli and a realization thereby of trance rapture, either with or without a sense of unqualified being. The positive method of the Buddha Realm, on the other hand, retains the supernormal image and develops it simultaneously in two directions: 1. toward the void of non-being (the Buddha Realm is a mere vision of the mind), and 2. toward actuality (the world of normal life is itself a Buddha Realm).

For example, when the Buddha Shakyamuni had taught the queen the first six meditations, there appeared, as though of itself, the vision of Amitayus. She had been taught to visualize, first, the sun; second, water; third, the land; and fourth, the wondrous jewel trees. Next, said the Buddha, the lotus-covered lakes of that Buddha Realm are to be seen: the waters of eight lakes, each being of seven jewels, soft and yielding, derived from the King of Jewels, the Wishing Gem. Those waters issue from that gem in fourteen luminous streams, each with the color of seven jewels, its channel being of gold, and its bed of variegated diamonds. In each lake are sixty million lotuses of seven jewels each, twelve yojanas in circumference, all of which gently rise and fall as the water ripples among them, melodiously sounding the lesson of "suffering," "non-existence," "impermanence," and "no self"; proclaiming also the signs, thirty-two in number, and the eighty minor marks of excellence. Moreover, golden rays pour from the Wishing Gem, becoming birds of the colors of a hundred jewels, harmoniously singing of the Buddha, the Law, and the Order. Such is the Fifth Meditation: on the eight waters of good qualities. And this, then, is fol-

lowed by a sixth and last meditation before the Buddha Amitayus
comes. One perceives that each division of that Buddha Realm has
jeweled galleries and stories to the number of five hundred million,
within each of which are innumerable deities playing heavenly
music. And numerous musical instruments hang, furthermore, like
jeweled banners in the open sky, resounding of themselves the re-
membrance of the Buddha, the Law, and the Order. And when this
meditation has been accomplished, one is said to have seen dimly
the jewel trees, jewel earth, jewel lakes, and jewel air of that Land
of Bliss. "The one who has experienced this," said the Buddha, "has
expiated all sins, such as would have led to numberless transmigra-
tions, and will surely be born in that Buddha Realm."

The mind has now been cleared of all connection with actual
trees, earth, lakes, and air, birds, banners, and gems; a visionary
theater has been set for the entry of Amida—and behold! he comes.

For even while the Buddha Shakyamuni, in the role of teacher,
was speaking to Queen Vaidehi, the Solar Buddha Amitayus appeared in the midst of the banner- and music laden jewel sky,
together with his two Great Bodhisattvas, Avalokiteshvara at his
left, Mahasthama at his right; and there was such a dazzling radiance that no one could clearly see. It was a hundred thousand times
greater than the radiance of gold. And the queen approached the
Buddha Shakyamuni and worshiped at his feet, who then explained
how all beings in the future were to meditate on the Buddha
Amitayus.

The reader will have seen the meditation described to the queen
reproduced in numerous Buddhist works of art, whether from
India, Tibet, China, Korea, or Japan. He will easily understand,
furthermore, that although the eye of the art connoisseur may judge
forms aesthetically, the eye of religion passes through and sees—
or at least strives to see—not stone, not wood or paint, not bronze,
but a ground of seven jewels supporting a lotus of innumerable
lights, each leaf exhibiting the colors of numerous jewels and
having eighty-four thousand veins, each vein emitting eighty-four
thousand rays. And there is a tower all of gems, whereon are four
posts with jeweled banners, each banner like a hundred thousand
cosmic mountains: over the banners a jeweled veil, like that of

the celestial palace of the Lord of Death, shining with five hundred million jewels, each with eighty-four thousand rays, each ray with eighty-four thousand golden colors, and the whole continually changing in appearance: now a diamond tower, now a pearl net, again clouds of many mixed flowers—which, as the Buddha Shakyamuni has been said to have declared, is the Seventh Meditation: on the flowery throne.

After which there comes the culminating thought: the jewel of all the great jewels in this jewel net; indeed, the one jewel of Asia that is to be held continually before the mind through all these amplitudes of metamorphic vision. Stage and throne have been established. Now the mind is to see Amitayus. And as to the nature of that Buddha, let the following be heard. Shakyamuni speaks.

"Every Buddha Thus Come [tathāgata] is one whose spiritual body is itself the inhabiting principle of nature [dharmadhātu-kāya: the body that is the principle, or support of the law of true being]. Hence he may enter into the mind of any being. Hence, also, when you have perceived that Buddha, it is in fact your own mind that is in possession of those thirty-two signs of perfection and eighty minor marks of excellence perceived in the Buddha. In sum: it is your own mind that becomes the Buddha. Nay! it is your own mind that is even now the Buddha. The ocean of true and universal knowledge of all the Buddhas derives its source from one's own mind and thought." [80]

In the light of this basic thought, set down in Sanskrit in the Kushana period, translated c. 424 A.D. into Chinese, and known to every modern temple of the solar Buddha Amitabha, whether in China, Korea, or Japan, the reader will know why it was that during the centuries following the first appearance of Buddha images, a rapid trend away from the realistically viewed, teaching Buddhas of both the early Greco-Roman Gandhara style and the native Indian style of Mathura * soon carried the form from the plane of waking life to that of the initiatory, visionary dream. The solar halo behind the Gandharan Buddha heads was originally an Iranian, Zoroastrian motif, which was appearing also in the West, at

* Supra, p. 300.

about the same time, in the Greco-Roman iconography of the early Christians. The image of Christ in the course of time, however, was to assume a character increasingly realistic, whereas that of the Buddha, on the other hand, was rapidly going the opposite way. In the Gandharan forms the dramatic play of the Greek drapery and Apollo-like distinction of the head were reduced in force: the figure, as it were, moved back a little, summoning the contemplative mind also to step back. As Heinrich Zimmer has declared: "Appearance was transmuted into apparition. No bodily being, only an essence that has become silently manifest, is what is seen in these later Gandharan forms." [81] And in the art of Mathura, too, in the great fifth century A.D.—which is the moment of apogee of classic India—the halo became glorious, suggesting the wonder of the lotus world. There followed across the whole of Asia a flowering of the arts of vision that is unmatched in the history of mankind. And within the realm of Mother India itself, the Buddhist inspiration ran, as by a chain reaction, into the new universe of post-Buddhistic Hinduism—which, having caught fire from the Buddhist spirit, was soon to come to view with its challenge, and, presently, assuming the lead, step away into a teeming voluptuous world of visionary beatitudes of its own.

> Entering a room containing Indian sculpture [wrote Dr. Zimmer], one is immediately struck by the stillness with which it is filled, even when the forms that it contains are vigorously active. They breathe an air of repose that takes possession of the beholder, slows his step, and brings him to silence, both without and within. These works of art do not inspire one to enthusiastic, appreciative conversation; they do not ask to be regarded and found beautiful. They dwell in a world of their own; and even the Buddha, who, with lifted or downward extended open hand, rather finds himself before us than deliberately stands there, fulfills in this gesture his own being within the field of his own aura, without addressing himself to our person. Before his tranquil being, we do not exist.[82]

Such a work is a precipitated vision, not in the subtle, self-radiant, jewel matter of a dream, but in the indurated mass of a rock, or in clay, wood, or bronze. One does not see or feel in it the effort of the artist. Nor is it an imitation of nature. It is a manifestation of mind—"thus come," *tathāgata*—from a depth, to address an equivalent depth, not a connoisseur. It is not to be judged even morally (as we soon shall have occasion to realize). For works of this kind are presentations from beyond the rational horizon, beyond the pale of social judgment, ethics and aesthetics; and the faculty of judgment, deriving its force from the fields of normal experience, is exactly the faculty from which they are intended to release us. Brought to bear against them, it can serve only as a barrier to our own entry into their fields of force. Or, phrased another way: it can serve only to protect us from the impact of a noumenal experience, shattering all of our self-congratulatory notions of discovered truth.

"In forming a perception of the Buddha Amitayus," said the Buddha Shakyamuni to the queen for whose mind there was no longer any prison, "you should first perceive the image of that Buddha—whether your eyes be open or shut—gold in color, sitting on that flower, and when you have seen that you will be able to see clearly and distinctly the glory of that Buddha Realm. And when you have seen that, you should form another great lotus flower on the left side, and another great lotus flower on the right side of that Buddha. On the left-hand flowery throne perceive an image of the Bodhisattva Avalokiteshvara emitting golden rays like those of the Buddha; and Mahasthama, equally, on the right. And when this perception has been achieved, one is to hear the Good Law being preached through a stream of water, a brilliant ray of light, numerous jewel trees, jewel ducks, jewel geese, jewel swans. Whether wrapped in meditation or no longer so enwrapped, one should ever hear the excellent Law." [83]

Moreover, of the two Great Bodhisattvas, each of whom is eight hundred thousand niyutas * of yojanas high, let it be seen that in the halo of Avalokiteshvara five hundred Buddhas blaze forth, each attended by as many Bodhisattvas, surrounding each of which are numberless gods, while in the front of his tiara sits the figure of a Buddha twenty-five yojanas high. From the curl of hair

---

* A *niyuta* is an integer variously defined as 100,000; 1,000,000; or 10,000 times 10,000,000.

between his eyebrows eighty-four kinds of rays pour forth, each emitting innumerable Buddhas attended by their Bodhisattvas, variously changing appearances and filling the worlds to the quarters. While in the crown of Mahasthama five hundred jewel flowers shine, each supporting five hundred jewel towers, in each of which all of the Buddha realms of the ten quarters are to be seen. When he walks, the ten quarters quake, and wherever the earth trembles there appear five hundred million jewel flowers. The palms of the hands of these two compassionate Bodhisattvas are multicolored, the tips of their fingers are endowed with eighty-four thousand pictures, each picture being of eighty-four thousand colors and each color of eighty-four thousand rays. And with those jewel hands they embrace all beings.[84]

That is the vision of the glory of the void of one's own non-being, which is to be known, now, as the ever-present glory of all things. The solid walls of our jail of matter melt. The jewel hands of the Bodhisattvas appear and the world that formerly meant bondage becomes a Buddha Realm. "A man should believe neither in the idea of a thing nor in the idea of a no-thing," we read in a widely read Mahayana text; and, continuing:

> Stars, darkness, a lamp, a phantom, dew, a bubble;
> A dream, a flash of lightning, and a cloud:
> Thus should we look upon the world.[85]

The lotus-goddess, lotus of the world, upon whose flowery throne of innumerable lights the Buddha appears, within whose calyx even the being of no achievement whatsoever, stupid, wicked, full of the guilt of many crimes, may attain the knowledge of his own glory, and who, furthermore, is incarnate in all of those female beings spurned by the Jains and the monks of the Hinayana, thus returns —transformed—to view. She appeared first, we have seen, in the works of earliest Buddhist art, as the most prominent single figure in the ornamentation of the sacred sites; for, as we read in a later Mahayana text:

> *sarvāsām eva māyānāṁ*
> *strīmāyaiva viśiṣyate*

"Of all the forms of illusion, woman is the most important." [86]
Her role, henceforth, is to increase, in the way, first, of vision,
but then, of actuality: as the very portal of release, the Buddha
Realm par excellence, in whose illusory nature is manifest the
compassion (*karunā*) of nirvana. For as the Buddha of the negative
way, so is she the prime symbol of the positive. As the living
image of the wonder of this world in which we live, she is the ferry
and the goal in one.

THE INDIAN GOLDEN AGE

++

1. The Heritage of Rome

In the year 399 A.D., Fa-hsien, the first of a notable series of Chinese Buddhist pilgrims, left the sumptuous capital Ch'ang-an, at the head of the Old Silk Road from China to Rome, to brave the waste lands of Lop Nor. He reached Taxila in the Punjab six years later, passed into India itself, and for another six years traversed the land from west to east, consulting and debating with the learned, visiting holy sites, and observing with delight the virtue of the people and beauty of the Buddhist shrines.

"In all the countries of India the dignified carriage of the priesthood and surprising influence of religion cannot be described," he wrote in his journal.

Down from the time of the Lord Buddha's Nirvana, the kings, chief men and householders have raised monasteries for the monks and have provided for their support by endowing them with fields, houses, gardens, servants, and cattle. These church-lands are guaranteed to them by copper-plate grants, which are handed down from reign to reign, and no one has had the temerity to cancel them. All the resident priests, who are allotted cells in the viharas, have beds, mats, food, and drink supplied to them; they pass their time in performing acts of mercy, in reciting the scriptures, or in meditation. When a stranger arrives at the monastery, the senior priests escort him to the guest house, carrying his robes and his alms-bowl for him. They offer him water to wash his feet, and oil for anointing, and prepare a special meal for him. After he has rested a while they ask him his rank in the priesthood and, according to his rank, they assign him a chamber and bedding. During the month after the rain-rest, the pious collect a united offering for the priesthood; and the priests in their turn hold a great assembly and preach the Law.[1]

Buddhism was burgeoning in the period of Fa-hsien, the period of the fabled Hindu monarch Chandragupta II (reigned 378–414 A.D.). In India the rock-carved monastic halls and chapels of Ajanta, the earliest of which date from c. 50 B.C., were increasing both in number and in the beauty of their sculptured ornament, showing numerous motifs unknown to earlier Indian art. The Buddhist cave temples of Chinese Turkestan were being chiseled into great cliffs. And in the year 414, the year of Chandragupta's death, work began on the Chinese Buddhist rock-cut caves of Yunkang. The Buddha image acquired its mathematically harmonious classic form in this period: colossal figures appeared both in stone and in bronze. And when our sturdy Chinese voyager, in the year 411, took ship from the port of Tamrilipti at the mouth of the river Ganges and in two weeks reached Ceylon, he found the Buddhist religion no less honored there than on the mainland.

However, of a day, the chance sight of a Chinese taffeta fan offered at a shrine so moved Fa-hsien that he burst into tears and decided to sail home by way of Java, which he reached in a large merchantman that carried in its hold two hundred passengers. He transferred there to a smaller ship, and with all his gear of Buddhist images and manuscripts reached the South China port of Kwan Chow in the year 414.

Fa-hsien had been on Buddhist ground all the way; and yet in India itself in his day, in spite of the magnitude and glory of the order both there and throughout greater Asia, the chief creative force was no longer Buddhism, but a resurgent, highly sophisticated Brahminism, lavishly patronized by the court and brilliantly developed by a generation of Brahmins who knew perfectly how to synthesize native and alien, high and primitive traditions, to create what can be termed without qualification the richest, most subtle and comprehensive mythological system—or rather, galaxy of systems—known to man.

One of the glories of this age was the Hindu poet Kalidasa, whose delicious play, Shakuntala, drew from Goethe the lines:

If you wish the blossom of the early years and fruit of the late,
Wish what is charming and exciting as well as nourishing and
    filling,
Wish to capture heaven and earth in one name:
I name for you Shakuntala, and all is said.[2]

A suddenly teeming enrichment of the whole range of Indian
life, art, literature, science, and religion comes to view in the
works remaining to us from this magical time of both the blossom
and the fruit, to which India has ever since looked back, imag-
inatively projecting its perfection far into the past, as though for
millenniums India had known the voluptuous grace and harmony
of this moment of its apogee. In fact, one of the most remarkable
features of the age was the tendency of those responsible for its
glory to attribute all of the new arts, sciences, theological, social,
and aesthetic regulations, not to their own genius, but to the gods
and sages of an imagined mythological past.

Such a tendency is, of course, not unique to India. We shall take
note of it in China. It inspired, also, the authors of the Pentateuch.
However, the magnitude and sophistication of the Indian fantasy of
the fifth century A.D. was something entirely exceptional; for not
only a renovation of religious belief and ritual, a moral order and
social system were involved, but also a blossoming of the visual
arts, literature, theater, music, and the dance, every aspect of which
was rationalized in such a way as to appear to represent a revival
of eternal India—whereas actually a great many of its antecedents
lay not in India at all, but in Rome.

"In no year," wrote the Elder Pliny (23–79 A.D.), "does India
drain us of less than 550,000,000 sesterces, giving back her own
wares, which are sold among us at fully 100 times their first cost." [3]

"Our ladies glory in having pearls suspended from their fingers,
or two or three of them dangling from their ears, delighted even
with the rattling of the pearls as they knock against each other;
and now, at the present day, the poorer classes are even affecting
them, as people are in the habit of saying that 'a pearl worn by a
woman in public is as good as a lictor walking before her.' Nay,
even more than this, they put them on their feet, and that not only
on the laces of their sandals but all over the shoes; it is not enough

to wear pearls, but they must tread upon them, and walk with them under foot as well." [4]

Evidence of this trade can be seen in the numerous Roman coins of the Madras Museum collection, bearing the seals of Tiberius, Caligula, Claudius, and Nero (42 B.C.–68 A.D.); less numerously, Vespasian and Titus (69–81 A.D.); and again abundantly, Domitian, Nerva, Trajan, and Hadrian (81–138 A.D.).[5] And there is also the log of an unknown Egyptian Greek, a Roman citizen, who had personally steered his merchant craft, in Pliny's time, from the Red Sea on a much traveled trade route to India and back, *The Periplus of the Eritrean Sea.*

"Muziris," he wrote, telling of the chief port of the Indian southwest, "abounds in ships sent there with cargoes from Arabia and by the Greeks." Pepper is named among the exports; also "great quantities of fine pearls, ivory, silk cloth, spikenard from the Ganges, malabathrum from the interior, transparent stones of all kinds, diamonds, sapphires and tortoise shell." [6] And among the imports: "wine, Italian preferred . . . ; copper, tin, and lead; coral and topaz; thin clothing . . . , bright-colored girdles a cubit wide; . . . gold and silver coin, on which there is a profit when exchanged for the money of the country; and ointment, but not very costly and not much. And for the king there are brought into those places very costly vessels of silver, singing boys, beautiful maidens for the harem, fine wines, thin clothing of the finest weaves, and the choicest ointments." [7]

"The inland country back from the coast comprises many desert regions and great mountains; and all kinds of wild beasts abound— leopards, tigers, elephants, enormous serpents, hyenas, and baboons of many sorts." However, there were also, as the author states, "many populous nations, as far as to the Ganges." [8]

Sir Mortimer Wheeler, in the mid-forties, unearthed on the southeastern, Coromandel coast of India the remains of a considerable Roman trading station of this period, Arikamedu. "Numerous sherds both of a red-glazed pottery known to have been made in Italy in the first centuries B.C.–A.D. and of the two-handled jars or amphoras characteristic of the Mediterranean wine-trade of the period, together with Roman lamps and glassware, combine to indicate," states Wheeler in his report, "that Arikamedu was one of the regular 'Yavana' or Western trading-stations of which both Greco-Roman and ancient Tamil writers speak." Bead manufacture was an industry of that port. "Gold, semi-precious stones and glass were used for this purpose, and two gems, carved with intaglio designs by Greco-Roman gem-cutters, and in one instance untrimmed, suggest the presence of Western craftsmen on the site." A couple of walled courtyards associated with carefully built tanks, supplied and drained by a series of brick culverts, suggest "the preparation of the muslin cloth which has from ancient times been a notable product of this part of India and is recorded by classical writers as an Indian export." [9] And three hundred miles to the north, at Amaravati, in the sculptured ornamentation of what in the first to third centuries A.D. was a richly decorated Buddhist stupa, several representations of Westerners appear, while some of the sculpture was clearly inspired by Hellenistic models.[10]

In other words, the signs are numerous of a lively Indian trade with Rome in the first centuries A.D., with a flow of cultural as well as commercial influences running both ways. At Alexandria, in Egypt, Indian scholars were a common sight: they are mentioned both by Dio Chrysostom (c. 100 A.D.) and by Clement (c. 200 A.D.).[11] In the north, where the Old Silk Road, Rome to China, had been opened c. 100 B.C., the Kushanas were cultivating, both in trade and in diplomacy, associations at both terms. An age had dawned of a systematically developed world trade, both by caravan and by ship, uniting with strands that would only continue to increase in complexity as well as strength the four great domains of the ancient world, from Rome (which by now included France and Britain) to the Far East.

All of which, however, is but the beginning of the tale; for, as Dr. Hermann Goetz, formerly Curator of the Museum of Baroda, has shown, there occurred an event of epochal importance for India at the beginning of the fifth century A.D., the first phase of which took place in Rome.

"The [Roman] cruelties committed against the Christian martyrs are well known," writes Dr. Goetz; "but when the tide turned, those against the heathens loyal to the faith of their fathers were no less marked. Under Theodosius I the old cults were systematically wiped out (379–395) in the face of an obstinate resistance, though they did not disappear completely before the end of the sixth century. The temples were systematically closed or destroyed, the heathen sacrifices suppressed under penalty of death, the priests expelled or killed." [12] But "refugees go wherever they can find asylum," and, as Dr. Goetz points out, "such a land was India, with old trade relations with the Mediterranean."

Hence it was that in tolerant India, in the period of Chandragupta II (378–414, which dates, it will be noted, include and follow those of Theodosius I), there occurred the sudden flowering of an immense and really wonderful constellation of architectural, sculptural, literary, social, religious, and philosophical forms, unknown to India before but bearing hundreds of points of relationship to Late Rome.

Let us pause to note a few details.

In the realm of architecture: a type of rectangular stone cella with a porch and colonnade, resembling a small Hellenistic *templum in antis,* which appeared abruptly in the period of Chandragupta II, and already in the period of his successor, Kumaragupta I (414–453), was supplanted by a modified type of stone cella with a somewhat pyramidal tower atop, derived from the inspiration of the ziggurat and associated with the introduction to India at this time of Babylonian-Hellenistic astronomy. Also from Roman art came the idea of statues placed in wall niches, a particular type of scroll-frieze decor in which Erotes play among intertwining creepers, another composed of a line of projecting cubes, still another of petals, another of four-or-more-petaled rosettes; further: torus moldings in the shape of a laurel or acanthus garland, certain new varieties of Buddha throne, garlands of pearl chains alternately hanging down and loosely joining two supports; a motif derived from Roman sarcophagi showing a half-opened door with a female peering out. Add certain types of chimeric water beast (*makara*), birdlike harpy (*kinnarī*), lion-mask (*kīrtimukha*), soaring divine couple (*gandharva*-and-*apsaras*), techniques of bronze casting with inlay, enamel, and glyptic art, and the number of analogues becomes too great to represent anything but a massive adaptation—which is to be recognized also, as Dr. Goetz precisely shows, in a multitude of other details, from modes of thought and literary form to ways of dance and of doing up the hair.

However—and here is the crucial point: "Though so many novel ideas, techniques and types were absorbed that practically a quite new and most important chapter of Indian art was opened, they were never taken over *en bloc.* . . . Everything was broken up, translated into Indian concepts and reconstructed on Indian principles." [13] Against the Hellenistic canon of the human body, an Indian one was set up. Against the Hellenistic-Roman typology, an Indian one was evolved, to serve a completely different life. Imported architectural and sculptural types were adapted to or replaced by analogous Indian ones: tritons by gandharvas; acanthus leaves by lotuses. Use was made of native folklore, which the Brahmins systematically (but never altogether consistently) adjusted to their own aims. And the result, once again to quote Dr. Goetz, was "a rewriting of history such as, in our own time, only Nazism and Communism have envisaged." [14] The real past was obliterated and a mythic past projected, by which the present, then, was to be validated, ostensibly for all time, against all heresy, all criticism, and all truth.

"The Gupta revolution succeeded on the slogan that it was bringing back the 'good old times' of the ancient rishis, heroes, and gods. In reality, however, a hectic cultural development was going on. But all innovations were introduced on the claim of having been proclaimed in the past, if possible by the gods themselves." [15]

And this, then, was the vivid age in which the bold Chinese pilgrim Fa-hsien arrived to marvel at India in its apogee: India at that golden moment when it became for a time the leading civilization of mankind.[16]

II. The Mythic Past

The chief mythological document of the Indian Golden Age is the epic Mahabharata, much of the material of which is indefinitely old, perhaps ante 400 B.C., but of which the final style and tone are rather of c. 400 A.D. and thereafter. The work is a kind of terminal moraine of all sorts of mythic, ritual, moral, and genealogical lore, eight times as long as the *Iliad* and *Odyssey* combined: "a conglomerate," to quote one learned authority, "of very different views, and, what is most important, of very different views repeated in immediate proximity to one another without any apparent sense of their incongruity." [17]

It would be a bore, and to no point, to offer here an outline of the plot of this massive work. But the legend of its supposed author, recounted in its first book, affords an excellent sampling of its fare. The great rishi Vyasa has been termed the Homer of India, but is in fact far more than that. He is what Homer would have been had he, besides singing of the Trojan War, also sired all its characters on both sides. The name itself, *vy-āsa,* means "distributing or letting go (*as*) in all directions (*vi-*)"—which could hardly be more apt. For this man was not only the author of the prodigious work itself and progenitor of all of its chief characters on both sides, but also the author of all eighteen or more of the Puranas (which are a series of lesser epics, dating from about the fourth to sixteenth centuries A.D.), collector and arranger of the four Vedas, creator of Vedantic philosophy, and a perfect forest recluse besides.

The typically Indian biography of this rishi begins in that more than golden age to which the poets of the period of Kanishka were already looking back, and which has supplied India with a past infinitely surpassing anything known to other parts of the world. For there was in that fabulous time a king, Vasu by name, who was devoted to virtue (*dharma*) but no less to the hunt; and of a time when a certain great mountain near his capital, having become maddened with desire for the river that was flowing at its foot, embraced and so enclosed that river that its waters no longer flowed past the city, the king went and gave that mountain a kick. The river came flowing from the indentation, but was now pregnant and, giving birth to a boy and girl, presented them in gratitude to the king, who made the boy his general and the girl his wife. She was called Girika, "Daughter of the Mountain." And when the season of her impurity came and passed, she told her husband of her state and went to the river to purify herself.

Now it is a principle of the dharma of all husbands that they must have intercourse with their wives immediately following the menstrual period, because—according to the infallible truth of Vedic revelation—this is the auspicious time for the begetting of a child. And so that king, having knowledge of the readiness of Girika, had knowledge also of his duty, to which he was devoted. But he was devoted equally, as we have heard, to the pleasures of the hunt; and so, when it came to pass, even while his wife was at the river, that a number of his elder relatives arrived to invite him to hunt deer, reasoning that an ancestor should be obeyed and heeding the filial, not the marital, dharma, he departed.

There were numerous flowering trees in the country that he entered. Moreover, the whole forest at that time was maddened with the cooing of birds and hum of intoxicated bees; for the season was spring, and the groves through which he moved were as fair as the gardens of the genii of the earth. He was put in mind of his marital dharma, and, overcome by desire, sat him down beneath a beautifully blossoming, heavily scented tree, where, when his mind had dissolved to madness, he was overcome by a crisis; following which he mused that his seed should not be lost and, gathering it up in a large leaf, he called to a hawk soaring above: "O my friend, do thou bear this to my wife, who is in her season."

The bird assumed the charge, but on the way a second hawk, supposing the burden to be meat, dove at it and it fell into the river Jumna, where it was immediately swallowed by a fish, who was actually a nymph under enchantment; and in the tenth month that unfortunate fish was taken by a fisherman, who, when he found a boy and girl within, was amazed. The boy presented to the king, became, presently, himself a king; but the girl, because of a perceptibly fishy smell with which she was endowed, was consigned to the fisherman to be his daughter. And the nymph, released, ascended to the sky.

Thus the first part of this tale of the lineage of the author of the Mahabharata.

The second now tells of the girl.

She was blessed with extraordinary beauty and gifted with all virtue. Satyavati, "Truth," was her name, but she was known as

Fishy Smell. And, serving her foster father, she plied a boat on the waters of the river Jumna, to which, one day, a great, a very great, yogi named Parashara came to be ferried to the other shore. And when he saw that girl with her tapering thighs smiling at him in that boat, he was suddenly mastered by desire. But she said: "O blessed saint, those other saints along the shores, waiting to be ferried: they would see."

The yogi thereupon brought down a fog by which they were obscured; seeing which, the girl was confused. "Know me to be a maid in her father's keep," she said. "O sinless saint without match, consider and behave."

Delighted by her character, the saint reassured her. "Timid girl, your virginity can be restored," he said. "Moreover, no wish of mine is ever without fruit. Ask of me anything you desire." She begged that her body should have a sweet smell; and so, their desires, mutually, were granted. Virginity returned; and the maid was known thereafter as Gandhavati, "Sweetly Scented," for men could smell the scent of her body from the distance of a league.

The yogi, on the yonder shore, departed for his hermitage, and the girl, in time, in secrecy, on a wooded isle in the middle of the holy river Jumna, whence she herself had come, gave birth to a boy. Once again virginity returned. And the infant, getting to his feet, walked away into the forest, saying as he left: "When you need me, think of me, Mother, and I shall appear." [18]

The reader will perhaps not be able to believe that this tale is quite precise as to fact. However, the son thus born was Vyasa; and we are reading his own account of these holy matters in his own great book—which goes on, now, with the adventure of the mother, still a virgin, to whose ferry there came, attracted by the scent, a certain great, a certain very great, king.

And this goodly man, no longer young, Santanu by name, had just bestowed the right of succession upon his excellent son Bhishma, born some years before of a lovely personage who had proved, to the king's amazement, to have been the goddess-river Ganges. Approaching now the holy river Jumna, and perceiving that extraordinary scent, the king, scouting for its source, arrived at the boat of this beautiful maid of the fisherman caste.

"O timid, lovely maid," he said, "who can you be?"

She answered: "I am the daughter, good sir, of the chief fisherman of this place, and in the service of my father I ferry pilgrims to the yonder shore."

The king went directly to the father; but the fisherman said to him: "If your desire is for my daughter lawfully, you must pledge to me that the son born to you of her shall be the sole successor to your throne." And when he heard that, the old king was unstrung. He returned to Hastinapur, his capital, and in sorrow, thinking only of that girl, began to waste away.

Then his excellent son, Bhishma, discovering the cause of his father's illness, went to that fisherman with a company of princes, saying, "My good man, I hereby vow before these princes that the son born to my father of your daughter shall be our king." But the fisherman answered: "I have no doubt, sir, of your vow. What, however, of the claims of your possible sons?" And the prince said, "I shall assume, then, a second vow: to live celibate for life." Whereupon the hair of that fisherman stood on end. He bowed. And the virgin of the river was bestowed.[19]

Thus we come to the tale of the ferrymaid's further sons; for the good king Santanu begot two. The elder succeeded to his throne, but was slain in battle, very young; and since the younger died of consumption, also very young, there were left two childless royal widows, beautifully tall, with flowing glossy hair, red nails, swelling breasts and mighty hips. And the widowed queen-mother, Satyavati, said to Bhishma, "The line is without issue. But you are learned in the Vedas, powerful, virtuous, and, I am sure, concerned for the preservation of this line; so I shall appoint you to a certain act. Ascend in majesty our throne, marry the girls according to our rites, and beget sons."

Bhishma simply recalled to her the vow that her father had extracted, and she thought, next, in her strait, of the infant who had walked away.

Vyasa now was a great sage, at work interpreting the Vedas, yet he appeared, as promised, when his mother addressed her mind to him.

"I shall produce sons like Yama and Varuna," he said, when she had bathed him with her tears and confronted him with her charge. "Only first, let the two young ladies keep for a year certain vows that I shall assign."

She answered, "But our kingdom is in danger. The work is to be done today."

"Well then," said he, "let them tolerate my ugliness, grim visage, foul body, terrible odor, and frightening garb. If they can do that they will bear sturdy sons. Let the elder be adorned. Let her wait for me in a bed in pure attire." And he disappeared.

The girl having been tactfully persuaded, bathed, and beautifully adorned, Satyavati led her to a large bed. "Here you will lie," she said, "and await the elder brother of your spouse." And the young widow, happily supposing Bhishma to be the elder brother meant, lay thoughtfully awake. The lamp burned. The door opened. A form entered. And what she saw, with a start, was an ascetic with black glowering face, blazing eyes, coppery piled-up matted hair, grim beard, and such an odor when he approached as she could hardly bear. She shut her eyes. And when he returned to Satyavati, "The boy," he said, "will be as strong as ten thousand elephants, father of a thousand sons; however, because of the failure of the mother, who at the moment of conception shut her eyes, he will be blind."

And the child was indeed blind. He became the great king Dhritarashtra ("He who supports," *dhṛta*, "the kingdom" *raṣṭra*), father of the Kauravas, the enemy party in the plot of the Mahabharata. But Satyavati, when she saw that child, once again thought of Vyasa, and when he appeared, bade him try again.

The second lovely widow was committed, unsuspecting, to the bed. The lamp in the large room burned. The door opened. A figure entered and her eyes stood wide; she went pale. The saint approached, and when he had done with her, he said, "Since you are pale, your son also will be pale. So you shall call him Pandu" (*pāṇḍu*: "white, yellow-white, pale").

And indeed, the son born was very pale. Yet he was the father of the Pandavas, the five hero brothers of the Mahabharata: Yudhishthira, Bhima, Arjuna, and the twins Nakula and Sahadeva. In other words, the epic war was to be in essence a conflict be-

tween the Sons of Darkness (a king who had been conceived with
the eyes closed) and the Sons of Light (one conceived with the
eyes open). But there was to be a third birth, besides; for Satyavati,
still dissatisfied, arranged a second occasion for the first of the two
young queens, who, however, contrived to put a slave girl in her
place. And when the yogi had accomplished Satyavati's will upon
that Shudra girl, she arose and paid him reverence; by which he
was greatly pleased. "O you amiable damsel, you shall no longer
be a slave," he said, "and your son shall be greatly endowed."
And indeed, her son was the sage Vidura, uncle-adviser of the
Pandavas, who, in the end, became illuminate as a yogi.[20]

Now the Light and Darkness motif, the reader recalls, appeared
in Iran c. 500 B.C., in the cosmic war of the Lord of Truth and
the Master of the Lie. In the Hebrew Dead Sea Scrolls of c. 175
B.C.–c. 66 A.D.,[21] it reappears in the war of the Sons of Light with
the Sons of Darkness. And in the various Gnostic literatures of
the first centuries A.D. other developments of the motif are to be
found. In all of these Levantine applications the argument is at
once ethical and ontological. The principle of truth and light represents both *virtue* and *true being*. It has both a social reference
and an absolute validity, and in the end will triumph on a cosmic
scale. No essential distinction is made in these systems between
social and metaphysical orders of judgment.

And in the Buddhist mythology of Amida, likewise, the principle
of light and true knowledge is at once ethical and substantial in
its reference. The ultimate victory of the light is not represented,
here, in cosmic terms; for in the Buddhist cosmos of unending
cycles there is no place for a time beyond time when the cycling
will have ceased: the Buddhist cessation is psychological, in the
way of a disengagement from the unimprovable round. Nevertheless, the principle of light is of an order truer and more substantial than that of the darkness of the round. The latter is a
mere function of ignorance and desire—and of action under their
binding, blinding spell. Consequently, just as in the Western systems the social and metaphysical orders are equated, so in that
of Amida, the psychological and metaphysical.

Something considerably more complex appears in the highly developed, apparently ridiculous, but actually extremely sophisticated symbolic game of the Brahmins by whom the physically impossible biography of Vyasa was devised. It is to be noted that in this eminently Indian version of the polar play of light and darkness in the battlefield of life, neither light nor darkness ultimately wins. Further, both powers derive from a single superior source, which is, namely, Vyasa. And although an ethical judgment is applied for and against, respectively, the Sons of Light and the Sons of Darkness, the verdict is by no means absolute. On the contrary, the two sides are equally of a secondary, dualistic order, functions of a certain circumstance, which it would be worth pausing a moment to regard; namely, the impatience of the queen for immediate, utilitarian results. This made impossible the preparation of the field, and so was the real cause of the shock of the two girls, and their opposed, equally innocent responses. The play of light and darkness in the field of human history thus appears to have been a function of human weakness; and, although ethical judgments can be rendered within the field of this play, both the virtue and the vice to which they refer belong to a secondary sphere. They are complementary. Compare the old Egyptian Secret of the Two Partners! There is a broader, higher point of view than that to which the cosmic shadow play of light and dark appears; and in the context of the Mahabharata it is represented by the progenitor and witness of the piece. Compare the figure, above discussed, of Ptah, the Mummy, begetter of the Apis bull, and Pharaoh, whose counterpart in the later Tantric symbolism of India is Shava, the Corpse, turned away from, yet in essence one with, the world-producing Shiva-Shakti pair (supra, p. 90, and Figure 21)! Compare the Self who said "I" and became two!

The late Brahminic system of the Mahabharata, in contrast to the Buddhist of Amida, comprehends involvement in the world of maya as well as escape from it. However, there is not implied in this involvement any such unqualified affirmation of the values of the world as our Western ethical positivism represents. The round cannot be improved; nor do its values refer beyond its own sphere. And yet—as the biography of Vyasa clearly shows—the world can be affirmed by the sage ironically: somewhat in the way of an adult's affirmation of a rather seriously played children's game.

And now, finally, the figure of the queen Satyavati, who represents the whole force in this tale of the irony of the play of maya,

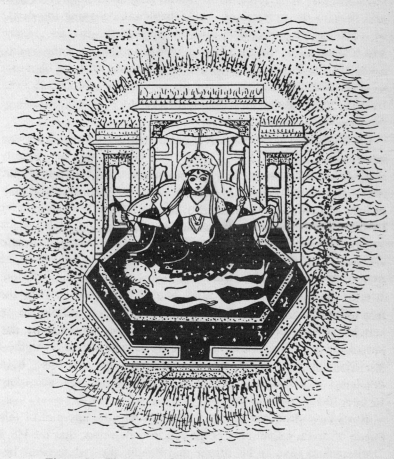

Figure 21. The Isle of Gems: India (Rajput), c. 1800 A.D.

is the mother both of Vyasa and of the two young kings who died. The cosmic mystery of maya has three powers. The first is that of obscuring brahman; the second, that of projecting the world-mirage; and the third, that of revealing brahman through the mirage. Satyavati in her ferry carried yogis to the farther shore and in that work represented the revealing power of maya; but she also ferried passengers from the yonder shore to this and thereby was obscuring and projecting. In the service of the desire of the good king Santanu, who remained with her on this shore, she became the activating force of the whole field and interplay of light and dark in the universe of the Mahabharata. Serving the desire of the not quite perfect yogi midway between the two shores, she was the mother of the great Vyasa, who, as collector of the Vedas, author of the Puranas, etc., provided the world with its literature of revelation, and as begetter of the two families produced, even on this hither shore, an essentially revelatory history, which, if read as merely factual, obscures.

Satyavati in her character as charmer of the king had a sweet scent, which, however, was not her true scent; nor was the virginity rendered to the king her true virginity. The scent repulsive to the world was her true scent, embraced with eagerness by the yogi— whose true goal, however, was beyond. And the ever-running river of life, out of which she had come, as all life, is throughout the literature of the Orient symbolic of the pouring of divine grace into the field of phenomenality. On one hand (one shore), it is the field of all joy and pain, virtue and vice, knowledge and delusion, but on the other hand (the other shore), traversed or read the other way, it leads beyond these complementary principles to an absolute that is beyond principles. And in the isle between, the isle of the great Vyasa's birth, is the world and source of myth— the Mahabharata—which in itself is both true and false, both revelatory and obscuring, and to be read, like life itself, according to one's talent, either way.

But I have promised not to attempt to rehearse the plot of this ocean of myth. I shall only point out, in conclusion, that the blind Dhritarashtra gave up his throne and Pandu, the "white one," became king; who, however, died young, so that the elder brother had to return. Dhritarashtra's numerous sons, the Kauravas, and the five excellent sons of Pandu, the Pandavas, then became engaged in a blood bath wherein the flower of the chivalry of the feudal age of Vedic India perished.

The last five books of the epic (Books 14 to 18) are of a

definitely post-heroic cast. Yudhishthira, the eldest of the Pandavas, performs a horse sacrifice by which all the sins of the battle are washed away. Old Dhritarashtra and his wife, completely bereaved of their thousand sons, retire to the forest. The divine incarnations of the god Vishnu—black Krishna and his white brother Balarama—who throughout the long course of the numerous ordeals have been of great comfort and assistance to the five brothers (who are symbolic of the five senses, the five elements) pass away, and the Pandavas themselves, together with the lovely Draupadi, their shared wife (the allure of life), set forth in bark clothing, with a dog at their heels, to climb afoot to heaven. They cross the Himalayas to the world mountain, Meru, which they ascend laboriously. On the way, Draupadi drops dead, and in sequence, Sahadeva, Nakula, Arjuna, and Bhima, so that Yudhishthira alone reaches the summit, accompanied only by his dog. The god Indra descends in his chariot to carry him beyond, but he demurs until promised that his wife and brothers will be found in the heavenly realm and that the dog, too, may come in. The animal, admitted, becomes the god Dharma. The brothers and wife, however, cannot be found, for they are in hell; whereas, sitting glorious on a throne is the leader of the dark Kauravas, the paramount villain. Indignantly, Yudhishthira quits heaven, descending to hell, where he discovers not his brothers only, but many friends in terrible distress. Then he learns (and so do we, at this point) that those who die with little sin go first to hell to be cleansed, and then to heaven, whereas those of little virtue ascend first to heaven for a brief enjoyment of their merit, and then are cast for a long and terrible term into hell.

The hell scene dissolves and the Pandavas all are in heaven as gods. Vyasa, however, their progenitor, still is at work down here on earth. A sort of eon has been run: the entire world of the Mahabharata, which had come into being out of himself, had disappeared into air, like a mirage. And he was now to render it into words, blessed words, the words of the truth of all things.

Now Vyasa had an acolyte, Vaishampayana by name, to whom he recounted the whole story; and this learned man then attended a great festival of snake magic, where a king, Janamejaya, took revenge for the death by snakebite of his father by causing all the serpents of the world to crawl to their death in a vast Vedic fire. And it was during the intervals between the stages of this ceremony that Vaishampayana recited the Mahabharata. A bard named Ugrashrava overheard it and was approached, later, by a company of saints to recount to them the entire thing—which he did. And that is the source of our present Mahabharata: from the words of a bard who had got it from the sage who had heard it from Vyasa himself,[22] who by now had departed from this world that he had brought into being and watched die, by a flight in yoga through the fiery door of the sun.[23]

III. The Age of the Great Beliefs: c. 500–1500 A.D.

Buddhism was in origin a doctrine of renunciation, typically represented by the shaven-headed, bowl-bearing monk who had retired to a monastery in quest of the yonder shore. The resurgent Brahminism of the Gupta restoration, on the other hand, was directed not to monastic ends alone, but equally to the maintenance of a secular society. And in this context, the term *dharma* did not refer primarily, as in Buddhism, to a doctrine of disengagement, but to the cosmic system of laws and processes by which the universe exists. It is a term derived from the verbal root *dhṛ,* "to hold up, support, maintain," and in meaning, as we have seen, accords with Egyptian *maat,* Sumerian *me.* Therefore, whereas in Buddhist mythology we hear nothing of the holy fashioning and maintenance of the world order, but only of the adventure of the biography of the Savior, from which the way to release from the sorrows of phenomenality is to be learned, in the mythologies of Brahminism a dual lesson is always served, both of dharma and of yoga, engagement and disengagement—both at once.

"O King," we read in the Mahabharata, "walk, as regards kingdoms, in the customary way trodden by all good men. What do you gain by living in the hermitage of the ascetics, deprived of the virtue (*dharma*) of your caste, and of both achievement (*artha*) and delight (*kāma*)?" [24]

In the Buddhist reading of the nature of existence all is absolutely void and without a self; the forms of phenomenality ride like a mirage over nothing at all, conjured up by the force of ignorance, and the sole interest is in its dissolution.

"From the arising of ignorance is the arising of the karma formations. From the stopping of ignorance is the stopping of the karma formations." That is the word of the Hinayana Pali Canon.[25]

"Form is the void and the void is the form. The void is nothing but form and form nothing but the void. Outside the void there is no form, and outside the form no void." That is the Mahayana wisdom of the yonder shore.[26]

In the orthodox Vedic-Brahminic-Hindu reading, on the other hand, all is the manifestation of a self-giving power (*brahman*) that is transcendent and yet immanent in all things as the self (*ātman*) of each. It has given of itself in the way of the Self that said "I," felt fear, then desire, and poured forth the world, of which we have already heard.* Hence, the generative power of that presence—not a void—is what is to be recognized and experienced in all beings. For, though unknown, it is everywhere.

> Though he is hidden in all things,
> That self does not shine forth.
> Yet he is seen by subtle seers
> With superior, subtle intellect.[27]

The way to the knowledge of this Being of beings may seem to resemble the Buddhist way; for it is conceived as an ego-sacrifice, wherein the I (*aham*) is abandoned.

> To him who has conquered himself by himself,
> His self is a friend.
> But to him who has not conquered himself by himself,
> His self is hostile, like a foe.[28]

However, what is to be achieved by this ego-sacrifice is a knowledge of identity, not with emptiness, but with that Being that is in its own sacrifice the wonder of the world.

There is therefore in Hinduism an essential affirmation of the cosmic order as divine. And since society is conceived to be a part of the cosmic order, there is an affirmation, equally, of the

* Supra, pp. 9–10.

orthodox Indian social order as divine. Furthermore, as the order of nature is eternal, so also is this of the orthodox society. There is no tolerance of human freedom or invention in the social field; for society is not conceived to be an order evolved by human beings, subject to intelligence and change, as it was in advanced Greece and Rome and as it is in the modern West. Its laws are of nature, not to be voted on, improved upon, or devised. Precisely as the sun, moon, plants and animals follow laws inherent in their natures, so therefore must the individual the nature of his birth, whether as Brahmin, Kshatriya, Vaishya, Shudra, or Pariah. Each is conceived to be a species. And as a mouse cannot become a lion, or even desire to be a lion, no Shudra can be a Brahmin; and desiring to be one would be insane. Hence the Indian word "virtue, duty, law," *dharma,* has a deep, a very deep reach. "Better one's own duty ill performed," we read, "than that of another, to perfection." [29] The Greek or Renaissance idea of the great individual simply does not exist within the pale of this system. One is to be, rather, a *dividuum,* divided man, a man who represents one limb or function of the great man (*puruṣa*), which is society itself: the Brahmin, priestly caste, being its head; the Kshatriya, governing caste, its arms; the Vaishya, financial caste, the belly and torso; while the Shudras, workers, are its legs and feet. The Pariahs, outcastes, meanwhile, are of another natural order entirely, and in connection with the human community can perform only inhuman, beastly chores.

The first severe blow to the integrity of this system fell in the Gupta period itself, in the year 510 A.D., when the Ephthalite Huns, under a young leader, Mihirgula, entered and ravaged the northwest and made the Guptas tributary. Their savage reign was short; for Mihirgula was defeated by a confederacy of princes 528 A.D., and retired to Kashmir, where he died. However, its consequences for India were decisive. "The curtain," as Professor H. G. Rawlinson writes of the transformed situation, "now rings down upon the scene for nearly a century"; and when it rises, we find in the Ganges Valley three prominent states continually at war. These were the Guptas of eastern Malwa, no doubt a branch of the imperial family of yore, the Maukharis of Kanauj, and the Vardhanas of Thanesar, a city north of Delhi. By about 612 the entire north was briefly united under Harsha, after whose murder, however, in the year 647, "the curtain once more descends," and when it rises two centuries later, the scene is altogether changed.[30]

"A new order of society has arisen, the central figures of which are the numerous clans of a race calling themselves Rajputs or 'Sons of Kings.' . . . The Rajputs claim to be the ancient Kshatriyas and found their ideals of conduct upon the heroes of the Hindu epics; but modern research shows that they are mainly the descendants of the Gurjara, Hun, and other Central Asian tribes who found their way across the northwest frontier in the fifth and sixth centuries. These invaders carved out kingdoms for themselves and eventually settled down in the country, taking Hindu wives." [31]

From the West, meanwhile, a number of new religious movements had arrived, among which the late Gupta cult of the sun-god Surya was of particular moment. This was a rich syncretic compound of elements derived from the late Roman imperial cult of Sol Invictus and Iranian Mithraism, a dash of Alexandrian planet worship, and a popular revival of the ancient Syrian rites of the great goddess Anahid-Cybele in a temple setting of ritual prostitution; [32] to all of which the famous sun-temple at Kanarak (thirteenth century A.D. in Orissa) is perhaps the best-known remaining witness.[33]

But the fervor, also, of an entirely new Levantine belief began to make itself felt in these years. Arab merchants had been frequenting for centuries the busy ports of the Indian west coast; their craft are mentioned already in the Periplus of the Eritrean Sea, first century A.D.* In the course of the seventh century the religion of Mohammed (570?–632 A.D.) gained the mastery of the whole Near East; and although its full impact was not felt in India until half a millennium later, the ports from Sind to Malabar were already familiar with its tenets by the year 712 A.D., when the first Mohammedan Arab colony settled in Sind. Indeed, a

* Supra, p. 324.

number of new movements within the Hindu fold itself were touched off by the proselytes of Islam; for, as a recent Indian author, P. N. Chopra, states the case:

> The belief in the brotherhood of man and theoretical equality of all believers, monotheism, and absolute submission to the will of God, which are characteristic of Islam, made a profound impression on the minds of certain Indian thinkers and reformers of the period. Contacts between Mussulmans and Hindus on both the Malabar and the Coromandel coasts worked as a leaven upon a considerable development of Indian thought and stimulated the renaissance of monotheistic and anti-caste movements in the South, which was the hearth of the religious reforms of the eighth to tenth centuries. Vishnuite and Shivaite saints founded schools of *bhakti* and such men of learning as Shankara, Ramanuja, Nimbaditya, Basava, Vallabhacharya and Madhva formulated their personal philosophical systems.[34]

In short, from the period of the Hunnish invasion a new spirit reigned on the Indian scene, characterized, on the one hand, by a multiplication of alien influences, but on the other, by a contrary effort to maintain the earlier Gupta classic forms. In the words of Dr. Goetz: "Following the terrible invasions of the Ephthalite Huns, Shulikas and Gurjaras, the fall of the Gupta empire, civil wars, military dictatorships, monetary disasters, declines of cities and collapse of the burgher class, Indian culture became definitively feudal-clerical: medieval. And what in the *earlier* Gupta period had been a disguised renaissance and return to aristocratic rule, now became a sacrosanct tradition: the indispensable model for an age defending its cultural heritage only with great effort against an increasing barbarization."[35]

The period corresponds to that of Gothic Europe, from the fall of Rome to the Renaissance. It is the period of the culmination of Byzantium and flowering of Islam, from the century of Justinian (483–565) to the fall, on the one hand, of Constantinople to the Turks (1453) and, on the other, of Moorish Granada (1492) to the patroness of Columbus. The parallel time in China extends from the Sui and T'ang dynasties to the middle of the Ming; while in Japan the entire development from the arrival of Buddhism in a frame of Chinese learning (552 A.D.) to the culmination of the Ashikaga period (1392–1568) was accomplished within the span of this millennium.

Broadly viewed, from East to West and West to East, the epoch is distinguished everywhere by a burgeoning of devotional religious arts: the Christian cathedral age, the world of the mosques of Islam, all the chief Brahminical monuments of India, and the Buddhist temple gardens of the Far East. Its ways of thought, by and large, were rather scholastic than creative, leaning back upon the paragons of an apotheosized past; little doubting; vehemently believing; attributing to eternity the revelations of time and to God the works of certain men. But while in India the temples grew in size and the pious books in bulk, their vitality gradually declined. Sentimentalism and clichés supplanted thought and emotion. Folk crafts and folk piety gained the field; and the arts, finally emptied of religious inspiration, became either slickly erotic or entirely expressionless. So that where formerly there had been a wonderful spirit of adventure, there was now but peasant piety, applied art, priestly routine, and a world of warring half-barbaric courts.

"Only in remote, backward regions like Nepal and Tibet," states Dr. Goetz, "has the Indian art tradition remained, to our own time, really alive in the medieval sense of an iconography. What is there can hardly be taken in its present state, however, as a measure of truly Indian art in all its vigor and wealth of forms." [36]

IV. The Way of Delight

For a final taste of the somewhat overripe late fruit of the tree of India, the obvious legend to be chosen is of the blue-black boy-savior Krishna, in his charming popular aspect as the moonlight lover of the Gopis: the young and middle-aged wives of a cow-herding folk, among whom, as their foster child, he was being reared.

The legend is of interest not only in itself but also from a comparative point of view; for when its overt celebration of adulterous love is contrasted with that of the poetry of the European troubadours and the romances of Lancelot and Guinevere, Tristan and

Iseult, it exhibits, on the one hand, a number of analogies, but on the other, a completely different spirit. Although its culminating document, "The Song of the Cowherd" (*Gītā Govinda*), by the court poet Jayadeva, is of a date (c. 1175) that lands it precisely in the century of the leading Tristan verse romances (from that of Thomas, c. 1165, to Gottfried von Strassburg, 1210) and is a work, furthermore, of an even more overt erotic definition than theirs, the atmosphere and argument throughout are of religion: as though the passion of Tristan and Iseult had been identified with the love, say, of Christ and Mary Magdalene in the mode of the Song of Songs. Moreover, whereas in the twelfth-century courtly disciplines of Europe the concentration of the lover was to be entirely on the qualities of one lady, the wonderful boy-savior Krishna, who could multiply himself boundlessly, achieved, in the course of the centuries of his legend (as the reader soon will see), an ecstasy of wanton rapture of the most prodigious spread; and to such a feat of yogic power the Occidental term *love* (at least in its courtly sense) cannot be applied.

We need not rehearse the legends of his miraculous birth and of the numerous childhood pranks played by the little blue-black boy, together with his white brother Balarama, among the wagons of the cowherds. Suffice to say that they were enough to make him well known to every girl and woman of the company; so that these were already very much his victims when they heard, one moonlit night, the strains of a solitary flute coming from the forest—distant music drifting to their hearts. The perfume of white waterlilies hung heavy in the air, and the Gopis all stirred in sleep. Their hearts opened, then their eyes, and one by one, they got up cautiously and, like so many shadows, slipped from their homes. One softly hummed an accompaniment to the flute; another, also running, listened; a third called out his name, then shrank, abashed; while a fourth, who, on stirring, had seen the seniors of her household still awake, shut her eyes again, but meditated with such effect on her beloved that she was joined with him forever—in death.

The boy professed surprise when he beheld his multitude arrive.

"But where," he asked, "are your fathers, brothers, husbands?" Shocked—and all greatly surprised, furthermore, to find the other Gopis present—some began to etch figures on the ground with their toes, and the eyes of all became lakes of tears. "We cannot move from thy lotus feet," they pleaded; and the god, when he had teased enough, began to move among them freely, playing still upon his flute. "O place thy lotus hands," they cried, "upon our aching breasts, upon our heads!" And the dance began.

Now there exist a number of versions of this dance, the *rāsa*, of Krishna and the Gopis, dating from the sixth to sixteenth centuries A.D.; so that there is available a rather full documentation of the growth of what was, on one side, a literary, but, on the other, a deeply religious tradition of erotic play. And it would be difficult to find a more convincing illustration of a certain universal principle in the history of religious thought, which is, namely, that, in proportion as poetic insight and sensibility decline, sensationalism, hackneyed formulae, and sentimentality increase.

In the earlier versions of the rasa, in the sixth-century Vishnu Purana and Harivamsa, the moonlight play of Krishna and the Gopis retains the atmosphere of a bucolic idyll. Its main event was a dance in which the women, holding hands, moved in a circle, each with her eyes closed, imagining herself to be Krishna's friend. "Each he took by the hand," states the Vishnu Purana,

> and when their eyes were shut by the magic of his touch, the circle formed. Krishna sang an air in praise of autumn. The Gopis responded, praising Krishna, and the dance began to the tinkle of their bracelets.
>
> Occasionally dizzied by the round, one or another would throw her arms about her beloved's neck and the drops of his perspiration then were like fertilizing rain, which caused the down to stand forth on her temples. Krishna sang. The Gopis cried "Hail, Krishna!" * Where he led, they followed; when he turned, they met; and for each, every moment was a myriad of years.
>
> Thus the Being Omnipotent assumed the character of a youth among the women of Vrindavan, pervading their natures and therewith, too, the natures of their lords; for, even

---

* Compare supra, p. 67: *Huree Bul!* Hari (i.e., Vishnu = Krishna), hail!

as in all creatures the elements are comprehended of ether, air, fire, water, and earth, so also is the Lord everywhere, within all.[37]

The idea of the immanence of the god transcendent is here the inspiring theme; and, as in all Indian mystic lore, the trend is to a depth wherein just that is realized and differentiations dissolve. The shut eyes of the Gopis indicate that the presence dwells within all, as the very being of each being, so that the rasa in this early version is a gently balanced symbol of the Indian orthodox Double Way, wherein the outer order of virtue (*dharma*) is maintained while within there is realized union (*yoga*) with a principle that both supports the order and transcends it, and with which every creature and particle of the universe is eternally one.

In the version of the Harivamsa—which is an appendix to the Mahabharata, stressing the divinity of the epic hero as an incarnation of Hari (Vishnu)—the rendition of the frolic of the dance leans rather more heavily than in the Vishnu Purana toward the mode of lascivious abandon which, in the end, was to gain the field.

"As she elephants, covered with dust, enjoy the frenzy of a great male," we read, "so those herding women—their limbs covered with dust and cowdung—crushed about Krishna and danced with him on all sides. Their faces, laughing, and their eyes, large and warm as those of dark antelopes, grew bright as they drank ravenously the wonder of their dear friend. 'Ahah!' he would cry out to startle them, and they would quiver with delight. And their hair, coming down, cascaded over their bounding breasts as the young god, thus among the Gopis, played, those nights, beneath the autumn moon." [38]

In the Bhagavata Purana of the tenth century A.D.—which is the chief work of meditation of Krishna-devotionalism to this day—the young god is master of the lover's art, and the balance now has shifted from introversion to a translation of *yoga* into *bhoga* ("physical enjoyment, possession"; from the root *bhuj,* "to enjoy a meal, to consume").

"Reaching out his arms," we read, "he caressed their hands, their flowing locks, thighs, waists and breasts; scratched them with his nails, pierced them with his glances; laughed, joked, and teased; gratified them with all the tricks of the Lord of Love." [39]

And as for the Gopis, they cried to him in rapture: "Pierced by those eyes and the wonder of those smiles, seeing those two magnificent arms, which give to all assurance of protection, and that chest that would kindle love in the heart of the Goddess of Fortune herself, we are determined to become thy slaves. Indeed, what woman in the heavens, on earth, or in the hells, would not forget the chastity of her nature when captured by thy flute and the beauty of thy form—which is the glory of the world, and seeing which, even cows, does, and the female birds brooding in the trees, feel the hairs and feathers of their bodies lift with delight." [40]

An episode now occurs, however, that delivers to the company a shock, and which, in the following centuries of religious worship and poetic celebration of Krishna and the Gopis, was to be developed as a leading theme and point of meditation. For when the women had been excited to a pitch of frenzy beyond bounds, their god abruptly disappeared, and they, now entirely mad, began to search for him from one forest to another, questioning the vines, trees, birds and flowers, shouting his name and praise, and amorously imitating his movements; whereupon, suddenly—behold! —one found his footsteps.

"Here," they all cried, "are the footsteps of our Lord!"

"But alas!" they cried again; for there were smaller footprints beside them; and then, those smaller footsteps disappeared.

"He must have carried her!" they cried. "See! his own now are deeper from the weight. And here he laid her down, to gather flowers. Here he sat, to braid the flowers in her hair. Who was she?"

In the Bhagavata Purana the favored Gopi is not named. Her adventure, however, is described.

She was the wife [we read] of a cowherd. Krishna had led her into the forest, leaving the rest, and she had thought herself the most blessed in the world. "Leaving the rest," she thought, "this beloved Lord of us all has chosen me for his delight"; and, becoming proud, she said to him: "My darling, I just can't walk another step. Do pick me up, once again, and carry me where you will." "Well then," said he, "climb onto my shoulder." But when she made to do so, he vanished and, stunned, she fell to the ground in a faint, where, presently, the others reached her and they all began desperately to cry.

"We have set our marriages at naught to come to thee; and thou knowest why, Deceiver! Who but thee would desert a woman, thus, at night?" Then immediately their mood changed. "Oh thy poor, poor feet," they cooed. "Are they not sore from all this running about? Come, let us place them on our soothing breasts." [41]

He appeared, laughing, and they all rose simultaneously, like plants at the touch of water. He was in yellow garments, dark and beautiful, garlanded with flowers, and many, seizing him by the arms, lifted him to their shoulders. One took from his mouth into her own the betel he was chewing; another placed his feet upon her breasts. And then all, removing their upper garments, spread these on the ground to create for him a seat where he sat while they took his feet into their laps and his hands to their breasts, massaging his legs and arms. As though in anger, they were saying to him, "Some people are attached to those devoted to them; others, to those not devoted; and again, there is a class attached to neither. So now, dear Krishna, please explain to us clearly the reason for these extraordinary manners."

To which the auspicious Lord Almighty answered, "Where people are mutually attached, each is prompted by his own interests, and so, they are attached, not to each other, but to themselves. And where there is attachment to those not so devoted, two classes of person are to be distinguished, namely, one: those who are kind, and two: those who are affectionate. The former gain religious merit and the latter gain a friend. And so, here again we find self-interest. But, as for those attached neither to those devoted to them nor to those not devoted, these, I would say, are of four classes; one: those finding solace in their own souls; two: those who have already attained the fruit of their desires; three: those selfishly ungrateful; and four: those who wish only to oppress. But now, my dear friends with lovable waists, I do not belong to any of these sects. When I refuse attachment to those devoted to me, my reason is, to make their devotion more intense. I disappeared so that your hearts should be so absorbed in me that you would be unable to think of anything else. You had already forsaken for me all sense of right and wrong, your relatives, husbands, and your duties. There is no blame in what you have done, my dears; nor is there blame in what I have done. I shall never be able to return to you the services you have rendered; they can find their return only in your own further service." [42]

He got up, and the Gopis, freed from all grief, arose and formed a circle. The Lord multiplied his presence and each felt that he embraced her by the neck. The sky above became filled with deities and their wives, gathering to watch; heavenly kettledrums sounded; showers of blossoms began to fall; and the ring of dancers commenced moving to the rhythmic sound of their own bangles, bracelets, and ankle bells. With measured steps, graceful movements of the hands, smiles, amorous contractions of the brows, joggling hips, bounding breasts, perspiration streaming and locks of hair coming down, then the knots of both hair and garments coming loose, the Gopis began to sing. And the Lord Krishna, sporting among them, wonderfully brilliant, cried, "Well done!" to one who had sung slightly out of tune, but loudly, giving the betel from his mouth to another who received it with her tongue, placing his lotus hands on the various breasts and letting his perspiration rain upon all.

They were beside themselves, their senses paralyzed, garments going out of place, garlands and ornaments dropping off. Above, the wives of the gods, gazing from the sky, were captured by the spell; the moon and stars brightened with amazement. And when a Gopi swooned beside him, Krishna in one of his presences wiped and soothed her face with his hand, while he kissed another in such a way that the down of her body lifted with delight. His nails, sharp as the arrows of the God of Love, were leaving their deadly marks upon all. The garlands of his neck were bruised by the crush and he was smeared with the saffron of their breasts. Like an elephant mad with passion, trumpeting mightily in a herd of equally mad she-elephants, ichor pouring from his temples, the god, followed by his whole company, went plunging to the river— and there, laughing, tumbling, sporting, screeching, they all splashed each other, right and left. And the god there, in the Jumna, was a dark blue, glorious lotus, swarmed upon by a multitude of black bees.

"But how then, O my Teacher," asked a king, who, in the text of this Purana, has been depicted as listening to the tale, "how, possibly, could the creator, expounder, and upholder of the laws of virtue have allowed himself to violate every order of religion by seducing others' wives?"

"My good King," replied the Brahmin who was recounting this sacred tale for the king's religious edification, "even the gods forget virtue when their passions are fully awake. But they are not to be blamed for this any more than fire when it burns. For what the gods teach is virtue—and that is for men to follow; but what the gods do is something else. No god is to be judged as a man."

That is lesson number one.

"Moreover," the text continues, "the greatest sages, too, as we all know, are beyond good and evil. Absorbed in devotion to their Lord, they are no longer fettered in their acts."

That is lesson number two. And the last?

"But finally," said the all-wise Brahmin, "Krishna was already present in the hearts of both the Gopis and their lords—as he is in the hearts of all living beings. His apparition as a man, the form of Krishna, was to rouse devotion to that presence. And all those who listen properly to his tale will find both devotion and understanding wakened in their hearts—as it was, of old, in the hearts of the Gopis of Vrindavan. For when that night of lunar rapture ended, the Gopis again were at their husbands' sides, and the men, who had thought them there all the while, were not jealous but only the more infatuated by the force within them of Vishnu's world-creating, world-supporting, sweet illusion." [43]

The contrast of this teaching with that of the legend of the young Future Buddha among his women in the groves or on the night of his Graveyard Vision could not, it would seem, be greater; and yet, in this period, Buddhist as well as Hindu sects were teaching the way to salvation, not only in terms of *neti neti,* "not that, not that," but also in those of *iti iti,* "it is here, it is here." We have seen that two negatives make a positive and that when dualistic thought is wiped away and nirvana therewith realized, what appears to be the sorrow and impurity of the world (*saṁsāra*) becomes the pure rapture of the void (*nirvāṇa*):

> The bound of nirvana is the bound of samsara.
> Between the two, there is not the slightest difference.[44]

> Everything seen is extinct: the procession is at rest.
> Never, anywhere, has the Law been taught to anyone by
>   a Buddha.[45]

This positive reading of nirvana led in the period of the great beliefs to the rise of a number of disparate yet related movements showing influences running back and forth between the Buddhist and Brahminic folds. And of these, one was the so-called Sahajiya, cult, which flourished in Bengal in the period of the Pala Dynasty (c. 730–1200 A.D.), wherein it was held that the only true experience of the pure rapture of the void was the rapture of sexual union, wherein "each is both." This was the natural path, it was declared, to the innate nature (*sahaja*) of oneself, and therewith of the universe: the path along which nature itself leads the way.

So we read: "The whole world is of the nature of sahaja; for sahaja is the 'proper form' (*svarūpa*) of all; and this precisely is nirvana to those who possess a perfectly pure intellect." [46] "This sahaja is to be intuited within." [47] "It is free from all sounds, colors, and qualities; can be neither spoken of nor known." [48] "Where the mind dies out and the vital breath is gone, there is the Great Delight supreme: it neither stands steady nor fluctuates; nor is it expressible in words." [49] "In that state the individual mind joins sahaja as water water." [50] "There is no duality in sahaja. It is perfect, like the sky." [51]

And again: "All external forms are to be recognized as pure void. The mind, also, is to be realized as pure void. And through this realization of the essencelessness of the objects, also of the subject, the sahaja reality is revealed of itself in the heart of the accomplished practitioner." [52] One knows then: "I am the universe: I am the Buddha: I am perfect purity: I am non-cognition: I the annihilator of the cycle of existence." [53]

In the Buddhist lamaseries of Tibet, which came into being in the period here discussed and remained until the recent arrival of the Chinese, the holy images and banners showed the various Buddhas and Bodhisattvas joined with their Shaktis in embrace, in the yogic posture known as Yab-Yum, "Father-Mother." And the great prayer of the old prayer wheels of Tibet OM *maṇi padme* HUM, "The jewel (*maṇi*) in the lotus (*padme*)," signifies, on one level: the immanence of nirvana (the jewel) in samsara (the lotus); another: the arrival of the mind (the jewel) in nirvana (the lotus); but also, as in the icon of the male and female joined: the lingam in the yoni. *Buddhatvam yoṣidyonisaṁśritam,* states a late Buddhist aphorism: "Buddhahood abides in the female organ."

And so it was that when the relatively intangible dream of Krishna's dance with the Gopis came in contact with this movement—which itself had become saturated with Shiva-Shakti lore —a certain new stress developed of which the beloved erotic poem of Jayadeva, "The Song of the Cowherd" (c. 1175 A.D.), is the document without peer. The center of the stage is held here, not by the herd of many Gopis, nor even by Krishna himself, but by the one whose footsteps were seen together with those of her Lord. She is given, now, a name and character. And with a boldness that, as far as I know, is unmatched in religious literature, an all too human woman is made the object of devotion to which even God, the Creator Himself, bows down.

She was Radha; married; somewhat older than the boy. And, as Jayadeva tells in his cherished poem (which is conceived in twelve odes, each to be sung to a particular measure and musical mode, in the manner of a lyric play), their romance commenced one evening in the glades of Vrindavan, when they had been out with Krishna's foster father Nanda, and the other elders of the clan, herding cows.

The sky grew dark; the forest too; and Nanda, turning to Radha, said: "The boy is afraid: see him home." She caught his hand; and he was guided that night, not home, but to love, on the bank of the Jumna.

"Hail to Vishnu!" the poet writes. "Hearing this song of Jayadeva, may He make it powerful to teach!"

A litany of the incarnations of Vishnu is rehearsed, of which
Krishna is the eighth; and the next we learn is that Radha, sick
with love, is roving helplessly with a maidservant amid the groves
of Vrindavan.

"I know," her companion sang to her when the two had paused
to rest; "I know where Krishna tarries: kissing one, caressing another, dashing for a third. Clothed in yellow, decked with garlands, he is dancing with his women, teasing them to madness, and
the prettiest of all is dancing with him now."

Radha, in a frenzy, hurling herself toward the grove, broke,
stark mad, into the company, and darting for Krishna's mouth,
passionately devoured him and cried, "Ah yes! Your mouth, dear,
is ambrosia."

And that is the end of Ode One of Jayadeva's song.

The second ode is called "The Penitence of Krishna":

For the god in his dance had continued unperturbed, and Radha,
repulsed, withdrew in a prodigious sulk to a bower. She sighed.
"Alas! My soul cannot forget Krishna." And her companion sang
to her this song:

"Oh let Krishna have his joy of me in all the ways of desire. Let
him lie close to me this night, incite me with his smiles, and having
clasped me in his arms, savoring my lips, sleep long upon my
breast in the flowery bed!" The song went on: "Let his nails dig into
my breast and, going beyond love's science, let him seize my hair
to ravish me, while the jewels on my limbs chatter and my girdle
comes apart! And oh! let me drop like a liana into his arms, stilled
by rapture, at the moment love's work is done.

"For even now," the song continued, "I see him pausing in his
dance. The flute drops from his hand: the play in the wood has
lost its charm. Recalling that brief glimpse of his beloved—her
breast, an arm, a lock of hair—his heart has turned away from his
dance. . . ."

The poem is lush, and by a critic today would be classed rather
with Shakespeare's "Venus and Adonis," as a kind of boudoir
piece, than with, say, Thomas a Kempis' *Imitation of Christ*. And

yet in India, where things are never quite what they seem to us to be, the *Imitation of Krishna* in the mystery of his union with Radha (as expressed in the name, for example, Radhakrishnan) has been, through the centuries following the first presentation of this work in the courts of the Pala kings, a matter of profound religious zeal.

Ode Three of the poem now tells of "Krishna Troubled":

He has departed from the Gopis and, having searched the wood for Radha, sits alone and sings in a thicket of bamboo, beside the Jumna.

"Alas! She is gone; for I let her go! What good to me now are friends; or life? I can see her brow, angry and offended. Yet I hold her in my heart. . . . But if I can hold her in my thoughts this way, can she be actually gone?"

Ode Four is called "Krishna Cheered":

Radha's servant girl comes to Krishna and sings to him of the yearning of his mistress. "For the pleasures of your embrace, she has prepared a flowery bed. How is she to live without you? Come! for she is sick with love."

Ode Five is "Krishna's Longing":

"Tell her," said he, "that I am here."

And the girl returned to Radha with a song of urging, without shame. "He has tuned the tones of his flute to your name. Oh, go to him in desire. On a couch of tender branches, letting part your robe and girdle, offer to him the luxury of your hips with the rich treasure between of their sweet receptacle of delight. He is impatient, watching everywhere for your appearance. It is time."

"Krishna Made Bolder," Ode Six:

But the woman, ravished by love, was too weak to move. The servant girl returned, therefore, to Krishna.

"And may this poem," adds the poet Jayadeva, "give to all lovers joy!"

"She waits amid flowers; lives only in dreams of your love; wonders why you hesitate; and is kissing mirages, weeping there alone. Every leaf that falls she thinks may be you and smoothes the bed. Why, then, do you tarry here?"

Ode Seven, "Krishna Supposed False":

The moon rose, but no Krishna came; and Radha, alone, lamented. "The hour has come and gone," she sighed. "Alas, I am erased from his heart!"

"But may this poem," sings Jayadeva, "live, O Reader, in your heart!"

"Another female has enmeshed him! The ornaments of her girdle chatter as she walks. Alluringly rocking with her haunches, they murmur of delight. Alas! I can see him lovingly placing pearls around her neck already branded by his nails. . . ."

"And may Vishnu, moved by this poem, suffuse all hearts!"

Ode Eight, "Krishna Reproved":

The lover sheepishly came; and though he bowed before her feet—He, the incarnation of the Lord who lives in all beings—the earthly woman tortured him in a rage. "Those heavy eyes! From weeping? Is it not, rather, from a night of luxurious excess? Go! Disappear! Follow the traces of the one who has brought you to this fatigue! Your teeth are black with the make-up of her eyes. Your body, marked with her nails, is the document of her victory. The imprint of her teeth on your lip pains my thought. O You! Your soul is even blacker than your body. You roam the forest only to eat up girls."

"O!" sings the poet. "O you sages! Listen to these laments of a young woman's heart!"

Ode Nine. "The End of Krishna's Trial":

The servant spoke: "O my dear Radha, your beautiful lover has now come. What greater pleasure is there on earth? Why do you render useless the bounty of your breasts, heavier than coconuts, to be culled with exquisite delight? Do not despise this delicious youth. Do not weep. Look at him. Love him. Eat him. Taste him, like a fruit."

"Oh, may this poem," the poet sings, "delight all lovers' hearts. And O, lovely Herdsman of Vrindavan, deign with the tones of your flute—which affect all women like a charm and break the bonds even of the gods—to remove from all of us the bondages of sorrow!"

Ode Ten, "Krishna in Paradise":

Thus pacified by her servant girl, Radha showed a gentler face; and Krishna, in the gathering dusk, spoke to her amid sighs and tears.

"The luster of your teeth, bright as the moon, scatters the darkness of my fear. The fire of desire burns in my soul: let me quench it in the honey of your lips. If you are angry, stab with your eyes, chain me in your arms, and rip me to tatters with your teeth. You are the pearl in the ocean of my being. You are the woman of my heart. Put away your fear of me, who inspired it. There is no power in my heart but love."

Eleven, "The Union of Radha and Krishna":

He moved away from her toward the flower couch she had made, and one of the Gopis present advised her.

"Dear, you are now to become his slayer. Approach with a slightly indolent walk, anklets languorously clashing, to let him know that your mood is now of sweetness. Bring to him those thighs, round as the trunks of elephants, letting your bosom be your guide, which now is yearning openly for his lips. Glorious, lovely woman, your majestic body is well equipped for this approaching night of war: march on, march on, to the drum beat of your jeweled, rocking belt; and having let the clank of your bracelets proclaim the pending attack, fall with sharp nails upon his breast. He waits—trembling, sweating there with joy. Embrace him fully in the dark of this perfect night."

Radha blushed; but the girl urged her on. "How can you be afraid of one whom you can buy as your slave for a pittance of joy, rendered as readily as a wink?"

And the woman, shining like the disk of the moon, arose in fear and delight, to move with anklets clanging toward the bower. And the Gopis who were there departed, covering their mouths to hide smiles; for she had already thrown off all shame.

Ode Last, "The God in the Yellow Garment Overwhelmed":

The Incarnation of God spoke to Radha. "Let me open that vest and press to my heart your breast, returning life to your slave who is dead." For a time they were delayed from close embrace by the honey of each other's eyes and lips; but when Radha seized the initiative, the battle of love began.

She made him captive with a sudden encirclement of arms, routed him with her bosom, mangled him with her nails and tore at his lower lip with her teeth; pummeled him with her haunches, dragged his head back by its hair, and then drowned him with the honey-mead of her throat. When her eyes closed and her breath began to come harder, however, the force of her arms relaxed and the great hip-zone grew still. The god then moved against the field. And when morning dawned, what the woman's divine lover beheld beneath him was her chest lacerated by the army of his nails, her eyes afire for lack of sleep, the color of her lips destroyed, her mashed garland tangled in her shattered hair, and her clothes dislodged from the jeweled girdle. The sight, like a volley of love's arrows, overwhelmed him.

"And—O Reader—may that god be your protection, who spread aside Radha's garment to gaze with ravished eyes upon the tumid pinnacles of her breast, while he sought to amuse her with a text from the Purana. 'When the gods and demons churned the Milky Ocean,' he said, 'for the butter of immortality, they churned for a thousand years; and there appeared first such a poisonous smoke that all operations had to cease until our greatest yogi, Shiva, took that poison into a cup and drank it off; which he held by yoga in his throat. You know, I have wondered why he did it. The poison turned his throat blue, so that we call him Blue Throat. But I think, now, that he drank because he knew, my dear, that when you came into being on the shore of the great milky sea, you would choose for your love not him but me.' "

And Radha, languorously happy, became gradually aware of the disorder of her person: hair in disarray, sweat on her face, cuts on her breast, and her belt where it should not have been. Mortified, she started up with her mashed garland; and with one arm shielding her breasts, the other at her groin, made off. When she returned, fatigued in all her members, with delight and admiration she begged her lover to help repair her dress.

"Krishna, my dear one, freshen with your beloved hand the sandal powder of my chest; now, the make-up on my eyes; here, the earrings; next—and do it prettily—these flowers for my hair: paint a nice tilaka on my forehead. And so now, the belt and

chain of pearls to enclose again these plump, succulent loins that
have presented a narrow pass for the elephant of love."

"O Reader," sings the poet, "listen to these lines of Jayadeva
with your heart!"

"Now enclose," she said, "my breasts; put the rings back on my
arms. . . ."

And her beloved did as she told him, though, indeed, he was
God Himself.

"O Reader—may the Lord, protecting you, multiply in the
world the signs of his omnipotence: Vishnu, the One Being of All,
who has passed into a myriad of bodies, drawn by his desire to
see with eyes myriadfold the lotus feet of the Daughter of the
Milky Ocean! May the learned extract from this poem all that is
in it of the art of those divine beings who in joy behold and celebrate the Lord! And may all those who love that Destroyer of
Sorrow bear forever on their lips this song of the great Jayadeva,
whose father was illustrious Banjadeva, and of whom Ramadevi
was the mother." [54]

Jayadeva was a poet. As a youth he had been a wandering
ascetic, but when a Brahmin offered his daughter, he wed; and it
was after his marriage that he wrote his song of divinity in love—
the god Krishna himself, we are told, lending him assistance when
he was at a loss to render Radha's beauty.[55]

But not all who wish to experience the divinity of love are endowed by nature with that quality of spirit which the troubadours
called the Gentle Heart; and so, as we have writing schools for
those who cannot write, there have been developed in India love
schools for those who cannot love, and their scholarship is divided
in three grades: 1. Beginner (*pravarta*), to be taught to repeat
God's name (*nāma*) and to recite certain charms (*mantra*);
2. Advanced Student (*sādhaka*), who has learned to experience
"divine emotion" (*bhāva*) and so is qualified to commence disciplines in the company of women, and finally 3. Perfected Master
(*siddha*), who, on realizing "love" (*prema:* from the root *pṛī*,
"to please, gladden, cheer; to show kindness, grace or favor; to
take pleasure in"), attains through it to "bliss" (*rasa:* "the sap, the
juice, the nectar; the taste").[56]

There have been reports of these schools of the so-called Left Hand Path (*vāmācarī;* from the words *vāma,* "reverse, adverse, left; bad, vile," but also, "beautiful, pleasing"; and *cārī,* "one who goes, proceeds, or walks a path"); for example, in the words of the German nineteenth-century observer, A. Barth: "The use of animal food and spiritous liquors, indulged in to excess, is the rule in these strange ceremonies, in which Shakti is worshiped in the person of a naked woman, and the proceedings terminate with the carnal copulation of the initiated, each couple representing Bhairava and Bhairavi (Shiva and Devi), and becoming thus for the moment identified with them. This is 'the holy circle' (*srī cakra*) or 'the complete consecration' (*purnābhiṣeka*), the essential act or rather foretaste of salvation, the highest rite of this delirious mysticism." [57]

The sacred texts of the Vamacharis belong to a type of religious scripture known as *Tantra* ("loom, web; vesture; discipline; textbook; correct way"), which date from the Gupta and later times, and are essentially technical supplements to the various Puranic scriptures of Vishnu, Shiva, and the Goddess, some being of the "right" (*dakṣiṇa*), others of the "left hand path"; and among the instructions of the latter we read:

> "I am Bhairava, the Omniscient I, endowed with qualities."
> Having meditated thus, let the devotee proceed to the Kula worship.[58]

> Wine, flesh, fish, woman, and sexual congress:
> These are the fivefold boons that remove all sin.* [59]

In such rites the sacred object is a naked dancing girl, female devotee, harlot, washerwoman, barber's wife, Brahminical or

---

* These five "boons" are known as the Five M's: wine (*madya*), meat (*mamsa*), fish (*matsya*), woman (*mudrā*), and sexual union (*maithuna*). In the so-called "substitutional rites" designed for those who have been advised by their gurus to worship the goddess in the attitude rather of children than of lovers, *madya* becomes coconut milk, *mamsa,* wheat beans, ginger, sesamum, salt, or garlic, *matsya,* red radish, red sesamum, masur (a kind of grain), the white brinjal vegetable, and paniphala (an aquatic plant), *mudrā,* wheat, paddy, rice, etc., and *maithuna,* childlike submission before the Divine Mother's Lotus Feet (Sir John Woodroffe, *Shakti and Shakta,* Madras and London: Ganesh and Company, 3rd ed., 1929, pp. 569–70).

Shudra female, flower girl, or milkmaid; and the time is to be midnight. The party is to be formed of a circle of eight, nine, or eleven couples in the roles of Bhairavas and Bhairavis. Appropriate mantras are pronounced, according to the class of person chosen to be Shakti, and she is then worshiped according to rule. She is placed, disrobed but richly ornamented, within or to the side of a circle of paired male and female devotees and by various mantras rendered pure. The radical sacred syllable of the occasion is thrice whispered in her ear; she is sprinkled over with wine, given meat, fish, and wine to bless with her touch, which then are shared; and to the tones of a symphony of sacred chanting, she then becomes the vessel of a sequence of sacramental acts preliminary to, and culminating in, the general consecration—"accompanied throughout," as H. H. Wilson writes, "with mantras and forms of meditation suggesting notions very foreign to the scene." [60]

Other manners of worshiping the Goddess involve, as we have learned, the sacrifice of human victims and even tasting of their flesh. Still others, for the gaining of magical powers, require of an accomplished yogi that he should meditate at midnight in a cemetery, burning ground, or place where criminals are executed, while seated on a corpse: and if he can accomplish this without fear, ghosts and female goblins will become his slaves.[61] Erotic exercises may accompany or culminate such rites. Certain devotees "pierce their flesh with hooks and spits, run sharp pointed instruments through their tongues and cheeks, recline on beds of spikes, or gash themselves with knives." [62] Others, called "Skull Bearers," smear themselves with ashes from a funeral pyre, hang a string of human skulls around the neck, weave their hair into matted braid, and wear a tiger skin about the loins, while bearing in the left hand a skull for a cup and in the right a bell, which is to be rung incessantly while they cry out: "Ho, the Lord and Spouse of Kali!" [63]

Generally, the sects of the "left-hand path" repudiate caste during the sacred time of the rite. "While the Bhairava Tantra is in session all castes are Brahmins," we read in a typical text. "When it is concluded, they are again distinct." [64] The rite is a form of yoga, a passage beyond the bounds of the sphere of dharma; and indeed, to such a point that in certain variants of this worship even incest-prohibitions must be disregarded. For example, in the so-called "bodice (*kanculi*) cult," the female votaries at the time of worship deposit their upper vests in a box in charge of the guru, and at the close of the preliminary ceremonies each of the males takes a vest from the box and the female to whom it belongs—"be she ever so nearly kin to him"—becomes his partner for the consummation. "The object," states H. H. Wilson in his presentation of this information, ". . . is to confound all the ties of female alliance, and not only to enforce a community of women amongst the votaries, but to disregard even natural restraints." For it is declared "that all men, and all women are of one caste and that their intercourse is free from fault." [65]

"Put away the idea of two and be of one body," we read in a song in celebration of the realization of this way: "Very difficult is this discipline of love." [66]

Both Jayadeva and the Tantric Shakti cults placed the human female in the center of the symbolic system. The later Puranic versions of Krishna and the Gopis, on the other hand, returned the lead to the male god and, even while adding Jayadeva's figure of Radha to the scene, expanded the rasa to an amplitude of dionysiac madness that is nowhere equaled—I believe—in the history of religious thought.

As we read in the fourteenth-century Brahmavaivarta Purana:

Within the forest, the circular place of that dance was tastefully sprinkled with aloe, saffron, sandal and musk. Numerous pleasure-lakes were in the area and gardens full of flowers; ganders, ducks, and other water fowl were swimming on the limpid surfaces; mangoes and plantain trees were all around: and Krishna, seeing that lovely glade and the cool waters in which the fatigues of passion could be laved away, smiled, and, to summon the Gopis to love, played upon his flute.

Radha, in her dwelling, hearing the melody, remained still, like a tree, her mind dissolving in one-pointed contemplation. When she recovered, hearing the sound of the flute again, she was extremely agitated. She got up. She sat down. Then, forgetting all her duties, she went rushing from the house and, glancing in all directions, hastened toward the point of sound, with the lotus feet of Krishna ever in mind. The luster of her body and shimmer of her jewels illumined the forest.

And the other Gopis also, her thirty-three companions, hearing the flute, were assailed with passion and, forgetting housewifely duties, made for the forest—the best of their race. They were equal in age, beauty, and dress, and were accompanied, each, by a following of many thousand: Sushila by sixteen thousand, Sashikala fourteen thousand, Chandramukhi thirteen thousand, Madhavi eleven thousand, etc., to the sum of nine hundred thousand. Many had garlands in their hands, others sandal, others fly-whisks, others musk; many carried gold, others saffron, others cloth. Along the way they sang out the name of Krishna, and when they reached the place of the dance, what they saw was lovelier than heaven, radiant with the pure light of the moon.

A gentle breeze carried the perfume of the flowers, bees were everywhere humming, and the cooing of the cuckoos would have seduced the hearts of saints. The women were discomposed. And the Lord Krishna saw with delight that Radha, like a jewel in the midst of her company, was approaching with arch glances. Her alluring walk, majestic as the gait of an elephant, would have unseated the mind of a yogi; for she was in the prime of her youth, ravishing, with loins and buttocks wonderfully great. The color of her skin was of the champak blossom; her visage was the autumn moon; her gleaming hair was held in place by a wreath of redolent jasmine; and when she saw that the youthful Krishna, beautifully dark, was observing her, she bashfully screened her face with the hem of her garment, yet returned his glance, again and again, and smitten deeply by Love's arrow, felt such a thrill of rapture that she nearly swooned.

But Krishna, too, was smitten. The flute, as well as a lotus with which he had been toying, dropped from his hand, and he stood as though turned to stone. Even the clothing dropped from his body. Yet in a trice, he recovered his wits, went to Radha, and embraced her, his touch restoring her strength. And the lord of her life, dearer than that life to her, then led her aside, the two continually kissing; and they proceeded to a pleasure house of flowers where they teased each other for a while, exchanging masticated betel from their mouths. But when she had swallowed what he had given, he asked to have it back and she became afraid, prostrating herself at his feet. Whereupon Krishna, full of love, his countenance radiant with desire, was joined with her on a flowery couch of delight.

Eight kinds of sexual intercourse—reverse and otherwise—Krishna, master of delights, practiced with his pulchritudinous Radha, scratching, biting, kissing, slapping, in all the ways known to love's science—ways that rob women of their minds. And with all the others too, simultaneously, Krishna rapturously was delighting himself, embracing every member of their impassioned bodies with his equally fervid limbs. Since he and Radha were savants of this pleasant sexual art, their war of love knew no intermission; yet even as they worked there, Krishna, assuming identical forms, entered into every chamber and enjoyed the bodies of the Gopis in the glorious sphere of the dance. Nine hundred thousand Gopis thus were enjoyed by as many cowherds, the full number of those there in rapture coming to one million eight hundred thousand. Everybody's hair was loose, clothing shattered, ornaments gone. The whole place resounded with bracelets, and mad with passion, everyone fainted. Then having done what they could on land, all headed for the lakes. And with these gambols they were presently exhausted. Whereupon they came out of the waters, put on their clothes, studied their faces in mirrors of gem, and after having applied sandal to their bodies, aloe, musk, and perfume, put on wreaths and were restored to their normal states.[67]

One need not go on to make the point. The dance continues for two more chapters; for, when it finally came to its height, the gods with their wives and companies, in golden cars, came together in the heavens to watch. Sages, saints, adepts, and the honored dead, the heavenly singers and nymphs, earth-demons, ogres, and various birdlike beings, gathered joyfully with their wives to see the great sight while in thirty-three forests for thirty-three days Krishna and his Gopis danced and sang, tore off each other's clothes, engaged in many more than the usual sixteen authorized types of sexual intercourse—passions mounting all the while, "like fire fed with clarified butter"—and when everything was done, the gods and goddesses, much amazed, eulogized the sight and retired to their homes.

However, the goddesses, who had fainted many times during the course of what they had seen, desiring knowledge of the master of the dance of Vrindavan, descended to earth and throughout India, were born as little girls in the palaces of kings.[68]

v. The Blow of Islam

The scimitars of the warriors of Allah—Praise and Glory be to His Name, the Most High, Who is full of Grace and Mercy—had already broached the ramparts of the Indian timeless dream when Jayadeva was celebrating his vision of Radha. Five centuries earlier—in the time of Harsha's reign (606–647 A.D.)—Mohammed, the messenger of the unity of God, had announced, for the guidance of those in whom God's love is great, the revelation of Islam, the path that is straight. And one of the wonders of world history is the miracle of the rapid spread of his one true community under God from the moment of its founding (date of the Hegira: 622). All of North Africa had succumbed by the year 710; Spain was entered 711; the Pyrenees were crossed 718; and the gates of Paris itself were at stake when Charles Martel met and broke the onrush in the battle of Poitiers, 732. Blazing eastward like a fire on a plain of sun-dried grass, the glory of the peace and blessing of Islam had taken Persia by 651, and the gates of India were at stake by 750. However, India had no Charles Martel. Allah's curse on the uncircumcised was delayed for two hundred years by internal struggles for power within the fold of Islam itself, but when it fell there was no let to His chastisement.

In the year 986 A.D. a former slave from Turkestan, Sabuktigin by name, who may or may not have been of Sassanian royal blood, led a raid for booty into the Punjab, and annually thereafter, in the cooler months commencing in October, raids of this kind into wealthy India became the rule. The leading Rajput prince of the area, Jaipal, managed by 991 to bring an army together, which was overwhelmed; Peshawar fell, and the raids went on.

In the year 997, Sabuktigin was succeeded by his son Mahmud al-Ghazni, who, continuing the custom of the raids, in the year 1001 delivered the *coup de grâce* to Jaipal—and to India therewith. There is an Islamic chronicle of his deed:

The enemy of God, Jaipal, together with his children, grand-children, nephews, the chief men of his tribe and his relations, were taken prisoners, and being strongly bound with ropes were carried before the Sultan, like as evildoers on whose faces the fumes of infidelity are evident, and who, being covered with the vapors of misfortune, are to be bound and carried to hell. Some had their arms forcibly tied behind their backs, some were seized by the cheek, some were driven by blows on the neck. A necklace was taken from the neck of Jaipal, composed of large pearls, shining gems, and rubies set in gold, of which the value was two hundred thousand dinars; and twice that value was obtained from the necks of those of his relations who were taken prisoners, or slain, and had become the food of the mouths of hyenas and vultures. Allah also bestowed upon his friends such an amount of booty as was beyond all bounds and calculations, including five hundred thousand slaves, beautiful men and women. The Sultan returned with his followers to his camp, having plundered immensely, by Allah's aid having obtained the victory, and thankful to Allah, the Lord of the Universe. For the Almighty had given him victory over a province of the country of Hind, broader and more fertile than Khurasan.[69]

Jaipal was released, but burned himself to death on a funeral pyre. The city of Kangra fell, Bulandshahr, Mathura, Kanauj, and the temple city of Shiva at Somnath.

Now in the great Shiva temple of Somnath there was enshrined, as Professor Rawlinson states in his vivid summary of the chronicles of the victory,

a massive stone lingam, five cubits in height, which was regarded as being of special sanctity and attracted thousands of pilgrims. It was bathed every day in water brought all the way from the Ganges, and garlanded with flowers from Kashmir. The revenue of ten thousand villages was assigned for its support, and a thousand Brahmins performed the daily ritual of the temple. The original shrine, like so many in ancient India, was built of wood: it was supported by fifty-six teak-wood pillars, coated with lead and inlaid with jewels. A chain of massive golden bells hung over the idol: jeweled chandeliers, images of pure gold and veils embroidered with precious stones were stored in the treasury. The temple, together with the buildings to accommodate the ministrants, formed a regular town, surrounded by a wall and strongly fortified.

Mahmud left Ghazni in December 1023 with 30,000 picked horsemen. He appeared suddenly before Multan, which surrendered. Here he obtained the necessary camels for the desert-crossing, and both Bikanir and Ajmir opened their gates to him. Six weeks' arduous marching brought him to Anhilvad and the raja, Bhima by name, fled at his approach. Mahmud probably marched against Somnath by the route running along the southern coast of Kathiawar. On Thursday, January 30th, he broke through the *enceinte* of fortresses surrounding the town and approached the walls of the sacred city. The inhabitants, confident in the power of the god, jeered at the invaders from the battlements. Next day the assault began. The Muslims, after a severe struggle, succeeded in gaining a footing on the ramparts, but were too exhausted to do more. And now the Hindus began to realize their peril. All night long the temple was thronged with wailing crowds, beating their breasts and calling upon the deity to come to the help of his own. But there was neither voice nor answer. At dawn the attack was renewed, and step by step the defenders were forced back through the narrow winding streets to the walls of the shrine itself. Here a last despairing stand was made until at length the Muslims, planting their scaling ladders against the walls, stormed them with loud cries of *Din! Din!* Fifty thousand Hindus were put to the sword; others tried to escape by sea and were drowned. The treasure taken exceeded two million dinars in value. According to one story, the Brahmins who had submitted begged to be allowed to ransom the lingam, but Mahmud would not listen. He refused, he said, to appear before the Judgment Seat as one who had taken money to spare an idol. The stone was broken in pieces and a portion of it buried in the threshold of the mosque of Ghazni, to be trodden under foot by true believers. . . .[70]

We need not go on. The sealed-off horizon of India's dream had been definitively broached and nothing could stop it now from dissolving before an order of reality of which it had not taken due account. The power of yoga to shape experience to the will of the introverted sage and of the wisdom of the Vedas to work magical effects was overcome by a mere detail of the sphere merely of maya—which now would have to be absorbed.

The holy Hindu city of Benares fell in 1194 and the entire Buddhist province of Bihar in 1199, where the university of Nalanda was utterly destroyed, its population of some 6000 monks summarily put to the sword, and the last ember of Buddhist light therewith quenched in India. In neighboring Bengal, the aged raja Lakshmanasena, the patron of Jayadeva, was so taken by surprise that he was at dinner when the officers of the army of Allah walked into his palace. And, having conquered thus the whole north, the scimitars of Islam began to carve their way southward, until the year 1565, when the brilliant city of Vijayanagar, the last remaining Hindu capital, collapsed.

Into a charge of Hindu cavalry the Moslem artillery had fired at close range bags of small copper coins with such terrible effect that the ranks broke. A charge of Moslem elephants then dashed into the screaming tumult, and the litter-bearers of the old Hindu raja Ramaraya ("ninety-six years old, but brave as thirty") dropped their royal charge and made off for their lives. The leading Moslem prince struck off the old man's head, which, mounted on a lance, was carried to the front line, where it struck panic in the Hindus, who broke and fled. Pursued in every direction, they were slaughtered—as Rawlinson writes—"till the Kistna ran red with blood" and "the plunder was so great that every private soldier was loaded with jewels, arms, horses, and slaves."

When the news of the terrible defeat reached the city, the princes who had been left behind to guard the capital packed up the contents of the royal treasury and made off. "It is said," states our author, "that over five hundred elephants were required to transport the treasures. On the tenth day the enemy arrived, and forced an entrance with little difficulty. They killed and plundered without mercy, and it is said that the work of destruction went on for three months. The magnificent stone-carving was smashed to pieces with crowbars and hammers, and where it defied human efforts, fires were lit to burst it open. . . ." [71]

And so perished forever the fabulous Hindu Empire of Vijayanagar, which, in its time, had stretched from sea to sea.

Part Three

THE MYTHOLOGIES
OF THE FAR EAST

CHINESE MYTHOLOGY

✦✦

i. The Antiquity of Chinese Civilization

"I used to feel extremely happy to know that I was born in a country whose history had already lasted 5000 years," wrote Dr. Li Chi of the National Taiwan University at the opening of his survey of *The Beginnings of Chinese Civilization.*

I say 5000 years because it was actually the figure given to the youthful mind of my generation. The Sumerian civilization and the Egyptian civilization, we were told, might have started earlier; but they were also dead long ago. The Hindus, too, enjoy a long tradition, but their men of learning, till recently, never seemed to think it worth while to put their tradition on written records. So when all these things have been considered, China is certainly the oldest country still existing on this earth, and possesses the longest—and this is important—continuous written history of all the nations. This was my understanding of China's past before the time of the Chinese Revolution [of 1912].

After the revolution, things began to change. There was a time when the reformers of China were skeptical about everything recorded in and about the past, including history itself. The Renaissance movement in the early twentieth century was essentially a rationalist movement, more or less akin in spirit to that of the classicists of the seventeenth century. Their slogan, "Show your proof," though destructive in nature, did bring about a more critical spirit in the study of ancient China. Thus, if one wants to pay excessive tribute to the Golden Age of Yao and Shun, well, show your proof; if one wishes to talk about the engineering miracles of the Great Yü of the third millennium B.C., proofs must also be given.

What must be considered in this connection is that written records alone were no longer accepted as valid proofs.

This proof-seeking movement created a great deal of havoc with the traditional learning and revolutionized the method of classical studies. Modern archaeology in China was born in this atmosphere.[1]

The actual archaeological enterprise through which the factual, as opposed to mythic, past of China began to appear was the work, not of a Chinese, but of an Occidental scientist—supported by the patronage of the Swedish Crown Prince (now King) Gustaf Adolf, the minds and learning of an extraordinary team of Austrian, Canadian, French, Swedish, and American, as well as young Chinese, men of learning, and, of course, a generous grant from the Rockefeller Foundation.

"It is well known that prehistoric researches in China started," Dr. Li Chi willingly concedes, "with the Swedish geologist, Dr. J. G. Andersson, who not only discovered the locality of Chou-kou-tien and the first trace of Peking Man but was also the first scientist to find the existence of a widely distributed prehistorical culture of the late Neolithic phase in North China." [2]

The work commenced in 1918, when Dr. Andersson began collecting the remains of prehistoric mammals in the hills around Chou-kou-tien, not far from Peking. In 1921 he found what appeared to be worked tools and in 1923 his friend and collaborator, an Austrian, Dr. Otto Zdansky, came across a couple of semi-human teeth. The crown prince arrived in 1926 and took an interest in the matter. In 1927 the scientific institutes of China, Sweden, and the United States contributed funds, and in 1928 the whole support of the now considerable enterprise—which continued till 1939—was taken over by the Rockefeller Foundation.[3]

Dr. Andersson's own summary of the results of his researches suggests the following schedule of basic prehistoric dates for the earliest Far East:

1,000,000 years ago: very uncertain traces of *Hominids*

More than 500,000 years: a fine flint implement (at Chou-kou-tien)

500,000 years: *Sinanthropus pekinensis* (at Chou-kou-tien)

Less than 500,000 years: *Hominid* mandible and large, well-made flint flakes (at Chou-kou-tien)

50,000 years: *Paleolithic Man* (abundant Ordos Desert finds)

25,000 years: non-Mongolian *Homo sapiens* (at Chou-kou-tien)

25,000–4,000 years ago: unexplained hiatus

c. 2000 B.C.: The Yangshao Culture: beautifully painted, fine ceramic wares: High Neolithic: proto-Chinese.[4]

Peking Man (*Sinanthropus pekinensis*, about 500,000 years ago), discussed already in my Primitive volume,[5] was a contemporary, roughly, of Java Man (*Pithecanthropus erectus*) and, in Europe, Heidelberg Man (*Homo heidelbergensis*), while his crudely chipped stone tools were of the heavy "chopper" type remarked above for the Soan Culture of India.* His eating habits included cannibalism,[6] and his brain case, to quote Dr. Andersson again, "was very low with exceedingly strong supraorbital ridges."[7] The chin, "slanting like that of the anthropoids," combined with these features of the forehead, must have presented a rather unpromising profile. And yet this lout—unless the evidence deceives—was the first creature on earth to make use of fire.

The Ordos Desert finds were of a considerably higher grade. "In type," states Dr. Andersson, "the majority of the implements are most closely connected with the cultural epoch known in Europe as Mousterian. . . . But there are also numerous resemblances to the next succeeding period, the Aurignacian. Exceptionally, we even find objects which in their perfection remind us of the still later culture which the French call the Magdalenian. In view of our limited knowledge of the Old Stone age of Eastern Asia it may, however, be too early to enter into detailed comparisons and we must content ourselves for the present with the suggestion that the Ordos discoveries most resemble in type the Mousterian-Aurignacian civilizations in Western Europe, that is, the middle of the Old Stone age."[8]

The observation of the non-Mongoloid traits of the earliest fully human (Homo sapiens) remains of the Far East is of interest not only anthropologically, but also with reference to the problems of

* Supra, pp. 150–52.

mythology, since it may (and I am saying only *may*) help to account for some (and I am saying only *some*) of the parallels to be noted between the myths and arts of the North American Indians and those of earliest China. Let me cite to this point the words of Dr. Walter A. Fairservis, Jr., of the American Museum of Natural History:

The evidence . . . indicates that at the close of the Pleistocene [the close of the Glacial Ages], North Asia, including northern China, was occupied by a paleo-caucasoid people probably much like the Ainu of Japan in physical form. The evidence also indicates that there were no Mongoloids in Southeast Asia until very much later. And since we have no Mongoloid types in this period for western Asia we must assume a northern place of origin . . .

It is claimed that [Mongoloid] physical attributes * are the result of an environment dominated by extreme cold. Such an environment must have existed in Siberia and eastern Central Asia during the Fourth Glacial Stage when ice-free areas existed as pockets between mountain glaciers and the Siberian ice sheets. These areas were extremely cold (frequently below —80° F) and swept by high winds. Man and animals must have had a terrible struggle to survive. Many men died off and the remainder, few in number, adapted their culture to the situation: sewed furs and skins into protective clothing (first tailored clothing?). This was one adaptation but another is of greater interest. The necessary exposure of the human face, particularly the nose, mouth, and eyes, required a physical change to protect those sensitive areas. The optimum situation for the operation of natural selection may have existed with these isolated limited groups of proto-Mongoloids (not identified). Such being the case, the anatomical changes for survival would have come about. . . .

The classic Mongoloid people who were released from their Ice Age habitat at the warming of the last glaciation probably began to spread from their homeland sometime after 8000 to 10,000 years ago. These people interbred with other races and produced in time the Mongoloid stocks that people the world today. By the second millennium B.C. the inhabitants

* These are: 1. stocky build, 2. small extremities, 3. flat face, 4. fat-padded epicanthus-shielded eyes, 5. coarse, straight hair with sparse growth on face and body.

ot North China and at least part of western China were essentially Mongoloids. . . .

In southwestern Siberia the Mongoloid type does not appear in the archaeological sequence until the period of the Minusinsk Kurgan culture (probably post-500 B.C.). This would indicate that the center of Mongoloid cultures was probably east of the Yenisei and that the greatest movement of that race was along a north-south axis, which would account for its earlier spread into China and possibly the New World.[9]

Four separate prehistoric backgrounds have, therefore, to be borne in mind as the particular forms of the Chinese mythological system begin to emerge:

1. The Lower Paleolithic, c. 500,000 B.C., with its primal derivation from the tropics (probable center in Southeast Asia: Java Man): a brood of apelike cannibals using heavy stone choppers, crudely chipped, and, at Chou-kou-tien, also fire.

2. The Middle and (possibly) Upper Paleolithic, c. 50,000–25,000 B.C., with superior chipped-stone tools suggesting the well-known series of Europe: Mousterian (Neanderthal Man), Aurignacian and Magdalenian (Crô-Magnon Man): here the rites and myths and customs of the northern culture world of the Great Hunt must have prevailed, such as we have discussed for both America and Eurasia in our Primitive volume.

3. A cut-off, highly specialized, hypothetical community of Arctic proto-Mongoloids, who, when released c. 8000–6000 B.C. from their isolated frigid hearth, somewhere northeastward of the Yenisei, drove southward on the one hand as a wedge through Mongolia and China, as far as Indonesia, and, on the other hand, into North and South America: we shall watch for signs that may tell us something of the mythic formulae of this circumpolar, proto-Mongoloid complex.

4. The great pottery cultures of the High Neolithic, which Dr. Andersson was the first to find in China in a rich series of sites in Kansu, Shansi, and Honan, and which emerge suddenly—as from nowhere.

The deeper we penetrate [states Dr. Andersson] into the study of those remote times, the more we are impressed by the inflexible riddles barring our way. Foremost of these is the "Neolithic hiatus," [of which] the facts are, in brief, as follows:

During the loess period (Palaeolithic time) the climate of Northern China was so arid that the region, apart from residual lake areas, may have been largely depopulated.

After the loess period there followed the P'an Chiao stage of vertical river erosion, during which the loess cover was largely dissected and locally small canyons were cut into solid rock. This period, which may correspond approximately to the Mesolithic and Early Neolithic, was a time of abundant rainfall, which in that part of the world must mean a genial climate. In other words, the region certainly abounded in game and must have formed a pleasant habitat for primitive Man. However, as far as I know . . . no indisputable Mesolithic or early Neolithic site has so far been found in northern China. . . .

Then suddenly, at the very end of the Neolithic, at a time only four thousand years distant from our own [i.e. about 2000 B.C.], the hitherto seemingly empty land becomes teeming with busy life. Hundreds, not to say thousands of villages occupy the terraces overlooking the valley bottoms. Many of these villages were surprisingly large and must have harbored a considerable population. Their inhabitants were hunters and stock-raisers, but at the same time agriculturalists, as is evidenced by their implements and by the finding of husks of rice in a potsherd at Yang Shao Tsun. The men were skilled carpenters and their womenfolk were clever at weaving and needlework. Their excellent ceramic, with few or no equals at that time, indicate that the then inhabitants of Honan and Kansu had developed a generally high standard of civilization. There must have been, by some means or other—new inventions or the introduction of new ideas from abroad—a rather sudden impetus that allowed the rapid spread of a fast-growing population.[10]

As for the likely dates, these have been given in my Primitive volume, as follows:

1. A coarse, unglazed pottery: hypothetically, this crude fabric, shaped by hand or by a coiling process, decorated with impressions ("cord- or mat-marked") or with lumps and strips of clay stuck on before firing, may be assigned to an (as yet unconfirmed) early neolithic stratum of c. 2500 B.C.: there is a considerable distribution of this kind of ceramic ware outside of China, from England to America, and its general hearth of origin would appear to have been the Nuclear Near East, c. 4500 B.C.

2. An elegant Painted Ware (Yangshao), c. 2200–1900 B.C.: showing undeniable affinities particularly with the painted wares, on the one hand, of the Danube-Dniester zone of Southeast Europe (the Aryan hearth), and on the other of northern Iran: conspicuous shared motifs are the double ax, spiral and swastika, meander and polygonal designs, concentric-circle and checker patterns, wavy-water lines, angular zigzags and organizations of bands; however, an interesting feature, peculiar, I believe, to China and pre-Columbian Mexico, is the so-called Li Tripod, a vessel composed, as it were, of three pendulous breasts, hollow within, standing as a tripod on the tips.

3. An elegant Black Polished Ware (Lungshan): typical rather of Shantung ("China's Holy Land") than of Honan; to be assigned, apparently, to c. 1900–1523 B.C.

4. An elegant White Ware (Shang): associated with bronze, the two-wheeled horse-drawn chariot, writing, and the concept of the hieratic city state: the Shang is the earliest of the classic dynasties of China and the dates now being assigned to it are c. 1523–1027 B.C.

Referring to the schedule that I have been using for a broad cross-reference of the mythologies of the higher civilizations, it is apparent that this Chinese series, far from being the earliest, actually is the latest of the lot. Our dates for the Nuclear Near East, it will be recalled, were these:

I. Proto-neolithic: c. 7500–5500 B.C.
II. Basal Neolithic: c. 5500–4500 B.C.
III. High Neolithic: c. 4500–3500 B.C.
IV. Hieratic City State: c. 3500–2500 B.C.

V. High Bronze Age: c. 2500–1500 B.C.
VI. Heroic Iron Age: c. 1500–500 B.C.
VII. Period of the Great Classics: c. 500 B.C.–500 A.D.
VIII. Period of the Great Beliefs: c. 500–1500 A.D.

India entered the story, we have seen, during Period V. China appears now in Period VI. However, as far as any actually available Chinese texts are concerned, we shall have to wait for Period VII. But by then, numerous signs will have already become evident of at least a remote intercourse with the West. The Rome-China Silk Road was in commercial use by 100 B.C. Alexander reached the Indus 327 B.C. Persia had been at the Indus two centuries before, and we have seen that iron reached India by way of Persia, c. 500 B.C. Iron reached China at about the same time.

The chief dates to be born in mind throughout this portion of our study are the following:

Shang (Basic Chinese High Bronze Age), 1523–1027 B.C.
Early Chou (period of developed feudalism), 1027–772 B.C.
Middle Chou (period of disintegrating feudalism), 772–480 B.C.

CONFUCIUS, 551–478 B.C.

Late Chou (period of the warring states), 480–221 B.C.
Ch'in (Burning of the Books: Great Wall), 221–206 B.C.
Han (Confucian bureaucracy established), 206 B.C.–220 A.D.
Six Dynasties (disunity: Buddhism established), 220–589 A.D.

BODHIDHARMA, 520 A.D.*

Sui (reunification of empire: Great Canal), 590–617 A.D.
T'ang (culmination of Chinese civilization), 618–906 A.D.
Sung (Neo-Confucianism: apogee of painting), 960–1279 A.D.
Yüan (Mongol dynasty: Jenghis Khan), 1280–1367 A.D.
Ming (Neo-Confucian restoration), 1368–1643 A.D.
Ch'ing (Manchu dynasty: disintegration), 1644–1911 A.D.

The periods of the Shang and the Early and Middle Chou Dynasties correspond generally, in character as well as in time, to India from the coming of the Aryans until the period of the Buddha. Comparably the eighth and following centuries B.C. saw the rise in China, as well as in India, of princely capital cities over a large area and a breakdown thereby of the earlier feudal order of life. It has been said that in Confucius' time there were no less

* This is probably a legendary character and certainly a legendary date.

than 770 contending princely states. However, Chinese thought, instead of giving up the fight and retreating to the forest when the world began to fall apart, put itself to the problem of repair. And so, instead of a high history of the ways of disengagement, Chinese philosophy is characterized by contending systems of orientation to the world in being—with what effect, we now turn to see.

II. The Mythic Past

Edgar Allan Poe once wrote a little piece called "The Imp of the Perverse," and I do believe that there must be in the fashioners of piously held beliefs, all over the world, an exceptionally strong strain of the faculty and impulse that he there describes; for it cannot be that they do not know what they are doing. Neither can it be that they regard themselves as deceivers. Nevertheless, they are seldom satisfied merely to brew for the moral nourishment of mankind an amusing little beer of what they know to be their own apocryphal fantasy, but they must needs present their intoxicant with deliberately pompous mien as the ambrosia of some well of truth to which they, in their state of soul, have been given access. It is exactly as my author, Poe, has said. "All metaphysicianism," as he terms such work, "has been concocted *a priori*. The intellectual or logical man, rather than the understanding or observant man, set himself to imagine designs—to dictate purposes to God. Having thus fathomed, to his satisfaction, the intentions of Jehovah, out of these intentions he built his innumerable systems of mind." [11] And with a curious strain of the same perversion by which the sages teach their designs, both the vulgar and the learned everywhere have been forever loath to see any such facts brought to light as might tend to inform them of the true nature of the brews by which they live, dream, and regulate their lives. Thus it has been, we know, in our own relation to the Bible. Thus it is, equally, in the Far East in the matters of the golden age of Yao and Shun, the engineering miracles of the Great Yü, and, above all, the written history of a China of five thousand years.

Actually, it is amazing how little we know of the writings of the Chinese before the period of Confucius (551–478 B.C.). And what to some will perhaps be still more amazing is the fact that from the period of Confucius onward there was such a doctoring of texts that even the most learned scholarship, whether of Europe, Japan, or China, has been at a loss, up to now, to reconstruct with assurance even the work of Confucius himself—not to mention whatever wisdom, mythic, philosophic, or other, may have gone before. Consequently, all of the myths (or rather, as we now have them, moralizing anecdotes) of the Chinese golden age have to be recognized as the productions rather of a Confucian forest of pencils than of any "good earth" or "forest primeval." And if gems or jades are to be found among them from the actual mythologies of Yangshao, Lungshan, Shang, or even Chou (anything earlier, that is to say, than Shih Huang Ti's burning of the books, 213 B.C.), we have to realize that they have been lifted from their primitive, and remounted carefully in a late, highly sophisticated setting, like an old Egyptian scarab mounted as a ring for some fine lady's hand.

In a work of enormous learning, the Swedish sinologist Dr. Bernhard Karlgren has attempted to reconstruct the mythic lore by which the Chinese—or at least some Chinese—lived before the scholiasts of the Han period began to apply their own brand of learning to the inheritance; and I am going to follow him in assuming that the materials presented in his pages are in large measure derived, as he takes them to be, from the ancestral legends of the princely houses of the Chou period.

The first point to be remarked is that there are no stories of creation, either in these early myths of the Chou period, or in the later Confucian classics. A few appear in later Han times, but these do not belong to the classic system and are associated largely with late Taoist thought. They do not tell us so much of China as of the world diffusion of themes in the period of the four great contiguous empires of Rome, Arsacid Persia, Kushana India, and Han China. They belong to the cosmopolitan mythology of the great sea and caravan ways. Nor do we find in the early Chinese material any such grandiose imagery of cosmic dissolution as appears throughout the mythologies of India. The world here is to be a much more solid thing than the Indian cosmic mirage. And finally, there is to be no sign whatsoever of the Great Reversal in its fundamental drive to the root of the will to live. The Chinese have maintained, through thick and thin (they have had much of both), an extraordinarily buoyant confidence both in themselves and in the simple goods of progeny, prosperity, and long years.

Now, in contrast to the rich fare that we have been wallowing in from India, this Chinese kitchen is going to seem, at first, a bit spare, I am afraid. But the courses—you will see—keep coming, and before long quite a banquet will have been served. The Chinese have a curious meandering way in their thinking as well as in their eating, and in spite of every effort on my part to present their mythology otherwise, the way of meandering has come through. And so, here we are, at the first stage of a curious road: the mythic past of China, as represented in the flotsam of a thoroughly wrecked mythology of the Early and Middle Chou periods, which has come down to us only in widely separated fragments, scattered through texts of the later, post-Confucian ages. The reader will note that there is no cosmogony, no world beginning here. The world is already solid under foot, and the work about to begin is the building of China.

PERIOD OF THE EARLIEST MEN

1. The Lords of the Birds' Nests. People in those days lived in birds' nests made in trees, to avoid the dangers threatening them on the ground.

2. The Lords, the Fire Drillers. Eating raw food, the people were ruining their stomachs. Some sages invented the fire drill and taught them how to cook.

3. The Deluge of Kung Kung. "After the time of the Fire Drillers, when Kung Kung was king, the waters occupied seven tenths and the dry land three tenths of the earth. He availed himself of the natural conditions and in the constrained space ruled the empire." [12]

It is to be observed that we already have an empire. We also have a Deluge. And a basic Chinese theme is announced in the final sentence, where it is said that Kung Kung "availed himself of the natural conditions." Virtue consists in respecting those conditions; competence, in making use of them.

In the later History Classic (*Shu Ching*), which is one of the fundamental texts of classical Chinese thought, this period of the earliest men is completely disregarded, and all good things commence with the golden age of Yao and Shun (below, page 385), while Kung Kung is deliberately transferred to that time and turned into an incompetent dignitary who was banished.

PERIOD OF HIGHEST VIRTUE

The name of this period suggests that it must have been of considerable importance in the old mythology. Nothing remains of it in extant texts, however, but the names of a dozen or so of its kings, one of whom, Jung Ch'eng, is termed the creator of the calendar, and another, Chu Jung, bears the name of the god of fire. Dr. Karlgren remarks that although the names of the kings of this shadowy period "tell us little," they underline the important fact that "in Chou-time China there must have existed any number of myths concerning primeval heroes." [13]

PERIOD OF THE GREAT TEN, CULMINATING WITH YAO, SHUN, AND THE GREAT YÜ

To this important age, which terminates in a Deluge, ten emperors were assigned in the early Chou-time mythology. Hence, it appears that what we are viewing here may be a local transformation of the series of the old Sumerian king list.* I shall present together with the names of its ten mythical monarchs a few items from their legends, such as seem to me to reinforce the argument for a Mesopotamian source; striving also to indicate, however, the characteristic Chinese inflections. They are as follows.

1. Fu Hsi; 2. Shen Nung. In the legends of the Chou period these two emperors played modest parts. Both acquired great importance, however, in the later "Book of Changes" (*I Ching*), where Fu Hsi is credited with the invention of the symbols on which that work is based (page 411), as well as with having taught the people to use nets for hunting and fishing, while Shen Nung, who "ruled the world," we are told, "for seventeen gener-

* Supra, p. 119.

ations," is supposed to have devised the plow and instituted markets.* [14]

3. Yen Ti. Following the long reign of Shen Nung, there came the short reign of Yen Ti, who was overcome by his glorious brother Huang Ti.

4. Huang Ti. This important mythic figure, the so-called Yellow Emperor, is supposed to have had twenty-five sons, from whom no less than twelve feudal families of the Chou period claimed descent; so that, as Karlgren observes, "sacrifices to Huang Ti must have been wide-spread in the feudal courts and not confined to the royal house." [15] Huang Ti invented the fire drill (already invented by the Fire Drillers), burned the forests on the hills, cleared the bush, burned the marshes, and drove out the wild beasts. Thus he made cattle-breeding possible. His virtue brought the barbarians of the four frontiers to allegiance, some of whom had holes in their chest, others long arms, and others deep-lying eyes. He consulted with his sages while deliberating on the Bright Terrace, ordered musical pitch pipes to be made and a console of twelve bells "to harmonize the five sounds"; and when he rode to assemble the spirits on the holy mount T'ai-shan, he drove in an ivory chariot drawn by six dragons. The wind-god ran ahead and swept; the rain-god sprinkled the road; tigers and wolves galloped before, spirits spirited behind, serpents streaked along the ground, and phoenixes flew above. [16]

Worth noticing here is a type of thought that I shall term *mythic ethnology*, which is typical not of Chinese philosophy alone but of all archaic system.† Beyond the pale of the Middle Kingdom are only barbarians, not quite human, whom it is China's cosmic mission to control—as we learn, for example, from the following admonishing message sent by the great Manchu Emperor of China, 1795, to King George III of Great Britain.

* It is worth noting that nineteenth-century Western scholarship generally agreed with the Chinese that these legendary kings must have been actual monarchs. Fu Hsi's dates were supposed to be 2953–2838 B.C.; Shen Nung's, 2838–2698 B.C. (Cf. E. T. C. Werner, *A Dictionary of Chinese Mythology* [Shanghai: Kelly and Walsh, 1932], p. 419.)

† Compare the Indian view, supra, pp. 227–28, heading B.

Swaying the wide world, I have but one aim in view, namely, to maintain a perfect governance and to fulfill the duties of the state. Strange and costly objects do not interest me. . . . I have no use for your country's manufactures. . . . It behooves you, O King, to respect my sentiments and to display even greater devotion and loyalty in the future, so that by perpetual submission to our throne, you may secure peace and security for your country hereafter. . . . Our Celestial Empire possesses all things in prolific abundance and lacks no products within our borders. There was, therefore, no need to import the manufactures of outside barbarians in exchange for our produce. . . . I do not forget the lonely remoteness of your island, cut off from the world by intervening wastes of sea, nor do I overlook your excusable ignorance of the usages of our Celestial Empire. . . . Tremblingly obey and show no negligence.[17]

Hoho!

5. *Shao Hao*. Little more is told of this monarch in texts available today than that he reigned for but seven years (ritual regicide motif?). But as the series of the Great Ten now approaches the classic golden age of Yao and Shun, texts become more abundant and flesh begins to appear on the bones:

6. *Chuan Hsü: known also as Kao Yang*. Kao Yang (Chuan Hsü) had eight talented sons, one of whom, Kun ("the Great Fish"), was the father of the Great Yü and his unsuccessful predecessor in dealing with the Deluge (see heading 8).[18]

7. *K'u*. This monarch had two wives, Chiang Yüan and Chien Ti, both of whom conceived miraculously. The first became pregnant when she trod on the big toe of God's footprint. She bore Hou Chi, "without bursting or rending," who, in the reign of Shun, became the Minister of Agriculture. "They laid him in a narrow lane, the oxen and the sheep nurtured him between their legs. They laid him on cold ice, birds covered and protected him." [19] (Virgin birth, infant exile, animal foster-parent: euhemerization of a deity of agriculture. Compare the nativity and manger of Christ.) The second pregnancy occurred when the two young ladies were in their pleasure tower of nine stories, enjoying wine, sweetmeats, and music. God sent them a swallow that sang, and the

two contested in catching it. They covered it with a basket, which, after a time, they lifted, and the bird flew off, leaving two eggs. Each swallowed one; Chien Ti conceived; and the child she bore became the father, centuries later, of the founder of the dynasty of Shang.[20] (The number nine here is worth noting. It is Dante's mystic number of Beatrice; [21] the number of the angelic choirs hymning God; and the number of strokes of the bell of the Angelus, celebrating Mary's conception of Christ by the Dove. Compare, also, Leda and the Swan.)

8. Yao. Ti Yao, Divine Yao, the most celebrated monarch of the Chinese golden age, is the model sagely man of all time. The great History Classic (*Shu Ching*) opens with a celebration of his character and reign:

"Examining into antiquity," it states, "we find Divine Yao, who, naturally and without effort, was reverential, intelligent, accomplished, thoughtful, sincerely courteous, and obliging. Moreover, the bright influence of these qualities was felt through the four quarters and reached both above and beneath. He distinguished the able and the virtuous, thence proceeding to a loving consideration of all in the nine classes of his kindred, who thereby became harmonious. He regulated and clarified the people, who all became luminously intelligent. He united and harmonized the many states. And the black-haired people thus were transformed. The result was universal accord." [22]

However, in spite of his great virtue and the cosmic influence of his sagely character, all was not quite perfect in the period of Yao; for there was a terrible spate of inundations, which no one seemed able to repair. The Minister of Works, having promised much, had accomplished little.

> Ti Yao said: "Who will search out for me a man according to the times, whom I can elevate and employ?"
>
> Fang Chi replied: "Your own heir and son Chu is exceptionally intelligent."
>
> Ti Yao said: "Alas! He is insincere and quarrelsome. Can he suffice?"
>
> Ti Yao said again: "Who will search out for me a man equal to the exigency of my affairs?"
>
> And his wicked counsellor Huan Tou replied: "Well, the

merits of the Minister of Works have been recently displayed on a large scale."

Ti Yao said: "Alas! When all is quiet, he speaks; but when employed, his acts turn out differently. He is worthy of respect only in appearance. Look! The floods are threatening the heavens!"

Ti Yao turned, therefore, to his Chief Minister: "My good Master of the Four Mountains, the floods in their spate are terrific. They embrace the hills and overtop the greatest heights, threatening even the heavens, so that the lower people groan and murmur. Is there no competent man at all, to whom I can assign the correction of this calamity?"

And all in the court then said: "Is there not Kun?"

Now Kun, as we have observed, was the father of the youth who was to become in time the Great Yü and was himself one of the talented eight sons of the earlier monarch (6) Chuan Hsü.

Ti Yao said: "Alas! How perverse that fellow is! Disobedient of orders, he tries to injure his peers."

The Master of the Four Mountains argued: "Yet, it might be well to let him try, just to see if he cannot succeed."

Accordingly, Kun was employed. Ti Yao said to him: "Go, and be reverent!" For nine years he labored; but the work remained undone.

Ti Yao then said to his Chief Minister: "So now, my good Master of the Four Mountains, I have been seventy years on this throne. You can carry out my orders: I shall resign to you my place."

But the other said: "I have not the virtue. I should be a disgrace in your place."

Ti Yao said to him: "Show me then someone among the illustrious or else set forth one among the poor and mean."

Whereupon all present said to the Ti: "There is an unmarried man among the lower people, named Shun."

Ti Yao said: "Yes, I have heard of him. What have you to say of him?"

The Master of the Four Mountains spoke: "He is the son of a blind man. His father was obstinately unprincipled; his stepmother insincere; his half-brother Hsiang was arrogant. He has been able, however, through his filial piety, to live with them in harmony and to lead them gradually to self-government, so that they no longer tend to great wickedness."

Ti Yao said: "I will try him. I shall wive him and observe thereby his behavior with my two daughters."

And Ti Yao arranged accordingly, sending his two daughters to the north of the river Kwei, to be wives in the family of Shun. And the Ti said to them: "Be reverent!" [23]

Thus the moment has arrived of the choice and accession of a new Ti, a new god-king, the point having been made that descent and worth are not genealogical but moral, which is a point that is eminently Confucian. Moreover, it has been rendered the more emphatic by the bad character given both to the emperor's own son and to the parents of the young Shun, whose filial piety is the chief and even only token of his eligibility to be the pivot of the universe. There is nothing comparable, as far as I know, in the mythologies of India, where the emphasis ever is on birth.

This highly characteristic Chinese motif of the monarch ceding his throne to the most worthy of his subjects without regard to station may be a vestige of an earlier matriarchal order, and even of something as violent as the murder-of-the-old-king theme discussed by Frazer in *The Golden Bough;* for Yao, we have seen— rather rashly—turns over to Shun both of his daughters. In fact, there is a line in one old book that carries just such a murderous tone, where it states: "Shun forced Yao; Yü forced Shun." [24] However, in this later, classic context, the archaic motif—if such it be—has been applied to a moral argument that is at the core of the Chinese ideal of the character of the good king, the sagely king, and thereby, the sagely man.

Yao tried Shun by various means: sent him, for example, into a forest at the foot of the wild hills; but not even violent wind, thunder, and rain could make him go astray.[25] So that here, once again, is a primitive theme; one common, for example, in the myths of North America: that of the tester, the ogre father-in-law. But again, the moral is Confucian. Or one might compare this trial of Shun in the forest, amid violent wind, thunder, and rain, with that of the Jain savior Parshvanatha *—whereupon the contrast of the Indian argument of absolute disengagement with the

* Supra, pp. 218–19.

Confucian of competence in constructive engagement becomes about as vivid as one could wish.

"The farmers of the Li-shan encroached upon each other's boundaries. Shun went there and farmed; and after a year the boundaries were correct. The fishermen on the Ho bank quarreled about the shallows. Shun went there and fished and after a year they gave way to their elders. The potters of the eastern barbarians made vessels that were coarse and bad. Shun went there and made pottery. After a year their vessels were solid." [26]

Ti Yao remained only three years more on his throne, when he invited Shun to accede; and the fine youth, of course, declined. "Nevertheless," states the History Classic, "on the first day of the first month Shun received Ti Yao's retirement in the temple of the Accomplished Ancestor." [27] (Compare the Sed Festival of the Pharaoh, timed to the commencement of the year!) And after Shun had reigned for twenty-eight years, Yao, at the age of 101, died on a journey toward the north to instruct the eight barbarian tribes of that quarter, among whom he was buried simply, with no tumulus, on the north side of the holy mountain of the North.[28]

9. *Shun.* As emperor vice-regent, Shun had already performed for twenty-eight years all of the great sacrifices, made tours of inspection every five years to the four quarters and there presented offerings to the mountains, received the feudal lords of the quarters every four years in his capital and examined their works, distributed tokens of investiture, corrected standards of measurement, divided the realm in twelve provinces, instituted penal codes, and punished those deserving to be punished.[29] He was bountiful, also, of awards. For instance, when his Keeper of Dragons, Tung Fu, proved to be an expert in attracting dragons to his barn by giving them food they liked, Shun was so appreciative that he bestowed on him a clan and family name, enfeoffed him, and established him as the ancestor of a great house.[30]

The chief problem still, however, was the flood, in the control of which Kun had miserably failed; for, according to the History Classic, he had made the mistake of violating nature in his work. "He dammed up the inundating waters and thereby threw into disorder the arrangement of the five elements. The Lord of Heaven was consequently roused to anger and did not give him the Great Plan with its nine divisions. Hence the unvarying principles of Heaven's method were allowed to go to ruin. Kun was made prisoner until his death; and his son Yü rose up and assumed his task." [31]

10. *Yü.* "To the Great Yü," our text goes on to say, "Heaven gave the Great Plan with its nine divisions, wherein the unchanging principles of its method were in due order set forth." [32] And this method was just the opposite of that which Yü's father had employed; for, as we learn from Mencius: "Yü dug the soil and led the water to the sea; drove out the snakes and dragons, relegating them to the marshes. The waters then had their courses through the middle of the land: the rivers Hsiang, Huai, Ho and Han. And when the obstacles had been cleared, the birds and beasts that had been molesting the people were driven off and the folk obtained ordered land, where they settled down." [33]

Yü had a long neck, a mouth like a raven's beak, and a face that was ugly too. The world followed him, however, considering him to be a sage, because of his devotion to learning.[34] A servant woman of the emperor, having made an excellent wine, brought him some; but when he tasted, finding it good, he sent her away. "In the future," said he, "there will be many who lose their states because of drink." And he refrained thereafter from all wine. His whole life, those years, was in his work, which he performed in accord with the natural conditions. When he entered the land of the naked, he stripped himself to accord with native custom. And he fared in his labors to the bounds of the earth. In the farthest East, he reached the place of the tree where the ten suns bathe and perch and whence they fly; in the farthest South, the country of the lacquer trees, the red grain, the boiling springs, the mountain of nine brilliances, the winged people, naked people, and the land of immortals; westward, the people who drink dew and live on air, the wizard's mountain, the mountain of accumulated gold, and the land of the people with three faces and one arm; in the North, the countries of the various barbarians, amassed waters, the holy mountain of the North, and the mountain of heaped stone.[35] And when his work was done, he came before Shun. As the History Classic tells:

> Shun said: "You must have some wonderful experiences to relate."
> Said Yü, doing obeisance: "I have been thinking only of my daily work. What can I say?"
> Said the Minister of Justice: "Oh come now! Will you not tell us anything at all?"
> Yü said: "The flooding waters seemed to assail Heaven; in their magnitude they embraced immense hills, overtoppled mighty mounds; and the people were bewildered, overwhelmed. So I mounted my four conveyances [carriages on land, boats on water, sledges in icy places, shoes with spikes when ascending hills] and along the hills I hewed down trees. At the same time, together with the Minister of Agriculture [see heading 7], I showed the multitude how to procure flesh to eat [by capturing fish, birds, and beasts]. I opened passages for the streams throughout the nine provinces and conducted them to the sea, sowing grain at the same time, together with the Minister of Agriculture; showing the multitudes how to procure the food of toil in addition to flesh meat. I urged them, further, to exchange what they had for what they had not, and to dispose of accumulated stores. In this way, all the people received grain to eat and the myriad regions began to come under good rule. . . .
> "When I married, I remained only four days together with my wife. And when my son wailed and wept, I paid no attention, but kept planning with all my might." [36]

"For ten years," states another text, "Yü did not see his home. On his hands there grew no nails. On his shanks there grew no hair. He contracted a sickness, furthermore, that made him shrivel in half the body, so that in walking he was unable to carry the one leg past the other. And people called this walk 'the walk of Yü.' " [37] "And were it not for Yü," said a prince of Liu in the year 541 B.C., "should we not all be fishes?" [38]

Which, in brief, is the tale of the great Chinese golden age that until some fifty years ago was taken seriously by scholars, even in the West, as representing China's claim to antiquity.

Let us pause to regard a few facts.

The first, already noted, is the obvious analogy of the ten Sumerian kings, biblical patriarchs, and Chinese monarchs, along with the shared legend of a Deluge overcome by the last of the series. It can be argued that the number ten of the Chinese series represents merely a coincidence; however, certain further points make the argument of coincidence a little difficult to maintain. For example, is it not remarkable that both Noah and the Great Yü, in the course of their labors during the Deluge, became lame? The biblical hero, states a popular Jewish legend, was injured by the lion (the solar beast) in the hold of his mighty craft. "One day in the ark," it is said, "Noah forgot to give his ration to the lion, and the hungry beast struck him so violent a blow with his paw that he was lame forever after, and, having a bodily defect, he was not permitted to do the offices of a priest." [39] Indeed, that is why, after the landing, it was Shem, not his father Noah, who served as priest at the family offering of an ox, a sheep, a goat, two turtle doves, and two pigeons.

Robert Graves, in *The White Goddess*, has a chapter on the figure of the lame king in early Levantine, Cretan, Greek, Celtic, and Germanic myth and legend, which is certainly worth reading in this connection. He points to Jacob's limp after wrestling with the angel at the ford (Genesis 32:24–32); the bull-foot of the god Dionysos: Hephaistos, the lame smith; and Wieland, also a lame smith. He reminds us, too, of the repeated falls of Christ bearing the cross. And if I have read his argument aright, it is based on the idea that the king, formerly killed, was in later rituals only lamed and emasculated. [40]

My own suggestion would be that the mythic image of the maimed king is related to the moon, which is normally—as we have found—the celestial counterpart of the sacrificed and resurrected bull-king. The moon is lame, first on one side, then on the other, and, even at the full, is marred by pocks of darkness. In my Primitive volume I have brought together a series of images of both a god and a tree of life that on one side are beautiful but on the other in decay. [41] The full moon, rising on the fifteenth day of its cycle, directly faces the orb of the setting sun. The direct light of the sun wounds the moon at that moment, which thereafter wanes.

Thus the lion wounded Noah, no doubt at the moment of the height of the Deluge, upon which he rode like the full moon upon its high tide. The moon, furthermore, is the heavenly cup of ambrosial liquor drunk by the gods; and we note that both Yü and Noah (Genesis 9:21) became drunk.

In any case, we have now before us three very different versions of the nature and meaning of the Deluge confronted by the tenth monarch of a mythic age. The first is of the ancient Sumerian cycle of the cosmic eon, mathematically inevitable, which ends in cosmic dissolution. The second is of the cosmic catastrophe brought about by a freely willing God; and this, we have seen, appears to represent the reflex of an essentially Semitic attitude of dissociation from, and guilt vis-à-vis, divinity. (Contrasted with this was the Aryan formula of the Vedic drought caused by a demon, where the gods were on the side of man.) And finally, in this Chinese version we see the catastrophe reduced from a cosmic to a local geographical event, with neither guilt nor mathematics invoked to rationalize the occurrence. "It is above all," as Dr. Karlgren has observed, "a *hero* legend: the preponderating theme is not so much the catastrophe of the inundation as its connection with a hero who copes with it." [42] And in the spirit of the basic Chinese—perhaps already Early Chou, but certainly Confucian—view of proper action, the virtue of the hero lies in his accord with the order of nature, as a consequence of which he is supported in his task by the mandate and revealed Great Plan of heaven itself.

PERIOD OF THE LEGENDARY HSIA DYNASTY

As Noah survived the Flood and therefore represents both the end of the old and beginning of the new eon, so also does the Great Yü. And as the age following the Flood, both in the Bible and in the old Sumerian king lists, approached gradually the plane of history, so also does the chronicle of China, following the period of Yü. He is supposed to have been the founder of the legendary Hsia dynasty, for which a number of serious scholars still believe some tangible evidence may yet be found. However, since none has yet appeared, we shall have to regard it as legendary still. The date of its founding is supposed to have been c. 2205 B.C.

and the date of the death of Yü, c. 2197 B.C.[43] A line of seventeen kings is supposed to have reigned for either 471 or 600 years (statements greatly differ). Following its fall, there rose the archaeologically well-validated dynasty of Shang. And as Yao, Shun, and Yü have stood in Chinese literature as models of the character of the good king, so the last legendary monarch, Chieh, of the Hsia dynasty has been the model of the bad.

Chieh, we are told, was a paragon of vice. In the winter he built no bridges, in the summer he made no rafts, just to watch the people freeze and drown. He let female tigers loose in the market, just to watch the people run. He had thirty thousand female musicians, who shouted and made music all night, so that it was heard through all the streets, and all were dressed in embroidered silk.[44]

Women, in particular, were his weakness. He attacked the land of Yu Shih and was placated when the people sent him a lady, Mo Hsi, who immediately won his favor. Then he attacked the land of Yu Min and the lord of that place sent him two ladies, Yüan and Yen, whose names he engraved on a famous jade; and Mo Hsi, rejected, was banished to the river Lo, where she nursed in her heart a resolve for revenge.

The legend tells next of another solitary lady, unnamed, dwelling by the river Yi, who, discovering herself pregnant, dreamed that night that a spirit spoke to her. "When water comes out of the mortar," it said, "start running east and do not look back." The next morning water was coming out of the mortar, and, warning her neighbors, she hurried east. But she paused to look back. Her city was under water. And she was turned into a mulberry tree.

This incident suggests the legend of Lot's wife. "Flee for your life," said the angels to Lot, his wife, and two daughters; "do not look back." But the woman paused to look back and saw that on the cities of Sodom and Gomorrah the Lord was raining fire and brimstone. They are now beneath the Dead Sea. And she was turned into a pillar of salt (Genesis 19:17–26).

Into the legend of the fall of the wicked monarch Chieh there now comes a third solitary young female. She was the daughter of the lord of a certain minor province, who was out culling mulberry leaves alone, when she found a baby boy in a hollow mulberry tree. She took it home and presented it to her father, who, in turn, gave it to the palace cook (a male). They named the child Yi Yin, after the river Yi. He grew to be exceeding wise. And his fame presently reached the ears of T'ang, the lord of the rising house of Shang, who sent an embassy to ask for him. But the lord of the minor province, whose daughter had discovered him, would not let the prodigy go. So the lord of Shang asked for a wife, and, as escort for the girl, Yi Yin was sent along—who, when he arrived, was seized by T'ang, who purified him in the temple, threw light upon him from the sacred fire, smeared him with the blood of a sacrificed pig, and the next day received him in audience as a member of his court.[45]

Now T'ang, the lord of Shang, in contrast to Chieh, the lord of Hsia, was a model of kingly virtue. He stored grain to save those who hungered and gave clothes to those who were cold. He mined metal and made coins of it, to redeem children sold by destitute parents.[46] And when there came a terrible drought, he went alone to a sacred mulberry grove and there, in prayer to God on High, tendered his own body as a sacrificial gift.[47]

The recurrent mulberry theme in this tale of the rise of the house of Shang and fall of the house of Hsia suggests very strongly an underlying vegetation myth. Dr. Karlgren has observed that two early monarchs of the series of The Great Ten—5, Shao Hao, and 6, Chuan Hsü—dwelt in a place called "The Hollow (k'ung) Mulberry Tree (sang)," which, as he declares, must have got its name "from some famous old mulberry tree, probably the center of a cult, a common phenomenon even in modern China." [48] The readiness of the virtuous lord T'ang to offer up his body in such a grove, expressly to produce rain, relates the legend to the matter of Frazer's Golden Bough and the world-restoring ritual regicide. (Compare the Indus Valley seal of Figure 17.) The mulberry grove and hollow tree are perfect counterparts of the Roman ritual grove at Nemi and its sacred oak tree of Diana.[49] And when to the symbolic (unconsummated) self-offering of T'ang in the mulberry grove there is added the virgin birth of Yi Yin from a k'ung *sang,* all the elements of a myth of death and resurrection by a holy tree (compare Christ on Holy Rood) stand before us.

We think of Osiris, tossed into the river Nile (compare the river Yi), who was found in the trunk of a tamarisk tree by his virgin sister-bride, the goddess Isis. There is the legend, also, of Adonis, the Greco-Syrian counterpart of Osiris and Tammuz, who was born from a tree, which had been a maid named Myrrha. Desiring her father, Myrrha seduced him and conceived; but then was turned into a myrrh tree. And, as Ovid tells her tale: "The tree cracked, the bark tore asunder, and gave forth its living burden, a wailing boy," which was received by the hands of Lucina, a goddess of birth.[50] The nymph Daphne, too, was turned into a tree when pursued by the sun-god Apollo. And, again considering Lot, we recall that when his wife, who had looked back, was turned into a pillar of salt, his daughters got him drunk and, seducing him, conceived; for they supposed that with the destruction of the two cities, the only remaining human beings were themselves and their bereaved father—as though a Deluge and new beginning of the world were in question.

"It is tempting," Dr. Karlgren writes, "to suspect an early hellenistic influence in the theme of the woman changed into a tree (Philemon and Baucis, Daphne)." [51]

Far more tempting, it seems to me, is the idea of the single fundamental myth of the end and rebeginning of an eon, which is part and parcel of the heritage of civilization itself. In its primary mythic form it produced the rites of Osiris and Tammuz; in the later, hellenistic modes of literary myth, the tales of Daphne, Myrrha, etc.; and in both the biblical and Chinese pseudo-historic chronicles, the legends of Noah, Lot, and—five thousand miles away—the Great Yü and the wonderful Yi Yin.

It is possible that in the culminating episodes of this legend actual echoes are to be heard of certain prehistoric scenes at the time of the victory of the bronze-bearing Shang people over the earlier Yangshao and Lungshan neolithic town and city states. The virtuous lord T'ang, we are told, sent his vizier Yi Yin to spy for him; who learned not only of the misery of the people under the wicked rule of Chieh, but also of the jealousy of the lady by the river Lo. And when the time came to attack, Heaven itself declared its will. The sun and moon missed their proper times. Cold and heat came promiscuously. The five kinds of grain were scorched and died. Demons howled in the land, cranes cried for more than ten nights, and the nine tripod caldrons that were the tokens of divine favor disappeared from Hsia and reappeared in Shang. The lady by the river Lo, Mo Hsi, kept the vizier Yi Yin apprised of all the omens and events within the palace; and when, finally, she informed him that the emperor Chieh had dreamed of two contending suns, one east, one west, of which the west had won, T'ang knew his day had dawned. A voice called to him: "Attack! I shall give you all the strength you need; for I have received for you Heaven's mandate." And the virtuous lord of Shang sent forth ninety war chariots in wild goose array and six thousand warriors devoted unto death.

Chieh, in his wickedness, had numerous giants who could tear apart a living rhinoceros or tiger and slay a man with the touch of a finger. But he could not escape the punishment of the gods. Chu Jung, the fire-god, flung down fire into the northwest corner of his city. T'ang's chariots struck; the warriors followed. Chieh fled with a party of five hundred and was banished. And the great model of all virtue, T'ang, then offered the royal seat to anyone who felt worthy to assume it. None dared. And so, he took it to himself to establish the great historical dynasty of Shang.[52]

III. The Chinese Feudal Age: c. 1500–500 B.C.

SHANG DYNASTY: c. 1523–1027 B.C.

The royal tombs of the actual first dynasty of China were unearthed in a series of excavations between the years 1928 and 1937, following the find by J. G. Andersson of the old Shang capital at Anyang; and, like the tombs at Abydos of the first dynasty of Egypt fifteen centuries before, they tell of a totally different spiritual order from that of any mythic golden age of philosophic thought. The normal form of the Shang tomb was of a large pit some 50 feet long, 40 feet wide, and 15 feet deep, in the

midst of which a central pit-grave had been excavated to a depth
of another 15 feet, and within this, still another, 8 feet more. A final
cavity then had been dug below this last, large enough for the
body of an armed warrior, and the whole affair, lined with logs,
had been regally furnished. All the tombs, of course, had been
plundered; yet enough remained to let us know what the order
of burial had been: a warrior with his halberd in the deepest pit;
a wooden coffin just above; in the great hall, ritual bronzes, jades,
carved bone, weapons, etc.; in the floors of the ramps and approaches, numerous buried horses, chariot teams, dogs and men;
and in the main pit, as in Egypt, the skeletons of men and women
of the court. The whole had been filled with pounded earth, and,
as a novelty surpassing Egypt, in this fill the skeletons of animals
—dogs, deer, monkeys, etc.—were strewn, together with human
skulls to the number, often, of a hundred or so.[53] Nor is it to be
thought that in the period of Confucius himself the archaic mythic
mimes documented in these tombs had been forgotten. As late as
420 B.C., the moralist Mo Tzu was complaining of the funeral rites
of the royalty of his day.

"Even when an ordinary and undistinguished person dies,"
wrote this philosopher of universal love, "the expenses of the
funeral are such as to reduce the family almost to beggary; and
when a ruler dies, by the time enough gold and jade, pearls and
precious stones have been found to lay by the body, wrappings of
fine stuffs to bind round it, chariots and horses to bury with it
in the tomb, and the necessary quantity of tripods and drums under
their coverings and awnings, of jars and bowls on tables and stands,
of halberds, swords, feather-work screens and banners, objects in
ivory and leather have been made . . . the treasuries of the State
are completely exhausted. Moreover in the case of an Emperor,
sometimes several hundred and never less than twenty or thirty of
his servants are slain to follow him; for a general or principal
minister sometimes twenty or thirty persons are slain, and never
less than four or five." [54]

There is no need to labor the point. The archaeology of China
reveals in the sequence above noticed of 1. early neolithic crude
pottery, 2. the fine painted ware of Yangshao, 3. the fine black

ware of Lungshan, and 4. the fine white pottery, bronzes, and tomb furniture of Shang, indisputable evidence of a late arrival in the Far East of that sequence of cultural mutations already long familiar in the Near East; while the fragments of early Chinese mythology that have come down to us, euhemerized and moralized by later Chinese scholars, reveal with equal clarity the primacy of the West-to-East cultural flow.

And yet, there is a no less eloquent array of facts pointing to another—perhaps older—cultural constellation represented in China in the period of the Shang tombs; for, as in India, so also here, signs are to be noted of a counterplayer—perhaps stemming, in this case, from the Mongoloid circumpolar hearth above suggested.* Many of the Shang bronzes, for example, are in form not circular, as though in imitation of ceramic wares, but boxlike, in imitation of wood; and the over-all ornamentation of these quadratic forms differs from anything known farther west. "The angular-bodied bronzes," states Dr. Li Chi, "not only inherited the shapes of the wooden prototypes but also carried on the method and patterns of decoration of the wood carvers, while the round-bodied articles cast in bronze, shaped mainly after the ceramic tradition, acquired their ornaments much later." [55]

A stylistic similarity has been noted, furthermore, between the decorative patterns of the Shang period and the arts of many tribes of North and South America; notably the totem-pole arts of the fishing peoples of the Northwest coast and the monuments of the Mayan-Aztec sphere (Figures 22 and 23). Among the most striking shared traits of this circum-Pacific style are: a piling up of similar forms in vertical series (principle of the totem pole), a way of splitting animal forms, either down the back or down the front, and opening them like a book (bilateral splitting), eyes and faces placed on joints and hands, and a particular way of organizing angular spirals and meanders.

Professor Robert Heine-Geldern has employed the term "Old Pacific Style" to designate this complex; and we may now think of it, hypothetically, as in some manner associated with the folk movement of the arctic Mongoloid population. Professors Joseph Need-

* Supra, pp. 373–75.

ham and Wang Ling in their encyclopedic *Science and Civilization in China* have remarked that in this context "certain traits are found which point to a wide community of culture throughout the northern latitudes below the Arctic Circle, i.e. Northern Asia and North America," and suggest that this whole area "could almost be called the Shamanism area."

> A typical implement common to all parts of this vast area [they write] is the rectangular or semilunar stone knife, quite unlike anything known in Europe or the Middle East, but found among Eskimos and Amerindians as among Chinese and in Siberia. . . . Such knives were common in the Shang dynasty, and continued to be made (of iron) down to recent times in China. Another characteristic of this northern culture area is the use of pit-dwellings or earth-lodges, the beehive shape of which may have descended to the peasants' houses of the T'ang period which may be seen painted on the frescoes of Tunhuang. The sinew-backed or composite bow seems to have been an invention of this area. If America was peopled by migrations across the Behring Straits at the beginning of the Neolithic, we might have an explanation of some of those strange similarities which exist between Amerindian and East Asian civilizations; but this is a very difficult problem. . . .[56]

Thus, in the now fairly well documented royal-tomb art of the Shang period, an interplay is to be recognized between a cultural tide stemming from the West, rooted in the bronze age and carried both by an early wave of neolithic potters (Yangshao, Lungshan) and by a later, chariot-driving warrior folk with evident Homeric-Aryan affinities, and a second, "shamanistic," circumpolar tide flowing south, also in waves, and of various Mongoloid strains.

Shamanism is an extremely prominent feature of both the Buddhism and the Shinto of Japan as well as of Chinese and Tibetan religious life; and a sign of its force already in the Shang period may be seen in the demonic animal-mask motif, termed *t'ao-t'ieh,* which appears prominently on the bronzes. In three of the five units of the carved bone design of Figure 22, t'ao-t'ieh masks appear; and in the other two units of the series the same monster is shown squatting profile. M. René Grousset, in his lively volume on *Chinese Art and Culture,* writes that "The absence of a lower

Figure 22. Old Pacific Style: *Left*, Bone Handle, China (Shang), c. 1200 B.C.; *Right*, Totem Pole, North America (Northwest Coast), recent

jaw in the t'ao-t'ieh, as in other zoomorphic monsters, is perhaps due to the fact that they may have been derived from the skin of an animal used as a disguise by sorcerers in certain magic dances, a skin of which the head, in order to 'cap' the shaman, had neces-

Figure 23. Old Pacific Style: *Above,* North America (Northwest Coast), recent; *Below,* Mexico (Tajin Style), c. 200–1000 A.D.

sarily to be reduced to the upper part." [57] "Claws sometimes flank the lower part of the animal's head on both sides, making the animal seem to be crouching, ready to spring. For it is indeed an animal, quite realistic initially. On several of our Shang bronzes, the t'ao-t'ieh is clearly the face of a bull, a ram, a tiger, or an owl (more rarely a stag)." [58] Marcel Granet, in his work on *The Dances and Legends of Ancient China,* states that "although by its name it appears to be an owl, it resembles a ram with a human head, tiger's teeth, human fingernails, and eyes in its armpits." [59] And let us note, besides, that both in certain Shang bronzes and in the arts of Yucatán and Mexico, there appears the shamanistic motif of a human (priestly or warrior) head capped by that of a beast.[60]

However, the Greek goddess Athene also wears a mask-like helmet high on her beautiful head, while on her shield there is the gorgon-mask of Medusa. Thus we are reminded that although shamanism was developed to a special pitch in the Mongoloid, circumpolar sphere, it has actually had a long, broadly flung history, from paleolithic times.[61] So that although in the obvious idiosyncrasies of the Shang ornamental style one may recognize the influence of an otherwise undocumented East Asian or Pacific culture hearth of that period, we cannot be sure that the actual mythic motifs rendered in this art were not brought thither from the West; for whether serpent, tiger, deer, dragon, or t'ao-t'ieh, the Shang motifs—though not the Shang style—are widely known.

The same can be said for the art of divination, to which a considerable Shang series of oracle-bone inscriptions bears witness; for example:

> Divining on the day Wu-wu,
> Ku made inquiry:
> "We are going to the chase at Ch'iu; any capture?"
>
> Hunting this day, we actually captured:
>   1 tiger
>   40 deer
>   164 foxes
>   159 hornless deer. . . .[62]

"The oracle bones were employed," states Professor Needham, "for a method of divination, 'scapulimancy,' which appears to have been peculiar to this culture area, and may have originated a little before the Shang. It consisted in heating the shoulder-blades of mammals or the carapaces of turtles with a live coal or a red-hot bronze poker, the reply of the gods being indicated by the shape or direction of the cracks produced. . . . Classifications have been made of the questions asked; among the most important were: (a) to what spirits should certain sacrifices be made; (b) travel directions, where to stop and how long; (c) hunting and fishing; (d) the harvest; (e) weather; (f) illness and recovery, etc." [63]

And so, here again, we find a particular style that is Chinese, yet an art that was already long developed in the nuclear Near East; for the interest in divination in Mesopotamia was obsessive. And just as in the patterns of the myths, so in this of the fathoming of the will of heaven by auspices, it was specifically with Sumer that the early Chinese connections appear to have been particularly close.

EARLY AND MIDDLE CHOU:
C. 1027–480 B.C.

The legends of the fall of the Shang dynasty and rise of Chou repeat the motifs already familiar from the fall of Hsia and rise of Shang. The History Classic (*Shu Ching*) then goes on to state that when the virtuous founder of the Chou dynasty, King Wu, became seriously ill, some two years after his victory, his younger brother, the Duke of Chou, conceived the idea of dying in his stead; and his ritual thereby, addressed to the ancestors of his line, is of considerable interest:

> The Duke of Chou reared three altars on a cleared space and, having made another altar on the south of these, facing north, he took there his own position. Having put a circular symbol of jade on each of the first three, and holding in his hands the long jade symbol of his own rank, he addressed the great three ancestral kings of his line. The grand historiographer had inscribed his prayer on tablets, to the following effect:
> "His Majesty, your great descendant, is suffering a severe and violent disease. If you three kings have charge in heaven of watching over him, Heaven's great Son, let me, Tan, be a substitute for his person. I was lovingly obedient to my father; I am possessed of many abilities and arts, which fit me to serve spiritual beings. Your great descendant, on the other hand, has not so many abilities and arts as I, and is not so capable of serving spiritual beings. Moreover, in the hall of the Lord of Heaven he was appointed to extend his aid throughout the kingdom, so that he might establish your descendants in this lower earth. The people of the four quarters all stand in reverent awe of him. Oh! do not let that precious Heaven-conferred appointment fall to the ground; the long line of our former kings will have one on whom they can ever rest at our sacrifices.
> "I shall now look for your determination in this matter from the great tortoise shell. If you grant my request, I shall take these symbols and this jade, and return and wait for your orders. If you do not grant it, I shall put them by."
> The duke then divined with three tortoise shells, and all were favorable. He opened with a key the place where the oracular responses were kept and looked at them, and they also were favorable. He said, "According to the form of the

prognostic, the king will take no injury. I, the little child, have obtained the renewal of his appointment from the three kings, by whom a long futurity has been prophesied. I have now to wait for the issue. They can provide for our One man."

When the duke returned, he placed the tablets of his prayer in a metal-bound coffer, and the next day the king got well.[64]

In the classic Book of Odes (*Shih Ching*) 305 pieces are preserved from the ritual lore and poetry of the feudal age. Many of these are Chinese counterparts, both in time and in sense, of the Vedas. Five are ascribed to the Shang dynasty, the rest are of Chou; the last being assigned to the reign of King Ting of Chou, 606–586 B.C.

> How admirable! How perfect!

So begins the first of the Shang series:

> Here are set our hand drums and drums: the drums resound, harmonious and loud, to delight our meritorious ancestor, the Lord T'ang.
> With this music, his descendant invites him: that he may soothe us with the realization of our thoughts, which have been addressed to him.
> Deep is the sound of our drums and hand-drums: shrilly sound the flutes; all harmonious, blending together.
> Oh! majestic is the descendant of T'ang: most admirable his music.
> The large bells and drums fill the ear: the various dances are grandly performed. We have with us the admirable visitors of the lines of Yao, Shun, and Hsia. They are pleased. They are delighted.
> From of old, before our time, the men of yore set us our example: how to be mild and humble from morning until night, and to be reverent in discharging the service.
> May he regard our seasonal sacrifices offered in this manner by the descendant of T'ang! [65]

One can hear the sound of those wonderfully beaten drums, shrilly calling flutes, and large bells, and see the grandly performed dances, with their decorously subdued shamanistic associations, in the Shinto shrines of Japan, to the present day. And this old hymn, when read with these contemporary sounds in one's ear, sends through the centuries a call of power that is far deeper, far more convincing in its force, than are the oddities of the later moralizing Confucian anecdotes of impossible things. The beautiful sacrificial bronzes, hardly matched for dignity, tell us of the lost majesty of those times.

"The clear spirits are in our vessels," states another hymn of the Shang heritage; "and there is granted to us the realization of our thoughts."

> There are also the well-tempered soups, prepared beforehand,
>   with their ingredients rightly proportioned.
> By these offerings we invite his presence without a word.
>
> He will bless us with the eyebrows of longevity; with the gray
>   hair and wrinkled face, in unlimited degree.
>
> With the naves of their wheels bound with leather and their
>   ornamented yokes, the eight bells of their horses' bits all
>   tinkling: the feudal princes come to assist at the offering.
> We have received the mandate in all its greatness, and from
>   Heaven is our prosperity sent down: fruitful years of
>   great abundance.
> Our ancestor will come. He will enjoy our offerings and con-
>   fer on us happiness without limit.[66]

And now a garland from the Odes of Chou:

> In his silken robes, clean and bright,
>   With his cap on his head, looking so respectful,
>   From the hall he goes to the foot of the stairs,
>   And from the sheep to the oxen:
> The officer inspects the tripods, large and small,
>   And the curved goblet of rhinoceros horn.
>
> The good spirits are mild, there is no noise, no insolence:
> An auspice, this, of great longevity.[67]

*   *   *

> They clear away the grass and the bushes;
> And the grass is laid open by their plows.
>   In thousands of pairs they remove the roots,
>   Some in the low wet land, some along the dikes.
>
> There are the master and his eldest son;
> His younger sons, and all their children;
> Their strong helpers and their hired servants.
>   How the noise of their eating the viands brought to
>   them resounds!

The husbands think lovingly of their wives;
The wives keep close to their husbands.

Then with their sharp plowshares
They set to work on the south-lying acres.
    They sow their various kinds of grain,
    Each seed containing in it a germ of life.

In unbroken lines rise the blades,
And, well nourished, the stalks grow long.
    Luxuriant looks the young grain,
    And the weeders go among it in multitudes.

Then come the reapers in crowds,
And the grain is piled up in the fields,
Myriads, and hundreds of thousands, and millions of stacks:
    For spirits and for sweet spirits,
    To offer to our ancestors, male and female,
    And to provide for all ceremonies.

Fragrant is their aroma: enhancing the glory of the state.
Like pepper is their smell: to give comfort to the aged.

It is not only here that there is this abundance;
It is not now only that there is such a time:—
    From of old it has been thus.[68]

                    *   *   *

On the trees go the blows chang-chang;
And the birds cry out ying-ying.
One issues from the dark valley and flies
    To the lofty tree; ying goes its cry,
    Seeking with its voice its companion.

Regard that bird: bird as it is,
Seeking with its voice its companion!
And shall a man not seek his friends?
    Spiritual beings will then hearken to him:
    He will have harmony and peace.[69]

In contrast to the Vedas, we find here predominantly agriculture, not herding; a worship directed to ancestors and not to the powers or gods of the natural world; and the leadership of kings, not priests, in the conduct of the rites: kings who were themselves descendants of the ancestors addressed.

Spengler in *The Decline of the West* has written of the contrast between "time thinking," in terms of a developing destiny, and "space thinking," in terms of timeless natural laws. The former is represented pre-eminently by the man of political tact, with a sense for the possible, who would himself become a destiny; the latter by the man of priestly or scientific knowledge, who would control effects through an application of eternally valid laws. Applied to the contrast of China and India in the main statements of their modes of thought and action, this contrast is illuminating. For in China it was the statesman and in India the priest who set his seal on the civilization; and we find, indeed, on the one hand a great stress placed on oracles investigating a changing destiny, *tao,* with a view to political achievement, and, on the other, a system of unchanging laws, *dharma,* epitomized in formulae of knowledge that are conceived to be of eternal truth: a sense of history, on the one hand, none whatsoever on the other; ancestor worship (direction in time) predominant in China; the gods of earth, air, and sky (the field of space) predominant in India: a sense, on the one hand, of significant engagement, and, on the other, of disengagement, as the greatest human aim.

And yet, in a way that is marvelous to observe, these two culture worlds develop through comparable periods of change almost simultaneously, from the period of the entry of the Aryans into India and of the Shang charioteers into China. The feudal Vedic Age concludes in a period of rising princely cities, roughly in the neighborhood of the eighth century B.C., and in China, too, at about that time, we enter upon a period of deep change of essentially the same kind.

In the year 776 B.C., on August 29, an eclipse of the sun was observed by the Chinese watchers for celestial auspices, and the bad times—which had already dawned—were recognized for what they were. The later pages of the Book of Odes (*Shih Ching*) present the poetry of a new mode for China, a pessimistic literature of lament: *

> At the conjunction of the sun and moon in the tenth month,
>   on the first day of the moon, the sun was eclipsed; a
>   thing of very bad omen.

* Cf. Supra pp. 137–44.

Before, the moon became small, and now, the sun became
    small;
Henceforth the lower people will be in very deplorable case.
The sun and moon announce evil, not keeping to their proper
    paths.
Throughout the kingdom there is no proper government, be-
    cause the good are not employed.
For the moon to be eclipsed is but an ordinary matter.
Now that the sun has been eclipsed: how terrible! [70]

*   *   *

Great Heaven, unjust, is sending down these exhausting dis-
    orders.
Great Heaven, unkind, is sending down these great miseries.
Let superior men come into office, and that would bring rest
    to the people's hearts.
Let superior men execute their justice, and the animosities
    and angers would disappear.

I yoke my four steeds, my four steeds, long-necked.
I look to the four quarters: distress is everywhere; there is no
    place to which I can drive.
Now your evil is rampant, and I can see your spears.
Anon you are pacified and friendly as if you were pledging
    one another.

From great Heaven is the injustice, and our king has no re-
    pose.
Yet he will not correct his heart, and goes on to resent en-
    deavors to rectify him.
I, Chia Fu, have made this poem, to lay bare the king's dis-
    orders.
If you would but change your heart, then would the myriad
    regions be nourished. [71]

The Chinese age of disintegrating feudalism and rise of contending princely states is known euphuistically as the Period of the
Great Protectors (771–480 B.C.). Mo Tzu's description of their
funerals, already quoted, suggests something of the nature of their
piety. The era traditionally is dated from the year when the emperor Yü was slain by one of his western vassals. P'ing, his successor moved the capital east to Loyang, and thereafter the only
major power remaining in the west was the relatively barbaric state
of Ch'in, which in the period following Confucius was to gain mas-

tery over all China, establish the first Chinese military empire, build the Great Wall, burn the books of the philosophers, and initiate in grand style that politics of despotism—alternately barefaced and masked—which has been the vehicle of Heaven's Mandate in the Middle Kingdom ever since.

We are to read in the following pages many fine phrases celebrating virtue in one or another of its aspects; but it must be realized meanwhile that in the actuality of Chinese history an explicit philosophy of altogether contrary kind has been the principal structuring force: that, namely, of the great Ch'in classic of the art of politics, The Book of the Lord Shang (*Shang Tzu*) which for disillusioned ruthlessness is equaled and surpassed only by its Indian counterpart, the Arthashastra. The latter (to quote the laudatory words of the modern Indian statesman and philosopher K. M. Pannikar) goes "far beyond the limited imagination of Machiavelli," and thus "enables Hindu thinkers to evolve a purely secular theory of state of which the sole basis is power." [72] But China too, as the following brief sampling will suffice to show, has a background for power politics in its own past.

The classic in question is a testament of the last years of the great Dynasty of Chou:

"If a country is strong and does not make war," we read, "there will be villainy within and the Six Maggots, which are, to wit: rites and music, poetry and history; the cultivation of goodness, filial piety and respect for elders; sincerity and truth; purity and integrity; kindness and morality; detraction of warfare and shame at taking part in it. In a country that has these twelve things, the ruler will not be able to make people farm and fight, with the result that he will become impoverished and his territory diminished." [73]

"Therefore I would have people told that if they want gain, it is only by plowing that they can get it; if they fear harm, it will only be by fighting that they can escape it. Then everyone within the borders of the land would know that he could get no happiness without first applying himself to plowing and warfare. The country might be small, but the grain produced would be much; the inhabitants might be few, but their military power would be great. A country that devoted itself to these two ends would not have to wait long before it established hegemony or even complete mastery over all other States." [74]

"A country where the virtuous govern the wicked will suffer from disorder, so that it will be dismembered; but a country where the wicked govern the virtuous will be orderly, so that it will become strong. . . ."

And as for such trivia as honor: "If things are done that the enemy would be ashamed to do, there is an advantage." [75]

IV. The Age of the Great Classics: c. 500 B.C.–500 A.D.

LATE CHOU: 480–221 B.C. (PERIOD OF THE WARRING STATES)

The highest concern of classical Chinese thought, in contrast to the Indian of social and cosmic disengagement, was political reform; and in such a context, the central problem is of the true seat of earthly influence and power. The above cited poem of lament accusing heaven actually turned, in the end, on the emperor; for according to the Chinese mythic view, there was a mutual influence operating between heaven, earth, and man: and within the sphere of man the central source of influence and power was the emperor, who, in the spirit of mythic subordination, was to regard himself as the son of heaven. Emperors, however, could lose their mandate; and so, the final social question was of the virtue by which the heavenly mandate of the emperor is retained.

The problem was complex, but, in the main, was viewed under a pair of aspects: 1. that of the macrocosmic order of time: the nature of the seasons, demands and possibilities of the hour, to be determined by auspices and omens; and 2. that of the microcosmic order of man: the recognition and use of the most effective power within the competence of the individual, for the harmonization of life on earth. "All Chinese philosophy," states Mr. Arthur Waley in his elegant introduction to the Tao Te Ching, "is essentially the study of how men can best be helped to live together in harmony and good order." "Every Chinese philosophy is formulated not as an abstract theory but as an art of ruling." [76] And the model for this order, which every one of the schools accepted and interpreted as fact, was the mythic golden age of Yao, Shun, and the Great Yü.

Now the chief Chinese document bearing on the first, or macrocosmic, aspect of the problem is The Book of Changes (*I Ching*), which on its practical side is an encyclopedia of oracles, based on a mythic view of the universe that is fundamental to all Chinese thought. The legend of its origin is that its basic elements were discovered by the first of the legendary Ten Emperors, Fu Hsi (see earlier, page 382, 1). These elements are two: an unbroken line (———) associated with the masculine *yang* principle, which is heavenly (light, dry, warm, active), and a broken line (— —) associated with the feminine *yin,* which is earthy (dark, moist, cold, passive). Primarily the terms *yang* and *yin* refer to the sunny and shady sides of a stream, mountain, or street. Spread an awning, step beneath it, and the yin (— —) qualities of the earth will be experienced; step away, and the yang (———) qualities of the sunny heaven will be felt. In all things, at all times, both yin and yang are operative, though in differing degrees; and the purpose of The Book of Changes was to provide an encyclopedia of the ways in which they may be related.

In the simplest possible combinations, four relationships are indicated: ═══ ══ ══ ══ . These are known as the four Emblematic Symbols. Fu Hsi is supposed to have arranged a series composed of three strokes: the eight trigrams, which have been named, arranged, and interpreted, as follows:

NAME	ATTRIBUTES	IMAGE	FAMILY ANALOGIES
1. ═══ Ch'ien, the Creative	strong	heaven	father
2. ≡ ≡ K'un, the Receptive	devoted, yielding	earth	mother
3. ═ ═ Chen, the Arousing	inciting movement	thunder	first son
4. ═══ K'an, the Abysmal	dangerous	water	second son
5. ═══ Ken, Keeping Still	resting	mountain	third son
6. ═══ Sun, the Gentle	penetrating	wind, wood	first daughter
7. ═══ Li, the Changing	light-giving	fire	second daughter
8. ═══ Tui, the Joyous	joyful	lake	third daughter

"The sons," states Richard Wilhelm in his commentary on this series, "represent the principle of movement in its various stages—beginning of movement, danger in movement, rest and completion of movement. The daughters represent devotion in its various stages—gentle penetration, clarity and adaptability, and joyous tranquillity." [77]

A further development of the signs and enrichment of their subtlety is attributed to King Wen (father of the founder of the Chou dynasty, King Wu) as the one who combined the trigrams to form sixty-four hexagrams; while his younger son, the Duke of Chou (the young man whom we have seen offering himself in his brother's stead), is supposed to have composed the text analyzing the force of each line in every combination. Confucius, it is said, supplied a commentary. In the course of time more commentaries were added. And in the holocaust of the Burning of the Books in the year 213 B.C., this particular book was spared as a practical work, not a maggot—so that it does, indeed, span the gamut of the schools.

The method of divining is to cast yarrow stalks six times and to construct a sign, line by line, from the bottom up, according to the way the sticks fall; after which a reference to the encyclopedia yields the prognostication. For example (just turning to one by chance):

7. Shih: The Army

≡ ≡ Above: K'un, the Receptive, Earth (the second trigram)
≡—≡ Below: K'an, the Abysmal, Water   (the fourth trigram)

This hexagram is made up of the trigrams *K'an,* water, and *K'un,* earth, and thus it symbolizes the ground water stored up in the earth. In the same way military strength is stored up in the mass of the people—invisible in times of peace but always ready for use as a source of power. The attributes of the two trigrams are danger inside and obedience outside. This points to the nature of an army, which at the core is dangerous, while discipline and obedience must prevail outside. . . .

Judgment: The army needs perseverance and a strong man. Good fortune without blame. . . .

The image: In the middle of the earth is water: the image of the army. Thus the superior man increases his masses by generosity toward the people. . . .[78]

The seeker is supposed to look for some sort of correspondence between all of this and his own case, the method of thought throughout being that of a broadly flung association of ideas. One has to feel, not think, one's way into these secrets, letting each symbol grow into a cosmos of associated themes. And underlying all is the elementary principle of a dialectic of two forces, yang and yin—which, in a way, is analogous to the Indian of the lingam and yoni. However, whereas in India the sexual suggestions of the duad are emphasized, the tendency in China has been toward an abstract mathematical (geometrical) style of symbolization. And these contrasting tendencies have colored every bit of the two mythologies: the Indian, lush, voluptuous, or in reaction, fiercely ascetic; the Chinese, either dryly practical or humorously symbolic, never extreme.

Nevertheless, in a fundamental way, the two systems match. Compare, for example, the Indian mythic image of the self-dividing Self with the following statement from the Great Appendix of The Book of Changes and the symbol of the Tao on page 24.

"There is the Great Extreme, which produced the two Elementary Forms. These two Forms produced the four Emblematic Symbols, which in turn produced the eight Trigrams. The eight Trigrams served to determine the good and evil issues of events, and from this determination there issued the prosecution of the great business of life." [79]

The Book of Changes, in a word, is a kind of geometry of mythology, referring particularly to the immediate present—the moment of the casting of the yarrow stalks. It tells of the readiness of time and the art of moving with its tides, rocking with the waves, and is the most important statement remaining to us of that aspect of ancient Chinese thought which relates the individual to the order of the outer world.

We turn now to the order of the inner world: the question of the most effective force within the competence of the individual for the harmonization of life on earth. Three points of view are to be noted (besides that of the already cited Book of the Lord Shang): that of Confucius, that of Mo Tzu, and that of the Taoists, in each of which there will appear a distinct, yet typically Chinese, view of the psychology—as opposed to cosmology—of myth.

Confucius, 551–478 B.C. The more one learns about Confucius, the more miragelike his figure becomes. It used to be supposed that he edited all the great classics. However, as Dr. Fung Yu-lan points out, "Confucius was neither the author, commentator, nor even editor of any of the classics." [80] It used to be supposed that we possessed certain writings from his hand; but, as Fung Yu-lan points out again, "The writing of books in a private rather than official capacity was an as yet unheard of practice which developed only after the time of Confucius." [81] The earliest extant biography of the sage appears in the forty-seventh chapter of the *Shih Chi* ("Historical Records"), China's first dynastic chronicle, which was completed c. 86 B.C.[82]—so that the reach of time between the dates of his actual life (551–478 B.C.) and his earliest known biography is the same as that between the dates of the Buddha (563–483 B.C.) and the earliest extant reports of his teaching in the Pali Canon (c. 80 B.C.).

The legend, briefly, is that Confucius was born in the unimportant small state of Lu, of a noble family descended from the imperial house of Shang (i.e., pre-Chou, as the Buddha's heritage was pre-Aryan). His father, a military officer, having died when he was three, he was brought up by his mother (Son-of-the-Widow motif: a euhemerizing folklore variant of the Virgin Birth).* He married when he was nineteen, advanced in office in the government of Lu, and at the age of about fifty became prime minister. However, when he noticed that his prince had begun to neglect state affairs to spend time and thought on a company of female dancers and musicians sent as a gift by a neighboring lord, Confucius, disillusioned and discouraged, resigned (the graveyard vision; the great departure) and, accompanied by disciples, wan-

* Compare Parsifal and Tristan.

dered, teaching, from one feudal estate to the next (Wandering Sage). He returned to Lu, to spend the last three years of his life in literary labors, and died apparently a failure. For his desire had not been, like that of the Buddha, to leave the guarding of the world to others,* but to become the adviser of a prince who should restore the righteous rule of the golden age of Yao, Shun, and the Great Yü.

Confucius called himself a transmitter, not originator; [83] and the doctrines to which his name are affixed are in fact to be found, in germ at least, in the classics. However, since these have themselves been largely doctored by later Confucians, it is impossible to know which came first, Confucianism or Confucius. The oft-repeated anecdote of his conversation with the older Lao Tzu is now generally rejected, since Lao Tzu is a *complete* mirage and the philosophy attached to his name belongs to the fourth and third centuries B.C., not to the sixth. The statement ascribed to Confucius in the Analects that if some years were added to his life he would apply fifty to the study of the Book of Changes and might then escape falling into great errors,[84] also has to be rejected: the passage is a late corruption.[85] The chief source of our knowledge of what is taken to be his thought, namely the Analects (*Lun Yu*), bears not a single stroke from his hand.[86] And so, as far as our present glance at his lore is concerned, we shall have to rest with the idea that what we are viewing is not Confucius but Confucianism.

Confucianism, then, regards "benevolence" (*jen*) as the most effective power for the harmonization of life on earth, and so stands at the opposite pole of Chinese thought to that philosophy of farming and fighting for which rites and music, poetry and history, the cultivation of goodness, filial piety and the rest, were the maggots that reduce the vital substance of a state to rot. The Chinese ideogram *jen* is composed of two elements: the sign meaning "man" and the sign meaning "two," which is translated roughly as benevolence or human feeling. The connotation is of relationship: benevolent, sincere, mutually respectful relationships between persons. In the Confucian texts five such relationships are announced: those be-

* Supra, p. 270.

tween prince and minister, between father and son, between husband and wife, between elder and younger brother, and between friends.

"Chung Kung asked about perfect virtue, we read in the Analects; and the Master said, 'It is when you go abroad to behave to everyone as if you were receiving a great guest; to employ people as if you were assisting at a great sacrifice; not to do to others as you would not wish done to yourself; to have no murmuring against you in the country, and none in the family.' " [87]

Benevolence, according to the orders of relationship, then, is the first great point of the Confucian system. And the second point, so that the relationships may be recognized, is what has been termed the rectification of names:

"The Master said: 'What is needed is to rectify names. . . . If names are not correct, language is not in accordance with the truth of things, affairs cannot be carried on to success. When affairs cannot be carried on to success, rites and music will not flourish. When rites and music do not flourish, punishments will not be properly awarded. When punishments are not properly awarded, the people do not know how to move hand or foot. Therefore, a superior man considers it necessary that the names he uses may be spoken appropriately, and also that what he speaks may be carried out appropriately. What the superior man requires is just that in his words there may be nothing incorrect.' " [88]

"The duke Ching of Ch'i asked Confucius about government.

"Confucius said: 'Let the ruler be ruler, the minister minister, the father father, and the son son.' " [89]

"In other words," writes in comment Dr. Fung Yu-lan, "every name contains certain implications which constitute the essence of that class of things to which the name applies. Such things, therefore, should agree with this ideal essence." [90]

But this idea is precisely that of the Indian view of sat ("being"), satya ("truth"), and the relation of these to the world-supporting, eternal dharma. As Heinrich Zimmer states in his Philosophies of India: "One either 'is' (sat) or one 'is not' (a-sat), and one's dharma is the form of the manifestation in time of what one is."
"The rules of the castes and professions are regarded as reflections

in the human sphere of the laws of the natural order; hence, when adhering to those rules the various classes are felt to be collaborating even when apparently in conflict. Each race or estate following its proper righteousness, all together do the work of the cosmos. This is the service by which the individual is lifted beyond the limitations of his personal idiosyncrasies and converted into a living conduit of cosmic force. . . . There are clean and unclean professions, but all participate in the Holy Power. Hence 'virtue' is commensurate with perfection in one's given role." [91]

In the Confucian classic known as The Doctrine of the Mean (*Chung Yung*), which is attributed to Confucius' grandson, Tzu Ssu, but is probably a work of the Ch'in or Han dynasty,[92] we read: "What Heaven confers (*ming*) is called the inborn nature (*hsing*). The following of this nature is called the Way (*tao*). The cultivation of this Way is called instruction." [93]

And going, now, one step further: "Sincerity (*ch'eng*) is the Way of Heaven. The attainment of sincerity is the Way of men." [94]

"It is only he who is possessed of the most complete sincerity that can exist under heaven, who can give its full development to his inborn nature. Able to give its full development to his own nature, he can do the same to the nature of other men. Able to give its full development to the nature of other men, he can give their full development to the natures of animals and things. Able to give their full development to the natures of creatures and things, he can assist the transforming and nourishing powers of Heaven and Earth. Able to assist the transforming and nourishing powers of Heaven and Earth, he makes with Heaven and Earth a series of three." [95]

Four cardinal points, then, are essential to this character-building Chinese system of thought: benevolence; regard for the order of relationships; the rectification of names, so that the relationships may be recognized; and sincerity, as a perfect cleaving to the inner nature, which has become known through the rectification.

Three important corollaries follow:

1. "The superior man does what is proper to the station in which he is; he does not desire to go beyond this. In a position of wealth and honor, he does what is proper to a position of wealth and

honor. In a poor and low position, he does what is proper in a poor and low position. Situated among barbarous tribes, he does what is proper to a situation among barbarous tribes. In a position of sorrow and difficulty, he does what is proper to a position of sorrow and difficulty. The superior man can find himself in no situation in which he is not himself." [96]

2. "The Master said: 'It is by poetry that the mind is aroused. It is by the rules of propriety (rituals, ceremonies, rules of proper conduct) that the character is established. It is from music that the finish is received.' " [97]

"Without recognizing the ordinances of Heaven, it is impossible to be a superior man. Without an acquaintance with the rules of Propriety, it is impossible for the character to be established. Without knowing the force of words, it is impossible to know men." [98] And, finally:

3. "The superior man comprehends righteousness (*i:* the 'oughtness' of a situation); the small man comprehends gain (*li:* profit)." [99]

The performance of one's duty without desire for the fruits (Sanskrit *karma-yoga*); the notion that the order of society provides guidance infallibly to the realization of one's inborn nature (Sanskrit *dharma*); and the belief that the virtue of such realization participates in the virtue of the reality of the cosmic order (Sanskrit *satya*): this, in essence, is the lesson of the early hieratic city state. And the chief difference between Manu and Confucius, India and China, in this view, lies simply in the local identifications of the duties to which the virtuous give heed: in India the regulations of caste; for Confucius, the proprieties of the five relationships. The metaphysics of the two systems are the same.

Mo Tzu, fl. c. 480–400 B.C. The first serious philosophical challenge to the system of Confucius came from that preacher of the doctrine of universal love whose complaint we have already quoted against the proprieties of the princely funeral rites of his time. Mo Tzu was born, apparently, about the time of Confucius' death, and so may be said to have flourished, roughly, about 480–400 B.C.

"Even those of long life cannot exhaust the learning required for Confucian studies," this challenger wrote. "Even people with the vigor of youth cannot perform all the ceremonial duties. And even those who have amassed wealth cannot afford music. The Confucianists enhance the beauty of the wicked arts and lead their sovereign astray. Their doctrine cannot meet the needs of the age, nor can their learning educate the people." [100]

"Mo Tzu asked a Confucian, saying: 'What is the reason for performing music?' The reply was: 'Music is performed for music's sake.' [The word for "music," *lo*, also means "pleasure": hence there is a pun here which Mo Tzu will miss.] Mo Tzu said: 'You have not yet answered. Suppose I asked: Why build houses? And you answered: It is to keep off the cold in winter and the heat in summer, and to separate men from women. Then you would have told me the reason for building houses. Now I am asking: Why perform music? And you answer: Music is performed for music's sake. This is like saying: Why build houses? And answering: Houses are built for houses' sake.' " [101]

"Since music is without practical use and so is to be eliminated," states Dr. Fung Yu-lan in exposition of the views of Mo Tzu, "all the other fine arts are naturally to be eliminated as well. Being products of the emotions, they are capable only of appealing to these emotions. . . . According to his positive utilitarianism, man's numerous emotions are not only of no practical value, but moreover of no significance. Hence they should be eliminated, so as not to be impediments to human conduct." [102]

"The Confucians tried to be correct in righteousness, without considering whether profit would result; tried to be pure in their principles, without considering whether this would bring material return. The Mohist school, on the other hand, laid exclusive emphasis on 'profitableness' (*li*) and 'accomplishment' (*kung*)." [103] "Anything must be of profit to the country and the people before it can possess value, and it is the wealth and populousness of a country, Mo Tzu believed, which constitute its greatest profit." [104]

The question of the order of society and the force by which it is to be structured, still is the question, as it was for Confucius; but faith in the power of decorum, arts, and the rites to activate and

develop the inborn nature has been lost. Moreover, all faith in
the inborn nature itself has been lost. For the Confucians the inborn nature had been conferred and sealed within each by heaven.
Awakened by the influence of poetry, the rites, decorum, etc., it
flowered naturally, in harmony with the tao. For Mo Tzu, however, there was no such hope.

> In the beginning of human life [states the *Mo Tzu*] when
> there was yet no law and government, the custom was:
> "Every man according to his own idea." Thus when there was
> one man there was one idea, when two men two ideas, and
> when ten men there were ten different ideas. The more people
> there were, the more were the different concepts. Hence each
> man approved of his own view and disapproved of that of
> others, and so there arose mutual disapproval among men.
> As a result, father and son, and elder and younger brothers
> became enemies and estranged from each other, and were
> unable to reach any agreement. The people of the world
> worked against each other with water, fire and poison. Surplus
> energy was not spent for mutual aid; surplus goods were
> allowed to rot without sharing; excellent teachings were kept
> secret and not taught to one another. The disorder in the
> human world was like that among birds and beasts. Yet it
> was evident that all this disorder was owing to the want of a
> ruler.
> Therefore there was a selection of the person in the world
> who was virtuous and able and he was established to be the
> Son of Heaven. . . . When the rulers were all installed, the
> Son of Heaven issued a mandate to the people, saying: "Upon
> hearing good or evil one shall report it to a superior. What
> the superior thinks to be right, all shall think to be right.
> What the superior thinks to be wrong, all shall think to be
> wrong." [105]

With the faith gone in the inner nature, the sole resort, then,
was despotism, sentimentalized as the mandate of heaven; and
the agency of enforcement was not music but espionage, fear of
punishment and desire for reward:

> Let the patriarch give laws and proclaim to the clan: "Who-
> ever discovers a benefactor to the clan shall report it; who-
> ever discovers a malefactor to the clan shall report it." Then
> whoever sees and reports a benefactor of the clan will be

equivalent to being a benefactor of the clan himself. Knowing him, the superior will reward him. Whoever fails to report a malefactor of the clan upon seeing one will be equivalent to being a malefactor to the clan himself. Knowing him, the superior will punish him; hearing of him, the group will condemn him. Thereupon all the members of the clan will wish to obtain reward and honor and avoid denunciation and punishment from their superior. . . . With the good rewarded and the evil punished, the clan will surely have order. Now, why is it that the clan becomes orderly? Just because the administration is based upon the principle of Agreement with the Superior (*shang t'ung*).[106]

And where, in the midst of all this, do we find the principle of universal love, for which Mo Tzu is celebrated?

The task of the human-hearted man is to procure benefits for the world and to eliminate its calamities. Now among all the current calamities of the world, which are the greatest? I say that attacks on small states by large ones, disturbances of small houses by large ones, oppression of the weak by the strong, misuse of the few by the many, deception of the simple by the cunning, and disdain toward the humble by the honored; these are the misfortunes of the world. . . . When we come to think about the causes of all these calamities, how have they arisen? Have they arisen out of love of others and benefiting others? We must reply that they have not. Rather we should say that they have arisen out of hate of others and injuring others. If we classify those in the world who hate others and injure others, shall we call them "discriminating" or "all-embracing"? We must say that they are "discriminating." So, then, is not "mutual discrimination" the cause of the major calamities of the world? Therefore the principle of discrimination is wrong. But whoever criticizes others must have something to substitute for what he criticizes. Therefore I say: "Substitute for discrimination all-embracingness." [107]

However, war to the limit in the name of this principle of all-embracing love is to be carried out without qualm.

Suppose [we read] there is a country which is being persecuted and oppressed by its rulers, and a Sage ruler in order to rid the world of this pest raises an army and sets out to punish the evildoers. If, when he has won a victory, he conforms to the doctrine of the Confucians, he will issue an order to his troops saying: "Fugitives are not to be pursued, an enemy who has lost his helmet is not to be shot at; if a chariot overturns you are to help the occupants right it—" if this is done, the violent and disorderly will escape with their lives and the world will not be rid of its pest. These people have carried out wholesale massacres of men and women, and done great harm in their day. There could be no greater injustice than that they should be allowed to escape." [108]

The Mohists themselves constituted, according to their own account, a strictly disciplined organization capable of military action. Their leader was called the "Great Master" (*Chu Tzu*). Mo Tzu himself was the first Great Master. And he had, we learn, "one hundred and eighty disciples, all of whom he could order to enter fire or tread on sword blades, and whom even death would cause to turn on their heels." [109]

Taoism, from c. 400 B.C. Now, given a world in which the order of society is composed, on one hand, of an exploited mass of ill governed "lower" people and, on the other, of an elite hurly-burly of ungovernable despots—either of the self-indulgent ilk whose incorrigibility caused even Confucius to give up, or of the self-righteous, brutally utilitarian stripe of the Mohists—shall we be surprised to learn that a large number of sensitive Chinese minds in the fourth and third centuries B.C. took to the woods? The epoch resembles, or at least suggests, that of the forest philosophers of India three or four centuries before, when the earlier feudal order there also was collapsing. Writing of one of the most famous of these uncooperative mountain sages, the Confucian philosopher Mencius states of him: "The principle of Yang Chu is: 'Each one for himself.' Though he might have benefited the whole empire by plucking out a single hair, he would not have done it." [110] And the unknown author of the third-century work known as the Han Fei Tzu describes the whole peaceful company as people who "walk apart from the crowd, priding themselves on being different from other men."

"They preach the doctrine of Quietism," states the author, "but their exposition of it is couched in baffling and mysterious terms.

. . . I submit that man's duty in life is to serve his prince and to nourish his parents, neither of which things can be done by Quietness. I further submit that it is man's duty, in all that he teaches, to promote loyalty, good faith, and the Legal Constitution. This cannot be done in terms that are vague and mysterious. The doctrine of the Quietists is a false one, likely to lead the people astray." [111]

Of course, however, the way of the men in the woods actually was at least as responsible to mankind and the ideal of a specifically human order of decency as that of the great liquidators of all who either opposed or sought to escape the rule by ukase of their own monolithic minds.

"A ruler," states another philosopher of the hard, so-called Legalist, school, "should not listen to those who believe in people having opinions of their own and in the importance of the individual. Such teachings cause people to withdraw to quiet places and hide away in caves or on mountains, there to rail at the prevailing government, sneer at those in authority, belittle the importance of rank and emoluments, and despise all who hold official posts." [112]

Actually, though, as Mr. Waley well shows,

the real reason why such persons refused to draw official salaries and insisted on living in their own way on the fruit of their own labor was that they thought society should consist of individuals each complete in himself, and it was against their consciences to be supported by 'hairs' drawn from the suffering head of the community at large. A certain Ch'en Chung was a scrupulous recluse of this class. He belonged to an important family in the land of Ch'i (now part of Shantung). His ancestors had held high office for many generations on end, and his elder brother administered a fief from which he received a revenue of 10,000 chung.* As it was against Ch'en Chung's principles to live on what he regarded as ill-gotten gains, he left his brother's house and set up at a remote place called Wu-ling. Here he supported himself by making hemp-sandals, his wife twisting the hemp thread. Their livelihood was very precarious and on one occasion Ch'en had nothing to eat for three days.[113]

* A tenth of the revenue of a prime minister (Waley's note).

Moreover, in their seclusion, practicing to various degrees disciplines of inward realization, these mavericks had hit upon something within that seemed to them to be a greater power for the benefit of mankind than either the food, clothing, and shelter which the Mohists thought were the fundament of virtue but which the mountain recluses themselves had to a degree renounced, or the main force of military and police might by which such material goods were to be assured to all; namely, the power and experience in deeply wonderful realization of the Tao, which, according to their experience, is the *actual* fundament of all things, all being, and of the true humanity of man.

"We know," writes Mr. Waley, "that many different schools of Quietism existed in China in the fourth and third centuries before Christ. Of their literature only a small part survives." [114] It is possible, though not proven, he states, that already in the formative period of this movement, in the fourth century B.C., outside influences were at work. However, in the following century, "such influences were demonstrably beginning to be of great importance." [115] The use of iron, use of cavalry in war and adoption of non-Chinese dress in connection with it, familiarity with new forms of disposal of the dead,[116] and the appearance in Chinese writings of motifs from India, combine to indicate that the period was one of considerable influx of exotic ideas. "All scholars are, I think, now agreed," states Waley, "that the literature of the third century is full of geographic and mythologic elements derived from India. I see no reason to doubt that the 'holy mountain-men' (*sheng-hsien*) described by Lieh Tzu are Indian *rishi;* and when we read in *Chuang Tzu* of certain Taoists who practised movements very similar to the *āsanas* of Hindu *yoga,* it is at least a possibility that some knowledge of the *yoga*-technique which these rishi used had also drifted into China." [117]

However, in the ultimate force and direction of the Chinese Quietist movement, as compared with that of India, there is a great contrast to be noted. In India, as we have seen, yoga enabled the ascetic to develop within himself certain "powers" (*siddhi*) by which all kinds of magical effects could be achieved. The true goal of the Indian exercise lay beyond those powers, however; so that, although Indian literature abounds in examples of the exercise of the *siddhi,* the dominant spiritual tradition requires that all interest in such should be abandoned. It is stated, for example, in a standard text of the Vedantic school, the fifteenth-century Vedantasara, that already at the beginning of his discipline, the candidate for yogic illumination must possess four requisites: 1. discrimination between things permanent and transient; 2. *renunciation of the fruits of action, both in this world and in the next;* 3. six spiritual treasures: control of the outgoing propensities, restraint of the external organs, discontinuance of appointed works, indifference to heat and cold, praise and blame, and all other pairs of opposites, concentration of the mind, faith in the spiritual teaching and task; and then 4. *a deep yearning for disengagement.*[118] In China, on the other hand, it was precisely in the powers (*tê*) that the interest lay. "*Tê* means a latent power, a 'virtue' inherent in something," Waley states.[119] *Tao tê,* then, is "the latent power (*tê*) of the Way, the order, of the universe (*tao*)," which the Quietist finds within, as well as without; since it is the "Mother of all things."

> The Valley Spirit never dies.
> It is named the Mysterious Female.
> And the Doorway of the Mysterious Female
> Is the base from which Heaven and Earth sprang.
>
> It is there within us all the while;
> Draw upon it as you will, it never runs dry.[120]

In the Chinese philosophy of the Tao, of which the classic statement is the Tao Te Ching, "the Book (*ching*) of the Power (*tê*) of the Way (*tao*)," it is maintained that a Quietist contemplation of the Tao "gives as the Indians say *siddhi,* as the Chinese say *tê,* a power over the outside world undreamt of by those who pit themselves against matter while still in its thralls." [121] And it was the firm belief of the Taoist writers that it must have been only through the power (*tê*) of their own inward experience of the Tao that the ancestral monarchs of the golden age held the order of society—and of the world—in form.

Of old those that were the best officers of Court
Had inner natures subtle, abstruse, mysterious, penetrating,
Too deep to be understood.
And because such men could not be understood
I can but tell of them as they appeared to the world:

Circumspect they seemed, like one who in winter crosses a
    stream,
Watchful, as one who must meet danger on every side.
Ceremonious, as one who pays a visit;
Yet yielding, as ice when it begins to melt.

Blank, as a piece of uncarved wood;
Yet receptive as a hollow in the hills.
Murky as a troubled stream—
Which of you can assume such murkiness, to become in the
    end still and clear?
Which of you can make yourself inert, to become in the end
    full of life and stir?

Those who possess this Tao do not try to fill themselves to
    the brim,
And because they do not try to fill themselves to the brim
They are like a garment that endures all wear and need never
    be renewed.[122]

*   *   *

Push far enough toward the Void,
Hold fast enough to Quietness,
And of the ten thousand things none but can be worked on
    by you.
I have beheld them, whither they go back.
See, all things howsoever they flourish
Return to the root from which they grew.
This return to the root is called Quietness;
Quietness is called submission to Fate;
What has submitted to Fate has become part of the always-so.
To know the always-so is to be Illumined;
Not to know it, means to go blindly to disaster.

He who knows the always-so has room in him for everything;
He who has room in him for everything is without prejudice.
To be without prejudice is to be kingly;
To be kingly is to be of heaven;

> To be of heaven is to be in Tao.
> Tao is forever and he that possesses it,
> Though his body ceases, is not destroyed.[123]

There is an anecdote recounted of the Taoist sage Chuang Tzu (fl. c. 300 B.C.); that when his wife died, the logician Hui Tzu came to his house to join in the rites of mourning but found him sitting on the ground with an inverted bowl on his knees, drumming upon it and singing. "After all," said Hui Tzu in amazement, "she lived with you, brought up your children, grew old along with you. That you should not mourn for her is bad enough; but to let your friends find you drumming and singing—that is really going too far!"

"You misjudge me," Chuang Tzu replied. "When she died, I was in despair, as any man well might be. But soon, pondering on what had happened, I told myself that in death no strange new fate befalls us. In the beginning we lack not life only, but form; not form only, but spirit. We are blent in the one great featureless, undistinguishable mass. Then a time came when the mass evolved spirit, spirit evolved form, form evolved life. And now life in its turn has evolved death. For not nature only but man's being has its seasons, its sequence of spring and autumn, summer and winter. If someone is tired and has gone to lie down, we do not pursue him with shouting and bawling. She whom I have lost has lain down to sleep for a while in the Great Inner Room. To break in upon her rest with the noise of lamentation would but show that I knew nothing of nature's Sovereign Law." [124]

"This attitude toward death," writes Mr. Waley of this scene, "exemplified again and again in Chuang Tzu, is but part of a general attitude toward the universal laws of nature, which is one not merely of resignation nor even of acquiescence, but a lyrical, almost ecstatic acceptance, which has inspired some of the most moving passages in Taoist literature. That we should question nature's right to make and unmake, that we should hanker after some role that nature did not intend us to play is not merely futile, not merely damaging to that tranquility of the 'spirit' which is the essence of Taoism, but involves, in view of our utter helplessness, a sort of fatuity at once comic and disgraceful." [125]

In the main, then, it can be said that Confucius and the Taoists agreed in centering the seat of the world-shaping power in man himself; they differed, however, as to its depth and the manner by which it might be awakened.

The Taoist honored introverted meditation as the method, "sitting with blank mind," "returning to the state of the uncarved block," where it would be found to lie deeper than the named, the formed, the honored, and the rejected, operating through antinomies. *Wu wei,* "non-assertion, not forcing," was their shibboleth, and the way of paradox (*fan-yen*) their teaching:

> "To remain whole, be twisted!"
> To become straight, let yourself be bent.
> To become full, be hollow,
> Be tattered, that you may be renewed.
> Those that have little, may get more,
> Those that have much, are but perplexed.
>
> Therefore the Sage
> Clasps the Primal Unity,
> Testing by it everything under heaven.
>
> He does not show himself, therefore he is seen everywhere.
> He does not define himself, therefore he is distinct.
> He does not boast of what he will do, therefore he succeeds.
> He is not proud of his work, and therefore it endures.
> He does not contend,
> And for that very reason no one under heaven can contend
>   with him.
> So then we see that the ancient saying "To remain whole be
>   twisted!" was no idle word; for true wholeness can be
>   achieved only by return.[126]

Confucius, on the other hand, had taught the extraverted way of sincere, respectful attention to the arts of music, poetry, ritual lore, and decorum as the awakeners of that sentiment of kindness, gentleness, or goodness (*jen*) which was acquired through—and endowed with grace—man's intercourse with men.

Whereas both of these, in their trust of nature, whether in its cosmic or in its inner human seat, stood diametrically apart from both Mo Tzu and the so-called Legalists or Realists of the way of thought represented in the Book of the Lord Shang, for both of whom the only effective power was main force, and the goods to be desired were food, shelter, and world rule. The Taoist maxim "Cling to the Unity," was in these divested of its metaphysical sense and turned into a political maxim; [127] and the principle of the uncarved block became that of the block carved square by the sword.

CH'IN DYNASTY: 221–207 B.C.

Nowhere had the Confucian doctrine of morality and kindness been so generally accepted as in the small State of Lu; yet in the year 249 B.C. Lu was invaded and destroyed.[128] By the year 318 B.C., the unphilosophical state of Ch'in, still practicing human sacrifice, had defeated a confederation of neighbors; in 312 the kingdom of Chu, in the Taoist southeast, was decisively defeated; in 292, Han and Wei collapsed, and in 260, Chao. By 256 B.C. the holdings of the Chou dynasty were entirely surrounded. In the year 246 B.C., King Ching assumed the Ch'in throne and in 230 annexed Han; in 228, Chao; in 226, Ch'i; in 225, Wei; in 222, Ch'u; in 221, he assumed the title Ch'in Shih Huang Ti, as the first emperor of China,[129] immediately commenced the building of the Great Wall, to protect the Empire from further inroads of barbarians such as himself, and in 213 issued his edict for the burning of the books.

Death was to be the doom of scholars discovered assembling for the reading or discussion of the classics; those found to possess copies thirty days following announcement of the ban were to be branded and sent to labor four years on the Great Wall; hundreds were buried alive.[130] In 210, however, Shih Huang Ti died; and in 207 the dynasty collapsed. (His career stands in contrast to that of his contemporary, Ashoka.) In 206 the capital was sacked, the fires burned for three months among the palaces, and what books the commissars of Shih Huang Ti had missed, the God Chu Jung of Fire destroyed.

HAN DYNASTY: 202 B.C.–220 A.D.

The Old Silk Road to Hellenistic Bactria, Buddhist India, Zoroastrian Parthia, and Rome was opened by the year 100 B.C.; and from this time onward the flow back and forth of currents of ideas between the four domains of Europe, the Levant, India, and the Far East, continually increasing in force, led to the development throughout the Eurasian land mass of a shared vocabulary of myth—applied, however, in each domain to a style of thought and feeling *sui generis,* which could be neither communicated nor effaced. The circumstance was analogous to that of our contemporary scene, where institutions, words, and ideals developed in the West have been diffused to Africa and Asia, where, in the fields of force of alien traditions, they are being applied to political practices, modes of feeling, and social goals that are in many cases precisely the opposite to—and in others altogether unassociated with —those to which the terms and instruments originally pertained. So likewise in the period of Rome, Parthian Persia, Kanishka's India, and Han China: a cross-cultural index of mythological motifs would show a common treasury of basic themes; yet in style, sentiment, and argument, the four domains held then—as they are holding now—to native patterns that, apparently, are to remain.

One is reminded of the Sartre play *No Exit.* A room in hell. The room is empty. A man is shown in by the bellboy. Then a woman; next another woman. That is all: they are there forever. And the hell of it is that not one of them can change. The man requires sympathetic understanding. The older woman could have supplied it, but she is a Lesbian who despises him and requires something of the younger, whose eyes are only for the man, whom she cannot possibly understand or release from his own self-absorption. At a later moment of the play the door opens for a time and they are free to escape from the hell that they are making for themselves. However, nothing can be seen outside but a void; and they are all so self-protective that not one dares step away into the unknown. The door shuts and they are there—as we are here, on this planet Earth: Europe (which now includes North America and Australia), the Levant (which, in the present view, includes Russia), India, the Far East—and now, South America and Africa. All have arrived. The room is full. All are wearing European dress: but what a variety of anthropologies within!

No one has been able to put his finger on the point of origin of the mythological notion of the five elements. My own guess, based on the distribution pattern, would be that evidences must appear, someday, in the tablets of Sumer and Akkad. The earliest known Greek system is represented in the fragments remaining from Anaximander (c. 611–547 B.C.), who names fire, air, earth, water, and the non-limited. The dating of the Indian system has, of course, not been established, but the series appears in the Taittiriya Upanishad (c. 600 B.C.?):

> From the Self (*ātman*) space arose;
> From space, wind;
> From wind, fire;
> From fire, water;
> From water, earth;
> And from the earth, herbs, food. . . .[131]

In the Sankhya system of Kapila, the five are linked to the five senses: respectively space or ether to hearing; wind or air to touch; fire to sight; water to taste; earth to smell.

The Chinese corresponding system first appears in the period of Han scholarship and is characteristically different, yet affiliated. The earliest authentic evidence occurs in a chapter of the History Classic (*Shu Ching*) called "The Great Plan or Norm" (*Huang Fan*), which is supposed to represent a communication of ancient lore to King Wu, founder of the Chou dynasty, by the Grand Master Chi of the fallen court of Shang, who attributes it—of course—to the Great Yü. "As to the actual date of the 'Grand Norm,' " writes Dr. Fung Yu-lan, however, "modern scholarship inclines to place it within the fourth or third centuries B.C." [132]

The five Chinese elements are water, fire, wood, metal, earth. "The nature of water is to soak and descend; of fire, to blaze and ascend; of wood, to be crooked and straight; of metal, to yield and change; while that of earth is seen in seed-growing and harvest. That which soaks and descends becomes salt; that which blazes and ascends becomes bitter; that which is crooked and straight becomes sour; that which yields and changes becomes acrid; and from seed-growing and harvest comes sweetness." [133]

The philosophers of the Han period made a great deal of this root system of five elements, building upon it a sort of pagoda of ideas, all associated by analogies of five, as, for example:

ELEMENTS:	Wood	Fire	Metal	Water	Earth
DIRECTIONS:	East	South	West	North	Center
SEASONS:	Spring	Summer	Fall	Winter	All
COLORS:	Green	Red	White	Black	Yellow
VIRTUES:	Goodness	Propriety	Justice	Good faith	Wisdom
NOTES:	Chiao	Chih	Shang	Yu	Kung *
GODS:	Kou Mang	Chu Jung	Ju Shou	Hsüan Ming	Hou T'u
EMPERORS:	T'ai Hao	Yen Ti	Shao Hao	Chuan Hsü	Huang Ti [134]

* Notes of the Chinese pentatonic scale.

It is clear at this point that the creative period of Chinese mythic thought was past, and that the work now being done was neither of poets nor of priests, but of systematizing scholar gentlemen, setting fragments of the past—broken jades, scattered jewels— into patterns drawn by rule. Their principle of order was: correlation by analogy. Their underlying theory was: that things of the same category energize each other. As in India, so here: there was no need to posit a creator behind the manifestation. The view was organic: within each thing in itself lay its life, its energizing tao. And, as it were by resonance, mutual influences touched the functioning life principles of all things, so that throughout the universe a wondrous harmony played, of which the laws, like those of music, might be learned and experienced in quiet wonder. Moreover, those laws, played upon skillfully by the man of learning—whether administrator of an empire, fashioner of swords, poet, lover, master athlete, or builder of a house—could be so enlivened that the work intended would evolve, as it were, of itself. And in its form it would then, of itself, be an illustration of those laws. So that nature and the world of Chinese art, architecture, gardening, and government were in spirit one.

The empire, shaped indeed by violence, now by learning was to be ordered in such a way that all its lineaments should be attuned to the order of the Tao. Of old, the principles of this order had been found. Now, by formula, they could be applied. Thus in the rich, majestic military empire of Han (which had been established in a flash, when its founder, the war lord Liu Pang, having made a treaty with his chief contender, Hsiang Chi, by which his captured father and wife were to be returned to him, broke the treaty as soon as they were safely back, and by surprise attained the mastery) the diligence of many reverent hands, functioning in accord in terms of a shared concept of accord, was to bring to form a civilization of such accord that in spite of reigns of force and cold brutality of incredible inhumanity, it should stand as the unwobbling pivot of the universe, the Middle Kingdom, for all time.

As Dr. Karlgren states in a superb paragraph, wherein the whole structure of this age comes to view:

Once we have passed the crucial date of 200 B.C. conditions are radically changed. The system of feudal kingdoms that had flourished for a millennium had entirely broken down. The barriers, both political and economical, between the various culture centers were abolished, new great highways connected the various parts of China with each other, the plebeian classes, farmers and merchants, obtained conditions of life quite different from those which prevailed during the feudal era, in short, the confederation of more or less independent small states was supplanted by a strong, centralized empire, in which the nivellation set in at a rapid pace, obviating the provincial contrasts and destroying the local customs and beliefs. The ancestral temples of the feudal lords were no longer the ritual and cultural centers, the *litterati* formed a social class independent of the patronage of feudal lords, the literature of the Chou era was seriously struck at by the famous burning of the books of 213 B.C., and the traditions and cults of the feudal kingdoms were no longer a living reality but a memory, beloved by a small class of scholars but forgotten and despised by the men in power, plebeian representatives sent out from the central Imperial Court in the Capital. In 250 B.C. the authors could still describe the cults they witnessed as living realities, in 100 B.C. they had to tell the story of how things were before the cataclysm of 221–211. (The cults of their own time were a conglomeration full of

innovations, many of them newly instituted by imperial order.)
At the same time the foreign influences multiplied. The
knowledge of Western Asiatic things gained ground rapidly,
but, above all, the Chinese of Han time came into close contact and carried on an exchange of ideas and customs with
the Nomad peoples of the North and North-west, and of the
cultures of the regions that now form Southern China, the
Chinese penetration and colonization of this region far south
of the Yang-tze making great strides in the course cf a couple
of centuries. The lore of the Han era is thus a mixtum composition far less homogeneous and less genuinely Chinese
than the lore of the Chou era.

Yet another great gulf gapes between the conditions of the
early Han and those of the second century A.D. Not only had
the first three centuries of Han rule revolutionized Chinese
life and thought, there was also another important difference.
In the first Han century the students were still not very far
remote in time from the feudal era: their masters' masters
lived in the last phase of that epoch, and though the customs
and cults were already badly shaken and certainly to a large
extent abolished, the knowledge about them could still be
kept alive to a certain extent, in the circles of the early Han
scholars. But a couple of centuries later, in the age of the
great scholiasts, Cheng Chung, Fu K'ien, Hsu Shen, Kia
K'uei, Ma Jung, Ching Hsuan, Kao Yu, and many others,
that knowledge was such as had passed through the chain
of many generations, it was no longer based on recent memories but the lore of ancient times." [135]

THE SIX DYNASTIES: 190/221–589 A.D.

Buddhism entered China in the Han period; perhaps c. 67 A.D.;
however, its influence on the mythic thought and therewith civilization of the empire became great only in the period of disorder
that followed the fall of the imperial house of Han. For nearly four
hundred years thereafter, war and devastation returned the land
to the condition that has been for the greater part of its long history
the Chinese reality of realities; and the serious quest for that
deeper Reality within, which had commenced in the period of
the collapse of the feudal order, recommenced. It is interesting
to note that every one of the ten Chinese Buddhist sects listed
by Professor Junjiro Takakusu in his volume on *The Essentials*

of Buddhist Philosophy was founded in this time "by those able men," as he writes, "who translated and introduced the texts." [136] We have already taken note of the pilgrimage to India of Fa-hsien, 399–414 A.D., and have remarked that it was on the year of his return home that work commenced on the rock-cut Chinese Buddhist cave temples of Yunkang.

But in the world of Taoist thought as well, there was a powerful enlivenment at this time. The hold of Confucianism on the minds of the literati had relaxed with the fall to ruin of the bureaucratic system of the ordered state, where advance and prestige had been achieved by way of learning in the Classics. Examinations were no longer held and a new term, the "dark learning" (*hsüan hsüeh*), came into use, suggesting the reference of all Taoist learning beyond the sphere of those names and forms to which the learning of Confucianism chiefly referred.

"There are four things," states a Taoist work of this age (the Lieh Tzu: third century A.D.), "that do not allow people to have peace. The first is long life, the second is reputation, the third is rank, and the fourth is riches. Those who have these things fear ghosts, fear men, fear power, and fear punishment. They are called fugitives. . . . Their lives are controlled by externals. But those who follow their destiny do not desire long life. Those who are not fond of honor do not desire reputation. Those who do not want power desire no rank. And those who are not avaricious have no desire for riches. Of this sort of men it may be said that they live in accordance with their nature. . . . They regulate their lives by internal things." [137]

One should live, declare these masters of the third and fourth centuries A.D., according to a principle termed *tzu-jan,* "self-so-ness, spontaneity, the natural," not according to *ming-chiao,* "institutions and morals." [138]

What the ear likes to hear is music, and prohibition of the hearing of music is called obstruction to the ear. What the eye likes to see is beauty, and prohibition of the seeing of beauty is called obstruction to sight. What the nose likes to smell is perfume, and prohibition of the smelling of perfume is called obstruction to smell. What the mouth likes to talk about is right and wrong, and prohibition of the talking about right and wrong is called obstruction to understanding. What the body likes to enjoy is rich food and fine clothing, and prohibition of the enjoying of these is called obstruction of the sensations of the body. What the mind likes to be is free, and prohibition of this freedom is called obstruction to the nature.

All these obstructions are the main causes of the vexations of life. To get rid of these causes and enjoy oneself until death, for a day, a month, a year, or ten years—that is what I call cultivating life. To cling to these causes and be unable to rid oneself of them, so as thus to have a long but sad life, extending a hundred, a thousand, or even ten thousand years —this is not what I call cultivating life.[139]

And now, as an example of the way this works:

"Wang Hui-chih [died c. 388 A.D.] was living at Shan-yin (near present Hangchow). One night he was awakened by a heavy snowfall. Opening the window, he saw a gleaming whiteness all about and suddenly thought of his friend T'ai K'uei. Immediately, he took a boat and went to see T'ai. It required the whole night for him to reach T'ai's house, but when he was just about to knock at the door, he stopped and returned home. When asked the reason for this act, he replied: 'I came on the impulse of my pleasure, and now it is ended, so I go back. Why should I see T'ai?' " [140]

The old roguism of these Taoist cronies is well brought out in the following anecdote of the sage Liu Ling (c. 221–c. 300 A.D.), who was one of a group known as the Seven Worthies of the Bamboo Grove. When he was in his room, Liu liked to be naked, and when he was criticized for this by a visitor he said: "I take the whole universe as my house and my own room as my clothing. Why, then, do you enter here into my trousers?" [141]

But there was another side of the Taoist way developing also at this time. Already in the late Han period one of the aims of Taoist enterprise had become the miracle of "transformation into a *hsien,*" that is to say a "mountain man," a mythological immortal. In other words, whereas in one direction (the one that philosophers like to write about) there was a wonderful lesson being learned in China at this time of living without aims, spontaneously, on the motivation of Tao; in the other corner of the bamboo grove there would have been found someone at work fashioning pills of immortality of cinnabar.

"Take three pounds of genuine cinnabar and one pound of white honey," wrote the great Taoist Ko Hung (c. 400 A.D.). "Mix them. Dry the mixture in the sun. Then roast it over a fire until it can be shaped into pills. Take ten pills the size of a hemp seed every morning. Inside of a year, white hair will turn black, decayed teeth will grow again, and the body will become sleek and glistening. If an old man takes this medicine for a long period of time, he will develop into a young man. The one who takes it constantly will enjoy eternal life, and will not die." [142]

"It is also dangerous for people who love life to rely on their own specialty," wrote this author again. "Those who know the techniques of the Classic of the Mysterious Lady and the Classic of the Plain Lady [books on sexual regimen no longer extant] will say that only the 'art of the chamber' will lead to salvation. Those who understand the method of breathing exercises will say that only the permeation of the vital power can prolong life. Those who know the method of stretching and bending will say that only physical exercise can prevent old age. And those who know the formulas of herbs will say that only medicine will make life unending. They fail in their pursuit of Tao because they are so onesided. People of superficial knowledge think they have enough when they happen to know of only one way and do not realize that the true seeker will search unceasingly even after he has acquired some good formulas." [143]

Thus—as so often happens in the Orient—two diametrically opposed ends were encompassed in a single movement: on one hand, no desire for long life and, on the other, exactly that.

Furthermore, at this time there was developing a system of organized religious Taoism, literally a church, with a patriarch, the Heavenly Teacher. The initiator of this movement was a character, Chang Ling, of the second century A.D., who collected from his followers tithes of five bushels of rice, so that his teaching was called the Tao of Five Bushels of Rice. Wei Po-yang, at about the same time (fl. 147–167 A.D.), sought to synthesize Taoist philosophy, alchemy, and the Book of Changes in a work named "The Three Ways of the Yellow Emperor, Lao Tzu, and the Book of Changes, Unified and Harmonized in the Latter" (*Ts'an-t'ung-ch'i*). And finally, Ko Hung—whose cinnabar recipe we have just read —combined with all of this a touch of Confucian ethics and what would appear to be a potion of India as well:

> Since Heaven and Earth are the greatest of things, it is natural from the point of view of universal principles that they should have spiritual power. Having spiritual power it is proper that they should reward good and punish evil. . . . As we glance over the Taoist books of discipline, all are unanimous in saying that those who seek immortality must set their minds on the accumulation of merits and the accomplishment of good work. Their hearts must be kind to all things. They must treat others as they treat themselves and extend their humaneness (*jen*) even to insects. . . . If, on the other hand, they hate good and love evil . . . the Arbiter of Human Destiny will reduce their terms of life by units of three days or three hundred days in proportion to the gravity of the evil. When all days are reduced, they will die. . . .
>
> Those who aspire to be terrestrial immortals should accomplish three hundred good deeds and those who aspire to be celestial immortals should accomplish 1,200. If the 1,199th good deed is followed by an evil one, they will lose all their accumulation and have to start all over. It does not matter whether the good deeds are great or the evil deed is small. Even if they do no evil but talk about their good deeds and demand reward for their charities, they will nullify the goodness of these deeds although the other good deeds are not affected.[144]

And the book further says: "If good deeds are not sufficiently accumulated, taking the elixir of immortality will be no help."

"As a religion of the masses," writes Professor Wing-tsit Chan, in discussion of these beliefs,

> Taoism . . . has one of the most thickly populated pantheons in the world, with deities representing natural objects, historical persons, the several professions, ideas, and even the whole and parts of the human body. It has a host of immortals and spirits, and a rich reservoir of superstitions in-

cluding an extensive system of divination, fortune-telling, astrology, etc. It developed an elaborate system of alchemy in its search for longevity which contributed much to material culture and scientific development in medieval China. It imitated Buddhism in a wholesale manner in such things as temples and images, a hierarchy of priests, monasticism, and heavens and hells. It has often been associated with eclectic sects and secret societies and so has been an important element in a number of popular uprisings. Today religious Taoism is rapidly declining and in the eyes of many is virtually defunct. However, its concentration on a good life on earth, its respect for both bodily and spiritual health, its doctrine of harmony with nature, its emphasis on simplicity, naturalness, peace of mind, and freedom of the spirit have continued to inspire Chinese art and enlighten Chinese thought and conduct. Even if unable to maintain its existence as an organized cult, it has enriched Chinese festivals with the romantic, carefree, and gay carnival spirit of its cult of immortals, and through its art symbols, ceremonies, and folklore has given to Chinese life a special color and charm.[145]

Thus, even before the Buddhist way had found solid footing on Chinese soil, a rival—somewhat in the manner of a parody of its own forms—had arisen to oppose its alien Middle Way.

K'ou Ch'ien-chih (died 432 A.D.) regulated the codes and ceremonies of the cult, fixed the names of its duties, and formulated its theology. Taoism, through his influence, was made the state religion 440 A.D.—and Buddhism was for a time suppressed.[146]

And yet again: it was to be from the other side of the Taoist bamboo grove that the very vocabulary of Chinese Buddhism was derived; so that in a subtle way, the teaching of the Buddha, who was known in Sanskrit as *tathāgata,* the one "thus come," became in Chinese *tzu-jan:* spontaneity itself; and the Buddha Way, the Middle Way, was understood to be precisely Tao.

v. The Age of the Great Beliefs:
c. 500–1500 A.D.

A systematic survey of the proliferation of schools within the Buddhist, Taoist, and Confucian folds cannot be added to our present task, which is to indicate in outline the chief currents and epochs of development in the mythological heritage of mankind. However, the question of the impact of sentiments and ideas carried from one domain to another, which is basic to our study, is so well illustrated by the annals of the settlement of Buddhism in China that a pause at this point is in order.

We have already had something to say of the pattern of inter-cultural impact-and-reaction in the India of this time: the influence on the Gupta courts of the contribution from Rome, the release therewith of native Indian energies already pressing for development, and the absorption by these of the alien suggestion; also, the invention thereby of a mythic past wherein the actual source-history was screened and the alien influence denied. In China, at about the same time, a comparable development was taking place, with reference to the Indian Buddhist contribution. We have made note of the following dates: Theodosius I, 379–395 A.D.; Chandragupta II, 378–414 A.D.; and the voyage to India of Fa-hsien, 399–414 A.D. This period in China was one of tremendous stress.

"Between 304 and 535," states Professor Needham, "no less than seventeen 'dynasties' contended with each other in the north —of these four were Hunnish, four Turkic (Tho-pa), six Mongol (Hsien-pi), and only three ruled by houses of Chinese stock. Nevertheless, throughout this time the 'barbarians' were Sinified much more than the northern Chinese were barbarized. Nomadic dress was doubtless widely adopted, but in general the Chinese agriculture and administration continued and barbarian customs were adapted to it; intermarriage was universal and encouraged, and even the polysyllabic names of the barbarian chieftains were exchanged for Chinese ones." [147]

And in the same way, the alien religion of the Buddha, which had now been established on Chinese soil for about five centuries, brought forth as native growths two completely Chinese phenomena: on the one hand, the popular Taoist parody above remarked, where the cruder folk aspect of the Buddhist system was rerendered (so to say) in Chinese, and, on the other hand, on a far more elevated plane, the Far Eastern Buddhist sect known as Ch'an or Ch'an-an (Japanese Zen; from the Sanskrit term *dhyāna,* "to contemplate"), where what are clearly Taoist thought and feeling were translated into imported Buddhist terms.

The origin of this interesting sect is attributed to the visit to China of a certain (probably legendary) Indian monk who is supposed to have been the twenty-eighth patriarch of the orthodox Buddhist Order. The twenty-eight are named as follows: [148]

1. Gautama Shakyamuni
2. Mahakashyapa
3. Ananda
4. Sanavasa
5. Upagupta
6. Dhritaka
7. Micchaka
8. Buddhanandi
9. Buddhamitra
10. Bhikshu Parshya
11. Punyayasas
12. Ashvaghosha
13. Bhikshu Kapimala
14. Nagarjuna
15. Kanadeva
16. Arya Rahulata
17. Samghanandi
18. Samghayasas
19. Kumarata
20. Jayata
21. Vasubandhu
22. Manura
23. Haklenayasas
24. Bhikshu Simha
25. Vasasita
26. Punyamitra
27. Prajnatara
28. Bodhidharma

The legend states that when he arrived in the year 520 A.D., Bodhidharma, himself the son of a king, was invited by the Emperor Wu of the Liang Dynasty to an audience in Nanking.

Wu Ti: "Since my enthronement I have built many monasteries. I have had many holy writings copied. I have invested numerous monks and nuns. How much merit have I gained?"

Bodhidharma: "None."

Wu Ti: "Why so?"

Bodhidharma: "Those are inferior deeds. They may conduce to favorable births in the heavens or on earth, but are of the world and follow their objects like shadows. They may seem to exist, but are non-entities. Whereas the true deed of merit is of pure wisdom, perfect and mysterious, in its nature beyond the grasp of man's intelligence, and not to be sought by way of material acts."

Wu Ti: "What, then, is the Noble Truth in its highest sense?"

Bodhidharma: "It is empty. There is nothing noble about it."

Wu Ti: "And who is this monk now facing me?"

Bodhidharma: "I do not know."

The Pivot of the Universe having missed the point, the saint crossed the Yangtze to the capital Loyang of the state of Wei, proceeded to the Shao-lin temple, and there sat for nine years facing a wall. A Confucian scholar, Hui K'e, approached him, asked for instruction, and, receiving no reply, stood for days without effect. Snow fell. It rose to his knees. He cut off his arm with his sword, to show that he was serious, and Bodhidharma turned.

Hui K'e: "I seek instruction in the doctrine of the Buddhas."

Bodhidharma: "This cannot be found through another."

Hui K'e: "I beg you, then, to pacify my soul."

Bodhidharma: "Produce it and I shall do so."

Hui K'e: "I have sought for it many years, but when I look for it, cannot find it."

Bodhidharma: "So there! It is at peace."

Hui K'e, thus taught, became the Second Patriarch of the order in the Far East; and when the First was about to leave, the disciples gathered.

Bodhidharma: "The time has come for me to leave. Let me judge of your attainments."

Tai Fu: "Truth is beyond yes and no. Thus it moves."

Bodhidharma: "You have my skin."

The nun Tsung Ch'ih: "It is like Ananda's view of the Buddha Realm of Akshobhya: seen once, it is never seen again."

Bodhidharma: "You have my flesh."

Tao Yu: "The four elements are void; the five constituents of form, sensation, conception, cogitation, and consciousness also are void. There is nothing to be grasped as real."

Bodhidharma: "You have my bones."

But Hui K'e, bowing to the Master, remained standing without a word.

Bodhidharma: "You have my marrow." [149]

The Buddha himself is supposed to have been the first to have taught in this enigmatic manner in a mythic scene on the mythic Vulture Peak. The god Brahma came to where he sat and, pre-

senting a kumbhala flower, begged that the Law should be taught
to all there assembled. And the Buddha, ascending the Lion Seat,
lifted the flower; whereupon only Mahakashyapa smiled with joy.
"Mahakashyapa," said the Buddha, "to you the doctrine of the
Eye of the True Law is herewith entrusted. Accept and pass it
on." [150]

The nature of the message thus passed by way of the silent
chain of the Patriarchs to the present day is summarized as follows:

> Special teaching, outside of scriptures,
> Not based on words and letters.
> Direct pointing to the heart of man.
> Seeing one's own nature. Reaching Buddhahood.[151]

And what became of Bodhidharma when he walked away from
his wall?

Nobody knows.

SUI DYNASTY: 581–618 A.D.

The long period of Chinese political disunity was terminated
by the brief but fearfully effective Sui Dynasty (581–618 A.D.),
whose second and last emperor, Yang Ti, is particularly celebrated
for his completion of a canal uniting the Yellow River and Yangtze.
"He ruled," states a writer of the Ming period, "without benevolence." [152]

"Some 5,500,000 workers," states Professor Needham, "including all commoners in certain areas between the ages of fifteen and
fifty, assembled, and worked under the guard of 50,000 police.
Every fifth family was required to contribute one person to participate in the supply and preparation of food. Those who could not
or would not fulfill the demands made on them were 'punished by
flogging and neckweights'; some had to sell their children. Over
two million men were said to have been 'lost.' " [153]

The great Chinese machine of "a million men with teaspoons"
did its work and the leap forward was achieved. The emperor
was captured in battle with a Turkic force, however, and the
dynasty collapsed. Nevertheless, just as the barbarities of Ch'in

had been followed by the civilization of Han, so was Sui by T'ang, "which," as Needham writes, "most historians, both Chinese and Western, have regarded as China's Golden Age." [154]

T'ANG DYNASTY: 618–906 A.D.

The first part of this richly cosmopolitan period saw the flowering, but the second part the shattering, of the Buddhist Order in China. Ch'an, the sect of silence, held the lead in the work of Sinicizing the doctrine. However, in the years 841–845 a Confucian-Taoist reaction brought about the leveling of more than 4600 monasteries, secularization of more than 260,000 monks and nuns, abolition of some 40,000 temples and shrines, confiscation of 1,000,000 acres of fertile Buddhist lands, and manumission of 150,000 monastery and temple slaves.[155]

It had been in the peaceful mountain monastery of the Yellow Plum that the greatest of the Ch'an Buddhist teachers, Hui-neng, who became the sixth and last patriarch of his sect, had achieved the realization that represents to this day the culminating synthesis of Indian spirituality and Chinese. The line of Far Eastern patriarchs, through his time, is supposed to have been as follows:

1. Bodhidharma: 520 A.D.
2. Hui K'e: 486–593
3. Seng-ts'an: died 606
4. Tao-hsin: 580–651
5. Hung-jen: 601–674
6. Hui-neng: 638–713

Hui-neng hailed from Hsin-chou in the South. His father had died when he was young. He had supported his mother by selling wood. And when he was standing one day before the door of a house, he heard a man within reciting the Diamond Sutra:

> Said the Buddha: "O Subhuti, what do you think? Is the Tathagata to be thought of as a body-form?"
> "No indeed, World-Honored One; he is not to be thought of as a body-form. And why? Because according to his own teaching, a body-form is not a body-form."
> Said the Buddha to Subhuti: "All that has form is illusory; and when it is perceived that all form is no-form, the Tathagata is recognized." [156]

The young woodseller Hui-neng got the idea, departed from his mother, walked for about a month, and when he reached the monastery of the Yellow Plum, the patriarch Hung-jen, who was there at the head of some five hundred monks, received him.

Hung-jen: "Where do you come from and what do you want?"
Hui-neng: "I am a farmer from Hsin-chou and I want to be a Buddha."
Hung-jen: "Southerners have no Buddha-nature."
Hui-neng: "Well, there may indeed be Southerners and Northerners, but as far as Buddha-nature goes, how can you find in it distinctions of that kind?"

The patriarch, pleased, sent him to the kitchen, to become the rice-pounder of the brotherhood, and when he had been there about eight months, the time came for the old patriarch to pass on the symbolic begging bowl and robe to a successor. The monks in competition were to summarize their concepts of the Law in verse on the wall of the meditation hall. And the one who wrote the best poem proved to be—as all had expected—a certain learned student of the Law, Shen-hsiu (d. 706 A.D.), as follows:

> This body is the Bodhi-tree,
> The mind, a mirror bright.
> Take care to wipe them always clean,
> Lest dust on them alight.

However, the kitchen boy, a mere illiterate layman, had the verse read to him by a friend that night and bade him write the following beside it:

> There never was a Bodhi-tree,
> Nor any mirror bright.
> Since nothing at the root exists,
> On what should what dust alight?

Discovered by the monks in the morning, this anonymous challenge set the monastery astir, and the patriarch, in a great show of wrath, took his slipper and erased it. But the next night he summoned the kitchen boy to his room, bestowed on him the begging bowl and robe, and in secret sent him off, to hide till the time should be ripe for him to appear. And there would be from that time no more handing on of bowl and robe; for with the insight of this layman the function of the monastic life had been surpassed.[157]

The news of Hui-neng's flight came out, and when he was overtaken at a mountain pass, he lay the robe on a rock and said to Ming, one of those who had arrived, "Here is the symbol of our faith. It is not to be gained by force. Take it if you wish."

But when the other sought to lift it, he found it heavy as a mountain. He fell on his face: "I come," he said, "for the faith; not for the robe."

And the Sixth Patriarch said to him: "If the faith is what you want, give up desiring. Do not think of good or evil. Find your own original face, right now, the face that was yours before you were born."

Ming said: "Besides the hidden meaning of these words, is there any further secret to be known?"

The Sixth Patriarch replied: "In what I have said there is no hidden sense. Look within. Find your own true face that was antecedent to the world. The only secret is inside yourself." [158]

But is not this the lesson of the Taoist school?

In the Tao Te Ching we have read of "the uncarved block." The knower of the Tao "returns to the Limitless"; "returns to the state of the Uncarved Block": [159]

> The Tao is eternal, but has no name:
> The Uncarved Block, though seemingly of small account,
> Is greater than anything under heaven.
> Once the block is carved, there will be names.[160]

"For Tao is itself the always-so, the fixed, the unconditioned, that which 'is of itself' and for no cause 'so,' " writes Mr. Waley. "In the individual it is the Uncarved Block, the consciousness on which no impression has been 'notched,' in the universe it is the Primal Unity underlying apparent multiplicity. Nearest then to Tao is the infant. Mencius, in whose system Conscience, sensitiveness to right and wrong, replaces the notion of Tao, says that the 'morally great man' is one who has kept through later years his 'infant heart.' The idea is one that pervades the literature of the third century [B.C.]." [161]

And by the eighth century A.D. it had coalesced with the gospel of nirvana. For the double negative expressed in the Buddha's realization that there is in the absolute sense neither an object nor a subject with which to be identified amounted, as we have seen, to an unqualified positive: a killing of all "thou shalts"; a killing of the dragon of the golden scales; and therewith a release of the child, the wheel rolling of itself, the Buddha-nature, *tathāgata: just-so-ness.* Likewise, in the teaching of the Tao, we have heard that when the arbitrary "obstructions" imposed by desirous thought are removed, the self-so (*tzu-jan*) becomes manifest. And these two—*tathāgatha* and *tzu-jan*—now were known as one.

Self-so-ness, however, is not always gentle, or, when rough, merely whimsical or roguish, as in the lives and illustrations of the sages of the self-realized Tao.

In the year 840 A.D., when the imperial throne of China became vacant on the death of the Emperor Wen-tsung (for he had previously, in fear of a plot, murdered his son, the crown prince), one of the most powerful eunuchs of the court, the mighty Ch'iu Shih-liang, Commissioner of Good Works for the Streets of the Left, aided the deceased monarch's brother, Wu-tsung, in the gaining of the throne. And when the latter had been thereby endowed with the mandate of heaven, he immediately slew—according to report—"over four thousand persons in the capital who had been favored in the time of the preceding Emperor." [162] The following year he began to show himself inclined to support the Taoist clergy against the Buddhist. And in the year 842 his enterprise commenced in earnest to extinguish on his sacred soil the alien light.

An edict was issued, commanding the Buddhist monasteries both to receive no more novices and to dismiss those of their monks and nuns not already registered with the government. A second edict the same year ordered all monks and nuns of questionable

* Supra, pp. 276–87.

habit to return immediately to lay life and those with money, grains, or fields to surrender these to the state. Monasteries in the capital were to keep their gates shut and their monks and nuns within. Furthermore, a monk might retain but one male and a nun but three female slaves. All others were to be returned to their homes, or, if they had none, were to be sold to the state.[163] In the year 843, a still more disturbing edict commanded the burning of the Buddhist scriptures in the palace and burial of the images of the Buddha, Bodhisattvas, and Heavenly Kings of the Four Quarters who had given the Buddha his fourfold begging bowl. Fires broke out thereafter in various quarters of the city and it was evident that a season of terror had begun.

Now by chance there had come to China at this time a Buddhist monk, Ennin, from Japan, whose diary—as Dr. Edwin O. Reischauer, its translator, states—leaves no doubt of the all-pervasiveness of Buddhism in his day.

"Rich and intellectually vigorous communities of monks," Reischauer writes, "were to be found throughout the cities and mountain fastnesses of the land; urban crowds thronged Buddhist festivals; laymen listened eagerly to religious lectures and services; monks and lay believers alike trod the rocky pilgrim trails. There had been earlier periods when the government had given Buddhism more vigorous support, and the Indian religion may have achieved its greatest popular appeal a few centuries later, but Ennin saw China at the moment when the already widespread faith of the masses and the still strong intellectual belief of the ruling classes perhaps combined to bring Buddhism to its apogee in China." [164]

Ennin was a member of the Japanese Tendai (Chinese T'ien-t'ai) sect, which is named after a mountain in South China where the founder, Chih-kai (531–597), had lived and taught; but his pilgrimage brought him to many other centers as well. And of all, the greatest was at Mount Wu-t'ai in the far northeast of what is now the province Shansi, where the Bodhisattva Manjushri was revered. Of old, he had appeared, Ennin was told, in the guise of monk before the Emperor; and when he had asked for and been granted as much land as a sitting-mat would cover, he spread a mat that covered five hundred li (about a hundred and sixty miles).

Maliciously the emperor scattered the seed of leeks over the area, but the monk replied with a scattering of orchid-like seeds that deprived the leeks of their smell; and in Ennin's day one could see over all the terraces both orchid-like flowers and leeks without smell. Five hundred poisonous dragons dwelt in the mountains round about, and these caused such a weather of clouds that, as Ennin wrote, the traveler never saw "a long stretch of clearness." But those dragons were not dangerous to man; for they were the subjects of a dragon king who had been converted by Manjushri to the Buddhist faith.

And again of old, as the pilgrim learned, there came to this land a monk of India, Buddhapala by name, attracted by its fame, who was met on the approaches by an old man who sent him back to India to fetch a certain esoteric text. And when he returned, the old man, who was Manjushri himself, led him to a grotto and bade him enter, which he did. The grotto closed, and he has been there ever since. "The rock wall," wrote the visiting Japanese, "is hard and has a yellow tinge, and there is a high tower [against the face of the cliff] where the mouth of the grotto would be. The grotto mouth is at the base of the tower, but no one can see it." [165] Within —as he was told and believed—there were, besides the Indian monk Buddhapala, three thousand kinds of musical instruments made of seven precious sorts of metal by a single saint, as well as a bell that would hold 120 bushels, and all who heard it toll obtained the four fruits of the first zone of enlightenment; also, a silver harp having 84,000 notes, each of which cured one of the worldly passions; furthermore, a treasured pagoda of 1300 stories; besides golden writing on silver paper of China and a billion forms of paper of the four continents.[166]

"When one enters this region of His Holiness Manjushri," wrote the pilgrim in his journal, "if one sees a very lowly man, one does not dare to feel contemptuous, and if one meets a donkey, one wonders if it might be a manifestation of Manjushri. Everything before one's eyes raises thoughts of the manifestations of Manjushri. . . ." [167]

And so, in the way of popular worship, the Buddha wisdom was taught that "all things are Buddha things."

However, at the court, meanwhile, there was brewing a veritable storm. A revolt of the regional commander of the army at Lu-chou (in southeastern Shansi) had made it necessary to send troops to that area; but the commander himself had escaped and was said to have disguised himself as a monk. Three hundred monks were therefore seized and executed, and the man's wife and children beheaded. An imperial edict was issued to say that whereas festivals had been held at Wu-t'ai and elsewhere celebrating various Buddha relics, no more pilgrimages to such sites were to be permitted. Anyone presenting offerings was to receive twenty strokes of the cane on his back; a monk or nun found at such a place was to receive twenty strokes of the cane on his back. The monks at those places were to be questioned and those lacking credentials executed on the spot. For it was feared that the fugitive commander of Lu-chou might be in hiding.

The crazily phantasizing emperor, far more solicitous for the safety of his own holy person than for anything else in the universe of which he was the sole support, summoned eighty-one Taoist priests and had built a ritual place of the Nine Heavens on the palace grounds. "Eighty benches," Ennin wrote, "were piled up high and covered with elegantly colored drapes, and throughout the day and night ceremonies were held and sacrifices made to the heavenly deities. . . . But since the place of ritual was not in a building and the ceremonies were performed in an open court, when it was clear the sun burned down on the priests and when it rained they were drenched, so that many of the eighty-one men fell sick. . . ." [168]

The army in battle with the Lu-chou rebels, meanwhile, was not having much success, and when the emperor importuned its officers for results, they began seizing the farmers and herdsmen of the region, sending them back to the capital as captured rebels. "The Emperor," Ennin tells, "bestowed ceremonial swords, and right in the streets the prisoners were cut into three pieces. The troops surrounded and slaughtered them. In this way they kept sending prisoners and there was no end of troops. The slaughtered corpses constantly littered the roads, while their blood flowed and soaked the ground, turning it into mud. Spectators filled the roads, and the Emperor from time to time came to see, and there was a great profusion of banners and spears. . . . The legionnaires each time they killed a man, cut out his eyes and flesh and ate them, and the people of the wards all said that this year the people of Ch'ang-an were eating human beings." [169]

> Another Imperial edict was issued [Ennin writes] ordering that throughout the land the mountain monasteries, the common Buddha halls, and the fasting halls at the public wells and in the villages which were less than a certain size and not officially registered, were to be destroyed and their monks and nuns all forced to return to lay life. . . . In the wards within the city of Ch'ang-an there are more than three hundred Buddha halls. Their Buddhist images, scripture towers, and so forth are as magnificent as those described in the Law, and all are the work of famous artisans. A single Buddha hall or cloister here rivals a great monastery in the provinces. But in accordance with the edict they are being destroyed. . . .
>
> Another Imperial edict called upon the University for Sons of the State, the Scholars, those who had achieved the status of Accomplished Literati of the Land, and those of learning, to take up Taoism, but so far not a single person has done so. . . .
>
> Beginning this year [the date is 844 A.D.] each time there was little rain the Commissioners of Good Works, on Imperial command, notified the various Buddhist and Taoist monasteries to read scriptures and pray for rain. But, when in response it rained, the Taoist priests alone received rewards, and the Buddhist monks and nuns were left forlorn with nothing. The people of the city laughingly said that, when they pray for rain they bother the Buddhist monks, but, when they make rewards, they give them only to the Taoist priests.[170]

The emperor went to a Taoist convent where there was an extremely pretty Taoist priestess, whom he summoned to his presence. He bestowed on her one thousand bolts of silk and ordered the convent reconstructed to connect with the palace. Then he went to a Taoist monastery and, presenting another thousand bolts, had installed there a figure of himself in bronze.[171]

It is indeed true, as Dr. Suzuki has told us: "There is something divine in being spontaneous and being not at all hampered by human conventionalities and their artificial sophisticated hypocrisies. There is something direct and fresh in this not being restrained by anything human, which suggests a divine freedom and creativity." [172]

"During the Eighth Moon," the pilgrim Ennin wrote in this fateful year 844, "the Empress Dowager died. . . . Because she was religious and believed in Buddhism, each time the monks and nuns were regulated, she admonished the Emperor. The Emperor killed her by giving her poisoned wine.

"The Empress of the I Yang Hall of the Hsiao family is the Emperor's half-mother and very beautiful. The Emperor ordered her to be his consort, but the Empress Dowager refused. The Emperor drew his bow and shot her. The arrow penetrated her bosom and she died." [173]

The great eunuch Ch'iu Shih-liang had now passed away, and his adopted son, one day, when drunk, was heard to say: "Although the emperor is so revered and noble, it was my father who set him up." Wu-tsung struck him dead on the spot, and an edict ordered that his wife and womenfolk should be seized, sent into exile, and, with hair shaved off, made to guard the imperial tombs. The palace officers were ordered to take over the wealth of the family. Elephant tusks filled the rooms; jewels, gold, and silver completely filled the storehouses; and the cash, silk, and goods were beyond count.[174]

The failure of the great Orient to evolve any order, either of social institutions or of expressly human ethical values, by which the divine nature of a despot could be controlled—or even judged and criticized—is cruelly manifest in such a time as that of the reign of the maniac Wu-tsung. The magical notion that benevolence, compassion, etc., work of themselves upon the universe left the entire East about where Egypt stood in the period of the Narmer palette, c. 2850 B.C. Beyond good and evil, the pieties of the mystics were of small use on the sheerly socio-political plane. When applied, they only served, either to support with mythological, or to condemn with ascetic, platitudes anything and everything taking place—either as divine or as merely material, according to whether a positive or a negative mode of verbalization was employed. All is Buddhahood; all is brahman; all is illusion; all is of the mind.

Nor did the various and numerous political philosophies of Confucian type effect any fundamental change. It is ironic that in the period of Wu-tsung himself there was an important revival of Confucianism, with a lot of fine writing about nature (*hsing*), the feelings (*ch'ing*), and the sage (*sheng*), self-cultivation, self-exertion, and the influence of virtue on the universe: for example, in the works of the Neo-Confucian masters Han Yü (768–824) and Li Ao (d. 844). Whereas on the coarse plane of dreadful fact, the well-being, not indeed of the universe but at least of the Chinese, hung finally on the disposition of the current monarch and the presence or absence in or near his palace of some military force by which he might be deposed. The archaic mythological celebration of his power as derived from and representing heaven's mandate served only to make his human will the more inhuman. He was great, and that was that. He was an "act of God," beyond the law, and yet the source, support, and very being of the law, who by his mere word brought to pass whatever came to pass.

The learned clergy of the Taoist church, that year of their victory, 844, in the ninth moon, issued to the Palace the following *summa contra gentiles* and pontifical request:

> The Buddha was born among the western barbarians and taught "non-birth." "Non-birth" is simply death. He converted men to Nirvana, but Nirvana is death. He talked much of impermanence, pain, and emptiness, which are particularly weird doctrines. He did not understand the principles of spontaneity and immortality.
>
> Lao Tzu, the Supreme, we hear, was born in China. In the Tsung-p'ing-t'ai-lo Heaven he roamed about and spontaneously and naturally became transformed. He concocted an elixir and, taking it, attained immortality and became one of the realm of spirits and produced great benefit without limit.
> We ask that a terrace of the immortals be erected in the

Palace where we may purify our bodies and mount to the heavenly mists and roam about the nine heavens and, with blessings for the masses and long life for the Emperor, long preserve the pleasures of immortality.[175]

And so it was that the final mad marvel of this year of Chinese metamorphosis came to pass. In the tenth moon, as Ennin tells the tale,

the Emperor ordered the two armies to build in the Palace a terrace of the immortals 150 feet high. . . . Each day he had three thousand legionnaires . . . transport earth to build it. The General Supervisors held sticks and oversaw the work. When the Emperor went to inspect it, he asked the Great Officials of the Palace who the men holding sticks were. Told, he said: "We do not want you to hold sticks and manage; you yourselves should be carrying earth. And he had them transport earth. Later the Emperor went again to the place where the terrace was being built and himself drew a bow and for no reason shot one of the General Supervisors, which was a most unprincipled act. . . ."

The terrace of the Immortals is 150 feet high. The area on top is level and big enough for the foundations of a seven bay building, and on top rises a five-peaked tower. People inside and outside the grounds can see it from afar, soaring like a solitary peak. They have brought boulders from the Chungnan Mountains and have made mountain cliffs on the four sides with grottoes and rocky paths. It is arranged most beautifully, and pines, arbor vitae, and rare trees have been planted on it. The Emperor was overjoyed with it, and there was an Imperial edict ordering seven Taoist priests to concoct an elixir and seek immortality on the terrace. . . .[176]

The emperor mounted twice to the top of the terrace. The first time, he wished to see a man pushed off, and when the individual ordered to give the shove demurred, he received twenty strokes of the cane on his back. The second time, wondering about the Taoist priests, he said, "Twice We have mounted the terrace, but not a single one of you, Our lords, has as yet mounted to Immortality. What does this mean?"

To which the witty Taoist priests replied, "Because Buddhism exists alongside of Taoism in the land, *li* ("sorrow") and *ch'i* ("breath") are in excess, blocking the way of the immortal. There-fore, it is impossible to mount to immortality." [177]

The emperor therefore announced, "The pit from which they took the earth [for the terrace] is very deep and makes people afraid and uneasy. We wish that it could be filled up. On a day for sacrifice to the terrace, you should falsely state that a maigre feast is being held to pay reverence to the terrace, gather all the monks and nuns of the two halves of the city, cut off their heads, and fill the pit with them."

A councilor said, however, "The monks and nuns basically are ordinary people of the state, and if they are returned to lay life and each makes his own living, it will benefit the land. I submit that you need not drive them to extinction. I ask that you order the offices concerned to force them all to return to lay life and to send them back to their places of origin to perform the local corvee."

The emperor nodded his head, and after quite a while he mur-mured, "As you say."

Wrote the Japanese, Ennin: "When the monks and nuns of the various monasteries heard about this, their spirits lost con-fidence, and they did not know where to turn." [178]

The cruel farce went on until, after numerous difficulties, Ennin left for home, and one of those seeing him off on his ship said to him, "Buddhism no longer exists in this land. But Buddhism flows toward the east. So it has been said since ancient times. I hope that you will do your best to reach your homeland and propagate Buddhism there. Your disciple has been very fortunate to have seen you many times. Today we part, and in this life we are not likely to meet again. When you have attained Buddhahood I hope you will not abandon your disciple." [179]

And it is said that the emperor, shortly after, died from an over-dose of immortality pills.

SUNG DYNASTY: 960–1279 A.D.

Buddhism in China never recovered from the blows of 841–845. It survived along with popular Taoism largely on the level of a crude folk religion, no longer developing, only serving in its own way the perennial needs of family and community life, providing colorful ceremonies for occasions of birth, marriage, and death; symbolic games to mark the passage and particular qualities of the seasons; solace for those sad and weary; mythic goals beyond, for those with none here; archaic answers to undeveloped questions about the mysteries of being; a literature of marvel; and supernatural backing for parental and governmental authority.

Specifically, the Chinese rendition of these services derives from the background of the Bronze Age and in that sense can be said indeed to represent in the modern world—along with India—a past of five thousand years. The basic level is that of the toiling, beautiful "lower" people of the patient earth. However, in contrast to the peasantry of India and of much of Europe, the Chinese were not in the deep past people of the soil. They were nomads of a race developed (apparently) in the northernmost habitable Arctic, who came south after the Glacial Age and displaced whatever people had preceded them. In their cults we find an interesting, characteristic combination of neolithic fertility elements, reverence for ancestors, etc., with an emphatically shamanistic factor. The phenomenon of possession is conspicuous throughout the Mongoloid terrain, both in private and in public cult. It serves to supplement divination as a means of learning—and even influencing—the will of the unseen. It supplements, also, the family cult of devotion to the ancestors, which is under the charge, fundamentally, not of the shaman, but of the paterfamilias. In Chinese thought the idea of the ancestor is on the one hand linked to the noble terms *Ti, Shang Ti,* and *T'ien,* which have been generally translated "God," but on the other to such terms as *shen,* "spirits," and *kuei,* "ghosts." The sphere of the shaman is properly the latter. The sphere of the paterfamilias centers about the family cult of his own ancestral line. And the sphere of the imperial cult is a development of the familial, with accretions from the shamanistic: the ancestral line of the emperor (the son of heaven) having been identified, practically, with "the deified being (*ti*) above (*shang*)," Shang Ti.

In relation to the cult of birth and death, two soul-like principles are recognized: the first, *p'o* (written with the character for "white" and that for "daemon," i.e., "white ghost"), is produced at the time of conception; the second, *hun* (written with the character for "clouds" and that for "daemon," i.e., "cloud daemon"), is joined to the *p'o* at the moment of birth, when the light-world is entered from the dark. The *p'o* in later thought was identified with the *yin*, the *hun* with the *yang*. At death, the *p'o* remains in the tomb with the corpse for three years (compare Egyptian *Ba*) and then descends to the Yellow Springs; or, if not set at rest it may return as a *kuei*, a ghost. On the other hand, the *hun*, which partakes of the principle of light, ascends to heaven, becoming a *shen*, a spirit.

It is now believed that the two terms Shang Ti (Lord Above) and T'ien (Heaven) derive from the periods, respectively, of the Shang and the Chou dynasties. The former term suggests a personality. The latter tends to the impersonal. Both imply a will, the will of heaven. However, this will is conceived, in accordance with the formula of the hieratic city state, in the way of a mathematically structured cosmic order (*maat, me, rta, dharma, tao*). And as everything in the history of Chinese thought and civilization shows, the realization of this order has been the chief concern of the Middle Kingdom, from the ages of its first appearance. Fundamentally, the idea is that the individual (microcosm), society (mesocosm), and the universe of heaven and earth (macrocosm), form an indissoluble unit, and that the well-being of all depends upon their mutual harmonization. As in India, so in China, there is no notion of an absolute creation of the world. In contrast, however, to India, where an accent is given to the dissolution-recreation motif, in China the main thought is of the present aspect of the world. And instead of a systematic sequence of four recurrent ages, ever growing worse, China presents in The Book of Changes a guide to the nuance of the present moment. Correspondingly— as Professor Joseph Kitagawa succinctly remarks—"How to realize Tao," more than "What is Tao?" is the problem that has been the chief concern of the Chinese—superstitious masses and lofty philosophers alike.[180]

And again in contrast to India, where a theoretically static system of caste represents the social aspect of the cosmic order and the individual is oriented to his duties by way of his broad caste alignment, in China the family and immediate kinship alignment dominates, and not devotion to a god but filial piety is the focal sentiment of the system. It is written in the Classic of Filial Piety (*Hsiao Ching*): "He who loves his parents will not dare to incur the risk of being hated by any man, and he who reveres his parents will not dare to incur the risk of being condemned by any man." [181] The philosophy of Mo Tzu of indiscriminate universal love ran against this fundamental sentiment, and so, until revived about 1950 by the Communists, with whose point of view this philosophy well accords, Mo Tzu played a relatively minor role in the shaping of the system of sentiments by which the civilization, from Han times on, was held together. Indeed, even the monarch was supposed to be regulated by the sentiment of filial piety.

"When the love and reverence of the Son of Heaven are thus carried to the utmost in the service of his parents," the Classic of Filial Piety continues, "the lessons of his virtue affect all the people, and he becomes a pattern to all within the four seas: this is the filial piety of the Son of Heaven." [182]

Thus it is that the Chinese religion—to cite once again Professor Kitagawa—never made a distinction between the sacred and the secular. "The religious ethos of the Chinese," he writes, "must be found in the midst of their ordinary everyday life more than in their ceremonial activities, though the latter should not be ignored. The meaning of life was sought in the whole life, and not confined to any section of it called religious." [183]

However, as we have seen, when the actual son of heaven forgot his posture of filial piety, there was nothing anyone could do about it. Spontaneity then was the rule—and with what result! Sociologically, that is to say, the Chinese may again, without demur, claim an age of five thousand years.

Following the orgy of Wu-tsung, the Buddhist community in China convalesced, and there developed what can be termed, for our purpose at any rate, the final form of the Chinese mythic order. The T'ang Dynasty, whose monarchs supposed themselves to be descended from the mythical sage Lao Tzu, collapsed 906 A.D., and after five decades of war lords (the so-called Five Dynasties), the politically weak but culturally wonderful Sung Dynasty arose (960–1279). Its founder sponsored the first printed edition of the Chinese Buddhist scriptures and its second monarch built a huge Buddhist stupa in the capital. Ch'an Buddhism, which, in one branch at least, namely that inspired by Hui-neng, had stepped away from the monastic ideal, was the chief Buddhist influence among the literati, and as a kind of synthesis of the Buddhist, Taoist, and Confucian vocabularies, Neo-Confucianism came into being.

"The ultimate purpose of Buddhism," states Dr. Fung Yu-lan,

> is to teach men how to achieve Buddhahood. . . . Likewise, the ultimate purpose of Neo-Confucianism is to teach how to achieve Confucian Sagehood. The difference between the Buddha of Buddhism and the Sage of Neo-Confucianism is that while the Buddha must promote his spiritual cultivation outside of society and the human world, the Sage must do so within these human bonds. The most important development in Chinese Buddhism was its attempt to depreciate the otherworldliness of original Buddhism. This attempt came close to success when the Ch'an Masters stated that "in carrying water and chopping firewood, therein lies the wonderful *Tao*." But . . . they did not push this idea to its logical conclusion by saying that in serving one's family and the state, therein also lies the wonderful *Tao*.[184]

As early as the days of Mencius (372?–289? B.C.) and Hsün Tzu (c. 298–238 B.C.) the two leading Confucians of pre-Han times, the fundamental principles had been well established upon which the consummate civilization (as opposed to the terrible history) of China has been established; namely:

1. Mencius: "The ten thousand things are complete within us. There is no greater delight than to realize this through self-cultivation. And there is no better way to human-heartedness (*jen*) than the practice of the principle of altruism (*shu*)."[185]

2. Hsün Tzu: "The sacrificial rites are the expression of man's affectionate longing. They represent the height of piety and faithfulness, of love and respect. They represent also the completion of propriety and refinement. Their meaning cannot be fully under-

stood except by the sages. The sages understood their meaning. Superior men enjoy their practice. They become the routine of the officer. They become the custom of the people.

"Superior men consider them to be the activity of man, while ordinary people consider them as something that has to do with spirits and ghosts. . . . They exist to render the same service to the dead as to the living, to render the same service to the lost as to the existing. What they serve has neither shape nor even a shadow, yet they are the completion of culture and refinement." [186]

"With this interpretation," states Fung Yu-lan, "the meaning of the mourning and sacrificial rites becomes completely poetic, not religious." [187]

And with this, we may add, on the side that I am calling civilization, the chasm is crossed from the way of religion to that of art.

JAPANESE MYTHOLOGY

++

I. Prehistoric Origins

When the eyes turn to Japan, four facts are immediately apparent. The first is that the period of the arrival of Buddhism, and with Buddhism the arts of a developed civilization, corresponds approximately to that of the Christianization of Germanic Europe; so that whereas both India and China may be looked upon as intrinsically fulfilled, burned out, or, as Spengler has termed them, Fellaheen, Japan is young, still dreaming, and able, as Nietzsche would say, "to give birth to a dancing star."

The second point is that, because of this youth, there was never in traditional Japan any such fundamental experience either of social or of cosmic disillusionment as we have noted for Egypt, Mesopotamia, India, and China; so that when Buddhism arrived, its first noble truth, "All life is sorrowful," may have met the ear but never reached the heart. Japan heard something quite different in the gospel of the Buddha.

The next point is that, as a comparatively primitive people, the Japanese at the time of their entry upon the stage of history were still endowed with that primary sense of the numinous in all things that Rudolf Otto has termed the mental state *sui generis* of religion.*

And the fourth fact is that Japan, like England, is an island world wherein a self-understood rapport exists by nature, from top to bottom of the social order; so that whereas on the mainland clashes of race, cultures, and mutually inconsiderate classes repre-

---

* Supra, pp. 35–36 and 45–46.

sent practically the norm of the social history, in Japan, even in days of the most brutal disorder, the empire functioned, in the main, as an organic unit. And with such effect that today, as nowhere else in the world, one has the sense there of a permeation of the social body by a spirit essentially heroic and aristocratic, endowed with the quality of honor, which has penetrated downward from the top, while, in counterplay, the sense of wonder and delight in the numinous just mentioned, which is generally lost in the sophistications of a developed civilization, remains significant in the structure of life, supported from beneath by the sensibilities of the folk, yet pervading the culture spectrum to the top.

The archaeology of Japan falls into five blocks. The first, largely hypothetical, is of paleolithic hunters of the period of Sinanthropus and Pithecanthropus, c. 400,000 B.C., when the islands appear to have been connected with the continent. There have been reports of finds of chopper-type tools and at least one possible fragment of a pithecanthropoid pelvis. Further discoveries are to be expected, but until they come there can be little more said than this of interglacial hominids in Japan.[1]

The second prehistoric block, also largely hypothetical, is of mesolithic hunters, possibly post-3000 B.C. There have been found in Honshu a few tiny artifacts, judged by some to be microliths, but again, the argument still is open and, in any case, for our present concern of no point.[2]

Block three, on the other hand, is of considerable point. The period is known as Jomon ("cord-marked") and, as the name indicates, is characterized by ceramic fabrics of a crude, hand-shaped, cord-marked type. The dating is from c. 2500 to c. 300 B.C., within which long span five phases are recognized: 1. Proto-, 2. Early, 3. Middle, 4. Late, and 5. Final. It is presumed that the earliest carriers of the culture were Caucasoid. Their probable descendants, the Ainus, are confined today to the northern island, Hokkaido, but at one time possessed all or most of Honshu as well. Fishing and sea-mammal hunting were the occupations of the north. In the south the foods were shellfish, deer, and acorns. Bone fishhooks, ground and chipped stone tools, semi-subterranean houses, flexed burials in or near the dwellings, and the absence of agriculture characterize the first three phases. During the fourth, ceramic figurines and well-conceived, rhythmically organized pottery designs appear that reflect Bronze Age influence from the continent. While in the final phase settled villages are established and an agriculture is developed of buckwheat, hemp, kidney beans, and gingili, together with a barnyard of cattle and horses.[3]

Block four, the Yayoi Period, is dated c. 300 B.C.–300 A.D., and represents the foundation of a culture properly Japanese. The sites, confined to Kyushu and southern Honshu, show that the arrivals were by way of Korea. The culture assemblage suggests pre-Shang China (Lungshan: black ware, c. 1800 B.C.). The Japanese dates, however, correspond to Chinese Ch'in and Han. Rice cultivation with the use of the flooded-terrace system, ceramics turned on the potter's wheel, pedestal vessels, and an early Chinese method of rice-steaming in a system of double jars, are the distinctive marks of this culture complex. The semilunar knife also appears (circumpolar assemblage); the quadrangular adze (which has a distribution from the Black Sea to Hawaii); wooden shovels, hoes, pestles, etc., and the high, single-ridgepole house. Copper and cast bronze weapons were known in the middle and late phases; also iron in small quantities. The culture, in short, was basically of a high neolithic style, and yet the dates were of imperial Han China and Rome.

Block five, the Yamato Period, which opens c. 300 A.D., represents a new penetration of Central Asians from Korea, via Kyushu, into Honshu. Earth-covered, mound-type tombs, circular, square, and keyhole-shaped, placed either in hills or amid rice fields, have earned the title "mound-burial complex" for this culture. By c. 400 A.D. the tombs reached immense size. One, traditionally attributed to a certain Emperor Nintoko, whose dates are given as 257–399 A.D. (sic),[4] covers about 80 acres of ground, is 90 feet high, 400 yards long, and on top carried shrines and buildings. A Chinese chronicle of c. 297 A.D. states of a queen named Pimiko (Japanese, Himiko, "Sun-daughter"), who was visited by a Chinese delegation in the year 238, that when she died "a great mound was raised more than a hundred paces in diameter and over a hundred male and female attendants followed her to the grave." [5] "Remaining unmarried," states another Chinese account (c. 445 A.D.), "she occupied herself with magic and sorcery and bewitched the populace. Thereupon they placed her on the throne. She kept one thousand female attendants, but few people saw her. There was only one man, who was in charge of her wardrobe and meals and acted as the medium of communication. She resided in a palace surrounded by towers and a stockade, with the protection of armed guards. The laws and customs were strict and stern." [6] Such a queen, as Professor Joseph Kitagawa points out, was a female shaman.[7]

The Chinese chronicles declare that the people of Japan divined by scorching bones, their diviners being men who neither combed their hair, rid themselves of fleas, washed their clothes, ate meat, nor approached women; also that, whenever anyone died, mourning was observed for more than ten days, during which period no meat was consumed. The chief mourners wailed and lamented, while the friends sang, danced, and drank; and when the rites were over, members of the family went into water for a bath of purification.[8]

An illuminating documentation of this age has recently appeared in the galaxy of *haniwa* ("clay image") figurines that have been unearthed from numerous sites. These hollow terra-cotta representations of armed warriors, saddled horses, etc., were placed in rows around the slopes of burial mounds as substitutes for living "death followers," in the way of the figures placed in Egyptian tombs three thousand years before. Swords, helmets, armor of slat and quilting, Central Asian bows and arrows, saddles, ring-stirrups, and reins are represented in these vigorously rendered little forms. Further, a number of actual iron weapons, ornaments, and elements of armor have been recovered from this earliest Yamato age.

In my Primitive volume I have discussed the shamanism, bear, fire, and mountain cults, burial and purification rites, of the Ainu. Culturally the blend from these to the more primitive aspects of Japanese Shinto is very smooth. The source land of both peoples was Northeast and North-Central Asia—a zone from which numerous entries into North America also were launched. And since continuous contributions from the same North Asiatic circumpolar sphere likewise flowed into northern Europe, astonishing affinities turn up throughout the native lore of Japan, touching fields of myth as widely separated as Ireland, Kamchatka, and the Canadian Northeast. The Iron Age reached Britain c. 450 B.C. with the Celts; c. 250 B.C. a second such wave arrived, distinguished by a developed (La Tène) type of decorated ironware, together with hero graves, chariots, hill forts, and stone-built towers. These dates and elements suggest those of Yamato Japan.

The chief linkage of the primitive lore of Japan is thus with the north. However, the mythology includes many elements suggesting Polynesia and coastal fishing folk as well. North Asiatic hunters, oceanic fishing folk, marginal neolithic agriculturalists and late waves of Bronze Age and finally Iron Age warrior folk, supply the ingredients of the Japanese compositum mythologicum. Tribal wars and a gradual pressing back of the Ainu (perhaps also Yayoi) brought the Yamato clans into dominance by c. 400 A.D. in the areas across from Korea. And it was through these that the boons of Chinese civilization arrived in force in the fifth and sixth centuries A.D.

II. The Mythic Past

Following a law that the reader will recognize, the Yamato rulers, in response to the Chinese inspiration, invented a past of their own, composed of local myths arranged as a world chronicle. However, in contrast to the dry-as-dust Confucians, who had considerably succeeded in de-mythologizing mythology without succeeding, however, in converting it into anything else, the freshly fledged literati of Japan still had the dew of youth upon them. Their model was, indeed, a legendary Chinese chronicle of the sort first composed in Sumer, telling of the origin of the universe and ages of the gods, the ages, then, of superhuman kings, and the ages, finally, of heroic men approximately of our own length of years. But the material that they dressed to this frame was of their own, comparatively childlike, folkloristic heritage, and the result was the most remarkable history of the world-as-fairytale that the literature of our subject knows—which, in a way, befits Japan, where, as remarked in the first pages of my Primitive volume (chapter on "The Lesson of the Mask"), the extraordinary earnestness and profound gravity of the ideal of life is masked by the fashionable fiction that everything is only play.

The first important Chinese influences were Confucian. These arrived possibly in the fourth, certainly by the fifth century A.D. The epochal date, however, is in the sixth century, 552 A.D., when a Korean king presented the Emperor Kimmei with a packet of sutras and a golden image of the Buddha. The arts of civilization thereafter poured into the country, and for the next three hundred years there was an avid assimilation in progress, which culminated in the Nara Period, 710–794 A.D., when two symbolic events took place: on the Buddhist side, the dedication of a colossal Buddha image in bronze that is today one of the wonders of the world, and on the side of the native Shinto heritage, the appearance by royal decree of two compilations of the genealogical lore of the royal house. These were the Kojiki ("Record of Ancient Matters"), 712 A.D., and the Nihongi ("Chronicles of Japan"), 720 A.D. As their names declare, they are recordings of native lore that formerly had been handed down only orally. In contrast to their Chinese model, they commence before the beginning of the world. And they maintain a thoroughly mythological mood while telling of the early godlike and later manly heroes of the great past. They bring kingship down from heaven to the house of Yamato and continue to within a few decades of their own day.

In the following, I present from the Kojiki the legends of 1. the earliest ages of the world, and 2. the descent of kingship to the land of Japan.

THE AGE OF SPIRITS

Now when chaos had begun to condense, but force and form were not yet manifest and there was nothing named, nothing done: who could know its shape? Nevertheless Heaven and Earth parted, and Three Spirits began the work:
1. The Spirit Master of the August Center of Heaven,
2. The August, High, Wondrously Producing Spirit,
3. The Divine, Wondrously Producing Ancestor.
These appeared spontaneously and afterward disappeared. But the young earth, like floating oil, now was drifting, and

there sprang up something like a reed shoot, from which two spirits emerged:

4. The Pleasant Reed-Shoot-Prince Elder, and

5. The Spirit Standing Eternally in Heaven: who likewise appeared and afterward disappeared.

And these were the five who separated Heaven and Earth.

Now there were born thereafter, spontaneously, the following pairs, who also appeared and then disappeared:

6. The Spirit Standing Eternally on Earth, and the Luxuriantly Integrating Master Spirit;

7. Mud-Earth Lord and his younger sister, Mud-Earth Lady;

8. Germ-Integrating Spirit and his younger sister, Life-Integrating Spirit;

9. Spirit Elder of the Great Place and his younger sister, Spirit Lady of the Great Place;

10. The Perfect-Exterior Spirit and his younger sister, the Awesome Lady; and

11. The Male Who Invites (*Izanagi*) and his younger sister, the Female Who Invites (*Izanami*).

Whereupon, all those Heavenly Spirits commanded the last pair to make, consolidate, and give birth to this drifting land, Japan; granting them a jeweled spear. And these two, standing on the Floating Bridge of Heaven, reached down with that jeweled spear and stirred with it. When they had agitated the brine until it went "curdlecurdle" [*koworokoworo*], they lifted the spear, and the brine that dripped from its end, piling up, became an island called Self-Condensed, onto which the august pair descended.

They attended there to the building of an August Heavenly Pillar and of a Hall of Eight Fathoms, after which His Augustness, the Male Who Invites, inquired of Her Augustness, the Female Who Invites, "In what manner is your body made?" She replied: "My body in its thriving grows, but there is one part that does not grow together." And His Augustness the Male Who Invites said to her: "My body in its thriving also grows, but there is one part that grows in excess. Therefore, would it not seem proper that I should introduce the part of my body in excess into the part of your body that does not grow together, and so procreate territories?"

Her Augustness the Female Who Invites said: "It would be well." And His Augustness, the Male Who Invites, said to her: "Let us then go round this August Heavenly Pillar, I and you, and when we shall have come together let us in august union join our august parts." She agreed, and then he said, "Do you, then, go around to the right and I shall go around to the left." They did so, and where they met, Her Augustness the Female Who Invites, said: "Ah! What a fair and lovely youth!" Whereupon His Augustness the Male Who Invites said: "Ah! What a fair and lovely maiden!"

But when these two utterances had been made, His Augustness said to his august sister: "It is not fitting that the woman should have spoken first."

Nevertheless, in the chamber they commenced, and begot a son named Leech, whom they placed in a boat of reeds and let float away. They gave birth next to Foam Island, which, since it also was a failure, is not reckoned among their offspring.

The two august spirits therefore took counsel. "The children to whom we have given birth are not good. We had best report this in the august place." They ascended. And when they had inquired of their Augustnesses, the Heavenly Spirits, the latter studied the matter by grand divination and commanded them to return. "The offspring were not good because the woman spoke first," they ordered; "go back and amend your words."

Descending, His Augustness the Male Who Invites and Her Augustness the Female Who Invites went around the august Heavenly Pillar as before. This time, however, His Augustness the Male spoke first: "Ah, what a fair and lovely maiden!" His august younger sister exclaimed: "Ah! What a fair and lovely youth!" And when they had thus corrected the utterance they were joined.

They begot, gave birth to, and named the eight islands of Japan. They begot next, gave birth to, and named, thirty august spirits of the earth, sea, and seasons, winds, trees, mountains, moors, and fire. The last, however, the Fire-Burning-Swift Male Spirit, scorched the august female parts of his mother as she gave birth to him, and Her Augustness the Female Who Invites grew sick and lay down.

The spirits that were born from her vomit were the Metal Mountain Prince and the Metal Mountain Princess; those from her faeces, the Prince Viscid Clay and Princess Viscid Clay; those from her urine, Spirit Princess Water and Young Wondrous Producing Spirit. But then, at length, Her Augustness the Female Who Invites retired.

And His Augustness the Male Who Invites said: "Oh! My

lovely younger sister! Alas, that I should have exchanged Your
Augustness for this one child!"

And as he crept weeping about her august pillow, and
crept weeping about her august feet, and wept, there was
born from his august tears the spirit that dwells at the foot of
trees on the slope of the spur of Mount Fragrant, the name of
whom is Crying Weeping Female Spirit. And he buried the
divinely retired August Spirit, the Female Who Invites, on
Mount Hiba, at the boundary of the lands of Izumo and
Hahoki.

And His Augustness the Male Who Invites drew his sword,
ten hand-grasps long, that was augustly girded on him, and he
cut off the head of his child, the Fire-Burning-Swift Male
Spirit. From the blood that clung to the point of the August
sword and bespattered and multitudinous rock masses, there
were born three spirits; from the blood on the upper part of
the august sword, which again bespattered the multitudinous
rock masses, again three; and from the blood that collected on
the hilt and leaked out between his fingers, there were born
two: eight in all. Additional spirits were born from the eight
body parts of the slain Fire Spirit: from his head, chest, belly,
genitalia, left and right hands, left and right feet. And the name
of the august sword itself was Heavenly Point Blade Extended.

Whereupon His Augustness, wishing to meet again and see
again his younger sister, descended into the Land of Night.
And when from the palace that was there, she raised the door
and came out to meet him, His Augustness the Male Who Invites said to her: "Oh my lovely younger sister! The lands that
I and you made are not yet finished. Do you therefore come
back!"

And Her Augustness the Female Who Invites answered:
"Lamentable, indeed, that you did not come sooner; for I
have eaten of the food of this place. However, since I am
overpowered by the honor of the entry here of Your Augustness, my lovely elder brother, I desire to return. Moreover,
I shall now discuss the matter with the spirits of this place.
But I beseech you not to look upon me." And she went back
within the palace.

But as she tarried there very long, His Augustness the Male
Who Invites could not wait, and he broke off one of the large
end teeth of the multitudinously close-toothed comb that was
stuck in the august left bunch of his hair. Setting it ablaze, he
went in and looked. She was rotting.

Maggots swarmed throughout her body. In her head dwelt

the Great Thunder, in her breast the Fire Thunder, in her belly the Earth Thunder, in her left arm the Young Thunder, in her right arm the Black Thunder; in her left leg, the Mountain Thunder; in her right leg the Moon Thunder; in her sex, the Cleaving Thunder: eight in all.

His Augustness the Male Who Invites, appalled at the sight, shrank back; and Her Augustness the Female Who Invites, his younger sister, said to His Augustness: "You have put me to shame!" She sent in pursuit of him as he fled, the Ugly Female of the Land of Night. But His Augustness the Male Who Invites took his black august headdress and cast it down behind him: it turned immediately into grapes.* And while she paused to pick these up and eat, he fled. She resumed pursuit, and he took and broke the multitudinously close-toothed comb in the right bunch of his hair and cast it down behind him: it turned instantly into bamboo shoots. And while she was pulling at these and eating, he fled on.

Her Augustness now sent after him the eight Spirit Thunders, together with warriors of that Land of Night to the number of one thousand five hundred, and he drew the ten-grasp sword that was augustly girded on him and, brandishing this behind, fled on. But as they all still pursued, he concealed himself at the foot of a large peach tree by the Flat Hill at the frontier line between the worlds of the living and the dead. And when they came on, he flung at them three peaches. Whereupon they all fled back.

And His Augustness the Male Who Invites announced, then, to those peaches: "Just as you have helped me, so must you help all living people of the Central Land of Reed Plains when they are in trouble and harassed." (This is the origin of the custom of keeping evil spirits away with peaches.) And he named them Their Augustness Great Divine Fruit.

But at last Her Augustness the Princess Who Invites came in pursuit of him herself. Whereupon he drew up a rock, which it would take a thousand men to lift, and setting this in the middle, blocked off the Level Pass of the Land of Night. So that from opposite sides of that rock the two exchanged leavetaking.

Her Augustness the Female Who Invites declared: "My lovely elder brother, Your Augustness! If you do thus, I shall every day strangle to death one thousand of the people of your land."

* Playing on a pun: *kuro-mi-katsura* (headdress), *ebi-katsura* (grapes).

His Augustness the Male Who Invites replied: "My lovely younger sister, Your Augustness! If you do thus, I will every day cause one thousand five hundred women to bear children."

Her Augustness the Female Who Invites is called, therefore, the Great Spirit of the Land of Night. And again, since she pursued and reached her elder brother, she is called the Road Reaching Great Spirit. And the rock by which he blocked up the Pass of the Land of Night is called the Great Spirit of the Road Turning Back, or again, the Great Blocking Spirit of the Door of the Land of Night.[9]

THE DESCENT OF KINGSHIP TO JAPAN

We read that, following his terrible adventure, the Male Who Invites purified himself by bathing in a stream; and as he did so, spirits sprang from each article of clothing as he flung it on the river bank. Likewise, from every part of his body spirits sprang. But of all, the most important to appear were three; namely, the Sun-Goddess Amaterasu Omikami (the Heaven Shining Great August Spirit), who was born as he washed his left august eye; the moon-god, Tsukiyomi-no-Mikoto (His Augustness Moon Night Possessor), who was born as he washed his right august eye; and an absolutely intractable storm-god, Susano-O-no-Mikoto (His Brave Swift Impetuous Male Augustness), who was born as he washed his august nose.[10]

And the last of these, rudely, one day, so greatly mortified his august sister Amaterasu Omikami, that she hid herself in a cave, whereupon both heaven and earth became dark; and, to entice her forth, the eight million spirits of the Plain of Heaven assembled trees before the cave, bedecked with jewels, lighted bonfires, and laughed aloud with such uproar at a raucous dance performed by a spirit-female named Uzume that the goddess in her cave, becoming curious, opened the door to peek out. They held a mirror before her, the first she had ever seen; she was drawn out, and the world again was alight.

But the culprit Susano-O, for his rudeness, was sent in exile from the heavenly plain to earth. And so this Brave Swift Impetuous Male, having descended to a place near the source of the river Hi in Izumo, saw at that time some chopsticks floating down the stream, and he thought, therefore, that there must be people above. Proceeding upward in quest of them, he discovered an old man and woman with between them a young girl. They were crying; and he deigned to ask who they were.

"I am an Earth Spirit," the old man said, "and my name is Foot-Stroking Elder. My wife's name is Hand-Stroking Elder. And this, our daughter's name is Mistress Head Comb."

The Brave-Swift Impetuous Male asked: "And what is the cause of the weeping?"

The old man said: "We had eight daughters, once. But there is an eight-forked serpent that comes each year and eats one. His time has come round again. That is why we weep."

The expelled Heaven Spirit asked: "And what is that serpent's form?"

"The eyes are as red as the winter cherry. It has one body with eight heads and tails. On that body moss grows, and conifers; the length extends over eight valleys and eight hills, and if one looks at the belly, it is constantly bloody and inflamed."

"This being your daughter, will you give her to me?" asked His Brave-Swift Impetuous Male Augustness.

The old man replied: "With reverence; however, I do not know your name."

"I am the elder brother of the Heaven Shining Spirit, who am descended here from heaven."

"That being so, with reverence, she is yours."

And His Swift Impetuous Male Augustness at once took that girl, changed her into a multitudinously close-toothed comb, and stuck her in his august hair bunch, while saying to the old pair: "Distill now a brew of eightfold refined liquor. Also, make a fence round about, and in that fence let there be eight gates; at each gate let there be eight platforms; and on each platform a liquor vat, into each of which pour the eightfold liquor, and wait."

They did just that. And the eight-forked serpent coming, it dipped a head into each vat. Then, having drunk deep, every one of those heads lay down and slept. And His Swift Impetuous Male Augustness drew his ten-grasp sword that was augustly girded on and cut the eight-forked sleeping serpent to bits. He built a palace in the land of Izumo, and appointing the old Foot-Stroking Elder to be his head steward, proceeded to beget children, who in turn begot children, to the sum precisely of eighty; all of whom except one left the land to pay suit to a certain distant princess of renown.[11]

The one remaining grandson, who was named the Spirit Master of the Great Land, begot on numerous wives a prolific progeny: and it was these, becoming uproarious and warlike, whom the Heaven Shining Great August Spirit thought to pacify by sending down to earth her august son. His name? His Augustness *Truly Conqueror, I Conquer Conquering, Swift Heavenly Great Great Ears,* who, standing on the Floating Bridge of Heaven, looking below, announced: "The luxuriant reed plains, the land of fresh rice ears of a thousand autumns, is painfully uproarious." And, having made this announcement, immediately he reascended.[12]

Three heavenly embassies now were sent to earth to arrange for the coming down of the solar monarch. However, all were seduced, one way or another, and it required a fourth to obtain submission of the Spirit Master of the Great Land of Izumo, who surrendering at the last to the inevitable, agreed to vacate his unruly throne if a palace were built for him below and he were appropriately worshiped for all time.[13]

Then the Heaven Shining Great August Spirit, Amaterasu Omikami, commanded and charged the Heir Apparent, His Augustness Great Great Ears; who, however, replied: "While I, your servant, have been getting ready, there has been born to me a son named His Augustness *Heaven Plenty, Earth Plenty, Heaven's Sun Height, Prince Ruddy Rice-Ear Plenty.* This child is the one who should be sent down."

His Augustness, the young prince, when told, replied: "I shall descend, according to your commands." And quitting his Heavenly Rock Seat, pushing asunder the eightfold heavenly spreading clouds, dividing a road with an august road-divider, he set off floating, shut up in the Floating Bridge of Heaven, descending to the peak of a certain mountain (not in Izumo, which is in the north, but) in Kyushu, which is in the south.

And when he had established himself in that country, in a palace, His Augustness Heaven Plenty, Earth Plenty, Heaven's Sun Height, Prince Ruddy Rice-Ear Plenty, met a beautiful person at the august cape called Kasasa and he asked her whose daughter she was.

"I am a daughter," she said, "of the Spirit Great Mountain Possessor; and my name is Princess Blossoming Brilliantly Like the Flowers of the Trees."

He asked: "Have you brothers? Have you sisters?"

She replied: "There is an elder sister. Her name is Princess Long as the Rocks."

And he said: "My desire is to lie with you. Now how do you feel about this?"

She said: "I am not the one to say. My father, the Spirit Great Mountain Possessor, is the one." [14]

So he sent her to her father, who, delighted, respectfully sent her back, together with the Princess Long as the Rocks, her elder sister. And the father caused merchandise to be carried on tables holding a hundred sorts of food and drink. But the elder sister was hideous. At the sight of her, Prince Ruddy Rice-Ear Plenty was alarmed. He sent her back; and he took to himself that night only the younger.

And the father, covered with shame when the Princess Long as the Rocks returned to him, sent a message to His Augustness.

"My reason for presenting my two daughters was that by virtue of the elder, Princess Long as the Rocks, the august offspring of the Heavenly Spirit—though snow fall and the wind blow—should have lived eternally, indestructible as the enduring rocks; and that by virtue of the younger, Princess Blossoming Brilliantly Like the Flowers of the Trees, they should have lived flourishingly, like the flowering of the blossoms of trees. However, since you have now returned the Princess Long as the Rocks, retaining only the Princess Blossoming Brilliantly Like the Flowers of the Trees, the august offspring of the Heavenly Shining Great August Spirit will be as perishable as the flowers of the trees."

And that is why the august lives of their Augustnesses, our August Heavenly Sovereigns, are not long.[15]

III. The Way of Spirits

There was an amusing story that went the rounds at the meetings of the Ninth International Congress for the History of Religions in Tokyo, 1958, which, whether true or no, illustrates the gulf that separates East and West in certain essential quarters of experience. It was told of two learned characters, one a Western sociologist, the other a Shinto priest. Both had read papers at the meetings; each supposed himself to have knowledge of the nature, history, and essential problems of mankind, and neither supposed for a minute that he was what in Chinese might have been termed a *chien,* which is to say, a fabulous bird with one eye and one wing: two of these birds must unite to fly.[16]

The learned Western bird, together with numerous others of the composite swarm of delegates from all quarters of the globe whom the Japanese Organizing Committee was miraculously trans-porting to every major Shinto shrine and Buddhist temple in the country, had—according to this joke—now witnessed seven or eight Shinto rites and gazed at numerous Shinto shrines. Such a place of worship is without images, simple in form, wonderfully roofed, and often painted a nice clear red. The priests, immaculate in white vesture, black headdress, and large black wooden shoes, move about in files with stately mien. An eerie music rises, reedy, curiously spiritlike, punctuated by controlled heavy and light drumbeats and great gongs; threaded with the plucked, harplike sounds of a spirit-summoning koto. And then noble, imposing, heavily garbed dancers silently appear, either masked or un-masked, male or female. These move in slow, somewhat dream-like or trancelike, shamanizing measure; stay for a time before the eyes, and retire, while utterances are intoned. One is thrown back two thousand years. The pines, rocks, forests, mountains, air, and sea of Japan awake and send out spirits on those sounds. They can be heard and felt all about. And when the dancers have retired and the music has stopped, the ritual is done. One turns and looks again at the rocks, the pines, the air and sea, and they are as silent as before. Only now they are inhabited, and one is aware anew of the wonder of the universe.

Nevertheless, it seems to be difficult for people of a certain thinking type to experience what is evoked for them by such art. "When compared with the great religions of the world," I have read, for example, "Shinto must be deemed perhaps the most rudimentary religious cult of which we have an adequate written record. It has not advanced beyond crude polytheism; its per-sonifications are vague and feeble; there is little grasp of the con-ception of spirit; it has scarcely anything in the shape of a moral code; it practically does not recognize a future state, and generally gives little evidence of deep thought or earnest devotion. . . ." [17]

Well—and so our friend the sociologist met his friend the Shinto priest at a lawn party in the precincts of an extensive Japanese garden, where paths, leading down among the rocks, turned to re-veal unforeseen landscapes, gravel lawns, craggy lakes, stone lanterns, trees curiously formed, and pagodas. And our friend the sociologist said to his friend the Shinto priest, "You know, I've now been to a number of these Shinto shrines and I've seen quite a few rites, and I've read about it, thought about it; but you know, I don't get the ideology. I don't get your theology."

And that Japanese gentleman, polite, as though respecting the foreign scholar's profound question, paused a while as though in thought. Then he looked, smiling, at his friend. "We do not have ideology," he said. "We do not have theology. We dance."

Which, precisely, is the point. For Shinto, at root, is a religion not of sermons but of awe: which is a sentiment that may or may not produce words, but in either case goes beyond them. Not a "grasp of the conception of spirit," but a sense of its ubiquity, is the proper end of Shinto. And just because this end is to an astonishing degree rendered, the personifications of Shinto are "vague and feeble" as to form. They are termed *kami,* which is a word that is ill translated either as "god," which is the usually given equivalent, or as "spirit," the term that I have used in the Kojiki passages above.

"You will, during your stay, hear a great deal about Japanese religions," said His Royal Highness Prince Takahito Mikasa to his guests at the Congress; "and you will undoubtedly come up against the English word 'god' or 'gods' used as a makeshift translation of the term 'kami,' the object of worship in the cult that is uniquely Japanese. You will also perceive in all probability that the Japanese 'kami' and 'god' are entirely different in essential nature.

"The object of worship of the Japanese Buddhist is 'hotoke' [the Buddha], and insofar as Buddhism is an imported religion, it would be logical to presume that 'hotoke' and 'kami' must be quite different. Nevertheless, it has become quite customary for the Japanese to link the two, and the term 'kamihotoke' is in common usage. Not only is there no contradiction sensed in this combination of what theoretically should be two separate concepts; there are any number of Japanese who can pray, without the slightest compunction, simultaneously to both 'kami' and 'hotoke.' This I believe can be explained in part by the psychology of the Japanese, which tends to favor the emotional rather than the rational. The Japanese take pleasure in sensing the atmosphere, so they tend rather easily to be swayed by environment.

"There is an ancient Japanese poem which in very free translation says:

Unknown to me what resideth here:
Tears flow from a sense of unworthiness and gratitude.

"These lines, it is said, were composed when their author was worshiping at the Grand Shrine of Ise; and I feel that they aptly reflect the religious feeling of many Japanese." [18]

A Shinto rite, then, can be defined as an occasion for the recognition and evocation of an awe that inspires gratitude to the source and nature of being. And as such, it is addressed as art (music, gardening, architecture, dance, etc.) to the sensibilities—not to faculties of definition. So that living Shinto is not the following of some set-down moral code, but a living in gratitude and awe amid the mystery of things. And to retain this sense, the faculties remain open, clean, and pure. That is the meaning of ritual purity. "The kami is pleased, by virtue and sincerity," states a thirteenth-century work compiled by the priests of the Outer Shrine of Ise. "To do good is to be pure; to commit evil is to be impure." [19]

Hence it is incorrect to say that Shinto lacks moral ideas. The basic moral idea is that the processes of nature cannot be evil. And to this there is the corollary that the pure heart follows the processes of nature. Man—a natural thing—is not evil inherently, but is in his pure heart, in his natural being, divine. The fundamental terms are "bright heart" (*akaki kokoro*), "pure heart" (*kiyoki kokoro*), "correct heart" (*tadashiki kokoro*), and "straight heart" (*naoki kokoro*). The first denotes the quality of a heart shining brightly as the sun; the second, a heart clear as a white jewel; the third, a heart inclined to justice; and the last, a heart lovely and without misleading inclinations. All four unite as *seimei shin:* purity and cheerfulness of spirit. [20]

Furthermore, in the inner sanctuaries of the chief shrines there have been preserved from of old—from far beyond the time of record—three symbolic talismans, borne to earth, it is said, by the august grandchild Heaven Plenty, Earth Plenty, Heaven's Sun

Height, Prince Ruddy Rice-Ear Plenty, when kingship descended to Japan. And these are, namely, a mirror (purity); divine sword (courage); and jewel necklace (benevolence).

In sum, then, Shinto, in its chief concern, is devoted to the cultivation of that sentiment which has been termed by Rudolf Otto the one essential of religion, "which, while it admits of being discussed cannot be strictly defined"; to wit: the sense of the numinous.[21] And with a particular inflection, not of fear, not of nausea, not of desire for release, but of experienced gratitude for its mystery. And so, once again: "Unknown to me what resideth here"—what resideth anywhere, in anything of our concern; "tears flow"—for I am actually moved; "from a sense of unworthiness"—as one not perfectly pure of heart; "and gratitude."

"What kami," we read in a fifteenth-century commentary by a learned scholar-statesman, "does Amaterasu Omikami worship in abstinence in the Plain of High Heaven? She worships her own Self within as kami, endeavoring to cultivate divine virtue in her own person by means of inner purity, and thus becoming one with that kami." [22]

And so now, finally, classifying, we may say, in regard to the actual functioning of the cult, that Shinto in old Japan was operative in four spheres: 1. domestic, centering in its gratitude upon the kami of the well, gate, family, garden plot, etc.; also (to quote Langdon Warner) "the recognized but unofficial spirits in cooking fire and cooking pot, the mysterious genius that presides over the process of aging going on in the household pickle jar and the yeast in beer"; [23] furthermore, the parents, the ancestors (a Confucian influence here), and, reciprocally, gratitude from the parent to the child; 2. the local community cult, in gratitude to both the natural phenomena of the scene in which one lives and the honored local dead, the ujigami (i.e., kami of the uji, the "local stock"); 3. the craft cults, honoring gratefully, in the very processes of work, the mysteries and powers of the tools, materials, etc. (It is to be recalled that seamstresses hold requiem services for lost and broken needles; and that the founder of the Japanese pearl industry, Mr. Kokichi Mikimoto [1858–1955], before his death held a requiem for the oysters through whose lives his fortune had been made.)

And then, finally, 4. the national cult, in gratitude to the emperor in his palace, the House of Awe, and to his world-preserving ancestors, the Great Kami of the Kojiki, of whom the greatest—born as the light of the universe from the left eye of the Male Who Invites, following his victory over impurity—is in particular mirrored here on earth at Ise, in the Grand Shrine: at the top of a long rise of majestically wooded land of great rocks and tall, arrow-straight conifers, to which the worshiper ascends by a broad, megalithic stair, as to a natural ziggurat.

IV. The Ways of the Buddha

The golden Buddha that came from Korea in 552 A.D. was not immediately a harbinger of peace. The king who had sent it—together with an assortment of flags, umbrellas, and Buddhist sutras—accompanied his gift with an interesting note. "This doctrine is, of all doctrines, the most excellent," he wrote, "but difficult to explain and to comprehend. Not even the Duke of Chou or Confucius attained to its knowledge. . . . Imagine a man possessing treasures to his heart's content, so that he might satisfy all his wishes in proportion as he used them. . . . Thus it is with the treasure of this wonderful doctrine. Every prayer is fulfilled and nothing lacking. . . . Thy servant, therefore, Myöng, King of Paekche, has humbly dispatched his retainer, so as to fulfill the recorded saying of the Buddha: 'My Law shall spread to the East.' " [24]

And the Emperor Kimmei, we read, leaped for joy; but was not sure what he should do. "The countenance of the Buddha is of a severe dignity," he said to the members of his council. "Should it be worshiped or should it not?"

Iname of the Soga clan replied, "All of the Western frontier lands, without exception, pay it worship; and shall Yamato alone refuse?"

But the leaders of the Mononobe and Nakatomi clans forcefully advised rejection. "Those who have ruled this Empire," they said, "have always taken care to worship, in spring, summer, autumn, and winter, the 180 Great Kami of Heaven and Earth, besides those of the local areas and of grain. But if we now begin to worship foreign kami in their stead, it is to be feared that we may incur the wrath of our own native kami."

The Buddha, that is to say, was being interpreted, not in Buddhist, but in Shinto terms; and the emperor in these simple terms decided. "Let it be given to Iname, who has shown his willingness to receive it. And as an experiment, let him pay it worship."

So Iname, overjoyed, knelt and, receiving the golden image, enthroned it in his house, retired from the world, purified his home, and transformed it into a temple. Whereupon, a pestilence broke out; many people died; no remedy was found and, as time went on, things got worse. The image of the Buddha was accordingly seized and flung into a canal. The temple was burned. But after that the heavens remained clear of clouds, no rain fell, drought ensued, and of a sudden the great hall of the palace broke into flames and was consumed. Then there was seen floating on the sea at night a log of camphor wood, shining brightly, and of this the emperor caused two radiant images of the Buddha to be made. Prodigies followed, some malignant, others benign; shrines arose; the same were destroyed—and with ever-mounting rancor between the Soga and Mononobe clans.[25]

For thirty years thereafter the feud continued until, in the year 587, Iname's son slew the entire Mononobe family; whereafter Buddhist temples arose in number. Five years later he slew the Emperor Sushun and enthroned the reluctant widow, who, as Empress Regnant Suiko (reigned 593–628), appointed to the regency the younger brother of her spouse. And it was only then that the promised blessings of the new Law began to appear. For this beloved Prince Shotoku (573–621) proved to be one of the great and noble rulers of all time.

His mother, it is said, bore him without pain while on a tour of inspection of the palace precincts. "When she came to the Horse Department and had just come to the door of the stables, she was suddenly delivered of him without effort.* He was able to speak as soon as born and when he grew up was so wise that he could attend to the suits of ten men at once and decide them all without error. He learned the Inner Doctrine (Buddhism), studied

* Compare discussion supra, p. 196.

the Outer Classics (Confucianism), and became in both branches proficient." [26] He fostered letters and the arts, prepared the first history of Japan (now lost), promulgated a system of laws and an organization of court ranks, and even before his death was honored by many as a Bodhisattva. In his reign, Buddhism, which in Japan had been the religion mainly of one clan, became a religion of the empire; and the branch of Buddhism favored—as in China—was the Mahayana.

"Concerning differences," wrote the prince, "between the Great and Little Vehicles: in the Great, one thinks primarily of those not seeking emancipation and tries to help them equally by drawing all toward the Buddhist goal; whereas in the Little, one seeks enlightenment for oneself alone, avoids teaching others like the plague, and rejoices in a false nirvana." [27]

In the year 621, second month, fifth day, in the middle of the night, the Imperial Prince Shotoku passed away; and there was sorrow in the palace; sorrow also in the village: the old, as if bereaved of a dear child, had no longer any taste for food, and the young, as though become orphans, filled the ways with sounds of lament. The farmer let go his plow, the pounding woman her pestle, and all said as one: "The sun and moon have lost their light; heaven and earth have gone to ruin. In whom, henceforth, can we trust?" [28]

NARA PERIOD: 710–794 A.D.

Buddhism in Japan had as yet produced no truly native thought. The situation was one simply of eclectic juxtaposition. The kami of the land were faced with a cosmopolitan pantheon of alien derivation, far more sophisticated than anything they themselves had ever represented—or, indeed, than the heart of Yamato could at that time have required. In the court, the new faith was the carrier mainly of a continental civilization that gave to life there a new fashionable tone, while among the folk it was a vehicle of solace. The period—we must note—was that of the fanatic onslaught of Islam across the Near and Middle East and into Europe (fall of Persia, 650; Spain, 711); also, of the far less bloody though no less fanatic cutting down of the Old Germanic sacred shrines and groves by the early Christian mission (Boniface, first Archbishop of Mainz, 732)—which latter deed of clumsy peda- gogy produced in the European psyche a mythic schizophrenia (Insania germanica: *Zwei Seelen wohnen, ach, in meiner Brust!*) that is deeply with us still, and to be analyzed in our volume next to come. Whereas in eighth-century Japan, with a quality of com- passion that in cults of the Levant has been rather talked about than illustrated in act, the Bodhisattvas joined in mutual support with the rustic spirits of the country.

The accord was achieved in four stages:

1. At Nara: period of the first Buddhist capital city of Japan, 710–794 A.D.: A stage when Chinese Buddhist art and thought were arriving in force. The chief symbolic event was the building of the great Todaiji Temple and consecration within it, in the year 752, of a colossal bronze seated Buddha on a lotus of bronze 68 feet in circumference—each petal 10 feet long, the figure it- self 53½ feet high and having a weight of 452 tons, with each eye nearly 4 feet long and each hand nearly 7; the right in the fear-not and the left in the boon-bestowing gestures of India.

2 and 3. At the second Buddhist capital, Heian (now Kyoto): 794–1185 A.D.: First, 794–894, a period of continuing Chinese influence, but with a new turn; for in the teachings of two Jap- anese monks, Dengyo Daishi (767–822) and Kobo Daishi (774– 835), the kami of Japan were recognized as local Bodhisattvas. Furthermore, in the school of the latter there was introduced a new strain of Tantric Buddhist doctrine derived from the Indian university at Nalanda—which at that time was at its peak, sending out developed doctrines of unfolding divine powers in missions northward to Tibet, southward to Indonesia, and eastward into China and Japan.

Next, 894–1185, continuing at Heian: diplomatic and cultural intercourse with T'ang China was discontinued, and in the elegant Fujiwara court described by Lady Murasaki (978–1015?) in her novel Genji Monogatari, an erotic flowery game of sensibility was played, much like that of the twelfth-century troubadours. Cut off from the continent, the Japanese now were developing a Buddhism of their own, which in the following period, of the Kamakura Shogunate, achieved maturity.

4. Kamakura Period: 1185–1392: an intense swing away from the delicate sensibility and aesthetic eroticism of the Fujiwara ladies and their nobles; four vigorous, specifically Japanese Buddhist schools were founded: Jodo, founded by Honen (1133–1212), and Shinshu, founded by his disciple Shinran (1173–1262), both of which were Amida sects; Zen, from the Chinese Ch'an school of Hui-neng but applied to new aims (chief founder, Eisai: 1141–1215); and lastly, the intensely personal, chauvinistic sect of the fisherman's son Nichiren (1222–1282).

It would be delightful to examine at length every aspect of the transformation in Japan of the Indian doctrine of disengagement into one of engagement, gratitude, and awe; but in a work of the present plan no more than the broadest lines can be indicated.

The first stage of the process, we have said, is symbolized in the Great Buddha of Todaiji—where the figure represented is not the Indian Gautama Shakyamuni, but a meditation Buddha, of no time, no place, no race. He is one of a group of five such Guardian Buddhas of the Planes of Meditation, who stand for aspects of the causal sphere, from which all Buddhas, Bodhisattvas, and indeed all beings of the visible universe, proceed. They appear before the inturned mind when it enters their domain of force. And the Sanskrit name of this particular one is Vairochana ("Belonging to, or coming from, the sun"; Japanese: *Dainichi-nyorai,* "Great Sun Buddha"). If we like, we may see in him evidence of an influence from the solar cult of Iran. However, there has never been, in Iran or in any other part of the world westward of the great cultural East-West divide, an ideology or theology with quite the accent of the Vairochana vision.

This mighty figure stands for an aspect of Buddhist realization that is taught in the Avatamsaka Sutra (Japanese: *Kegon,* "Flower Garland"), to which the vast Javanese Buddhist stupa at Borobudur (eighth century A.D.) also bears witness.[29] It is a teaching that is supposed to have been enunciated by the Buddha Gautama directly after enlightenment. But since no one listening could understand a word, he began afresh and taught the simpler dualistic Hinayana, which in time would render the mind eligible to grasp the Mahayana. And in time, indeed, there was such a one, a youth, Sudhana by name, who departed on a pilgrimage (which is represented in the panels of the second and third galleries of the stupa at Borobudur), in the course of which he addressed himself to fifty-three great teachers. Some of these were living men and women; others were Meditation Buddhas. And what he learned was this wonderful teaching of the Flower Garland.

The doctrine is central to all of the Buddhist sects of Japan and requires an attempt on our part, therefore, to represent at least one or two of its most suggestive points. What it represents, in the main, is a further application of the primary doctrine of the Buddha summarized above in the twelve-linked chain of causation, which, it will be recalled, proceeds from 1. ignorance, 2. action, 3. new inclinations, etc., . . . on to 11. rebirth, and 12. old age, disease, and death.* All beings, according to this law, were self-creating in as much as 11, rebirth, was seen to be the result of 1, ignorance. As presented in this twelve-linked chain, the teaching of the Buddha gives stress to the idea of a sequence in time: first this, then that, then the next; or as they say, "derivation from an antecedent." In the further extension of this teaching in the Wreath, the idea is added of an interdependence equally in space: the universe, that is to say, is correlative, is generally interdependent and thus "mutually originating": no single being exists in and of itself. Or, in the words of the learned Professor Junjiro Takakusu: "We can call it the causation by the common action-influence of all beings." [30]

So that the problem of causation now is read in terms of both time and space simultaneously; which together constitute what is known as the matrix of the thus-come (*tathāgata garbha*), the way of the being of things, within which the Buddha, *tathāgata,* is concealed—but simultaneously revealed. This is the wreath, the circle of petals, within which the colossal Solar Buddha sits, with one of his hands saying "Fear not" while the other is rendering all the boons of being. And the Japanese people pouring into this

* Supra, pp. 273–74.

temple, gazing at the Buddha, bowing in humility, circulating in gratitude, and going out again, are themselves flowers of the garland through which he is both concealed and revealed.

This teaching is called the Doctrine of the World of Totalistic Harmony Mutually Relating and Penetrating; and to elucidate its insight "Ten Profound Theories" have been taught, of which four will suffice for our present view:

1. The Profound Theory of Correlation, according to which all things coexist, simultaneously arising. They coexist, furthermore, not only in relation to space, but also in relation to time; for past, present, and future include each other. "Distinct as they are, and separated as they seem to be in time, all beings are united to make one entity—from the universal point of view." [31]

2. The Profound Theory of Perfect Freedom, according to which all beings, great and small, commune with one another without obstruction; so that the power of each partakes of that of all and so is limitless. *"Even in a hair there are innumerable golden lions."* [32] One act, however small, includes all acts.

5. The Profound Theory of Complementarity, according to which both the hidden and the manifest constitute the whole by mutual reinforcement. "If one is inside, the other will be outside, or vice versa." [33] By complementarity they constitute a unit.

10. The Profound Theory of the Completion of the Common Virtue, according to which a leader and his following, the chief and his retinue, work together harmoniously and brightly; for, "according to the one-in-all and all-in-one principle, they really form one complete whole," [34]—permeating each other by inter-reflection.

And so that is the wonderful teaching of the Flower Wreath Sutra, known in Japan as Kegon, the object of which is the establishment of a harmonious totality of all beings, as a garland around the Buddha-nature of each. And the sense of it all is in the active body no less than in the meditating mind, so that the practice of religion is life. But to *realize* this, two things are needed: the Vow of Bodhisattvahood (*praṇidhāna*), which is, to work without cease to bring all beings—oneself included—to the realization of Buddhahood, and equally, compassion (*karuṇā*).[35]

HEIAN PERIOD: 794–1185 A.D.

The second major step toward an essentially Japanese Buddhist realization was taken when Dengyo Daishi (767–822) and Kobo Daishi (774–835), set sail in the year 804 for China.

The priestly order founded by the former on his return is called Tendai (Chinese, T'ien-t'ai), after the mountain monastery in South China founded by Chih-kai (531–597),* who is supposed to have been a disciple of Bodhidharma. But Bodhidharma, if historical, was in China c. 520–528(!).

The basic doctrine of Tendai is that the Buddha Mind is in all things—which, of course, we have heard now a thousand times. But the particular thought here, which gives to this order its own character and has made it a very strong force in the shaping of the popular Buddhism of later Japan, is the following: that the Lotus Sutra, "The Lotus of the True Law" (*Saddharmapuṇḍarīka*) is itself the Buddha. For the Buddha in the course of his career taught numerous ways to various groups. He taught the way of boundless giving, the way also of the Hinayana, the way of the Great Delight, and at the end of his days, most profoundly, the Lotus of the True Law. Moreover, at the moment of his passing, the Buddha said to those about him: "Do not grieve, saying 'Our Master has passed away!' *What I have taught will be your Master after my death*. If you hold to and practice my teachings, will that not be as though my Law Body were remaining here forever?" [36] But the Lotus of the True Law, the culminating doctrine, is the summary of the rest. Therefore, the Lotus Sutra is the Law Body of the Buddha.

But now we must add to this one further thought: that between eternity and time—Law Body and Phenomenal Body, that and this—there is no distinction. One is not to suppose that there exists anywhere an abiding, motionless Buddha Substance around which the qualities of reality move and change. On the contrary: the "true" state which is no state may be regarded provisionally as opposite to "this state" which is phenomenal; however, the middle, the Middle Way, is over and above, nay, is identical with both.

* Supra, p. 448.

The Living Buddha and his Law Body were not different from each other; nor is the Law Body other than the Lotus Sutra. But things equal to the same thing are equal to each other; and so, the Lotus Sutra is the Living Buddha.

Something considerably more complex arrived, however, with the return of the second voyager, Kobo Daishi, who in China had studied the Indian Tantric mystery known as the "True Word" (Sanskrit, *mantra;* Chinese, *Chen Yen;* Japanese, *Shingon*). The basic concept here is comparable to that of the Roman Catholic Mass, where, by pronouncing properly the solemn words of consecration, the anointed priestly celebrant actually changes bread and wine into the body and blood of Christ. The appearances remain, but the substance changes into God. In the Buddhist-Hindu Tantric schools, as well, the idea prevails that the "True Word" can work such effects. There is the additional idea there, however, which is essential to all Oriental thought, that the sphere of divinity, the Buddha sphere, is within the celebrant himself: the miracle takes place within the celebrant; it is he—or she—that is transubstantiated.

The celebrant, therefore, is to assume the posture of the Buddha-principle invoked. He is thereby placed in accord with that principle at once in thought (*dhyāna*), word (*mantra*), and body posture (*mudrā*). Thus this very body of ours becomes the Buddha.

Furthermore, in line with the Hindu-Buddhist notion of numerous degrees, orders, or forms of divine manifestation, numerous symbolic images have become associated with this development, offering models, so to say, for the posture system associated with the mantras. And these are classified in two large categories: 1. those of the circle of the diamond or thunderbolt body (*vajra*), representing aspects of the realm of the indestructible, true, or diamond state, the pivotal figure of this group being the great Solar Buddha, Vairochana, surrounded by his emanations; and then 2. those of the circle of the womb (*garbha*), symbolizing the order of the changing world, which was termed above the matrix of the thus-come, and is symbolized in Indian Buddhist art by the goddess-lotus of the world.*

* Supra, pp. 301–302.

Kobo Daishi assigned the kami of his native land to membership in the womb circle; so that whereas formerly the Buddhas had been viewed as kami, now the kami could be viewed as Buddhathings. A two-way interplay was thereby achieved. In addition, the Indian Tantric magic became combined with the Japanese shamanistic tradition, and again, a two-way interplay was achieved. This powerful, popular as well as elite, dual order was known as *Ryobu Shinto,* "Two Aspect Shinto." The Tendai sect joined the movement, terming its own approach "One Reality Shinto" (*Ichijitsu Shinto*). So that even before the intercourse with China was discontinued, Japan had begun to make Buddhism its own.

It was only in the second phase of the Heian Period, however, that Japan began to exhibit its own style through every aspect of its newly assimilated higher culture stage. Professor Langdon Warner, in a sensitive discussion, points out, for example, that by the tenth and eleventh centuries, "almost suddenly, and certainly without debt to foregoing schools of painting, the Japanese were producing long horizontal scrolls of such narrative as the world had never seen. While the Chinese of those decades, and later, gave you moods of landscape and of weather charged with all they can imply for human beings who are sensitive to nature, the Japanese showed peopled narratives beyond compare. . . .

"The main difference," he concludes, "is the fact that the Chinese were largely interested in matters of philosophy, while the Japanese emphasized Man and what happened in the material world at a particular time." [37]

We have already remarked that in China the vocabulary of Taoism associated the idea of the Tao with the order of nature, in heaven and on earth; so that the ideal of the sage was of a man who, like the mythical mystic Lao Tzu himself, had escaped from the social sphere to nature, where his own nature had developed amid the noble influences of mountains, waters, trees, and wonderful mists. For among these, the mysteries announced in the Book of Changes were everywhere variously apparent, and by a principle of spiritual resonance, one's own nature there recovered spontaneity. Whereas in India, on the other hand, the ideal aim had been of release (*mokṣa*), not merely from the human sphere but from the cosmic as well.

The learned Professor of Oriental Philosophy, Dr. Hajime Nakamura, of Tokyo University, made an extremely important point in a talk delivered in Rangoon in 1955. The concept of *freedom* is rendered in Chinese and Japanese, he pointed out, by the same two ideograms: those denoting *self* and *cause* (self-cause, self-motivation, or spontaneity, would seem to be the sense). "But," as he then observed, "while in China 'freedom' meant *liberation from the human nexus* (Pu-hua, for example, acting like a madman, constantly ringing his bell, was an idiot sage), in Japan it meant *compliance with the human nexus*—through devotion to secular activities." [38]

We have followed the course in China of the transformation of the Indian Buddhist doctrine of release into one of spontaneity —in the doctrine of the Ch'an school of Hui-neng. We have now to watch a further shift of accent in Japan to the world of men and to men of the world: or rather, we have already seen the accent shift. For already in the words of Prince Shotoku we have heard the keynote sounded; and in the one-in-all, all-in-one doctrine of the World of Totalistic Harmony Mutually Relating and Penetrating, this note was expanded to a fortissimo in concerto. In fact, all that need now be said is that the remainder of the history of Buddhism in Japan is, by and large, the reflex of the differing human nexuses to which the doctrine has been applied.

The Indian Buddhist was disillusioned in the universe, the Chinese in society, the Japanese—not at all. So that, whereas the Indian retreat was to the Void and the Chinese either to the Family (Confucius) or to Nature (Lao Tzu), the Japanese did not retreat but stood exactly where he was, simply magnified his kami into Buddha-things, and saw this world itself, with all its joy as well as oddities and sorrow, as the Golden Lotus World, right here and now.

And one of the first of the various human nexuses in Japan to take on the radiance of the Golden Lotus was the palace-world of the Heian court.

It was an age [writes Professor Masaharu Anesaki] of the "cloud gallants" and the "flower maidens," of the luxurious nobles and ladies who moved amidst the romantic and artificial surroundings of the Imperial court. It was an epoch of aestheticism and sentimentalism, in which free rein was given to emotions that were refined and cultivated by the somewhat enervating atmosphere of the Imperial capital. Every member of this picturesque society, man or woman, was a poet, sensitive to the charm of nature and eager to express every phase of feeling in verse. Their intimate feeling for nature and for the varied emotions of the human heart was expressed in the word *aware,* which meant both "pity" and "sympathy." This sentiment had its source in the tender romanticism of the age; it owed much, too, to the Buddhist teaching of the oneness of existences, of the basic unity that joins together different beings, and which persists through the changing incarnations of one individual. That conviction of the continuity of life, both in this existence and hereafter, deepened the sentimental note and widened the sympathetic reach of *aware.* It is not strange that the reign of *aware* produced many romances of love, both in actual life and in the stories of the period.[39]

The Western reader will recognize in *aware* a quality properly comparable to the twelfth-century courtly troubadour ideal of the gentle heart, susceptible to the pure, ennobling sentiment of love. However, in Japan, as Professor Anesaki shows, the sentiment was opened out to include all of nature and the universe.

"Buddhism," he writes, "impressed on the 'cloud gallants' and 'flower maidens' of that time a sense of the oneness of life."

Their sentiment, *aware,* is therefore actually an echo, very gentle, of the deep pang of the young Prince Gautama in his own palace period of the realization of death. There is a phrase, *mono no aware wo shiru:* "to be aware of the pity of things." However, instead of a graveyard vision, the gallants and maids of the Fujiwara garden of life saw in the world, rather, a festival of the beauty of falling blossoms.

KAMAKURA PERIOD: 1185–1333 A.D.

When the Heike were routed at Ichi no tani, and their nobles and courtiers were fleeing to the shore to escape in their ships, Kumagai Naozane came riding along a narrow path onto the beach, with the intention of intercepting one of their captains. Just then his eye fell on a single horseman who was attempting to reach one of the ships in the offing. The horse he rode was dappled-gray, and its saddle glittered with gold mounting. Not doubting that he was one of the chief captains, Kumagai beckoned to him with his war fan, crying out: "Shameful! to show an enemy your back. Return! Return!"

The warrior turned his horse and rode back to the beach, where Kumagai at once engaged him in mortal combat. Quickly hurling him to the ground, he sprang upon him and tore off his helmet to cut off his head, when he beheld the face of a youth of sixteen or seventeen, delicately powdered and with blackened teeth, just about the age of his own son and with features of great beauty. "Who are you?" he asked. "Tell me your name, for I would spare your life."

"Nay, first say who you are," replied the young man.

"I am Kumagai Naozane of Musashi, a person of no particular importance."

"Then you have made a good capture," said the youth. "Take my head and show it to some of my side, and they will tell you who I am."

"Though he is one of their leaders," mused Kumagai, "if I slay him it will not turn victory into defeat, and if I spare him, it will not turn defeat into victory. When my son Kojiro was but slightly wounded at Ichi no tani this morning, did it not pain me? How this young man's father would grieve to hear that he had been killed! I will spare him."

Just then, looking behind him, he saw Doi and Kajiwara coming up with fifty horsemen. "Alas! look there," he exclaimed, the tears running down his face, "though I would spare your life, the whole countryside swarms with our men, and you cannot escape them. If you must die, let it be by my hand, and I will see that prayers are said for your rebirth in Paradise."

"Indeed it must be so," said the young warrior. "Cut off my head at once."

Kumagai was so overcome by compassion that he could scarcely wield his blade. His eyes swam and he hardly knew what he did, but there was no help for it; weeping bitterly, he cut off the boy's head. "Alas!" he cried, "what life is so hard as that of a soldier? Only because I was born of a warrior family must I suffer this affliction! How lamentable it is to do such cruel deeds!" He pressed his face to the sleeve of his armor and wept bitterly. Then, wrapping up the head, he was

stripping off the young man's armor when he discovered a
flute in a brocade bag. "Ah," he exclaimed, "it was this youth
and his friends who were amusing themselves with music
within the walls this morning. Among all our men of the Eastern Provinces I doubt if there is any one of them who has
brought a flute with him. How gentle the ways of these
courtiers!"

When he brought the flute to the Commander, all who saw it
were moved to tears; he discovered then that the youth was
Atsumori, the youngest son of Tsunemori, aged sixteen
years.—From this time the mind of Kumagai was turned
toward the religious life.[40]

The date is 1184; the occasion, the extinction of the Taira
(Heike) clan by the Minamoto (Genji); the period the opening
of four and a quarter centuries of feudal strife, parallel to those
of Europe from the brilliant Third Crusade to the murder of
Mary Queen of Scots; and the sentiment is *awaré:* "alas!"

The warriors of Islam are now disintegrating India; the Mongols
are in China and the Golden Horde in the Russias; on the waters
of the Pacific, eastward of Japan, Polynesian warrior kings are
pressing claims to every circle of palms on the broad sea; and beyond, two military, priestly empires, Inca and Aztec, are being
built on crushed flesh and bone. The characteristic foci of all the
religions of the age are the sumptuous moated palace and armed
camp; the peasant's hut and illiterate village; magical temples and
cathedrals, which in this period are brought to a climax of icono-
graphic splendor; and the gradually growing, raucous towns. As
in Europe, so in Japan, we discover the gallantry of the flower
of knighthood, banditry, *awaré* and the gentle heart, military
monks, meditating cloisters, and ladies with their pillow books.

We hear also of a new breed of friars, donning sandals and
ragged robes, to move among and minister to the poor: in Europe,
Dominic (1170–1221) and Francis (1182–1226), and in Japan,
Honen (1133–1212) and Shinran (1173–1262).

Buddhism in the Kamakura Period (1185–1333)—the moment
of its maturation in Japan—was of two trends: *jiriki,* "own strength,
self-reliance"; and *tariki,* "other's strength, salvation by interces-

sion." The latter was represented principally by the cult of Amida; the former by Zen. The chief teachers of the latter were the saints Honen and Shinran; of the former, Eisai (1141–1215) and Dogen (1200–1253). And the social spheres in which the latter flourished were largely the chambers of the gentlewomen and villages of the poor, while those of the former were the manly warrior camps.

The simple act of calling upon Amida had been known in Japan for many years. Ennin, from whose diary of the Chinese persecution we have quoted, was on his return to Japan a devotee and propagandist of Amida. Many wandering folk priests among the villages also had taught his name. The formal establishment of a specific Pure Land (Jodo) Sect as a churchly religion within the Mahayana fold, however, with its own monks, nuns, and temples, was the work of the saintly Honen, carrier of the message of the Buddha's paradise to the poor. *Namu Amida Butsu,* "Praise Amida Buddha," as a pious aspiration pronounced repeatedly in every circumstance as well as in special religious services amid the inspiration of lights, bells, incense, and the rest, became established through his mission as a fundamental tradition of prodigious influence in the religious life of Japan. And the goal was not Buddhahood or enlightenment here on earth, but an afterlife in beatitude, through which, in due course, nirvana would be achieved. The method was not the practice of any self-reliant disciplines, but thoughtful, pious invocation, in reliance on the Buddha's vow. And the earthly benefit was a change of heart, as an effect of this simple religious practice readily available to all.

Honen was but eight years old when his father was slain, dying with the wish that his son should seek not revenge but the Buddha; and the boy that year joined the Tendai order as a priest. At the age of forty-two he was seized with the idea of devotion to Amida's name, and thereafter, for the remainder of his life, carried his message to a people suddenly assailed with slaughter, war cries, and heroes on every side.

But the full translation of Amida into the secular living of Japan was achieved only by his chief disciple Shinran—who had been bereaved of his father when he was three, mother when he was eight, became a child priest of the Tendai order, and when twenty-eight met Honen, who died when Shinran was thirty-nine. The innovation that Shinran achieved in the worship of Amida was twofold. In the first place, rejecting the monastic ideal as invalid for Japan, he left the monastery, assumed the layman's role, and married. The lesson of this act was that worship is not a special task or way, but coextensive with life, identical with one's daily task whatever it may be. And in the second place, he gave stress not to the vow and paradise of Amida, but to a crisis of awakening within the worshiper himself, which he termed "the awakening of faith," the sense of which was an actual realization (which might, however, remain unconscious while transmuting every aspect of one's thought, speech, and action) of the reality of the truth of the Flowery Wreath, that one is all and all are one. Coextensive with this awakening is gratitude to the world; and the calling of the name thereafter is in thanksgiving. Indeed, the method now is not, as in the Jodo of Honen, the calling of the name, but living life and listening to the teaching in an attitude of gratitude, cultivating faith in the mystery symbolized in the figure of the Solar Buddha Amida. And the awakening comes, not through effort, but of itself.[41]

In Zen, on the other hand, which in the period of its introduction to Japan became the Buddhism of the samurai, an essentially non-theological view is taken of the problem of illuminated life. All things are Buddha things. Buddhahood is within. Look within, the Buddha will be found. Act in this orientation and Buddhahood will act. *Freedom* ("self-motivation," "spontaneity") is itself the manifestation of the Solar Buddha, which egoity, anxiety, fear, forcing, reasoning, etc., only impede, distort, and block. In India, in the yoga system of Patanjali, the aim of yoga was described as "the intentional stopping of the spontaneous activity of the mind-stuff." * In Zen, on the contrary, the aim is, rather, to let the mind stuff proceed in all its motility spontaneously.

> Sitting quietly, doing nothing,
> Spring comes, and the grass grows by itself.

* Supra, p. 27.

"This 'by itself,' " as Alan W. Watts observes, "is the mind's and the world's natural way of action, as when the eyes see by themselves, and the ears hear by themselves, and the mouth opens by itself without having to be forced apart by the fingers." [42]

And in the nexus of warcraft: "Perfection in the art of swordsmanship is reached," wrote Eugen Herrigel in his *Zen in the Art of Archery,* "when the heart is troubled by no more thought of I and You, of the opponent and his sword, of one's own sword and how to wield it—no more thought even of life and death. 'All is emptiness: your own self, the flashing sword, and the arms that wield it. Even the thought of emptiness is no longer there.' From this absolute emptiness, states Takuan, 'comes the most wondrous unfoldment of doing.' " [43]

To a certain degree, any great athlete or performer will recognize this last as, what we term, being "in form." Zen, it might be said, is the art of being "in form" for everything, all the time. There is no blocking: all perfectly flows. And Buddhahood is in this, in so far as no intrusive egoity is in play. Egoity is in play only in the neophyte, the amateur, the dub; in the perfectly trained professional it does not exist. And so, in Zen we find, so to say, the Buddhahood of competence in art. In the art of the samurai, it was applied to warcraft. In the later periods and other spheres of life in Japan, its principles were applied to all or any of the arts: in monasteries, to the art of meditation; in the tea room, to the art of serving tea; comparably in painting, calligraphy, etc., to the act "in form."

And now, finally, one more important movement is to be noted: that of the fiery son of a fisherman, Nichiren, who asked himself in his fifteenth year, "What was the Truth taught by the Buddha?" and in his quest decided that a revival of Tendai would represent the nearest approach to that truth. For it is there that the idea is stressed of that ultimate principle of Buddhahood which is eternal, the Buddha of immeasurable ages, ever acting as the Enlightener, of whom the historical Buddhas, Meditation Buddhas, Bodhisattvas, and the rest, are but the modes of appearance. The terms "Buddha of Original Position," and "Buddha of Trace-leaving

Manifestation," epitomize the dichotomy. Nichiren denounced all
the other ways being taught, therefore, as deluding devotions to
the mere traces. They are of the realms of *upāya,* "approaches,"
"masks," or "expediencies," whereas the final, "one vehicle for
all," of the last half of the Lotus Sutra shows the teaching of the
Realm of Origin itself.

Nichiren condemned Honen as an enemy of all the Buddhas,
scriptures, sages, and people of all time, and asked the government to take a hand to terminate his heresy: Jodo is hell; Zen,
the devil; Shingon, national ruin. Nichiren himself was mobbed,
and banished; but returned. He saw Japan as the land of Buddhist
destiny, for the restoration of Buddhism and therewith illumination of the world. The Chinese Mongol dynasty was at that time
seriously threatening an invasion of Japan. Nichiren, whose name
means Sun (*nichi*) Lotus (*ren*), declared that his religious reform would save the day. "I will be the pillar of Japan; I will be
the eyes of Japan; I will be the vessel of Japan," he wrote, and
he began to think of himself as the Bodhisattva Vishishtacharita
("Distinguished Action"), to whom the Buddha had entrusted the
work of protecting the truth.[44]

In his cult, as in the Tendai, it is the Lotus Sutra that receives
the worship, and the prayer that is repeated, even shouted, to the
beat—dondon dondoko dondon—of a drum, is *Namu Myōhō-
renge-kyō:* "Hail to the Lotus of the True Law!" And of himself,
in the end, alone in a mountain hermitage, he wrote: "I know
that my breast is the place where all the Buddhas are immersed
in contemplation; know that they turn the Wheel of Truth upon
my tongue; that my throat is giving birth to them; and that they
are attaining Supreme Enlightenment in my mouth. . . . As the
Truth is noble, so is the man who embodies it; as the man is noble,
so is the place where he resides." [45]

The numbers in Japan professing to be adherents of the sects
we have reviewed are today about as follows: [46] Amida (Shinshu
and Jodo), 13,238,924; Nichiren, 9,120,028; Shingon, 7,530,531;
Zen (Rinzai and Soto), 4,317,541; Tendai, 2,141,502; Kegon,
57,620; all other Buddhist sects, 608,385.

v. The Way of Heroes

"We were invited to follow the Japanese witness into the *hondo* or main hall of the temple, where the ceremony was to be performed. It was an imposing scene." So begins A. B. Mitford's account of a Japanese ritual suicide.

A large hall with a high roof supported by dark pillars of wood: From the ceiling hung a profusion of those huge gilt lamps and ornaments peculiar to Buddhist temples. In front of the high altar, where the floor, covered with beautiful white mats, is raised some three or four inches from the ground, was laid a rug of scarlet felt. Tall candles placed at regular intervals gave out a dim mysterious light, just sufficient to let all the proceedings be seen. The seven Japanese took their places on the left of the raised floor, the seven foreigners on the right. No other person was present.

After the interval of a few minutes of anxious suspense, Taki Zenzaburo, a stalwart man thirty-two years of age, with a noble air, walked into the hall attired in his dress of ceremony, with the peculiar hempen-cloth wings which are worn on great occasions. He was accompanied by a *kaishaku* and three officers, who wore the *jimbaori* or war surcoat with gold tissue facings. The word *kaishaku*, it should be observed, is one to which our word executioner is no equivalent term. The office is that of a gentleman: in many cases it is performed by a kinsman or friend of the condemned, and the relation between them is rather that of principal and second than that of victim and executioner. In this instance the *kaishaku* was a pupil of Taki Zenzaburo, and was selected by friends of the latter from among their own number for his skill in swordsmanship.

With the *kaishaku* on his left hand, Taki Zenzaburo advanced slowly towards the Japanese witnesses, and the two bowed before them, then drawing near the foreigners they saluted us in the same way, perhaps even with more deference; in each case the salutation was ceremoniously returned. Slowly and with great dignity the condemned man mounted onto the raised floor, prostrated himself before the high altar twice, and seated himself on the felt carpet with his back to the high altar, the *kaishaku* crouching on his left hand side. One of the three attendant officers then came forward, bearing a stand of the kind used in the temple offerings, on which, wrapped in paper, lay the *wakizashi,* the short sword or dirk of the Japanese, nine inches and a half in length, with a point and an edge as sharp as a razor's. This he handed, prostrating himself, to the condemned man, who received it reverently, raising it to his head with both hands, and placed it in front of himself.

After another profound obeisance, Taki Zenzaburo, in a voice which betrayed just so much emotion and hesitation as might be expected from a man who is making a painful confession, but with no sign of either in his face or manner, spoke as follows:

"I, and I alone, unwarrantably gave the order to fire on the foreigners at Kobe, and again as they tried to escape. For this crime I disembowel myself, and I beg you who are present to do me the honor of witnessing the act."

Bowing once more, the speaker allowed his upper garments to slip down to his girdle, and remained naked to the waist. Carefully, according to custom, he tucked his sleeves under his knees to prevent himself from falling backward; for a noble Japanese gentleman should die falling forwards. Deliberately, with a steady hand he took the dirk that lay before him; he looked at it wistfully, almost affectionately; for a moment he seemed to collect his thoughts for the last time, and then stabbing himself deeply below the waist in the left-hand side, he drew the dirk slowly across to his right side, and turning it in the wound, gave a slight cut upwards. During this sickeningly painful operation he never moved a muscle of his face. When he drew out the dirk, he leaned forward and stretched out his neck; an expression of pain for the first time crossed his face, but he uttered no sound. At that moment the *kaishaku,* who, still crouching by his side, had been keenly watching his every movement, sprang to his feet, poised his sword for a second in the air; there was a flash, a heavy, ugly thud, a crashing fall; with one blow the head had been severed from the body.

A dead silence followed, broken only by the hideous noise of the blood throbbing out of the inert head before us, which but a moment before had been a brave and chivalrous man. It was horrible.

The *kaishaku* made a low bow, wiped his sword with a piece of paper which he had ready for the purpose, and retired from the raised floor; and the stained dirk was solemnly borne away, a bloody proof of the execution.

The two representatives of the Mikado then left their places, and crossing over to where the foreign witnesses sat, called to us to witness that the sentence of death upon Taki Zenzaburo had been faithfully carried out. The ceremony being at an end, we left the temple.[47]

We have come a long way since the period of the hieratic city states and the royal tombs of Ur—and yet, not; for the basic principle here, as there, is that of the full and solemn identification of the individual with his socially assigned role. Life in civilization is conceived as a grandiose, noble play, enacted on the world stage; and the function of each is to render his part without blockage through any fault of the personality. Taki Zenzaburo, on a certain occasion, had misplayed. There was, however, a formal style of exit from the stage, which, in its rigor, provided him with an occasion to prove that his fundamental identification was not with the character responsible for the accident (namely, himself as a freely acting individual), but with his part. And in the same spirit, we read innumerable accounts in the Japanese annals of totally gallant men and women who in the character of their roles have gone even eagerly to death—most impressively in the ritual act known as *junshi,* dead-following.

The haniwa figures placed around the mound-tombs of the Yamato period were substitutes for live victims; yet the custom of the living following the dead has continued in Japan to the very present. In the period of the great feudal wars it was revived in force, and at the death of a daimyo, fifteen or twenty of his retainers would disembowel themselves. For centuries thereafter, even against the firm rulings of the Tokugawa Shogunate (1603–1868), heroic players of the old school insisted on playing on. Against orders, for example, a certain Uyemon no Hyoge disemboweled himself in the late seventeenth century at the death of his lord, Okudaura Tadamasa; and the government promptly confiscated the lands of his family, executed two of his sons, and sent the rest of the household into exile. Other loyal followers, when their lords died, would shave their heads and become Buddhist monks.[48] But even as late as 1912, the general Count Nogi, hero of Port Arthur, committed suicide at the precise hour of the burial of the Mikado, Meiji Tenno; and his wife, the Countess Nogi, then killed herself to accompany her spouse.[49]

The proper conduct of the female in such a case was to cut her throat, after having tied her legs together with a belt, so that whatever the agonies of her death might be, her body would be found properly composed.[50]

And there is an interesting brief poem celebrating the suicide of Count Nogi, composed by the editor, Ruiko Kuroiwa, of the newspaper *Yorozo Choho,* which reads as follows:

> Falsely, I thought him
> An old soldier:
> Today, I confess him
> God Incarnate.[51]

Bushido, "the Way (*do;* Chinese *tao*) of the Warrior (*bushi*)," has been called the soul of Japan. I would say, in larger view, that it is the soul of the Orient; and, larger still, of the archaic world. For it is the hieratic ideal of the mighty play.

vi. The Way of Tea

We have found that in Mesopotamia, c. 2500 B.C., a psychology of mythic dissociation broke the old spell of the identity of man and the divine, which division was inherited by the later mythic systems of the West, but that this did not occur either in Egypt or in the Orient eastward of Iran. Japan participates in the Oriental system and is, in fact, its most vital representative in the modern world.

But there is something no less important, which Japan shares with the West, which I would delineate in terms rather of time than of geography; for, though at the opposite margins of the Asiatic continent, Japan and Western Europe matured about simultaneously and at the same pace. The Yayoi Period (300 B.C.–300 A.D.) can be compared with the European Celtic and the Yamato with the period of Germanic Völkerwanderung; the age of the entry and early propagation of Buddhism, from the reception of the Korean gift to the termination of intercourse with T'ang China (552–894) can be compared with the contemporary Merovingian–Carolingian European age (c. 500–900). Likewise, the centuries of courtly Heian aestheticism suggest in many ways the flowering in Europe of the arts of courtly love. while in both domains a number of culminating religious movements appear in the thirteenth century (Honen, Shinran, Eisai, Nichiren: Dominic, Francis, Aquinas); whereafter, in Japan until 1638 (expulsion of the Jesuits) and Europe until 1648 (end of Thirty Years' War), comparable periods of disintegrating feudal ties and increasingly fierce dynastic and religious struggles supervened.

It might even be worth noticing that in fourteenth-century Japan things came to such a pass that from 1339 to 1392 there were two Mikados, each supported by a great feudal house, while in Europe from 1378 to 1418 there were two, and finally three, Popes excommunicating one another. Langdon Warner has remarked in Japanese art and life during the late fourteenth and early fifteenth centuries, a new "half-secular tendency." "For, as in the European Renaissance, there was an end to the ancient tradition that all the arts were essentially handmaidens to religion." [52] Nor is Warner the only Western scholar to have noticed such analogies. A French observer of some fifty years ago, M. de la Mazelière, wrote as follows:

> Toward the middle of the sixteenth century, all was confusion in Japan, in the government, in society, in the church. But the civil wars, the manners returning to barbarism, the necessity for each to execute justice for himself, formed men comparable to those Italians of the sixteenth century in whom Taine praises "the vigorous initiative, the habit of sudden resolutions and desperate undertakings, the grand capacity to do and to suffer." In Japan as in Italy "the rude manners of the Middle Ages made of man a superb animal, wholly militant and wholly resistant." And this is why the sixteenth century displays in the highest degree the principal quality of the Japanese race, that great diversity which one finds there between minds as well as between temperaments. While in India and even in China men seem to differ chiefly in degree of energy or intelligence, in Japan they differ by originality of character as well. . . . Using an expression dear to Nietzsche, we might say that in continental Asia, to speak of humanity is to speak of its plains, while the analogy for Japan as for Europe is, above all, of its mountains. [53]

Also to be remarked is the fact that in the matter of landscape Japan, like Europe, lacks those immense inhuman wastes that in

Asia impress the human spirit with the sublime indifference of the universe to man. The gentle, charming landscapes, where the four seasons—autumn coloring and all—exhibit themselves to man's delight, suggest a world, rather, fitted to humanity; a world that has a power even to humanize humanity. This may have facilitated the Japanese shift of focus from the nature landscapes of the great Chinese masters to peopled countrysides and lively city and town scenes. The breach between the ways of man and nature were in Japan not so great or perceptible as in China.

In any case, the final point that I would make in this brief survey of the functioning and transformations of mythology in Japan, is that in the course of four grim centuries of feudal disintegration, there was produced, as from a highly fired kiln, an extraordinary glass-hard yet intensely poignant civilization, wherein the qualities of the entire religious inheritance of the Far East have become transmuted to secular ends. The world feeling of Shinto, that the processes of nature cannot be evil, together with its zeal for purity, and the clean house as well as heart, where the processes become manifest unencumbered: the recognition of ineffable wonder in little things, and then the Buddhist lesson of the Flower Wreath that all is one and one is all, mutually arising—which adds to the Shinto mystique a magnitude: the Taoist feeling for the order of nature and Confucian for the Tao in human relationships, along with the Buddhist of the One Way that all things are following to the Buddhahood that is already theirs: the idea of the leader and his retinue, and therewith, the Buddhist recognition of sorrow, not with a violent revulsion (Hinayana), but with affirmative compassion, sympathy, pity, and "an awareness of the sigh of things" (*mono no awaré wo shiru*): [54] the lesson of Shinran that the way for Japan was not asceticism but the normal layman's life lived properly in gratitude, toward an awakening of faith in the reality of the Flower Wreath, which will occur of itself; and the further stress in Zen upon tenacity in discipline with a view to pristine spontaneity in action—through all of which the basic hero virtues of the gallant Warrior Way are fostered, of loyalty with courage, veracity, self-control, and benevolence, together with a willingness to play fully one's given role in the masquerade of life: these were the viable lessons drawn from their remarkably composite yet firmly synthesized mythological inheritance by the Japanese.

And from the fourteenth century onward, these produced an array of mutually enriching secular, folk as well as elite, arts, through all of which an aesthetic order prevailed of enchantment. Gardens were devised that brought nature itself into the manifoldly symbolic play, not as merely its theater, but as an active participant, evoking at every turn a recognition both of humanity and of something else which is yet the same: great gardens, opening to vistas of far villages; little gardens, within doors. We catch the savor of the Zen verse:

A long thing is the long Body of the Buddha;
A short thing is the short Body of the Buddha.[55]

A number of highly styled types of theater came into being, numerous new arts, games, and manners of festival. The enchanted geisha world developed—to remind Japan of a point little stressed by the shaven Indian monks, namely that when the Buddha, at the age of eighty (and so, well seasoned in the wisdom of the Farther Shore), was about to leave the fond city of Vaisali for the last time, to pass into utter extinction, the reigning princes of the ancient Licchavi family had hoped to entertain him at a farewell dinner: but the most elegant courtesan of the capital had presented her invitation first. And when the Buddha then departed from that city, together with his cousin Ananda, he paused to rest on a neighboring hill and, looking back over the pleasant scenery with its numerous sanctuaries, holy trees, and shrines, said to Ananda: "Colorful and rich, resplendent and attractive is India; and lovable, charming, is the life of men." [56]

But a central discipline of all this urbane spirituality was tea. For the act of drinking tea is a normal, secular, common day affair; so also is sitting in a room with friends. And yet, consider what happens when you resolve to pay full attention to every single aspect of the act of drinking tea while sitting in a room with friends, selecting first your best, most appropriate bowls, setting these down in the prettiest way, using an interesting pot, sharing with a few friends who go well together, and providing things for them to look at: a few flowers perfectly composed, so that each will shine with its own beauty and the organization of the group also will be radiant: a picture in accord, selected for the occasion: and perhaps an amusing little box, to open, shut, and examine from all sides. Then, if in preparing, serving, and drinking, every phase of the action is rendered in such a gracefully functional manner that all present may take joy in it, the common affair might well be said to have been elevated to the status of a poem. And, in fact, in the writing of a sonnet, words are used that are quite normal, secular, common day tools. Just as in poetry, so in tea: certain rules and manners have been developed as a consequence of ages of experience; and through a mastery of these, immensely heightened powers of expression are achieved. For as art imitates nature in its manner of operation, so does tea. The manner of nature is spontaneity, but at the same time organization. Nature is not for the most part mere protoplasm. And the more complex the organization, the greater is the manifestation of the range and force of spontaneity. The mastery of tea, then, is the mastery of the principle of freedom (self-motivation) within the nexus of a highly complex, glass-hard, rule-bound civilization, for every one of whose contingencies only gratitude is to be felt, if one is to live as a man.

TIBET: THE BUDDHA AND
THE NEW HAPPINESS

++

In a document entitled "The Black Wickedness of the Deceiving
Reactionaries Belonging to Religious Establishments Is Quite In-
tolerable," the following account appears of the life of the Buddha.

"At that time there were many kingdoms in India, and the kingdom where Shakyamuni was born was the largest and most beastly
of these kingdoms. It was always oppressing the neighboring
smaller kingdoms. When Shakyamuni was ruling, all the people of
his kingdom were opposed to him and afterwards the neighboring
kingdom joined with them and rose against him; eventually
Shakyamuni was defeated, but he escaped from the midst of the
surrounding armies. As he had nowhere to go, he went to a forest
hermitage, and having meditated, he invented the Buddhist religion. Thus having induced regrets and weaknesses into the strong
hearts of the people, he came back to impose his authority on
ordinary folk. This is clearly the beginning of religion." [1]

The author of this Revised Version is said to have been a
Tibetan monk before he was transported to China and introduced
to the light of modern objective scientific research. And at the
conclusion of his testament, he states proudly: "If there are those
who talk about gods, the god I believe in is Communism. If I be
asked why, it is because Communism will bring us a life of happiness. So, cleaning up the frontiers from these reactionary monastic
potentates, I shall continue to follow Communism, as long as I
live." [2]

And so, let us turn for a deeper knowledge of his lore, to his master.

"The gods? They may quite deserve our worship. But if we had no peasant association but only the Emperor Kuan and the Goddess of Mercy, could we have knocked down the local bullies and bad gentry? The gods and goddesses are indeed pitiful; worshiped for hundreds of years, they have not knocked down for you a single local bully or a single one of the bad gentry!

"Now you want to have your rent reduced. I would like to ask: How will you go about it? Believe in the gods, or believe in the peasant association?" [3]

So, Mao Tse-tung.

The dialectical world outlook had already emerged in ancient times both in China and in Europe [Mao wrote in his work *On Contradiction*]. But ancient dialectics has something spontaneous and naïve about it; being based upon the social and historical conditions of those times, it was not formulated into an adequate theory, hence it could not fully explain the world, and was later supplanted by metaphysics. The famous German philosopher Hegel, who lived from the late eighteenth century to the early nineteenth, made very important contributions to dialectics, but his is idealist dialectics. It was not until Marx and Engels, the great men of action of the proletarian movement, made a synthesis of the positive achievements in the history of human knowledge and, in particular, critically absorbed the rational elements of Hegelian dialectics and created the great theory of dialectical materialism and historical materialism, that a great, unprecedented revolution took place in the history of human knowledge. Later Lenin and Stalin have further developed this great theory. Introduced into China, this theory immediately brought about tremendous changes in the world of Chinese thought.

This dialectical world outlook teaches man chiefly how to observe and analyze skillfully the movement of opposites in various things, and, on the basis of such analysis, to find out the methods of solving the contradictions. Consequently, it is of paramount importance for us to understand concretely the law of contradiction in things.[4]

The first point of interest here for the student of mythology is that there has taken place a juncture between the old Chinese yin-yang dichotomy and the dialectical materialism of Marx. And, as many manifestations in the modern Orient suggest, there is in the Oriental mind a sense of deep affinity with the Marxist view; which, I believe, must be founded in the fact that in the Marxist dogma of an irreversible law of history the idea of *maat, me, dharma, tao,* has been applied to the order of man on earth. The notion of a cosmic law is disregarded as irrelevant, but that of a law in human affairs is retained: a law to be known and followed, without the necessity or even possibility of individual choice and freedom of decision. So that, whereas formerly it was the priest, the reader of the stars, who knew and taught the Law, now it is the student of society. Thus the possibility seems to be offered of moving into the modern period in wholly modern terms, without having to face the crucial Occidental problem of what Dr. C. G. Jung has termed individuation; or an earlier vocabulary, free will: the responsibility of each individual, not to obey, but to judge and to decide.

"The Englishman talks about free will," said the Indian saint Shri Ramakrishna. "But those who have realized God are aware that free will is a mere appearance. In reality, man is the machine and God its Operator. Man is the carriage and God its Driver." [5]

Beyond the law-bound order of the world of names and forms there is no mythology in the Orient of a transcendent, antecedent seat of individuality of eternal character and worth, but only the void, non-dual brahman, the empty other face of Tao. Or, phrased another way: in the Orient that peculiar entity has never been conceded to exist who is not God but man, and yet of eternal worth none the less; or rather, not man, but this particular man, that or this woman here, who, when free, is not a mere manifestation of cosmic spontaneity, but its subject, its initiator. "Show me the face that you had before you were born!" That we have heard from the Orient: the idea of the uncarved block. But what about the block being carved through a series of unprecedented creative decisions?

One of the most important, mythologically conditioned facts

of the world scene today is that, whereas every call of the West to individual freedom sounds to the Oriental ear like an advertisement of the very devil itself (*aham,* "I," which created the world —and indeed it did!), the song of the Marxian Flower Wreath sounds like the inevitable modern transformation of a theme long revered as deeply spiritual, mysterious, and holy. There is no idea that men can *decide* what kind of world they want and then bring it to pass.

And so, as we all today well know, this new development of the idea of a superordinated law to which all human minds must bow was carried, in the most recent decade, to Tibet—where, if anywhere on earth, the way of the older Orient was still in form: brittle, aged, and decrepit, perhaps, yet in viable, still pleasant form. Let the reader consult, for example, the view of Tibetan life before the catastrophe, given by Marco Pallis in his *Peaks and Lamas.*[6] Or let him study the very carefully weighed view of the Legal Inquiry Committee on Tibet, of the International Inquiry Commission of Jurists, published in Geneva, 1960. "The picture of the Tibetan people," we are here informed, ". . . is of a sturdy, cheerful and self-reliant nation living in peace with its neighbors and seeking to a remarkable degree to cultivate the faith and mysticism which is known to so few people outside Tibet."[7]

The Buddhism of Tibet represented in the main the Indian Mahayana schools of the tenth to twelfth centuries A.D.: a development largely of the order of Shingon, with a psychological emphasis of great sophistication—as even a brief study of the marvelous Tibetan Book of the Dead will suffice to show.[8]

And then, suddenly, there fell upon this people an immediate materialization of the spiritual scenes of their own Hell of the Wrathful Deities, such as must be putting to an absolutely final test the power of Mahayana Buddhist meditation to recognize in all beings, all things, all acts, mutually arising, the presence—thus come—of the Buddha. It is a test, however, that the Buddhist world has met before—the test, I dare say, out of which it was born. And the scenes, incredible as they may seem, must be, in the main, reproductions in modern dress of motifs already rehearsed— for example, in the season of 844 A.D.

A monk, aged thirty-seven, who had escaped to Nepal from Thrashak, Nyarong village, testified that in March 1955 all the people and monks of his village were summoned to a meeting and asked where their leaders had got their wealth and whether those leaders treated them badly.

The reply was that no one had been ill-treated and that there was no complaint against the leaders. In the meeting the Chinese asked for arms and ammunition. Then the monks were asked what sort of crops, property and wealth they had and who were the good and bad leaders. The reply was that their leaders were good and treated them well. The Chinese then told the monks they were all spoiled and that they ought to marry. Those who refused to marry were put into prison and he himself saw two lamas, Dawa and Naden, who were amongst them, crucified by nails and left to die. A lama named Gumi-Tsering was pricked through the thigh with a pointed instrument like an awl, the thickness of a finger. He was tortured in this way because he refused to preach against religion. The Chinese called his fellow lamas and monks to carry him. They also took part in torturing him and he died. It is not known whether they were forced to do so or not. After this many monks and villagers ran away. As far as the informant knows, no monk agreed to marry and he heard that twelve others had been crucified. The crucifixions were carried out in the monasteries and he heard of this because fugitives came back at night to find out what was happening. . . . They saw many Chinese inside and horses had been taken inside the temple. The Chinese brought women inside but the monks refused to take them. These were Khamba women who were brought in groups surrounded by armed Chinese. Scriptures were turned into mattresses and also used for toilet paper. A monk named Turukhu-Sungrab asked the Chinese to desist and his arm was cut off above the elbow. He was told that God would give him back his arm. The Chinese told them there was no such thing as religion, the practice of which was a waste of one's life and of one's time. Because of religion people did not work.[9]

A farmer, aged fifty-two, from Ba-Jeuba, hearing a disturbance in his brother's house, looked through the window and, as he said, "saw his brother's wife's shouts being stifled by a towel. Two Chinese held her hands and another raped her, then the other two raped her in turn and left." In 1954 * forty-eight babies of this village below the age of one year were taken to China,

> in order, the Chinese said, that their parents could do more work. Many parents pleaded with the Chinese not to take the babies. Two soldiers and two civilians with a few Tibetan collaborators came into the house and took the babies from the parents by force. Fifteen parents who protested were thrown into the river by the Chinese and one committed suicide. All the babies came from the middle and upper classes. . . . Children were encouraged to submit their parents to indignities and to criticize their parents if they did not conform to the Chinese ways. Indoctrination had begun. One indoctrinated youth saw his father with a prayer-wheel and rosary and began to kick him and abuse him. The father began to hit the boy, he fought back and a number of people came to stop this. Three Chinese soldiers arrived and stopped these people from intervening, telling them that the boy had a perfect right to do this. The boy continued to abuse and beat his father, who then and there committed suicide by jumping into the river. The father's name was Ahchu and the boy's Ahsalu, aged about eighteen or nineteen. . . .

In 1953 this same informant was called to witness the crucifixion in his village of Patung Ahnga, a man from a well-to-do family.

> A fire was lit underneath him and he saw his flesh burn. Altogether twenty-five people from the wealthy classes were crucified and he saw them all. When he left Tibet in January 1960 fighting was still going on at Trungyi. . . . By this time the monasteries in that part had completely ceased to exist as religious institutions. They were being used as quarters for Chinese soldiers and the lower floors were used as stables. Some time after the children had been sent to China he saw twenty-five people killed in Jeuba by having nails driven into their eyes. Again the people were called to witness this. They were middle-class people and the Chinese stated that this was being done because they were not going on the road to Communism, having expressed their unwillingness to cooperate and to send their children to school.[10]

"All Power," writes Mao Tse-tung, "to the Peasant Association!"

---

* Compare the date of the Sino-Indian Agreement on Trade with Tibet and "Five Principles of Peaceful Coexistence"; supra, p. 311, note.

The peasants attack as their main targets the local bullies and bad gentry and the lawless landlords, hitting in passing against patriarchal ideologies and institutions, corrupt officials in the cities, and evil customs in the rural areas. In force and momentum, the attack is like a tempest or hurricane; those who submit to it survive, and those who resist it perish. As a result, the privileges which the feudal landlords have enjoyed for thousands of years are being shattered to pieces. The dignity and prestige of the landlords are dashed to the ground. With the fall of the authority of the landlords, the peasant association becomes the sole organ of authority, and what people call "All power to the peasant association" has come to pass. Even such a trifle as a quarrel between man and wife has to be settled at the peasant association. Nothing can be settled in the absence of people from the association. The association is actually dictating in all the matters in the countryside, and it is literally true that "whatever it says goes." The public can only praise the association and must not condemn it. The local bullies and bad gentry and the lawless landlords have been totally deprived of the right to have their say, and no one dares mutter the word "No." [11]

"In 1956 the Chinese surrounded Litang monastery while a special ceremony was going on, and the witness (a nomad, aged 40, from Rawa, one day's journey away), together with other outsiders, was attending the ceremony inside the monastery. The Chinese told the monks that there were only two possible ways: socialism and the old feudal system. If they did not surrender all their property to socialism the monastery would be completely destroyed. The monks refused. . . . For sixty-four days, with the witness still inside, the monastery was besieged. The Chinese charged the walls and the monks fought with swords and spears. On the sixty-fourth day planes bombed and machine-gunned the monastery, hitting the surrounding buildings but not the main temple. That night about two thousand escaped and two thousand or so were captured. . . ." One lama was crucified, another burned to death, two others were shot and wounded, then over one boiling water was poured and he was strangled, while the other was stoned and hit on the head with an ax.[12]

A village headman from Ba-Nangsang was told to stop at Minya to see what happened to people who opposed reform. "A man named Wangtok was arrested and taken to a large hall where Tibetans had been assembled for the purpose of seeing what happened. Beggars who had become soldiers in the Chinese army beat him with sticks and poured boiling water on his head. He then admitted having nine loads of gold (which never turned up, the witness says). He was tied and slung up by his thumbs and big toes. Straw was burned under him and he was asked where his gold was. He could not answer this because, according to the witness, he had none. A red-hot copper nail was then hammered into his forehead, the nail being between ¾ to 1 inch long. He was then carried into a truck and taken away. The Chinese said that he had been taken to Peking." [13]

The feet of the lama Khangsar, the abbot of Litang, were chained together, and a pole was placed across his chest and arms. "Then his arms were bound with a wire. He was suspended by a heavy chain around his neck and hanged, although the people asked for his release. The *uza* (prayer reciter) was arrested, stripped naked and burned on the thighs, chest, and under the armpits with a red-hot-iron about two fingers thick. This was done for three days, with applications of ointments between the sessions. When the witness left after four days the *uza* was still alive." [14]

At Sakya monastery, near Sikkim, the mother of the wife of a lama of the red-hat sect (in which the clergy marry) had her hair pulled out in public.[15] At Derge Dzongsar the daughter of a village leader, aged about forty, was first of all abused as an exploiter of the people; then her mouth was stuffed with hay, she was harnessed and saddled, and the riff-raff rode on her back, making her crawl around on all fours; then the Chinese did the same.[16] In a village of the province of Amdo, Rigong, where the people were assembled to watch their leaders being killed, "one man was shot in stages working up the body, there being about nine stages in all. Another man was asked whether he would prefer to die standing up or lying down. He preferred standing. A pit was dug and he was placed inside it. Then the pit was filled with mud and compressed. This continued even after he had died until his eyes protruded from his head and were then severed by the Chinese. Four others were made to recount the faults of their own parents, that they were devoted to religion, etc., then these four were shot in the back of their heads. As their brains spattered the Chinese called them the flowers in bloom." [17]

"Let a hundred flowers bloom," wrote Mao Tse-tung, "and let a hundred schools of thought contend." [18]

"Identity, unity, coincidence, interpermeation, interpenetration, interdependence (or interdependence for existence), interconnection or cooperation—all these different terms mean the same thing and refer to the following two conditions: first, each of the two aspects of every contradiction in the process of development of a thing finds the presupposition of its existence in the other aspect and both aspects coexist in an entity; second, each of the two contradictory aspects, according to given conditions, tends to transform itself into the other. This is what is meant by identity." [19]

"The agrarian revolution we have carried out is already and will be such a process in which the land-owning landlord class becomes a class deprived of its land, while the peasants, once deprived of their land, become small holders of land. The haves and the have nots, gain and loss, are interconnected because of certain conditions; there is identity of the two sides. Under socialism, the system of the peasants' private ownership will in turn become the public ownership of socialist agriculture; this has already taken place in the Soviet Union and will take place throughout the world. Between private property and public property there is a bridge leading from the one to the other, which in philosophy is called identity, or transformation into each other, or interpermeation." [20]

In the Amdo region, again at Rigong, three very high lamas had their hair pulled out before the people, their shoes were removed, and they were beaten, then made to kneel down on the gravel. "They were asked: 'Since you are lamas did you not know that you were going to be arrested?' Three pits were dug and the lamas were placed inside. The public were then made to urinate on them.

The Chinese then invited the lamas to fly out of the pit. Then they were taken off to prison and they were chained together around the neck and made to carry human dung in baskets." [21]

A man, aged twenty-two, from Doi-Dura in the Amdo region was told by the Chinese that he required treatment to make him more intelligent. The Chinese at that time were telling Tibetans that they were a stupid inferior race and would have to be supplanted by Russians and Chinese. They took blood tests of this man, his wife, and many others, and there are a number of corresponding reports from different parts of Tibet detailing the sort of operation to which this young man and his wife were the next day forced to submit. They were both taken to the hospital. "He was completely undressed, placed on a chair and his genital organs were examined. Then a digital rectal examination was carried out and the finger was agitated. He then ejaculated a whitish fluid and one or more drops fell on a glass slide which was taken away. After this a long pointed instrument with handles like those of scissors was inserted inside the urethra and he fainted with pain. When he came round the doctors gave him a white tablet which they said would give him strength. Then he received an injection at the base of the penis where it joins the scrotum. The needle itself hurt but the injection did not. He felt momentarily numb in the region until the needle was removed. He stayed ten days in hospital and then a month in bed at home. . . . He had been married for only two years and prior to this treatment had very strong sexual feelings. . . . Afterwards he had no sexual desire at all. . . ."

Meanwhile, his wife "was undressed and tied down. Her legs were raised and outstretched. Something very cold which became painful was inserted inside the vagina. She saw a kind of rubber balloon with a rubber tube attached, the end of which was inserted inside the vagina. The balloon was squeezed and his wife felt something very cold inside her. This caused no pain and only the tube and not the balloon was inserted. She remained conscious throughout. Then she was taken to bed. The same procedure was carried on every day for about a week. Then she went home and stayed in bed for about three weeks," and thereafter she had neither sexual feeling nor menstruation.[22]

"The district officer of Tuhlung ran away and was captured after about two days. His lips were cut off and he was bound and brought back naked to Tuhlung. The Chinese were not satisfied with his rate of progress; being a fat man he could not walk very fast and he was poked with bayonets to make him walk faster. The witness saw him covered with bayonet wounds. The Chinese tied him to a tree and invited Tibetans to go and beat him, accusing him of cruelty. They were told not to beat him to death since he would benefit by this. . . . He was in fact beaten by the Chinese and died after eight days. His lips were cut off after he had begged rather to be shot than tortured." [23]

And finally—though the reports go on and on—there was a nomad, aged forty-nine, formerly the owner of twenty or thirty yaks and a dweller in tents, who saw two of his comrades burned alive in public. He next saw all the wealthy people in the Kham area executed, and then the lamas and monks. The last were gathered from the monasteries in the district and about a thousand were executed in public. The informant saw them clearly from the slope of a hill where he was hiding. "He saw five strangled by a rope with a heavy image of the Buddha providing the necessary force. . . . And he saw Dzorchen Rimpoche, one of the most famous lamas in Kham, tied down to four pegs and slit all the way down the abdomen. The accusation made against the lamas was of deceiving and exploiting the people." [24] At Doi, Amdo, in 1955, the monks "were taken to the fields, yoked together in pairs, pulling a plow, under the supervision of a Chinese who carried a whip." [25]

Throughout the scenes of the Tibetan Book of the Dead, whether of heavenly or of infernal kind, the soul is advised by its attendant lama to recognize all the forms beheld as projections of its own consciousness; and when the hell scenes are to be met, the lama says: "Fear not, fear not, O nobly born! The Furies of the Lord of Death will place around your neck a rope and drag you along; cut off your head, extract your heart, pull out your intestines, lick up your brains, drink your blood, eat your flesh, and gnaw your bones; but in reality, your body is of the nature of voidness; you need not be afraid. . . ." [26]

"Be not terrified; be not awed. If all existing phenomena shining forth as divine shapes and radiances are recognized to be emanations of one's own intellect, Buddhahood will be obtained at that very instant of recognition. . . . If one recognizes one's own thought-forms, by one important act and by one word, Buddhahood is obtained." [27]

And with this sobering, terrible vision of the whole thing come true, the materialization of mythology in life, I shall close—in silence; for no Western mind can comment on these two aspects of the one great Orient in terms appropriate to the Orient itself, which, as far as any words from its leading contemporary minds would seem to show, is rather proud and hopeful of both.

The old doctrine of Egypt of the Secret of the Two Partners, the Mahayana of Voidness, Mutual Arising and the Flower Wreath, the Taoist of the complementarity of *yang* and *yin,* the Chinese Communist of interpermeation, and the Tantric lore of the presence within each being of all the gods and demons of all the storied heavens and hells: these, it would seem, variously turned and phrased, represent the one timeless doctrine of eternal life— the nectar of the fruit of the tree in the garden that Western man, or at least a notable number of his company, failed to eat.

REFERENCE NOTES
INDEX

REFERENCE NOTES

PART ONE: THE SEPARATION OF EAST AND WEST

CHAPTER 1: THE SIGNATURES OF THE FOUR GREAT DOMAINS

1. Sir James George Frazer, *The Golden Bough* (New York: The Macmillan Company, one-volume edition, 1922), pp. 264 ff.

2. Sir Charles Leonard Woolley, *Ur of the Chaldees* (London: Ernest Benn Ltd., 1929), pp. 33 ff., cited and discussed in *The Masks of God: Primitive Mythology*, (New York: Viking, 1959), pp. 405–11. Woolley's dating of his find, c. 3500 B.C., is now recognized as about a millennium too early.

3. Duarte Barbosa, *Description of the Coasts of East Africa and Malabar in the Beginning of the Sixteenth Century* (London: The Hakluyt Society, 1866), p. 172; cited by Frazer, op. cit., pp. 274–275, and Joseph Campbell, *The Masks of God: Primitive Mythology*, pp. 165–66.

4. E. A. Gait, "Human Sacrifice (Indian)," in James Hastings, *Encyclopaedia of Religion and Ethics* (New York: Charles Scribner's Sons, 1928), Vol. VI, pp. 849–53.

5. Ibid.

6. *Kālikā Purāṇa*, Rudhirādhyāya; translation adapted from W. C. Blaquiere, *Asiatic Researches*, Vol. V, 1797, pp. 371–91, and Gait, loc. cit.

7. *Bhagavad Gītā* 2:22.

8. For a dating c. 1000 B.C. and general discussion of the problem, cf. G. B. Gray and M. Cary, in *The Cambridge Ancient History*, Vol. IV (Cambridge: The University Press, 1930), pp. 206–207 and 616–17; and for a dating c. 550 B.C., A. T. Olmstead, *History of the Persian Empire* (Chicago: The University of Chicago Press,

Phoenix Books, 1948), pp. 94 ff.

9. *Yasna* 44:3.

10. *Yasna* 30:9.

11. Rabbi Bahia ben Asher, *Commentary on the Pentateuch* (Warsaw, 1853), on Genesis 2:9; as cited by Louis Ginzberg, *The Legends of the Jews* (Philadelphia: The Jewish Publication Society of America, 1925), Vol. V, p. 91.

12. *Bṛhadāraṇyaka Upaniṣad* 1.4.1–5.

13. Genesis 2:21–22.

14. Isaiah 2.20.

15. Ibid., 8:9–10.

16. *Śvetāśvatara Upaniṣad* 6:20.

17. Isaiah, 40:5.

18. *Kena Upaniṣad* 1.3.

19. *Bṛhadāraṇyaka Upaniṣad* 1.4.7.

20. Genesis 3.8.

21. *Kena Upaniṣad* 1.

22. *Chāndogya Upaniṣad* 6.11.

23. C. G. Jung, *Das Unbewusste im normalen und kranken Seelenleben*, first edition 1916, second, 1918, third: Rascher Verlag, Zurich, 1926; reprinted in *Two Essays on Analytical Psychology* (London: Bailliere, Tindall and Cox, 1928; New York, The Bollingen Series XX, *The Collected Works of C. G. Jung*, Vol. 7, 1953).

24. Sigmund Freud, *Jenseits des Lustprinzips* (Leipzig, Wien, Zurich: Internationaler Psychoanalytischer Verlag, 1920).

25. *Jātaka* 1.68–71, following (with slight alteration) the translation of Henry Clarke Warren, *Buddhism in Translations* (Cambridge, Mass.: Harvard University Press, 1922), pp. 75–76.

26. Aśvaghoṣa, *Buddhacarita* 13–14 (abridged), following largely the

519

translation of E. B. Cowell, *Sacred Books of the East,* Vol. XLIX (Oxford: The Clarendon Press, 1894), pp. 137–58.

27. *Tao Tê Ching* 1.1–2. James Legge, *The Sacred Books of the East,* Vol. XXXIX (Oxford: The Clarendon Press, 1891); Paul Carus, *The Canon of Reason and Virtue* (La Salle, Illinois: The Open Court Publishing Co., 1913); Dwight Goddard, *Laotzu's Tao and Wu Wei* (New York: Brentano's, 1919); Arthur Waley, *The Way and Its Power* (New York: The Macmillan Company, London: George Allen and Unwin, Ltd., 1949).

28. Waley, op. cit., p. 30.

29. Marcel Granet, *La Pensée chinoise* (Paris: La Renaissance du Livre, 1934), p. 280, n. 2.

30. *Tao Tê Ching* 1.3.

31. *Kuan Tzu,* P'ien 12, beginning (Waley's note).

32. Ibid., P'ien 36, beginning (Waley's note).

33. Ibid., P'ien 36 (Waley's note).

34. Waley, op. cit., pp. 46–47.

35. *Jātaka* 1.76.

36. Sir Monier Monier-Williams, *A Sanskrit-English Dictionary* (Oxford: The Clarendon Press, 1888), p. 528.

37. James Haughton Woods, *The Yoga System of Patañjali* (Cambridge, Mass.: The Harvard University Press, 1927), p. xx, suggests c. 650–850 A.D., which, however, Dr. M. Winternitz, *Geschichte der indischen Litteratur,*

Vol. III (Leipzig: C. F. Amelangs Verlag, 1920), p. 461, seriously questions, suggesting the earlier placement, c. 350–650 A.D., as the more likely.

38. Woods, op. cit., pp. xxi–xxii.

39. Winternitz, loc. cit.

40. Woods, op. cit., p. xix.

41. *Yogasūtras* 1.2.

42. *Chuang Tzu,* Book VI, Part I, Section VI. 2–3; translation by James Legge, op. cit., pp. 238–39.

43. *Tao Tê Ching* 25.5–6; following Legge, op. cit., pp. 67–68.

44. *Aṣṭavakra-saṁhitā* 19.3.

45. *Symposium* 189D ff.; following the Benjamin Jowett translation, *The Dialogues of Plato* (Oxford: The Clarendon Press, 1871).

46. F. M. Cornford, *Greek Religious Thought from Homer to the Age of Alexander* (London: J. M. Dent and Sons, Ltd.; New York: E. P. Dutton and Co., 1923), pp. xv–xvi.

47. Job 2:3.

48. Job 40:4; 42:2 and 6.

49. Aeschylus, *Prometheus* 11.938–939. Translation by Seth C. Benardete, in David Green and Richmond Lattimore (eds.), *The Complete Greek Tragedies* (Chicago: The University of Chicago Press, 1959), Vol. I, p. 345.

50. Friedrich Nietzsche, *Menschliches Allzumenschliches: Ein Buch für freie Geister,* Nietzsche's *Werke,* Bd. II (Leipzig: Alfred Kroner Verlag, 1917), Aphorism No. 23.

51. Ibid., Vorrede 2 (p. 5).

CHAPTER 2: THE CITIES OF GOD

1. Rudolf Otto, *The Idea of the Holy,* translated by John W. Harvey (London: Oxford University Press, 1925).

2. Ibid., p. 4.

3. Discussed in *The Masks of God: Primitive Mythology,* Chapters 3 and 10, pp. 140–144 and 402–404.

4. H. R. Hall, *A Season's Work at Ur, al-'Ubaid, Abu Shahrain (Eridu), and Elsewhere* (London: Methuen and Co., 1919); H. R. Hall and C. Leonard Woolley, *Ur Excavations I, Al-'Ubaid* (London: Oxford University Press, 1927); P. Delougaz, "A Short Investigation of the Temple at Al-'Ubaid," *Iraq,* V, Part 1 (1938), pp. 1–12.

5. Julius Jordan, Arnold Nöldeke, E. Heinrich, et al., "Vorläufige Bericht über die von der Notgemeinschaft der deutschen Wissenschaft in Uruk-Warka unternommenen Ausgrabungen," *Preussische Akademie der Wissenschaften zu Berlin. Abhandlungen, 1929,* Nr. 7; *1930,* Nr. 4; *1932,* Nr. 2, Nr. 6; *1933,* Nr. 5;

1935, Nr. 2, Nr. 4; *1936*, Nr. 13; *1937*, Nr. 11; *1939*, Nr. 2.

6. Hall, op cit., pp. 187–228; Seton Lloyd and Fuad Safar, "Eridu," *Sumer* III, No. 2 (1947), pp. 85–111; IV, No. 2 (1948), pp. 115–127; VI, No. 1 (1950), pp. 27–33.

7. Henri Frankfort, "Preliminary Reports on Iraq Expeditions," *Chicago University, Oriental Institute. Communications,* Nos. 13, 16–17, 19–20 (1932–1936); also Delougaz, op. cit., p. 10, Fig. 1.

8. Seton Lloyd and Fuad Safar, "Tell Uqair," *Journal of Near Eastern Studies,* II, No. 2 (1943), pp. 132–58.

9. M. E. L. Mallowan, *Twenty-five Years of Mesopotamian Discovery (1932–1956)* (London: The British School of Archaeology in Iraq, 1956), pp. 27–31.

10. André Parrot, *Ziggurate et Tour de Babel* (Paris: Albin Michel, 1949), p. 167.

11. H.R.H. Prince Peter of Greece and Denmark, "The Calf Sacrifice of the Todas of the Nilgiris (South India)." *Selected Papers of the Fifth International Congress of Anthropological and Ethnological Sciences, Philadelphia, 1956* (Philadelphia: University of Pennsylvania, 1960), pp. 485–89.

12. Stanzas of a hymn to the Goddess in her aspect as "Ruler of the World" (*Bhuvaneśvarī*), from the *Tantrasāra*. Cf. Arthur and Ellen Avalon, *Hymns to the Goddess* (London: Luzac and Co., 1913), pp. 32–33.

13. Henri Frankfort, *Cylinder Seals* (London: The Macmillan Company, 1939), p. 17.

14. Ernest de Sarzec, *Découvertes en Chaldée* (Paris: Ernest Leroux, 1884–1912), Vol. I (*Texte*), pp. 319–20; Vol. II (*Planches*), Pl. 30 bis, No. 21.

15. Compare the ritual murder in connubium and subsequent cannibalistic meal of the Marind-anim of New Guinea, described in *The Masks of God: Primitive Mythology,* pp. 170–71.

16. Or perhaps better stated in this context: the scorpion represents the same principle as the serpent of Figure 2 and the man with a weapon of Figure 4; that is to say, the principle of death.

17. In dating I am following Alexander Scharff and Anton Moortgat, *Ägypten und Vorderasien im Altertum* (Munich: Verlag F. Bruckmann, 1950, 1959).

18. Gudea, Cylinder B, 5, 11 ff., reproduced in de Sarzec, op. cit., Pl. 37.

19. Frankfort, op. cit., pp. 75–77.

20. Ibid., p. 77.

21. *The Masks of God: Primitive Mythology,* pp. 405–11, citing Sir Charles Leonard Woolley, *Ur of the Chaldees* (London: Ernest Benn Ltd., 1929), pp. 46–65.

22. Scharff and Moortgat, op. cit., p. 214.

23. Otto, op. cit., p. 7.

24. Carl G. Jung, *The Integration of the Personality,* translated by Stanley M. Dell (New York and Toronto: Farrar and Rinehart, 1939), p. 59.

25. Otto, op. cit., p. 8.

26. E. A. Wallis Budge, *Osiris and the Egyptian Resurrection* (London: Philip Lee Warner; New York: G. P. Putnam's Sons, 1911), Vol. I, pp. xiv–xv and passim; also, *The Gods of the Egyptians* (London: Methuen and Co., 1904), Vol. I, pp. xiv–xv, 7 ff., etc.

27. John A. Wilson, *The Culture of Ancient Egypt* (Chicago: University of Chicago Press, 1951), pp. 27 and 22–23.

28. J. E. Quibell, *Hierakonpolis,* Egyptian Research Account No. 4 (London: Bernard Quaritch, Part I, 1900; Part II, 1902), Part II, pp. 20–21 and Plate LXXV.

29. George Andrew Reisner, *The Development of the Egyptian Tomb down to the Accession of Cheops* (Cambridge, Mass.: Harvard University Press, 1936), p. 1.

30. Ibid., p. 13.

31. Quibell, op. cit., p. 20.

32. Helene J. Kantor, "The Chronology of Egypt and Its Correlation with That of Other Parts of the Near East in the Periods before the Late Bronze Age," in Robert W. Ehrich (ed.), *Relative Chronologies in Old World Archeol-*

ogy (Chicago: University of Chicago Press, 1954), p. 6.

33. The suggestion was first made by Sethe and Garstang (*Denkmäler Narmers: Hierakonpolis;* see also Capart); Eduard Meyer thought it not unlikely (*Kulturgeschichte des Altertums,* Vol. I, Part 2, Section 208, note), and it is accepted by Henri Frankfort, *Ancient Egyptian Religion* (New York: Columbia University Press, 1948), p. 159.

34. I am following the dating system of Alexander Scharff and Anton Moortgat, op. cit., p. 38. For 3100 B.C., cf. Wilson, op. cit., p. 319; for 3000 B.C., Samuel A. B. Mercer, *The Pyramid Texts* (New York, London and Toronto: Longmans, Green, 1952), Vol. IV, p. 225; and for 2400 B.C., P. van der Moer, in *Orientalia Neelandica* (1948), pp. 23–49. Carbon-14 datings from a Dynasty I tomb have yielded the following ranges: 3010 ± 240 B.C. and 2852 ± 260 B.C. (W. F. Libby, *Radiocarbon Dating* [Chicago: University of Chicago Press, 1952], pp. 70–71), i.e., a total range of likelihood from c. 3250 to c. 2592 B.C.

35. Herodotus II. 99.

36. Henri Frankfort, *Kingship and the Gods* (Chicago: University of Chicago Press, 1948), p. 171.

37. W. Max Müller, *Egyptian Mythology. The Mythology of All Races,* Vol. XII (Boston: Marshall Jones Company, 1918), pp. 38–39.

38. Frankfort, *Kingship and the Gods,* loc. cit.

39. Thomas Mann, "Freud and the Future," in *Life and Letters Today,* Vol. XV, No. 5, 1936, pp. 90–91.

40. Frankfort, *Kingship and the Gods,* p. 18.

41. Frankfort, *Kingship and the Gods,* p. 51, citing A. H. Gardiner, in *Proceedings of the Society of Biblical Archaeology,* London, XXXVIII, p. 50.

42. Henri Frankfort, *The Birth of Civilization in the Near East* (London: Williams and Norgate, 1951), p. 102.

43. Oswald Spengler, *The Decline of the West* (New York: Alfred A. Knopf, 1926 and 1928), translation by Charles Francis Atkinson, Vol. II, p. 16.

44. Ibid., Vol. I, pp. 166–67.

45. Ibid., Vol. II, p. 163.

46. Auguste Mariette, *Catalogue général des monuments d'Abydos* (Paris: Imprimerie Nationale, 1880); Émile Amélineau, *Les Nouvelles Fouilles d'Abydos* (Paris: Ernest Leroux, Vol. I, *1895–96* [1899], Vol. II, *1896–97* [1902], Vol. III, *1897–98* [1904]); W. M. Flinders Petrie, *The Royal Tombs of the First Dynasty* (London: The Egypt Exploration Fund, Part I, 1900, Part II, 1901).

47. Petrie, op. cit., Part II, pp. 5–7 and Plate LIX.

48. Ibid., p. 5 and Meyer, op. cit., Vol. I, Part 2, p. 132; also, Scharff and Moortgat, op. cit., pp. 40–41.

49. Petrie, op. cit., Part II, p. 24.

50. Meyer, op. cit., Vol. I, Part 2, p. 208.

51. George A. Reisner, *Excavations at Kerma,* Harvard African Studies, Vol. V (Cambridge, Mass.: Peabody Museum of Harvard University, 1923), pp. 65–66.

52. Ibid., pp. 68–70.

53. Kewal Motwani, *India: A Synthesis of Cultures* (Bombay: Thacker and Company, 1947), p. 253.

54. *Rg Veda* 1.153.3; 8.90.15; 10.11.1.

55. A. A. Macdonell, *Vedic Mythology. Grundriss der Indo-Arischen Philologie und Altertumskunde* III Band, 1. Heft A (Strassburg: Karl J. Trübner, 1897), p. 122.

56. *Rg Veda* 1.136.3.

57. Ibid., 5.46.6.

58. Ibid., 8.25.3; 10.36.3; 10.132.6.

59. Ibid., 4.18.10; 10.111.2.

60. Heinrich Zimmer (ed. Joseph Campbell), *The Art of Indian Asia* (New York: Pantheon Books, The Bollingen Series XXXIX, 1955), Vol. II, Plates 294–95.

61. Cf. Heinrich Zimmer (ed. Joseph Campbell), *Philosophies of India* (New York: Pantheon Books, The Bollingen Series XXVI, 1951), p. 133 and note.

62. Reisner, *Excavations at Kerma*, pp. 70–71.

63. The Rev. William Ward, *A View of the History, Literature, and Religion of the Hindoos* (first edition Serampore: The Baptist Mission Society, 1815; second edition, abridged and improved, London: Black, Parbury and Allen, Booksellers to the Hon. East India Company, Vols. I and II, 1817, Vols. III and IV, 1820). The excerpt is from Vol. I (1817), pp. lxxi–lxxiii, note.

64. Reisner, *Excavations at Kerma*, pp. 99–102.

65. Ibid., pp. 78–79.

66. *The Masks of God: Primitive Mythology*, Chapters 4, 5, and 10.

67. *The Masks of God: Primitive Mythology*, pp. 406–409, citing Sir Charles Leonard Woolley, *Ur of the Chaldees*, p. 57.

68. British Museum No. 29, 777; reproduced in E. A. Wallis Budge, *Osiris and the Egyptian Resurrection* (London: Philip Lee Warner; New York: G. P. Putnam's Sons, 1911), Vol. I, p. 13; also, in Joseph Campbell, *The Hero with a Thousand Faces*, Bollingen Series XVII (New York: Pantheon Books, 1949), p. 54.

69. Henri Frankfort, "Gods and Myths on Sargonid Seals," *Iraq*, Vol. I, No. 1 (1934), p. 8; cited in *The Masks of God: Primitive Mythology*, p. 411.

70. Petrie, op. cit., Part II, pp. 16–17.

71. Reisner, *The Development of the Egyptian Tomb down to the Accession of Cheops*, p. 354.

72. Petrie, op. cit., Part I, pp. 14–16.

73. Walter B. Emery, "Royal Tombs at Sakkara," *Archaeology*, Vol. 8, No. 1 (1955), p. 7.

74. Frazer, op. cit., p. 286.

75. *The Masks of God: Primitive Mythology*, pp. 144–50.

76. Supra, p. 5, and *The Masks of God: Primitive Mythology*, pp. 144–69.

77. See *The Masks of God: Primitive Mythology*, pp. 144–69.

78. Petrie, op. cit., Part I, p. 22.

79. Frankfort, *Kingship and the Gods*, p. 79.

80. *The Masks of God: Primitive Mythology*, pp. 151–69.

81. Frankfort, *Kingship and the Gods*, p. 85.

82. Frankfort, *Kingship and the Gods*, p. 86.

83. Petrie, op. cit., Part I, p. 22.

84. Frankfort, *Kingship and the Gods*, pp. 83–87.

85. Cf. Joseph Campbell, *The Hero with a Thousand Faces*.

86. I have followed, for the details of the festival, the reconstruction presented by Frankfort, *Kingship and the Gods*, pp. 85–88.

87. Spengler, op. cit., Vol. I, p. 12.

88. Petrie, op. cit., Part II, p. 31.

89. Frankfort, *Kingship and the Gods*, pp. 21–22.

90. James Henry Breasted, "The Philosophy of a Memphite Priest," *Zeitschrift für ägyptische Sprache und Altertumskunde*, Vol. XXXIX, 39.

91. G. Maspero, "Sur la toute puissance de la parole," *Transactions of the Ninth International Congress of Orientalists*, London, 1891; Vol. III.

92. Adolf Erman, "Ein Denkmal memphitischer Theologie," *Sitzungsbericht der Königlichen Preussischen Akademie*, 1911, XLIII, pp. 916–50.

93. Meyer, op. cit., Section 272, p. 245; Frankfort, *Kingship*, notes to Chapter 2, pp. 352–53; John A. Wilson, "Egypt," in Henri Frankfort et al., *The Intellectual Adventure of Man* (Chicago: University of Chicago Press, 1946); Pelican Books edition: *Before Philosophy*, 1949, p. 65.

94. Pyramid Text 1248; translation from Samuel A. B. Mercer, *The Pyramid Texts* (New York, London, Toronto: Longmans, Green, 1952), Vol. I, p. 206.

95. Pyramid Text 1652 (Mercer, op. cit., I, p. 253).

96. Pyramid Text 447b (ibid., p. 100).

97. Pyramid Text 1655 (ibid., p. 253).

98. James Henry Breasted, *Development of Religion and Thought in Ancient Egypt* (London: Hodden and Stoughton, 1912), p. 45, n. 2.

99. My rendition is based on Breasted, *Development*, pp. 44–46; Frankfort, *Kingship*, pp. 29–30; and John A. Wilson, "The Memphite Theology of Creation," in

James B. Pritchard (ed.), *The Ancient Near East* (Princeton: Princeton University Press, 1958), pp. 1–2.

100. Meyer, op. cit., Vol. I, Section 272, p. 246.

101. "The Destruction of Men," E. Naville, *Transactions of the Society of Biblical Archaeology,* Vol. IV (1876), pp. 1–19; Vol. VIII (1885), 412–20. Also, von Bergmann, *Hieroglyphische Inschriften,* Plates LXXV–LXXVII.

102. Reisner, *Development,* p. 122.

103. Ibid., p. 348.

104. Meyer, op. cit., Section 230, p. 169.

105. Cecil M. Firth and J. E. Quibell, *Excavations at Saqqara: The Step Pyramid* (Cairo: Imprimerie de l'Institut Français

d'Archéologie Orientale, 1936), Vol. I, passim.

106. Meyer, op. cit., Vol. I, Sections 233 and 247, pp. 177 and 200; Reisner, *Development,* p. 357.

107. Meyer, op. cit., Vol. I, Section 236, p. 182.

108. Ibid., Section 234, p. 178.

109. Ibid., Section 248, p. 200.

110. Ibid., Section 219, p. 152.

111. Abdel Moneim Abubakr, "Divine Boats of Ancient Egypt," *Archaeology,* Vol. 8, No. 2, 1955, p. 97.

112. Meyer, op. cit., Vol. I, Section 238, pp. 185–86.

113. Sir G. Maspero, *Popular Stories of Ancient Egypt* (London: H. Grevel and Co.; New York: G. P. Putnam's Sons, 1915), pp. 36–39.

114. Meyer, op. cit., Section 252, pp. 207–208.

CHAPTER 3: THE CITIES OF MEN

1. Wilson, *The Culture of Ancient Egypt,* p. 160.

2. Morris Jastrow, Jr., *Aspects of Religious Belief and Practice in Babylonia and Assyria* (New York and London: G. P. Putnam's Sons, 1911), pp. 143–264.

3. Samuel Noah Kramer, *Sumerian Mythology* (Philadelphia: The American Philosophical Society, 1944), pp. 8–9.

4. Parrot, *Ziggurat et Tour de Babel,* pp. 148–55.

5. Cf. H. V. Hilprecht, *Die Ausgrabungen im Bêl-Tempel zu Nippur* (Leipzig: J. C. Hinrich'sche Buchhandlung, 1903).

6. W. Andrae, *Das Gotteshaus und die Urformen des Bauens im alten Orient,* Studien zur Bauforschung, Heft 2 (Berlin: Hans Schoetz und Co., 1930).

7. Stephen Henry Langdon, *Semitic Mythology. The Mythology of All Races,* Vol. V (Boston: Marshall Jones Company, 1931), pp. 103–106.

8. Samuel Noah Kramer, *From the Tablets of Sumer* (Indian Hills, Colorado: The Falcon's Wing Press, 1956), pp. 172–73; Langdon, op. cit., pp. 194–95.

9. Kramer, *From the Tablets of Sumer,* pp. 77–78.

10. Hesiod, *Theogonia* 176.

11. Kramer, *From the Tablets of Sumer,* pp. 101–144; also, Kramer, *Sumerian Mythology,* pp. 68–72; and Thorkild Jacobsen, "Mesopotamia," in Henri Frankfort et al., *Before Philosophy* (Harmondsworth: Penguin Books, 1949), pp. 175–78, 202–207.

12. Pyramid Text 1 (Mercer, op. cit., Vol. I, p. 20).

13. Pyramid Text 842 (ibid., Vol. 1, p. 156).

14. Pyramid Text 2171 (ibid., Vol. I, p. 315).

15. Pyramid Text 1321 (ibid., Vol. I, p. 215).

16. Pyramid Text 1142 (ibid., Vol. I, p. 194).

17. Kramer, *From the Tablets of Sumer,* p. 77.

18. Ibid., p. 177; Arno Poebel, *Historical Texts* (University of Pennsylvania, Philadelphia; The University Museum: Publications of the Babylonian Section, Vol. IV, No. 1, 1914), p. 17.

19. Kramer, *From the Tablets of Sumer,* pp. 92–93.

20. Ananda K. Coomaraswamy, *The*

Transformation of Nature in Art (Cambridge, Mass.: Harvard University Press, 1934), p. 31.

21. Dante Alighieri, *Divina Commedia: Paradiso* I, 103–105.

22. Thomas Aquinas, *Summa Theologica* I–II, Question 21, Article 4, Reply 1. Translation of the Fathers of the English Dominican Province (London: Burns, Oates and Washbourne, 1914), Vol. 6, p. 276.

23. *Grimnismol* 23; translation by Henry Adams Bellows, *The Poetic Edda* (New York: The American-Scandinavian Foundation, 1923), p. 93.

24. *Mahābhārata* 3.188.22 ff.; also, 12.231.11 ff., and *Mānava Dharmaśāstra* 1.69 ff. Discussion by H. Jacobi, "Ages of the World (Indian)," Hastings (ed.), op. cit., Vol. I, pp. 200–201.

25. J. L. E. Dreyer, *A History of the Planetary Systems from Thales to Kepler* (Cambridge, England: Cambridge University Press, 1906), pp. 203–204. The annual precession actually varies between the limits of $50'' \cdot 2015 \pm 15'' \cdot 3695$ (ibid., p. 330).

26. H. V. Hilprecht, *The Babylonian Expedition of The University of Pennsylvania, Series A: Cuneiform Texts*, Vol. XX, Part I (Philadelphia: University of Pennsylvania, University Museum, 1906), p. 31.

27. Alfred Jeremias, *Das Alter der babylonischen Astronomie* (Leipzig: J. C. Hinrechs'sche Buchhandlung, 2 aufl., 1909), p. 68, n. 1.

28. Ibid., pp. 71–72.

29. V. Scheil, notice in *Revue d'assyriologie et d'archéologie orientale*, Vol. 12, 1915, pp. 195 f.

30. Erich F. Schmidt, *University of Pennsylvania, The Museum Journal*, Vol. 22 (1931), pp. 200 ff.

31. E. Heinrich, "Vorläufige Bericht über die von der Notgemeinschaft der deutschen Wissenschaft in Uruk-Warka unternommenen Ausgrabungen," *Preussische Akademie der Wissenschaften zu Berlin. Abhandlungen 1935*, Nr. 2, Tafel 2.

32. Sir Charles Leonard Woolley, *Ur of the Chaldees* (Harmonsworth: Penguin Books, 1929), pp. 17–18.

33. L. C. Watelin and S. Langdon, "Excavations at Kish IV," *Field Museum–Oxford University Joint Expedition to Mesopotamia, 1925–1930*, pp. 40–44. See, also, Jack Finegan, *Light from the Ancient Past* (Princeton University Press, 1959), pp. 27–28.

34. Respectively from Arno Poebel, *Historical Texts* (Philadelphia: University of Pennsylvania, 1914), The University Museum Publications of the Babylonian Section, Vol. IV, No. 1, p. 17, and Langdon, op. cit., p. 206. A third interpretation of the line is offered by Kramer, *From the Tablets of Sumer*, p. 177: "To Nintu I will return the . . . of my creatures."

35. Poebel, Langdon, and Kramer, loc. cit.

36. I have followed primarily Poebel, op. cit., pp. 17–20, but with considerable help from the later renditions of Langdon, op. cit., pp. 206–208, and Kramer, *From the Tablets of Sumer*, pp. 179–81.

37. Kramer, *From the Tablets of Sumer*, p. xix: "the first half of the second millennium B.C."

38. Poebel, op. cit., p. 70.

39. Obituary, *Journal of the Royal Asiatic Society*, 1906, pp. 272–77.

40. Julius (Jules) Oppert, "Die Daten der Genesis," *Königliche Gesellschaft der Wissenschaften zu Göttingen. Nachrichten*, No. 10 (May 1877), pp. 201–23.

41. Ibid., p. 209.

42. Daisetz T. Suzuki, "The Role of Nature in Zen Buddhism," *Eranos-Jahrbuch 1953* (Zurich: Rhein-Verlag, 1954), pp. 294 and 297.

43. Thorkild Jacobsen, *The Sumerian King List*, (University of Chicago, 1939), pp. 77–85.

44. Edward J. Harper, *Die babylonischen Legenden von Etana, Zu, Adapa, und Dibbara* (Leipzig: August Pries, 1892), pp. 4–10; Morris Jastrow, Jr., "Another Fragment of the Etana Myth," *Journal of the American Oriental Society*, Vol. XIII, 1909–10, pp. 101–29; Stephen H. Langdon, op. cit., pp. 168–73.

45. Jastrow, "Another Fragment of the Etana Myth," pp. 127–28.
46. Ibid., p. 126.
47. Ibid., p. 128.
48. Ibid., p. 129.
49. *Bhagavad Gītā* 2:20.
50. Wilson, *The Culture of Ancient Egypt*, pp. 78–79.
51. Breasted, *Development of Religion and Thought in Ancient Egypt*, p. 188, following Adolf Erman, "Gespräch eines Lebensmüden mit seiner Seele," *Abhandlungen der königlichen Preussischen Akadamie*, 1896, translating a Middle Kingdom papyrus, Berlin P. 3024; here greatly abridged.
52. Aquinas, *Summa Contra Gentiles*, Book III, Chapter XLVIII, Paragraph I.
53. Nietzsche, *Also Sprach Zarathustra*, Part I, Ch. 3.
54. Bilingual historical inscription in Sumerian and Akkadian, c. 2350 B.C. George A. Barton, *The Royal Inscriptions of Sumer and Akkad* (New Haven: Yale University Press, 1929), pp. 101–105.

55. Translation (abridged) following Morris Jastrow, "A Babylonian Parallel to Job," *Journal of Biblical Literature*, Vol. XXV, pp. 135–91; also François Martin, "Le juste souffrant babylonian," *Journal Asiatique*, 10 series, Vol. xvi, pp. 75–143; and Simon Landersdorfer, "Eine babylonische Quelle für das Buch Job?" *Biblische Studien*, Vol. xvi, 2. Following the observations of these authorities, I have restored the name Enlil in the final verses, where a later scribe placed that of the later god of the city of Babylon, Marduk. The name of the king itself, Tabi-utul-Enlil, speaks for the propriety of this restoration.
56. "The Counsels of King Intef," transl. Allan H. Gardiner, in Charles F. Horne (ed.), *The Sacred Books and Early Literature of the East* (New York and London: Parke, Austin and Lipscomb, 1917), Vol. II, "Egypt," pp. 98–99.

PART TWO: THE MYTHOLOGIES OF INDIA

CHAPTER 4: ANCIENT INDIA

1. Ananda K. Coomaraswamy, *Yakṣas, Part II* (Washington, D.C.: Smithsonian Institution, Publication 3059, 1931), p. 14.
2. Donald E. McCown, "The Relative Stratigraphy and Chronology of Iran," in Ehrich (ed.), *Relative Chronologies in Old World Archeology*, pp. 59 and 63; Stuart Piggott, *Prehistoric India* (Harmondsworth: Penguin Books, 1950), pp. 72 ff.
3. V. Gordon Childe, *New Light on the Most Ancient East* (New York: D. Appleton-Century Company, 1934), p. 277.
4. Robert Heine-Geldern, "The Origin of Ancient Civilizations and Toynbee's Theories," *Diogenes*, No. 13 (Spring 1956), pp. 96–98.
5. Piggott, op. cit., pp. 126–27.
6. Walter A. Fairservis, Jr., *Natural History*, Vol. LXVII, No. 9.

7. Piggott, op. cit., p. 127.
8. See *The Masks of God: Primitive Mythology*, pp. 360–65 and 392–394.
9. Piggott, op. cit., p. 33. The Summary of stone-age finds on which my account is based will be found, together with notes and bibliography, pp. 22–41.
10. Leo Frobenius, *Monumenta Terrarum* (Frankfurt am Main: Frankfurter Societäts-Druckerei, 2. Aufl., 1929), pp. 21–25.
11. Leo Frobenius, *Indische Reise* (Berlin: Verlag von Reimar Hobbing, 1931), pp. 221–22.
12. W. Norman Brown, "The Beginnings of Civilization in India," *Supplement to the Journal of the American Oriental Society*, No. 4, Dec. 1939, p. 44.
13. Kewal Motwani, *Manu Dharma Śāstra: A Sociological and His-*

torical Study (Madras: Ganesh and Co., 1958), pp. 223–29.

14. Sri Aurabindo, *On the Veda* (Pondicherry: Srī Aurabindo Āsram, 1956), p. 11; cited by Motwani, op. cit., p. 215.

15. Sir Mortimer Wheeler, *Early India and Pakistan* (New York: Frederick A. Praeger, 1959), p. 98.

16. Ibid., pp. 109–10.

17. Piggott, op. cit., pp.146–47.

18. Ibid., p. 148.

19. Jules Bloch, "Le Dravidien," in A. Meillet and Marcel Cohn (eds.), *Les Langues du monde* (Paris: Centre National de la Recherche Scientifique, 1952), pp. 487–91.

20. Piggott, op. cit., pp. 145–46.

21. *Rg Veda* 7.21.5.

22. Wilhelm Koppers, "Zum Ursprung des Mysterienwesens in Lichte von Völkerkunde und Ethnologie," *Eranos-Jahrbuch 1944* (Zurich: Rhein-Verlag, 1945), pp. 215–75.

23. Frazer, op. cit., pp. 435–37.

24. G. E. R. Grant Brown, "Human Sacrifices near the Upper Chindwin," *Journal of the Burma Research Society*, Vol. I; cited by Gait, loc. cit.

25. *The Masks of God: Primitive Mythology*, esp. pp. 176–83.

26. *The Gospel of Srī Ramakrishna*, translated into English with an Introduction, by Swami Nikhilananda (New York: Ramakrishna-Vivekananda Center, 1942), pp. 135–36.

27. Sir John Marshall (ed.), *Mohenjo-Daro and the Indus Civilization* (London: Arthur Probesthain, 1931), Vol. I, p. 52.

28. Marshall, op. cit., Vol. I, pp. 61–63.

29. Piggott, op. cit., pp. 132 ff.; Marshall (ed.), op. cit., Vol. I, pp. 28–29; Wheeler, op. cit., pp. 93 ff.; Ernest Mackay, *The Indus Civilization* (London: Lovat Dickson and Thompson, Ltd., 1935), pp. 21 ff.

30. *The Masks of God: Primitive Mythology*, p. 199, citing Ananda K. Coomaraswamy, *The Rg Veda as Lánd-Náma-Bok* (London: Luzac and Co., 1935).

31. Sir Leonard Woolley, *Ur: The First Phases* (London and New York: The King Penguin Books, 1946), p. 31.

32. Childe, op. cit., pp. 181–82.

33. Harold Peake and Herbert John Fleure, *The Horse and the Sword. The Corridors of Time*, Vol. VIII (New Haven: Yale University Press, 1933), pp. 85–94.

34. *Rg Veda* I. 35, verses 1, 2, 9, 3, and 11; translation based on Arthur Anthony Macdonell, *A Vedic Reader* (London: Oxford University Press, 1917), pp. 10–21.

35. C. C. Uhlenbeck, "The Indogermanic Mother Language and Mother Tribes Complex," *American Anthropologist*, Vol. 39, No. 3 (1937), pp. 391–93.

36. The Vedic references for each of these statements will be found in Macdonell, *Vedic Mythology*, pp. 22–27.

37. Hermann Oldenberg, *Die Religion des Veda* (Stuttgart and Berlin: J. G. Cotta'sche Buchhandlung Nachfolger, 3rd and 4th eds., 1923), pp. 195 97.

38. Nikhilananda (translator), op. cit., p. 136.

39. *Rg Veda* V. 80, verses 2, 5. 6.

40. *Rg Veda* VIII. 48, verses 1, 3, 5, and 6; following Macdonell, *A Vedic Reader*, pp. 157–58.

41. *Rg Veda* I. 32A, verse 3.

42. *Rg Veda* I. 32A, verses 7 and 8.

43. Winternitz, op. cit., Vol. I, p. 70; citing *Rg Veda* VIII. 14. 1–2.

44. *Mahābhārata* 12.281.1 to 282.20.

45. *Māṇḍūkya Upaniṣad* 1.

46. *Aitareya Brāhmaṇa* 3.3, translation by Arthur Berridale Keith, *Rigveda Brahmanas;* Harvard Oriental Series, Vol. 25 (Cambridge, Mass.: Harvard University Press, 1920), pp. 166–67, abridged.

47. Ibid., 2.37.

48. *Satapatha Brāhmaṇa* 2.2.2.6; 4.3.4.4.

49. Ibid., 12.4.4.6.

50. *Mānavadharma Sāstra* 9.319.

51. *Aitareya Brāhmaṇa* 5.28.

52. Frazer, op. cit., pp. 11–37.

53. *Taittirīya Saṃhitā* 7.4.5.1; cited by J. J. Meyer, *Trilogie altindischer Mächte und Feste der Vegetation*

(Zurich & Leipzig: Max Niehans Verlag, 1937), Part III, pp. 238–239.

54. K. Geldner, article "Aśvamedha," in Hastings (ed.), op. cit., Vol. II, p. 160.

55. Śatapatha Brāhmaṇa 13.2.1.2–5; Taittirīya Brāhmaṇa 3.8.14; Apastamba Śrautasūtra 20.10.5, et al.; cited by Meyer, op. cit., Part III, pp. 239–40.

56. Ṛg Veda I.162.2–4; 163.12; cited by Oldenberg, op. cit., p. 472, note 1.

57. Mahābhārata 14.88.19–36 (abridgment).

58. The Sanskrit sources for this rite are Śatapatha Brāhmaṇa 13.1–5; Taittirīya Brāhmaṇa 3.8–9; and the Śrautasūtras of Katyāyana 20. Apastamba 20, Aśvalāyana 10.6 ff., Sānkhyāna 16. I have followed the readings of Meyer, op. cit., Part III, pp. 241–46. For a discussion of variant readings of the Śatapatha text, cf. Julius Eggeling, The Śatapatha Brāhmaṇa, Sacred Books of the East, Vols. XII, XXVI, XLI, XLIII, XLIV (Oxford: The Clarendon Press, 1882–1900), Vol. XLIV, pp. 321–322, note 3.

59. Ibid., p. 246.

60. Ibid., p. 248.

61. Ṛg Veda IV.39.6.

62. Ṛg Veda X.9.1–3.

63. Mahābhārata 14.89.2–6 (slightly abridged).

64. Uno Holmberg, Finno-Ugric Mythology. The Mythology of All Races, Vol. IV, Part I (Boston: Marshall Jones Company, 1927), pp. 265–81.

65. E. J. Rapson, "Peoples and Languages," in E. J. Rapson (ed.), The Cambridge History of India, Vol. I, Ancient India (New York: Macmillan, 1922), p. 46.

66. A. Berriedale Keith, "The Age of the Rigveda," in Rapson (ed.), op. cit., p. 81.

67. Bṛhadāraṇyaka Upaniṣad 2.1.

68. The Masks of God: Primitive Mythology, p. 424.

69. Chāndogya Upaniṣad 5.3–10 abridged; translation largely from Robert Ernest Hume, The Thirteen Principal Upanishads (Lon-

don and New York: Oxford University Press, 1921), pp. 230–34.

70. Other kingly gurus teaching Brahmins were: King Ashvapati Kaikeya (Chāndogya Upaniṣad 5.11–24), King (?) Atidhanvan (ibid., 1.9.3), and a perhaps mythical Sanatkumara, who gave instruction to the legendary student-sage Narada (ibid., 7.1–25).

71. Paul Deussen, Die Philosophie der Upanishad's (Leipzig, F. A. Brockhaus; first edition, 1899; fourth edition, 1920), p. 19.

72. Kena Upaniṣad 3.1 to 4.1; following Zimmer, The Art of Indian Asia, Vol. I, pp. 108–109.

73. Kena Upaniṣad 4.2.

74. Zimmer, The Art of Indian Asia, Vol. I, pp. 109–10.

75. Zimmer, Philosophies of India.

76. Atharva Veda, passim.

77. Mircea Eliade, Yoga: Immortality and Freedom (New York: Pantheon Books, The Bollingen Series LVI, 1958), pp. 337–39.

78. Oldenberg, op. cit., p. 64.

79. Macdonell, Vedic Mythology, p. 34, citing Yāska (c. 700–500 B.C.?); also J. Muir, Original Sanskrit Texts, Vol. V (London: Trübner and Co., 1870), p. 165, citing Yāska, Nirukta 10.31. Cf. Lakshman Sarup, The Nighaṇṭu and the Nirukta (London: Oxford University Press, 1921), English Translation and Notes, p. 164.

80. Ṛg Veda I.35.6.

81. Ibid., I.35.5.

82. Cf. Macdonell, Vedic Mythology, pp. 32–35, for Ṛg Veda references.

83. Ṛg Veda II.33.3.

84. Ṛg Veda I.154.3 and 5; following Macdonell, A Vedic Reader, pp. 33 and 35.

85. Mahā-Vagga 1.21.1–2.

86. Taittirīya Upaniṣad 3.10.6; following Hume, op. cit., p. 293.

87. Bṛhadāraṇyaka Upaniṣad 1.1.1.

88. Mahā-Vagga 1.21.2–4; translation by Henry Clarke Warren, Buddhism in Translations, Harvard Oriental Series, Vol. III (Cambridge, Mass.: Harvard University Press, 1896), pp. 352–53.

89. Arthaśāstra, Book XIV, "Secret

Means," Chapter III, "The Application of Medicines and Mantras," Item 418; from the translation by R. Shamasastry (Mysore: Sri Raghuveer Printing Press, 4th ed., 1951), p. 450.

90. Ibid., Item 422; Shamasastry, p. 453.

91. *Viṣṇu Purāṇa* 4.2–3; translation based on H. H. Wilson, *The Vishnu Purāna* (London: The Oriental Translation Fund of Great Britain and Ireland, 1840), pp. 363–68.

92. Zimmer, *Philosophies of India*, p. 183.

93. Cf. Mrs. Sinclair Stevenson, *The Heart of Jainism* (London: Oxford University Press, 1915), pp. 272–74; Hermann Jacobi, article "Jainism," in Hastings (ed.), op. cit., Vol. VII, p. 466; Zimmer, *Philosophies of India*, pp. 182–83; Helmuth von Glasenapp, *Der Jainismus* (Berlin: Alf Hager Verlag, 1925), pp. 244 ff.; A. Guérinot, *La religion djaina* (Paris: Paul Geuthner, 1926), pp. 140–41.

94. Cf. Monier-Williams, op. cit., p. 823.

95. My chief source for this presentation of the Jain orders of the monad has been Guérinot, op. cit., pp. 186–205.

96. Cf. Monier-Williams, op. cit., pp. 448 and 1168.

97. Spengler, op. cit., Vol. I, pp. 57, 83, 63.

98. *Uttarādhyayana Sūtra* 30.5–6; Hermann Jacobi, *The Gaina-Sūtras, Part II*, Sacred Books of the East, Vol. XLV (Oxford: The Clarendon Press, 1895), p. 174.

99. Kunda-kunda Acharya, *Pravacana* III.2–3, 7–9, 20; translation by Barend Faddegon, F. W. Thomas (ed.), Jain Literature Society Series, Vol. I (Cambridge University Press, 1935), pp. 152–55; 157–59; 165.

100. *Tātparya-vṛtti* III.24b, 4–5, 7–8; translation by Faddegon in Thomas (ed.), op. cit., p. 202.

101. *Pravacana-sāra* I.44; ibid., p. 27.

102. For the full life story of Parshva, see Maurice Bloomfield, *The Life and Stories of the Jaina Savior Parçvanātha* (Baltimore: The Johns Hopkins Press, 1919); also, Zimmer, *Philosophies of India*, pp. 181 ff. For the stages of the way, Stevenson, op. cit. Bloomfield's source is Bhavadevasuri's *Parśvanātha Carita* (ed. Shravak Pandit Hargovinddas and Shravak Pandit Bechardas, Benares, 1912); Zimmer's, in part, Laksmivallabha's commentary to *Uttarādhyayana-sūtra* (Calcutta, 1878), pp. 682 ff.

CHAPTER 5: BUDDHIST INDIA

1. Miguel Asín y Palacios, *La Escatologia musulmana en la Divina Comedia* (Madrid: Imprenta de Estanislao Maestre, 1919; 2nd ed., Madrid-Granada: Escuelas de Estudios Árabes, 1943).

2. Ibid. (1943), pp. 166–68.

3. Langdon, *Semitic Mythology*, pp. 94–102, 161–62.

4. Zimmer, *Philosophies of India*, pp. 237–38.

5. *Yasna* 30:2; translation from L. H. Mills, *The Zend Avesta, Part III*, Sacred Books of the East, Vol. XXXI (Oxford: The Clarendon Press, 1887), p. 29.

6. *Vendidad* 4.47–49. Translation from James Darmesteter (*Sacred Books of the East*, Vol. IV, *The Zend-Avesta*, Part I; Oxford: The Clarendon Press, 1880), pp. 46–47.

7. Darmestetter, op. cit., p. lxxvi.

8. N. G. L. Hammond, *A History of Greece* to 322 B.C. (Oxford: The Clarendon Press, 1959), p. 75.

9. *Rg Veda* 2.12.4.

10. Wheeler, op. cit., pp. 117 and 125.

11. Ibid., pp. 26–28.

12. Ibid., p. 132.

13. Ibid., pp. 132–33.

14. *Timaeus* 30 D.

15. Definition of the term "mythogenetic zone," from *The Masks of God: Primitive Mythology*, p. 387.

16. Karl Kerényi, "Die Orphische Kosmogonie und der Ursprung

der Orphik," *Eranos-Jahrbuch 1949* (Zurich: Rhein-Verlag, 1950), p. 64.

17. Matthew 16:23; *Mahāparinibbāna-Sutta* 61.

18. *Sāṅkhya-sūtras* 4.1. (Transl., Zimmer, *Philosophies of India,* pp. 308–309.)

19. *Mahābhārata* 3.107.

20. Vijñānabhikṣu, commentary to *Sāṅkhyasūtra* I.146, cited by Richard Garbe, *Die Saṃkhya-Philosophie* (Leipzig: H. Haessel Verlag, 2nd ed., 1917), p. 387.

21. Vijñānabhikṣu, commentary to *Sāṅkhyasūtra* II.34; Garbe, loc. cit.

22. Nietzsche: *Die Geburt der Tragödie,* p. 7, paragraph next to last.

23. Aśvaghoṣa, *Buddhacarita,* Books 2–15, greatly abridged.

24. *Dīgha-nikāya* II.55.

25. Arrian, *Anabasis of Alexander,* VII.2.4; Strabo, *Geography,* XV, c. 714 f. and Plutarch, *Alexander* 65; as cited by E. R. Bevan, "Alexander the Great," in Rapson (ed.), op. cit., pp. 358–59.

26. Arrian VII.3 and Strabo XV, c. 717; Bevan, op. cit., p. 381.

27. *Tattvārthadhigama Sūtra* 4 (*Sacred Books of the Jaina,* Vol. II), pp. 6–7.

28. *Thera-gāthā* 62 (Vajji-putta); translation, Mrs. Rhys Davids, *Psalms of the Early Buddhists II. —Psalms of the Brethren,* Pali Text Society (London: Henry Froude, 1913), p. 63.

29. Compare Rapson, "The Scythian and Parthian Invaders," in Rapson (ed.), op. cit., pp. 581–82 (78–123 A.D.) and H. G. Rawlinson, *India: A Short Cultural History* (New York and London: D. Appleton–Century, 1938), pp. 93–94.

30. Aśvaghoṣa, *Buddhacarita* 16.57–129 (abridged).

31. Hpe Aung, "Buddhist Ethics, Buddhist Psychology, and Buddhist Philosophy, from Buddhadesana," in *Proceedings of the IXth International Congress for the History of Religions, Tokyo and Kyoto, 1958* (Tokyo: Maruzen, 1960), pp. 311–13.

32. *Vajracchedikā* (*The Diamond-Cutter*), 5 and 16.

33. *Yoga Sūtras* 4.34.

34. Friedrich Nietzsche, *Also sprach Zarathustra,* Part I, Zarathustra's Speeches, Section One. Translation by Walter Kaufmann, *The Portable Nietzsche* (New York: The Viking Press, 1954), pp. 137–139.

35. Albert Schweitzer, *Indian Thought and Its Development,* translated by Mrs. Charles E. B. Russell (London: Hodder and Stoughton, 1936), p. 13.

36. *Aṣṭavakra Saṃhitā* 18, verses 57 and 49.

37. The New World phases were as follows. In Middle America: Pre-Mayan Chicanel (424 B.C.–57 A.D.), Early Mayan Tzakol (57–373 A.D.), Late Mayan Tepeuh (373–727 A.D.). In Peru: Salinar and Gallinazo (c. 500–c. 300 B.C.), Moche, Nezca, and Early Tiahuanaco (c. 300 B.C.–c. 500 A.D.). See *The Masks of God: Primitive Mythology,* p. 213.

38. Rapson (ed.), op. cit., pp. 467–73.

39. Wheeler, op. cit., pp. 172–73. See also E. Diez, *Die Kunst Indiens* (Potsdam: Akademische Verlagsgesellschaft Athenaion, n.d.), p. 11, and Benjamin Rowland, *The Art and Architecture of India: Buddhist, Hindu, Jain. The Pelican History of Art* (London, Melbourne, Baltimore: Penguin Books, 1953), pp. 44–45. For illustrations, Zimmer, *The Art of Indian Asia,* Vol. I, Plates B7a and b, and Vol. II, Plate 4; or Rowland, op. cit., Plates 8, 9, 10, and 11.

40. Zimmer, *The Art of Indian Asia,* Vol. I, p. 257 and Plate B4c.

41. A. Dupont-Sommer, "Une inscription greco-araméenne du roi Asoka récemment découverte en Afghanistan," *Proceedings of the IXth International Congress for the History of Religions, Tokyo and Kyoto 1958* (Tokyo: Maruzen, 1960), p. 618.

42. Ibid.

43. Matthew 5:39; 8:22.

44. Rock Edict XIII; Vincent A. Smith, *The Edicts of Asoka* (Broad Campden: Essex House Press, 1909), p. 21.

45. Rock Edict IX; Smith, op. cit., p. 15.
46. Minor Rock Edict I (Rupuath Text); Smith, op. cit., p. 3.
47. Rock Edict VI; Smith, op. cit., p. 12.
48. Rock Edict XIII; Smith, op. cit., pp. 20–21.
49. Rock Edict XII; Smith, op. cit., p. 17.
50. Rock Edict XII; Smith, op. cit., p. 20.
51. R. E. M. Wheeler, "Brahmagiri and Chandrawelli 1947: Megalithic and Other Cultures in the Chitaldrug District, Mysore State," Ancient India, No. 4, pp. 181–310.
52. Kauṭilya's Arthaśāstra. Kauṭilya is supposed to have been the adviser and vizier of Chandragupta Maurya; cf. Zimmer, Philosophies of India, pp. 87–139.
53. Zimmer, Philosophies of India, pp. 503–504, citing Rapson (ed.), op. cit., p. 558.
54. E. J. Rapson, "The Successors of Alexander the Great," in Rapson (ed.), op. cit., pp. 540 ff.
55. Ibid., p. 551.
56. Winternitz, op. cit., Vol. II, pp. 140–41. Books IV–VII are missing from the Chinese translation, made between 317–420 A.D., and so are judged to be of later date.
57. The Questions of King Milinda, transl. by T. W. Rhys Davids, Sacred Books of the East, Vols. XXXV and XXXVI (Oxford: The Clarendon Press, 1890, 1894).
58. For the dates 78–123, see E. J. Rapson, "The Scythian and Parthian Invaders," in Rapson (ed.), op. cit., pp. 582–83; and for 120–162, H. G. Rawlinson, India: A Short Cultural History (New York and London: D. Appleton–Century, 1938), pp. 93–94.
59. Zimmer, The Art of Indian Asia, Vol. II, Plate 61.
60. D. C. Sircar, "Inscriptions in Sanskritic and Dravidian Languages," Ancient India, No. 9, 1953, p. 216.
61. Zimmer, The Art of Indian Asia, Vol. II, Plate 9.
62. Ibid., Plate 11b.
63. Sutta Nipāta 5.7.8.
64. Zimmer, The Art of Indian Asia, Vol. II, Plates 62–67.
65. Ibid., Plates 71–73.
66. Ibid., Vol. I, p. 340.
67. Quoted from rules of the order (Vinaya) by Edward Conze, Buddhism, Its Essence and Development (New York: Philosophical Library, no date), p. 58.
68. Zimmer, The Art of Indian Asia, Vol. II, Plate 27.
69. Ibid., Plate 12.
70. Ibid., Plates 9, 15, 22.
71. Aṣṭasāhasrikā Prajñāpāramitā 1; Zimmer, Philosophies of India, p. 485.
72. Cf. K. L. Reichelt, Truth and Tradition in Chinese Buddhism (Shanghai: Commercial Press, 1927), pp. 9–12.
73. Buddhacarita 15.11–12.
74. Amitāyur-dhyāna Sūtra, Part III, Paragraph 22, following the translation of Junjiro Takakusu, in Buddhist Mahāyāna Texts, Sacred Books of the East, Vol. XLIX (Oxford: The Clarendon Press, 1894), Part II, p. 188.
75. Amitāyur-dhyāna Sūtra, Part III, Paragraph 30; Takakusu, op. cit., pp. 197–99.
76. Marie-Thérèse de Mallmann, Introduction à l'étude d'Avalokiteçvara (Paris: Civilizations du Sud, 1948), pp. 90–91.
77. See the discussion of this figure in Pierre Lambrecht, Contributions à l'étude des divinités celtiques (Brugge: Rijksuniversiteit te Gent, 1942), pp. 56–60.
78. Amitāyur-dhyāna Sūtra, Part I, paragraphs 1–7; Takakusu, op. cit., pp. 161–67.
79. Ibid., Part II, Paragraphs 1–12; Takakusu, op. cit., pp. 169–73.
80. Ibid., Part II, Paragraph 17; Takakusu, op. cit., p. 178.
81. Zimmer, The Art of Indian Asia, Vol. I, p. 343.
82. Heinrich Zimmer, Kunstform und Yoga im indischen Kultbild (Berlin: Frankfurter Verlags-Anstalt, 1926), p. 12.
83. Amitāyur-dhyāna Sūtra, II.17; Takakusu, op. cit., pp. 178–79.
84. Ibid., 19; Takakusu, op. cit., pp. 181–85.
85. Vajracchedikā 31 and 32.
86. L. de la Vallée Poussin, Boud-

dhisme (Paris: Gabriel Beauchesne, 3rd ed., 1925), p. 403; cited by Albert Grünwedel, *Mythologie des Buddhismus in Tibet und der Mongolei* (Leipzig: F. A. Brockhaus, 1900), p. 142.

CHAPTER 6: THE INDIAN GOLDEN AGE

1. Fa-hsien (Fa Hian), *Fo-kwo-ki*, translated by Samuel Beal, *Travels of Fah-Hian and Sung-Yun* (London: Trübner and Co., 1869), pp. 55–58.
2. Goethe, *Sämtliche Werke*, Jubiläumsausgabe (Stuttgart and Berlin: J. G. Cotta'sche Buchhandlung Nachfolger, 1902–1907), Vol. I, p. 258.
3. Pliny, *Natural History*, VI.26,101; cited by Wilfred H. Schoff, *The Periplus of the Erythraean Sea: Travel and Trade in the Indian Ocean by a Merchant of the First Century*, translated from the Greek and annotated (New York: David McKay Company, 1916), p. 219.
4. Ibid., IX.57, 114; cited by Schoff, op. cit., p. 240.
5. Schoff, op. cit., p. 220.
6. *Periplus*, paragraphs 54 and 56; Schoff, op. cit., pp. 44–45.
7. Ibid., paragraph 49; Schoff, p. 42.
8. Ibid., paragraph 50; Schoff, op. cit., p. 43.
9. Wheeler, with Ghosh and Deva, op. cit. (*Ancient India*, No. 2, 1946), p. 17.
10. Hermann Goetz, "Imperial Rome and the Genesis of Classical Indian Art," *East and West*, New Series, Vol. 10, Nos. 3–4, Sept.–Dec., 1959, p. 180.
11. Rawlinson, op. cit., p. 98.
12. Goetz, op. cit., p. 262.
13. Ibid., p. 264.
14. Ibid., p. 264.
15. Ibid., p. 265.
16. Ibid., pp. 262 and 264–68.
17. A. Berriedale Keith, *The Sāmkhya System*, The Heritage of India Series (Calcutta: Association Press; London: Oxford University Press, no date), p. 30.
18. *Mahābhārata* 1.63.1–85, abridged.
19. Ibid., 1.100.40–101, abridged.
20. Ibid., 1.101–106, abridged.
21. Millar Burrows, *The Dead Sea Scrolls* (New York: The Viking Press, 1955), pp. 222–23.
22. *Mahābhārata* 1.
23. Ibid., 12.333.
24. Ibid., 3.33.2.
25. *Samyutta-nikāya* 2.43.
26. *Prayñāpāramitā-sūtra*.
27. *Kaṭha Upaniṣad* 3.12; Hume, op. cit., p. 352.
28. *Bhagavad Gītā* 6.6.
29. Ibid., 3.35.
30. Rawlinson, op. cit., p. 111.
31. Ibid., pp. 199–200.
32. Goetz, op. cit., pp. 262–63.
33. Zimmer, *The Art of Indian Asia*, Vol. II, Plates 348–375.
34. P. N. Chopra, "Rencontre de l'Inde et de l'Islam," *Cahiers d'histoire mondiale*, Vol. VI, No. 2 (1960), pp. 371–72.
35. H. Goetz, "Tradition und schöpferische Entwicklung in der indischen Kunst," *Indologen-Tagung, 1959*, Verhandlungen der Indologischen Arbeitstagung in Essen-Bredeney, Villa Hügel (Göttingen: Vandenhoeck und Ruprecht, 1959), p. 151.
36. Ibid., p. 152.
37. *Viṣṇu Purāṇa* 5.13, somewhat abridged; following Wilson, op. cit., pp. 531–35.
38. *Harivaṁsa* 75.
39. *Bhagavatā Purāṇa* 10.29.46.
40. Ibid., 10.29.39–40.
41. Ibid., 10.30–31.
42. Ibid., 10.32.
43. Ibid., 10.33.
44. *Mādhyamika Śāstra* 25.20 (Tibetan version).
45. Ibid., 25.24. From Max Walleser, *Die Mittlere Lehre des Nāgārjuna, nach der tibetanischen Version übertragen* (Heidelberg: Carl Winter's Universitätsbuchhandlung, 1911), pp. 163–64.
46. *Hevajra Tantra* (Calcutta: Manuscript in library of Royal Asiatic Society of Bengal), p. 36 (B); cited by Shashibhusan Dasgupta, *Obscure Religious Cults as Background of Bengali Literature* (University of Calcutta, 1946), p. 90.

47. Dasgupta, op. cit., p. 91.
48. Ibid., p. 94, citing Saraha-pāda, Dohākoṣa.
49. Ibid., p. 93, citing same.
50. Ibid., p. 93, citing same.
51. Ibid., p. 95, citing same.
52. Ibid., p. 97, citing same.
53. Ibid., p. 100, citing Tillo-pāda, Dohākoṣa.
54. Jayadeva, Gītāgovindakāvyam, considerably abridged; ed. C. Lassen (Bonn, 1836).
55. Winternitz, op. cit., Vol. III, p. 127.
56. Dasgupta, op. cit., p. 164.
57. A. Barth, translated by J. Wood, The Religions of India (Boston: Houghton, Mifflin and Company, 1882), pp. 205–206.
58. Śyāma Rahasya; as cited in H. H. Wilson, "Essays on the Religion of the Hindus," Selected Works (London: Trübner and Company, 1861), Vol. I, p. 255, note 1.
59. Ibid.; as cited by Wilson, "Essays on the Religion of the Hindus," p. 256, note 1.

60. Wilson, "Essays on the Religion of the Hindus," pp. 258–59, note 1; citing the Devī Rahasya.
61. Ibid., p. 257.
62. Ibid., p. 265.
63. Ibid., p. 264, note 1, citing Ānandagiri, Savikara Vijāya.
64. Ibid., p. 262, note 1; citing Śyāma Rahasya.
65. Ibid., p. 263.
66. Dasgupta, op. cit., p. 166, citing Candidas.
67. Brahmavaivarta Purāṇa, Kṛṣṇajanma-khaṇḍa, 28.12–82.
68. Ibid., 28.84–181; also 29 and 30.
69. Sir H. M. Elliot (ed. by J. Dowson), The History of India as Told by Its Own Historians; 8 vols. (London: Trübner and Co., 1867–1877), Vol. II, p. 26; cited by Rawlinson, op. cit., pp. 206–207.
70. Rawlinson, op. cit., pp. 208–209, citing Elliot, op. cit., Vol. IV, pp. 180–83.
71. Rawlinson, op. cit., pp. 277–78.

PART THREE: THE MYTHOLOGIES OF THE FAR EAST

CHAPTER 7: CHINESE MYTHOLOGY

1. Li Chi, The Beginnings of Chinese Civilization (Seattle: University of Washington Press, 1957), pp. 3–4.
2. Ibid., p. 12.
3. The reader will find an excellent summary view of this enterprise in the lively volume of Herbert Wendt, translated from the German by James Cleugh, In Search of Adam (Boston: Houghton Mifflin, 1956), pp. 455–66.
4. J. G. Andersson, "Researches into the Prehistory of the Chinese," Bulletin of the Museum of Far Eastern Antiquities, No. 15, 1943, p. 25.
5. The Masks of God: Primitive Mythology, pp. 360–61, 392–95.
6. Andersson, op. cit., p. 24.
7. Ibid., p. 23.
8. Ibid., p. 30.
9. Walter A. Fairservis, Jr., The Origins of Oriental Civilization (New York: The New American Library of World Literature, Inc.; A Mentor Book, 1959), pp. 73–76, abridged.
10. Andersson, op. cit., pp. 296–97.
11. Edgar Allan Poe, Works (New York: Thomas Nelson and Sons, 1905), Section I, Part IV, pp. 27–28.
12. Bernhard Karlgren, "Legends and Cults in Ancient China," Bulletin of the Museum of Far Eastern Antiquities, No. 18, 1946, pp. 218–19, citing Kuan Tzu.
13. Ibid., p. 221.
14. Ibid., pp. 276–77 and 212, citing Lü Shih Ch'un Ch'iu.
15. Karlgren, op. cit., p. 278.
16. Ibid., pp. 278–80; citing Kuan Tzu, Lü Shih Ch'un Chin, and Han Fei Tzu.
17. E. T. Backhouse and J. O. P. Bland, Annals and Memoirs of the Court of Peking (London: W. Heinemann, 1914), p. 322; as cited by Adda B. Bozeman, Poli-

tics and Culture in International History (Princeton University Press, 1960), pp. 145–46.

18. Karlgren, op. cit., p. 211; citing *Tso Chuan.*

19. Ibid., p. 257, note 1, citing *Shih Ching,* ode 245.

20. Ibid., p. 211, citing *Lü Shih Ch'un Ch'iu.*

21. Dante, *Vita Nuova,* 2, 3; also 6.

22. *Shu Ching* 1.1; following James Legge, *The Sacred Books of China: The Texts of Confucianism, Part I,* Sacred Books of the East, Vol. III (Oxford: The Clarendon Press, 2nd ed., 1899), pp. 32–33.

23. *Shu Ching* 1.3; following Legge, op. cit., pp. 34–36.

24. *Han Fei Tzu* as cited by Karlgren, op. cit., p. 295.

25. *Shu Ching* 2.1.2; Legge, op. cit., p. 38.

26. *Han Fei Tzu,* Nan 1, as cited by Karlgren, op. cit., p. 297.

27. *Shu Ching,* 2.1.2; Legge, op. cit., p. 38.

28. Karlgren, op. cit., pp. 292–93, citing *Mo Tzu.*

29. *Shu Ching* 2.1.3; Legge, op. cit., pp. 38–40.

30. Karlgren, op. cit., p. 298, citing *Tso Chuan.*

31. *Shu Ching* 5.4.1; Legge, op. cit., pp. 139–40.

32. Loc. cit.

33. *Mencius* 3.1.4.7; following Karlgren, op. cit., p. 303.

34. Karlgren, op. cit., p. 306, citing *Shih Chi.*

35. Ibid., p. 305, citing *Lü Shih Ch'un Ch'iu.*

36. *Shu Ching* 2.4.1; following Legge, op. cit., pp. 57–60.

37. Karlgren, op. cit., p. 303, citing *Shih Chi.*

38. Loc. cit., citing *Tso Chuan.*

39. Louis Ginzberg, op. cit., Vol. I, pp 163–66; and Vol. V, p. 187.

40. Robert Graves, *The White Goddess* (New York: Creative Age Press, 1948), p. 272.

41. *The Masks of God: Primitive Mythology,* pp. 118–22.

42. Karlgren, op. cit., pp. 303–304.

43. E. T. C. Werner, *A Dictionary of Chinese Mythology* (Shanghai: Kelly & Walsh, 1932), p. 597.

44. Karlgren, op. cit., pp. 326–27, citing *Kuan Tsu.*

45. Ibid., p. 329, citing *Lü Shih Ch'un Ch'iu.*

46. Ibid., p. 327, citing *Kuan Tzu.*

47. Ibid., p. 328, citing *Lü Shih Ch'un Ch'iu.*

48. Ibid., p. 329, note 1.

49. Frazer, op. cit., pp. 1–2, and *passim.*

50. Ovid, *Metamorphoses* X, lines 512–13.

51. Karlgren, op. cit., p. 329, note 1.

52. Ibid., pp. 331–33, citing largely *Mo Tzu.*

53. Fairservis, op. cit., pp. 127–28.

54. Translation by Arthur Waley, *Three Ways of Thought in Ancient China* (New York: The Macmillan Company, 1939; Garden City, N.Y.: Doubleday Anchor Books, 1956), p. 123.

55. Li Chi, op. cit., p. 32.

56. Joseph Needham and Wang Ling, *Science and Civilization in China* (Cambridge, England: Cambridge University Press, 1954), Vol. I, p. 81.

57. René Grousset, translated from the French by Haakon Chevalier, *Chinese Art and Culture* (New York: The Orion Press, 1959), p. 17.

58. Ibid.

59. Marcel Granet, *Danses et légendes de la Chine ancienne* (Paris: Felix Alcan, 1926), p. 491, note 2; cited by Grousset, op. cit., p. 18, note 37.

60. See, for example, the series of illustrations in Miguel Covarrubias, *The Eagle, the Jaguar, and the Serpent* (New York: Alfred A. Knopf, 1954), pp. 48–49.

61. *The Masks of God: Primitive Mythology,* pp. 229 ff.

62. Li Chi, op. cit., p. 23.

63. Needham and Wang Ling, op. cit., Vol. I, p. 84.

64. *Shu Ching* 5.6.1; Legge, op. cit., pp. 152–54.

65. *Shih Ching,* "The Sacrificial Odes of Shang," Ode 1; following Legge, op. cit., pp. 304–305.

66. *Shih Ching,* "The Sacrificial Odes of Shang," Ode 2; Legge, op. cit., p. 306.

67. *Shih Ching,* "The Sacrificial Odes

of Chou," Decade 3, Ode 7; Legge, op. cit., p. 334.

68. Ibid., Decade 3, Ode 6; Legge, op. cit., pp. 331–32.

69. Ibid., "The Minor Odes of the Kingdom," Decade 1, Ode 5, Stanza 1; Legge, op. cit., p. 347.

70. *Shih Ching*, "The Minor Odes of the Kingdom," Decade 4, Ode 9 (in part); Legge, op. cit., p. 355.

71. *Shih Ching*, "The Minor Odes of the Kingdom," Decade 4, Ode 7, abridged; Legge, op. cit., p. 353.

72. K. M. Panikkar, "Indian Doctrines of Politics," First Annual Lecture at the Harold Laski Institute of Political Science at Ahmedabad, July 22, 1955; cited by Bozeman, op. cit., p. 264. For an insight into the classical Indian philosophy of politics, the reader is referred to Zimmer, *Philosophies of India*, pp. 87–127; for the Chinese, Waley, *Three Ways of Thought in Ancient China*, pp. 152–88; and for a survey of these views in relation to the history of political thought in Asia, Adda B. Bozeman, *Politics and Culture in International History* (Princeton University Press, 1960), pp. 118–161.

73. *Shang Tzu* 8.2a and 13.8b; translation from Waley, *Three Ways of Thought in Ancient China*, pp. 167–68, and J. J. L. Duyvendak, *The Book of the Lord Shang: A Classic of the Chinese School of Law* (London: Arthur Probsthain, 1928), pp. 236 and 256.

74. Ibid., 25.11b (Duyvendak, op. cit., p. 326); transl. Waley, op. cit., p. 167.

75. Ibid., 4.11a and b (also 20.3b); Duyvendak, op. cit., pp. 196, 199–200 (also p. 305); Waley, op. cit., p. 173.

76. Arthur Waley, *The Way and Its Power*, pp. 64 and 41.

77. Richard Wilhelm, translation by Cary F. Baynes, *The I Ching or Book of Changes* (New York: Pantheon Books, Bollingen Series XIX, 1950), Vol. I, p. xxxi.

78. Ibid., Vol. I, pp. 32–34, abridged.

79. *I Ching*, "Great Commentary"; translation by James Legge, *The Sacred Books of China: The Texts of Confucianism, Part II, The Yi King. Sacred Books of the East*, Vol. XVI (Oxford: The Clarendon Press, 1899), pp. 12 and 373.

80. Fung Yu-lan, *A Short History of Chinese Philosophy*, edited by Dirk Bodde (New York: The Macmillan Company, 1948), p. 39.

81. Ibid., p. 40.

82. Ibid., p. 38.

83. *Analects* 7.1.

84. Ibid., 7.16.

85. Needham and Wang Ling, op. cit., Vol. II, p. 307.

86. Fung Yu-lan, op. cit., p. 39.

87. *Analects* 12.2; James Legge, *The Four Books*, p. 157.

88. Ibid., 13.3, 5–6; Legge, *The Four Books*, p. 176.

89. Ibid., 12.11; Legge, *The Four Books*, pp. 165–66.

90. Fung Yu-lan, op. cit., p. 41.

91. Zimmer, *Philosophies of India*, pp. 162–63.

92. Fung Yu-lan, *A History of Chinese Philosophy* (Princeton University Press, 1952), Vol. 1, p. 370.

93. *Chung Yung* 1.1; Legge, *The Four Books*, p. 349.

94. Ibid., 20.18; Legge, *The Four Books*, p. 394.

95. Ibid., 22; Legge, *The Four Books*, pp. 398–99.

96. Ibid., 14.1–2; Legge, *The Four Books*, p. 367.

97. *Analects* 8.8; Legge, *The Four Books*, p. 100.

98. *Analects* 20.3; Legge, *The Four Books*, p. 306.

99. *Analects* 4.16; Legge, *The Four Books*, p. 44, and Fung Yu-lan, *A Short History*, p. 42.

100. *Mo Tzu* 39; translation from Fung Yu-lan, *A Short History*, p. 52.

101. *Mo Tzu* 48; transl. Fung Yu-lan, *A History of Chinese Philosophy*, Vol. I, p. 86.

102. Fung Yu-lan, *History*, Vol. I, p. 90.

103. Ibid., p. 84.

104. Ibid., p. 87.

105. *Mo Tzu* 11; Fung Yu-lan, *History*, Vol. I, p. 100.

106. *Mo Tzu* 13; Fung Yu-lan, *History*, Vol. I, pp. 101–102.
107. *Mo Tzu* 16; translation, Fung Yu-lan, *A Short History*, p. 54.
108. *Mo Tzu;* 9.39; translation, Waley, *Three Ways of Thought*, p. 131.
109. Fung Yu-lan, *A Short History*, pp. 50–51.
110. *Mencius* 7.26.1; translation, Legge, *The Four Books*, p. 956.
111. *Han Fei Tzu* 51; translation by Waley, *The Way and Its Power*, p. 43.
112. *Kuan Tzu* 65; translation by Waley, op. cit., p. 37.
113. Waley, *The Way and Its Power*, pp. 37–38, citing *Mencius*, 3.2.10; cf. Legge, *The Four Books*, pp. 681–85.
114. Waley, *The Way and Its Power*, p. 46.
115. Ibid., p. 114.
116. Ibid., p. 52.
117. Ibid., pp. 114–15.
118. *Vedāntasāra* 15–25.
119. Waley, *The Way and Its Power*, p. 32.
120. *Tao Tê Ching* 6; translation, Waley, *The Way and Its Power*, p. 149.
121. Waley, *The Way and Its Power*, pp. 45–46.
122. *Tao Tê Ching* 15; Waley, p. 160.
123. *Tao Tê Ching* 16; Waley, p. 162.
124. *Chuang Tzu* 18.2; translation by Waley, *The Way and Its Power*, pp. 53–54.
125. Waley, *The Way and Its Power*, pp. 54–55.
126. *Tao Tê Ching* 22; Waley, *The Way and Its Power*, p. 171.
127. Waley, *The Way and Its Power*, p. 84.
128. Ibid., p. 72.
129. Needham and Wang Ling, op. cit., Vol. I, pp. 97–98.
130. Legge, *The Sacred Books of China: The Texts of Confucianism*, pp. 6–7.
131. *Taittīriya Upaniṣad* 2.1.
132. Fung Yu-lan, *A Short History of Chinese Philosophy*, pp. 131–132.
133. *Shu Ching* 5.4; Legge, *The Sacred Books of China: The Texts of Confucianism*, pp. 139–41.
134. Karlgren, op. cit., p. 222; Fung Yu-lan, *A History of Chinese Philosophy*, Vol. II, pp. 7–30.
135. Karlgren, op. cit., pp. 200–201.
136. Junjiro Takakusu, *The Essentials of Buddhist Philosophy*, ed. W. T. Chan and Charles A. Moore (Honolulu: University of Hawaii, 1947, second ed., 1949), pp. 14–16.
137. *Lieh Tzu*, chapter Yang Chu (*Yang Chu's Garden of Pleasure*, translation by Anton Forke), cited by Fung Yu-lan, *A Short History*, pp. 232–33.
138. Fung Yu-lan, *A Short History*, p. 233.
139. *Lieh Tzu*, loc. cit.; transl. Fung Yu-lan, *A Short History*, p. 234.
140. *Shih Shuo* 23; in Fung Yu-lan, *A Short History*, pp. 235–36.
141. *Shih Shuo* 23; Fung Yu-lan, p. 235.
142. *Ko Hung* (called also *Pao-p'u Tzu*), *Nei P'ien*, 7, translation from Obed Simon Johnson, *A Study of Chinese Alchemy* (Shanghai, 1928), p. 63.
143. *Pao-p'u Tzu* 6.42; translation from Wm. Theodore de Bary, Wing-tsit Chan, and Burton Watson, *Sources of Chinese Tradition* (New York: Columbia University Press, 1960), p. 301.
144. Ibid., 6.5b–7a and 3.10a–b; from *Sources*, pp. 302–304.
145. Wing-tsit Chan, in *Sources*, p. 298.
146. Ibid., p. 297.
147. Needham and Wang Ling, op. cit., vol. I, p. 119.
148. Daisetz Teitaro Suzuki, *Essays in Zen Buddhism (First Series)* (New York, London, etc.: Rider and Company, n.d.), p. 168.
149. Suzuki, op. cit., pp. 186–89; Takakusu, op. cit., p. 159; citing Tao Hsüan, *The Records of the Transmission of the Lamp* (composed 1004 A.D.).
150. Suzuki, op. cit., p. 165; Takakusu, op. cit., pp. 158–59.
151. Suzuki, op. cit., p. 174; Alan W. Watts, *The Way of Zen* (New York: Pantheon Books, 1957), p. 88.
152. Yu Shen-Hsing, as quoted in Fu Tse-Hung, *Golden Mirror of the Flowing Waters (Hsing Shui-Chin Chien)*, 92; cited by

Needham and Wang Ling, op. cit., Vol. I, p. 123.
153. Needham and Wang Ling, op. cit., Vol. I, pp. 123–24.
154. Loc. cit.
155. Edwin O. Reischauer, *Ennin's Travels in T'ang China* (New York: copyright 1955, The Ronald Press Company), p. 227.
156. *Vajracchedikā* 5.
157. Suzuki, op. cit., pp. 203–206; Watts, op. cit., 91–92.
158. Suzuki, op. cit., pp. 208–209.
159. *Tao Tê Ching* 28.
160. Ibid., 32, abridged; translation, Waley, *The Way and Its Power*, p. 183.
161. Waley, *The Way and Its Power*, p. 55.
162. Reischauer, op. cit., p. 235.
163. Ibid., pp. 238–39.
164. Ibid., p. 211.
165. Edwin O. Reischauer, *Ennin's Diary* (New York: Copyright 1955, The Ronald Press Company), pp. 246–47.
166. Ibid., pp. 247–48.
167. Reischauer, *Ennin's Travels in T'ang China*, p. 196.
168. Reischauer, *Ennin's Diary*, p. 341.

169. Ibid., p. 345.
170. Ibid., pp. 347–48.
171. Ibid., pp. 343–44.
173. Ibid., pp. 347–48.
174. Ibid., pp. 350–51.
175. Ibid., pp. 351–52.
176. Ibid., pp. 352–53.
177. Ibid., p. 357.
178. Ibid., pp. 358–59.
179. Reischauer, *Ennin's Travels in T'ang China*, p. 262.
180. Joseph M. Kitagawa, *Religions of the East* (Philadelphia: The Westminster Press, 1960), p. 44.
181. *Hsiao Ching* 2; translation, Legge, *The Sacred Books of China: The Texts of Confucianism*, Part I, p. 467.
182. Loc. cit.
183. Kitagawa, op. cit., p. 50.
184. Fung Yu-lan, *A Short History of Chinese Philosophy*, p. 271.
185. *Mencius* 7.1.4; translation from Fung Yu-lan, *A Short History*, p. 77; Legge, *The Four Books*, pp. 935–36.
186. *Hsün Tzu* 19; translation from Fung Yu-lan, *A Short History*, pp. 149–50.
187. Fung Yu-lan, loc. cit.

CHAPTER 8: JAPANESE MYTHOLOGY

1. Fairservis, op. cit., pp. 145–46, citing J. Maringer, "Einige faustkeilartige Geräte von Gongenyama (Japan) und die Frage des Japanischen Paläolithikums," *Anthropos* VI, 1956, pp. 175–93; ibid., "A Core and Flake Industry of Paleolithic Type from Central Japan," *Artibus Asiae*, Vol. XIX, 2, pp. 111–25; and R. K. Beardsley, "Japan Before Prehistory," *Far Eastern Quarterly*, Vol. XIV, 3, 1955, p. 321.
2. Ibid., p. 146, citing J. E. Kidder, "Reconstruction of the Pre-pottery Culture of Japan," *Artibus Asiae*, XVII, 1954, pp. 135–43.
3. Ibid., pp. 148–50, citing J. E. Kidder, *The Jomon Pottery of Japan*, Supplement 17, *Artibus Asiae*, 1957, pp. 150–51.
4. *The Japan Biographical Encyclopedia and Who's Who* (Tokyo: The Rengo Press, 1958), p. 1050.

5. *Wei Chi* ("History of the Kingdom of Wei"), translation from Ryusaku Tsunoda and L. Carrington Goodrich, *Japan in the Chinese Dynastic Histories*, Perkins Asiatic Monograph No. 2 (South Pasadena: P. D. and Ione Perkins, 1951), pp. 8–16.
6. *Hou Han Shu* ("History of the Latter Han Dynasty"), Tsunoda and Goodrich, op. cit., p. 3.
7. Joseph M. Kitagawa, article "Japan: Religion," *Encyclopaedia Britannica*, 1961.
8. *Hou Han Shu* and Kitagawa, loc. cit.
9. *Kojiki* 1, Preface and 1–9; following Basil Hall Chamberlain, *Ko-ji-ki: "Records of Ancient Matters,"* Supplement to Vol. X, *Transactions of the Asiatic Society of Japan*, pp. 1–41, abridged and modified, with elements from Post Wheeler, *The*

Sacred Scriptures of the Japanese (New York: Henry Schuman, Inc., 1952), pp. 1–17.

10. *Kojiki*, 1.10.

11. Ibid. 1.18–21; Chamberlain, op. cit., pp. 71–81.

12. Ibid. 1.26–30; Chamberlain, op. cit., pp. 98–113.

13. Ibid. 1.31–32; Chamberlain, op. cit., pp. 114–28.

14. Ibid. 1.33–34; Chamberlain, op. cit., pp. 128–38.

15. Ibid. 1.37; Chamberlain, op. cit., pp. 140–43.

16. *Mathews' Chinese-English Dictionary*, revised American edition (Cambridge, Mass.: Harvard University Press, second printing, 1960), p. 114, entry 833.

17. W. G. Aston, article, "Shinto," in Hastings (ed.), op. cit., Vol. XI, p. 463.

18. Address by Prince Takahito Mikasa, in *Proceedings of the IXth International Congress for the History of Religions*, Tokyo and Kyoto, 1958, pp. 826–27.

19. *Shinto Gobusho;* as cited by Genchi Kato, *What Is Shinto?* (Tokyo: Maruzen Company, 1935), pp. 45 and 43.

20. *An Outline of Shinto Teachings*, compiled by Shinto Committee for the IXth International Congress for the History of Religions (Tokyo, 1958), p. 31; also *Basic Terms of Shinto*, compiled and published by same, p. 52.

21. Otto, op. cit., p. 7.

22. Ichijo Kaneyoshi (1402–1481), *Nihonshoki Sanso;* cited by Kato, op. cit., p. 46.

23. Langdon Warner, *The Enduring Art of Japan* (New York: Grove Press, 1952), p. 18.

24. *Nihongi* 19.34–35; W. G. Aston, *Chronicles of Japan: From the Earliest Times to* A.D. 697 (London: George Allen and Unwin, 1956; reprint from Supplement to Transactions and Proceedings of the Japan Society, 1896), Part II, p. 66.

25. Ibid., 19.35–38; Aston, op. cit., Vol. II, pp. 60–68.

26. Ibid., 22.2; Aston, op. cit., Part II, p. 122.

27. Shotoku, *Shomangyo-gisho;* trans-

lation following Shinsho Hanayama, "Japanese Development of Ekayana Thought," in *Religious Studies in Japan*, edited by Japanese Association for Religious Studies and Japanese Organizing Committee of the Ninth International Congress for the History of Religions (Tokyo: Maruzen Company, Ltd., 1959), p. 373.

28. *Nihongi* 22.32–33; Aston, op. cit., Part II, p. 148.

29. For a study of the Borobudur series, cf. Zimmer, *The Art of Indian Asia*, Vol. I, pp. 301–12, and Vol. II, Plates 476–94.

30. Takakusu, op. cit., p. 114.

31. Ibid., p. 120.

32. Philipp Karl Eidmann, "The Tractate of the Golden Lion," translation and commentary (unpublished).

33. Takakusu, op. cit., p. 120.

34. Ibid., p. 121.

35. I want to recognize with gratitude at this point, five months of discussion with Professors Shinya Kasugai and Karl Philipp Eidmann at Chion-in and Nishi Honganji, Kyoto.

36. *Nirvāna sūtra*. Takakusu, op. cit., pp. 127–28.

37. Warner, op. cit., pp. 29–30.

38. Hajime Nakamura, "The Vitality of Religion in Asia," in *Cultural Freedom in Asia*, Proceedings of a Conference Held at Rangoon, Burma, Feb. 17–20, 1955 (Rutland, Vermont, and Tokyo: Charles E. Tuttle Company, 1956), p. 56.

39. Masaharu Anesaki, *Japanese Mythology. The Mythology of All Races*, Vol. VIII, Part II (Boston: Marshall Jones Company, 1928), p. 296.

40. *Heike Monogatari* (*The Tale of Heike: The Death of Atsumori*), translation by A. L. Sadler, in Donald Keene (ed.), *Anthology of Japanese Literature*, UNESCO Collection of Representative Works (New York: Grove Press, 1955), pp. 179–81.

41. Philipp Karl Eidmann, et al., *The Lion's Roar*, Vol. 1, No. 3 (April 1958), *passim*, and Takakusu, op. cit., pp. 166–75.

42. Alan W. Watts, *The Way of Zen* (New York: Pantheon Books, 1957), p. 134.

43. Eugen Herrigel, *Zen in the Art of Archery* (New York: Pantheon Books, 1953), p. 104.

44. Takakusu, op. cit., pp. 176–84.

45. Masaharu Anesaki, *Nichiren, the Buddhist Prophet* (Cambridge, Mass.: Harvard University Press, 1916), p. 129.

46. *Religions in Japan at Present* (Tokyo: Institute for Research in Religious Problems, 1958), p. 54.

47. A. B. Mitford, *Tales of Old Japan* (London: Macmillan and Co., 1871), pp. 232–36; cited by Inazo Nitobé, *Bushido: The Soul of Japan* (Tokyo: Teibi Publishing Company, 17th edition, revised and enlarged, 1911), pp. 106–11.

48. Lafcadio Hearn, *Japan* (New York: Grosset and Dunlap, 1904), pp. 313–14.

49. Cited in *The Masks of God: Primitive Mythology*, p. 419.

50. Nitobé, op. cit., pp. 129–30.

51. Cited from Genchi Kato, *Shinto in Essence, as Illustrated by The Faith in a Glorified Personality* (Tokyo: The Noki Shrine, 1954), p. 12.

52. Warner, op. cit., p. 58.

53. Cited by Nitobé, op. cit., pp. 19–20.

54. For this particular paraphrase of the idea I thank Alan W. Watts (personal communication).

55. Zenrin verse cited by Watts, op. cit., p. 126.

56. Zimmer, *The Art of Indian Asia,* pp. 189–90.

Chapter 9: TIBET: THE BUDDHA AND THE NEW HAPPINESS

1. *Tibet and the Chinese People's Republic,* A Report to the International Commission of Jurists by Its Legal Inquiry Committee on Tibet (Geneva: International Commission of Jurists, 1960), p. 59.

2. Ibid., p. 63.

3. Mao Tse-tung, *Selected Works,* Vol. I (New York: International Publishers, 1954), p. 49.

4. Mao Tse-tung, *On Contradiction* (New York: International Publishers, 1953), p. 14.

5. Nikhilananda, op. cit., pp. 379–80.

6. Marco Pallis, *Peaks and Lamas* (London: Cassell, 1939; New York: Alfred A. Knopf, 1949).

7. *Tibet and the Chinese People's Republic,* p. VIII.

8. W. Y. Evans-Wentz, *The Tibetan Book of the Dead* (New York: Oxford University Press, A Galaxy Book, 1960).

9. *Tibet and the Chinese People's Republic,* Statement No. 45, p. 278.

10. Ibid., Statement No. 1, pp. 222–223.

11. Mao Tse-tung, *Selected Works,* Vol. I, p. 23.

12. *Tibet and the Chinese People's Republic,* Statement 26, p. 254.

13. Ibid., Statement No. 11, p. 235.

14. Loc. cit.

15. Ibid., Statement No. 4, p. 225.

16. Ibid., Statement No. 5, p. 226.

17. Ibid., Statement No. 7, p. 229.

18. Mao Tse-tung, *Let a Hundred Flowers Bloom* (New York: The New Leader, 1958), ed. by G. F. Hudson, p. 44.

19. Mao Tse-tung, *On Contradiction,* p. 42.

20. Ibid., pp. 44–45.

21. *Tibet and the Chinese People's Republic,* Statement No. 7, pp. 229–30.

22. Ibid., Statement No. 2, p. 223. Other examples of this treatment appear in Statements No. 7 (p. 230), 10 (p. 234), 36 (p. 267), 37 (p. 269), 38 (p. 269), 39 (p. 271), 44 (p. 277), and *passim.*

23. Ibid., Statement No. 32, p. 260.

24. Ibid., Statement 44, p. 276.

25. Ibid., Statement 35, p. 266.

26. Evans-Wentz, op. cit., p. 166.

27. Ibid., p. 147.

INDEX

Penguin Books about Mythology

THE NATURE OF GREEK MYTHS
G. S. Kirk

What are myths? Theories abound. They have been seen as echoes of cosmological and meteorological events; as attempts to explain some of the odder natural phenomena—a sort of primitive science; as stories to validate existing customs or institutions; as justification for primitive rituals. Professor Kirk examines such universal theories and admits they are all illuminating but points out that none is adequate by itself. His general analysis of the nature of myth is followed by a splendid account of the Greek myths.

MIDDLE EASTERN MYTHOLOGY
S. H. Hooke

Professor Hooke has provided an absorbing account, based on first-hand sources, of the fascinating mythologies of the Egyptians, Babylonians, Assyrians, Hittites, Canaanites, and Hebrews. In addition he discusses the nature and function of myth and devotes a chapter to the important subject of the place of myth in Christianity.

GODS AND MYTHS OF NORTHERN EUROPE
H. R. Ellis Davidson

Recent research in archaeology and mythology has added to what was already a fairly consistent picture of the principal Scandinavian divinities. This study—the first popular treatment of the subject to appear in English for many years—describes the more familiar gods of war, of fertility, of the sky and the sea and the dead, and also discusses the most puzzling figures of Norse mythology, Heimdall, Balder, and Loki. The author has endeavored to relate their cults to daily life and to see why these pagan beliefs gave way in time to the Christian faith.

Books of Mythology Published by Penguin Books

BEOWULF, *a prose translation by David Wright*
BEOWULF, *a verse translation by Michael Alexander*
EGIL'S SAGA, *translated by Herman Pálsson and Paul Edwards*
THE EPIC OF GILGAMESH, *English version by N. K. Sandars*
THE GREEK MYTHS (2 vols.), *Robert Graves*
HINDU MYTHS, *translated by Wendy O'Flaherty*
HRAFNKEL'S SAGA, *translated by Herman Pálsson*
THE ILIAD, *Homer, translated by E. V. Rieu*
KING HARALD'S SAGA, *translated by Magnus Magnusson and Herman Pálsson*
LAXDAELA SAGA, *translated by Magnus Magnusson and Herman Pálsson*
LE MORTE D'ARTHUR (2 vols.), *Sir Thomas Malory, introduced by John Lawlor and edited by Janet Cowen*
THE MABINOGION, *translated by Jeffrey Gantz*
THE METAMORPHOSES, *Ovid, translated by Mary M. Innes*
THE NIBELUNGENLIED, *translated by A. T. Hatto*
NJAL'S SAGA, *translated by Magnus Magnusson and Herman Pálsson*
THE ODYSSEY, *Homer, translated by E. V. Rieu*
SIR GAWAIN AND THE GREEN KNIGHT, *translated by Brian Stone*
TALES FROM THE THOUSAND AND ONE NIGHTS, *translated by N. J. Dawood*
THE VINLAND SAGAS: THE NORSE DISCOVERY OF AMERICA, *translated by Magnus Magnusson and Herman Pálsson*

Ted Lippa *7/22/88*

PENGUIN BOOKS

THE MASKS OF GOD:
ORIENTAL MYTHOLOGY

Joseph Campbell has been interested in mythology since his childhood in New York, when he read books about American Indians, frequently visited the American Museum of Natural History, and was fascinated by the museum's collection of totem poles. He earned his B.A. and M.A. degrees at Columbia in 1925 and 1927 and went on to study medieval French and Sanskrit at the universities of Paris and Munich. After a period in California, where he encountered John Steinbeck and the biologist Ed Ricketts, he taught at the Canterbury School, then, in 1934, joined the literature department at Sarah Lawrence College, a post he retained for many years. During the 1940s and '50s, he helped Swami Nikhilananda to translate the Upanishads and *The Gospel of Sri Ramakrishna.* The many books by Professor Campbell include *The Hero with a Thousand Faces, Myths to Live By, The Flight of the Wild Gander,* and *The Mythic Image.* He has edited *The Portable Arabian Nights, The Portable Jung,* and other works.